Class

CLASS

THE ANTHOLOGY

*Edited by Stanley Aronowitz
and Michael J. Roberts*

WILEY Blackwell

Registered Offices
John Wiley & Sons, Inc., 111 River Street, Hoboken, NJ 07030, USA
John Wiley & Sons Ltd, The Atrium, Southern Gate, Chichester, West Sussex, PO19 8SQ, UK

Editorial Office
9600 Garsington Road, Oxford, OX4 2DQ, UK

For details of our global editorial offices, customer services, and more information about Wiley products visit us at www.wiley.com.

Wiley also publishes its books in a variety of electronic formats and by print-on-demand. Some content that appears in standard print versions of this book may not be available in other formats.

Limit of Liability/Disclaimer of Warranty
While the publisher and authors have used their best efforts in preparing this book, they make no representations or warranties with respect to the accuracy or completeness of the contents of this book and specifically disclaim any implied warranties of merchantability or fitness for a particular purpose. No warranty may be created or extended by sales representatives or written sales materials. The advice and strategies contained herein may not be suitable for your situation. You should consult with a professional where appropriate. Neither the publisher nor authors shall be liable for any loss of profit or any other commercial damages, including but not limited to special, incidental, conse-quential, or other damages.

Library of Congress Cataloging-in-Publication data is available for this book.

ISBN 9780631224983 (hardback), 9780631224990 (paperback)

Cover Design: Wiley
Cover Image: © Young Sam Green / EyeEm/Gettyimages

Set 10.5/12.5pt Ehrhardt by SPi Global, Pondicherry, India

Printed in Singapore by C.O.S. Printers Pte Ltd

10   9   8   7   6   5   4   3   2   1

Contents

Part Three The Capitalist Class

General Introduction

Stanley Aronowitz and Michael J. Roberts

This volume of documents, classic articles and original analysis by the editors remains controversial on several grounds. Despite the growing evidence that the global economy is dominated by a handful of leading corporations and the very rich individuals who control them, the conventional wisdom is that we live in a world of mom and pop enterprises. Accordingly, most citizens of the most industrially developed countries are termed "middle class." For those who do not own their own businesses, we measure class by income and by consumption. Beneath this vast social group is the relatively small corps of the poor, a diminishing proportion of the population.

Mainstream political science insists that there is no ruling class or power elite in the functions of the state. Following the dictum, most forcefully established in the late 1950s by Yale political scientist Robert Dahl, whose book *Who Governs?* remains a bible for many, American politics consists of a plurality of organizations, including business, political parties, pressure groups on single issues, and unions, none of which, in advance, constitutes the leading edge of governance. This idea of American classlessness can be traced back to the immensely influential book *Why There is No Socialism in the United States* (1906) by the German economist and sociologist Werner Sombart. Sombart advanced the thesis that the workers were not a class in the European sense. They did not exhibit solidarity as a class because America is really the land of opportunity. It had no feudal tradition and possessed unlimited natural and economic resources. The urban political machines address and often solve the most pressing issues facing workers outside the workplace. Yet in subsequent years, especially the 1930s, 1940s and 1960s, American workers engaged in some of the sharpest strikes, factory occupations and demonstrations of any working class in advanced industrial capitalism, most of which were unauthorized by law.[1] Even so, conventional social science remains adamant that class plays a subordinate or no role in the conduct of politics and the political economy. According to this view, the United States is a middle class society with a tiny stratum of the rich and a slightly larger underclass of the poor, who are declining over time. And the poor are poor because their families are dysfunctional or they lack the energy and the will to take advantage of prevailing opportunities to lift themselves out of poverty. Some anthropologists and sociologists advanced the theory that the poor wallow in a "culture of poverty" that effectively cuts them off from mainstream society. In the absence of outside intervention, either by the state or by private philanthropies this culture, it is held, is self-reproducing. Among the leading scholars of this position were Daniel Patrick Moynihan and Nathan Glazer, whose book *Beyond the Melting Pot* stirred fierce debate in the 1960s when the question of poverty commanded the nation's attention and became a subject of national policy.

However, the most disputed idea that underlies this project is that we declare that our societies are constituted by three classes: a capitalist ruling class consisting of the tycoons of finance, the top political managers, the corporate elite, and in the United States what C. Wright Mills termed the "warlords" at the pinnacle of the military; a middle class of small business owners and salaried professionals and technical operatives who still enjoy some autonomy in the performance of their work; and the working class, employed or not, with decent or low income, who have little or no control over their labor.[2] More, we argue that class and class conflict has riven society throughout the history of capitalism and, indeed, constitutes how capitalism has developed. Capital accumulation is not an automatic process initiated solely by investment. It is spurred by economic and social struggles. When force does not work, the demands of labor are often met by capitalists through the introduction of job-destroying technologies that may yield higher wages, but to fewer employees. Capitalism has penetrated agriculture in these societies, so that there is no longer a peasantry. Capitalist agriculture is almost entirely industrialized; it imposes a factory-like division of labor, hours of work and forms of supervision. Most people who work the land are either a diminishing group of small producers, seasonal laborers on middle sized farms, many of whom are immigrants, often undocumented, or workers for giant agricultural corporations. The developing world, which still has billions of peasants – small owners, tenant farmers, subsistence farmers, workers on state or privately-owned industrial farms – has experienced, over the last 40 years, an explosion in manufacturing industry. The primary site for the industrialization is China. Following the death in 1977 of Mao, the revolution's key figure, the leadership of the Communist Party began a major program of industrialization. In predominantly peasant society, its first task was to create a working class. With a population of over a billion, it adopted the most extensive enclosure in human history. The expulsion of farm labor from the countryside made the parallel effort of the British seventeenth and eighteenth centuries look like a tea party. In the 1980s and 1990s, 150 million people were driven from the land into China's major cities.[3] There they were employed in construction, factories and urban service industries, and some remained unemployed pending economic expansion. Second, under state control, the government invited foreign private capital to establish industrial plants and other enterprises. Third, the state began a program of expanded vocational and higher education to train skilled workers, scientific and technical personnel and managers. In contrast to the years following the conquest of power in 1949, the party and the government were eager to learn from the capitalist West, and to import its technologies. For example, scientists, engineers and students were sent abroad to acquire knowledge and training in their respective fields and western consultants were brought to China to train the indigenous population in management skills and technical fields.

By 2000 China was already a major global industrial power. It quickly overtook western countries in the production of textiles, shoes and clothing, but moved beyond light manufacturing to heavy machinery such as construction vehicles, electronics (computers, telephones and other equipment), petrochemicals and, within a few years, automobiles. Much of its industrial production was destined for export; its main internal market was among the growing middle class of small producers and professionals. The regime retained a substantial state sector, but the emphasis on attracting private capital marked a new phase in the country's history. China's exports to the United States and Europe far exceeded its imports. By 2010, China was supplying inexpensive cars to the growing middle class of Southeast Asia and was beginning to penetrate the African and Latin American markets.

Working and living conditions in the private sector were, in the main, abysmal. The 1990s witnessed the beginning of a steady wave of worker protest against these conditions. Workers demanded higher wages, but also fought for decent working conditions and housing. The state permitted strikes and demonstrations against private sector employers, but strictly forbid industrial action against state enterprises. Its argument was that because the Chinese state is a workers' state, workers cannot strike against themselves. Yet the past 20 years have been rife with class conflict. Since the early 1990s, official reports count the number of protests each year at about 7000; in recent years the number has reached nearly twice that amount.[4] In some instances the government and the private employers have responded by instituting reforms. In other cases, conditions have not materially improved. Workers are often required to labor for 12–16 hours a day and occasionally are forced to spend 30 hours or more on the job. Beyond the factory the government's vast urban development program has been met with resistance. As the government tore down thousands of residential buildings to make way for industrial plants and middle class housing, residents responded by what the official press termed "riots," which obliged the authorities to promise relocation to alternative housing, a promise not always fulfilled. Will the great proletarian revolution break out in China?

Following World War Two, experts left, right and center have, with numbing regularity, declared the era of class and class struggle at an end. In the advanced societies, workers enjoyed rising living standards brought about by a combination of economic growth in Western Europe and North America and the legalization of collective bargaining and state-sponsored social benefits. The strike weapon proved potent, providing upward pressure for change. While Europeans hesitate to call this phenomenon a symptom of the "bourgeoisification" of the working class, sociologists in the United Kingdom and the United States argued that workers had become "middle class" and the concept of struggle between classes was permanently overcome by welfare capitalism.[5] State and private pensions insured the continuation of economic security beyond employment; unemployment compensation effectively tided over those temporarily afflicted by recession or labor market instability. And in the years following the failure of Congress to enact national health insurance in 1949, unions incorporated health coverage in collectively-bargained contracts, and most, but not all non-union employers offered some kind of health plan to their workers in order to prevent further union organization. In addition, with the assistance of the Federal Government, many working class families were able, for the first time, to purchase single or two household homes.

The post-war boom which left millions behind lasted until about 1973. This was the year that President Richard Nixon took the United States off the gold standard in order to spur the economy, which after 1969 was stagnating. Already, in the late 1960s America was experiencing capital flight to developing countries and the US South, leaving New England, parts of the Midwest, and the Middle Atlantic states in an apparently permanent condition of decline. The new challenges to the US economy were wrought by the emergence of Japan and Europe as global economic powers and by the militancy of a considerable, highly unionized industrial labor force which fought against speedup and other productivity measures.[6] In the wake of declining productivity due, chiefly, to worker resistance, US capital went on strike. It fought the workers by destroying jobs in two ways: outsourcing and, perhaps more important, introducing a new wave of technological innovation led by computerization of manual labor. In automobile manufacturing, machine tool manufacturing, steel, textiles, oil refining and chemical production, corporations shed workers even when they did not close plants. But they closed plants, too.

Once prosperous industrial cities like Homestead, PA, Detroit, Flint, Toledo, Akron, Youngstown and many others were either suddenly or gradually deindustrialized. The remaining labor force was reduced by as much as 60–70%, even as production levels did not suffer. For example, the basic and fabricating US steel labor force was 600,000 in 1960. By 2000 it had been reduced to slightly over 100,000, with no loss of tonnage production. The big three auto corporations had employed 750,000 workers in 1970; by 2000, threatened in part by foreign imports and by their own computerization on the production lines, they had no more than 200,000 workers and continued to shed workers in the early years of the twenty-first century, even as the industry revived from its doldrums in 2010. In 1960, there were 180,000 refinery workers in the oil industry. By 2010, even as production remained high, less than 40,000 were still employed.[7]

In Europe, Spain has a 20% unemployment rate, joblessness is rising in Italy and Portugal, and in Greece the economy is close to collapse. The demands of the European Union's financial managers for severe austerity measures in these countries as a price for bailout funds for the banks and other institutions of the financial system have met with varying degrees of resistance. Trade unions and Left parties have argued that the austerity is directed, much like US austerity, at workers' living standards. Already in Greece, for example, pensions for state employees, including academics, have been cut in half. Private sector wages have also suffered and social benefits are threatened everywhere. Among these countries, Greece is experiencing ongoing protest. The parties of the Left won a clear majority in the 2012 parliamentary elections, and the coalition of the groups calling itself Syriza enjoyed a stunning victory in the January 2015 election and is now leading Greece against the austerity programs designed by the captains of finance capital.[8] In Spain, the anti-austerity party Podemos was on the verge of winning national elections there, as Pablo Iglesias had a good chance of becoming the next Prime Minister.[9] Podemos lost ground in a recent election in June of 2016, but it is too soon to know if they can regain the ground that they lost.[10] The French elections resulted in the first Socialist government in 18 years, a victory that can only be ascribed to resistance to the austerity program of the previous Center-Right government of Sarkozy. Still, it remains to be seen whether the new Socialist regime will chart an independent course or submit to the harsh conditions set by the European Union's managers and by the conservative German Chancellor. Recent events have revealed that the Socialist government is suffering from internal strife, as strikes by workers resisting changes in the country's labor laws have significantly complicated the ability of the Socialist government to mediate class conflict.[11] Italy's technocratic regime that has been installed to administer austerity is highly unstable. From the Right as well as the Left, there have been challenges to the idea that the people must pay for the perfidy of the banks and other institutions of finance capital.

But America was not immune from protest against austerity from below. In 2006 a million marchers took to the streets of American cities and towns to demand immigration reform.[12] The protesters, who were composed, largely, of undocumented as well as legal immigrants, believed that their action would force the Federal government to enact a plan to legalize 11 million undocumented immigrants. Indeed, the administration of the Republican president, George W. Bush, called for changes in both statute and the practice of government expulsion. But Congress was slow to act. The marchers could be confident that a new Democratic president and a Democratic Congress would heed their call. However, the 2008 Democratic sweep of the White House and Congress failed to fulfill the immigrant dream of citizenship. The newly elected president Barack Obama did not view his victory as a mandate for change. From the start, he assumed a defensive posture, as if he had barely squeaked through, despite a commanding majority in the poll. Most of the undocumented were working as low-paid laborers in various service industries or in the hugely important agricultural sector and were no burden on the public treasury. Nor did citizens clamor to take dishwashing jobs in restaurants or opportunities to pick apples, vegetables, strawberries and cotton. But these facts failed to deter the administration from undertaking a fierce campaign of deportation that far exceeded that of the previous Bush era. Indeed, according to *The Nation* magazine, Obama expanded an existing deportation program by 3,600 percent.[13]

Spring 2011 was a season of global discontent. In quick succession mass demonstrations in Tunisia, Egypt, Libya and other Arab countries removed long-ruling dictators from their thrones.[14] The democratic impulse ran deep among all subordinate classes of society. But US media all but ignored the working class strikes and demonstrations that preceded and accompanied the protests in the center of Cairo.[15] For these media, the so-called "Arab Spring" was clearly a middle class series of events. If there was any difference within the movement it was termed religious versus secular, the army against the democrats, but the class struggle was conveniently left out. The fact that many workers walked out from the workplace and took to the streets was due, largely, to years of political and social repression and impossibly low wages reinforced by state-run trade unions as much as the government. Egypt, the largest country in North Africa and the Middle East, faced the problem of a military take-over that threatened to undermine and ultimately cancel the effect of liberal democratic elections, and the re-introduction of anti-working class force. In an unstable situation in 2012 it remained to be seen whether liberal democracy and an autonomous labor movement would survive.

After four years of economic slump, a new movement of protest and resistance emerged in the United States. The first sign of struggle occurred in Madison, Wisconsin. Following the shellacking sustained by the Democrats in the 2010 elections where the Republicans captured the House of Representatives and many statehouses and state legislatures changed hands as well, the newly elected right-wing Wisconsin governor Scott Walker, following the lead of his Indiana counterpart, Mitch Daniels, proposed abolition of collective bargaining for state employees, except on wages. In the spring of 2011, the labor movement, students and community activists responded with mass demonstrations at the state capital, including an occupation of the capital. It was not a one-day demonstration. Day after day up to 125,000 demonstrators showed up at the capital; teachers left their classrooms and students at the university stopped attending classes. Fourteen Democratic senators left town, depriving Walker of a quorum to pass the legislation.[16] As the movement gained momentum the Democrats proposed to recall four Republican senators and the governor. The forward march of direct action was diverted to electoral strategy. The Democrats regained a senate majority but the recall failed to topple the governor. But, after years of torpor, a section of the American labor movement had removed the scales from its eyes, for at least a moment. The Wisconsin struggle, which failed to reverse the anti-collective bargaining legislation, reverberated throughout the country. In Ohio, in a referendum, voters repealed a similar measure as Labor flexed its considerable muscle.

In September 2011, the class movement from below entered a new phase. Occupy Wall Street, without offering a list of specific demands, occupied Zuccotti Park, a sliver of land in the Wall Street area. The occupation, which gathered mostly young people, many of whom were unemployed college graduates, advanced only a single slogan, "We are the 99%," and opposed themselves to the "1%," who they claimed ran the economic and political institutions of the globe and had ruthlessly imposed a series of bank bailouts that would be paid for with working class and middle class tax dollars, a merciless transfer of wealth from the 99% to the 1%. A few weeks later the 200 occupiers, now supplemented by at least 500 others, attempted to block the Brooklyn Bridge. The demonstration was quickly met with a cordon of New York City riot police that beat some of the protesters and arrested more than 70 of them. The exhibition of police coercion electrified youth and activists throughout the United States and spread around the globe. Within days at least 110 American cities and smaller communities had Occupy movements: Boston, Philadelphia, Chicago, Saint Louis, Detroit, Los Angeles, San Francisco, Portland, Seattle and Providence, among others. In Oakland, dockers who were members of the International Longshore and Warehouse Union shut down the port in sympathy with the occupation, and in New York a demonstration and march of 20,000 pro-occupiers, many of whom were organized union members, filled the streets of the downtown area.[17]

Occupy movements sprouted in some Canadian, European and Southeast Asian cities such as London, Toronto and Hong Kong, and in Latin America in Mexico City, Santiago and Buenos Aires, among others. By late fall, 2011, the class nature of global power was exposed to public view. Occupy Wall Street organizers resisted calls from liberal supporters to advance specific demands, enter the electoral arena, and negotiate with city and state authorities. President Obama expressed sympathy with the movement, but did not come to the Washington Occupy site, let alone any of the more than 100 others. Mayors in some leading cities hesitated to break the occupation until in late November a conference call was convened among 18 mayors of cities where the occupation was particularly effective and visible. They decided, probably advised by the US Attorney General, to apply force to disperse the sites. Accordingly, under the pretext of security and sanitary concerns, a coordinated police action was implemented and dozens of sites were cleared. The Occupy movement did not entirely disappear but it was set back, in part, because the organizers did not seem to have a "plan B" to meet the eventuality that they would be removed from public space.

What differentiates the Occupy movement from other social movements? In the first place, the activists remained skeptical about suggestions made by their liberal supporters that they frame a specific series of demands. Their suspicion was motivated by a reading of the history of American social movements. Feminist, black freedom and environmental movements of recent vintage have sought amelioration of very pressing but relatively easy grievances for the power structure to address. Although the mass struggle for black civil rights was conducted over several decades of the twentieth century, its resolution was not genuine equality but two significant but limited legislative victories. The Voting Rights Act prohibited by law discriminatory state measures to exclude blacks from the vote. These included literary tests, poll taxes and outright coercion. The Civil Rights Act was more far-reaching. For the first time since Reconstruction, the Federal government would enforce employment, housing and public accommodation discrimination, and the right of citizens to organize for their interests without facing the organized violence of the state. Similarly, women fought for and, in 1973, won abortion rights and anti-discrimination measures at the Federal level on questions of employment. But abortion rights were granted by the Supreme Court rather than Congress. In Roe v. Wade, Justice Harry Blackmun, writing for the majority, invoked the privacy doctrine, not the equal protection under the 14th amendment, which Ruth Bader Ginsburg argued would have been a stronger rationale because it would have recognized women as a class.

The publication of Rachel Carson's *Silent Spring* in 1962 was the intellectual event that spurred the emergence of the contemporary environmental movement. Within a decade, activists in Greenpeace and other organizations engaged in direct action against polluters, especially power companies that used fossil fuels, the US Navy, public institutions and some politicians. Their force was sufficiently potent to influence the Nixon administration to establish an Environmental Protection Agency with some enforcement powers. In subsequent years, the Agency faced strong opposition from conservatives and some unions, especially in the energy sector that was invested in coal and oil. As scientific evidence mounted in the 1980s and 1990s that showed the planet was experiencing severe climate change (global warming, sea level rise, tornadoes, drought, etc.) that would eventually threaten the supply of food and potable water and rain physical destruction on entire communities, the subject became a major public issue. The Right greeted the ecological crisis with systematic denial. The Left remained divided: while it did not repudiate the claim of global deterioration, it remained preoccupied with issues of economic justice, the definition of which grew narrower after 2000 as the employment and financial crises became endemic to all industrially advanced societies. As always, the progressive liberals vacillated between their reliance on political parties which they believed could enact legislative remedies, and institutions such as the United Nations which enjoyed the legitimacy of international law and public opinion.

The brilliant success of the political center was to persuade all of the major social movements, including the disability movement, to follow the playbook of the unions. Even though their most successful results had been won by direct action rather than electoral politics, at least initially, one by one they formed caucuses within the Democratic Party at the national and state levels. While not entirely renouncing direct action, especially in times of dire emergency, they largely surrendered their independence. Consequently, as the Democrats moved to the center, they pulled the unions, civil rights, feminist and environmental organizations away from confrontation toward compromises that frequently amounted to defeat. For example, as black and Latino joblessness officially grew to double digits even as the general unemployment rates were about 8% or less, the black and Latino organizations did not entertain the idea that they should learn from the example of Madison Labor or the Occupy movement. They had become so tied to the electoral and legislative process that placing their faces against the wheel became virtually unthinkable. While Martin Luther King Jr. remained an icon and events like the Montgomery bus boycott, the Birmingham mass demonstrations that faced down police violence, the March on Washington for Jobs and Freedom and the fight for unionization of Memphis garbage workers are worn proudly by the leadership, these organizations have largely remained passive as poverty has spread throughout many black and Latino communities. Nor have the women's organizations been able to counter the steady deterioration of abortion at the state and local level. And at the global and local level the struggle for sustainable ecology is at a standstill, even as the icecaps melt, incidents of climate instability multiply, and unseasonable drought spreads throughout the American Midwest that threatened the 2012 corn crop and other grains. Efforts to reach a global agreement to stem the deleterious efforts of climate change have failed because some of the leading powers like the United States and the emerging economies like China have effectively vetoed the entreaties of scientists and activists to heed the call to action.

The failure of the Bernie Sanders campaign to topple the Clinton–Obama machine that dominates the Democratic Party is the most recent example of how the political center continues to thwart challenges from the Left. In some ways, the Sanders campaign provided an avenue for Occupy Wall Street to enter mainstream politics, but the attempt failed. It might be, as Robert Reich has recently argued, that the Left needs to seriously consider once again a third party, like the Green Party led by Jill Stein, as a more effective vehicle for progressive change, because the Clinton campaign proved unable to hold onto voters in the rustbelt states who voted for Obama in 2012, then flipped to Trump in 2016. There is pressure on Bernie Sanders to lead such a movement during the next cycle of elections after 2016.[18] In the meantime, the Trump administration seeks to push through legislation and policy changes that will continue to redistribute wealth upwards, betraying working-class voters who were persuaded that he was the best candidate to take on the twin powers of Washington and Wall Street.[19] In all likelihood Trump's proposals will worsen the economic crisis that led to the discontent that put him in the White House as he seeks to repeal the Dodd-Frank Wall Street Reform and Consumer Protection Act, which includes the Volker rule that prevents investment banks from speculating with other people's money.[20]

Class politics extends beyond the shop floor. What is lacking today in most industrialized countries are middle class and working class movements that include, but are not limited to, workplace and other economic issues. For example, the quality of public education in the United States has deteriorated over the past 20 years. Of course, budget cuts play a significant role in producing bloated classrooms, frayed facilities and teacher layoffs. But the problems of schooling are evident in the curriculum, too. Many urban high schools lack laboratories, computers and other basic technologies of science. The shortage of qualified math teachers has forced schools to assign humanities and social science teachers to fill the gap and they have been unable to offer advanced placement math such as calculus or even trigonometry. And the issues go beyond science and math. As is well known, Texas, whose politics have become extreme right, sets the standard for textbooks of all sorts; most publishers simply will not commission texts that take controversial positions on history, or other social science subjects. Thus, labor history is virtually absent in high school history textbooks. The struggles of the black freedom movement, if addressed at all, are cleansed and the key achievements of feminism and ecology are treated with deafening silence. In the wake of this retrograde situation there is no important movement for curriculum reform in the United States.

Given the strong tendency of some state administrations to even deny the climate crisis, the incidence of humanly caused environmental disasters is concentrated in states and regions where measures to ameliorate, if not solve, the environmental crisis are systematically refused. We can see the consequences of this refusal in Louisiana and other Gulf States where Hurricane Katrina and subsequent tornadoes in Alabama and Mississippi resulted in a level of devastation of lives and resources that was due largely to neglect. As recently as 2015, New Orleans' lower ninth ward is still in ruins, more than nine years after Hurricane Katrina.[21] The effects of Hurricane Irene are still being felt on the Atlantic coast. Joplin, MO, was all but flattened by a brief tornado, and some communities of New York State are still digging their way out of the destruction wrought in the wake of Hurricane Irene, in 2011. In 2012, New Jersey, New York and Connecticut suffered the horrendous effects of Hurricane Sandy, an event that left coastal communities devastated and proved that government agencies were ill-prepared to deal with the disaster. The class dimension of these disasters is evident: most communities that were the most deeply affected have working class majorities, often black.

Finally, the financial crisis of 2007 is still with us. The cutting edge of the crisis was in housing mortgages. As is well known, from the 1990s banks were encouraged to make loans to borrowers with little or no equity. They were made at variable interest rates and many required the lender to pay only on the interest rate. In time, the bubble burst: the borrowers were hit suddenly with exorbitant payment requirements, even as the value of the property crashed. As many as four million homes were in payment arrears. The borrowers found themselves with a debt that was greater than the value of the houses. Some fled the homes, leaving only the keys behind. Most were served with eviction notices. Although the Federal government started a rescue program to prevent evictions, its terms were so stringent that only 700,000 borrowers were saved. More than three million houses went on the market at severely reduced prices in comparison to their last purchase prices. Home prices fell precipitously in the midst of America's first depression since 1939. It takes no Einstein to realize that most of those who lost their homes were working class.[22]

Like Katrina and other "natural disasters" of recent vintage, the working class has paid the price for the crisis, and the middle class – small farmers, some professionals, public employees – are not far behind. With mass layoffs in the public sector and an economy that is all but at a standstill, living standards have plunged; there is a housing "shortage" even as millions of homes are vacant. Homelessness among families with working parents as well as the unemployed has become one of the consequences of the housing crisis. Still, the Bush and Obama administrations and most European states bailed out the banks as their top priority. In short, with more than 14 million officially unemployed and stagnant wages, a weak labor movement and social movements that are tied to conventional electoral politics, the situation worsens with each passing day. And the workers and middle class pay for the profits and income of the financial corporations and the very rich. Moreover, even as the stock and commodities markets boomed and the Obama administration declared a recovery, good jobs remained hard to find for credentialed workers as well as those with less schooling. And the jobless rate remains stubbornly high.

There is good reason to believe that the long night of denial is reaching its end. What is missing are the forces that are prepared to reverse the one-sided class war being waged against the people by a tiny formation of financiers and their political supplicants. It is open to question whether the putative forces of opposition are prepared to join the battle. At this juncture it is premature to make predictions, but what is certain is that there are signs from the base of society that we are in the winter of our discontent.

This reader is, in many ways, unique.

Notes

1 See Martin Glaberman, *Wartime Strikes* (Bewick Editions, 1980), Art Preis, *Labor's Giant Step* (Pathfinder Press, 1972), Jeremy Brecher's *Strike!* (PM Press, 2014), Mario Tronti, *Operai e Capitale [Workers and Capital]* (Einaudi, 1996), George Lipsitz, *Rainbow and Midnight* (University of Illinois Press, 1994), Michael Roberts, *Tell Tchaikovsky the News* (Duke University Press, 2014), and Stanley Aronowitz, *False Promises* (Duke University Press, 1992) and the *Death and Life of American Labor* (Verso, 2014).

2 The underlying assumption of the contents of this reader is the classical three-class model of social structure, based on the social relations of production suggested by Karl Marx and many who follow his perspective. We want to call attention to the relatively recent work of one of the editors, Stanley Aronowitz, who in his book *How Class Works* (Yale, 2003) argues, from a framework of social and

political power, that classes emerge when a social formation – women, racialized groups, workers and so forth – forces society to address their demands. Aronowitz also claims that under these conditions "classes" emerge and disappear as classes if they fail to impose their demands or, having achieved a measure of success, are re-integrated into the prevailing power relations.

3 See Pun Ngai, *Made in China: Women Factory Workers in a Global Workplace* (Duke University Press, 2005).

4 See the article "Behind China's Wildcat Strike Wave" in *Labor Notes*, http://www.labornotes. org/blogs/2014/10/review-behind-chinas-wildcat-strike-wave, the *Atlantic Magazine* article "Rising Protests in China" http://www.theatlantic.com/photo/2012/02/rising-protests-in-china/100247/, and "China's Workers Are Getting Restless" in *Bloomberg Business* http://www. bloomberg.com/bw/articles/2014-10-15/chinas-workers-are-getting-restless

5 See Ralf Dahrendorf, *Class and Class Conflict in Industrial Society* (Stanford University Press, 1959), for a good example of this point of view.

6 See *Rebel Rank and File* edited by Brenner et al. (Verso, 2010).

7 See David Brody, *Steel Workers in America: The Non Union Era* (University of Illinois Press, 1988), and in the *New York Times*, "The Wage that Meant Middle Class," http://www.nytimes. com/2008/04/20/weekinreview/20uchitelle.html?pagewanted=all&_r=0

8 See the article published in *The Guardian*, "Anti-Austerity Syriza Party Sweeps to Stunning Victory," http://www.theguardian.com/world/2015/jan/25/greece-election-vote-austerity-leftwing-syriza-eu

9 See the coverage in *The Nation* magazine: http://www.thenation.com/article/195129/can-podemos-win-spain#

10 See the recent coverage in *The Guardian* here: https://www.theguardian.com/commentisfree/ 2016/jun/28/podemos-spanish-elections-spain-anti-austerity-party and here: https://www. thenation.com/article/has-spains-podemos-party-squandered-its-prospects/

11 See the coverage in *The Guardian* here: https://www.theguardian.com/law/2016/jun/04/what-are-french-strikes-about-and-will-they-affect-euro-2016. See also coverage in the *New York Times* here: http://www.nytimes.com/2016/05/13/world/europe/france-hollande-no-confidence-vote.html?_r=0

12 See coverage in the *Washington Post*, http://www.washingtonpost.com/wp-dyn/content/ article/2006/03/25/AR2006032501352.html

13 See coverage in *The Nation* magazine here: https://www.thenation.com/article/the-deportation-machine-obama-built-for-president-trump/

14 See Paul Mason, *Why It's Still Kicking Off Everywhere* (Verso, 2013).

15 See Michael Yates' piece in the *New Labor Forum* on this issue. http://newlaborforum.cuny. edu/2013/03/06/we-are-the-99-the-political-arithmetic-of-revolt/

16 For more on the situation in Wisconsin, see Michael Yates' book, *Wisconsin Uprising* (Monthly Review Press, 2012).

17 For more on the Occupy movement see Todd Gitlin, *Occupy Nation* (It Books, Original Edition, 2012).

18 See coverage in *Salon* here: http://www.salon.com/2016/03/27/robert_reich_this_is_a_working_class_revolt_partner/

19 See the coverage in the *New York Times* here: https://www.nytimes.com/2016/12/02/opinion/ seduced-and-betrayed-by-donald-trump.html?_r=0

20 See the coverage in the *Financial Times* here: https://www.ft.com/content/7dec9a66-faa2-11e6-9516-2d969e0d3b65

21 See the coverage in *The Guardian* here: https://www.theguardian.com/us-news/2015/jan/23/ new-orleans-lower-ninth-ward-condos-gentrification

22 See David Dayen's reporting for Bill Moyers on this topic here: http://billmoyers. com/2015/02/14/needless-default/

How to Read This Book

Michael J. Roberts

What makes this anthology unique in relation to other readers that address the issue of class is its multi-disciplinary approach. We have brought together texts drawn from three distinct epistemological traditions of academic research: political economy, social history and cultural studies. Each of these theoretical orientations provides a particular way to understand the phenomenon of class. The three main parts of this reader, The Working Class, The Middle Class and The Capitalist Class, include chapters drawn from all three of these theoretical orientations, although the perspective of political economy dominates The Capitalist Class, while the orientations of social history and cultural studies constitute the majority of chapters in The Working Class and The Middle Class. We also approach class in terms of intersectionality by including chapters by David Roediger, Nan Enstad, Mariarosa Dalla Costa and Selma James, and Jonathan Cutler that look at the ways in which class is mediated by race and gender and vice versa.

The most distinctive aspect of our book is that we embed the concept of class within the larger theoretical framework of the labor question, which means that class must be understood in terms of conflicts over and about work. As Hannah Arendt argued in her definitive text, *The Human Condition*, work is primarily characterized by the relationship between rulers and ruled. For us, this phenomenon must be included in what counts as class. Scholars and commentators who conceptualize class in terms of income and consumption frequently ignore the workplace and the asymmetrical power relations that structure it. This is a serious mistake. We agree with women's-studies scholar Kathi Weeks, who argues in her recent book, *The Problem with Work*, that "political theorists tend to be more interested in our lives as citizens and noncitizens, legal subjects and bearers of rights, consumers and spectators, religious devotees and family members, than in our daily lives as workers" (p. 2). In short, the reification of work permeates our culture. This book should be seen as contributing to the project of bringing the critique of work back into the analysis of class, a point of view which has been neglected in recent years. A critique of work not only questions the way in which work is organized, it also *imagines the possible liberation from work*.

One of the principal theoretical perspectives emphasized in this reader is that class, as a phenomenon, must be understood as a *relationship* rather than as a location. This way of looking at class is explained in great detail by E.P. Thompson in his classic work, *The Making of the English Working Class*. Thompson's perspective has provided a significant influence upon how we have organized this anthology. In terms of the organization of this reader, we have constructed The Working Class and The Capitalist Class parts so that certain chapters from each should be read together as a means to get a flavor for how class must be understood as a relationship constituted by the conflict between labor and capital. In particular, the chapters in The Working Class by E.P. Thompson, Mike Davis, Art Preis, Michael J. Roberts, Jonathan Cutler, Ryan Moore and Robin D.G. Kelley should be read alongside the chapters in The Capitalist Class by Sven Beckert, Harry Braverman, Rhonda Levine, Benjamin Klinne Hunnicutt and Jefferson Cowie. Other selections in all three parts complement these ones as well as move in directions that provide unique ways to look at class in *cultural* terms.

In addition to the inter-disciplinary character of this reader, we have organized the reader so as to follow a rough chronology of key moments or periods in the history of class relations in the United States. We lead off The Working Class and The Capitalist Class with selections that look at the origins of capitalism in Western Europe, then move our focus to the US experience where we include chapters that examine important developments in the history of class struggle in the United States including: the conflict over the emergence of the wage-labor system in the early nineteenth century, the relationship between slavery and industrialization and its impact on race relations, the intersection between class and gender in the division of labor, the emergence of the fight for the 8-hour workday, the tumultuous period known as the "Gilded Age," the emergence of scientific management and the concomitant struggle between capitalists and workers over control of the shop-floor, the political fight that produced the New Deal set of legislation followed by the Taft–Hartley Act in 1947, the influence of the counterculture on the labor movement in the 1960s, the corporate assault on the labor movement beginning in the 1970s, and automation and the jobless future. We then turn to globalization and the global crisis of capitalism in the twenty-first century in the chapter by Foster and McChesney on the global reserve army of labor. This chapter complements issues that we introduced in the general introduction, namely the emergence of a new form of class conflict in China and the explosion of the Arab Spring and the global Occupy Wall Street movement as responses to the meltdown of the global financial services industry. While most of the selections focus on the American experience, we have pointed beyond the US context by including selections from Kristin Lawler, Siegfried Kracauer and Serge Mallet that consider the contexts of Europe. It is our contention that a theoretical perspective which gives historical context to these new developments is crucial for an adequate understanding of the contemporary global capitalist system and the changing class relations that we are experiencing today. Below we discuss the three theoretical orientations that constitute the unique perspective of this reader.

The tradition of political economy situates the concept of class within a framework that seeks to understand the macro-structural dynamics of capitalist development. The selections in this reader that exemplify the point of view of political economy include the chapters by Harry Braverman, Karl Marx, Rhonda Levine, John Bellamy Foster and Robert W. McChesney, Teresa Ghilarducci, Stanley Aronowitz and William DiFazio, and Stanley Aronowitz. Political economy is necessary to, if not sufficient for, an adequate understanding of class because unlike many theoretical perspectives on the issues of class and "stratification," political economy makes explicit what these paradigms do not: namely, the capitalist-economic *context* within which class distinctions are created and reproduced. Many academic treatments of class as stratification discuss the issues in terms of "occupational ladders" that seem to exist independently of the particular dynamics of a capitalist economic system. In other words, the treatments of class that define the phenomenon in terms of stratification reify the distribution of wealth and income in both ahistorical and universalistic terms. The specific dynamics of capitalism are ignored in mainstream discussions of class that discuss the issue in vague generalities like "upper class," "middle class" and "lower class," as if all societies irrespective of place and time exhibit these characteristics. Perhaps the best example of this problem is in the field of sociology where the reification of class found its most sophisticated form within structural functionalism, including the now canonical text by Davis and Moore, "Some Principles of Stratification" (*American Sociological Review*, Vol. 10, No. 2, 1944, pp. 242–249).

Part of what separates political economy (PE) from mainstream economics is that PE seeks to identify the specific features of capitalism that separate it from other modes of production, i.e. feudalism and socialism, at the same time as it explains how capitalism is rent with contradictions that keep the system in a constant state of crisis. Perhaps most important for the purposes of this reader, PE seeks to show how capitalism creates the conditions for its own transcendence through contradictions that are internal to, and constitutive of its development. As Marx argues in the *Grundrisse*, capitalists seek to use labor-saving technology to control workers, increase surplus value and expand the dynamics of capitalist accumulation to all corners of the globe not yet exposed to capitalism. The irony of this development is that this very same technology makes possible the radical reduction of time spent at work, which meant for Marx the possibility of a vast expansion of the so-called "leisure class." Capitalist development points toward a future where robots will be doing more and more of the work in advanced "post-industrial" societies.

The possibility of working less depends upon the course of the class struggle, specifically whether or not workers can successfully fight for the shorter hours of work, which is an historical and political question that cannot be answered by an analysis which seeks to examine the dynamics of capitalist accumulation. In other words, a major theoretical problem at the heart of PE is the framing of labor as a dependent variable: capitalist development, it is often argued, happens at the expense of workers, who by definition are constituted theoretically as a mere category or variable in a framework which situates labor as an instrument used by capital. The theoretical framework of PE is unable to explain how workers constitute themselves as a class that opposes capitalist interests and the logic of capitalist accumulation. This brings us to the second epistemological perspective in this book: history.

Social history addresses the main problem with the intellectual tradition of PE: namely, its inability to explain how working people have responded and contributed to the development and history of capitalism on the one hand, and how capitalists have constituted themselves as a class opposed to workers on the other hand. In the tradition of PE, a major theoretical problem has been its neglect of everyday life, especially the ways in which working people and the power elite make sense of their situation inside capitalist social relations. Intellectuals working in the tradition of social history and labor history have sought to fill in the gaps created by PE through looking at the particular ways in which working people have played an important role in the various phases of capitalist development and the ways in which the capitalist class, in turn, has constituted itself in opposition to the labor movement. The chapters in this volume that are drawn from history include those by E.P. Thompson, Sven Beckert, Lawrence Glickman, David Roediger, Roy Rosenzweig, Nan Enstad, Robin D.G. Kelley, Benjamin Kline Hunnicutt and Jonathan Cutler.

The main focus in these chapters is on how class is something that "happens" in history, as individuals become aware of themselves as members of a class that exists in antagonism to another class: workers on the one side, capitalists on the other. What is crucial about these selections from social and labor history is that they reveal how the development and history of capitalism does not produce class relations in any direct, or determined way as if a *telos* were present in history that directs the classes toward their destiny independently of the actions of actual individuals. In other words, capitalist development does not produce classes in a logical, predetermined fashion. Historians like E.P. Thompson have been careful to note that classes can only emerge if individuals develop a sense of class consciousness. The selections from E.P. Thompson, David Roediger and Lawrence Glickman focus on how workers came to understand themselves as a "class," while the selections from Sven Beckert, Rhonda Levine and Jefferson Cowie look at how the capitalist class developed its identity as a capitalist class against the interests and actions of the working class. Class can also be undone, as the selection by Ryan Moore demonstrates, when workers lose their class consciousness for complicated reasons having to do with culture.

Other selections by Stanley Aronowitz, Siegfried Kracauer, Magali Larson, Andrew Hoberk, Serge Mallet, Justin Myers, and Andrew Ross examine the position of the middle class in relation to the working and capitalist classes, and how the middle class can, under certain historical conditions, identify with either workers or capitalists. Thus, while capitalist development has included the tendency to "proletarianize" the middle class, this does not mean that individuals from the middle class will automatically lose their sense of middle-class consciousness. In short, class consciousness is an historical phenomenon that can never be deduced from the structural location of individuals within the division of labor structured by capitalism. Class has a cultural dimension that is relatively independent of the economic dimensions in a given social formation of capitalism. This brings us to the epistemological orientation of cultural studies.

In some ways, cultural studies evolved out of labor history, especially the work of E.P. Thompson, but cultural studies emphasizes the aspects of everyday life that much of labor history has neglected, which followed from the narrow focus upon the institution of the labor union. Understanding the culture of the working class required an expansion of the field of vision beyond unions. Cultural studies seeks to look at the everyday life of workers in leisure spaces, in schools, in the political formation of the state and the family. Chapters in this volume that draw on cultural studies include selections from Robin D.G. Kelley, Nan Enstad, Michael J. Roberts, Ryan Moore, Roy Rosenzweig, Kristin Lawler and Sven Beckert. Here the focus is on the cultural dimension of class, namely the formation of the capitalist work ethic and the struggle against work that constitutes much of working-class culture. Cultural studies examines the ways in which changes in the political economy are handled in cultural terms by the working class, the middle class and the capitalist class.

Most important for the purposes of this book, cultural studies insists that class struggle is never fought *exclusively* on the economic terrain. Of course class struggle *is* about the fight over control of the labor process, the conflict over wages and the distribution of wealth more generally. However, the perspective of cultural studies has opened up a new dimension for analysis – the cultural dimension of class struggle – which is to say that language and lifestyle practices are also the site, or terrain, of class struggle. This leads to the other important contribution to cultural studies, literary criticism. The chapter by Andrew Hoberk in The Middle Class is a good example of how to study the phenomenon of class from the reading of novels. Among the novelists Hoberk examines as a way to understand the class consciousness of the middle class is Ayn Rand. David Roediger's chapter in this volume looks at how the language used to describe class distinctions changed as the United States entered the period of industrialization, while E.P. Thompson looks at how the phenomenon of *time itself* became the terrain of class struggle. The chapters by Roberts and Moore look at how forms of popular music are intimately linked to class struggle, but from different historical periods. The selection from Kristin Lawler looks at how the political-economic strategy of austerity in Europe must be understood as an attack on working-class culture. By bringing together the social sciences and the humanities, cultural studies provides a powerful framework for the investigation of class that fills in the gaps left by conventional research.

It is through such a multi-disciplinary approach that we seek to provide an alternative, more historically oriented and comprehensive way of examining the phenomenon of class, especially in light of the current crisis in global capitalism and the new forms of resistance we see today. We hope that our reader will provide a powerful theoretical orientation that will help activists and students who are struggling to make sense of the current crisis in our global capitalist system.

PART ONE
The Working Class

CHAPTER 1

Representing the Working Class

Michael J. Roberts

The sometimes confusing array of ways in which the class relations in society are interpreted is not only a problem in the news media and the other various representations produced by the culture industry. The problem exists in the social sciences as well. In the social sciences, research on the American working class has been, to a large extent, framed by the contrast between the conceptual framework of historical materialism (the western Marxist tradition) and the dominant paradigm in social science, which includes foundational texts by Max Weber and Emile Durkheim. In the theoretical framework of historical materialism, the concept of class must be deployed within the wider philosophical and political context concerning the normative issue that is sometimes referred to as the "labor question", whereas for conventional social scientists working in the dominant tradition the theoretical context that frames the analysis of the concept "class" plays a much more limiting role. In conventional social-science discourse, the issue of class is often distilled down to questions of description, method and accuracy of measurement. Indeed, the sometimes contentious discursive exchanges between those working within the framework of historical materialism and their interlocutors in the social sciences frequently get displaced through, and encoded by, academic debates concerning methodological procedures and techniques for measurement of empirical phenomena.

In conventional social science, the concept of class is typically separated, analytically, from the concept of work so that class is understood as an *outcome*, in order to frame the issue more generally within a theoretical context that is designed to map patterns of inequality in distributions of wealth and income.[1] In historical materialism, on the other hand, class is conceptually fused together with work, so that class is conceptualized in terms of *activity* rather than outcome. This difference approaches what Thomas Kuhn, in the *Structure of Scientific Revolutions*, refers to as a paradigmatic incommensurability, because the manifestation of these differences reveals that in contrast to the framework of historical materialism, social scientists working within the dominant paradigm deny the existence of a working class that exists in antagonism with a capitalist or ruling class. A relationship of that kind simply does not appear in the research results produced by the dominant paradigm in social science.

To return to the normative dimension, it is also important to note that historical materialism does not break from the humanities, because to focus on production and work involves an examination of the *un*freedom which pervades the workplace in capitalist

Class: The Anthology, First Edition. Edited by Stanley Aronowitz and Michael J. Roberts.
© 2018 Stanley Aronowitz and Michael J. Roberts. Published 2018 by John Wiley & Sons Ltd.

social formations. The critique of unfreedom in the workplace animates much of the research on the working class within the paradigm of historical materialism. While class and class struggle are core concepts for those working in the Marxist tradition, it is important to note that historical materialism is not itself a unified discourse in the social sciences, as there are several distinct intellectual trajectories that have developed in response to particular empirical problems. Failure to acknowledge these distinctions leads many conventional social scientists to incorrectly claim that the Marxist point of view suffers from crude economic determinism. Part of the problem is that conventional social science relies almost exclusively upon a reading of the *Communist Manifesto* to construct its understanding of the Marxist concept of class, ignoring all of Marx's more nuanced analyses of class relations and intra-class fractions, like *The Eighteenth Brumaire of Louis Bonaparte* and *The Class Struggles in France*, to say nothing of the sophisticated appropriation of Georg Hegel in the *Grundrisse* and the three volumes of *Capital: A Critique of Political Economy*. A truncated reading of Marx leads Weberians like John R. Hall, the editor of *Reworking Class*, to claim that "the once dominant Marxist theory that predicted a historically decisive struggle in the capitalist world between two classes – workers and owners – is widely recognized as inadequate" (p. 1). This volume should be seen as an attempt both to provide an alternative view of class as well as to correct some misinterpretations of the Marxist view on class.

I

On the one hand, *what* is being studied differs from one paradigm of social research to another. For reasons having to do with methodological training in their disciplines, professional social scientists working in the dominant paradigm tend to ignore both the asymmetrical structural relations that constitute the labor *process* as well as the history of the transformation of the social relations of production. Instead, the preferred objects constituted for analysis are income, education and status levels – what mainstream sociologists refer to collectively as socio-economic status or "SES" for short. SES is the central organizing concept in the field of inequality studies in conventional social science, referred to as "social stratification." It is important to emphasize that the modifying term "economic," in the concept SES, is severely restricted to only indicate levels of income and wealth, phenomena that are said to allow for the expanded exercise of power in the *marketplace*. The legacy of narrowing the viewpoint of stratification studies to the space of markets was forged by Max Weber's attempts to merge sociological analyses with the marginal utility theory developed by the Austrian School of Economics, which included important figures such as Carl Menger, Friedrich von Wieser and Eugen Bohm von Bawerk. The reification of market interactions within conventional social science means that most stratification research focuses exclusively upon lifestyle differences, "life chances," and the unequal distribution of resources, but *not* on how wealth is produced in the first place. Weber himself argues in volume two of *Economy and Society* that "class situation is…ultimately market situation…the market is the decisive moment…" (1978, p. 928). This difference in orientation regarding the concept of class leads Weberians to construe class in terms of questions such as "What does an individual have?," and "What is an individual likely to obtain?", whereas in the tradition of historical materialism the questions are "What does the person do?", "What is the individual likely to do?" and "Will they maintain or change the existing social relations?"

In short, what happens at work during production is outside of the ordinary conceptual framework in the social studies of class inequality. For example, the so-called "occupational ladder" theorized by conventional sociology is understood as a continuum of social *status* ranks leading from one rung of the ladder up to the next all the way from bottom to top, leaving no conceptual room for understanding a break in the structure of the ladder that would separate individuals into distinct classes (and class fractions) with contradictory interests based upon their relation to the process of production as well as their opposing relationship to one another. Viewing class in terms of a status location on a continuous vertical ladder involves a conceptual process that constructs the phenomenon "class" as a *thing* that can be located in social space, whereas in historical materialism class is understood as an antagonistic *relationship* that takes place in time, as a phenomenon that *happens*. The difference between viewing class as a thing and understanding class as a relationship that develops historically turns upon epistemological differences that orient the direction and content of social research. This dissimilarity between the concept of *class* in historical materialism and the social-science concept of *SES* is only partly explained by methodological differences due to the preference for historical analysis among Marxists, and the preference for survey research and statistical methodology among conventional sociologists. The differences go *beyond* the contrast in methodology. Class and SES are notions that differ from one another in the sense described by Thomas Kuhn, where competing concepts exist within a larger context of incommensurable theoretical paradigms. In short, the issues at hand regarding class versus status are not reducible to questions regarding the proper procedures of measurement. Measuring is ultimately not the issue.

Rather than beginning and focusing the analysis upon the conditions of poverty and inequality (outcomes) as in the conventional paradigm, the tradition of research in historical materialism begins with laboring *activity* in the analysis of capitalist society because this way of fusing the concepts of class and work places an emphasis on the *agency* of individuals. By setting the focus on the practices of working people, the researcher is able to reveal the ways in which workers exercise a certain amount of power within the struggles that condition the forms of the workplace and their everyday life outside the workplace. The conventional focus on class as an outcome, however, implicitly assumes a relative disempowerment of workers, since they are mapped onto the bottom of the distribution of wealth, power and status. Mapping and measuring class as outcome conceals and silences working-class agents.

Exploring the region beyond the "market" is the *raison d'être* for historical materialism. This is not to say that Marxists ignore market dynamics, especially labor market formations, but to ignore the moment of production results in a one-sided point of view on economic activity in general that distorts the understanding of the class relation in capitalist social formations. In an effort to address this weakness in conventional social science, contemporary Marxists continue to analyze the process of proletarianization: namely, the de-skilling of workers in all segments of the economy through the relentless separation of mental and manual labor that follows from the application of specific forms of technology designed to dominate workers on the shop-floor of the workplace, in both blue- and white-collar working environments. The knowledge of the production process as a whole is wrested away from the minds of workers on the assembly line (as well as office workers isolated in cubicles) and situated within the manuals and computer programs of engineers and computer programmers working for management. Ultimately, this knowledge *itself* becomes a force of production as it is objectified within machines that displace workers on the factory floor and position them as mere appendages of the machines. Key figures in this tradition of sociology include Harry Braverman and Michael Burawoy, who, despite being recognized in the field of sociology, still constitute the minority perspective in the field of stratification and inequality studies.[2]

The process of proletarianization is not limited to manufacturing sectors in the economy. White-collar workers, service-sector workers, and skilled workers in the bio-tech fields have all been subject to the process of proletarianization. In recent decades, medical doctors who work for health-maintenance organizations (HMOs) have organized themselves into unions as a response to the relative proletarianization of their field. Doctors are among the groups of workers who have shown the fastest rate of growth in new union membership in the United States, as they resist the growing bureaucratic structures of HMOs that threaten to diminish the autonomy of doctors working on the hospital floor. In 1972, one of the first unions for physicians was organized, which today includes dentists under the name Union of American Physicians and Dentists (UAPD). The UAPD exists under the umbrella of the American Federation of State, County and Municipal Employees (AFSCME). There is also the Doctors Council in New York City, which is affiliated with the Service Employees International Union (SEIU). Both of these cases demonstrate that income and education (SES) do not determine or constitute class, for while professional physicians as a whole earn an average yearly income of roughly $270,000, these doctors' unions have been organized to fight against employers for better working conditions, which is a fundamental issue for the labor movement more generally. Professional physicians have very good "life chances" in the Weberian sense, but they also sometimes constitute themselves as a class in terms of their activity; namely, they see their interests as workers to be in conflict with the interests of their employers (HMOs). This phenomenon is far outside the purview of the dominant paradigm in social science, which is incapable of explaining how medical doctors actively seek collective representation of their interests *against* their employers. In a rather rudimentary manner, conventional social science understands "doctor" as merely a status position near the top of the occupational ladder.

This does not mean, however, that Weberian themes are incommensurate with historical materialism. On the contrary, as we will argue below, there is a way to displace the age-old Weber/Marx antinomy concerning the concept of class within sociology by shifting the analysis *away* from concerns about measurement and occupational ladders, and *toward* framing an understanding of how workers resist work and challenge the power of capitalists to organize the economy throughout various changes in the social formation of capitalism. When the sociological lens shifts to a focus upon the cultural struggle against work, the conceptual wall between Weber and Marx becomes rather porous. We will return to this shift in analysis later, in section III of this essay.

From the point of view of historical materialism, the process of proletarianization is a *tendency* within capitalist development, not a *telos* in an Hegelian sense, or a "law" of motion within a framework of social physics as developed by Auguste Comte and his followers. Because proletarianization is a contingent aspect of capitalist development, Marxists focus on historical analysis to explain the particular conditions that make possible the emergence of various processes of proletarianization in particular sectors of the economy. This tendency is referred to as part of the *logic of capital accumulation*, and because class is understood within historical materialism as a relationship and not a thing, the logic of capital exists in perpetual tension with the *counter-logic of labor*, i.e. resistance exercised by workers against capitalist working conditions, if not against work *as such*. The epic struggle for shorter hours of work, which developed into an international labor movement during the final two decades of the nineteenth century, is a leading example of the counter-logic of labor. Indeed, the struggle against work is understood by many Marxists to constitute many cultural forms produced by the working class. (This part of the reader contains many selections by scholars who have studied the cultural struggle against work.) Furthermore, developments of particular technologies that are key variables in the process of proletarianization must be understood as a *response* of capitalists to recalcitrant workers. Technology is never deployed in a neutral social environment. The very form and content of technology is the historical product of class struggle. The chapter by Stanley Aronowitz and William Difazio and the chapters by Mike Davis and Harry Braverman address these issues.

Many conventional social scientists, on the other hand, have argued that "Marxism" is an antiquated methodology, lacking the proper tools needed to accurately describe post-industrial or post-modern society. Professional researchers working in the dominant paradigm often turn to questions of method and measurement in an attempt to "prove" that Marxist concepts do not square with empirical reality. In this way, political differences between competing traditions in the social sciences are said to be resolved by an appeal to "truth." The move here is to attempt to demonstrate that concepts used in the paradigm of historical materialism do not accurately represent the "real" world, in an effort to relegate the Marxist project as a whole to the garbage can of history. The problem, however, is that it is impossible to move from one paradigm to another without radically changing concepts that frame the issues at hand. The question of *how objects of knowledge get produced in the first place* is left out of disciplinary maneuvers within what Kuhn might refer to as "normal" social science. The group of intellectuals sometimes referred to as the Frankfurt School points to the irony of this strategy; namely, that debates concerning measurement turn our attention away from the matter at hand: social class. From the efforts of professional methodologists we learn a lot about how to do certain kinds of research and the correct ways to conduct measurement with certain kinds of instruments, but not so much about the phenomenon itself, "class." As a result, in many of these discourses on method, the means become the ends. Conventional social scientists working within the dominant paradigm very rarely reflect upon their categories of knowledge that produce the object of analysis in the first place. Ironically, the discipline of sociology has under its own umbrella of various discourses a rich tradition of such reflection in both the sociology of knowledge and Critical Theory.[3] The sociological discourses on stratification and SES, however, are largely at epistemological odds with those two traditions, because Critical Theory demands reflection on the constitution of facts within scientific discourse, whereas in much of stratification research the emphasis is placed upon technical questions regarding how to follow certain steps in the correct procedural manner when applying instruments of measurement.

As Critical Theorists like Herbert Marcuse and Theodor Adorno point out, methodology and/or measurement is ultimately not the issue; rather, the concept of class cannot be adequately understood unless it is embedded within the *labor question*, which transcends the positivistic frame of mind that attempts to separate values and facts.[4] Not only must the sociological analysis of class consider the transformation of the labor process – which cannot appear inside the methodological imperative within mainstream social science that focuses on voting data and market interactions outside of the space of actual production – but in addition, the concept of class must be deployed in a *normative* framework which focuses upon exploitation *and*, most importantly, the possible liberation from work, what Marx refers to in *Capital Vol. 3* as the movement from the "realm of necessity" to the "realm of freedom."[5]

Key figures in the history of conventional sociology like Durkheim, on the other hand, argue that happiness can be found *within* work, and that "too much" free time causes anxiety among and within individuals, a condition that he coined "anomie." Following Plato's theory of justice in the *Republic*, Durkheim believed that inside the social division of labor there exists – *in advance* – a location uniquely designed to match the aptitudes of every individual in society.[6] As long as each individual is able to "freely" locate their occupational niche in the division of labor, then we can claim that we have arrived at a "just" society. Society functions properly and as it *should*, while individuals find meaning in their lives through attachment to the division of labor. Contemporary followers of Durkheim like William Julius Wilson (in the book *When Work Disappears*) continue the neo-functionalist line of reasoning which assumes, *a priori*, that individuals without work suffer from anomie. The argument here is that people need structure in their lives, since on their own they are incapable of controlling their insatiable desires, which left unchecked by the major institutions of society cause the individual to suffer under the crushing weight of their own infinite/unreasonable wants. For Durkheim, workers must not be exposed to too much education and leisure, because if they were, then they would lose their appetite for work, which would throw society into a state of chaos and dysfunction.[7] The question of income and material standard of living as it relates to work is secondary in this line of reasoning because structuring human activity is the main focus.

Indeed, Durkheim's emphasis on society as a moral community revealed an animosity toward material needs and desires. This particular Durkheimian perspective on the individual who is said to need order as a means to find happiness as well as to be able to function properly in society is a *metaphysical* view, based upon the philosophy of Plato's *Republic*, but the metaphysics of Durkheim's description of the needs of the anomic individual in modern capitalist society remains *unconscious* in much of the research conducted in professional sociology today. It is understood *a priori* that the said individual needs his/her free time filled up with structured activity. Research on the class/labor question in the Durkheimian tradition assumes this rather dogmatic perspective on what it means to be human. Thus it exists as an ontology that lurks below the sociology. Furthermore, by identifying constraint as the essence of the social *per se*, and by looking to bolster social authority whenever it seems to sag, Durkheimian sociology tends toward political conservatism through its apologetic stance on the relationship between power, domination and social class within the capitalist division of labor.

Historical materialism draws upon Aristotle rather than Plato. Aristotle's argument that *unstructured* leisure time – what Edmund Husserl in the *Phenomenology of Internal Time Consciousness* described as the phenomenology of constituting time on your own hands – is necessary for an authentic, gratifying human existence seems to have been lost upon Durkheimian sociologists, but it was a central organizing principle for leaders of the American labor movement during much of the nineteenth century, many of whom, like Samuel Gompers, were familiar with the writings of Marx. Gompers was a cigar roller. It was common practice for cigar rollers to pay individuals referred to as "lectors" to read books out loud to give the rollers something to think about while they worked. Perched atop a makeshift platform in the center of the factory, the lector would read the news in the morning and then shift to literary and political texts in the afternoon including texts by Dostoyevsky, Goethe and Marx among many others. Such activity would be condemned by Durkheim, since he believed that broadening the "horizons" of workers too much would make it impossible for a worker to adjust to and "freely" accept very narrow and specialized tasks as the condition of his or her existence, and therefore create instability in the division of labor.

Marx, of course, drew many of his questions for social research from the Aristotelian tradition. For the workers who built the international movement for shorter hours of work, the problem was *too much* work, not too little. In the late nineteenth century, the workweek was six days long, and the workday was typically 12, sometimes 14 hours long. In the United States, the 40-hour workweek and the eight-hour workday were not achieved until passage of the 1938 Fair Labor Standards Act by Congress during the New Deal era. The epic struggle for shorter hours of work, which drove the labor movement for nearly a century, is a topic that remains alien territory for conventional stratification studies. It is interesting that Durkheim ignored the struggle for shorter hours of work while writing the *Division of Labor in Society*, which was published in 1893 and later became a foundational text in the field of sociology.

For Marxists on the other hand, the struggle against work is understood to occupy a central place in the content of working-class culture as well as being one of the driving forces that contributes to the development of particular social formations. Included in this part of the reader is an excerpt from Aronowitz and DiFazio's book *Jobless Future*, which tells the story of union workers who secured a deal with management that instituted a guaranteed annual wage *without* work, in exchange for agreeing to management's plan to implement new technologies at the workplace. The excerpt is based upon DiFazio's earlier case study of dock workers in his book *Longshoremen: Community and Resistance on the Brooklyn Waterfront*. Against arguments made by the followers of Durkheim, DiFazio reveals that individuals who lack work, but who *have* income, do not fall into the abyss of social disorganization, deviance and anomie. On the contrary, the experience of these union members demonstrates that free time with an income translates into both more happiness among individuals and stronger social bonds within the community. These are social bonds formed largely *outside* of work, in leisure spaces like the pub, the bowling alley and the billiards hall.

II

Within the dominant paradigm in sociology the emphasis has been, and continues to be, on the perceived absence of class consciousness among working people in the United States. The dominant view in recent years has been that American workers either remain relatively conservative when compared to their European counterparts or that class is simply not a significant factor in the process of identity construction among American workers. According to sociologists like Paul Kingston (*The Classless Society*) and Jan Pakulski and Malcolm Waters (*The Death of Class*), race, ethnicity and gender are more salient identity markers than class when looking at how post-industrial workers understand themselves. Historians like Lizabeth Cohen, however, have revealed that the opposite is the case. In her important book, *Making a New Deal*, Cohen argues that during the Great Depression workers developed a sense of community based upon their class identity precisely because they could not rely on their ethnic communities to support them in times of profound economic crisis. Because the Great Depression overwhelmed their ethnic network of economic support, workers in Chicago and other parts of the country took it upon themselves to *make* a "new deal," in part by fighting against corporate interests in the struggle to shape the contours of the new Keynesian welfare state.

Furthermore, if we keep the concept "class" fused together with the concept of working activity, then we have a much richer analysis of identity formations. Pakulski's claim that class is not relevant to how individuals construct their identities only makes sense if we separate the concept of class from working activity. When we keep the focus on work when thinking about the concept of class, we see that the problem of work crosses the identity boundaries created by race, gender, sexual preference, occupational status and so on. Unfortunately, most sociological studies on the social construction of identity fail to consider the phenomenon of work as a contributing factor.

According to Robin Leidner, whose chapter "Identity and Work," appears in the edited volume, *Social Theory at Work*, "relatively few contemporary theorists have put work at the center of their analyses of identity in late or postmodernity" (p. 424). The concept of class that Pakulski works with is a static notion of class, which in part explains why some conventional sociologists seek to jettison the concept altogether. If class is understood as process rather than as a thing, then the theoretical paradigm shifts significantly. We agree with Kathi Weeks, who argues in her important book *The Problem With Work*, that "the politics of and against work has the potential to expand the terrain of class struggle to include actors well beyond that classic figure of traditional class politics, the industrial proletariat" (p. 17).[8] In short, we take the point of view that when the concept of class is fused together with the concept of work activity, then we see class not as a location, or a category assigned to individuals. Rather, class is something we do, something we perform as a significant part of our everyday life activities.

The most recent attempts to jettison the concept of class in sociology depend on particular interpretations of history. The position of sociologists like Pakulski and Kingston is frequently combined with two older arguments: (1) property and wealth have been widely redistributed in the United States, leading to economic conditions that alleviate the struggle between classes, and (2) class conflict has been further resolved through the institutionalization of negotiations between labor and management inside the structure of the modern state. These two points explain why Durkheimian sociologists see labor disputes as merely "industrial" problems that require *technical* solutions, which can be achieved by tinkering with the existing system through "helping" workers to fit into the system of production.

Marxists, on the other hand, see such phenomena as revolts against the logic of capital, which point beyond mere technical questions and toward normative questions about the purpose and experience of work as well as the possible transcendence of alienation and unhappiness that is produced by work. Marxists inspired by Aristotle always have an eye on the possible expansion of the sphere of *leisure*, which informs their analysis of working conditions and the class relations that constitutes the very possibility of capitalism as a mode of production.

For sociologists like Kingston, evidence for the lack of class consciousness among American workers is said to exist on the basis of voting behavior, where it is argued that if working-class individuals do not vote in terms of what mainstream sociologists consider to be "real" class issues, then a consciousness of class among workers is supposedly not present, ostensibly because they are satisfied. In contrast, recent scholarship in labor history by historians like Jefferson Cowie reveals the lack of complexity in analyses like Kingston's, which relies too heavily on voting patterns. In his book *Stayin' Alive: The 1970s and the Last Days of the Working Class*, Cowie has convincingly argued that voting for a Republican candidate during the key decade of the 1970s did *not* mean that working-class Americans lacked class consciousness *per se*. Cowie has revealed that in some cases working-class voters (primarily union members) in the 1970s believed that either a socially conservative candidate *or* a communist candidate would be more willing to stand up to corporate power than a liberal one. In the words of a truck driver quoted by Cowie, "I'm either for him [Wallace] or the Communists, I don't care, just anybody who wouldn't be afraid of the big companies." Here we see a willingness to vote in two quite divergent directions, and this difference can only be explained by careful historical analysis that goes beyond examination of voting records. Cowie reveals a peculiar form of class consciousness in the 1970s that was interwoven with right-wing populism and racism. Unique cultural and political-economic conditions help explain how working-class consciousness merged with conservative populism in this period of US history.

What historical studies like Cowie's have demonstrated is that class consciousness is historically variable and only historical analysis can explain how it emerges and what particular form it takes within certain cultural and political-economic conditions which are shaped by conflict. If a researcher were to observe only a vote cast for a conservative like Wallace, then the possibility for understanding that the same person was considering casting their vote for a communist would be missed. Class consciousness is not a static thing that corresponds to a hypostasized category of knowledge existing in a reified social-science discourse. In short, there is no universal class consciousness. Rather, class consciousness is always over-determined by other factors including the social constructions of race, gender, sexual preference and other such phenomena. Furthermore, class consciousness must also be analyzed in relation to specific political opportunities. If the structure of power relations does not provide an avenue for the expression of working-class consciousness within the state, we cannot conclude that such a consciousness does not exist. Voting behavior must be seen as one aspect among many variables in understanding the history of class politics in the United States. Indeed the very concept of politics must be expanded to include the realm of the mundane, everyday life experience of working-class people. Again, this involves going outside the boundaries of conventional social science. Given specific historical circumstances, contradictions may exist both in the social relations of production and *within* individuals. Critical Theory places an emphasis upon how these kinds of contradictions and complexities do not fit neatly within a static form of concepts and research protocols that assume a logical form which is unable to adequately grasp contradictions that exist in our society.[9]

Another very important issue to consider is that since the early part of the twentieth century, the disciplinary preference in sociology has been for the concepts of "status" and "strata" over class because these concepts point to the existence of inequality but the *absence* of either exploitation of workers or antagonism between classes in capitalist society. Furthermore, the concepts of strata and status fit into a logical schema that exists prior to the conduct of research. This line of inquiry stems from Max Weber's famous statement – found in his essay "Class, Status, Party" – that "classes are not communities." Weber sought to point out that class as a concept can only describe social divisions in terms of the unequal distribution of power and wealth in society, rather than shared cultural affiliations, because such affiliations are said, *a priori*, not to exist. Weber made this argument in part because he was profoundly influenced by neo-classical economics, especially the Austrian marginalist school, which in turn meant that he focused exclusively on the labor *market*, to the exclusion of the labor *process*.

For Weberians, workers are understood in terms of isolated individuals competing against one another for jobs in a marketplace, rather than as individuals who labor together in the process of production, or as individuals constituting a cultural community that seeks to find cooperative strategies to gain power and leverage against their employers, or as a community constituted in leisure spaces that cannot be reduced to the economic realm. A prime example of the latter phenomenon is the rich history of the struggle for shorter hours of labor initiated by US workers and their unions, which became a vibrant international labor movement that existed more or less at the same time that Weber was claiming that there was no such working-class community. The struggle for shorter hours of work was both a labor-market strategy and a point-of-production strategy. Reducing the amount of hours worked was a market strategy to extract higher wages and better working conditions from employers (because working shorter hours drives down unemployment), but in order to achieve that goal workers used the strike weapon as a means to exploit their leverage at the point of production. The struggle against work was also an *end in itself*, because the expansion of free time, what workers in the labor movement referred to as "8 hours for what we will," was seen as a valuable cultural good. Against Weber, class did become a community formed around the struggle for shorter hours of work. The intellectual tradition that both denies the empirical existence of class consciousness and therefore by extension the very concept of class and class conflict in the United States began in earnest with Weber's colleague, Werner Sombart, and the publication of Sombart's 1906 book, *Why Is There No Socialism in the United States?*

According to Sombart, if it could be demonstrated that socialism has not been able to gain traction in the United States, then it is reasonable to suggest further that class consciousness is absent from most American workers, and as class consciousness goes, so does class as a useful concept for sociologists. Sombart attempted to demonstrate that workers in the United States were better off than their European counterparts, and that this relative affluence explains why socialist ideas have not been able to enjoy as much influence in American society as they have in Europe. Sombart's famous passage, "all socialist utopias founder on apple pie and roast beef," encapsulates his attempt to demonstrate that capitalism was able to deliver the goods to the American working class, thereby derailing any possibility of the development of a community of working-class individuals existing in antagonism with the capitalist class. Sombart's emphasis on "apple pie" and "roast beef" reveals an irony, namely that it is Sombart and his anti-Marxist followers who are guilty of economic determinism, not the Marxists. Furthermore, Sombart wrote these words in the midst of a vigorous socialist movement in the United States spearheaded by Eugene V. Debs, who received 6 percent of the vote in the 1912 presidential election. Debs was also active in the organization and creation of the Industrial Workers of the World (also known as the "wobblies") in 1905, a year prior to Sombart's infamous observation. At their peak, the wobblies mobilized more than 300,000 workers in various labor conflicts across the country and had more than 100,000 members. For more on the wobblies, see Chapter 6 by Mike Davis.

The other key figure in the field of sociology who has influenced those seeking to discredit the Marxist perspective on the phenomenon of class is Ralf Dahrendorf, whose book *Class and Class Conflict in Industrial Society* (published in 1959) bridges the gap between the generation of Sombart and more contemporary sociologists like Kingston and Pakulski. In fact, Pakulski explicitly draws upon Dahrendorf's view that class conflict was overcome during the development of capitalism in the twentieth century via integration and mitigation of class conflict within the Keynesian welfare state, which was said to have been able to appeal to the rational side of capital and labor, since both sides shared a mutual interest in economic growth. Like Dahrendorf, Pakulski argues that capitalism has passed through the phase of class conflict as the state has been able to diminish the conflicts between industrial workers and industrialists. Sociologists working against Marxism prefer the Durkheimian term "industrial society" over "capitalism" as a means to shift attention away from antagonism between classes on the one hand, and the condition of alienation among workers on the other hand. For Critical Theorists like Max Horkheimer and Theodor Adorno, however, the integration of the labor movement into the Keynesian welfare state indicated that modern capitalism in the United States and Europe had become a "totally administered society," rather than a rational, social-democratic society based upon the peaceful resolution of class conflict. As was the case with Sombart, Dahrendorf's analysis proved to be flawed when, in roughly a decade after publication of his book, American workers led one of the largest revolts against work in the history of the modern working class. For several generations, professional social scientists have sounded the death knell of class conflict, and yet their prognostications ring hollow in the ears of actual workers laboring in the global capitalist system of production.

The other major flaw in the Weberian and Durkheimian traditions has to do with the fact that while conventional sociologists cannot deny the extreme inequality of wealth distribution in western societies, they have been unwilling to examine just how wealth gets produced in the first place. Marxists focus on the point of production in capitalist society precisely for this reason: to demonstrate how wealth is created through the exploitation of workers. As Erik Olin Wright has correctly observed in his collection of essays in *Approaches to Class Analysis*, part of what sets historical materialism at paradigmatic odds with the dominant perspective in sociology is its emphasis upon exploitation, which in turn is based upon normative commitments not shared by the other traditions in sociology. The dominant traditions in sociology cling to the methodological imperative that leaves no room for normative evaluation in a putatively scientific discourse on the contours of inequality. This difference is what makes Marxism a form of Critical Theory, insofar as the inclusion of norms into scientific discourse points to the transformation of society as much as to the mere representation of it among a constellation of concepts.

Wright's emphasis on the spatial location of different classes in relation to the production process does *not*, however, exhaust the research pursuits of Marxists in the social sciences, nor does his definition of the normative dimension of historical materialism. Wright's analysis has been criticized for failing to account for *cultural* aspects of class formation over time, and his reduction of Marxism's normative perspective to "radical egalitarianism" is also too limiting. There also exists a commitment to freedom and libertarianism in the tradition of historical materialism, but this side of the conceptual framework is less well known among social scientists.

The libertarian perspective in historical materialism is best articulated as the freedom *from* work, a phenomenon which has been emphasized by Critical Theorists like Antonio Negri, Herbert Marcuse and Theodor Adorno, among others. One distinctive characteristic of Critical Theory is an engagement with philosophical traditions that rarely cross the path of social science discourse, including the tradition in philosophy that has the labor question as its object of thought. The theoretical link between the concept of class and the labor question that plays such an important role in historical materialism can be traced back to Aristotle. In Book One, Section 4 of *The Politics*, Aristotle argued that if machines "worked all by themselves" there could be no masters and no servants as we know them. In the words of Aristotle, "If every instrument could accomplish its own work, obeying or anticipating the will of others, like the statues of Daedalus, or the tripods of Hephaestus, which, says the poet, of their own accord entered the assembly of the Gods; if in like manner, the shuttle would weave and the plectrum touch the lyre, *chief workmen would not want servants, nor masters slaves*" (emphasis ours).[10]

The class division constituted by the relationship between masters and servants turns upon the labor question: who will do the necessary work, and under what conditions will they work? But if there is no work to be done (or very little as in an automated post-scarcity environment) the bond between master and servant cannot exist, or at the very least the bond is radically transformed. Due to the application of labor-saving technology, the class relation (as constituted by the yoke between masters and servants) has taken on various forms in the long history of the various transformations of the labor process over the millennia. At certain points in time, this history leads in the direction of the abolition of the relationship itself, as Aristotle speculated. It ultimately depends on the historical conditions of class struggle. The question that still reveals the wildcard of this specific history is: how will workers respond to proletarianization, globalization and automation?

It is also important to note that Marx's understanding of the abolition of work is *not* merely a utopian dream, because the process of proletarianization within capitalism is *already* moving in the direction of reducing the amount of labor time necessary to reproduce the expanding wealth of society. As the leaders of capitalist industries often make clear, capital turns to automation when workers become intractable (see Chapter 15 by Roberts for more on this issue). This phenomenon is always indeterminate, based upon the contingencies of class struggle. Therefore, Marx was analyzing an existing tendency in the historical development of actually-existing, empirical capitalism. Studying the empirical history of class struggle does not, however, mean that speculation has no role to play, which is why Marx insists on the continuing relevance of the humanities like, for example, the philosophy of Hegel and Aristotle.

Marx's link to Aristotle is most clearly articulated in the famous "fragment on machines" section in the *Grundrisse,* where Marx describes how the worker in capitalism eventually "steps to the side of the production process," as *techno-science,* which is objectified in labor-saving machines and computers, becomes the principal power of production. It is at this point that knowledge displaces muscle power as the prime mover of the capitalist production processes. It is with Aristotle's argument in mind that Marx claimed that abolishing class divisions in society necessarily involved the abolition of work. In Volume Three of *Capital,* Marx argued that labor's fight for shorter hours of work was the *prerequisite* for the potential transformation of the class relation and the expansion of the "realm of freedom." His Aristotelian point of view is best captured on page 325 of the *Grundrisse* (Notebook III in the "Chapter on Capital"). There Marx argues that the historic destiny of class struggle could only be fulfilled if and

> when the development of the productive powers of labor, which capital incessantly whips onward with its unlimited mania for wealth, and of the sole conditions in which this mania can be realized, have flourished to the stage where the possession and preservation of general wealth require lesser labor time of society as a whole, and where the laboring society relates scientifically to the process of its progressive reproduction, its reproduction in a *constantly greater abundance;* hence *where labor in which a human being does what a thing [robot] can do has ceased.* [emphasis ours][11]

In this passage, Marx has described how science itself has become a force of production. The radical transformation of the labor process that has followed from the application of computer-based technologies in recent years is further evidence that Marx was on the correct path in understanding the *tendency* toward the abolition of work under capitalism when workers successfully fight against capitalists over the conditions and duration of work itself. This history is contingent, as it depends upon a manifold of social, political and cultural particularities. The jobless future can go in different directions, either toward unemployment and relative deprivation among masses of workers, or the future can bring more leisure time and a higher standard of living. It all depends on the past, present and future of the labor movement. Abolishing work is the necessary if not sufficient condition for eradicating class domination. Workers must also constitute themselves as a class, which cannot emerge automatically from the historical transformation of the labor process (see Chapter 13 by Aronowitz and DiFazio and Chapter 15 by Roberts for more on this issue).

III

In the field of history, Marxists have had more influence than in sociology, especially in the field of labor history. Historians have also corrected mistakes made by some Marxist political economists who have tended to reduce labor to a dependent variable in the history of the development of capitalism. Marxists who have focused their attention on proletarianization have described and explained the transformation of the labor process in great detail, but most of these analyses – Harry Braverman's *Labor and Monopoly Capital* is probably the best example here – have overlooked the reactions and practices of workers. This problem follows from the fact that the working class constitutes itself, in large part, *outside* of the production process. Analyses that focus on proletarianization cannot, by definition, explain the emergence of class consciousness, because this perspective situates labor *a priori* as a dependent variable in the history of the development of capitalism. It has been the task of labor historians to show how and when class consciousness has happened.

As in sociology, Sombart's question also generated discussion and debate in the field of American labor history, but unlike in American sociology, which has more or less given up on the concept of class in favor of the concepts of "status" and "strata," labor historians have developed research perspectives that point to the continuing relevance of the Marxist concept of class, although there are significant differences in how labor historians frame the important issues surrounding the labor question.

In the early decades of the twentieth century, labor historians like Selig Perlman (whose book *A Theory of the Labor Movement* appeared in 1928) accepted Sombart's thesis that American workers were not interested in socialism, which indicated to Perlman a certain kind of conservatism that he referred to as "pure and simple" unionism. The peculiar form of syndicalism among American workers was interpreted by Perlman as conservative when compared to European workers who advocated for their representatives to seek power and representation within the state apparatus. Perlman leaned on this conception to explain why America was the exception to the rule regarding the question of why socialist ideas and policies have had a significant influence in every western democracy except the United States. The argument here was that while American workers do sometimes join unions, they do so only for economic reasons, i.e.

bigger paychecks and better working conditions, rather than political reasons like seizing state power through building a separate labor party. Perlman was convinced that because workers did not seek to intervene in state politics like their European counterparts, the conclusion must be that American workers were not as "radical," or at the very least, much less "political." Perlman argued that American workers were satisfied with incremental gains within capitalism and had no desire to challenge the system itself. The generation of labor historians who followed Perlman (sometimes referred to as the "new" labor historians) responded to Perlman's argument in three distinct ways.

First, many of the new labor historians agreed with Perlman that any move away from a strategy to seize the state apparatus signified a lack of radical class politics, but generations of labor historians after Perlman argued that it was the leadership of the labor movement that became relatively conservative, not the rank and file. This position led many labor historians to follow the lead of Herbert Gutman in order to find class consciousness and radical politics among workers in places *beyond* the formal institution of the labor union itself.[12] Gutman, like E.P. Thompson before him, emphasized the need to focus on *culture*, in order to examine how the working class constitutes itself outside of the labor process. Labor historians began investigating the school, the bar, and other spaces in the public sphere as a means to excavate a class consciousness among regular workers not in charge of the direction of the official labor movement. (See Chapter 15 by Roberts and Chapter 17 by Rosenzweig.) Workers *un*organized by labor unions were also considered a very important part of the story. In short, the view among generations after Perlman was that the formal structure of the labor union itself was, and in some cases still is, a barrier to the expression of the true consciousness of rank-and-file working people.

Ironically, it was Max Weber who provided labor historians with a new way to construe class, and in turn reconfigure historical materialism, while forging a critique of Sombart and Perlman. In Weber's classic essay *The Protestant Ethic and the Spirit of Capitalism*, historians found new ways to frame class consciousness *not* as the desire to take over the state, or manage the means of production; rather, class consciousness emerges from the practice of *resisting work*. One of Weber's keen insights in his essay was that in order for the Puritan work ethic to gain hegemony in western culture, the "traditionalism" of European workers would have to be destroyed. By "traditionalism," Weber means the common practice of workers to find ways to work the minimum amount necessary in order to enjoy the culturally and historically defined material standard of living in a given society. In Weber's (2001) words, "the opportunity of earning more was less attractive than *working less*... Wherever modern capitalism has begun its work of increasing the productivity of human labour by increasing its intensity, it has encountered the immensely stubborn resistance of this leading trait of pre-capitalist labour" (italics ours, p. 24).[13]

Gutman's emphasis on culture and everyday life of workers outside of the formal dealings of the institution of the labor union, and E.P. Thompson's path-breaking analyses of the cultural dimensions of class were inspired by Weber's analysis of the problem of "traditionalism" among European workers, that is to say a problem for the capitalist class, insofar as "traditionalism" was a cultural phenomenon that stood opposed to the capitalist work ethic.[14]

Thompson's focus upon culture and class has led to the flowering of an entire generation of scholars working under the rubric of cultural studies who have produced a myriad of new ways to study working-class consciousness including studies of representations of class in popular music, film, paperback-trade novels, as well as studies of the significance of clothing styles, and the expansion of working-class leisure activities in the twentieth century more generally. This development has resulted in a relative break from the epistemological point of view dominant in labor history before E.P. Thompson that focused almost exclusively on the institution of the labor union. In short, the school of thought that became known as British Cultural Studies, including the works of Stuart Hall, Raymond Williams, Paul Willis and Dick Hebdige, revolutionized the study of the working class by expanding the scope of how and where to look for working-class consciousness.

A key development in this shift of focus was to look at micro-level resistances, what the anthropologist James Scott refers to as "hidden transcripts," a kind of resistance practice that is much less visible than a strike or an election.[15] According to Scott, hidden transcripts are forms of resistance that are purposely constructed to fly under the radar, so as to escape the attention of the manager and/or employer, and other figures of authority. A strike, on the other hand, is understood by Scott to be a "public" transcript, for it exists for everyone in society to examine, read and interpret. Crafty and sometimes deceitful forms of resistance, however, not only remain hidden from public view, but are much more frequent and intimately interwoven into the fabric of everyday life among working people. For example, - Robin D.G. Kelley, author of the book *Race Rebels: Culture, Politics and the Black Working Class*, focuses his first chapter on workers at McDonald's finding ways to resist work through a myriad of micro-tactics including: slowing down the pace at work, blasting music and dancing while flipping hamburgers, creating and wearing hair styles that signify a counter-culture, walking a certain way (gangsta limp) while working, creating games to accompany food preparation, leaving work early and handing out free cheeseburgers to friends who happen to stop by the store. These are good examples of the application of the concept of "hidden transcripts" to the ubiquity of micro-resistance practices that constitute a significant portion of working-class everyday life and culture. Scott refers to the hidden transcript as an "art" of resistance because it involves an aesthetic dimension, which is captured quite nicely by Robin Kelley's description of the *styles* of resistance created by his former co-workers.

These practices of micro-level resistances help focus our attention on the struggle against work as the crucial element of working-class everyday life activity, rather than the organized strategies of the official labor union institutions. In short, just because workers are not on strike, or are not active at the voting polls does not indicate that there is a lack of class consciousness among workers. The combination of public and hidden transcripts of resistance constitutes what we call in this reader the "counter-logic of labor," which exists in opposition to the logic of capital. Many of the selections are largely organized around precisely this concept (Kelley, Davis, Enstad and Roberts).

The second direction of research for the new labor historians looking for ways to respond to Perlman's assessment of American workers was to examine the history of other labor unions besides the American Federation of Labor (AFL) like the Knights of Labor (KoL) and the Industrial Workers of the World (IWW) because these institutions posed a serious challenge to the AFL under the leadership of Samuel Gompers. The strategy for historians like Leon Fink and Kim Voss was to challenge Perlman's claim that American workers were conservative on the grounds that Perlman focused too much attention on the AFL as the true representative of working-class consciousness.[16] The Knights of Labor and the IWW were seen as more radical unions because they sought to seize the means of production, and during the late nineteenth and early twentieth century the AFL had to vigorously compete with these other unions for the hearts and minds of American workers. Most labor historians point to structural barriers that prevented the Knights and the IWW from winning the battle against the AFL, and that if it were not for certain structural barriers such as US labor law, and the superior capacity for violence on the part of the capitalist state, these other institutions might have had more success in organizing American workers. In short, the argument against Perlman was that American workers have had plenty of class consciousness, but so far political opportunities have not allowed workers to prevail in their struggle against capital. (For more on the IWW, see Chapter 6 by Mike Davis.)

Third, there is yet another position taken by labor historians who agree with Perlman that American workers are relatively conformist. This time the blame for their relative conservatism is placed upon consumerism and mass media institutions that developed in the twentieth century, rather than on the leadership of the AFL. This position holds that workers succumbed to capitalist ideology during the rise of consumer capitalism, the phase of capitalism also referred to as monopoly capitalism. Not only did American workers have to struggle against the violence of the capitalist state (in the form of the police and the army) but in addition workers and unions have had to struggle against capitalist ideology, which emanates from a different segment of the state, what Louis Althusser refers to as the "ideological state apparatuses," including schools, the media, church, etc.[17] This narrative, constructed by historians like Sean Wilentz, describes American workers as, once upon a time, radical in the ante-bellum period when they resisted the emergence of the waged-labor system and the discipline of factory work, but by the late nineteenth century accepting of the waged-labor system because they found compensation for declining political power in the buying of more commodities.[18] The rise of advertising and the emergence of a new class of capitalist henchmen in the early twentieth century (what Stuart Ewen refers to as the "captains of consciousness") derailed the socialist project by distracting workers with expanded shopping opportunities as well as mass media forms like film and recorded music, which taken together create an ideological bulwark that is said to keep workers from focusing on the serious business of building a socialist state.[19] It is assumed in this perspective that consumption is a relatively frivolous activity, which diverts workers from the more serious project of working toward a socialist state. But more recent work by historians like Nan Enstad and Lizabeth Cohen challenges this point of view by situating popular culture not as a distraction produced by the culture industry, but rather as an important resource for workers seeking to organize resistance to the demands of their employers, while also creating a political bloc to influence the shape of the state (see Chapter 8 by Enstad and Chapter 15 by Roberts).

In some ways, the perspective in the new labor history which sees popular culture and consumerism as a problem privileges the discourse of the ante-bellum labor movement, referred to as "artisan republicanism," because this early form of the labor movement resisted the development of the wage system and argued that the growth of waged labor threatened the very possibility of independence and therefore freedom and democracy. The "good" society was understood by artisan republicanism to be one consisting of a myriad of small producers who each owned their means of production, which in turn would guarantee both their independence as well as their moral virtue, secured through hard, meaningful work. In short, the new labor historians tended to romanticize the early form of the labor movement due to a perspective that views consumption and leisure activities as relatively trivial compared to the traditional socialist project of seizing the state. The work of Sean Wilentz in particular seems to measure radicalism by the standard of artisan republicanism, the discourse of the ante-bellum labor movement.

A key feature of Wilentz's communitarian discourse is the emphasis upon moral virtue and the value of the work ethic. One major problem with this rather romantic view of the discourse of artisan republicanism follows from its place in history, a time *before* work had been thoroughly divided up into monotonous, meaningless tasks. For most workers laboring in industries after the Civil War, work had lost whatever meaning and gratification it may once have had in the artisan, craft traditions. Daniel Rodgers' book *The Work Ethic in Industrial Society* demonstrates that the Calvinist work ethic lost much of its cultural appeal after the rise of proletarianization during the Industrial Revolution radically transformed the labor process. Second, Wilentz's communitarian celebration of work and civic virtue remains at odds with the libertarian impulse that animated the movement for shorter hours of work. Under conditions where work is imposed from without and lacks both intrinsic satisfaction and moral value, working-class culture shifts to a quest for happiness and pleasure *beyond* work, and breaks from abstractions like citizenship based upon moral virtue derived from artisanal forms of work. Finally, a major contradiction in the history of artisan republicanism that is mostly ignored in Wilentz's analysis is the question of race. As David Roediger has demonstrated in his book *Wages of Whiteness*, the ante-bellum labor movement was animated by racism as much as it was animated by the opposition to waged labor. Indeed, the American working class developed its class identity as producers by creating an identity of "whiteness" in opposition to "black," which signified slave labor. Whiteness came to be associated with "free" labor in opposition to slaves (see Chapter 4 by Roediger).

In short, all three of these responses seek to challenge Perlman's thesis, but each one has an argument that details when and how the American labor movement failed in its quest for socialism. Recent work by historians like Howard Kimeldorf, Lawrence Glickman, Nan Enstad and Jonathan Cutler has sought to challenge the narrative that the post-bellum labor movement "sold out" to consumer capitalism, allowing for the development of a conservative American working class.[20] There has been a shift of focus away from the question of "when and how labor lost," to reinterpreting the politics of the post-bellum labor movement. A change in perspective seems appropriate especially when one examines the great labor upheavals during World War II, the late 1960s and early 1970s. One such change in perspective is the argument that legitimate worker radicalism has had a home for a long time in the movement for shorter hours for work, which should not be interpreted as somehow less political than strategies for re-capturing the means of production and seizing state power.

The issue turns upon the conceptual divide that developed within the labor movement after the Civil War which, according to Lawrence Glickman, has created two distinct perspectives in both the labor movement and American politics more broadly: namely, what he calls "producerism" and "consumerism." For Glickman, in both these perspectives, the central question regarding the goal of the labor movement remains the same: how is democracy, freedom and independence possible in industrial (and now post-industrial perhaps) society? In the discourse of "producerism" freedom and independence can only be possible when individuals have access to, and control over, the means of production. The key archetypes in this discourse are the ante-bellum yeoman farmer and the heroic artisan master-craftsman, as both of these figures were able to produce their own means of subsistence through control over the means of production. Furthermore, when ante-bellum yeoman farmers and master-craftsmen interacted in the marketplace, these types of producers secured an exact equivalent for their labor. They understood that they spent a certain amount of time and resources on making a product and when they took it to market they got all of the proceeds from their sale. This narrative viewed all non-producers, including merchants, bankers, absentee owners/ employers, slave owners and speculators, as parasites living off the labor of producers, the people whose work is the foundation of society.

The explosion of the system of waged-labor in the early nineteenth century radically changed the political-economic environment. If individuals depend on others in order to provide their subsistence (wages), then said individuals fall into a relationship of dependence, which in this conception is fundamentally at odds with a democratic form of government, because democracy presupposes universal independence among the citizenry. Furthermore, workers who labor for a wage do not get an exact equivalence for their labor, as they are forced to share the wealth produced by their labor with their master/employer. In short, from the point of view of the discourse on artisan republicanism, a true and legitimate democracy is only possible in a society where all individuals have the capacity to produce their own subsistence through access to and control over the means of production.

In the "consumerist" discourse of the late nineteenth century American labor movement on the other hand, the assumption is that relentless proletarianization has made it impossible to turn the clock back to a society of small-scale independent producers. Under monopoly capitalism, labor needs a new strategy focused on the shorter hours of labor. The shorter-hours movement anticipated the relentless universal drive of proletarianization and developed a strategy to reduce the demand for labor as the appropriate response to elimination of jobs that is concomitant to proletarianization and automation.

Another key element in the labor-movement discourse on shorter hours is that because the technological transformation of the labor process has boosted productivity to such enormous levels, there exists the very real possibility of achieving a relative post-scarcity environment. This way of looking at the issues should be considered a version of left-libertarianism, as opposed to Glickman's awkward and imprecise term "consumerism." The left-libertarian discourse on shorter hours stipulates that workers must fight to enjoy the fruits of rising levels of productivity. The most effective way to wage this struggle is to tighten labor markets by withdrawing the participation in work through the application of shorter hours of work, which after the Civil War was expressed in the movement for the eight-hour workday. The incredible wealth produced by the application of technology to the labor process signaled the possibility of an expanded rise in the standard of living. "More" became the slogan of the "post-bellum" labor movement under Samuel Gompers: more leisure time, more pianos in the homes of workers, more homes owned by working people, more newspapers read by workers, more fine clothes and foods, etc.

Consuming goods and expanding leisure activity does not, by definition, exist in opposition to the "serious" business of building a labor movement. Private recreation has a *political* dimension, revealed in the phrase: "picnics one day did not preclude strikes the next." New research by labor historians like Nan Enstad and Michael J. Roberts (see Chapters 8, 10 and 15) has demonstrated that consumption of previously thought to be trivial items like rock-and-roll records, fancy hats and shoes did *not* distract workers from the serious business of organization and political action. In fact, Enstad has demonstrated the opposite: namely, women workers who had developed a taste for fine hats and fancy shoes were among the most militant workers of the early twentieth century. Women who desired to consume popular culture were also the most willing to go on strike.

Glickman also argues that, in the discourse on shorter hours of work, workers can be free, and democracy is a distinct possibility if workers have ample leisure time and a high standard of living, which would allow for more education and more involvement in civic life. The goal was to keep demanding more and more leisure time, while simultaneously fighting for higher wages and better working conditions until work as we know it becomes a thing of the past. Asking for "more," then, was fundamentally a political and cultural act, not "merely" an economic demand.

Finally, within the tradition of historical materialism, it is understood that the refusal of work, as the core of class struggle, has the potential of transforming capitalism from the inside out. If workers are able to fight successfully for shorter hours "all the way down" so to speak, then would it make any sense to continue calling our political-economic system "capitalism," if people are only working, say, one day a week? These are the stakes raised by Marx's analysis in the *Grundrisse* when he scrutinizes the implications of new forms of technology that are continually shaped by class struggle. Herein lies the true radicalism of the fight for shorter hours. It is for these reasons that we argue for a reformulation of the concept "class" that focuses upon work and the fight against work, for what is ultimately at stake is freedom. As Kathi Weeks argues in her book *The Problem With Work*,

> rather than develop a politics of class focused primarily on issues of economic redistribution and economic justice – particularly a politics that seeks to alter wage levels to redraw the map of class categories – the politics that…[we are] interested in pursuing also investigates questions concerning the command and control over the spaces and times of *life*, and seeks the freedom to participate in shaping the terms of what collectively we can do and together what we might become…the politics of work that [we] would like to see elaborated would also levy a critique at its unfreedoms. [p. 23, italics ours]

This, then, is what Critical Theory, historical materialism and cultural studies offer as an alternative to conventional social science. Rather than focus only on how to measure "class," should we not also insist upon a critique of the unfreedom at the core of the phenomenon we call class? What about the spaces and times of *life* beyond work? Doesn't that matter? Otherwise, why pursue this kind of research?

Notes

1 For more on the methodological differences in the study of class in sociology, see Erik Olin Wright, *Approaches to Class Analysis* (New York and London: Cambridge University Press, 2005).
2 See Harry Braverman, *Labor and Monopoly Capital* (New York: Monthly Review Press, 1998) and Michael Burawoy, *Manufacturing Consent* (Chicago: University of Chicago Press, 1982).
3 See for example, David Bloor, *Knowledge and Social Imagery* (Chicago: University of Chicago Press, 1991), Bruno Latour, *Science in Action* (Cambridge, MA: Harvard University Press, 1988), Adorno T. et al., *The Positivist Dispute in German Sociology* (New York: Ashgate Publishing, 1981), Jurgen Habermas, *Knowledge and Human Interests* (Boston: Beacon Press, 1972), Ludwig Fleck, *Genesis and Development of a Scientific Fact* (Chicago: University of Chicago Press, 1981).
4 See Herbert Marcuse, *One-Dimensional Man* (Boston: Beacon Press, 1991).
5 See Karl Marx, *Capital: Volume 3*, translated by David Fernbach (New York: Penguin Classics, 1993), p. 949.
6 See Emile Durkheim, *The Division of Labor in Society* (New York: The Free Press, 1997).
7 Durkheim argued that "no doubt it is good for the worker to be interested in art, literature, etc…who cannot see, moreover that two such forms of existence are too opposed to be reconciled, and

cannot be followed by the same individual! If a man has become accustomed to vast horizons, total views, and fine abstractions, he cannot be confined within the strict limits of a specialized task without becoming frustrated." (*Selected Writings*, Cambridge University Press, 1972), pp. 178–9.

8   Kathi Weeks, *The Problem with Work* (Durham: Duke University Press, 2011).

9   Adorno T. et al., *The Positivist Dispute in German Sociology* (New York: Harper Torchbooks, 1976).

10 See *The Complete Works of Aristotle, Volume Two*, edited by Jonathan Barnes (Princeton University Press, 1984), p. 1989.

11 See Karl Marx, the *Grundrisse*, translated by Martin Nicolaus (New York: Vintage Books, 1973).

12 See Herbert Gutman, *Work, Culture, and Society in Industrializing America, 1815–1919* (New York: Vintage Books, 1977).

13 Max Weber, *The Protestant Ethic and the Spirit of Capitalism*, translated by Talcott Parsons (New York: Routledge Classics, 2nd Edition, 2001).

14 See E.P. Thompson, *The Making of the English Working Class* (New York: Vintage, 1966).

15 James Scott, *Domination and the Arts of Resistance: Hidden Transcripts* (New Haven: Yale University Press, 1992).

16 See Leon Fink, *Working Men's Democracy* (Urbana: University of Illinois Press, 1985) and Kim Voss, *The Making of American Exceptionalism* (Ithaca: Cornell University Press, 1994).

17 See Louis Althusser, "Ideology and Ideological State Apparatuses," in *Lenin and Philosophy and Other Essays* translated by Ben Brewster (New York: Monthly Review Press, 2001).

18 See Sean Wilentz, *Chants Democratic* (New York: Oxford University Press, 2004).

19 See Stuart Ewen, *Captains of Consciousness* (New York: Basic Books, 2001).

20 See Howard Kimmeldorf, *Battling for American Labor* (University of California Press, 1999), Lawrence Glickman, *A Living Wage* (Ithaca: Cornell University Press, 1999), Nan Enstad, *Ladies of Labor, Girls of Adventure* (New York: Columbia University Press, 1999), Jonathan Cutler, *Labor's Time* (Philadelphia: Temple University Press, 2004).

CHAPTER 2

The Realm of Freedom and The Magna Carta of the Legally Limited Working Day

Karl Marx

On the Realm of Necessity and the Realm of Freedom

[49]We have seen how the capitalist process of production is an historically specific form of the social production process in general. This last is both a production process of the material conditions of existence for human life, and a process, proceeding in specific economic and historical relations of production, that produces and reproduces these relations of production themselves, and with them the bearers of this process, their material conditions of existence, and their mutual relationships, i.e. the specific economic form of their society. For the totality of these relationships which the bearers of this production have towards nature and one another, the relationships in which they produce, is precisely society, viewed according to its economic structure. Like all its forerunners, the capitalist production process proceeds under specific material conditions, which are however also the bearers of specific social relations which the individuals enter into in the process of reproducing their life. Those conditions, like these social relations, are on the one hand the presuppositions of the capitalist production process, on the other its results and creations; they are both produced by it and reproduced by it. We also saw that capital, in the social production process appropriate to it – and the capitalist is simply personified capital, functioning in the production process simply as the bearer of capital – pumps out a certain specific quantum of surplus labour from the direct producers or workers, surplus labour that it receives without an equivalent and which by its very nature always remains forced labour, however much it might appear as the result of free contractual agreement. This surplus labour is expressed in a surplus-value, and this surplus-value exists in a surplus product. Surplus labour in some form must always remain, as labour beyond the extent of given needs. It is just that in the

Original publication details: Karl Marx, "On the Realm of Necessity and the Realm of Freedom," and "Magna Carta of the Legally Limited Working Day", from *Capital: A Critique of Political Economy*, Vol 3, tr. David Fernbach, pp.4–6 and 414–416. Penguin Books in association with New Left Review, 1981. Reproduced with permission from New Left Review.

Class: The Anthology, First Edition. Edited by Stanley Aronowitz and Michael J. Roberts.

capitalist, as in the slave system, etc., it has an antagonistic form and its obverse side is pure idleness on the part of one section of society. A certain quantum of surplus labour is required as insurance against accidents and for the progressive extension of the reproduction process that is needed to keep pace with the development of needs and the progress of population. It is one of the civilizing aspects of capital that it extorts this surplus labour in a manner and in conditions that are more advantageous to social relations and to the creation of elements for a new and higher formation than was the case under the earlier forms of slavery, serfdom, etc. Thus on the one hand it leads towards a stage at which compulsion and the monopolization of social development (with its material and intellectual advantages) by one section of society at the expense of another disappears; on the other hand it creates the material means and the nucleus for relations that permit this surplus labour to be combined, in a higher form of society, with a greater reduction of the overall time devoted to material labour. For, according to the development of labour productivity, surplus labour can be great when the total working day is short and relatively small when the total working day is long. If the necessary labour-time is 3 hours and surplus labour also 3 hours, the total working day is 6 hours and the rate of surplus labour 100 per cent. If the necessary labour is 9 hours and the surplus labour 3 hours, the total working day is 12 hours and the rate of surplus labour only $33\frac{1}{3}$ per cent. It then depends on the productivity of labour how much use-value is produced in a given time, and also therefore in a given surplus labour-time. The real wealth of society and the possibility of a constant expansion of its reproduction process does not depend on the length of surplus labour but rather on its productivity and on the more or less plentiful conditions of production in which it is performed. The realm of freedom really begins only where labour determined by necessity and external expediency ends; it lies by its nature beyond the sphere of material production proper. Just as the savage must wrestle with nature to satisfy his needs; so must civilized man, and he must do so in all forms of society and under all possible modes of production. This realm of natural necessity expands with his development, because his needs do too; but the productive forces to satisfy these expand at the same time. Freedom, in this sphere, can consist only in this, that socialized man, the associated producers, govern the human metabolism with nature in a rational way, bringing it under their collective control instead of being dominated by it as a blind power; accomplishing it with the least expenditure of energy and in conditions most worthy and appropriate for their human nature. But this always remains a realm of necessity. The true realm of freedom, the development of human powers as an end in itself, begins beyond it, though it can only flourish with this realm of necessity as its basis. The reduction of the working day is the basic prerequisite.

The Magna Carta of the Legally Limited Working Day

In the United States of America, every independent workers' movement was paralysed as long as slavery disfigured a part of the republic. Labour in a white skin cannot emancipate itself where it is branded in a black skin. However, a new life immediately arose from the death of slavery. The first fruit of the American Civil War was the eight hours' agitation, which ran from the Atlantic to the Pacific, from New England to California, with the seven-league boots of the locomotive. The General Congress of Labour held at

Baltimore in August 1866 declared: 'The first and great necessity of the present, to free the labour of this country from capitalistic slavery, is the passing of a law by which eight hours shall be the normal working day in all States of the American Union. We are resolved to put forth all our strength until this glorious result is attained.'[63] At the same time (the beginning of September 1866), the Congress of the International Working Men's Association, held at Geneva, passed the following resolution, proposed by the London General Council: 'We declare that the limitation of the working day is a preliminary condition without which all further attempts at improvement and emancipation must prove abortive ... the Congress proposes eight hours as the legal limit of the working day.'*

Thus the working-class movement on both sides of the Atlantic, which had grown instinctively out of the relations of production themselves, set its seal on the words of the English factory inspector, R. J. Saunders; 'Further steps towards a reformation of society can never be carried out with any hope of success, unless the hours of labour be limited, and the prescribed limit strictly enforced.'

It must be acknowledged that our worker emerges from the process of production looking different from when he entered it. In the market, as owner of the commodity 'labour-power', he stood face to face with other owners of commodities, one owner against another owner. The contract by which he sold his labour-power to the capitalist proved in black and white, so to speak, that he was free to dispose of himself. But when the transaction was concluded, it was discovered that he was no 'free agent', that the period of time for which he is free to sell his labour-power is the period of time for which he is forced to sell it, that in fact the vampire will not let go 'while there remains a single muscle, sinew or drop of blood to be exploited'. For 'protection' against the serpent of their agonies, the workers have to put their heads together and, as a class, compel the passing of a law, an all-powerful social barrier by which they can be prevented from selling themselves and their families into slavery and death by voluntary contract with capital. In the place of the pompous catalogue of the 'inalienable rights of man' there steps the modest Magna Carta of the legally limited working day, which at last makes clear 'when the time which the worker sells is ended, and when his own begins'. *Quantum mutatus ab illo!***

Notes

[49]   This is where Chapter 48 begins in the manuscript. – Frederick Engels.

[63]   'We, the workers of Dunkirk, declare that the length of time of labour required under the present system is too great, and that, far from leaving the worker time for rest and education, it plunges him into a condition of servitude but little better than slavery. That is why we decide that eight hours are enough for a working day, and ought to be legally recognized as enough; why we call to our help that powerful lever, the press;. and why we shall consider all those that refuse us this help as enemies of the reform of labour and of the rights of the labourer' (Resolution of the Working Men of Dunkirk, State of New York, 1866).

*   This resolution was drafted by Marx himself. (See 'Instructions for Delegates to the Geneva Conference', printed in *The First International and After*, Pelican Marx Library, 1973, p. 87.)

**   'What a great change from that time' (Virgil, *Aeneid*, Bk 2, line 274).

CHAPTER 3

Time, Work–Discipline, and Industrial Capitalism

E.P. Thompson

It is commonplace that the years between 1300 and 1650 saw within the intellectual culture of Western Europe important changes in the apprehension of time.[1] In the *Canterbury Tales* the cock still figures in his immemorial rôle as nature's timepiece: Chauntecleer —

> Caste up his eyen to the brighte sonne,
> That in the signe of Taurus hadde yronne
> Twenty degrees and oon, and somwhat moore,
> He knew by kynde, and by noon oother loore
> That it was pryme, and crew with blisful stevene....

But although "By nature knew he ech ascensioun/Of the equynoxial in thilke toun", the contrast between "nature's" time and clock time is pointed in the image —

> Wel sikerer was his crowyng in his logge
> Than is a clokke, or an abbey orlogge.

This is a very early clock: Chaucer (unlike Chauntecleer) was a Londoner, and was aware of the times of Court, of urban organization, and of that "merchant's time" which Jacques Le Goff, in a suggestive article in *Annales*, has opposed to the time of the medieval church.[2]

I do not wish to argue how far the change was due to the spread of clocks from the fourteenth century onwards, how far this was itself a symptom of a new Puritan discipline and bourgeois exactitude. However we see it, the change is certainly there. The clock steps on to the Elizabethan stage, turning Faustus's last soliloquy into a dialogue with time: "the stars move still, time runs, the clock will strike". Sidereal time, which has been present since literature began, has now moved at one step from the heavens into the

Original publication details: E.P. Thompson, "Time, Work-Discipline, and Industrial Capitalism" from *Past and Present*, No. 38 (Dec 1967), pp. 56–97. Reproduced with permission from Oxford University Press.

home. Mortality and love are both felt to be more poignant as the "Snayly motion of the mooving hand"[3] crosses the dial. When the watch is worn about the neck it lies in proximity to the less regular beating of the heart. The conventional Elizabethan images of time as a devourer, a defacer, a bloody tyrant, a scytheman, are old enough, but there is a new immediacy and insistence.[4]

As the seventeenth century moves on the image of clock-work extends, until, with Isaac Newton, it has engrossed the universe. And by the middle of the eighteenth century (if we are to trust Laurence Sterne) the clock had penetrated to more intimate levels. For Tristram Shandy's father — "one of the most regular men in everything he did … that ever lived" — "had made it a rule for many years of his life, — on the first Sunday night of every month … to wind up a large house-clock, which we had standing on the back-stairs head". "He had likewise gradually brought some other little family concernments to the same period", and this enabled Tristram to date his conception very exactly. It also provoked *The Clockmaker's Outcry against the Author*:

> The directions I had for making several clocks for the country are countermanded; because no modest lady now dares to mention a word about winding-up a clock, without exposing herself to the sly leers and jokes of the family … Nay, the common expression of street-walkers is, "Sir, will you have your clock wound up?"

Virtuous matrons (the "clockmaker" complained) are consigning their clocks to lumber rooms as "exciting to acts of carnality".[5]

However, this gross impressionism is unlikely to advance the present enquiry: how far, and in what ways, did this shift in time-sense affect labour discipline, and how far did it influence the inward apprehension of time of working people? If the transition to mature industrial society entailed a severe restructuring of working habits — new disciplines, new incentives, and a new human nature upon which these incentives could bite effectively — how far is this related to changes in the inward notation of time?

It is well known that among primitive peoples the measurement of time is commonly related to familiar processes in the cycle of work or of domestic chores. E.E. Evans-Pritchard has analysed the time-sense of the Nuer:

> The daily timepiece is the cattle clock, the round of pastoral tasks, and the time of day and the passage of time through a day are to a Nuer primarily the succession of these tasks and their relation to one another.

Among the Nandi an occupational definition of time evolved covering not only each hour, but half hours of the day — at 5–30 in the morning the oxen have gone to the grazing-ground, at 6 the sheep have been unfastened, at 6–30 the sun has grown, at 7 it has become warm, at 7–30 the goats have gone to the grazing-ground, etc. — an uncommonly well-regulated economy. In a similar way terms evolve for the measurement of time intervals. In Madagascar time might be measured by "a rice-cooking" (about half an hour) or "the frying of a locust" (a moment). The Cross River natives were reported as saying "the man died in less than the time in which maize is not yet completely roasted" (less than fifteen minutes).[6]

Pierre Bourdieu has explored more closely the attitudes towards time of the Kabyle peasant (in Algeria) in recent years: "An attitude of submission and of nonchalant indifference to the passage of time which no one dreams of mastering, using up, or saving ... Haste is seen as a lack of decorum combined with diabolical ambition". The clock is sometimes known as "the devil's mill"; there are no precise meal-times; "the notion of an exact appointment is unknown; they agree only to meet 'at the next market'". A popular song runs:

It is useless to pursue the world, No one will ever overtake it.[7]

J.M. Synge, in his well-observed account of the Aran Islands, gives us a classic example:

While I am walking with Michael someone often comes to me to ask the time of day. Few of the people, however, are sufficiently used to modern time to understand in more than a vague way the convention of the hours and when I tell them what o'clock it is by my watch they are not satisfied, and ask how long is left them before the twilight.[8]

The general knowledge of time on the island depends, curiously enough, upon the direction of the wind. Nearly all the cottages are built ... with two doors opposite each other, the more sheltered of which lies open all day to give light to the interior. If the wind is northerly the south door is opened, and the shadow of the door-post moving across the kitchen floor indicates the hour; as soon, however, as the wind changes to the south the other door is opened, and the people, who never think of putting up a primitive dial, are at a loss....

When the wind is from the north the old woman manages my meals with fair regularity; but on the other days she often makes my tea at three o'clock instead of six....[9]

Such a disregard for clock time could of course only be possible in a crofting and fishing community whose framework of marketing and administration is minimal, and in which the day's tasks (which might vary from fishing to farming, building, mending of nets, thatching, making a cradle or a coffin) seem to disclose themselves, by the logic of need, before the crofter's eyes.[10] But his account will serve to emphasize the essential conditioning in differing notations of time provided by different work-situations and their relation to "natural" rhythms. Clearly hunters must employ certain hours of the night to set their snares. Fishing and seafaring people must integrate their lives with the tides. A petition from Sunderland in 1800 includes the words "considering that this is a seaport in which many people are obliged to be up at all hours of the night to attend the tides and their affairs upon the river".[11] The operative phrase is "attend the tides": the patterning of social time in the seaport follows *upon* the rhythms of the sea; and this appears to be natural and comprehensible to fishermen or seamen: the compulsion is nature's own.

In a similar way labour from dawn to dusk can appear to be "natural" in a farming community, especially in the harvest months: nature demands that the grain be harvested before the thunderstorms set in. And we may note similar "natural" work-rhythms which attend other rural or industrial occupations: sheep must be attended at lambing time and guarded from predators; cows must be milked; the charcoal fire must be attended and not burn away through the turfs (and the charcoal burners must sleep beside it); once iron is in the making, the furnaces must not be allowed to fail.

The notation of time which arises in such contexts has been described as task-orientation. It is perhaps the most effective orientation in peasant societies, and it remains important in village and domestic industries. It has by no means lost all relevance in rural parts of Britain today. The peasant or labourer appears to attend upon what is an observed necessity [...] — the working-day lengthens or contracts according to the task — and there is no great sense of conflict between labour and "passing the time of day". To men accustomed to labour timed by the clock, this attitude to labour appears to be wasteful and lacking in urgency.[12]

Such a clear distinction supposes, of course, the independent peasant or craftsman as referent. But the question of task-orientation becomes greatly more complex at the point where labour is employed. The entire family economy of the small farmer may be task-orientated; but within it there may be a division of labour, and allocation of rôles, and the discipline of an employer-employed relationship between the farmer and his children. Even here time is beginning to become money, the employer's money. As soon as actual hands are employed the shift from task-orientation to timed labour is marked. It is true that the timing of work can be done independently of any time-piece — and indeed precedes the diffusion of the clock. Still, in the mid-seventeenth century substantial farmers calculated their expectations of employed labour (as did Henry Best) in "dayworkes" — "the Cunnigarth, with its bottomes, is 4 large dayworkes for a good mower", "the Spellowe is 4 indifferent dayworkes", etc.;[13] and what Best did for his own farm, G. Markham attempted to present in general form:

> A man … may mow of Corn, as Barley and Oats, if it be thick, loggy and beaten down to the earth, making fair work, and not cutting off the heads of the ears, and leaving the straw still growing one acre and a half in a day: but if it be good thick and fair standing corn, then he may mow two acres, or two acres and a half in a day; but if the corn be short and thin, then he may mow three, and sometimes four Acres in a day, and not be overlaboured....[14]

The computation is difficult, and dependent upon many variables. Clearly, a straightforward time-measurement was more convenient.

This measurement embodies a simple relationship. Those who are employed experience a distinction between their employer's time and their "own" time. And the employer must *use* the time of his labour, and see it is not wasted: not the task but the value of time when reduced to money is dominant. Time is now currency: it is not passed but spent.

Attention to time in labour depends in large degree upon the need for the synchronization of labour. But in so far as manufacturing industry remained conducted upon a domestic or small workshop scale, without intricate subdivision of processes, the degree of synchronization demanded was slight, and task-orientation was still prevalent.[15] The putting-out system demanded much fetching, carrying, waiting for materials. Bad weather could disrupt not only agriculture, building and transport, but also weaving, where the finished pieces had to be stretched on the tenters to dry. As we get closer to each task, we are surprised to find the multiplicity of subsidiary tasks which the same worker or family group must do in one cottage or workshop. Even in larger workshops men sometimes continued to work at distinct tasks at their own benches or looms, and — except where the fear of the embezzlement of materials imposed stricter supervision — could show some flexibility in coming and going.

Hence we get the characteristic irregularity of labour patterns before the coming of large-scale machine-powered industry. Within the general demands of the week's or fortnight's tasks — the piece of cloth, so many nails or pairs of shoes — the working day might be lengthened or shortened. Moreover, in the early development of manufacturing industry, and of mining, many mixed occupations survived: Cornish tinners who also took a hand in the pilchard fishing; Northern lead-miners who were also smallholders; the village craftsmen who turned their hands to various jobs, in building, carting, joining; the domestic workers who left their work for the harvest; the Pennine small-farmer/weaver.

It is in the nature of such work that accurate and representative time-budgets will not survive.

The work pattern was one of alternate bouts of intense labour and of idleness, wherever men were in control of their own working lives. (The pattern persists among some self-employed — artists, writers, small farmers, and perhaps also with students — today, and provokes the question whether it is not a "natural" human work-rhythm.) On Monday or Tuesday, according to tradition, the hand-loom went to the slow chant of *Plen-ty of Time, Plen-ty of Time*: on Thursday and Friday, *A day t'lat, A day t'lat*.[16] The temptation to lie in an extra hour in the morning pushed work into the evening, candle-lit hours.[17] There are few trades which are not described as honouring Saint Monday: shoemakers, tailors, colliers, printing workers, potters, weavers, hosiery workers, cutlers, all Cockneys. Despite the full employment of many London trades during the Napoleonic Wars, a witness complained that "we see Saint Monday so religiously kept in this great city … in general followed by a Saint Tuesday also".[18]

Saint Monday, indeed, appears to have been honoured almost universally wherever small-scale, domestic, and outwork industries existed; was generally found in the pits; and sometimes continued in manufacturing and heavy industry.[19] It was perpetuated, in England, into the nineteenth — and, indeed, into the twentieth[20] — centuries for complex economic and social reasons. In some trades, the small masters themselves accepted the institution, and employed Monday in taking-in or giving-out work. In Sheffield, where the cutlers had for centuries tenaciously honoured the Saint, it had become "a settled habit and custom" which the steel-mills themselves honoured (1874):

> This Monday idleness is, in some cases, enforced by the fact that Monday is the day that is taken for repairs to the machinery of the great steelworks.[21]

Where the custom was deeply-established, Monday was the day set aside for marketing and personal business. Also, as George Duveau suggests of French workers, "le dimanche est le jour de la famille, le lundi celui de l'amitié"; and as the nineteenth-century advanced, its celebration was something of a privilege of status of the better-paid artisan.[22]

> Saint Monday brings more ills about,
>   For when the money's spent,
> The children's clothes go up the spout,
>   Which causes discontent;
> And when at night he staggers home,
>   He knows not what to say,
> A fool is more a man than he
>   Upon a fuddling day.

This irregular working rhythm is commonly associated with heavy week-end drinking: Saint Monday is a target in many Victorian temperance tracts. But even the most sober and self-disciplined artisan might feel the necessity for such alternations. "I know not how to describe the sickening aversion which at times steals over the working man and utterly disables him for a longer or shorter period, from following his usual occupation", Francis Place wrote in 1829; and he added a footnote of personal testimony:

> For nearly six years, whilst working, when I had work to do, from twelve to eighteen hours a day, when no longer able, from the cause mentioned, to continue working, I used to run

from it, and go as rapidly as I could to Highgate, Hampstead, Muswell-hill, or Norwood, and then "return to my vomit" … This is the case with every workman I have ever known; and in proportion as a man's case is hopeless will such fits more frequently occur and be of longer duration.[23]

We may, finally, note that the irregularity of working day and week were framed, until the first decades of the nineteenth century, within the larger irregularity of the working year, punctuated by its traditional holidays and fairs. Still, despite the triumph of the Sabbath over the ancient saints' days in the seventeenth century, the people clung tenaciously to their customary wakes and feasts, and may even have enlarged them both in vigour and extent.[24]

How far can this argument be extended from manufacturing industry to the rural labourers? On the face of it, there would seem to be unrelenting daily and weekly labour here: the field labourer had no Saint Monday. But a close discrimination of different work situations is still required. The eighteenth- (and nineteenth-) century village had its own self-employed artisans, as well as many employed on irregular task work.[25]

The irregular labour rhythms described in the previous section help us to understand the severity of mercantilist doctrines as to the necessity for holding down wages as a preventative against idleness, and it would seem to be not until the second half of the eighteenth century that "normal" capitalist wage incentives begin to become widely effective.[26] The first is found in the extraordinary Law Book of the Crowley Iron Works. Here, at the very birth of the large-scale unit in manufacturing industry, the old autocrat, Sir Ambrose Crowley, found it necessary to design an entire civil and penal code, running to more than 100,000 words, to govern and regulate his refractory labour-force. The preambles to Orders Number 40 (the Warden at the Mill) and 103 (Monitor) strike the prevailing note of morally-righteous invigilation. From Order 40:

> I having by sundry people working by the day with the connivence of the clerks been horribly cheated and paid for much more time than in good conscience I ought and such hath been the baseness & treachery of sundry clerks that they have concealed the sloath & negligence of those paid by the day.…

And from Order 103:

> Some have pretended a sort of right to loyter, thinking by their readiness and ability to do sufficient in less time than others. Others have been so foolish to think bare attendance without being imployed in business is sufficient.… Others so impudent as to glory in their villany and upbrade others for their diligence.…
>
> To the end that sloath and villany should be detected and the just and diligent rewarded, I have thought meet to create an account of time by a Monitor, and do order and it is hereby ordered and declared from 5 to 8 and from 7 to 10 is fifteen hours, out of which take 1½ for breakfast, dinner, etc. There will then be thirteen hours and a half neat service.…

This service must be calculated "after all deductions for being at taverns, alehouses, coffee houses, breakfast, dinner, playing, sleeping, smoking, singing, reading of news history, quarelling, contention, disputes or anything forreign to my business, any way loytering".

We are entering here, already in 1700, the familiar landscape of disciplined industrial capitalism, with the time-sheet, the time-keeper, the informers and the fines. Some 70 years later the same discipline was to be imposed in the early cotton mills (although the machinery itself was a powerful supplement to the time-keeper). Lacking the aid of machinery to regulate the pace of work on the pot-bank, that supposedly-formidable disciplinarian, Josiah Wedgwood, was reduced to enforcing discipline upon the potters in surprisingly muted terms. The duties of the Clerk of the Manufactory were:

> To be at the works the first in the morning, & settle the people to their business as they come in, — to encourage those who come regularly to their time, letting them know that their regularity is properly noticed, & distinguishing them by repeated marks of approbation, from the less orderly part of the workpeople, by presents or other marks suitable to their ages, &c.
>
> Those who come later than the hour appointed should be noticed, and if after repeated marks of disapprobation they do not come in due time, an account of the time they are deficient in should be taken, and so much of their wages stopt as the time comes to if they work by wages, and if they work by the piece they should after frequent notice be sent back to breakfast-time.[27]

These regulations were later tightened somewhat:

> Any of the workmen forceing their way through the Lodge after the time alow'd by the Master forfeits 2/-d.[28]

and Wedgwood wrestled with the problem at Etruria and introduced the first recorded system of clocking-in.[29] But it would seem that once the strong presence of Josiah himself was withdrawn the incorrigible potters returned to many of their older ways.

It is too easy, however, to see this only as a matter of factory or workshop discipline, and we may glance briefly at the attempt to impose "time-thrift" in the domestic manufacturing districts, and its impingement upon social and domestic life. Almost all that the masters *wished* to see imposed may be found in the bounds of a single pamphlet, the Rev. J. Clayton's *Friendly Advice to the Poor*, "written and publish'd at the Request of the late and present Officers of the Town of Manchester" in 1755. "If the *sluggard hides his hands* in his bosom, rather than applies them to work; if he spends his Time in Sauntring, impairs his Constitution by Laziness, and dulls his Spirit by Indolence ..." then he can expect only poverty as his reward. The labourer must not loiter idly in the market-place or waste time in marketing. Clayton complains that "the Churches and Streets [are] crowded with Numbers of Spectators" at weddings and funerals, "who in spight of the Miseries of their Starving Condition ... make no Scruple of wasting the best Hours in the Day, for the sake of gazing ...". The tea-table is "this shameful devourer of Time and Money". So also are wakes and holidays and the annual feasts of friendly societies. So also is "that slothful spending the Morning in Bed":

> The necessity of early rising would reduce the poor to a necessity of going to Bed betime; and thereby prevent the Danger of Midnight revels.

Early rising would also "introduce an exact Regularity into their Families, a wonderful Order into their Oeconomy".

The catalogue is familiar, and might equally well be taken from Richard Baxter's *The Poor Man's Family Book* in the previous century. If we can trust Bamford's *Early Days*,[30] Clayton failed to make many converts from their old way of life among the weavers. Nevertheless, the long dawn chorus of moralists is prelude to the quite sharp attack upon popular customs, sports, and holidays which was made in the last years of the eighteenth century and the first years of the nineteenth.

One other non-industrial institution lay to hand which might be used to inculcate "time-thrift": the school. Clayton complained that the streets of Manchester were full of "idle ragged children; who are not only losing their Time, but learning habits of gaming", etc. He praised charity schools as teaching Industry, Frugality, Order and Regularity: "the Scholars here are obliged to rise betimes and to observe Hours with great Punctuality".[31] William Temple, when advocating, in 1770, that poor children be sent at the age of four to work-houses where they should be employed in manufactures and given two hours' schooling a day, was explicit about the socializing influence of the process:

> There is considerable use in their being, somehow or other, constantly employed at least twelve hours a day, whether they earn their living or not; for by these means, we hope that the rising generation will be so habituated to constant employment that it would at length prove agreeable and entertaining to them....[32]

Powell, in 1772, also saw education as a training in the "habit of industry"; by the time the child reached six or seven it should become "habituated, not to say naturalized to Labour and Fatigue".[33]

The onslaught, from so many directions, upon the people's old working habits was not, of course, uncontested. In the first stage, we find simple resistance.[34] But, in the next stage, as the new time-discipline is imposed, so the workers begin to fight, not against time, but about it. The evidence here is not wholly clear. But in the better-organized artisan trades, especially in London, there is no doubt that hours were progressively shortened in the eighteenth century as combination advanced. By the end of the eighteenth century there is some evidence that some favoured trades had gained something like a ten-hour day.

In all these ways — by the division of labour; the supervision of labour; fines; bells and clocks; money incentives; preachings and schoolings; the suppression of fairs and sports — new labour habits were formed, and a new time-discipline was imposed. It sometimes took several generations (as in the Potteries), and we may doubt how far it was ever fully accomplished: irregular labour rhythms were perpetuated (and even institutionalized) into the present century, notably in London and in the great ports.[35]

Throughout the nineteenth century the propaganda of time-thrift continued to be directed at the working people, the rhetoric becoming more debased, the apostrophes to eternity becoming more shop-soiled, the homilies more mean and banal. In early Victorian tracts and reading-matter aimed at the masses one is choked by the quantity of the stuff. But eternity has become those never-ending accounts of pious death-beds (or sinners struck by lightning), while the homilies have become little Smilesian snippets about humble men who by early rising and diligence made good. The leisured classes began to discover the "problem" (about which we hear a good deal today) of the leisure of the masses. A considerable proportion of manual workers (one moralist was alarmed to discover) after concluding their work were left with

> several hours in the day to be spent nearly as they please. And in what manner ... is this precious time expended by those of no mental cultivation? ... We shall often see them just simply annihilating those portions of time. They will for an hour, or for hours together ... sit on a bench, or lie down on a bank or hillock ... yielded up to utter vacancy and torpor ... or collected in groups by the road side, in readiness to find in whatever passes there occasions for gross jocularity; practising some impertinence, or uttering some jeering scurrility, at the expense of persons going by....[36]

This, clearly, was worse than Bingo: non-productivity, compounded with impertinence. In mature capitalist society all time must be consumed, marketed, put to *use*; it is offensive for the labour force merely to "pass the time".

But how far did this propaganda really succeed? How far are we entitled to speak of any radical restructuring of man's social nature and working habits? I have given elsewhere some reasons for supposing that this discipline was indeed internalized, and that we may see in the Methodist sects of the early nineteenth century a figuration of the psychic crisis entailed.[37] By the 1830s and 1840s it was commonly observed that the English industrial worker was marked off from his fellow Irish worker, not by a greater capacity for hard work, but by his regularity, his methodical paying-out of energy, and perhaps also by a repression, not of enjoyments, but of the capacity to relax in the old, uninhibited ways.

There is no way in which we can quantify the time-sense of one, or of a million, workers. But it is possible to offer one check of a comparative kind. For what was said by the mercantilist moralists as to the failures of the eighteenth-century English poor to respond to incentives and disciplines is often repeated, by observers and by theorists of economic growth, of the peoples of developing countries today. Thus Mexican paeons in the early years of this century were regarded as an "indolent and child-like people". The Mexican mineworker had the custom of returning to his village for corn planting and harvest:

> His lack of initiative, inability to save, absences while celebrating too many holidays, willingness to work only three or four days a week if that paid for necessities, insatiable desire for alchohol — all were pointed out as proof of a natural inferiority.

He failed to respond to direct day-wage incentives, and (like the eighteenth-century English collier or tinner) responded better to contract and sub-contract systems:

> Given a contract and the assurance that he will get so much money for each ton he mines, and that it doesn't matter how long he takes doing it, or how often he sits down to contemplate life, he will work with a vigour which is remarkable.[38]

In generalizations supported by another study of Mexican labour conditions, Wilbert Moore remarks: "Work is almost always task-orientated in non-industrial societies ... and ... it may be appropriate to tie wages to tasks and not directly to time in newly developing areas".[39]

The problem recurs in a dozen forms in the literature of "industrialization". For the engineer of economic growth, it may appear as the problem of absenteeism — how is the Company to deal with the unrepentant labourer on the Cameroons plantation who declares: "How man fit work so, any day, any day, weh'e no take absen'? No be 'e go die?" ("How could a man work like that, day after day, without being absent? Would he not die?")?[40]

> ... the whole mores of African life, make a high and sustained level of effort in a given length of working day a greater burden both physically and psychologically than in Europe.
> Time commitments in the Middle East or in Latin America are often treated somewhat casually by European standards; new industrial workers only gradually become accustomed to regular hours, regular attendance, and a regular pace of work; transportation schedules or the delivery of materials are not always reliable....[41]

The problem may appear as one of adapting the seasonal rhythms of the countryside, with its festivals and religious holidays, to the needs of industrial production:

> The work year of the factory is necessarily in accord with the workers' demands, rather than an ideal one from the point of view of most efficient production. Several attempts by the managers to alter the work pattern have come to nil. The factory comes back to a schedule acceptable to the Cantelano.[42]

What needs to be said is not that one way of life is better than the other, but that this is a place of the most far-reaching conflict; that the historical record is not a simple one of neutral and inevitable technological change, but is also one of exploitation and of resistance to exploitation; and that values stand to be lost as well as gained.

It is a problem which the peoples of the developing world must live through and grow through. One hopes that they will be wary of pat, manipulative models, which present the working masses only as an inert labour force. And there is a sense, also, within the advanced industrial countries, in which this has ceased to be a problem placed in the past. For we are now at a point where sociologists are discussing the "problem" of leisure. And a part of the problem is: how did it come to be a problem? Puritanism, in its marriage of convenience with industrial capitalism, was the agent which converted men to new valuations of time; which taught children even in their infancy to improve each shining hour; and which saturated men's minds with the equation, time is money.[43] One recurrent form of revolt within Western industrial capitalism, whether bohemian or beatnik, has often taken the form of flouting the urgency of respectable time-values. And the interesting question arises: if Puritanism was a necessary part of the work-ethos which enabled the industrialized world to break out of the poverty-stricken economies of the past, will the Puritan valuation of time begin to decompose as the pressures of poverty relax? Is it decomposing already? Will men begin to lose that restless urgency, that desire to consume time purposively, which most people carry just as they carry a watch on their wrists?

If we are to have enlarged leisure, in an automated future, the problem is not "how are men going to be able to *consume* all these additional time-units of leisure?" but "what will be the capacity for experience of the men who have this undirected time to live?" If we maintain a Puritan time-valuation, a commodity-valuation, then it is a question of how this time is put to *use*, or how it is exploited by the leisure industries. But if the purposive notation of time-use becomes less compulsive, then men might have to re-learn some of the arts of living lost in the industrial revolution: how to fill the interstices of their days with enriched, more leisurely, personal and social relations; how to break down once more the barriers between work and life. And hence would stem a novel dialectic in which some of the old aggressive energies and disciplines migrate to the newly-industrializing nations, while the old industrialized nations seek to rediscover modes of experience forgotton before written history begins:

> ... the Nuer have no expression equivalent to "time" in our language, and they cannot, therefore, as we can, speak of time as though it were something actual, which passes, can be wasted, can be saved, and so forth. I do not think that they ever experience the same feeling of fighting against time or of having to co-ordinate activities with an abstract passage of time because their points of reference are mainly the activities themselves, which are generally of a leisurely character. Events follow a logical order, but they are not controlled by an abstract system, there being no autonomous points of reference to which activities have to conform with precision. Nuer are fortunate.[44]

Of course, no culture re-appears in the same form. If men are to meet both the demands of a highly-synchronized automated industry, and of greatly enlarged areas of "free time", they must somehow combine in a new synthesis elements of the old and of the new, finding an imagery based neither upon the seasons nor upon the market but upon human occasions.

Notes

1   Lewis Mumford makes suggestive claims in *Technics and Civilization* (London, 1934), esp. pp. 12–18, 196–9: see also S. de Grazia, *Of Time, Work, and Leisure* (New York, 1962), Carlo M. Cipolla, *Clocks and Culture 1300–1700* (London, 1967), and Edward T. Hall, *The Silent Language* (New York, 1959).

2   J. le Goff, "Au Moyen Age: Temps de L'Egliste et temps du marchand", *Annales, E.S.C.*, xv (1960); and the same author's "Le temps du travail dans le 'crise' du XIVe Siecle: du temps médiéval au temps moderne", *Le Moyen Age*, lxix (1963).

3   M. Drayton, "Of his Ladies not Comming to London", *Works*, ed. J. W. Hebel (Oxford, 1932), iii, p. 204.

4   The changes are discussed in Cipolla, *op. cit.*; Erwin Sturzl, *Der Zeitbegriff in der Elisabethanischen Literatur* (Wiener Beitrage zur Englischen Philologie, lxix, Wien-Stuttgart, 1965); Alberto Tenenti, *Il Senso della Morte e l'amore della vita nel rinanscimento* (Milan, 1957).

5   Anon., *The Clockmaker's Outcry against the Author of ... Tristram Shandy* (London, 1760), pp. 42–3.

6   E. E. Evans-Pritchard, *The Nuer* (Oxford, 1940), pp. 100–4; M. P. Nilsson, *Primitive Time Reckoning* (Lund, 1920), pp. 32–3, 42; P. A. Sorokin and R. K. Merton, "Social Time: a Methodological and Functional Analysis", *Amer. Jl. Sociol.*, xlii (1937); A. I. Hallowell, "Temporal Orientation in Western Civilization and in a Pre-Literate Society", *Amer. Anthrop.*, new ser. xxxix (1937). Other sources for primitive time reckoning are cited in H. G. Alexander, *Time as Dimension and History* (Albuquerque, 1945), p. 26, and Beate R. Salz, "The Human Element in Industrialization", *Econ. Devel. And Cult. Change*, iv (1955), esp. pp. 94–114.

7   P. Bourdieu, "The attitude of the Algerian peasant toward time", in *Mediterranean Countrymen*, ed. J. Pitt-Rivers (Paris, 1963), pp. 55–72.

8   J. M. Synge, *The Aran Islands* (Dublin, 1907), p. 179: "Spanish Americans do not regulate their lives by the clock as Anglos do. Both rural and urban people, when asked when they plan to do something, gives answers like: 'Right now, about two or four o'clock'".

9   J. M. Synge, *Plays, Poems, and Prose* (Everyman edn., London, 1941), p. 257.

10 The most important event in the relation of the islands to an external economy in Synge's time was the arrival of the steamer, whose times might be greatly affected by tide and weather. See Synge, *The Aran Islands* (Dublin, 1907), pp. 115–6.

11 Public Rec. Off., W.O. 40/17. It is of interest to note other examples of the recognition that seafaring time conflicted with urban routines: the Court of Admiralty was held to be always open, "for strangers and merchants, and seafaring men, must take the opportunity of tides and winds, and cannot without ruin and great prejudice attend the solemnity of courts and dilatory pleadings" (see E. Vansittart Neale, *Feasts and Fasts* [London, 1845], p. 249), while in some Sabbatarian legislation an exception was made for fisherman who sighted a shoal off-shore on the Sabbath day.

12 Henri Lefebvre, *Critique de la Vie Quotidienne* (Paris, 1958), ii. pp. 52–6, prefers a distinction between "cyclical time" — arising from changing seasonal occupations in agriculture — and the "linear time" of urban, industrial organization. More suggestive is Lucien Febvre's distinction between "Le temps vécu et le temps-mesure", *La Problème de L'Incroyance an XVIᵉ Siècle* (Paris, 1947), p. 431. A somewhat schematic examination of the organization of tasks in primitive economies is in Stanley H. Udy, *Organization of Work* (New Haven, 1959), ch. 2.

13 *Rural Economy in Yorkshire in 1641... Farming and Account Books of Henry Best*, ed. C. B. Robinson (Surtees Society xxxiii, 1857), pp. 38–9.

14 G. Markham, *The Inrichment of the Weald of Kent*, 10th edn. (London, 1660), ch. xii : "A general computation of men, and cattel's labours: what each may do without hurt daily", pp. 112–8.

15 For some of the problems discussed in this and the following section, see especially Keith Thomas, "Work and Leisure in Pre-Industrial Societies", *Past and Present*, no. 29 (Dec. 1964). Also C. Hill, "The Uses of Sabbatarianism", in *Society and Puritanism in Pre-Revolutionary England* (London, 1964); E. S. Furniss, *The Position of the Laborer in a System of Nationalism* (Boston, 1920: repr. New York, 1965); D. C. Coleman, "Labour in the English Economy of the Seventeenth Century", *Econ. Hist. Rev.*, 2nd ser., viii (1955–6); S. Pollard, "Factory Discipline in the Industrial Revolution", *Econ. Hist. Rev.*, 2nd ser., xvi (1963–4); T. S. Ashton, *An Economic History of England in the Eighteenth Century* (London, 1955), ch. vii; W. E. Moore, *Industrialization and Society* (UNESCO, 1963).

16 T. W. Hanson, "The Diary of a Grandfather", *Trans. Halifax Antiq. Soc.*, 1916; p. 234.

17 J. Clayton, *Friendly Advice to the Poor* (Manchester, 1755), p. 36.

18 *Report of the Trial of Alexander Wadsworth against Peter Laurie* (London, 1811), p. 21. The complaint is particularly directed against the Saddlers.

19 It was honoured by Mexican weavers in 1800: see Jan Bazant, "Evolution of the textile industry of Puebla, 1544–1845", *Comparative Studies in Society and History*, viii (1964), p. 65. Valuable accounts of the custom in France in the 1850s and 1860s are in George Duveau, *La Vie Ouvrière en France sous le Second Empire* (Paris, 1946), pp. 242–8, and P. Pierrard, *La Vie Ouvrière à Lille sous le Second Empire* (Paris, 1965), pp. 165–6. Edward Young, conducting a survey of labour conditions in Europe, with the assistance of U.S. consuls, mentions the custom in France, Belgium, Prussia, Stockholm, etc. in the 1870s: E. Young, *Labour in Europe and America* (Washington, 1875), pp. 576, 661, 674, 685, &c.

20 Notably in the pits. An old Yorkshire miner informs me that in his youth it was a custom on a bright Monday morning to toss a coin in order to decide whether or not to work. I have also been told that "Saint Monday" is still honoured (1967) in its pristine purity by a few coopers in Burton-on-Trent.

21 E. Young, *op. cit.*, pp. 408–9 (Report of U.S. Consul). Similarly, in some mining districts, "Pay Monday" was recognized by the employers, and the pits were only kept open for repairs: on Monday, only "dead work is going on", *Report of the Select Committee on the Scarcity and Dearness of Coal, P.P.*, 1873, x, QQ 177, 201–7.

22   Duveau, op. cit., p. 247. "A Journeyman Engineer" (T. Wright) devotes a whole chapter to "Saint Monday" in his *Some Habits and Customs of the Working Classes* (London, 1867), esp. pp. 112–6, under the mistaken impression that the institution was "comparatively recent", and consequent upon steam power giving rise to "a numerous body of highly skilled and highly paid workmen" – notably engineers!

23   F. Place, *Improvement of the Working People* (1834), pp. 13–15 ; Brit. Mus., Add. MS. 27825. See also John Wade, *History of the Middle and Working Classes*, 3rd edn. (London, 1835), pp. 124–5.

24   Clayton, *op. cit.*, p. 13, claimed that "common custom has established so many Holy-days, that few of our manufacturing works-folks are closely and regularly employed above two-third parts of their time". See also Furniss, *op. cit.*, pp. 44–5, and the abstract of my paper in the *Bulletin for the Society for the Study of Labour History*, no. 9, 1964.

25   "We have four or five little farmers… we have a bricklayer, a carpenter, a blacksmith, and a miller, all of whom… are in a very frequent habit of drinking the King's health… Their employment is unequal; sometimes they are full of business, and sometimes they have none; generally they have many leisure hours because… the hardest part [of their work] devolves to some men whom they hire…", "A Farmer", describing his own village in 1798. "A Farmer", Observations on Taken-Work and Labour", *Monthly Magazine*, September 1798, May 1799.

26   The change is perhaps signaled at the same time in the ideology of the more enlightened employers: see A. W. Coats, "Changing attitudes to labour in the mid-eighteenth century", *Econ. Hist. Rev.*, 2nd ser., xi (1958–9).

27   MS. instructions, *circa* 1780, in Wedgwood MSS. (Barlaston), 26. 19114.

28   "Some regulations and rules made for this manufactory more than 30 years back", dated *circa* 1810, in Wedgwood MSS. (Keele University), 4045.5.

29   A "tell-tale" clock is preserved at Barlaston, but these "tell-tales" (manufactured by John Whitehurst of Derby from about 1750) served only to ensure the regular patrol and attendance of night-watchmen, etc. The first printing time-recorders were made by Bundy in the U.S.A. in 1885. F. A. B. Ward, *Handbook of the Collections illustrating Time Measurement* (London, 1947), p. 160; Charles Babbage, *On the Economy of Machinery and Manufacturers* (London, 1835), pp. 28, 40; E. Bruton, *The Longcase Clock* (London, 1964), pp. 95–6.

30   Samuel Bamford, *Early Days* (London: Simkin, Marshall, & Co and All Booksellers, 1849).

31   Clayton, *loc, cit.*, pp. 19, 42–3.

32   Cited in Furniss, *op. cit.*, p. 114.

33   Anon. [Powell], *A View of Real Grievances* (London, 1772), p. 90.

34   The best account of the employers' problem is in S. Pollard, *The Genesis of Modern Management* (London, 1965), ch. v, "The Adaptation of the Labour Force".

35   There is an abundant literature of nineteenth-century dockland which illustrates this. However, in recent years the casual labourer in the ports has ceased to be a "casualty" of the labour market (as Henry Mayhew saw him) and is marked by his preference for high earnings over security: see K. J. W. Alexander, "Casual Labour and Labour Casualties", *Trans. Inst. of Engineers and Shipbuilders in Scotland* (Glasgow, 1964). I have not touched in this paper on the new occupational time-tables introduced in industrial society — notably night-shift workers (pits, railways, etc.): see the observations by "Journeyman Engineer" [T. Wright], *The Great Unwashed* (London, 1868), pp. 188–200; M. A. Pollock (ed.), *Working Days* (London, 1926), pp. 17–28; Tom Nairn, *New Left Review*, no. 34 (1965), p. 38.

36   John Foster, *An Essay on the Evils of Popular Ignorance* (London, 1821), pp. 180–5.

37   E. P. Thompson, *The Making of the English Working Class* (London, 1963), chaps. xi and xii.

38   Cited in M. D. Bernstein, *The Mexican Mining Industry, 1890–1950* (New York, 1964), ch. vii, see also M. Mead, ed. *Cultural Patterns and Technical Change* (New York, UNESCO, 1953), pp. 179–82.

39   W. E. Moore, *Industrialization and Labor* (Ithaca, 1951), p. 310 and pp. 44–7, 114–22.

40   F. A. Wells and W. A. Warmington, *Studies in Industrialization: Nigeria and the Cameroons* (London, 1962), p. 128.

41   Edwin J. Cohn, "Social and Cultural Factors affecting the Emergence of Innovations", in *Social Aspects of Economic Development* (Economic and Social Studies Conference Board, Istanbul, 1964), pp. 105–6.

42   Manning Nash, "The Recruitment of Wage Labor and the Development of New Skills", *Annals of the American Academy,* cccv (1956), pp. 27–8. See also Manning Nash, "The Reaction of a Civil-Religious Hierarchy to a Factory in Guatemala", *Human Organization*, xiii (1955), pp. 26–8, and B. Salz, *op. cit.*, pp. 94–114.

43   Suggestive comments on this equation are in Lewis Mumford and S. de Grazia, cited note 1 above; Paul Diesing, *Reason in Society* (Urbana, 1962), pp. 24–8; Hans Meyerhoff, *Time in Literature* (Univ. of California, 1955), pp. 106–19.

44   E. Evans-Pritchard, *op. cit.*, p. 103.

CHAPTER 4

The Wages of Whiteness
Race and the Making of the American Working Class

David R. Roediger

W.E.B. Du Bois's *Black Reconstruction* continually creates jarring, provocative theoretical images, mixing race and class by design. Black reconstruction is, for Du Bois, the key to the story of 'our [the US] labor movement'. The book is organized around the activities of workers, but those workers function, for Du Bois tragically, within racial categories: the first chapter is entitled 'The Black Worker' and the second 'The White Worker'. White labor does not just receive and resist racist ideas but embraces, adopts and, at times, murderously acts upon those ideas. The problem is not just that the white working class is at critical junctures manipulated into racism, but that it comes to think of itself and its interests as white.[1]

Du Bois regards the decision of workers to define themselves by their whiteness as understandable in terms of short-term advantages. In some times and places, he argues, such advantages showed up in pay packets, where the wages of white, native-born skilled workers were high, both compared with those of Blacks and by world standards.[2] But vital for the white workers Du Bois studied most closely was, as he puts it in a brilliant, indispensable formulation, that even when they 'received a low wage [they were] compensated in part by a ... public and psychological wage.' Here Du Bois not only emphasizes status but the extent to which status was bound up with real social gains. He continues:

> They were given public deference ... because they were white. They were admitted freely, with all classes of white people, to public functions [and] public parks. ... The police were drawn from their ranks and the courts, dependent on their votes, treated them with leniency. ... Their votes selected public officials and while this had small effect upon the economic situation, it had great effect upon their personal treatment. ... White schoolhouses were the best in the community, and conspicuously placed, and cost anywhere from twice to ten times colored schools.[3]

Original publication details: David Roediger "Neither Servant Nor a Master am I," and "Class, Coons and Crowds in Antebellum America", from *The Wages of Whiteness: Race and the Making of the American Working Class*, pp. 12–14; 43–50; 52–53; 55–57; 66–67; 87; 95–100; 103–105; 107; 118–119. Verso Press, 1991. Reproduced with permission from Verso Press.

As important as the specifics are here, still more important is the idea that the pleasures of whiteness could function as a 'wage' for white workers. That is, status and privileges conferred by race could be used to make up for alienating and exploitative class relationships, North and South. White workers could, and did, define and accept their class positions by fashioning identities as 'not slaves' and as 'not Blacks'.

When they did so, Du Bois argued, the wages of whiteness often turned out to be spurious. America's 'Supreme Adventure ... for that human freedom which would release the human spirit from lower lust for mere meat, and set it free to dream and sing' gave way to a racism that caused 'capitalism [to be] adopted, forwarded and approved by white labor' and that 'ruined democracy'. Race feeling and the benefits conferred by whiteness made white Southern workers forget their 'practically identical interests' with the Black poor and accept stunted lives for themselves and for those more oppressed than themselves.[4]

Du Bois argued that white supremacy undermined not just working class unity but the very *vision* of many white workers. He connected racism among whites with a disdain for hard work itself, a seeking of satisfaction off the job and a desire to evade rather than confront exploitation. Du Bois held that this would have been a better and more class-conscious nation and world had the heritage of slavery and racism not led the working class to prize whiteness.[5]

In its broadest strokes, this book argues that whiteness was a way in which white workers responded to a fear of dependency on wage labor and to the necessities of capitalist work discipline. As the US working class matured, principally in the North, within a slaveholding republic, the heritage of the Revolution made independence a powerful masculine personal ideal. But slave labor and 'hireling' wage labor proliferated in the new nation. One way to make peace with the latter was to differentiate it sharply from the former. Though direct comparisons between bondage and wage labor were tried out ('white slavery'), the rallying cry of 'free labor' understandably proved more durable and popular for antebellum white workers, especially in the North. At the same time, the white working class, disciplined and made anxious by fear of dependency, began during its formation to construct an image of the Black population as 'other' – as embodying the preindustrial, erotic, careless style of life the white worker hated and longed for. This logic had particular attractions for Irish-American immigrant workers, even as the 'whiteness' of these very workers was under dispute.

The insights, and considerable drama, of recent histories of early labor derive largely from a focus on the remaking of republicanism by labor. The new labor history illuminates the question of how workers creatively pursued the vision of a republic of small producers in which, in [Walt] Whitman's words, 'I will be even with you, and you shall be even with me', even as the United States became a land whose citizens increasingly worked 'in shops they did not own and control, at a pace ... often determined by others.'[6]

But labor republicans in the United States did not only attempt to abolish mastery and servanthood among white Americans. Many of them also acquiesced in the even sharper social divisions between Black Americans and slavemasters. Thus Whitman: 'Slaves are [probably] there because they must be – when the time arrives for them not to be ... they will leave.'[7] Moreover, republicanism itself carried a strong suspicion of the powerless, not just of the powerful, and a fear that the top and bottom in society would unite against the 'producing classes' in the middle. As virtually all working whites were included in the 'producing classes', that suspicion could fall heavily on slaves and free Blacks. *All* labor republicans existed in a society that offered the opportunity for white workers to measure their situations not only against the dream of a republic of small producers but also against the nightmare of chattel slavery. If early languages of class have already been located by historians within the context of republican thought and accelerating working class formation, they need also to be located within a *slaveholding* republic in which the constant, even increasing, presence of slavery was, as the Black abolitionist H. Ford Douglass remarked, 'completely interwoven into the passions of the ... people.'[8]

In 1814, Francis Scott Key wrote, in a verse of 'The Star-Spangled Banner' not sung before baseball games, 'No refuge could save the hireling and the slave/From the terror of flight or the gloom of the grave.' The significant pairing of 'hireling and slave' would echo even into the 1850s as the status of white workers was debated. For Key's original audience the pair of words carried meanings within the context of the War of 1812. Britain prosecuted that war using hated mercenary or 'hireling' soldiers. Also in the British ranks were about three hundred former slaves, promised freedom and protection by British commanders in exchange for their military service. Some of these exslaves helped to burn the White House in 1814.[9] But Key's words also carried much broader meanings, embodying what a young, republican nation hated and perhaps feared that it might become.

In castigating 'hirelings', Key used a word that captures much of what republicans despised. A nation that depended on hirelings simply could not be a republic. Anglo-American usages of *hireling* current by the early nineteenth century connected a hireling soldier with a propensity to flee under fire. More broadly, hirelings in various fields, but particularly in politics, behaved as the very opposite of self-sacrificing republican citizens. They made 'reward or material remuneration the motive of [their] actions'; They were prostitutes – indeed Noah Webster's 1829 dictionary of American English gives 'prostitute' as a synonym for *hireling* and further defines *hirelings* as 'perjurers by virtue of their avarice'. As an adjective, *hireling* typically meant both 'venal' and 'mercenary'. In usage it was often preceded by *press* and *politicians*, adumbrating various aspects of the critique of British corruption that had been a staple of American republican rhetoric since before the Revolution.[10] As Steve Watts's *Republic Reborn* demonstrates, Americans by 1814 had substantial doubts, and substantial reasons to doubt, with regard to their nation's ability to preserve a republican vision against 'hireling' corruption.[11]

But *hireling* conjured up yet another threat to republican liberty, one perhaps less easily conquered in the long run than the mercenary soldier or even than the acid of corrupt self-interest. *Hireling* meant, of course, 'one who is hired or serves for wages'. That usage, as the *Oxford English Dictionary* observes, was 'opprobrious', with 'serving for hire or wages' being all too nearly synonymous with 'to be had for hire'.[12] The term was especially opprobrious for American republicans. In particular, the artisanal follow-ers of Tom Paine and Thomas Jefferson held that a free government required 'independent' small producers who owned productive property and therefore were nei-ther cowed nor mercenary, as lifelong 'hirelings' would inevitably be. For Paine, 'freedom [was] destroyed by dependence' and *servant* was an opprobrious term. Hirelings and slaves were sometimes connected in popular logic, as in the observation that those who labor for others become 'mere Negroes [growing] lazy, and careless' and in the frequent references to sailors, the outstanding occupational group of waged adult males, as children and as slaves.[13]

Thus, the gradual transition to wage labor from 1800 to 1860 (and beyond) was an extremely serious matter for labor republicans. There were, of course, elements within republican thought that discouraged panic and encouraged long-term faith in republican solutions. From Tom Paine to Abraham Lincoln ran a line of thought that held that wage labor was not degrading *per se* – for Paine, man was free in large part because he held 'property in his own labor'. Wage labor could then be a rite of passage on the road to the economic independence of free farming or of self-employed craft labor.[14] Moreover, many labor republicans shared with their British counterparts the view that political plots – the corruption and machination of the powerful and the acquiescence of the servile – gave rise to social inequality. In a republic of freemen, these political evils could be identified and checked, in the long run if not the short.[15]

It was impossible to think about dependency on wages merely in comparison with the position of labor in an ideal republic; the comparison with the truly enslaved also loomed. Such a comparison cut hard, and it cut in two ways. On the one hand, the spectre of chattel slavery – present historically in no other nation during the years of significant working class formation – made for a remarkable awareness of the dangers of dependency and a strong suspicion of paternalism. On the other hand, hard thought about 'the hireling and the slave' could make the position of hireling comparatively attractive. The white hireling had the possibility of social mobility as the Black slave did not. The white hireling was usually a political freeman, as the slave, and with very few exceptions the free Black, were not. The comparison could lead to sweeping critiques of wage labor as 'white slavery' but it also could reassure wage workers that they belonged to the ranks of 'free white labor'. In their early attempts to develop a language of labor, working Americans therefore expressed soaring desires to be rid of the age-old inequalities of Europe and of any hint of slavery. They also expressed the rather more pedestrian goal of simply not being mistaken for slaves, or 'negers' or 'negurs'. And they saw not nearly so great a separation between these goals as we do.

As early as 1807, the British investor Charles W. Janson published the indignant replies he had received when he visited an acquaintance in New England and asked the maid who answered the door. 'Is your master home?' Not only did the maid make it clear that she had 'no master' but she insisted, 'I am Mr. ___'s *help*. I'd have you to know, *man*, that I am no *sarvant*; none but *negers* are *sarvants*.' The *Massachusetts Spy* in 1815 reported that exactly such exchanges occurred frequently, when visitors attempted to address *servants* or to ask about *masters*. Two decades later, a more celebrated observer of American life, Frances Trollope, lamented the difficulty of 'getting servants' in Ohio, but then corrected herself to write 'getting help'. She explained that in the United States, 'It is more than petty treason to the republic to call a free citizen a *servant*.' One of her own 'help' anxiously expressed to Trollope the hope that she would not think whites in service to be 'just as bad as if we are negurs.'[16]

Trollope and Janson were among many foreigners and American citizens to note such avoidance of the term *servant* and the reasons for such avoidance. As the American lawyer John Bristed put it in 1818, 'There is no such relation as *master and servant* in the United States: indeed the name is not permitted.' In explaining the disappearance of these terms, especially among farm and domestic laborers, Bristed commented on the tendency of US citizens toward 'confounding the term *servant* with that of *slave*.' There was good reason for such confounding, dating from the early imprecisions of colonial usages of *slave* and *servant* right through Noah Webster's inconsistent distinctions between the two terms in his dictionary of 1828 and the tendency in the South to apply *servant* overwhelmingly to slaves in the antebellum years. Yet another complicating factor was that free Blacks often worked as domestic servants, with the result that the degradations suffered by slaves, by Blacks generally and by domestics all came to be associated under the heading *servant*.[17]

The *Oxford English Dictionary* counts 'hired man, woman, girl [and] people' all as Americanisms of probable early nineteenth-century origins. It stresses connections with slavery, finding the words to have been coined to be 'applied to free men or women engaged as servants (the latter word being formerly used to include slaves).' The *OED* adds that the terms particularly applied to workers 'on a farm' and in or 'around a house'.[18] Albert Matthews's close study of American usages of *hired man* and *help* shows the words to be more complex and even more interesting than the *OED* allows. Matthews establishes some colonial examples of the terms and, in the former case, some British antecedents. But he emphasizes an increase in their popularity in the early nineteenth century and attributes that increase both to a desire to be set apart from Blacks and to postrevolutionary ideals. This juxtaposition of the search for a language of freedom and for a language that would simply set apart and racially stigmatize the wholly unfree makes the popularity of terms like *hired man* and *help* extremely suggestive.

In one sense the developing language of labor was certainly egalitarian; it was largely the creation of those who worked. Daniel Rodgers, in an interesting short passage on antebellum labor and language, argues that euphemistic terms like *help* were inventions of the employers and 'reflected the vain hope that labels would rectify the anomaly of dependence in a society in which self-employment was the moral norm.' He adds that capitalists 'had good reason for the evasion' because they wanted to avoid associating the 'worker who labored at the will ... of another [with] the oldest, bluntest and most troubling word of all: "slave".'[19] Whether words like *help* functioned in the way Rodgers argues is a fascinating question. Whether they came into being through upper-class initiatives is quite another. On the latter score, the evidence from the early nineteenth century, when *help* and *hired man* became popular evasions, does not support Rodgers's point. Virtually all primary accounts show the new usages being enthusiastically initiated by those whose work was being described. James Fenimore Cooper, who hated the new terms as 'subterfuges', regarded them as creations of the workers themselves: of *help*, he snickered, 'A man does not usually hire his cook to *help* him cook his dinner, but to cook it herself.' The British traveller Charles Mackay similarly counted the new words for *servant* as marks of self-assertion, however quaint, among whites who did domestic work, and even suggested that the now-familiar 'help wanted' ads took that wording to avoid ruffling the racial and republican sensibilities of those who worked as servants.[20] The *Dictionary of American English* aptly summarizes a range of usages substituting *helps* and *hands* for *servants* by saying that the substitutions reflect what the employed 'chose to call themselves'. White female household workers in particular 'resisted' the designation *servant*, in favor of 'helps, helpers or hands'.[21]

In popularizing such new words, farm and household workers were not simply becoming racists, but neither were they simply being militant republicans. Rather, they were becoming *white workers* who identified their freedom and their dignity in work as being suited to those who were 'not slaves' or 'not negurs'. White workers were not slaves, and there were excellent reasons, quite without manipulation by employers, for their not wanting to be considered 'like a slave'. Not all these reasons had to do immediately with race. The first recorded instance of an American objecting to being called a servant, in 1784, reflected the sentiments of a white freeman who apparently hated being compared to indentured *whites*. US republicans, moreover, were used to railing against those who sought to enslave others, and several primary accounts of the rise of substitutes for *servant* set the changes squarely in the context of a quest for 'republican liberty' and a desire to be rid of models that had been inherited from 'slavish Europe'.[22]

But in a society in which Blackness and servility were so thoroughly inter-twined – North and South – assertions of white freedom could not be raceless. To criti-cize Europe as 'slavish' or full of 'dastardly slaves' inevitably called to mind chattel slavery and in several cases high republicanism and high race feeling cohabit on the same page.[23] James Flint, a British visitor in the second decade of the nineteenth century, noted that among the poor in the free states that bordered slaveholding states 'certain kinds of labour are despised as being the work of slaves.' He counted shoeblacking and, at times, 'family manufactures' as tabooed and told of paupers in an Ohio poorhouse who 'refused to carry water for their own use' for fear of being considered 'like slaves'.[24] We can see in such actions both the frayed strands of republican self-assertion and a sense of whiteness that could at times be self-defeating.

The existence of slavery (and increasingly of open Northern campaigns to degrade free Blacks) gave working Americans both a wretched touchstone against which to meas-ure their fears of unfreedom and a friendly reminder that they were by comparison not so badly off. It encouraged an early language of labor that was at once suffused with concern for 'republican liberty' and at the same time willing to settle for what Rodgers calls 'evasions'. Amidst much assertion of independence, the term *hired* subtly became one to be embraced. As *hired* was increasingly placed in front of *man, woman* and *girl*, it was also placed before the old term *hand*, especially when referring to farm laborers. In the latter usage – apparently first commented upon when James Flint observed in 1818 that where he visited in the North, 'Laborers are not *servants*, all are hired *hands*' – labor is clearly a commodity, separable from its owner and for sale.[25] Some of the sting had been taken from the connection between *hireling* and *slave*.

Even with these complications, *mechanic* was a term that survived healthily, especially when interspersed with references to the rights of 'American Freemen'.[26] But journey-men mechanics had *masters*, according to time-honored usage, and it was here that republican values, worries about wage labor, and anxieties about being compared to slaves conspired to change the language of labor. So long as the master was called by that term because of his craft skills, no violation of republican principles occurred. As Marx observed, the master typically owned the tools used in production and the product and therefore was a capitalist. 'But it is not as a capitalist that he is a *master*', Marx went on. 'He is an artisan in the first instance and is supposed to be a master of his craft. Within the process of production he appears as an artisan, like his journeymen, and it is he who initiates his apprentices into the mysteries of his craft.'[27]

But real changes in small workshops in the US in the early nineteenth century, changes often caused by pressures from merchant capitalists, made many masters act like masters of men rather than of crafts.[28] As the masters sought greater production and lower costs in a postrevolutionary and slaveholding society, their motivations were closely scruti-nized by journeymen whose reactions mixed republicanism and whiteness. It was par-ticularly difficult to be mastered by someone who was not a master of his craft. Thus the Philadelphia General Trades Union in 1836 complained that the 'veriest *botch*' among craftsmen too often assumed '*kingly supremacy* to himself the very moment he becomes a "MASTER MECHANIC".' Earlier and smaller labor organizations had made similar points. During 1806, in the Philadelphia journeymen shoemakers' conspiracy case, a labor appeal referred to 'these masters, as they are called, and who would be masters and tyrants if they could.'[29] Well before the term *wages slavery* came into common use, journeymen criticized *masters* as so-called 'after the slavish style of Europe'. A very early carpenters' organization scored the 'haughtiness and overbearance' of masters as more appropriate to those who 'give laws to slaves ... depriving free men of their just rights.'[30]

If republicanism meant different things to different groups, it still carried a resonance; and white supremacy was widely shared, if also variously interpreted. In such a society it was desirable, even imperative, not to be taken for a slave or anything like one. Conventions of *Black* reformers declared, 'To be dependent, is to be degraded.' A *hired hand* could claim and perhaps insist upon small privileges that a *servant* could not. He could see himself in a different way. White native-born Americans not only changed the language of domestic service but also, by the 1830s, in fact largely abandoned domestic service as a job. Avoidance of connections to dependency and to blackness paid, in Du Bois's language, 'public and psychological' wages.[31] But there were costs as well, not only in terms of race relations but also the wedding of labor to a debased republicanism.

If there was a 'manly' Jacksonian-era alternative to the kinds of workers' self-identification that Cooper deplored, it was *freeman*. The evolution of this long-used term illustrates the impossibility of avoiding race in constructing a class identity. The evolution of *freeman* also richly suggests the payoffs of whiteness and the tendency of those payoffs to prove spurious – spurious, that is, if we regard an attack on lifelong wage labor to have been a legitimate goal of labor republicanism.

Freeman continued to carry the double meaning of economic and political independence. Webster's 1829 dictionary gave as its first definition of *freeman* 'one who enjoys liberty ... one not a slave or a vassal', and as its second 'one who enjoys or is entitled to a franchise'.[32] Before the Revolution, these various freedoms were only imperfectly linked to whiteness amidst patterns of deference, varied forms of economic vassalage among whites, colonial status and limits on suffrage. By the Age of Jackson, the correspondence between who was white and who was a freeman has become a far closer one.

Blackness meanwhile almost perfectly predicted lack of the attributes of a freeman. In 1820, 86.8 percent of African-Americans were slaves – in 1860, 89 percent. Free Blacks in the South lacked political rights, as they did in the North to a nearly equivalent extent. As white manhood suffrage became the norm, perhaps one free Black male in fourteen could legally vote in the North by 1860, with tradition barring the participation even of many of these who were technically so qualified. With jury duty, militia service and other civil responsibilities and rights barred to Black Northerners, the typical 'free' Black had, as the historian Jean Baker has tellingly observed, a single accepted public role: that of the victim of rioters.[33]

That Blacks were largely noncitizens will surprise few, but it is important to emphasize the extent to which they were seen as *anticitizens*, as 'enemies rather than the members of the social compact.' As such they were driven from Independence Day parades as 'defilers' of the body politic and driven from their homes by Sons of Liberty and Minute Men.[34] The more powerless they became, the greater their supposed potential to be used by the rich to make freemen unfree. Thus, it was necessary to watch for the smallest signs of power among Blacks, and, since Blacks were defenseless, it was easy to act on perceived threats. We shall see this dynamic very much at work later in discussions of antebellum race riots, but worth considering here are the vehement and usually successful popular objections to any hint that Blacks could be freemen, objections that at times also bolstered white workers' labor market positions.

Use of terms like *white slavery* and *slavery of wages* in the 1830s and 1840s presents an intriguing variation on the theme of American exceptionalism. US labor historians are usually pressed to explain why American workers have historically lacked the class consciousness said to have existed elsewhere in the industrializing world. But if the antebellum US labor movement was exceptional in its rhetoric, it was exceptionally militant as it critiqued evolving capitalist social relations as a kind of slavery. France, with a revolutionary tradition that forcefully used metaphors regarding slavery to press republican attacks on political oppression, apparently saw but slight use of phrases such as *wage slavery* before the Revolution of 1848. The German states, though they produced a great popularizer of the concept of wage slavery, likewise did not witness frequent use of the term. Only Britain, where the metaphoric term *wage slavery* apparently originated in the second decade of the nineteenth century, rivalled the US in producing a discourse that regarded white hirelings as slaves. But since the spread of the metaphor in Britain was as much associated with the Tory radical politician Richard Oastler as with its use by working class Chartists, one might regard the antebellum US labor movement as exceptional in being the world leader in militant criticisms of wage work as slavery.[35]

Of course, concern over 'slavery' was very much in the air in Jacksonian America, whose citizens worried variously that Catholics, Mormons, Masons, monopolists, fashion, alcohol and the national bank were about to enslave the republic. Nonetheless, the use of the white slave metaphor for wage workers ought not be dismissed as merely another example of the 'paranoid' style of antebellum politics.[36] It might instead be profitable to view the paranoid style itself as a republican tradition much enlivened by the horrific example of chattel slavery and fears engendered by the growing failure of the American republic to produce a society of independent farmers and mechanics among whites.

All this suggests that David Brion Davis's provocative ideas concerning antislavery and the acceptance of wage labor need to be pushed further still. Davis has argued that attacks on chattel slavery made 'free labor' (that is, wage labor) more easily acceptable during the first half of the nineteenth century. But in looking at US working class history, it is clear that the existence of *slavery*, not just of antislavery, stalled the development of a telling critique of hireling labor – a critique that might have built on and transcended the republican heritage. It was not just the abolitionists and Republicans who failed to produce such a critique. Also failing were the often proslavery laborites who argued that workers were white slaves. As long as slavery thrived, any attempt to come to grips with wage labor tended to lapse into exaggerated metaphors or frantic denials of those metaphors. Only with Black emancipation could a more straightforward critique of wage slavery, and a fierce battle over the meaning of *free labor*, develop. By that time, the importance of a sense of whiteness to the white US worker was a long-established fact, not only politically but culturally as well.[37]

George Rawick, in his enormously suggestive conclusion to *From Sundown to Sunup*, argues that racism grew so strongly among the Anglo-American bourgeoisie during the years America was colonized because blackness came to symbolize that which the accumulating capitalist had given up, but still longed for. Increasingly adopting an ethos that attacked holidays, spurned contact with nature, saved time, bridled sexuality, separated work from the rest of life and postponed gratification, profit-minded Englishmen and Americans cast Blacks as their former selves. Racism, according to Rawick, served to justify slavery but also did more than that. Racists still pined for older ways, and even still practiced older styles of life, guiltily. All of the old habits so recently discarded by whites adopting capitalist values came to be fastened onto Blacks. As Rawick wonderfully puts it, Englishmen and profit-minded settlers in America 'met the West African as a reformed sinner meets a comrade of his previous debaucheries.' The racist, like the reformed sinner, creates 'a pornography of his former life. … In order to insure that he will not slip back into the old ways or act out half-suppressed fantasies, he must see a tremendous difference between his reformed self and those whom he formerly resembled.' Blackness and whiteness were thus created together.[38]

During the last two decades, 'new labor historians' following in the footsteps of Herbert Gutman and E.P. Thompson have shown how dramatically capitalist labor discipline reshaped the lives of American workers in the period from the War of 1812 until the Civil War. Gutman and his students – and in a broad sense virtually all recent labor historians have been his students – have chronicled capital's increasing demands for regular, timed and routinized labor and for 'industrial morality' off the job. Industrial capitalism and speedups in smaller shops joined cultural initiatives to eliminate holidays, divorce the worker from contact with nature, bridle working class sexuality, separate work from the rest of life and encourage the postponing of gratification. Even skilled workers in small shops and nominally self-employed artisans in the sweated trades were far from immune to such pressures.[39] Using and recasting the traditions of their crafts and their communities, workers often contested, and at some times successfully resisted, these new disciplines. But much of the new discipline was also internalized, both by those who used punctuality, regularity and habits of sacrifice to further labor organization and by those who saw the same values as necessary to accumulate wealth and move out of the ranks of wage labor.[40]

There was plenty of anxiety to go around. Those who sought to succeed by giving up traditional holidays and the 'social glass' surely were tempted to create 'a pornography of their former lives'. Those who continued to gamble, drink or take 'Saint Monday' off – the picturesque 'traditionalists' whom historians often have portrayed as holdouts resisting labor discipline – also had reason to fret. They faced social pressures, unemployment and even the poorhouse. Although historians try to draw lines between hard-plugging 'loyalists', hard-protesting 'rebel mechanics' and hard-drinking 'traditionalists', individual workers were pulled in all three directions, and changed categories often, especially during hard times. It was possible to feel guilty for taking a drink with a fellow journeyman at work on Monday and for refusing to do so on Tuesday.[41] The changes were staggering, as Sidney Pollard, a historian of the growth of industrial discipline in Britain, observes in a passage equally applicable to the United States:

> There was a whole new culture to be absorbed and an old one to be … spurned, there were new surroundings, often a different part of the country, new relations with employers, and new uncertainties of livelihood, … new marriage patterns and behavior patterns of children within the family and without.[42]

Just as the languages of class that developed in the United States in the early nineteenth century were shaped at every turn by race, so too did racial language reflect, in a broad sense, changes and tensions associated with class formation. In 1767, a featured Black performer in the first musical to be published in America sang a variation of what was to become 'Yankee-Doodle' as he portrayed a character called Raccoon, an 'old debauchee'.[43] Seventy years later, the white entertainer George Washington Dixon had popularized Zip Coon as the blackface minstrel embodiment of the irrepressible, irresponsible, dandified free Black in the North. Seventy years after that, at the end of the nineteenth century, the 'coon song' craze swept the nation, with individual racist songs selling as many as three million copies in sheet music. Probably the best-known of the 'coon songs', Ernest Hogan's 'All Coons Look Alike to Me', bore a title that suggested how thoroughly dehumanizing racist stage stereotypes could be.[44]

And yet even amidst this lineage of seemingly unrelieved prejudice, the 'coon' image carried a substantial and striking complexity during most of the years between 1767 and 1900. A song like 'All Coons Look Alike to Me' could, quite simply, not have been written before 1848, because human *coons* were typically *white* until that point. It is true that Zip Coon and Raccoon strutted on early American stages, but the word *coon* referred to a white country person, to a sharpster or, in phrases like a *pretty slick coon*, to both.[45]

Only gradually did *coon* emerge as a racial slur, with the first clear case of such usage coming in 1848. That it first found racist use mainly on the minstrel stage suggests that the slur evolved from Zip Coon, and in the context of the many references to coon-hunting and eating coons in blackface songs.[46] An alternative explanation is that *coon* derived from the corruption of *barracoon*, from the Spanish *barracon*, which came into increasing use to describe the 'enclosures in which slaves [were] temporarily enclosed after escape or during travel' in the years just before the Civil War.[47] Whatever the derivation, all coons decidedly did not look alike in the 1850s. Lewis Garrard's *Wah-to-Yah; or, The Taos Trail* of 1850, for example, introduces a frontiersman who says of himself, 'This coon ... had made Injuns go under some.' He quickly adds, 'This child's no nigger.[48]'

The ambiguities of meaning in *coon* were not lost on Herman Melville, who brilliantly explored the mutability and the social construction of race, and even the deleterious effects of whiteness, in such works as *Benito Cereno, Moby Dick*, 'Paradise of Bachelors and Tartarus of Maids' and 'The Encantadas'. The racial dimensions of his work have received penetrating treatment from such scholars as Sterling Stuckey, Joshua Leslie and Carolyn Karcher. Karcher particularly observes that Melville's enigmatic masterpiece, *The Confidence-Man* (1857), mocks any firm distinction between black and white. She sees Melville's repeated characterization of the book's most disgusting character as a 'coon' as one key to the racial ambiguities of the novel.[49] The character, an outspoken antiabolitionist and probably a child molester, is of questionable color himself. 'My name is Pitch and I stick to what I say', he says at one point. By calling him a 'coon' Melville emphasizes the uncertainty as to his race.[50] If we add to Karcher's analysis the knowledge that *coon* itself was racially ambiguous in the 1850s and that it could in fact refer to a rural white or to a white confidence man, the layers of Melville's playfulness and seriousness become clearer.

Such words as *coon*, *buck* and *Mose* had more than ambiguous or multiple meanings: they had trajectories that led from white to black. More than that, each of them went from describing particular kinds of whites who had not internalized capitalist work discipline and whose places in the new world of wage labor were problematic to stereotyping Blacks. Rustics and con-men, fops and 'fascinators of women', brawlers and 'sentinels of the new army of the unemployed' – all of these proved easier to discuss when blacked up.[51] Such an evolution of language suggests that some use of the concept of projection is necessary to understand the growth of a sense of whiteness among antebellum workers, who profited from racism in part because it enabled them to displace anxieties within the white population onto Blacks. But the process of projection was not abstract. It took place largely within the context of working class formation and addressed the specific anxieties of those caught up in that process.

As late as the early 1800s, Black excellence in and centrality to popular entertainment was frequently remarked upon by white Americans. But that centrality could only be episodically asserted in the urban North on those occasions when the color line was not drawn. By the 1830s, Alexis de Tocqueville observed that, particularly in the North, Blacks did not 'share ... the recreations of whites'. Even so, the association of Blacks with preindustrial joys, with entertainment prowess and with 'natural humor' continued.[52] Blackface literally stepped in as a popular entertainment craze at the very moment that genuinely Black performers and celebrations were driven out.[53]

Nor was blackface confined to the minstrel stage. White crowds repeatedly colored *themselves*, replacing excluded Blacks from within their own ranks. Of course, some care must be exercised here. Body-painting is often a part of popular festivity. There is no shortage of examples of Africans painting themselves white ceremonially and, as George Lipsitz has shown, the African-American 'Mardi Gras Indians' of Louisiana have promiscuously crossed racial lines to create one of America's richest popular traditions. Within the Anglo-American tradition there was also a substantial tradition of blacking the skin or of dressing up as Indians on occasions of festivity, rebellion and 'misrule'.[54] The revolutionaries dumping tea into Boston harbor, Constance Rourke argues, combined racial disguise, revelry and revolt so thoroughly that 'it may well be a question whether the participants enjoyed more dumping the tea ... or masquerading in war paint and tomahawks.'[55]

Nonetheless, in the racially charged atmosphere of antebellum America, blacking up (or redding up) was not simply traditional, joyous or decorative. It also usually involved a conscious declaration of whiteness and white supremacy, even as it identified celebration and popular justice with adopting a racial disguise. Indian impersonation, common among volunteer fire companies, was also often a feature at militia days, where half the participants sometimes 'became' Indians to stage a mock battle from an anti-Indian war.[56] The antirent protesters in New York between 1839 and 1845 so frequently adopted 'redface' disguises as they drove off sheriffs and rent collectors that the state government outlawed dressing up as Indians. But the antirent rebels do not seem to have experienced the exhilaration Rourke imputes to the tea-dumpers of Boston harbor. Instead, their spokesmen apologized for having to wear Indian disguises and reassured listeners that 'although they were obliged to darken their faces they had hearts like their white brethren.'[57]

Nor were the rebelliousness and preindustrial joyousness of crowds in blackface separable from the (usually conscious) white supremacy pervading that form of masking. The context in which popular blackfacing emerged and the purposes to which it was directed ensured as much. Blackface crowds apparently came into prominence in the Age of Jackson, even as truly mixed popular celebrations were waning and as minstrelsy was taking off in popularity. According to the fullest local study, Susan G. Davis's superb account of 'street theater' in Philadelphia, blackened white crowds were overwhelmingly young, male and working class. They borrowed freely from the minstrel stage, moving in bands known as the 'Jim Crows' and the 'Strut-Some Guards'.[58]

Blackface served not only to identify the white crowd with the excellence of Black popular culture but also to connect its wearers with the preindustrial permissiveness imputed to African-Americans. It reemphasized that the Christmas night or the militia day was a time of celebration and license, of looseness, drinking and promiscuity. But even in the midst of revelry and even given the real desires of the crowds to 'act black', the celebrants needed to underscore continually the point that they were still white. That chimney sweeps were part of the crowds adds a curious twist to this drama, in that sweeps faced the daily problem that their occupation and the involuntary blacking up it entailed might lead to their being identified with Blacks.[59]

Just as the minstrel stage held out the possibility that whites could be 'black' for awhile but nonetheless white, it offered the possibilities that, via blackface, preindustrial joys could survive amidst industrial discipline. Even the 'rough' culture of young, rowdy traditionalist artisans and unskilled workers could lie down with the 'respectable' norms of striving, upwardly mobile skilled workers.

To black up was an act of wildness in the antebellum US. Psychoanalytically, the smearing of soot or blacking over the body represents the height of polymorphous perversity, an infantile playing with excrement or dirt. It is the polar opposite of the anal retentiveness usually associated with accumulating capitalist and Protestant cultures. Painting oneself hearkened back to traditional popular celebrations and to paint oneself as a Black person, given American realities at the time, was to throw reason to the winds. It is no accident that the early minstrel show was sometimes called a 'nigger festival'.[60]

Similarly assuaged was the tension between a longing for a rural past and the need to adapt to the urban present. The blackface wore rather thin when, for example, Irish minstrels sang laments by 'slaves' involuntarily removed from home and family. Other immigrants, migrants from rural to urban areas in the United States and migrants to the frontier, could likewise identify with the sentiments in 'Carry Me Back to Ole Virginny' or 'Dixie'.[61] So could almost any American involved in what Alexander Saxton has called the nation's 'endless outward journey' of expansion. Minstrelsy likewise idealized the preindustrial pastimes familiar to its white and often formerly rural audience. Hunting, especially of coons and possums, was a recurring delight during blackface performances, which also featured the joys of crabbing, eel catching, eating yellow corn, fishing and contact with animals not about to be killed. 'Niggas', one song had it, 'live on clover.[62]'

But the identification with tradition and with preindustrial joy could never be complete. It was, after all, 'niggers' who personified and longed for the past. Contradictions abounded.

Notes

1   W.E.B. Du Bois, *Black Reconstruction in the United States, 1860–1880*, New York 1977 (1935), 727 and passim.
2   Ibid., 30 and 633–34.
3   Ibid., 700–701.
4   Ibid., 30 and 700.
5   Du Bois, *Black Reconstruction*, 27–30, 347, 633–34 and 700–701. See also Du Bois, 'Dives, Mob and Scab, Limited', *Crisis* 19 (March 1920): 235–36.
6   Walt Whitman, *Leaves of Grass*, Boston 1860, 144. For a good recent synthesis reflecting the impact of an approach that stresses labor's republicanism, see Bruce Laurie, *Artisans into Workers: Labor in Nineteenth-Century America*, New York 1989.
7   Lorenzo D. Turner, 'Walt Whitman and the Negro', *Chicago Jewish Forum* 15 (Fall 1956): 8; Rowland Berthoff, 'Free Blacks, Women and Corporations as Unequal Persons', *Journal of American History* 76 (Dec. 1989): 760.
8   Quoted in Eric Foner, *Reconstruction: America's Unfinished Revolution, 1863–1877*, New York 1988, 26.
9   Robin Blackburn, *The Overthrow of Colonial Slavery, 1776–1848*, London 1988, 288–89.

10   *Oxford English Dictionary*, 2nd edn (OED2), Oxford 1989, 5:299–300; Noah Webster, *An American Dictionary of the English Language*, New York 1829, 412.

11   Robin Blackburn, *Colonial Slavery*, 289.

12   *OED2*, 5:300.

13   Quoted in Eric Foner, *Tom Paine and Revolutionary America*, New York 1976, 134, and in David Brody, 'Time and Work during Early American Industrialism', *Labor History* 30 (Winter 1989): 13–15. See also Edward Countryman, *The American Revolution*, New York 1985, 61–62, and Marcus Rediker, *Between the Devil and the Deep Blue Sea: Merchant Seaman, Pirates and the Maritime World, 1700–1750*, Cambridge, Mass. 1987, 111. On Paine and *servant*, see Elizabeth Blackmar, *Manhattan for Rent, 1785–1850*, Ithaca, N.Y., 1989, 116.

14   E. Foner, *Tom Paine*, 40 and 143–44. On Lincoln, see Eric Foner, *Free Soil, Free Labor, Free Men: The Ideology of the Republican Party before the Civil War*, New York 1970, 23, 29–30. On the extent of the transformation to wage labor by the time of the Civil War, see David Montgomery, *Beyond Equality, Labor and the Radical Republicans, 1862–1872*, New York 1967, 25–31.

15   John Ashworth, *'Agrarians and Aristocrats': Party Political Ideology in the United States, 1837–1846*, London 1983, 25 and 40–41; Sean Wilentz, *Chants Democratic: New York City and the Rise of the American Working Class, 1788–1850*, New York 1984, 243.

16   Charles W. Janson, *The Stranger in America*, New York 1946 (1807), 88; Richard H. Thornton, ed., *An American Glossary, Being an Attempt to Illustrate Certain Americanisms on Historical Principles* (hereafter *AG*), Philadelphia 1912, 1:428; Frances Trollope, *Domestic Manners of the Americans*, New York 1839, 45.

17   John Bristed, *American and Her Resources*, London 1818, 460. Compare Adam Ferguson, *Practical Notes Made during a Tour in Canada and a Portion of the United States*, London 1833, 233–34. See Webster, *American Dictionary*, 743; *OED2*, 5:508; and Christopher Tomlins, 'The Ties That Bind: Master and Servant in Massachusetts, 1800–1850', *Labor History* 30 (Spring 1989), passim, for the complexities of usage but also an argument that *servant* did have more or less precise, limited legal meanings in colonial Massachusetts. See Edmund Morgan, *American Slavery, American Freedom: the Ordeal of Colonial Virginia*, New York 1975, 327–32; Winthrop Jordan, *White over Black: American Attitudes toward the Negro, 1550–1812*, Chapel Hill, N.C. 1968, 80–81; Albert Matthews, 'The Terms Hired Man and Help', *Publications of the Colonial Society of Massachusetts* 5 (1898), esp. 229–38; Thomas Hamilton, *Men and Manners in America*, Edinburgh 1834, 1:104; and *AG*, 1:428; See also Blackmar, *Manhattan*, 116–22.

18   *OED2*, 5:299, and *A Dictionary of American English, On Historical Principles* (DAE), Sir William A. Craigie and James R. Hulbert, ed. Chicago 1938, 2:1250.

19   Daniel T. Rodgers, *The Work Ethic in America, 1850–1920*, Chicago 1979, 30–31. See Matthews, 'Hired Man', 243–54, on *help*.

20   James Fenimore Cooper, *The American Democrat; or, Hints on the Social and Civic Relations of the United States of America*, Cooperstown, N.Y. 1838, 122; Charles Mackay, *Life and Liberty in America*, London 1859, 2:45–46; Trollope, *Domestic Manners*, 44–45; Janson, *Stranger*, 88. A partial exception is Francis J. Grund, *The Americans in Their Moral, Social and Political Relations*, Boston 1837, which sees the employer and employed both acting to find substitutes for *servant* out of a shared republicanism. The labor leader Seth Luther satirizes *help* in Appendix H of his *Address to the Workingmen of New England*, Boston 1832.

21   *DAE*, 1:288 and 2:1236. See also Christine Stansell, *City of Women: Sex and Class in New York, 1789–1860*, New York 1986, 272 n. 7.

22   Matthews, 'Hired Man', 229; Janson, *Stranger*, 88; Trollope, *Domestic Manners*, 44–45; Grund, *Americans*, 236.

23   Webster, *American Dictionary*, 262; Bristed, *America*, 460; Trollope, *Domestic Manners*, 44–45.

24   James Flint, *Letters from America, 1818–1820*, London 1822, 218.

25   Ibid., 98. On *hired hand* see also *DAE*, 2:1212 and 1250, and David E. Schob, *Hired Hands and Plowboys: Farm Labor in the Midwest, 1815–60*, Urbana, Ill. 1975.

26   Perhaps the most vivid such a combined appeal to 'Brother Mechanics' and 'American Freemen' is the Boston 'Ten-Hour Circular' of 1835, reprinted in John R. Commons et al., *A Documentary History of American Industrial Society*, Cleveland 1910, 6:94–99.

27 Karl Marx, *Capital* Volume 1, trans. Ben Fowkes, London 1976, 1029. The passage is not in Marx's *Capital* as first published but is from a projected, and dropped, Part Seven, of Volume 1 of that work. Fowkes's is the first published English translation.

28 John R. Commons et al., *History of Labour in the United States*, New York 1918–35, 1:103ff, remains useful on this point. See also Alan Dawley, *Class and Community: The Industrial Revolution in Lynn*, Cambridge, Mass. 1972, 20–32.

29 The 1836 quote is from *The Pennsylvanian*, 31 March 1836, emphasis in the original as cited in Richard A. McLeod, 'The Philadelphia Artisan, 1828–1850' (Ph.D. dissertation, University of Missouri-Columbia, 1971), 192; 1806 quote from Anthony Bimba, *The History of the American Working Class*, New York 1927, 79.

30 Mark Lause's forthcoming book on early labor organizations records the first two uses while the third is from Howard B. Rock, 'The Independent Mechanic: The Tradesmen of New York City in Labor and Politics during the Jeffersonian Era' (Ph.D. dissertation, New York University, 1974), 94.

31 Quoted in Leon F. Litwack, *North of Slavery: The Negro in the Free States, 1790–1860*, Chicago 1961, 174; W.E.B. Du Bois, *Black Reconstruction*, 700; Stansell, *City of Women*, 155–58.

32 Webster, *American Dictionary*, 359.

33 Ira Berlin, *Slaves Without Masters: The Free Negro in the Antebellum South*, New York 1974, 137: Jean Baker, *Affairs of Party: The Political Culture of Northern Democrats in the Mid-Nineteenth Century*, Ithaca, N.Y. 1983, 244–45.

34 Flint, *Letters from America*, 122; Baker, *Affairs of Party*, 246.

35 Marcus Cunliffe, *Chattel Slavery and Wage Slavery: The Anglo-American Context, 1830–1880*, Athens, Ga. 1979, 9–13; on France, see David Geggus, 'Racial Equality, Slavery and Colonial Secession during the Constituent Assembly', *American Historical Review* 94 (December 1989): 1291, and William H. Sewell, Jr., *Work and Revolution in France: The Language of Labor from the Old Regime to 1848*, Cambridge 1980; on Germany, I am indebted to Prof. Jonathan Sperber for discussing usages through 1848; on Britain, see Dorothy Thompson, *The Chartists*, London 1984, 226 and passim; Alfred Plummer, *Bronterre: A Political Biography of Bronterre O'Brien, 1804–1864*, London 1971, 194–97; Gareth Stedman Jones, *Languages of Class: Studies in English Working Class History, 1832–1982*; Cambridge 1983, 146.

36 Richard Hofstadter, *The Paranoid Style in American Politics and Other Essays*, New York 1966.

37 David Brion Davis, *Slavery and Human Progress*, New York 1984, 15 and 254; see also Thomas L. Haskell, 'Capitalism and the Origins of Humanitarian Sensibility, Part One', *American Historical Review* 90 (April 1985); 350 n59.

38 George P. Rawick, *From Sundown to Sunup: The Making of the Black Community*, Westport, Conn. 1972, 132–33.

39 Herbert G. Gutman, *Work, Culture and Society in Industrializing America*, New York 1977, esp. 3–78; E.P. Thompson, 'Time, Work-Discipline and Industrial Capitalism', *Past and Present* 38 (December 1967): 56–97; Paul Faler, 'Cultural Aspects of the Industrial Revolution: Lynn, Massachusetts Shoemakers and Industrial Morality, 1826–1860', *Labor History* 15 (Summer 1974): 367–94; Bruce Laurie, "Nothing on Compulsion": Life Styles of Philadelphia Artisans, 1820–1860', *Labor History* 15 (Summer 1974); David R. Roediger and Philip S. Foner, *Our Own Time: A History of American Labor and the Working Day*, London 1989, 2–42.

40 Paul Faler and Alan Dawley, 'Working Class Culture and Politics in the Industrial Revolution', *Journal of Social History* 9 (June 1976); 466–80; Paul Johnson, *A Shopkeeper's Millennium: Society and Politics in Rochester, New York, 1815–1837*, New York 1978; Barbara M. Tucker, "Our Good Methodists": The Church, the Factory and the Working Class in Antebellum Webster, Massachusetts', *Maryland Historian* 8 (Fall 1977); 26–37.

41 Faler and Dawley, 'Working Class Culture', 466–80; Gutman, *Work, Culture and Society*, esp. 5 and 19–32; Bruce Laurie, *Working People of Philadelphia, 1800–1850*, Philadelphia 1980, 40–42, 116–19, 124, 139–47 and 201–2.

42 Quoted in Gutman, *Work, Culture and Society*, 14.

43 James H. Dorman, 'Shaping the Popular Image of Post-Reconstruction American Blacks: The "Coon Song" Phenomenon of the Gilded Age', *American Quarterly* 40 (December 1988): 451;

Alan W.C. Green, "Jim Crow", "zip Coon": The Northern Origins of Negro Minstrelsy', *Massachusetts Review* 11 (Spring 1970): 385.

44 Dorman, 'Popular Image', 453 and 459.

45 The best source is Frederic G. Cassidy, ed. *Dictionary of Regional English [DARE]*, Cambridge, Mass. 1985, 1:763. But see also *DA*, 1:388–89; *DAE*, 1:611–12; *OED2*, 2:962 and *OED2* supplement (1972), 1:630–31.

46 See for example, *DARE*, 1:763; *DA*, 1:388; *OED2*, supplement, 1:630–31; *Ethiopian Serenaders' Own Book*, Philadelphia 1857, 8 and 37; *Christy's New Songster*, New York n.d., 35; *Ethiopian Glee Book*, Boston 1849, 24, 72–73, 103, 160; *Howe's 100 Ethiopian Songs*, Boston and Chicago 1877, 224; Harold Wentworth and Stuart Berg Flexner, eds, *Dictionary of American Slang*, New York 1975, 122.

47 *OED2*, 1:679; Tamony Papers, University of Missouri-Columbia; Charles R. Shrum, quoted in 'Editorial Notes', *American Mercury* 9 (October 1926).

48 Lawrence H. Garrard, *Wah-to-Yah; or, The Taos Trail*, Norman, Okla. 1955 (1850?), 117, 163, 208, 216, 226, 228, 238, and for the quote, 190. Compare Robert Montgomery Bird, *Nick of the Woods*, New York 1939 (1837), 84–85.

49 Carolyn Karcher, *Shadow over the Promised Land*, Baton Rouge, La. 1980, 256–57; Joshua Leslie and Sterling Stuckey, 'The Death of Benito Cereno: A Reading of Herman Melville on Slavery', *Journal of Negro History* 67 (Winter 1982): 287–301.

50 Herman Melville, *The Confidence-Man; His Masquerade*, New York 1971 (1857), 101, 121, and 98–120 passim.

51 Sean Wilentz, *Chants Democratic*, 301.

52 Joseph Boskin, *Sambo: The Rise and Demise of an American Jester*, New York 1986, 69, which includes de Tocqueville's quote.

53 Herbert Marshall and Mildred Stock, *Ira Aldridge: The Negro Tragedian*, Carbondale, Ill. 1958, 37.

54 George Lipsitz, *Time Passages: Collective Memory and American Popular Culture*, Minneapolis, Minn. 1990, 233–53; Susan G. Davis, *Parades and Power: Street Theatre in Nineteenth-Century Philadelphia*, Philadelphia 1986, 77–111; Bryan D. Palmer, 'Discordant Music; Charivaris and White Capping in Nineteenth-Century North America', *Labour/Le Travailleur* 3 (September 1973): 5–62, esp. 31 and 49.

55 Quoted in Albert Murray, *The Omni-Americans: Black Culture and the American Experience*, New York 1970, 15.

56 Telfer H. Mook, 'Training Day in New England', *New England Quarterly* 11 (December 1938); 689; Davis, *Parades and Power*, 145.

57 Donald B. Cole, *Martin Van Buren and the American Political System*, Princeton, N.J. 1984, 407–8; David Maldwyn Ellis, *Landlords and Farmers in the Hudson-Mohawk Region, 1790–1850*, Ithaca, N.Y. 1946, 242–50; *Working Man's Advocate*, 17 August 1844.

58 Susan G. Davis, *Parades and Power*, 106 and 108.

59 Susan G. Davis, "Making Night Hideous": Christmas Revelry and Public Disorder in Nineteenth-Century Philadelphia', *American Quarterly* 34 (Summer 1982): 192; Paul A. Gilje, *The Road to Mobocracy: Popular Disorder in New York City, 1763–1843*, Chapel Hill, N.C. 1987, 254.

60 Sandor Ferenczi, 'The Origins of Interest in Money', in Richard C. Badger, ed., *Contributions to Psychoanalysis*, Boston 1916; Otto Fenichel, 'The Drive to Amass Wealth', *Psychoanalytical Quarterly* 7 (1938).

61 'Interview with Leni Sloan', "Irish Mornings and African Days on the Old Minstrel Stage: An Interview with Leni Sloan," Callahan's Irish Quarterly 2 (Spring 1982): 49–53.

62 Alexander Saxton, 'Blackface Minstrelsy and Jacksonian Ideology', *American Quarterly* 27 (March 1975): 28 and 12; *The Ethiopian Glee Book*, 182.

CHAPTER 5

A Living Wage
American Workers and the Making of Consumer Society

Lawrence B. Glickman

Wage labor seems almost a natural aspect of the world, a system of remuneration so ingrained that it is difficult to imagine an alternative. Wage levels are hotly contested, to be sure; even in this era of weakened trade unionism, the struggle for decent wages continues. But that workers, however well or ill paid, earn wages seems only a matter of common sense. "This is a wage labor society," Susan Willis notes. "If you do not work for a wage, you are not felt to be a worker."

This was not always the case. At the inception of the system in England during the first industrial revolution, workers "fought desperately to avoid the abyss of wage labor." Nor did nineteenth-century American workers wish to live in a "wage labor society." Although most proudly accepted the label "worker," they did not want to work for wages. The "simple fact of employment," Daniel T. Rodgers points out, "deeply disturbed … many Americans." Wage labor represented a dangerous, demeaning, and debilitating departure from traditional modes of financial reward. The ideal for these workers lay in a semimythical artisanal past or in an uncertain cooperative future.

Even after the independent craftsman had become more a symbol deeply etched in labor's collective memory than an accurate description of working-class reality, many workers continued to challenge the legitimacy of wage labor. For most of the nineteenth century, workers hoped to become independent producers, not permanent employees. They claimed that wage labor denied workers the "full fruits" of their labor and reduced the proud American citizen-worker to a "wage slave"—a derisive term popularized in the Jacksonian era as the incipient crisis of wage labor led to the rise of the organized labor movement. Free workers did not want to be identified with lifelong "hirelings," whom they saw as little different from slaves.

Original publication details: Lawrence Glickman, *A Living Wage: American Workers and the Making of Consumer Society*, pp. 1–7; 24–27; 29; 68–71; 76–77. Cornell University Press, 1997. Reproduced with permission from Cornell University Press.

In the decades after the Civil War, however, a striking transformation began, as many workers for the first time considered the possibilities of wage labor. The unanimous aversion characteristic of the antebellum period splintered. Some in the labor movement continued to condemn wage labor as a form of slavery, but a far greater number began to accept wages as permanent and to view them in a positive light.

This change in perspective was born of necessity; late nineteenth-century workers had little power to avoid wage labor. Fleeting political movements, successful unionization efforts, waves of strikes (of which there were approximately thirty-seven thousand between 1881 and 1905), and the formation of cooperatives indicated workers' strength, resolve, and fierce opposition to debilitating economic transformations. But these efforts did not stop the momentum toward proletarianization brought on by business consolidation and an adversarial state. In the period between the Civil War and World War I, workers learned to accept wages and to identify themselves as wage earners because they had no alternative.

While acknowledging the encroaching reality of a "wage labor society," wage earners and their advocates refused to accept the meaning of wage earning as fixed and inevitable. "The question of wages," noted Ira Steward, a labor theorist, was "one of the most disputed points in Political Economy." He was only one of many workers to offer an alternative theory of wage labor. Rejecting the defeatist political economy of the "iron law of wages" as well as the "free labor" condemnation of wage workers as moral failures, living wage proponents struggled to make this new wage labor regime consistent with working-class notions of justice and democracy. A wage labor society, in their view, had no predetermined meaning; it could be inhabited by degraded "wage slaves," or in the version they preferred, it could be constituted by proud citizen-workers earning living wages.

In coming to accept the necessity of wages, then, workers also redefined wage earning to make it consistent with their vision of a just world. They began to interpret wages not as slavery but as a potential means of escape from slavery. George Gunton, a pamphleteer for the American Federation of Labor (AFL) eight-hour campaign, declared, "Wages are not a badge of slavery, but a necessary and continual part of social progress." While not all labor leaders shared Gunton's utopian vision, almost all of them participated in the redefinition of wage labor from slavish to liberating.

The linchpin of this transformation was the demand for a "living wage," usually defined as remuneration commensurate with a worker's needs as citizen, breadwinner, and consumer. The AFL president Samuel Gompers, for example, declared in a well-publicized 1898 debate that a living wage should be "sufficient to maintain an average-sized family in a manner consistent with whatever the contemporary local civilization recognizes as indispensable to physical and mental health, or as required by the rational self-respect of human beings." Although others put forth very different definitions, all proponents of the living wage shared a new, positive vision of wage labor. Instead of contrasting wage labor with freedom, they contrasted low wages with high ones. The living wage, proponents held, should offer to wage earners in the postwar years what independent proprietorship had promised in the antebellum era: the ability to support families, to maintain self-respect, and to have both the means and the leisure to participate in the civic life of the nation. Far from condemning the wage system, Gompers called the level of wages "the barometer which indicates the social, political and industrial status" of a society. High wages became a benchmark of freedom, independence, and citizenship.

From the start, reformers, politicians, and religious leaders joined labor in debating the meaning of the living wage. By the 1890s, it became impossible for Americans to comment on the "wage question" without invoking the phrase that, according to one observer, had already "found its way in everyday language." The living wage became central to social and political issues of national importance, including Progressive Era minimum wage legislation and New Deal economic policy. For Herbert Croly, a Progressive, "the most important single task of modern democratic social organization" was to determine "if wage earners are to become free men." Workers had wrestled with this question long before Progressives posed it; nonetheless, input from religious leaders, politicians, and social reformers became crucial in shaping the twentieth-century conception of the living wage.

Explaining changing attitudes toward wage labor in American culture is by no means a simple undertaking. Conceptions varied widely, affected by such variables as class, political persuasion, race, and gender. In addition, the acceptance of wage labor was a process as uneven as the actual proletarianization of the work force. Some in the middle classes trumpeted the promise of wage labor in the antebellum years. Many trade unionists did so shortly after the Civil War. Some continued to reject the legitimacy of the "wage system" well into the twentieth century.

There is also a historiographical difficulty: although labor historians have identified the trend toward wage labor as, after emancipation, the defining event of the nineteenth century, they have tended to focus on opposition to it rather than acceptance. Placed alongside the usual fare of labor history, the living wage demand appears mundane and materialistic. Compared with strikes, organizing campaigns, and political activities, where heroes proliferate, the living wage has been interpreted as a distressing sign of the conservative business unionism that triumphed in the late nineteenth century, "an inclination," as John Bodnar writes, "to seek practical goals ... rather than the loftier ideals which prevailed in the protest of earlier times."

By deemphasizing demands for living wages, however, historians have neglected an area in which workers demonstrated an abiding political interest. Like the Chicago workers in the 1920s and 1930s, whose concerns, Lizabeth Cohen notes, were both "material and ideological," living wage advocates did not draw a distinction between economics and politics. Samuel Gompers stressed in 1919 that, as political freedom was intimately linked with economic freedom, high wages were necessary for workers "to be free." Conceding that trade unions "have been derided as materialistic and lacking in idealism because they concentrate their forces upon securing higher wages," he responded that "no nation can retain its power when the masses of its citizenship are existing upon inadequate wages." As early as the 1870s, Ira Steward denounced "an atmosphere of cheap labor" as "eminently un-American." Good wages, he claimed, were as integral to the success of American democracy as the "frequency and freedom of elections." A half century later, a union journal maintained that high wages enabled American workers to "become self-respecting citizens in an industrial democracy."

Acceptance of the wage system does not constitute proof of the eclipse of working-class consciousness. Certainly, opponents of the living wage demand from the 1870s through the present have viewed it as a dangerous political threat, a challenge to the laws of the market and an affront to capitalist property relations. "When we resist employers reducing our wages below a living basis," declared Gompers, "we are called Anarchists." Wage labor enabled workers to see themselves as a unified class rather than as a loosely related group of craftspeople, inevitably known for most of the nineteenth century in the plural as the "producing classes." The "modern experience of class," according to David Montgomery, "had its origin in the encounter with wage labor." John Bray noted in 1876 that "the wages class" could for the first time be described as "a unit." A dozen years later, the leaders of the AFL became the first American trade unionists to declare that "wage workers ... are a distinct and practically permanent class of modern society; and consequently, have distinct and permanently common interests." Few workers, of course, viewed the causes of this newfound unity as an altogether good thing. What brought them together, some believed, was nothing more than the misery of wage labor. The demand for living wages, nonetheless, produced new solidarities since it linked all workers by virtue of their status as wage earners, rather than on the basis of craft or ethnicity. As a British commentator noted in 1913, it was no accident that "permanent wagedom" and "trade unionism" came into existence simultaneously.

"Most Americans once identified themselves as producers whose labor created wealth," Michael Kazin has noted. "Now they see themselves primarily as consumers—or have let themselves be defined that way." This observation, frequently made by historians and contemporary commentators, implies both passivity and defeat. I contend, on the contrary, that workers played an active role in creating a consumerist identity and a consumerist political economy. This "consumerist turn," I believe, occurred in the postbellum years, much earlier than is usually supposed. It was during this period that workers began to think about themselves as consumers and to ponder the power of consumer organizing, while they were developing the idea of the living wage; the two ideas, in fact, developed in tandem.

In late twentieth-century America it may be hard to imagine how a progressive vision could be built around high wages and consumerism. The influence of such critics as Christopher Lasch, who argued that consumer society creates a "restless, bored" populace uninterested in politics, makes it difficult to conceive how such a focus could be anything other than "therapeutic" escapism. The living wage ideology, however, developed in a very different context, when consumer society was nascent and ill defined.

Labor's "consumerist turn" in the late nineteenth century was as much ideological as practical; it reflected new conceptions of identity and economics as well as a new conception of power. Well before most workers were able to enjoy the fruits of mass consumption, living wage advocates theorized about the positive benefits of high wages, consumer activism, purchasing power, and leisure, and they explicitly associated all these with a class-conscious consumerism. They defined what Warren Susman has called "the utopian possibilities in the culture of abundance" in political rather than therapeutic terms. Workers made the new consumer society not just by participating in commercial amusements; far more significant was the consumerist realignment of class consciousness, working-class identity, and, ultimately, economic and social policy.

The consumerist turn did not entail abandonment of "producerism." In order for workers to maintain their special status in the republic, living wage advocates argued, they needed to recognize and empower themselves as consumers because in the new world of wage labor, consumption and production were intimately linked. As an article in the *Journal of United Labor* noted in 1884: "We have been led to suppose that the producer and the consumer were totally separate individuals, with separate and distinct interests, when in reality all producers are consumers." Proponents of the consumerist turn maintained that the productive human being was equal parts *Homo faber* and *Homo consumens*.

For most workers in the period between 1865 and the 1930s, wages sufficient to provide for a well-maintained home, plentiful food, and some discretionary spending money—demands that Gompers grouped under the rubric of "more of the comforts and necessities of life"—were prerequisites for citizenship. Living wage advocates promoted consumption unapologetically, not as a site of embourgeoisement but as a locus of political power. The Boston labor leader George McNeill argued in the 1870s that the class struggle could be reduced to the demand of the capitalists that the worker "produce more." Instead, McNeill declared, "we say make him consume more."

Workers continued to think of economics in moral terms even after they accepted wage labor, but instead of understanding justice and liberty from the perspective of small producers whose class consciousness manifested itself at the point of production, they understood themselves as wage earners, demanded remuneration commensurate with their needs, and articulated a notion of class which centered as much in the realm of consumption as production. While it shared with the eighteenth-century moral economy what E. P. Thompson calls a "highly-sensitive consumer-consciousness," the "social economy" under examination in this book situated itself within, not against, the market. Interpreting spending as productive rather than wasteful, proponents of the living wage renounced thrift and the fetishization of work. Class consciousness moved from the shop floor to the storefront.

The living wage enabled workers to reground a republican morality in the modern world of the wage labor economy. If proprietorship and production had once been the hallmarks of citizenship, living wage advocates reconstructed citizenship around high wages and consumption. In this process, workers helped construct American consumer society. Even as the literal term "living wage" faded from view from the 1930s to the 1970s—only to be revived in the 1980s and 1990s—its underlying ideas became central to the political economy of the New Deal era and beyond.

Producerist and Consumerist Forms

Defenders of the wage slavery metaphor argued that economic deprivation inevitably damaged both the person and the polity and that wages necessarily produced economic injustice, usually conceived as a kind of robbery. But what exactly was the nature of this injustice? Were all wages inherently unjust or only particular kinds of wages? The vocabulary employed suggested a consensus about the immoral economics of wages. The wage system, critics railed, did not provide an "exact equivalent," a "just return," the "full fruits of one's labor," "fair remuneration," or simply, "one's worth." Most used these terms interchangeably; few actually defined them. Ultimately, however, the crucial differences among them reveal fissures in the seemingly monolithic edifice of opposition to wage slavery. The persistence of the slavery metaphor masked the fact that the meaning of the term had changed significantly since the Civil War.

There were, in fact, two related but fundamentally distinct ways of thinking about wage slavery and the worth of labor: producerism and consumerism. According to the producerist argument, wage slavery resulted from the difference in value between what workers produced and what they earned in wages, which was often said to have been stolen from them. The consumerists were more concerned about the inadequacy of wages that did not meet the needs of workers as family supporters, citizens, and consumers, and they condemned the wage system for its seeming inability to reward the nation's producers with a comfortable republican lifestyle. This distinction is critical. The producerist rhetoric predominated during the first years after the Civil War, but as the nineteenth century waned and workers redefined and ultimately accepted wage labor, the critique shifted from the producerist to the consumerist version.

The producerist critique conveyed the commonsense meaning of the metaphor for much of the nineteenth century. The language used by the *Journal of United Labor* in 1884 was most familiar: "The real essence of slavery is the coercing of one man by another in such a way as shall compel him to yield up the fruits of his labor ... without the power or opportunity or freedom to extract a return which shall be a just equivalent for such service." On this definition, since the wage system could not possibly accord workers the full productive value of their labor, a "just equivalent" in wages was not simply unlikely but altogether unreachable. Accordingly, the "system of paying wages to workers is a system of slavery." In a 1904 letter to the editor of the *Railroad Telegrapher*, "Alphega," extending this producerist argument, suggested that the extent of inequivalence marked the degree of enslavement: "If you produce wealth equivalent to $1,000 per year and receive a wage of $500, then you are one-half a slave. If a profit of 10% is made on your labor, then you are one tenth a slave. If you get only your living out of a year's continuous toil, then you are as much a slave as ever a black man in the antebellum days." By this standard of equivalence, the key to the producerist definition of wage slavery, workers could never be fully rewarded and therefore would always be at least partial slaves. No "considerable improvement can take place in [workers'] circumstances as long as they remain simply wage workers," announced Charles Pope, secretary of the Shoe Makers Union of San Francisco, in 1879. For Pope, robbery was an inherent aspect of wage labor, since "the producers receive but a portion of their earnings in the form of wages." Wage slavery, on this view, was an inevitable concomitant of wage labor.

The consumerist view, which eventually displaced the producerist view, was in many ways more relevant to a republic of wage earners. Its defining concept was the notion of a "just reward," rather than "exact equivalence." Although superficially similar, the concepts turned out to be crucially different. Unlike the producerist schema, which insisted that anything less than exact equivalence was inherently unfair, the consumerist idea of just reward implied, at least theoretically, that workers under the wage system could be free and fairly remunerated. It required only a short leap from the concept of the "just reward" to "just wages," and from "just wages" to "living wages."

One of the first hints of the consumerist argument came in an 1870 report by the Massachusetts Bureau of Statistics of Labor, which denounced wage slavery in the strongest possible terms: "Not a single workman working at day wages has acquired a competence." Only by "thrift and injustice," by denying himself and his family the "necessaries of life" could a worker survive. The "wage system," the report concluded, "has proved to be adverse to the general good." While the report employed the prevailing producerist wage slavery metaphor, it used the term in a new way, condemning the wage system not because it robbed workers of an equivalence but because it denied them what they needed to live as family men and citizens. The focus was shifting from equivalence to needs, from production to consumption.

No one in the labor movement did more than Ira Steward to promote the view that it was inability to consume rather than failure to receive an exact equivalence which constituted wage slavery. Raised in antebellum Massachusetts. Steward retained the abolitionist spirit of reform. Even after the Civil War abolition remained a leitmotif in his writings, guiding his vision of political economy, especially with respect to wage labor.

Arguing that American workers had uniquely cultivated wants and needs, Steward believed that a denial of these lay at the heart of this new slavery. "To surround a very poor man with what seems to him abundance is to surround him with temptations," he noted. "The only safety therefore when the laboring classes are limited to the most barren, dreary and cheerless physical necessities is chattel slavery."

Another New Englander, the young reformer Edward Bellamy, articulated a consumerist understanding of wage slavery in an address at the Chicopee Falls Village Lyceum in 1871. After condemning the payment to workers of a "bare subsistence" for their "painful labors," he went on to describe as slavery the perpetuation of a system in which the few enjoy the consumerist benefits of "the abundance created by labor." For Bellamy, lack of leisure and wages too low to meet family needs and workers' wants constituted slavery.

The consumerist emphasis on needs did not entirely supplant the producerist focus on equivalence, however. The two strands coexisted throughout the late nineteenth century. In an 1886 article titled "Wants," for example, the *Journal of United Labor* posited a natural connection between "the full fruits of their toil" and "legitimate wants." A "just wage" represented both the value of labor and the needs of the worker.

The shift from a producerist to a consumerist critique of wage slavery registered a significant change in the relation between economics and politics. For producerists, rewards could be fair only if they amounted to the full fruits of one's labor; for consumerists, rewards could be just if they met one's needs. Equivalence called for productive payment. Wants and needs required consumerist payment. Both versions linked economic autonomy to political freedom: but whereas for producerists, an economic concept—equivalence—was inextricably tied to a political vision, for consumerists, a political concept—justice—informed the economic.

Toward the Living Wage

Negotiating the postbellum definition of freedom, which was central to the wage slavery metaphor, necessitated coming to terms with wage labor and challenging the conception that subsumed all wage earners under the rubric of wage slavery. This negotiation had several components.

First, in an increasingly market-oriented and market-dominated country, it became difficult to maintain a definition of slavery that included wage workers. In late nineteenth-century America almost no one existed outside the market, and such existence had come to seem a sign not of independence but of isolation from the benefits of freedom. Many workers, stressing the allure of the market, claimed that withdrawal from it led to stagnation and depression and that the attempt to avoid it signaled savagery. Even George McNeill, who in 1877 famously denounced the selling of labor as slavery, put forth a much more positive view of wage labor in his eight-hour pamphlet a decade later. Employing the rhetoric of the market, he described wage earners as "the merchants of time," marking as the key issue not the sale of human labor as such but the price that could be extracted.

The living wage marked a critical shift toward a positive view of wage labor, a "Copernican Revolution" in labor ideology, as Ira Steward called it. In defining fair wages, Steward linked them not to productive value but only to the things that such wages could "secure" for the worker. A living wage was a new concept because it was

Figure 1 "Don't Be a Wage Slave," *International Socialist Review* (August 1911), 128. Courtesy Charles H. Kerr and Company.

based on a consumerist view, not the just price for the products of labor but remuneration commensurate with the needs of workers and their families. Basing remuneration on needs was a startlingly new idea.

The emphasis on consumption engendered a subtle but important shift in the meaning of the link between wages and production. While placing unprecedented stress on needs and desires as the basis of wages, living wage advocates did not neglect the relation between wages and production, which they acknowledged lay at the root of wealth. Despite the consumerist emphasis of his definition, Samuel Gompers also described the living wage as workers' "fair share of the product of their toil." But advocates invoked "fair share" in a new way. Whereas proponents of "fair" or "honest" or "just" wages described them as a return for individual labor yields, those who favored living wages described them in collective terms, as the worker's rightful "share in the products of common toil."

Challenging the notion that it was possible to measure the full fruits of individual labor, living wage proponents collectivized the value of labor. While proponents still described the living wage as a claim on the products of labor, it was no longer an individual claim. In rejecting the idealized—and in their view no longer valid—economy assumed by the notion of "just wages," advocates of the living wage developed a new conception of value. Max Weber succinctly described how the collectivization of the value of labor initiated a trajectory from producerist to consumerist theories of value, which culminated in the living wage:

> Quite generally, where the return is determined by the sale of the product in a freely competitive market, the content of the right of the individual to the full value of his product loses its meaning. There simply is no longer an individual "labor yield," and if the claim is to make any sense it can be only as the collective claim of all those who find themselves in a common class situation. In practice, this comes down to the demand for a "living wage," i.e., to a special variant of "the right to the standard of living as determined by traditional need."

This collective claim was based on needs—the realm of consumption—as much as production, and thus the new wage equation sanctioned and reinforced, rather than undermined, the new emphasis on consumption.

Living wage advocates refused to separate remuneration from production, although their critics accused them of doing so. The living wage, however expansively construed, was a demand for wealth earned by the sweat of workers' brows, and therefore Samuel Gompers insisted that it should be understood as an "entitlement" rather than "charity." Economic justice depended on this producerist side of the equation; living wages derived from wealth that workers themselves created. As the radical Bob Ingersoll framed it, the living wage was not a claim for unearned wealth but a way to establish economic justice in the classic producerist sense. "Why should labor fill the world with wealth and live in want?" he asked in 1882.

Living wage proponents usually qualified the emphasis on production in a number of ways, however. First, they claimed that the fruits of production had become so vast in America as to constitute an almost infinite pool of wealth from which to draw wages. The "power of consumption has not increased in proportion to the increase in productive power," declared Gompers. The living wage had become feasible only in the "last generation," John Mitchell claimed in 1903; because of the productive power of industrial capitalism, for the first time "it is possible to give the workingman a wage upon which he may live with reasonable comfort and decency, and with which he may obtain the necessaries and some of the pleasures of life, which in the past society was too poor to provide for him." Proponents of the living wage tended to agree with the Reverend John Chadwick's claim that industrial production in America had produced "enough for all." They also argued that workers had been denied their full fruits for so long that the living wage could be justified as redress of past wrongs. As an 1892 article in a labor newspaper declared, "The great question that agitates the civilized world is—how much shall the wage worker receive for his labor and how much shall the capitalist retain for his profit. The wage worker produces all the wealth of the country and has grown tired of providing all and receiving comparatively nothing."

It was one thing to demand that wages reflect the rightful share of the common toil, but what was the rightful share? Labor's faith in the nearly infinite capacities of production made bold claims for high wages commonplace. Although acknowledged in theory as a limiting factor, as a practical matter, production presented no real limits as far as most workers were concerned since, as Samuel Gompers put it, "the workman has created, creates, and will continue to create, in excess of his ability to consume." In addition, higher wages would spur production; the expansion of needs would expand both production and wage levels. Beyond subsistence, B. W. Williams noted, the laborer "should receive as much more as the profits of the business will justly allow," suggesting that wages could exceed basic needs. Gompers insisted that it was impossible for a worker to "demand more than an equivalent for his services" and claimed that "the wealth augmented by the additional result of his labors above his ability to consume" legitimated living wage demands.

Without abandoning the view that wages were determined in part by production, then, many workers came to define them largely in consumerist terms. Rather than as exploitation that inevitably fell short of full compensation, wages came to be defined positively in need-based language. Even relatively modest living wage demands were framed in terms of need. One proponent wrote in 1895 that the living wage "should enable [the wage earner] with economy and sobriety to maintain a comfortable and healthful home, under conditions which make possible the cultivation of virtue." Despite this stress on thrift, the demand is for more than subsistence. Some recognized that producerism was being abandoned. The Massachusetts labor activist Frank Foster declared in 1900, "It is not ... the value of what is produced which determines the wage rate, but the nature and degree of the wants of the workers."

In promulgating this innovative consumerist theory of wages, proponents fought conventional wisdom on several fronts. Not only did they modify producerist conceptions, they also challenged the increasingly popular view that wages were a product of the operations of the market, in particular the "laws" of supply and demand. A critic of this view explained: "The theory of orthodox political economy ... is that if laborer and employers are left absolutely free to make whatever contracts they like, the wages of labor will be fixed by the law of supply and demand, and the rate thus determined will be, according to one school, just; according to the other school, absolutely necessary, whether just or not." Proponents of the living wage charged that the wages being paid were neither just nor necessary. Instead of the market-based law of supply and demand, living wage advocates suggested that the proper criterion was what the labor pamphleteer and politician William Howard called the "natural law" of need. In redefining the value of labor, Howard articulated two principles, one negative and one positive, which became central to living wage claims. First, labor could not be properly rewarded on the basis of the market categories of supply and demand. Second, only human needs formed a valid basis for wage determinations. This rejection of market-based wage determinations in favor of a standard of needs had contradictory implications. On one level, needs, based on the political concepts of natural law and inalienable rights, trumped the impersonal and amoral machinations of the market, but in a more fundamental sense, need-based wages were utterly dependent on the market. The living wage discourse reflected an unprecedented working-class engagement with the market, which became understood as a site where needs were satisfied, not blocked. Although claiming to be rejecting the principles of the market, living wage advocates were in fact reinterpreting it. They politicized the market by challenging the notion that it was a "natural" force governed by immutable laws. Instead, the essence of "natural law" as they defined it mandated a very different type of market, one subject to working-class control.

Rather than place limits on this need-based conception of wages, living wage advocates argued unapologetically for continual expansion. John Mitchell claimed that "no limit should be set to the aspirations of the workingmen, nor to the demands for higher wages." Since "the consuming power of the community" rested on the backs of workers, wrote George Gunton, it was their duty to "unite and struggle" continually for the "expansion of human desires and necessities." In this rhetoric, needs tended to grow rather than shrink. By 1913 the AFL treasurer John Lennon announced that "the labor movement has now reached the point where we insist that every man and woman in the world performing useful labor is entitled to a living wage." Silent on what counted as useful labor, Lennon insisted that a living wage was not one "upon which they can merely exist." Rather, it was a combination of retirement plan, workmen's compensation program, and family trust fund.

Fundamental to the concept of the living wage for most proponents was the belief that needs were ever expanding, that wages should grow correspondingly, and that the limitless capacity of production made continual growth possible. The living wage had "elevated the standard of living of the American workman and conferred upon him higher wages and more leisure," declared Mitchell, and it should continue to do so indefinitely. Wages should reflect the expanding consumption habits of the workers. "The American of today," noted George McNeill, "wants something today that yesterday knew nothing of: tomorrow he will have a new want." Stressing the consumerist dimension in his well-publicized 1898 defense of the living wage, Samuel Gompers demanded a wage that would enable workers to maintain the American standard of living; it should, he declared, prevent the breadwinner from becoming what he called a "non-consumer." Gompers refused to be pinned down to a specific definition since, as he put, "a living wage today may be denounced as a starvation wage in a decade." Placed in this context, Gompers's famous demand for "more, more" emerges as part of a long working-class tradition of political economy. The notion of the ever-increasing living wage was an ideal to which all groups of workers aspired.

CHAPTER 6

The Stop Watch and The Wooden Shoe
Scientific Management and the Industrial Workers of the World

Mike Davis

Taylor and the "Art of Sweating" (1)

According to the founding father of modern industrial management, the "conscious restriction of output" or "soldiering" has always been the original sin of the working class. "The natural laziness of men is serious," Frederick W. Taylor wrote, "but by far the greatest evil from which both workmen and employers are suffering is the systematic soldiering which is almost universal."[1] Taylor's lifelong crusade against the "autonomous and inefficient" worker was the crystallization of his personal experiences as a foreman at the Midvale Steel Company in Philadelphia. For three years he waged a relentless campaign against the machinists and laborers whom he accused of collectively restricting plant output. He was finally able to break up the group cohesion of the workers and reduce "soldiering" only after a ruthless dose of fines and dismissals. This pyrrhic victory took "three years of the hardest, meanest, most contemptible work of any man's life ... in trying to drive my friends to do a decent day's work." It convinced Taylor that repression alone was an inadequate foundation for management control over the conditions of production.[2]

After further years of experimentation in the steel industry and in tool-and-die shops, and with the occasional backing of key corporate leaders from Bethlehem Steel and other large companies, Taylor systematized his theories in a series of books. Of his several works, however, his bluntly written *Principles of Scientific Management* popularized his ideas most effectively. Eventually, after being translated into a dozen languages, this book became a bible to "efficiency men" all over the world. Here Taylor proposed effective solutions to the problems of reduced output and "soldiering."

The traditional basis of soldiering, he explained, was the degree of job control exercised by skilled workers through their mastery of the production process. Craft

Original publication details: Davis, 1975.

Class: The Anthology, First Edition. Edited by Stanley Aronowitz and Michael J. Roberts.
© 2018 Stanley Aronowitz and Michael J. Roberts. Published 2018 by John Wiley & Sons Ltd.

exclusivism, maintained by control over entry into workforce and the monopolization of skills almost as an artisanal form of property, blocked the operation of free-market forces upon both the wage scale and employment.[3]

Taylor, moreover, recognized that the submission of the work force to the new discipline of the assembly line would not automatically resolve these problems as long as even a minority of the personnel preserved the right to define a "fair day's work." He emphasized that the crucial precondition of complete management power was the appropriation from the skilled workers of the totality of their craft secrets and traditions. The techniques of time and motion study developed by Taylor (and later perfected by others) were precise methods for analyzing the content of craft skills involved in the production process. These "scientific" studies conducted by the new-fangled production engineers and acolytes of Taylorism became the basis for undermining the autonomy of craft labor. Knowledge of the production process would be monopolized by management, while craft skills were simultaneously decomposed into simpler, constituent activities.

Skilled workers immediately perceived the twin menace of scientific management: the loss of craft control and the radical polarization of mental and manual labor. In 1916 a leader of the Molders' Union incisively analyzed the deteriorating position of American craftsmen as a whole:

> The one great asset of the wage worker has been his craftsmanship. … The greatest blow that could be delivered against unionism and the organized workers would be the separation of craft knowledge from craft skill. Of late this separation of craft knowledge and craft skill has actually taken place in an ever widening area and with an ever increasing acceleration. Its process is shown in the introduction of machinery and the standardization of tools, materials, products, and processes, which makes production possible on a large scale …. THE SECOND FORM, MORE INSIDIOUS AND MORE DANGEROUS THAN THE FIRST, is the gathering up of all this scattered craft knowledge, systematizing and concentrating it in the hands of the employer and then doling it out again only in the form of minute instructions, giving to each worker only the knowledge needed for the mechanical performance of a particular relatively minute task. This process, it is evident, separates skill and knowledge even in their narrow relationship. When it is completed, the worker is no longer a craftsman in any sense, but is an animated tool of the management. (My emphasis) [4]

While scientific management demanded the progressive "dequalification" of labor's craft aristocracy, it also signaled a new slavery for unskilled workers. As Taylor recognized, even gangs of common laborers, unorganized and lacking a property right in a craft, frequently were able to convert the solidarity of their work group into an effective brake on increased output. Management, he argued, had to aim at destroying the solidarity of all functional work groups, skilled or unskilled.

A good deal has been written about the American Federation of Labor's response to scientific management, from its initial strong opposition to its eventual conciliation (or capitulation).[5] However, the response to Taylorism among unskilled or immigrant workers has been explored only recently. And very little is known about the reaction of the radical Industrial Workers of the World. Although the Wobblies have received much attention in the last decade, they have not been taken as seriously as they should. In contrast to the AFL's narrow defense of endangered craft privileges, the Wobblies attempted to develop a rank-and-file rebellion against the rationality of Taylor and the speed-up. In fact, they were virtually unique among American labor organizations, in their time or any other, in their advocacy of a concrete plan for workers' control.

Nothing illustrates the specificity of I.W.W. industrial unionism better than the I.W.W.'s role in the wave of mass strikes initiated by Eastern industrial workers from the first detonation at McKees Rocks, Pennsylvania in 1909 through the Detroit auto strikes of 1913. Historians have yet to put these strikes in their proper perspective.

I.W.W members recognized that the industrial working class would not be organized in one single leap forward. Instead, the Wobblies saw the need for the forging of a "culture" of struggle among immigrant workers and the creation of a laboratory to test the tactics of class struggle. These years saw a vigorous debate on industrial strategy both within the I.W.W. and between its partisans and the rest of the American left. Having traced some of the origins of the pre-war strike wave to the impact of scientific management, it is time to consider the famous, somewhat enigmatic controversy over "sabotage" and its relationship to I.W.W. practice in the Taylorized mills and plants.

The I.W.W. Turns to Guerilla Warfare

Historians have tended to agree that "sabotage" was an indelible mark of I.W.W infatuation with European syndicalism. Philip Foner, an "old left" historian whose volume on the I.W.W. remains the most carefully crafted account of the Wobblies' "heroic period," is firmly convinced that sabotage is the "one doctrine which the I.W.W. borrowed directly from the French syndicalists."

A careful reading of the I.W.W. literature concerning sabotage in this period reveals the striking mixture of old ideas and new which can be analytically reduced in each case to three fundamental and differing meanings of "sabotage." These three dimensions of "sabotage," in turn, correspond to different, historically specific tactics of the labor movement.

First, there is the meaning frequently assigned by Bill Haywood that sabotage was only the frank, open advocacy of the same "universal soldiering" practiced by most workers. In this sense, "the conscious withdrawal of the workers' industrial efficiency" boils down to the familiar and inherently conservative tactic which had been one of the main bases of craft unionism. Moreover, it was precisely this traditional form of job control through conscious self-regulation of the pace which, as we have seen, Taylorism and speed-up were dissolving through the transfer of total control over working conditions to management. It was in Europe, where industry was less rationalized, that the old conservative application of soldiering was still a ubiquitous safeguard of traditional worker prerogatives.

Second, "sabotage" sometimes carried that inflammatory connotation which so terrified right-wing socialists like Victor Berger — who thought he saw the ghost of anarchist bomber Johann Most in the I.W.W. The retaliatory destruction of capitalist property (and occasionally persons) was an unspoken but familiar tactic in American labor struggles. Undoubtedly the I.W.W. had some first-hand knowledge of the efficacy of the match or fuse in Western labor struggles involving brutally terrorized miners, agricultural laborers, or lumberjacks. Workers in these industries had a long international tradition — "Captain Swing," "Molly Maguires," Asturian and Bolivian "Dynameteros," etc. — of using "sabotage" as a last resort against the daily experience of employer violence. In contrast, the Wobblies, while far from being pacifists, channeled the rebellion of Western workers into industrial unionism and new, essentially non-violent forms of struggle like the free-speech campaigns. These tactics helped break down the isolation

of the casual laborer from workers in the towns and turned the migrant into a sophisticated and self-sufficient political agitator.

In urban, industrial strikes, moreover, the I.W.W. used violence or property destruction far less often than the AFL. because of its greater reliance on passive resistance and
mass action. It is truly a remarkable fact that the Commission on Industrial Relations
could attribute only $25 property damage to the Paterson I.W.W. strikers during the
whole course of that bitter struggle.[6] In fact, the principal reason for continued agitation
around the idea of the workers' right to employ retaliatory property destruction as a
tactic, whether actually used or not, was to demystify the sanctity of property and teach
workers the methods of protracted struggle. There are many examples where the mere
threat of sabotage (in this sense) taught an invaluable lesson in political economy and
actually strengthened the strikers' position. For example:

> In Lawrence one of the reasons for the settlement of the strike on terms favorable to the
> strikers was the fact that the employers feared that the cloth might not be produced in
> the best of conditions by workers who were entirely dissatisfied. This knowledge, shared by
> the strikers, gave to the toilers the feeling that they were a necessary portion of the social
> mechanism and brought them that much nearer the time when the workers as a class shall
> feel capable of managing industry in their own interests.[7]
>
> During the important I.W.W.-led New York Waiters Strike of 1913, Joe Ettor electrified
> the hotel and restaurant owners with his straightforward advice to beleaguered strikers: "If
> you are compelled to go back to work under conditions that are not satisfactory, go back
> with the determination to stick together and with your minds made up that it is the unsafest
> proposition in the world for the capitalists to eat food prepared by members of your
> union." (!)[8]

It appears that the Wobblies rarely went ahead and actually brought the "fire next
time," in the form of retaliatory destruction, down upon the heads of the bosses. Their
typical emphasis in discussing sabotage was on a third meaning of the word, as a mass
tactic requiring some form of continuing, although clandestine, mass organization in the
plant or mill. Sabotage is clearly defined as a flexible family of different tactics which
effectively reduce output and efficiency. Old-fashioned soldiering or the retaliatory
destruction of capitalist property are merely potential applications, under specific
conditions, of a much more diverse strategy which also included the "open mouth strike"
(purposeful disruption by observing every rule to the letter) and (above all) the hit-and-
run slowdown. The essence of the Wobbly advocacy of sabotage was to encourage the
creativity of the workers in the discovery of different tactics. When moulded to the
particularities of specific industries, these tactics could be applied directly on the job with
maximum effect (whether or not union organization was recognized) and with a minimum danger of company retaliation against individual workers. Although little is really
known about the history of unofficial job actions, there is good reason to believe that the
I.W.W. focused especially on systematic sabotage through repeated slowdowns and short,
sporadic strikes. The relationship of these tactics to the overall Wobbly strategy is forcefully summed up by Elizabeth Gurley Flynn: "Sabotage is to the class struggle what guerrilla warfare is to the battle. The strike is the open battle of the class struggle, sabotage is
the guerrilla warfare, the day-to-day warfare between two opposing classes."[9]

Furthermore, the I.W.W. press offers abundant proof that this industrial "guerrilla
warfare" was a direct response to scientific management and that sabotage in fact provided the only soundly based alternative to workers in the most rationalized industries.

In addition to regular articles about scientific management, the *Industrial Worker* repeatedly editorialized the need to counteract the stop watch with prudent use of the wooden shoe:

> Many who condemn sabotage will be found to be unconscious advocates of it. Think of the absurd position of the "Craft Union Socialists" who decry sabotage and in almost the same breath condemn the various efficiency systems of the employers. By opposing "scientific management" they are doing to potential profits what the saboteurs are doing to actual profits. The one prevents efficiency, the other withdraws it. Incidentally, it might be said that sabotage is the only effective method of warding off the deterioration of the worker that is sure to follow the performance of the same monotonous task minute after minute, day in and day out. … Sabotage also offers the best method to combat the evil known as "speeding up." None but the workers know how great this evil is.[10]

The close correlation between the introduction of scientific management and the appearance of the famous black cat of sabotage was widely appreciated by contemporary observers, whether friend or foe of the I.W.W. For instance there is the testimony of P. J. Conlon, international vice-president of the International Association of Machinists, before the Commission on Industrial Relations:

> … we believe that it (scientific management) builds up in the industrial world the principle of sabotage, syndicalism, passive resistance, based on economic determinism. We did not hear of any of these things until we heard of scientific management and new methods of production. … we find that when men can not help themselves, nor can they get any redress of grievances, and are forced to accept that which is thrust upon them, that they are going to find within themselves a means of redress that can find expression in no other way than passive resistance or in syndicalism.[11]

Conlon's perception is amplified by William English Walling in his widely read *Progressivism and After*. Walling, in this period a leading spokesman of the Socialist left, possessed a rich understanding of the I.W.W.'s actual practice and the trajectory of its strategic thought. After discussing the false identification of sabotage with violence Walling explains:

> But many representatives of the labouring masses, including well-known I.W.W. members, either attach little importance to such extreme methods or positively oppose them. To withdraw the "efficiency from the work," that is, to do either slower or poorer work than one is capable of doing, is also a mere continuation and systematization of a world-wide practice which has long been a fixed policy of the unions of the aristocracy of labor. But its object in their hands was merely to enable the workers to take things easy, to increase the number of employed, and so to strengthen the monopoly of skilled craftsmen.[12]

Having carefully distinguished these two traditional forms of sabotage, Walling goes on to classify methods of "poor and slow" work which, because of their specificity to Taylorized production, carry an entirely new and different meaning:

> The laboring masses have now completely revolutionized the motive as well as the method. In order to influence employers the output can no longer be restricted on all occasions. The work must be good and fast when the employer does what labor wants. It is a pity, then, that there is for this practice not some middle expression between the old term, ca' canny, which

means intermittent restriction of output, and the new term, sabotage, which often means almost any kind of attack on the employer or his business.

But what I want to emphasize at this point is that, in proportion as the scientific methods of increasing efficiency are applied in industry, one of the laborers' best and most natural weapons is the scientific development of methods of interfering with efficiency, which methods, it seems, are likely to be lumped together with entirely different and often contradictory practices under the common name of sabotage.[13]

Walling also analyzed the strategy he saw emerging from the mass strike movement and described a system of "provisional agreements," unbound by legal contracts, and enforced by intermittent strikes. Despite the fact that the Wobblies would almost certainly have rejected his introjection about sometimes encouraging workers to do their jobs "good and fast," *Progressivism and After* captures a deeper aspect of I.W.W. tactics, particularly the degree to which a bold and coherent action strategy was emerging on premises radically different from the liberal goal of "institutionalized collective bargaining."

The larger conception of revolutionary industrial unionism in which sabotage appeared as a tactic was vigorously discussed and debated in the pages of the *Industrial Worker* during the 1909–1914 period. Fellow Worker Will Fisher provided a succinct definition:

FIRST.......... Avoid labor contracts.

SECOND....... Don't give long notices to the employer what you intend to do.

THIRD .... Avoid premature moves and moves at the wrong time.

FOURTH....... Avoid as far as possible the use of violence.

FIFTH. .... Use force of public education and agitation; the union is an agitational and educational force for the workers.

SIXTH. .... Boycott.

SEVENTH. .... Passive strikes and sabotage, irritant strikes.

EIGHTH. ..... Political strikes.

NINTH. ...... General strikes.

TENTH .... Where possible seizure of warehouses and stores to supply strikers or locked out men.[14]

It is important to remember that at this time the formal labor contract and time agreement was one of the methods by which craft unions had preserved their control over the work place. The Wobblies pointed out that "... the time agreement under which the workers of each craft union are given a closed shop is often as bad for the workers as a whole as an open shop, because, under its terms, contracting craftsmen are bound to scab on the other workers."[15] At McKees Rocks, New Castle, Akron and Paterson, the immigrant workers had seen their struggles broken by the native, skilled workers who signed independent agreements with the bosses and used them as legal cover to break strikes.[16]

In contrast to the maintenance of the closed shop by legal agreement amd external compulsion, the I.W.W. proposed an entirely different concept of shop control based on voluntary self-organization and shop-floor direct action (sabotage) to resolve grievances and preserve conditions won in previous strikes. During the Brooklyn Shoe Strike of 1911 the Wobblies introduced the "shop committee." "The I.W.W. shop organization developed technical knowledge in the working class and prepared it to take over technical management."[17] Furthermore, the I.W.W. local union, borrowing and extending the European precedent of the MAISON DU PEUPLE, functioned as a high-energy agitational and educational force: "not only a union hall but an educational and social center."[18] Finally, by building entirely upon a basis of voluntary membership and rank-and-file activism, with a minimal full-time staff, the Wobblies told astonished questioners that they were "… doing away with the professional labor leader."[19]

This model of shop organization pivoted around sabotage, intermittent slowdowns, one-day wildcats, and walkouts was, in turn, a prototype of industrial unionism as a "culture of struggle":

> … we have the partial strike, the passive strike, the irritant strike, and the general strike — one continual series of skirmishes with the enemy, while in the meantime we are collecting and drilling our forces and learning how to fight the bosses. [20]
>
> The short strike is not only to pester the employer; it is like army drill, to become the school of practice in preparation for the coming general or universal strike.[21]

Sabotage was thus conceived as both a means of achieving some degree of shop control in scientifically managed factories, and also as an integral part of the "greviculture" (strike culture) preparing the American working class for the Social Revolution. Unfortunately we know very little about the actual development of job-action tactics and sabotage within the concrete context of individual factories. The daily building of collective organization on a plant level and the ceaseless guerrilla warfare against management's despotism constitute a "terra incognita" for historians. Staughton Lynd's ground-breaking interviews with rank-and-file steel workers, which challenge so many

PUNCHIN' TH' CLOCK

bi Woody Guthrie

Figure 6.1

accepted theories of the C.I.O., demonstrate how vital this dimension of labor history is for a real understanding of the struggle to build industrial unionism.[22]

Judging the importance or "marginality" of the I.W.W. in the Progressive Era by the Wobblies' failure to actually construct the One Big Union or to found permanent locals ignores the fact that the mass strikes of 1909–1913 transmitted a valuable arsenal of new tactics and organizational weapons to the industrial working class. Though the I.W.W. failed to reach many workers struggling against scientific management within the AFL, the Wobblies' dual unionism allowed them to take a new course in developing direct-action strategies that would be used in later industrial struggles. Without romanticizing the I.W.W., we should take it seriously as the only major labor organization in the U.S. which seriously and consistently challenged the capitalist organization of production. In our own time, when "virtually all manufacturing operations in the industrial world are based on an application of scientific management rules"[23] and when workers from Lordstown to Lip are actually struggling to break those rules and to challenge the managers who make them, the old confrontation between the stop watch and the wooden shoe still has living significance.

Notes

The author thanks Paul Worthman and James Green for their help on this article.

1 Frederick W. Taylor, *Principles of Scientific Management* (New York, 1911), p. 13.
2 Taylor before the Commission on Industrial Relations, April 13, 1914. *Report and Testimony, Vol. 1* (Washington, 1916), p. 782. For a description of Taylor's aberrant personality, including his habit of chaining himself at night to "a harness of straps and wooden points," see Samuel Haber, *Efficiency and Uplift: Scientific Management in the Progressive Era*, 1890–1920, Chicago, 1964.
3 For a provocative description of the degree of job control exercised by skilled workers before the advent of rationalization, see Katherine Stone, "Origin of Job Structures in the Steel Industry," *Radical America*, Nov.–Dec. 1973.
4 John P. Frey, "Modern Industry and Craft Skills," *American Federationist* (May 1916), pp. 365–66. Cf. Andre Gorz's summary: As a whole, the history of capitalist technology can be read as the history of the dequalification of the direct procedures." Andre Gorz, "The Tyranny of the Factory," *Telos* (Summer 1973), pp. 61–68.
5 Haber, op. cit.; Milton Nadworny, *Scientific Management and The Unions* (Cambridge, 1955); and Jean McKelvey, *AFL Attitudes Toward Production* (Ithaca, 1952).
6 Commission on Industrial Relations, op. cit., Vol. 1, p. 55. Philip Foner, *The Industrial Workers of the World* 1905–1917 (New York, 1965) p 160.
7 Industrial Worker, May 15, 1912.
8 Melvyn Dubofsky, *When Workers Organize: New York City in the Progressive Era* (Amherst, 1968), p. 124.
9 Elizabeth Gurley Flynn, *Sabotage* (Chicago, n.d.), p. 4.
10 *Industrial Worker*, Feb. 6, 1913. See also Editorial, Dec. 28, 1911, and the articles by Covington Hall, Nov. 16, 1911, and B.E. Nilsson, April 24, 1913.
11 Commission on Industrial Relations, op. cit., Vol. 1, pp. 874–77.
12 William English Walling, *Progressivism and After* (New York, 1914), pp. 301–302.
13 Ibid.
14 Will Fisher, "Industrial Unionism, Tactics and Principles," *Industrial Worker*, March 12, 1910.
15 Fisher, op. cit., March 19, 1910.
16 "The more I see of the old unions the more I am convinced that we must fight them as bitterly as we fight the bosses; in fact, I believe they are a worse enemy of the One Big Union than the bosses, because they are able to fight us with weapons not possessed by the bosses." E.F. Doree, "Shop Control and the Contract: How They Affect the I.W.W.," reported in the Stenographic Minutes

of the Tenth Convention, 1916. Doree's sectarianism must be seen in the light of the innumerable instances of strikebreaking by AFL unions; the second walkout at McKees Rocks, for instance, was broken by armed native workers affiliated to the Amalgamated. (See Ingham, op. cit.) In other steel mills AFL men gave the bosses the names of suspected Wobbly sympathizers. (Industrial Worker, Feb. 19, 1912.)

17   Justus Ebert, The I.W.W. In *Theory And Practice*, 5th Revised Edition (Chicago, 1937), pp. 126–27.

18   Fisher, op. cit., March 12, 1910.

19   Joe Ettor, *Commission on Industrial Relations*, op. cit., Vol. 2, p. 1555.

20   *Industrial Worker*, Feb. 5, 1910.

21   James Brooks, *American Syndicalism: The I.W.W.* (New York, 1913), p. 135.

22   Staughton Lynd, ed., "Personal Histories of the Early C.I.O.," Radical America, May-June 1972.

23   George Friedmann, *The Anatomy of Work* (New York, 1961).

CHAPTER 7

The Power of Women and the Subversion of the Community

Mariarosa Dalla Costa and Selma James

These observations are an attempt to define and analyze the "Woman Question," and to locate this question in the entire "female role" as it has been created by the capitalist division of labor.

We place foremost in these pages the housewife as the central figure in this female role. We assume that all women are housewives and even those who work outside the home continue to be housewives. That is, on a world level, it is precisely what is particular to domestic work, not only measured as number of hours and nature of work, but as quality of life and quality of relationships which it generates, that determines a woman's place wherever she is and to whichever class she belongs. We concentrate here on the position of the working class woman, but this is not to imply that only working class women are exploited. Rather it is to confirm that the role of the working class housewife, which we believe has been indispensable to capitalist production, is *the* determinant for the position of all other women. Every analysis of women as a caste, then, must proceed from the analysis of the position of working class housewives.

In order to see the housewife as central, it was first of all necessary to analyze briefly how capitalism has created the modern family and the housewife's role in it, by destroying the types of family group or community which previously existed.

The day-to-day struggles that women have developed since the second world war run directly against the organization of the factory and of the home. The "unreliability" of women in the home and out of it has grown rapidly since then, and runs directly against the factory as regimentation organized in time and space, and against the social factory as organization of the reproduction of labor power. This trend to more absenteeism, to less respect for timetables, to higher job mobility, is shared by young men and women workers. But where the man for crucial periods of his youth will be the sole support of a new family, women who on the whole are not restrained in this way and who must always consider the job at home, are bound to be even more disengaged from work discipline, forcing disruption of the productive flow and therefore higher costs to capital. (This is one excuse for the discriminatory wages which many times over make up for capital's loss.)

Original publication details: Mariarosa Dalla Costa and Selma James, *The Power of Women and the Subversion of the Community*, pp. 1–2; 5–6; 10–12; 16–19; 21–25. Falling Wall, 1975.

It is this same trend of disengagement that groups of housewives express when they leave their children with their husbands at work.[1] This trend is and will increasingly be one of the decisive forms of the crisis in the systems of the factory and of the social factory.

The Origins of the Capitalist Family

In pre-capitalist patriarchal society *the home and the family* were central to agricultural and artisan production. With the advent of capitalism the socialization of production was organized with *the factory* as its center. Those who worked in the new productive center, the factory, received a wage. Those who were excluded did not. Women, children and the aged lost the relative power that derived from the family's dependence on their labor, *which was seen to be social and necessary*. Capital, destroying the family and the community and production as one whole, on the one hand has concentrated basic social production in the factory and the office, and on the other has in essence detached the man from the family and turned him into a *wage laborer*. It has put on the man's shoulders the burden of financial responsibility for women, children, the old and the ill, in a word, all those who do not receive wages. From that moment began the expulsion from the home of all those who did not *procreate and service those who worked for wages*. The first to be excluded from the home, after men, were children; they sent children to school. The family ceased to be not only the productive, but also the educational center.[2]

To the extent that men had been the despotic heads of the patriarchal family, based on a strict division of labor, the experience of women, children and men was a contradictory experience which we inherit. But in pre-capitalist society the work of each member of the community of serfs was seen to be directed to a purpose: either to the prosperity of the feudal lord or to our survival. To this extent the whole community of serfs was compelled to be co-operative in a unity of unfreedom that involved to the same degree women, children and men, which capitalism had to break.[3] In this sense the *unfree individual*, the *democracy of unfreedom*,[4] entered into a crisis. The passage from serfdom to free labor power separated the male from the female proletarian and both of them from their children. The unfree patriarch was transformed into the "free" wage earner, and upon the contradictory experience of the sexes and the generations was built a more profound estrangement and therefore a more subversive relation.

The Exploitation of the Wageless

To the extent to which capital has recruited the man and turned him into a wage laborer, it has created a fracture between him and all the other proletarians without a wage who, not participating directly in social production, were thus presumed incapable of being the subjects of social revolt.

Since Marx, it has been clear that capital rules and develops through the wage, that is, that the foundation of capitalist society was the wage laborer and his or her direct exploitation. What has been neither clear nor assumed by the organizations of the working class movement is that precisely through the wage has the exploitation of the non-wage laborer been organized. This exploitation has been even more effective because the lack of a wage hid it. That is, the wage commanded a larger amount of labor than appeared in factory bargaining. *Where women are concerned, their labor appears to be a personal service outside of capital.* The woman seemed only to be suffering from male chauvinism, being pushed around because capitalism meant general "injustice" and "bad and unreasonable behavior"; the few (men) who noticed convinced us that this was "oppression" but not exploitation. But "oppression" hid another and more pervasive aspect of capitalist society. Capital excluded children from the home and sent them to school not only because they are in the way of others' more "productive" labor or only to indoctrinate them. The rule of capital through the wage compels every ablebodied person to function, under the law of division of labor, and to function in ways that are if not immediately, then ultimately profitable to the expansion and extension of the rule of capital. That, fundamentally, is the meaning of school. *Where children are concerned, their labor appears to be learning for their own benefit.*

Proletarian children have been forced to undergo the same education in the schools: this is capitalist levelling against the infinite possibilities of learning. Woman on the other hand has been isolated in the home, forced to carry out work that is considered unskilled, the work of giving birth to, raising, disciplining, and servicing the worker for production. Her role in the cycle of social production remained invisible because only the product of her labor, *the laborer*, was visible there. She herself was thereby trapped within pre-capitalist working conditions and never paid a wage.

And when we say "pre-capitalist working conditions" we do not refer only to women who have to use brooms to sweep. Even the best equipped American kitchens do not reflect the present level of technological development; at most they reflect the technology of the 19th century. If you are not paid by the hour, within certain limits, nobody cares how long it takes you to do your work.

This is not only a *quantitative* but a *qualitative* difference from other work, and it stems precisely from the kind of commodity that this work is destined to produce. Within the capitalist system generally, the productivity of labor doesn't increase unless there is a confrontation between capital and class: technological innovations and co-operation are at the same time moments of attack for the working class and moments of capitalistic response. But if this is true for the production of commodities generally, this has not been true for the production of that special kind of commodity, labor power. If technological innovation can lower the limit of necessary work, and if the working class struggle in industry can use that innovation for gaining free hours, the same cannot be said of housework; to the extent that she must *in isolation* procreate, raise and be responsible for children, a high mechanization of domestic chores doesn't free any time for the woman. She is always on duty, for the machine doesn't exist that makes and minds children.[9] A higher productivity of domestic work through mechanization, then, can be related only to specific services, for example, cooking, washing, cleaning. Her workday is unending not because she has no machines, but because she is isolated.[10]

Surplus Value and the Social Factory

At this point then we would like to begin to clear the ground of a certain point of view which orthodox Marxism, especially in the ideology and practice of so-called Marxist parties, has always taken for granted. And this is: when women remain outside social production, that is, outside the socially organized productive cycle, they are also outside social productivity. The role of women, in other words, has always been seen as that of a psychologically subordinated person who, except where she is marginally employed out-side the home, is outside production; essentially a supplier of a series of use values in the home. This basically was the viewpoint of Marx who, observing what happened to women working in the factories, concluded that it might have been better for them to be at home, where resided a morally higher form of life. But the true nature of the role of the housewife never emerges clearly in Marx. Yet observers have noted that Lancashire women, cotton workers for over a century, are more sexually free and helped by men in domestic chores. On the other hand, in the Yorkshire coal mining districts where a low percentage of women worked outside the home, women are more dominated by the fig-ure of the husband. Even those who have been able to define the exploitation of women in socialized production could not then go on to understand the exploited position of women in the home; men are too compromised in their relationship with women. For that reason only women can define themselves and move on the woman question.

We have to make clear that, within the wage, domestic work produces not merely use values, but is essential to the production of surplus value.[12] This is true of the entire female role as a personality which is subordinated at all levels, physical, psychical and occupational, which has had and continues to have a precise and vital place in the capitalist division of labor, *in pursuit of productivity at the social level*. Let us examine more specifi-cally the role of women as a source of social productivity, that is, of surplus value making. Firstly within the family.

The Productivity of Wage Slavery Based on Unwaged Slavery

It is often asserted that, within the definition of wage labor, women in domestic labor are not productive. In fact precisely the opposite is true if one thinks of the enormous quantity of social services which capitalist organization transforms into privatized activity, putting them on the backs of housewives. Domestic labor is not essentially "feminine work"; a woman doesn't fulfill herself more or get less exhausted than a man from washing and cleaning. These are social services inasmuch as they serve the reproduction of labor power. And capital, precisely by instituting its family structure, has "liberated" the man from these functions so that he is completely "free" for direct exploitation; so that he is free to "earn" enough for a woman to reproduce him as labor power.[13] It has made men wage slaves, then, to the degree that it has succeeded in allocating these services to women in the family, and by the same process controlled the flow of women onto the labor market. In Italy women are still necessary in the home and capital still needs this form of the family. At the present level of development in Europe generally, in Italy in particular, capital still prefers to import its labor power – in the form of millions of men from underdeveloped areas – while at the same time consigning women to the home.[14]

And women are of service not only because they carry out domestic labor *without a wage and without going on strike*, but also because they always receive back into the home all those who are periodically expelled from their jobs by economic crisis. The family, this maternal cradle always ready to help and protect in time of need, has been in fact the best guarantee that the unemployed do not immediately become a horde of disruptive outsiders.

The organized parties of the working class movement have been careful not to raise the question of domestic work. Aside from the fact that they have always treated women as a lower form of life, even in factories, to raise this question would be to challenge the whole basis of the trade unions as organizations that deal (a) only with the factory; (b) only with a measured and "paid" work day; (c) only with that side of wages which is given to us and not with the side of wages which is taken back, that is, inflation. Women have always been forced by the working class parties to put off their liberation to some hypothetical future, making it dependent on the gains that men, limited in the scope of their struggles by these parties, win for "themselves".

In reality, every phase of working class struggle has fixed the subordination and exploitation of women at a higher level. The proposal of pensions for housewives[15] (and this makes us wonder why not a wage) serves only to show the complete willingness of these parties further to institutionalize women as housewives and men (and women) as wage slaves.

Now it is clear that not one of us believes that emancipation, liberation, can be achieved through work. Work is still work, whether inside or outside the home. The independence of the wage earner means only being a "free individual" for capital, no less for women than for men. Those who advocate that the liberation of the working class woman lies in her getting a job outside the home are part of the problem, not the solution. Slavery to an assembly line is not a liberation from slavery to a kitchen sink. To deny this is also to deny the slavery of the assembly line itself, proving again that if you don't know how women are exploited, you can never really know how men are. But this question is so crucial that we deal with it separately. What we wish to make clear here is that by the non-payment of a wage when we are producing in a world capitalistically organized, the figure of the boss is concealed behind that of the husband. He appears to be the sole recipient of domestic services, and this gives an ambiguous and slavelike character to housework. The husband and children, through their loving involvement, their loving blackmail, become the first foremen, the immediate controllers of this labor.

The husband tends to read the paper and wait for his dinner to be cooked and served, even when his wife goes out to work as he does and comes home with him. Clearly, the specific form of exploitation represented by domestic work demands a correspondingly specific form of struggle, namely the women's struggle, *within the family*.

The possibility of social struggle arises out of the *socially productive character* of women's work in the home. It is not only or mainly the social services provided in the home that make women's role socially productive, even though in fact at this moment these services are identified with women's role. But capital can technologically improve the conditions of this work. What capital does not want to do for the time being, in Italy at least, is to destroy the position of the housewife as the pivot of the nuclear family. For this reason there is no point in our waiting for the automation of domestic work, because this will never happen: the maintenance of the nuclear family is compatible with the automation of these services. To really automate them, capital would have to destroy the family as we know it; that is, it would be driven to *socialize* in order to *automate* fully.

A New Compass for Class Struggle

If women demand in workers' assemblies that the night-shift be abolished because at night, besides sleeping, one wants to make love – and it's not the same as making love during the day if the women work during the day – that would be advancing their own independent interests as women against the social organization of work, refusing to be unsatisfied mothers for their husbands and children.

But in this new intervention and confrontation women are also expressing that their interests as women are not, as they have been told, separate and alien from the interests of the class. For too long political parties, especially of the left, and trade unions have determined and confined the areas of working class struggle. To make love and to refuse night work to make love, *is in the interest of the class*. To explore why it is women and not men who raise the question is to shed new light on the whole history of the class.

To sum up: the most important thing becomes precisely this explosion of the women's movement as an expression of the specificity of female interests hitherto castrated from all its connections by the capitalist organization of the family. This has to be waged in every quarter of this society, each of which is founded precisely on the suppression of such interests, since the entire class exploitation has been built upon the specific mediation of women's exploitation.

Electric appliances in the home are lovely things to have, but for the workers who make them, to make many is to spend time and to exhaust yourself. That every wage has to buy all of them is tough, and presumes that every wife must run all these appliances alone; and this only means that she is frozen in the home, but now on a more mechanized level. Lucky worker, lucky wife!

The question is not to have communal canteens. We must remember that capital makes Fiat for the workers first, then their canteen.

For this reason to demand a communal canteen in the neighborhood without integrating this demand into a practice of struggle against the organization of labor, against labor time, risks giving the impetus for a new leap that, on the community level, would regiment none other than women in some alluring work so that we will then have the possibility at lunchtime of eating shit collectively in the canteen.

We want them to know that this is not the canteen we want, nor do we want play centers or nurseries of the same order.[17] We want canteens too, and nurseries and washing machines and dishwashers, but we also want choices: to eat in privacy with few people when we want, to have time to be with children, to be with old people, with the sick, when and where we choose. To "have time" means to work less. To have time to be with children, the old and the sick does not mean running to pay a quick visit to the garages where you park children or old people or invalids. It means that we, the first to be excluded, are taking the initiative in this struggle so that all those other excluded people, the children, the old and the ill, can re-appropriate the social wealth; to be re-integrated with us and all of us with men, not as dependents but autonomously, as we women want for ourselves; since their exclusion, like ours, from the directly productive social process, from social existence, has been created by capitalist organization.

The Refusal of Work

Hence we must refuse housework as women's work, as work imposed upon us, which we never invented, which has never been paid for, in which they have forced us to cope with absurd hours, 12 and 13 a day, in order to force us to stay at home.

We must get out of the house; we must reject the home, because we want to unite with other women, to struggle against all situations which presume that women will stay at home, to link ourselves to the struggles of all those who are in ghettos, whether the ghetto is a nursery, a school, a hospital, an old-age home, or asylum. To abandon the home is already a form of struggle, since the social services we perform there would then cease to be carried out in those conditions, and so all those who work out of the home would then demand that the burden carried by us until now be thrown squarely where it belongs – onto the shoulders of capital. This alteration in the terms of struggle will be all the more violent the more the refusal of domestic labor on the part of women will be violent, determined and on a mass scale.

The working class family is the more difficult point to break because it is the support of the worker, but as worker, and for that reason the support of capital. On this family depends the support of the class, the survival of the class – but *at the woman's expense against the class itself.* The woman is the slave of a wage-slave, and her slavery ensures the slavery of her man. Like the trade union, the family protects the worker, but also ensures that he *and she* will never be anything but workers. And that is why the struggle of the woman of the working class against the family is crucial.

To meet other women who work inside and outside their homes allows us to possess other chances of struggle. To the extent that our struggle is a struggle against work, it is inscribed in the struggle which the working class wages against capitalist work. But to the extent that the exploitation of women through domestic work has had its own specific history, tied to the survival of the nuclear family, the specific course of this struggle which must pass through the destruction of the nuclear family as established by the capitalist social order, adds a new dimension to the class struggle.

Notes

1   This happened as part of the massive demonstration of women celebrating International Women's Day in the US, August 1970.

2   This is to assume a whole new meaning for "education", and the work now being done on the history of compulsory education – forced learning – proves this. In England teachers were conceived of as "moral police" who could 1) condition children against "crime" – curb working class reappropriation in the community; 2) destroy "the mob", working class organization based on family which was still either a productive unit or at least a viable organizational unit; 3) make habitual regular attendance and good timekeeping so necessary to children's later employment; and 4) stratify the class by grading and selection. As with the family itself, the transition to this new form of muni control was not smooth and direct, and was the result of contradictory forces both within the class and within capital, as with every phase of the history of capitalism.

3   Wage labor is based on the subordination of all relationships to the wage relation. The worker must enter as an "individual" into a contract with capital stripped of the protection of kinships.

4   Karl Marx, "Critique of Hegel's Philosophy of the State", *Writings of the Young Marx on Philosophy and Society*, ed. and trans. Lloyd D. Easton and Kurt H. Guddat, N.Y., 1967, p.176.

9   We are not at all ignoring the attempts at this moment to make test-tube babies. But today such mechanisms belong completely to capitalist scientific control. The use would be completely against us and against the class. It is not in our interest to abdicate procreation, to consign it to the hands of the enemy. It is in our interest to conquer the freedom to procreate for which we will pay neither the price of the wage nor the price of social exclusion.

10 To the extent that not technological innovation but only "human care" can raise children, the effective liberation from *domestic work time*, the *qualitative change of domestic work*, can derive only from a movement of women, from a struggle of women: the more the movement grows, the less men and first of all political militants – can count on female babyminding. And at the same time the new social ambiance that the movement constructs offers to children social space, with both men and women, that has nothing to do with the day care centers organized by the State. These

are already victories of struggle. Precisely because they are the *results* of a movement that is by its nature a struggle, they do not aim to *substitute* any kind of co-operation for the struggle itself.

12   Some first readers in English have found that this definition of women's work should be more precise. What we meant precisely is that housework as work is *productive* in the Marxian sense, that is, is producing surplus value.

We speak immediately after about the productivity of the entire female role. To make clearer the productivity of the woman both as related to her work and as related to her entire role must wait for a later text on which we are now at work. In this the woman's place is explained in a more articulated way from the point of view of the entire capitalist circuit.

13   Labor power "is a strange commodity for this is not a thing. The ability to labor resides only in a human being whose life is consumed in the process of producing… To describe its basic production and reproduction is to describe women's work."

14   This, however, is being countered by an opposite tendency, to bring women into industry in certain particular sectors. Differing needs of capital within the geographical sector have produced differing and even opposing propaganda and policies. Where in the past family stability has been based on a relative-standardized mythology (policy and propaganda being uniform and officially uncontested), today various sectors of capital contradict each other and undermine the very definition of family as a stable, unchanging, "natural" unit. The classic example of this is the variety of views and financial policies on birth control. The British government has recently doubled its allocation of funds for this purpose. We must examine to what extent this policy is connected with a racist immigration policy, that is, manipulation of the sources of mature labor power; and with the increasing erosion of the work ethic which results in movements of the unemployed and unsupported mothers, that is, controlling births which pollute the purity of capital with revolutionary children.

15   Which is the policy, among others, of the Communist Party in Italy who for some years proposed a bill to the Italian parliament which would have give a pension to women at home, both housewives and single women, when they reached 55 years of age. The bill was never passed.

17   There has been some confusion over what we have said about canteens. A similar confusion expressed itself in the discussions in other countries as well as Italy about wages for housework. As we explained earlier, housework is as institutionalized as factory work and our ultimate goal is to destroy both institutions. But aside from which demand we are speaking about, there is a misunderstanding of what a demand is. It is a goal which is not only a thing but, like capital at any moment, essentially a stage of antagonism of a social relation. Whether the canteen or the wages we win will be a victory or a defeat depends on the force of our struggle. On that force depends whether the goal is an occasion for capital to more rationally command our labor or an occasion for us to weaken their hold on that command. What form the goal takes when we achieve it, whether it is wages or canteens or free birth control, emerges and is in fact created in the struggle, and registers the degree of power that we reached in that struggle.

CHAPTER 8

Ladies of Labor, Girls of Adventure
Working Women, Popular Culture, and Labor Politics at the Turn of the Twentieth Century

Nan Enstad

Introduction

Mud in Our French Heels

At a recent American Studies Association conference, I attended a session entitled, "Does Cultural Studies Neglect Class?" The panelists presented a variety of views, but one argued "yes," and urged historians and cultural critics to make sure we have "materialist mud on our boots." This fashion metaphor captured my attention, immersed as I was in researching the fashions of working women at the turn of the twentieth century. That brief phrase conjured in my mind a very specific image of boots: *work* boots, with tough, thick soles and heavy leather uppers, a man's boots, well worn from labor and the "mud" of daily life. The presenter argued that, as scholars, we wear boots, and they ought not be clean and pretty. This suggested to me an ideal of a strong identification between scholar and working-class subject. The presenter warned that cultural studies threaten to remove us from the materialist mud, as scholars lose touch with the suffering of workers in favor of the fun of popular culture studies.

Because of my research, I experienced a dissonance with the opposition between "materialist mud" and "cultural studies" this metaphor created. The most stylish working women at the turn of the twentieth century wore cheap French heels, not boots, which they bought for one or two dollars on pushcarts in urban, working-class neighborhoods. French heels signaled Americanization and "ladyhood" for these mostly immigrant women. Young women often chose the pretty shoes as one of their first purchases in the United States, and proudly wore them for work and leisure. The middle class disdained

Original publication details: Nan Enstad, *Ladies of Labor, Girls of Adventure: Working Women, Popular Culture, and Labor Politics at the Turn of the Twentieth Century*, Introduction; 48–52; 54–55; 57–61; 63–65; 68–75; 77–78; 81–83. Columbia University Press, 1999. Reproduced with permission from Columbia University Press.

these delicate high heels; the style was worn predominantly by the wealthy and the working classes. The French heels seemed woefully flimsy and too pretty to carry the "materialist mud" of the presenter's metaphor. When I tried to substitute them in my imagination for the boots in the metaphor, I realized that my mind had supplied an entire archetypical image of a worker wearing such muddy boots: a large male with muscular arms, engaged in physically demanding labor. While there was nothing in the presenter's words that overtly coded a gender or race connotation to these boots, my mind drew on well-established labor iconography and supplied an image of a white male worker. French heels lacked the connotations of labor and heroic hard struggle that the boots conveyed to me.

I would like to suggest, however, that French heels provide an apt metaphor for how historians should approach class and cultural studies. Women's French heels represented both the promises and limitations of American capitalism. Working women wore them and declared themselves "American ladies." They invested French heels with great meanings of entitlement and belonging: they actively rejected the class ideologies that excluded women from the privileged label of "lady," and embraced America's promise that immigrants could escape the oppression and caste systems of the "old country." At the same time, the cheap shoes had paper-thin soles that could not withstand the walking and standing that women's work required. The grit from the streets quickly wore through, so that women literally had mud *in* their shoes. The capitalist marketplace both offered working women utopian promises and contained painful limitations. Indeed, the two cannot be separated. To see French heels simply as part of working women's "culture," which threatens to divorce us from their material life, is to pull apart aspects of daily life that the women necessarily experienced together. Indeed, by understanding the contradictions and connections between the promises and the limitations of consumer culture we can recover a rich matrix of meanings in working women's daily lives. As historians, perhaps we should metaphorically keep French heels on our feet, attuned to the tangible connections between the pleasures and the pains of consumer capitalism.

The American Studies Association panelist's fear that popular culture will take us away from serious class politics is an old one, and is reflected in the labor history sources I examine here. Labor leaders in the International Ladies Garment Workers Union (ILGWU) and the Women's Trade Union League (WTUL) routinely chastised working women for their ceaseless pursuit of fashion, their avid dime novel reading about working heroines who married millionaires, and their "affected" style, which included aristocratic airs and accents. While these practices had an array of diverse meanings, most leaders saw them as wholly negative. Leaders feared that such practices kept women from serious and practical concerns like labor organizing, and exacerbated middle-class perceptions of working women as too frivolous to be taken seriously as workers or political actors. Leaders urged working women to adopt a more serious demeanor and more sensible shoes. In doing so, they were asking women to more closely fit ideals of "worker" and "political actor" already deeply entrenched in U.S. culture.

Closely related ideals structured the raced and gendered image my mind supplied to the panelist's metaphor. While the word "worker" appears not to exclude but simply to describe, the *ideal* of "worker" in the nineteenth century was male. In addition, it was often *as workers* that working-class people claimed access to the political process, either through union representation or through the vote. As Judith Butler has argued, the dominant understanding of political action is that it requires a coherent and fixed identity already in place. That is, many assume that people must first fully identify with the category "worker" before they will engage in political action around working conditions. But Butler and others have noted that this idea of a coherent subjectivity, traceable to Enlightenment thought, carries an inherent tyranny. Identity categories such as "workers" or "women" are necessarily based in exclusions: as they define the inside they also define the outside. In doing so, they establish a new norm that becomes oppressive when they exclude others, or when they require people to fit themselves to the fiction of the category in order to be included. Far more than simple descriptions, labels shape identities and experiences.

The phrase "the worker" has had an insidious role in the labor movement: this seemingly descriptive category is also based in exclusions, ways in which some workers can seem less serious than others and less deserving of the name. As David Roediger argues, male labor unions in the antebellum era developed a heroic category of "worker" for white males, in direct contrast to "slave labor." Their language of class, according to Roediger, formed around concepts of "manly" and "free" labor that explicitly excluded African American laborers and all women. The long-term impact of this was to grant dignity to the name "worker" but reserve it for "serious" (white, male, and usually skilled) laborers. By the late nineteenth century, most unions sought the advancement of the working classes by advocating a living wage for men, who served as heads of families. In this ideal, male wages were sufficient to support women and children, removing the necessity for their employment. Though the ideal of the living wage was never realized, the notion of the worker became more intricately tied to masculinity. For example, when Samuel Gompers of the American Federation of Labor talked about the rights of "workers" in the early twentieth century, he usually meant white, male, skilled industrial workers. Gompers overtly identified this most privileged group as the true backbone of the working class, and the AFL limited its organizing largely to this group. Correspondingly, many leaders believed women lacked dedication to their jobs and desired only marriage. In other words, many people did not consider women *real* workers, and they therefore did not expect political action from them. Clearly, the category of the worker carried gender and race assumptions that replicated dominant hierarchies and undermined the oppositional potential of the labor movement.

Working women's participation in consumer culture exacerbated the perception of them as frivolous and their exclusion from the category of worker. Consumer culture can seem inherently opposed to serious political subjectivity. As Tania Modleski argues, our ways of thinking about consumer culture are intricately connected to conceptions of the feminine. The nineteenth-century white middle class saw consumption as the feminine counterpart to productivity, a valued ideal associated with masculinity. Labor and production formed the basis of male identity and workers' dignity; consumer culture was seen as feminized, unproductive, irrational, and even emasculating. Of course, the dichotomy was false: this ideal formulation obscured men's consumption as well as women's productive activities in and out of the home. A man's work boot is as much a commodity as is a French heel, but high heels are typically associated with commodity culture while men's boots are associated with work. When working women engaged in consumer activities, they threatened their already provisional status as workers by participating in a part of culture associated with femininity.

Many contemporary scholars accept and extend the opposition between production and consumption. However, as Modleski points out, they differ on whether a "feminine" consumer culture is positive or negative. Historian Ann Douglas argues that the advent of a mass culture at the turn of the century "feminized" all of American society. She decries this transition for undermining the best Calvinist values of work and for obfuscating the process of industrial production. Critic Michel de Certeau, in contrast, celebrates the potentials of consumer culture but fundamentally agrees with Douglas's acceptance of that culture as feminine. The logic of the realm of popular culture, claims de Certeau, is not linear and rational; rather it is more "natural," "primitive," and "feminine," which allows it to resist the regimented "logic" of industrial capitalism. As Modleski notes, these very different critics maintain and perpetuate the nineteenth-century construction of consumerism as feminine. It is little wonder then that women have been most often the symbol of the mindless consumer, from the turn of the century to today. Little wonder too that radicals at the turn of the century might mistake women with pretty hats for women with empty heads.

However, women workers in the early twentieth century went on strike in very large numbers. How can we account for this? Clearly, their participation in consumer culture did not preclude their political activism. Although contemporaries consistently bemoaned working women's consumer culture activities as detrimental to their identification and acceptance by others as serious workers, women did take political action in their workplaces and on public streets[…]it was not so much clear and coherent identities as workers that supported women's political consciousness and actions, but the very contradictions they experienced as they found themselves excluded or only provisionally included in powerful cultural categories such as "worker," "lady," or "American." The dissonance between their experiences and the categories available to describe them proved to be a source of creativity as they fashioned a particular form of radicalism and their own gender and class language.

The very interests in fashion, film, and fiction that labor leaders condemned became resources as women wrested identities from the contradictions they faced. The dissonance and contradictions they experienced, while painful, were not their only liability. An additional liability was that the radicalism they shaped was unintelligible to many contemporaries and has continued to be unintelligible to historians. Thus, it failed to transform dominant understandings of political activism at the time. Working women's politics remains misconstrued if we look only to how and when women acted according to our preconceived idea of political subjectivity and within our established category of worker.

Consumer culture offered working-class women struggling with extremely difficult material and ideological constraints a new range of representations, symbols, activities, and spaces with which to create class, gender, and ethnic identities. Working women embraced these new resources and created practices that were in themselves a form of politics, in that they shifted the cultural terrain to the women's interests.

Women's labor historians have not tended to view women's popular culture activities as potential political resources. Rather, like the labor leaders of the time, they have been suspicious of consumerism's trivializing effects. In an effort to defend the legitimacy of women as *workers*, most women's labor historians writing about this time period marginalize evidence about the centrality of popular culture to working-class women. At the same time, Kathy Peiss's important book about working women's popular culture activities in New York does not address the fact that this same cohort of pleasure-seeking women produced some of the most dramatic strikes of the century. Indeed, the labor histories that stress the seriousness of the strikers and Peiss's documentation of a world of pleasure-seeking seem so at odds that it is hard to believe these books are about the same women.

Ladies of Labor: Fashion, Fiction, and Working Women's Culture

Lillian Wald, founder of the Henry Street Settlement House on the Lower East Side of New York City, described in her memoirs her frustration with one young working woman who longed for fine clothes. The woman lived in a crowded tenement, had begun working at age eleven, and failed to demonstrate the interest in self-improvement that Wald attempted to foster through Settlement work. Despite her long, tedious work hours and her bleak tenement apartment, Wald wrote, "her most conscious desire was for silk underwear; at least it was the only one she seemed able to formulate!" Wald decried "this trivial desire" for fashion in the young women she served, as she felt it deflected them from more serious pursuits: education in English, the arts, work skills, and union organizing. For others, working women who wore the latest fashions and perhaps exceeded them "dressed beyond their station," and thus confounded her efforts to bestow charity on a class of women unambiguously "lower" than herself.

Reformers and union leaders also despaired at some working women's habit of dime novel romance reading, which they found as trivial as the pursuit of fashion, particularly because it offered a fantasy of magnificent wealth bestowed on the working-girl heroine through a secret inheritance and marriage to a millionaire. Journalist Rose Pastor admonished women workers:

> With our free circulating libraries what excuse is there other than ignorance for any girl who reads the crazy phantasies from the imbecile brains of Laura Jean Libbey, The Duchess, and others of their ilk! ... I appeal to you— if you read those books— stop! stop!

Critics feared that the books instilled in readers a vague "hope that some man or some chance will come to change the monotony of their lot" and would therefore deflect women from union activity. Perhaps most disturbing was that working women incorporated their consumption of fashion and fiction into a social practice of calling and presenting themselves as ladies, complete with an affected style of speech, walk, and manners.

But Wald was mistaken when she dismissed the desire for silk underwear as entirely trivial. There was a system of meaning at work that was incomprehensible to her, bent as she was on extending bourgeois values of self-improvement to the working class. Judith Butler argues that some kinds of agency are, in fact, unrecognizable as such when they operate outside of the epistemology of those trying to understand them. Whereas Wald looked for the kind of subjectivity that *to her* meant empowerment and improvement, working women exhibited subjectivities based on a variety of consumer practices with their own cultural configurations of gender, class and ethnicity and did not exhibit the "self-interest" Wald expected. Working women's use of consumer goods was intensely invested with meanings, but they were unintelligible to Wald.

In order to understand this arena of meaning rooted in commodities, we first need to recognize that commodity consumption is not a single, discrete event. Film critic Jane Gaines has recently noted that the word "consumption" refers to many events, not just one, so cultural critics should distinguish among buying, having, and using as aspects of the meaning-making process. Likewise, Janice Radway has called for a distinction between the activity of reading within a particular social context, and the actual meaning readers make from the narrative itself. Exploring when and where people read, argues Radway, makes us better prepared to use textual interpretation to understand how people might read to gratify needs, perhaps those that prompted their choice of texts.

This chapter therefore looks at three aspects of working women's consumption of fashion and fiction: the act of purchasing or otherwise acquiring the products, the acts of reading the dime novels and wearing the clothing, and the imaginative interactions with a narrative or an outfit. The first two aspects, the acts of purchasing, and reading/wearing, occurred in a social context and became part of working women's collective culture. Women's memoirs, reformers' and union records, and periodicals reveal these aspects of women's consumption. The imaginative experience of a narrative or an outfit, while shaped by the workplace culture, was necessarily more internal and idiosyncratic. "Textual" analysis of the stories and clothing, embedded in this social context, reveals the ways products could support the practice of "ladyhood." The meanings that women created through all three of these aspects of consumption operated together to imbue the commodities with significance.

Specifically, working women's consumption of fiction and fashion engaged their identities as workers, as women, and as immigrants. Through their purchases, women used the money they had earned, thus participating in consumption *as workers*. They bought fashion products and books written in English in part to mark themselves as "American." They used both types of products at their workplaces in ways that refused the terms of subordination they experienced on the job and created another, imaginative reality in which they were highly valued. In addition, some quite literally appropriated work skills, and sometimes materials and time, in order to make their own clothes, and in this way avoided being entirely subordinated to the needs of capital.

Finally, women could use the narratives and the specific clothing to create themselves as "ladies," a signifying practice that allowed them to occupy a creative space of cultural contradiction and to affirm their lived experiences as workers, as women, and as immigrants. The practice of working ladyhood engaged gender, class, and ethnic exclusions that working women daily experienced in a society that saw the heroic worker as male, the heroic woman as middle class, and the heroic American as a native-born Anglo-Saxon. Working ladyhood was a set of consumption-based conventions and practices through which individuals variously constructed particular subjectivities. Thus, the practice of working ladyhood created a site of multiplicity, a shifting identity which played off a range of cultural contradictions and instabilities in turn-of-the-century society.

The practice of working ladyhood built on a shared firsthand knowledge of the daily injustices of women's labor, but it was not a self-conscious political strategy and it did not contain a specific, articulated political critique. The phenomenon did have ramifications for organized labor politics. But I do not argue that these practices necessarily functioned as a step along the path to organized political activism. Rather, I argue that working women could *use* the cultural resources of ladyhood to construct formal political subjectivities. Furthermore, working ladyhood had political significance in itself because when working-class women made themselves into ladies, they rejected the denigration they experienced at work and in public and replaced it with pride and dignity. As Robin D. G. Kelley writes, "Still missing from most examinations of workers are the ways in which unorganized working people resisted the conditions of work, tried to control the pace and amount of work, and carved out a modicum of dignity at the workplace." A broader examination of politics requires understanding the systems of meanings that sustained workers on a day-to-day level. In particular, bringing into view working ladies' particular cultural configurations of gender, class, and ethnicity reveals a key terrain of subjectivity formation that was in some ways connected to, and certainly as important as, the subjectivity formation of women who became labor leaders. Working women's subjectivities, however, were rendered invisible by contemporary organized politics and historical analyses, both of which searched for political actors who matched preconceived cultural ideals.

Because working ladyhood was rooted in both fashion and fiction consumption, the two forms of popular culture must be studied in tandem. Popular culture activities exist in isolation only in academic studies. For historical actors, the fashion they wore was related to the dime novel they read in the same day or evening, creating a weave of meanings. To isolate products based on academic distinctions between "literature" and "clothing" would analytically sever the meanings working women themselves created from both. Conversely, intertextuality, or looking across different kinds of "texts," guided by the lived experience of working women, allows greater insight into the meanings of both types of consumer products.

The consumption of fiction and fashion products also operated as what Colin Campbell calls "imaginative" events in the lives of working women. Fashion is commonly seen as a way that an individual "sends a message" about themselves to the larger society. However, as Fred Davis has argued, this reduces a complex process to a simplistic single meaning. While at times people wear clothing to publicly communicate membership in a particular group, pleasure in clothing also stems from the personal and imaginative process of creating oneself within a range of recognizable social meanings. Similarly, the reading of dime novels is best understood not simply as the reception of messages by the reader from the text, but as the creation of meaning imaginatively by the reader via the text. Contradictions within the text and the various cultural contexts that the reader brings to the reading process make reading as much an imaginative event as fashion. Indeed, the reader may *consume* a book, in that she purchases and uses it, but she *produces* a text as she reads, through her interaction with the book's narrative.

For analytical purposes, this chapter separates three aspects of consumption: purchasing, wearing/reading, and imaginative interactions with the products. However, these three aspects are intricately related. For example, the imaginative experience of both fiction and fashion can exceed the boundaries of the physical interaction with the goods themselves through daydreaming and conversations about the products with others. Thus, the meanings women made with the texts themselves became closely related to the meanings created collectively in their uses of the products. In this way, working ladies formed what literary critics call an "interpretive community," partly within what historians call "workplace culture." To borrow Walter Benjamin's language, women experienced and shaped an imaginative "dream world" through the collective imaginative acts of purchasing and using dime novels and clothing. Thus, the concept of the "dream world of commodities" should be broad enough to encompass all three aspects of consumption.

Dime novels were accessible for working women partly because of their low price. The romances cost ten cents each, which was not an insignificant amount of money for young women who earned as little as $3.50 per week while learning a job, and typically five or six dollars per week as regular pay. Very few women had much spending money. Many turned their pay over to their mothers as their needed contribution to the family economy; others supported themselves, living as boarders or in furnished rooms. Some saved to bring other relatives over to America. Nevertheless, women saved money by walking to work rather than taking the streetcar, and by skimping on lunches.

Working women also purchased dime novels because they were available. Only some kinds of literature were both inexpensive enough for women to buy and available for purchase in working-class neighborhoods. This accessibility was crucial, particularly for immigrants who might not have been familiar with stores and institutions off their beaten path from neighborhood to workplace. While Rose Pastor asked why women did not use "our free, circulating libraries" in making their choice of reading material, Rose Schneiderman explained in her memoir that dime novels, despite their cost, were more accessible to her than books available free of charge from the library:

> I knew nothing about going to a public library and taking out any book my heart desired …
> I did not even know about the College Settlement House which was only a block away.

Pushcarts and newsstands put dime novels into the hands of working women without first requiring other cultural competencies.

Dime novels were so common a part of workplace discussions that women expected co-workers to have at least a cursory familiarity with the narratives. Dorothy Richardson recounted one conversation about dime novel romances in which her unfamiliarity with the novels became a point of ridicule. Richardson worked in factories but had a middle-class background. She wrote about her experiences in 1905, and it is unclear whether she had to work or whether she worked, like many middle-class women, to gain material for a book. When the fact that she had never read a dime novel romance was revealed one worker cried in surprise and disgust, "Oh, mama! Carry me out and let me die!" Another clutched her throat and cried, "Water! Water! … I'm going to faint!" At this point both workers gave way to laughter at Richardson's expense. They later hastened to help her overcome her deficiency by including her in their discussions of plots and heroes, and recounted the story of one Laura Jean Libbey novel. Dime novels were so important in working women's collective experience of daily life and work itself that they were part of the process of *becoming* a working woman. That is, the romances, as valued objects, played a role in subjectivity formation.

Working women's act of reading at work, during their thirty- to forty-minute lunch hours, was a rejection of the relentless tedium of the work-place. Factory workers usually labored at highly repetitive tasks that required concentration, dexterity, and physical endurance. Because of the rationalization of the production process, creativity or intelligence was largely irrelevant, and after one mastered the task at hand, learning ceased. Employers paid women by the piece, which meant that only great speed ensured an adequate wage. Women regularly reported that the repetitive yet demanding piecework left them exhausted in mind and body. In this context, reading allowed women to engage another, fictitious world in which working-girl heroines embarked on sensational adventures. As Janice Radway has argued, the "act of picking up a book is a form of social behavior that permits the reader to suspend momentarily all connection with the outside world." Because of time constraints, workers often physically could not leave the factories or shops for lunch, and employers rarely provided lunchrooms. Workers stayed at their benches or sat on the floor among the work materials scattered about, sharing sandwiches and pickles. Reformer Gertrude Barnum remarked upon the readers' intense absorption in the novels: "A pale little paper box maker will sit on the floor of her factory at the noon hour lost to the world behind the cover of her book." Dorothy Richardson recalled that in her workplace, "Although we had a half-hour, luncheon was swallowed quickly by most of the girls, eager to steal away to a sequestered bower among the boxes, there to lose themselves in paper-backed romances." By reading at work, women literally changed the shop itself during the lunch hour to a place that could provide relief from labor. In addition, by reading women refused to act like machines. They engaged their minds with thrilling adventures, and some simultaneously practiced their English literacy skills. Indeed, the narratives in which working heroines were ladies offered a counterpoint to the real-life devaluation of the workers. The practice of reading and discussing the novels, then, actively rejected the terms of women's subordination through the piecework system.

For some women, identification with the working-girl heroine who became a lady was so strong that, according to Dorothy Richardson, they took on aristocratic names from the dime novels. Richardson recounted one worker trying to convince her to adopt a new name:

> All the girls do it when they come to the factory to work. It don't cost no more to have a high-sounding name. ... Georgiana Trevelyan and Goldy Courtleigh and Gladys Carringford and Angelina Lancaster and Phoebe Arlington—them girls all got [their names] out of stories.

By taking on new names, women moved the internal imaginative process that occurred while reading into the collective space of work-place culture. Furthermore, when workers changed their names they shed their family names and the ethnic and class associations that went with them. Experience had taught them that such associations were liabilities in the United States, and they adopted aristocratic-sounding English names instead. This practice certainly reveals that the dime novels encouraged women to obscure their race and ethnic identities and to identify with the dominant culture. At the same time, however, when women adopted "rich"-sounding names from dime novels they resisted the depersonalization that occurred at the workplace. Because piecework, as a method of labor control, reduced the skill and creativity required for jobs, workers were rather interchangeable. Bosses and supervisors reflected this fact in the ways that they treated and addressed them. In some factories, supervisors assigned and called workers by numbers to keep track of their piecework production. Elizabeth Hasanovitz remembers her forelady often calling, "*Hundred and twelve*, what happened to you?" Supervisors also regularly used derogatory names, such as "stupid animal," as Sadie Frowne was called. Women used the dime novel fantasies to insist on their own worth when they took on names like "Rose Fortune," the name given Richardson by her co-worker.

Just as "high-sounding" names countered the implicit message of piecework production that women were merely stupid cogs in a machine, the elaborate fashion women wore asserted their worth in a context that denied it. Through fashion, women borrowed from the cultural values placed on objects they produced to dignify their own devalued labor. Working women knew from daily experience that owners subjugated workers' health and welfare to the needs of industry in exchange for a wage that was usually inadequate. Whatever their view of unions, workers in factories, sweatshops, and laundries complained of long hours and unpaid overtime, unfair fines for lateness and botched work, sexual harassment, work speedups, and unventilated, unhealthy, and unsafe working conditions. Women workers lost a great deal of time to illness, and after years of factory work many suffered from malnutrition, exhaustion, and sometimes serious chronic diseases. Working–class immigrant women daily learned what United States society had to teach them: the clothes they made, laundered, or sold were more important than they were themselves. When they borrowed the signifying logic of the display window to increase their own worth, they claimed a cultural franchise they would other-wise lack. This act held particular resonance for the many women who labored to produce, maintain, or sell fashion commodities.

Just as work experiences taught women that they held less value than the products they made, their social interactions taught them that, in the United States, appearance mattered more than character. Working women's encounters with bosses, wealthier Americans, and men in general shaped their understanding of the ethnic, class, and sexual economies in which they had to find a place, all of which involved clothing. Many historical accounts record this generation of urban immigrants' embrace of American fashion as a sign of Americanization. Historians have focused primarily on the differ-ences between customs in the United States, where ready-made clothing made it possi-ble for most to dress with style, and in the "old country," where fine dress often still signaled nobility. Indeed, in parts of Eastern Europe only women of the upper class could wear hats, coding a rigid caste system. When both Jewish and Italian immigrants embraced American fashions, they imbued them with meanings rooted in a collective memory of oppression. But the social meanings of clothing also came from day-to-day practices and hierarchies in the United States.

When working women purchased clothing, they exercised their new entitlement as workers. As females, women had traditionally worked to maintain the household; when they worked for pay, they owed the whole of their wages to the family economy. Parents expected daughters to hand over pay envelopes to the household financial manager, which in Italian and Jewish households was usually the mother. In return, most received a small allowance. Fathers and sons, however, could justly open their own envelopes before returning home and extract sums for their own leisure. Many sons simply paid "board" to their mothers and kept the remaining money for themselves. Breadwinning was still associated with a male role, and male breadwinning earned this right.

Turn-of-the-century sources are filled with accounts of working women struggling to change this system and lay full and equal claim to the name of "worker" in their families. They did so in part through demanding more of their paychecks for their own use. In one case, a Jewish immigrant named Jean found a blouse she wished to buy for three dollars on Grand Street on New York's Lower East Side. However, her mother only allowed her a two-dollar allowance from her wages of eleven dollars per week. Her mother suggested she choose a cheaper blouse; Jean refused. Jean kept her pay envelope unopened for four weeks, withholding it from the family economy. Finally, her father suggested a solution usually reserved for sons: Jean was to pay one dollar per day for room and board and keep the remaining four dollars per week for her own use. Jean's later fashion purchases doubtlessly were symbolic of the status that she had won as a breadwinner. "I used to go out on Clinton Street and get a hat for twenty-five dollars … and my mother used to say, 'What's on this hat, gold?'" Filomena Moresco also dis-missed the allowance system and kept money from her pay envelope. She spent twenty-five dollars, nearly a month's wages, on a "pretty party dress, a beaver hat and a willowed plume." When women claimed their pay envelopes to purchase clothing they laid claim to the status of "worker," enjoyed by their brothers but often denied to them, and made clothing a badge of their own labor.

While purchasing clothing could serve as an enactment of women's identities as work-ers, women also drew upon the skills and the knowledge of styles they gained at work to make and alter clothing. As stated earlier, working women could rarely do *all* of their own sewing: a tailored suit, jacket, or dress was complicated and laborious, demanding more time, and often more skill, than the women possessed. Nevertheless, working women often made shirtwaists and underwear and applied trimmings, lace, feathers, and other decorations to dresses and hats. Thus, they rescued from their labor additional personal value, and inflected their consumer practices with an element of their own creative production. As one journalist wrote in 1900, "In the matter of dresses it is natural that the East Side should be strictly up to date, for does it not furnish clothes for the rest of the town?"

The consumption of dime novels and fashion, then, consisted of a number of related social practices of buying and having that shaped the place of particular texts and clothing items in women's lives. These practices all had imaginative elements in themselves. Purchasing a fashionable dress from a brightly lit pushcart, dreaming together of dime novel heroes or a coveted outfit, and taking on "rich" names from dime novel heroines all served to create a collective dream world of consumption that was rooted in the painful limitations of daily life and labor. Women's imaginative experiences of reading the narratives and putting on the articles of clothing articulated to these social practices. While individual idiosyncrasies and the multiple possibilities for interpretation meant that not all women "read" the fashions or the novels in exactly the same ways, a close look at the texts of the dime novel formula and the typical clothing worn by working women can reveal more about the contours of their collective dream world.

When working women dressed with "gentility" and read about working-girl heroines who became "ladies," they engaged the "wish images" embedded in the products—a term Walter Benjamin used to describe the utopian element present in much of popular culture. For Benjamin, products such as fashion pleased because they offered a fleeting fulfillment that anticipated a potential, emancipatory reality. While such products could not emancipate people from oppressive labor or class structures, as wish images they engaged a potentially revolutionary or egalitarian impulse within the imagination. Benjamin argued that wish images were spurred by the new but rooted in the old, in culturally sedimented images remaining from unfulfilled desires. Fictional figures of gentility operated in this way: the "ladies" of the dime novels evoked a past era of nobility even as they referenced middle-class privilege from which working-class women were excluded in daily life. The elaborate fashion worn by working women likewise evoked a fairy-tale princess's grace and status even as it was spurred by the latest signifiers of glamour. (Indeed, a popular style worn by working women at the turn of the century was the "princess dress.") While Benjamin did not see wish images as radical in themselves, he did see a utopian imagination as a necessary component of social change.

Working women, however, did not simply *imbibe* wish images embedded in the dime novel narratives and the fashion products; they *enacted* wish images when they made themselves into ladies. In this way, the wish images of the commodities became part of a much larger, socially materialized practice. Women acted as ladies through "aristocratic pretensions" similar to those played out by African Americans of the same time period when competing in the cake walk. They adopted an exaggerated walk, mocked by Dorothy Richardson as "nervous, jerky, [and] heavy-footed," along with elaborate manners. Working women bowed hello or good-bye with "grace put on," and "fine flourishes" of the arms. Taking a seat could be a "fine art," a "great, grand effort to sit down with all ease and grace." This "vulgar vanity," as the middle class saw it, was matched by aristocratic speech. The working woman, complained Gertrude Barnum, "will search her brain for long words and high-sounding phrases, and use them in a grandiloquent style which expresses nothing but ignorance and affectation." Middle-class judgments notwithstanding, working women clearly enacted a commodity display that wove the wish image of the lady in dime novels and fashion into a social practice. But what kind of wish image was available in those products themselves?

Working women who already participated in some of the social practices related to ladyhood would bring particular cultural competencies, or what Radway has called "social grammars," to their dime novel reading experience. However, the cultural competencies of working women learning to be ladies could promote certain readings over others. Specifically, working ladies could read the dime novel romances as melodramatic defenses of women's position as wage earners. The novels offered narrative fantasies of social recognition that allowed them to briefly bridge painful cultural contradictions that assigned heroic worker status to men and heroic "lady" status only to middle- and upper-class white women.

The structure of the dime novel narrative prompted a different mode of reading than did that of the bourgeois novel. The narrative formula begins with the working girl becoming orphaned, homeless, and jobless, usually within the first ten pages of the novel. The long series of adventures and calamities that follow comprise the bulk of the narrative. The working girl gains a secret inheritance near the middle of the book, and finally marries the rich hero at the end. The novels followed the "adventure-romance" (or aristomilitary romance) tradition, in which the protagonist must survive a series of contests that prove her/his worth and grant her/him a valorized position in the group as well as a reward. As in the adventure-romance, heroines in dime novels did not change through the stories: they were already perfect. But their worth had to be proven to the outside world to become recognized as valid. Dime novels invited a highly visceral identification with heroines who met rapid successions of suspenseful adventures.

The bourgeois novel, in contrast, centered around personal growth through education or inner struggle, often to solve a problem or gain mastery over an external situation. Therefore, it relied narratively on character development, while the dime novel romance did not. Chance also played a very different role in the two types of books. In the bourgeois novel, a character often must find a way to grow and gain mastery over a problem in spite of the vagaries of chance. For example, in *Little Women*, the government required the father to leave home and serve in the Civil War. This element outside of personal control sets up the premise of the book: the "little women" have to grow up and become virtuous, caring women without a male authority figure. They must try all the harder to master themselves and be good because father is absent; they must develop in spite of circumstances. The orphaned dime novel heroine is similarly without a father, but she hardly has time to notice that before she loses her job, is abducted, poisoned, trapped in a building that is on fire, etc. The dime novels are not about the exertion of will over chance but about meeting a string of challenges and responding to each one. Thus, the dime novel heroine changes in a very different way than do protagonists of bourgeois novels. Gaining a secret inheritance makes the dime novel heroine magically a "lady," which she unknowingly has been all along. Her change is dramatic and sudden, yet merely a manifestation of what was already true. Both types of novels validated the protagonists' selves in the social world, but according to quite different narrative mechanisms.

Dime novels solicit readers' identification largely by first prompting indignation on the heroine's behalf or a suspenseful anxiety for the heroine. Film critic Elizabeth Cowie has argued that readers identify with characters not when they share specific characteristics with them, but when they have common "structural relations of desire." That is, readers do not identify simply because they are "like" a character, but because they can associate the desire of the character with one of their own—so they come to desire with, or on behalf of, the character. The dime novels entice such correspondence first by regularly making readers privy to conversations about the heroine that she herself does not hear, or by making readers the witnesses to grossly unfair treatment. For example, the romances routinely include a conversation between members of the hero's wealthy family about the working heroine, in which someone invariably voices common middle- and upper-class pretensions and prejudices. As one rich villainess put it, "Can he, who is the patrician through and through, care for a girl who actually works with her hands?" Another says, "How horribly ill-bred she must be!" These conversations set up a key theme of the dime novel while inviting readers to align their resentment of class distinctions— or other distinctions—with the heroine's.

The different narrative structures of dime novel romances and bourgeois novels thus could promote quite different experiences and pleasures of reading, and understanding them can help explain why some critics could find the dime novels so disempowering to women, while many working women loved them. Someone reading the dime novels for character development and the expectation that the heroine would grow might well find the heroines "weak" or "vapid," as have some scholars and contemporary critics. This is not to argue that the character traits of the heroine are irrelevant, but rather that working women might take different narrative cues and form different impressions. In fact, the formula introduces the heroines as both vulnerable and strong. One heroine is described as at once physically small and courageous: "'I don't care *who* hears me!' she cried, snapping her little white fingers and stamping a mite of a foot. 'I'll stick up for my rights. No one shall run over *me*!'" Readers could feel anxious or indignant on behalf of the vulnerable heroine *and* thrill to her successful adventures and thus her power.

The first thing that happens to every dime novel heroine is that her established identity is suspended when she becomes an orphan. In the first chapter of almost every novel, the working girl labors to support a sick sister or father, who invariably immediately dies. The heroine then loses her job, perhaps because she misses work when she attends her sister's funeral or because the boss wants to make her his mistress. Here, the novels always invoked some injustice that working women typically experienced: unfair fines for botched work (or work claimed by the boss to be botched), sexual harassment, no time off to care for family members.

The heroine then loses her home, perhaps because she does not have rent money due to her boss' unfairness, or perhaps because someone falsely reports to the landlady that she has compromised her virtue. Orphaned, jobless and homeless, the heroine finds herself cast into the city, the epitome of vulnerability, with villains and seducers hot on her trail.

The heroine's extreme vulnerability was crucial to the adventure element of the novels, but her orphan status served other functions as well. Heroines who were orphaned were not only vulnerable, but also free of the class and ethnic associations that accompanied their family identity, and free of the patriarchal or paternal supervision working-class women typically experienced in their parents' homes, some boarding houses, and at work. Women's class identity derived not solely from their labor, but also from the class status of the male producers (fathers or husbands) in their families. In order to provide a fantasy of a new class identity, the dime novel romances had to rid the heroine of her old family connection and provide her with a freedom to move about the city that most women could not claim.

The orphaned working girl heroine also could signal freedom to women who experi-enced a paternalism at work that overtly capitalized on women's subservient place in the family. Employers baldly denied women a living wage because they assumed them to be secondary wage earners, in part supported by their parents. Some employers went so far as to refuse to employ women who did not live with parents, because their wages could not support someone even at barest subsistence. Employers often supported building boarding homes for working women, to keep them from being driven to "vice," but would not raise wages. Such paternalistic authority drew the ire of working-class women. One complained of an employer's interest in working-girl "homes":

> What the employer has got to learn and learn quickly is that women are going to have a living wage, enough to let them live where and how they like. There has been too much of this father idea to working women. We would like the freedom of being orphans for a while.

To a working-class reader, the heroine could epitomize a familiar vulnerability and oppression, but also an exhilarating freedom from the oppressive and intertwined con-straints of work and family. The romances barely mention work or the workplace after these first ten to twenty pages. However, the novels were about *being* a female worker throughout. The attacks the heroine encounters are always in the context of her status as worker. Key to the dime novel plot is the question: Can a worker be a lady? That is, does work indeed degrade, spoil one's virtue, make one coarse and masculine? The heroine's adventures make her the victim of male villains who believe her status as worker makes her "lower" and therefore available for their pleasure. They usually try to force her into marriage with them. The hero, of course, thinks that "a woman may work with her hands and yet have a soul like snow," because he can see her inner, unchanging worth. The hero and heroine, however, are torn apart through misunderstanding, usually plotted by the villains, and the hero goes away, often to Europe, for most of the book. When heroines fend off villains, they demonstrate their own worth as workers, without the aid of the hero, though occasionally they are rescued by others.

When working-girl heroines encountered challenges, their task was not simply to endure, or to wait to be rescued by someone. On the contrary, they proved their brav-ery as much as their virtue, and often saved themselves. Indeed, heroines showed that they were "really" ladies by accomplishing dramatic and daring physical feats. They escaped from compromised positions by breaking glass windows with their fists, unty-ing their own bound wrists, and physically fighting with villains. One abducted hero-ine rebukes a stolen kiss "with a stinging blow, just as she had done once before for the same offense, straight upon his aristocratic face with her little clinched white hand." When he persists, this heroine struggles with the villain "with almost superhuman strength" until he (accidentally) falls off the bridge on which they have been standing. These scenarios celebrated the powerless overcoming the powerful, much as people cheered Houdini for his masteries of escape during the same time period. Furthermore, dime novel heroines did not simply react to peril: they also actively sought challenges. Another heroine discovered that her kidnappers ran a counterfeiting ring in a tunnel that connected to the room where she was kept: "For a moment, Gay stood as if rooted to the spot, but she was a brave, daring girl, and in a trice she had quickly recovered her composure, the love of adventure which was keen within her, leading her on."

While heroines exhibited great vulnerability, their success in adventures signaled their bravery and physical strength.

The dime novel formula clearly held powerful resonances for working-class women who dressed and acted as ladies. The heroines not only encountered the kinds of oppression with which working women were familiar, they also enacted a transformation to ladyhood that provided continued adventures, lavish fashion, and the opportunity to attend upscale balls. Working-class female readers could easily see the dime novel heroine as engaging in activities similar to their own. Furthermore, just as the women who wore encumbering fashions to work demonstrated that labor did not masculinize them or lower their status, the heroine could, to these women, show that someone could be physically active and yet deserving of the highest valuation. The heroine's inherent virtue and physical strength in fighting off villains could be read as validating women's labor, while the secret inheritance could affirm an unassailable, *inner* worth of women workers.

A close look at the content of working women's fashion choices reveals a parallel utopian impulse to the dime novels. Working women dressed in fashion, but they exaggerated elements of style that specifically coded femininity: high-heeled shoes, large or highly decorated hats, exceedingly long trains (if trains were in style), and fine undergarments. In addition, they used more color than was considered tasteful by the middle class to dress up their garments and heighten the element of display in their clothing.

Let us return, finally, to the young woman who, to Lillian Wald's dismay, desired only silk underwear. While it might be difficult to wholly celebrate this desire, it is possible to understand it. Silk petticoats were a key element, albeit hidden, in the creation of oneself as lady because of the distinctive sound that they made when one walked. This sound was in itself a very fashionable "frou frou," marking wealth that could not be seen. Bertha Richardson was offended in part by a "rustle of silk petticoats" among the working girls she wished to "uplift." Thus, "silk underwear" signaled the invisible, interior ladyhood, similar to that promised by the dime novels, to which working women laid claim.

As part of the subculture of working ladies, the woman who desired silk underwear participated in a series of cultural practices that constituted a highly utopian commodity display. Ladyhood created a space for a differently gendered class identity, a counterpoint to the masculine versions women typically encountered in labor unions and to the classist assumptions of some well-meaning reformers. Imagined through the dream world of fashion and fiction commodities, and played out in the daily lives of working women, it offered a gratifying image of emancipation from oppression, which was fundamentally populist. Expressed through commodities, ladyhood was itself a wish image. Within the social practices of working women's daily lives it became an identity category that allowed them to negotiate the exclusive categories of "worker," "American," and "woman."

But ladyhood served political functions in another respect: it provided for solidarity, resistance, and identity formation in relation to the larger society. It was part of how working women maintained dignity and self-worth in a highly exploitative and degrading context of selling their labor and their time. But precisely because most people did not understand the system of meaning inherent in ladyhood, few recognized its cultural practices as political in nature. Like Wald, most found the flamboyant display bewildering, epistemologically unintelligible. And since they did not see the sense of such practices, like Wald most declared them nonsensical.

When more than 20,000 New York shirtwaist makers walked off their jobs in November 1909, they engaged in an action that the wider society *did* recognize as political. Of course, many of the strikers visibly did so as *ladies*; they could not do otherwise. The practices of ladyhood had shaped who they were and had centrally formed their public identities. The dramatic shirtwaist strike captured public attention in New York City and the nation at large. For the majority of observers, however, it did not appear to be an extension of working women's already-formed public identities, but a surprising, almost inexplicable emergence of working women onto the public stage.

CHAPTER 9

Three Strikes That Paved the Way

Art Preis

The National Industrial Conference Board, in a survey of collective bargaining under the National Recovery Act (NRA), could boast in March 1934 of "the relatively small proportion of employees found to be dealing with employers through an organized labor union." At the same time, said the board, "Employee representation [company unions] appears to have made considerable progress" and "it is clear that individual bargaining has not in any way been eliminated by Section 7(a) of the Recovery Act."

In that same month, the *American Federationist*, organ of the top American Federation of Labor (AFL) leadership, complained: "In general there has been no increase in real wages…The codes will not safeguard real wages…The government monetary policy points toward diminishing real wages."

Worst of all, the wave of strikes following the enactment of the NRA in June 1933 was ending in a series of defeats. Where the union leaders themselves did not rush the workers back on the job without gains—not even union recognition, the strikes were smashed by court injunctions and armed violence. Behind the legal restraining orders and the shotguns, rifles and machine guns of police, deputies and National Guardsmen, the scabs and strikebreakers were being herded into struck plants almost at will.

It was at this stage, when strike after strike was being crushed, that the Toledo Electric Auto-Lite Company struggle blazed forth to illuminate the whole horizon of the American class struggle. The American workers were to be given an unforgettable lesson in how to confront all the agencies of the capitalist government — courts, labor boards and armed troops—and win.

Toledo, Ohio, an industrial city of about 275,000 population in 1934, is a glass and auto parts center. In June 1931, four Toledo banks had closed their doors. Some of the big local companies, including several suppliers to the auto industry, had secretly transferred their bank accounts to one big bank. These companies did not get caught in the crash.

But thousands of workers and small business men did. They lost their lives' savings. One out of every three persons in Toledo was thrown on relief, standing in lines for food handouts at a central commissary. In 1933, the Unemployed League, led by followers of A. J. Muste, head of the Conference for Progressive Labor Action (later the American Workers Party), had organized militant mass actions of the unemployed and won cash relief.

Original publication details: Art Preis, "Three Strikes that Paved the Way", from *Labor's Giant Step: 20 Years of the CIO*, pp. 19–27; 29–33. Pioneer Publishers, 1964.

The League made it a policy to call for unity of the unemployed and employed workers; it mobilized the unemployed not to scab, but to aid all strikes.

On February 23, 1934, the Toledo Auto-Lite workers, newly organized in AFL Federal Local 18384, went on strike. This was quickly ended by the AFL leaders with a truce agreement for negotiations through the Regional Labor Board of the National Labor Board, which had been set up under the NRA.

Refusing to be stalled further by the labor board or to submit to the special Auto Labor Board, which Franklin D. Roosevelt had set up in March to sidetrack pending auto strikes and which had upheld company unionism, the Auto-Lite workers went on the picket lines again on April 13.

The company followed the usual first gambit in such a contest. It went to a friendly judge and got him to issue an injunction limiting picketing. The strike had begun to die on its feet when a committee of Auto-Lite workers came to the Unemployed League and asked for aid.

The unexampled letter sent by the local Unemployed League to Judge Stuart deserves to be preserved for posterity. It is an historic document that ranks in its way with the great declarations of human freedom more widely known and acclaimed. The letter read:

May 5, 1934

His Honor Judge Stuart
County Court House
Toledo, Ohio

Honorable Judge Stuart:

On Monday morning May 7, at the Auto-Lite plant, the Lucas County Unemployed League, in protest of the injunction issued by your court, will deliberately and specifically violate the injunction enjoining us from sympathetically picketing peacefully in support of the striking Auto Workers Federal Union.

We sincerely believe that this court intervention, preventing us from picketing, is an abrogation of our democratic rights, contrary to our constitutional liberties and contravenes the spirit and the letter of Section 7a of the NRA.

Further, we believe that the spirit and intent of this arbitrary injunction is another specific example of an organized movement to curtail the rights of all workers to organize, strike and picket effectively.

Therefore, with full knowledge of the principles involved and the possible consequences, we openly and publicly violate an injunction which, in our opinion, is a suppressive and oppressive act against all workers.

Sincerely yours,
Lucas County Unemployed League
Anti-Injunction Committee

Sam Pollock, Sec'y

By May 23, there were more than 10,000 on the picket lines. County deputies with tear gas guns were lined up on the plant roof. A strike picket, Miss Alma Hahn, had been struck on the head by a bolt hurled from a plant window and had been taken to the hospital.

By the time 100 more cops arrived, the workers were tremendously incensed. Police began roughing up individual pickets pulled from the line. What happened when the cops tried to escort the scabs through the picket line at the shift-change was described by the Associated Press.

"Piles of bricks and stones were assembled at strategic places and a wagon load of bricks was trundled to a point near the factory to provide further ammunition for the strikers... Suddenly a barrage of tear gas bombs was hurled from upper factory windows. At the same time, company employees armed with iron bars and clubs dragged a fire hose into the street and played water on the crowd. The strike sympathizers replied with bricks, as they choked from gas fumes and fell back."

But they retreated only to reform their ranks. The police charged and swung their clubs trying to clear a path for the scabs. The workers held their ground and fought back. Choked by the tear gas fired from inside the plant, it was the police who finally gave up the battle. Then the thousands of pickets laid siege to the plant, determined to maintain their picket line.

The workers improvised giant slingshots from inner tubes. They hurled whole bricks through the plant windows. The plant soon was without lights. The scabs cowered in the dark. The frightened deputies set up machine guns inside every entranceway. It was not until the arrival of 900 National Guardsmen, 15 hours later, that the scabs were finally released, looking a "sorry sight," as the press reported it.

Then followed one of the most amazing battles in U.S. labor history. "The Marines had landed" in the form of the National Guard but the situation was not "well in hand." With their bare fists and rocks, the workers fought a six-day pitched battle with the National Guard. They fought from rooftops, from behind billboards and came through alleys to flank the guardsmen. "The men in the mob shouted vile epithets at the troopers," complained the Associated Press, "and the women jeered them with suggestions that they 'go home to mama and their paper dolls.'"

But the strikers and their thousands of sympathizers did more than shame the young National Guardsmen. They educated them and tried to win them over. Speakers stood on boxes in front of the troops and explained what the strike was about and the role the troops were playing as strikebreakers. World War I veterans put on their medals and spoke to the boys in uniform like "Dutch uncles." The women explained what the strike meant to their families. The press reported that some of the guardsmen just quit and went home. Others voiced sympathy with the workers. (A year later, when Toledo unionists went to Defiance, Ohio, to aid the Pressed Steel Company strike, they found that eight per cent of the strikers had been National Guardsmen serving in uniform in the Auto-Lite strike. That was where they learned the lesson of unionism.)

On May 24, the guardsmen fired point-blank into the Auto-Lite strikers ranks, killing two and wounding 25. But 6,000 workers returned at dusk to renew the battle. In the dark, they closed in on groups of guardsmen in the six-block martial law zone. The fury of the onslaught twice drove the troops back into the plant. At one stage, a group of troops threw their last tear gas and vomit gas bombs, then quickly picked up rocks to hurl at the strikers; the strikers recovered the last gas bombs thrown before they exploded, flinging them back at the troops.

A monster rally on the evening of June 1 mobilized some 40,000 workers in the Lucas County Courthouse Square. There, however, the AFL leaders, frightened by this tremendous popular uprising, were silent about the general strike and instead assured the workers that Roosevelt would aid them.

By June 4, with the whole community seething with anger, the company capitulated and signed a six-month contract, including a 5% wage increase with a 5% minimum above the auto industry code, naming Local 18384 as the exclusive bargaining agent in the struck plants. This was the first contract under the code that did not include "proportional representation" for company unions. The path was opened for organization of the entire automobile industry. With the Auto-Lite victory under their belts, the Toledo auto workers were to organize 19 plants before the year was out and, before another 12 months, were to lead the first successful strike in a GM plant, the real beginning of the conquest of General Motors.

While the Auto-Lite strike was reaching its climax, the truck drivers of Minneapolis were waging the second of a series of three strikes which stand to this day as models for organization, strategy and incorruptible, militant leadership.

Minneapolis, with its twin city St. Paul, is the hub of Minnesota's wheat, lumber and iron ore areas. Transport —rail and truck—engages a relatively large number of workers. In early 1934, Minneapolis was a notoriously open-shop town. The Citizens Alliance, an organization of anti-union employers, ruled the city.

On February 7, 8 and 9, 1934, the Citizens Alliance got the first stunning blow that was to shatter its dominance. Within three days the union of coal yard workers, organized within General Drivers Local Union 574, AFL International Brotherhood of Teamsters, had paralyzed all the coal yards and won union recognition.

The February 24, 1934 *Militant* reported that Local 574 "displayed a well organized, mobile, fighting picket line that stormed over all opposition, closed 65 truck yards, 150 coal offices and swept the streets clear of scabs in the first three hours of the strike."

"One of the outstanding features of the strike," the original *Militant* report stated, "was the Cruising Picket Squad. This idea came from the ranks and played a great role in the strike." This "cruising picket squad" was the original of the "flying squadrons" that were to become part of the standard picketing techniques of the great Congress of Industrial Organizations (CIO) strikes.

The Dunne brothers (Vincent, Miles and Grant), Carl Skoglund and their associates proved to be a different and altogether superior breed of union leaders compared to the type represented by the craft-minded bureaucrats of the AFL who were content to build a little job-holding trust and settle down for life to collecting dues. After the first victory they set out to organize every truck driver and every inside warehouse worker in Minneapolis. A whirlwind organizing campaign had recruited 3,000 new members into Local 574 by May.

On Tuesday, May 15, 1934, after the employers had refused even to deal with the union, the second truck drivers strike began. Now 5,000 strong, the organized drivers and warehousemen promptly massed at a large garage which served as strike headquarters. From there, fleets of pickets went rolling by trucks and cars to strategic points.

All trucking in the city was halted except for milk, ice and beer drivers who were organized and who operated with special union permits. The city was isolated from all truck traffic in or out by mass picketing. For the first time anywhere in connection with a labor struggle, the term "flying squads" was used—the May 26, 1934 *Militant* reported: "Flying squads of pickets toured the city."

The Local 574 leaders warned the membership over and over to place no reliance or hope in any government agents or agencies, including Floyd B. Olsen, the Farmer-Labor Party governor, and the National Labor Board. They preached reliance only on the mass picket lines and militant struggle against the employers.

The next day some 35,000 building trades workers declared a strike in sympathy with the truck drivers. The Central Labor Union voted its support. Workers, many from plants which weren't even organized, stayed off their jobs and flocked to join the pickets.

On May 21 and 22 there was waged a two-day battle in the City Market that ended with the flight of the entire police force and special deputies in what was called by the strikers "The Battle of Deputies Run."

Word had come to the strike headquarters that the police and bosses were planning a "big offensive" to open the City Market to scab trucks on Monday and Tuesday. The strike leaders pulled in their forces from outlying areas and began concentrating them in the neighborhood of the market.

On Monday, a strong detachment of pickets was sent to the market. These pickets managed to wedge between the deputized business men and the police, isolating the "special deputies." One of the strikers, quoted in Charles Walker's *American City*, a stirring and generally reliable study of the Minneapolis struggle, described the ensuing battle:

"Then we called on the pickets from strike headquarters [reserve] who marched into the center of the market and encircled the police. They [the police] were put right in the center with no way out. At intervals we made sallies on them to separate a few. This kept up for a couple of hours, till finally they drew their guns. We had anticipated this would happen, and that then the pickets would be unable to fight them. You can't lick a gun with a club. The correlation of forces becomes a little unbalanced. So we picked out a striker, a big man and utterly fearless, and sent him in a truck with twenty-five pickets. He was instructed to drive right into the formation of cops and stop for nothing. We knew he'd do it. Down the street he came like a bat out of hell, with his horn honking and into the market arena. The cops held up their hands for him to stop, but he kept on; they gave way and he was in the middle of them. The pickets jumped out on the cops. We figured by intermixing with the cops in hand-to-hand fighting, they would not use their guns because they would have to shoot cops as well as strikers. Cops don't like that.

"Casualties for the day included for the strikers a broken collar bone, the cut-open skull of a picket who swung on a cop and hit a striker by mistake as the cop dodged, and a couple of broken ribs. On the other side, roughly thirty cops were taken to the hospital."

The strikers were victorious in another sense: no trucks moved.

The blood, however, was drawn by the other side. Police and employers deliberately planned to lure isolated picket trucks into an ambush and shoot down the unarmed workers without warning. This was to be a pretext for sending in the National Guard to break the strike.

The trap was sprung on the fifth day of the strike—"Bloody Friday," July 20. *American City* quotes a strike picket on what happened that day in the wholesale grocery district:

"For two hours we stood around wondering what was up for there was no truck in sight. Then as two P.M. drew near a tensing of bodies and nervous shifting of feet and heads among the police indicated that something was up. We were right, for a few minutes later about one hundred more cops hove into view escorting a large yellow truck. The truck, without license plates and with the cab heavily wired, pulled up to the loading platform of the Slocum-Bergren Company. Here a few boxes were loaded on… At five past two the truck slowly pulled out … It turned down Sixth Avenue and then turned on Third Street toward Seventh Avenue. As it did a picket truck containing about ten pickets followed. As the picket truck drew near the convoy, the police without warning let loose a barrage of fire. Pickets fell from the trucks, others rushed up to pick up their wounded comrades; as they bent to pick up the injured, the police fired at them… One young worker received a full charge of buckshot in the back as he bent to pick up a wounded picket.

"The rain of bullets then became a little heavier so I and three other pickets hopped a fence and walked to headquarters… Pickets by the dozens lying all over the floor with blood flowing from their wounds, more coming in and no place to put them. The doctor would treat one after another who urged him to treat others first.

"The Minneapolis papers printed hundreds of lies about what had happened but none was brazen enough to claim that the strikers had any weapons at all."

This was substantially confirmed by the Governor's own investigating committee which, after the strike, found that the police had planned the attack in advance and fired to kill on unarmed pickets.

One worker, Harry Ness, died shortly after the shooting. Another, John Belor, died a few days later in the hospital. Some 55 workers were wounded. Within 20 minutes of the massacre, the National Guard rolled into the area. It was their signal.

But if this terrorism was expected to smash the strike, the bosses got an unpleasant surprise.

All union-driven taxicabs, ice, beer and gasoline trucks, which had continued to operate by union permit, immediately went on strike. The police were cleared from all areas near the strike headquarters. Then, when Harry Ness was buried, the whole working class of Minneapolis turned out in an historic demonstration for his funeral. Some 40,000 marched in the funeral cortege. They took over the streets. Not a cop was in sight. The workers themselves directed traffic.

On August 22, after five weeks of the toughest battling against all the forces of the employers and government, the strikers won. The bosses capitulated and signed an agreement granting the union its main demands. This included the right to represent "inside workers," which the employers had threatened to fight to the bitter end as industrial unionism.

While the Minneapolis truck drivers were battling their way to victory, the San Francisco general strike—involving 125,000 workers at its peak—carried the American class struggle to new heights.

On May 9, 1934, from 10,000 to 15,000 West Coast members of the AFL International Longshoremen's Association went on an "unauthorized" strike. Soon the strike included 25,000 workers, many of them members of seamen's organizations who joined in sympathy.

The original demands had been for a coast-wide agreement, union control of hiring halls and a closed shop. The strikers added demands for $1 an hour instead of 85 cents and the 30-hour week instead of 48.

From the start, the strike was waged with great militancy. Frederick J. Lang, in his book *Maritime: A historical sketch and a workers' program*, wrote: "It was a real rank-and-file strike, with the 'leaders' swept along in the flood. It encountered every weapon then in the arsenal of the employers. The shipowners hired their own thugs who tried to work the docks and man the ships. The city police of every port on the Coast were mobilized on the waterfronts to hunt down the strikers. The newspapers, launching a slander campaign against the strikers, called on the citizenry to form vigilante committees to raid strike headquarters, the actual organization of this dirty work being entrusted to the American Legion and other 'patriotic' societies."

ILA President Joseph Ryan hastily flew into San Francisco from New York in an effort to squelch the strike. Over the heads of the strikers and their local leaders, he signed an agreement giving up the main demand—the union-controlled hiring hall. He was repudiated by the strikers in a coast-wide poll.

The chief strike leader was the then unknown Harry Bridges.

Ryan — a consort of shipowners, stevedore bosses, gangsters and Tammany politicians, who 20 years later was to be dumped by these elements when he was no longer useful to them — tried to split the strike by making separate settlements in each port. He succeeded only in Seattle. AFL President William Green joined in denouncing the strike and yelling "reds" and "communists."

On July 5 the bosses tried to smash the strike by attacking its strategic center, San Francisco's waterfront, with calculated force and violence. At the "Battle of Rincon Hill" the police blasted away with tear gas, pistols and shotguns at the waterfront pickets. They killed Howard Sperry and Nick Bordoise and wounded 109 others. As in the third Minneapolis strike and the Toledo Auto-Lite battle, the deliberate massacres perpetrated by the police were the signal for sending in the National Guard.

The murder and wounding of strikers did not crush the workers. Instead, San Francisco labor answered with a tremendous counter-attack—a general strike. For two days, the working class paralyzed the city. The workers took over many city functions, directing traffic and assuming other municipal tasks. On the third and fourth days, the general strike petered out when the AFL leaders, who were swept along in the first spontaneous protest against the killings, ordered an end to the stoppage.

The bosses and police, with the aid of organized vigilantes, vented their fear and hatred of the workers on the small radical organizations, not daring to hit directly at the unions. Thirty-five gangs of vigilantes, heavily armed, raided headquarters of Communist, IWW and Socialist groups. They smashed furniture, hurled typewriters and literature out the windows, beat up many defenseless workers. In some instances, the police who arrived after the vigilantes left completed the work of destruction. They jailed more than 300 persons.

After 11 weeks, the longshore strike was ended on July 31 with an agreement to arbitrate. It was a poor settlement, but the workers returned to the job in an organized body. Within a year, in job action after job action, they won the union hiring hall up and down the Coast. Their struggle gave impetus to maritime organization on the East Coast, leading in 1937 to establishment of the CIO National Maritime Union, and opened the way for organization of West Coast industrial labor.

Too little credit has been given to the Toledo, Minneapolis and San Francisco strikes for their effect on the subsequent industrial union movement, the CIO. But had these magnificent examples of labor struggle not occurred, in all likelihood the CIO would have been delayed or taken a different and less militant course.

It was these gigantic battles—all led by radicals—that convinced John L. Lewis that the American workers were determined to be organized and would follow the leadership that showed it meant business.

"Lewis watched the unrest and flareups of violence through the summer of 1934. He saw the Dunne brothers of Minneapolis lead a general strike of truck drivers into a virtual civil war. Blood ran in Minneapolis," wrote Sal Alinsky in his *John L. Lewis—An Unauthorized Biography*.

"In San Francisco a general strike spearheaded by Harry Bridges' Longshoremen's Union paralyzed the great western city for four days.

"Before that year was out, seven hundred thousand workers had struck. Lewis could read the revolutionary handwriting on the walls of American industry. He knew that the workers were seething and aching to be organized so they could strike back. Everyone wanted to hit out, employer against worker and worker against employer and anyone else who they felt was not in their class. America was becoming more class conscious than at any time in its history..."

Of course, "civil war" was going on in towns and cities from coast to coast and blood was being spilled in scores of other places besides Minneapolis, Toledo and San Francisco. These latter cities were unique, however, in this: *they showed how the workers could fight and win. They gave heart and hope to labor everywhere for the climactic struggle that was to build the CIO.*

CHAPTER 10

Jukebox Blowin' a Fuse
The Working-Class Roots of Rock-and-Roll

Michael J. Roberts

In 1943, the popular jump blues bandleader Louis Jordan and his band, the Tympany Five, recorded a hit single for Decca Records called "Ration Blues." Through the use of risqué double entendres, the lyrics of the song present a humorous satire of the experience of the sudden and serious misfortune of enforced austerity implemented by the War Production Board, an agency created by the federal government to assist in the colossal effort of reorganizing the economy after the entrance of the United States into World War II. In the third verse, Jordan sings, "They reduced my meat and sugar/And rubber's disappearing fast/You can't ride no more with poppa/'Cause Uncle Sam wants my gas." In the song, Jordan plays the part of a lamenting profligate who once enjoyed the good life but who now has to cope with lowered expectations given the shortages of certain goods that prevailed during the war. In addition to complaining about giving up "meat," Jordan laments giving up his "jelly." These two terms were commonly used in the vernacular of the urban working class as code for indulging in the carnal pleasures. "I like to wake up with my jelly by my side," sings Jordan. "Since rationing started, baby, you just take your stuff and hide." At the end of the song, Jordan's character resorts to appropriating the "meat" of his partner as a means of coping with the problem of government-enforced austerity. "I'm gonna steal all your jelly, baby/And rob you of your meat/I've got the ration blues, blue as I can be."

The use of sexual innuendo in the lyrics of rhythm and blues songs from the 1940s and early 1950s has been duly noted by historians of rock 'n' roll music who have chronicled the ways in which rhythm and blues and rock 'n' roll culture contributed to the transformation of the norms that govern sexual relations in American society. Much less attention has been given to the ways in which the situation of class and class conflict mediated the formation of sexual practices within rhythm and blues culture. In "Ration Blues," however, we see how risqué double entendres are layered within a discourse of working-class grievances about enforced scarcity upon workers, a situation which was widely seen as unjust at the time, since big business was allowed to enjoy large,

Original publication details: Michael J. Roberts, "Jukebox Blowin' a Fuse: The Working-Class Roots of Rock-and-Roll", from *Tell Tchaikovsky the News: Rock 'n' Roll, the Labor Question, and the Musician's Union, 1942–1968*, pp. 41–46; 48–58; 64–68; 75–77; 93–96. Duke University Press, 2014. Reproduced with permission from Duke University Press.

very lucrative contracts with the federal government during and after the war. Jordan recorded "Ration Blues" in the midst of widespread discontent among the American working class over the double standard set up by the federal government that allowed corporations to garner windfall profits during the expansion of the wartime economy, while the working class was expected to renounce wage increases and cut back on "luxury" goods, including food items like meat, butter, and sugar and clothing material like silk, nylon, and wool.

Between the years 1940 and 1944 the government turned over more than $175 billion in military contracts to approximately 1,800 companies, marking the beginning of the phenomenon that President Eisenhower, in his famous speech from 1960, referred to as the military-industrial complex. The money was far from evenly distributed among the 1,800 companies that held contracts with the Pentagon. Of the 1,800 companies involved, 100 walked away with $117 billion. The U.S. economy almost doubled in size during the war, and yet President Roosevelt called for a wage freeze for workers, while companies were allowed to raise prices—in spite of so-called price regulations—during the wartime era of increasing aggregate demand. Widespread awareness among workers of these severe inequities led to the largest working-class revolt in American labor history.

"Ration Blues" is a good example of how rhythm and blues culture during the 1940s presented sexual practices as part of a *totality* of pleasures that constitute the construction of working-class identity, a totality which exists in *opposition* to surplus repression and unjust austerity, conditions which follow from the unequal distribution of wealth and power. Jordan cut a similar hit record in 1946 called "Inflation Blues," which also lampooned the federal government for allowing corporations to raise prices and garner huge profits during and immediately after the war, while workers were forced to cope with stagnant wages and while returning soldiers were dealing with the problems associated with finding relatively "meaningful" and well-paid work during the reconversion of the American political economy from a war-oriented system to a peacetime market.

Among the American working class in general, a significant pent-up demand was beginning to put pressure on the establishment to respond to their growing expectations for both more income and more leisure. The tension was particularly acute during 1945–46 as workers in the millions went on strike all over the country in response to the problems associated with restructuring the economy. At the end of the war, as production was severely curtailed, nearly one-quarter of all workers lost their jobs, many of them women who were unfairly expected to give up their relatively well paying jobs to men returning from war. By October 1945 some 2 million workers were unemployed, and they would have to compete for jobs with the 10 million service men and women returning from overseas. Mediating the general tension between workers and capital during this period was a growing impatience among the black working class with the status quo of racial discrimination in the United States. Black soldiers returning from the war—in addition to civil rights activists who did not fight overseas and young men who refused to fight and found ways to dodge the draft—were even more critical of the stark hypocrisy of the government, which was willing to fight a war abroad, ostensibly in the name of saving democracy and defeating racist ideology, while allowing racism to thrive at home. The general mood of American workers that included pent-up demand and the grievances having to do with economic injustice, combined with the more specific grievances of black workers having to do with racial discrimination, gave shape to the content and form of rhythm and blues music during the 1940s. The music of Louis Jordan and his influence on the development of rhythm and blues and rock 'n' roll provides us with a good example of this phenomenon, since much of his music and that of his peer group expressed resistance to the pressures of the changing conditions of capital accumulation and racial injustice. Rhythm and blues culture also provided the working class with images produced by utopian desires for a better future based on more leisure time and an improved material standard of living.

Jordan and his generation of rhythm and blues musicians of the 1940s created a culture that was mediated by class and class conflict. Rhythm and blues in turn shaped the development of the content of rock 'n' roll music during the 1950s, giving the new music a form and content that continued to express the struggle against work and authority. The influence of class on the emergence and expansion of rock 'n' roll remains relatively neglected in most historical accounts of the music. Class as a concept that signifies "status" as a position in the hierarchical social structure often figures as an important background context in many histories of rock 'n' roll, but class *conflict* rarely does. Usually class as *status* figures as a biographical detail associated with an individual who may struggle against poverty and finally make it as a recording star in the music business. In these histories, class is important as an indication of the status of an individual, but not as a structural phenomenon that shapes the organization of social relations in society. In short, class coded as status usually follows the familiar American myth of rags to riches in most histories of rock 'n' roll that address the phenomenon. Class conflict and class as a collective phenomenon are rarely considered, especially as forces that shape the music, rather than merely describe the status of the individual musician. The consideration of class conflict as a variable that contributes to the creation of popular culture provides a framework to interpret Louis Jordan's music and the rhythm and blues culture of his era as a form of resistance.

Historians of American labor like Herbert Gutman have demonstrated that popular cultural traditions that were formed in preindustrial times presented a serious obstacle to merchant capitalists who were seeking to impose a new way of life on agrarian workers who filled the first factories in the United States, a life oriented toward endless work and the hours on the clock rather than the natural rhythms of the day and of the seasons. Workers who were unwilling to give up their leisure time activities developed in preindustrial times resisted these changes, and although proletarianization and industrialization eventually destroyed the agrarian way of life, certain features of preindustrial working-class culture—especially resistance to the Protestant work ethic—continued to exist in the forms and images of popular culture. The development of rhythm and blues in the 1940s presents a good case study of this phenomenon, because as workers left their agrarian way of life in search of work in the urban areas of the country during the war, they brought their culture with them, one that has consistently been at odds with the demands of capital accumulation. Structural changes in the economy during the war provided a unique opportunity for workers to gain leverage in their struggle with capital during this period, and the increasing political power of workers is reflected in the urban music of both rhythm and blues and honky-tonk. Older, preindustrial images of leisure remained in the culture, but a new popular culture developed in the urban areas as rural cultures from different parts of the country collided in the cities. The structural opportunities that followed from the changing economy gave the urban working class a reason to develop rising expectations, and these new expectations made their way into the utopian images of the new popular culture. This chapter is an investigation of working-class images, both old and new, in the popular music of this period, through the analysis of key figures in the emergence of rhythm and blues and honky-tonk music and how these forms influenced the shape and content of rock 'n' roll music.

Images of Work and Resistance in Rock 'n' Roll

Historians of rock 'n' roll frequently make use of terms like *dangerous, mysterious*, and *rebellious* to describe what it is that is unique to rock 'n' roll during the early years in the development of the music and culture, but these terms are usually used in a context that focuses on the subversion of norms that govern race and sexual relations, or the conflict between generations, at the relative expense of an analysis that considers class conflict. In other places in these texts it seems that the "danger" signified by rock 'n' roll culture seems to hang in the air all by itself with no adequate explanation for what gave content to the menace posed by rock 'n' roll culture. The relative mystification of the early years of rock 'n' roll can be explained in part as *reification*, which follows from either a complete erasure of class conflict from the history of rock 'n' roll or a displacement of class onto other categories like race. I use the phrase "class struggle" very broadly to include not only the clash between labor and capital during these years but also the struggle for racial equality and the specific ways in which black workers had to fight on two fronts. On the one hand, they fought alongside white workers for better working conditions, better pay, and more leisure time. On the other, they fought over these issues within a larger social context of racial discrimination and violence, making their struggle against capital much more complicated and difficult than that of their white contemporaries.

In short, there is no scholarly account of the history of rock 'n' roll that approaches the topic of class in a rigorous manner such as Bill Malone's excellent book on country music, *Don't Get Above Your Raisin': Country Music and the Southern Working Class*. Malone's book is the only sustained analysis of the impact of social class on the formation of popular music in the United States. For Malone, country music was particularly relevant for people like his father, whose "life as a tenant farmer on the worn-out cotton fields of East Texas, working on someone else's land and under someone else's terms, did not permit much in the way of self-assertion." Country music was and continues to be, according to Malone, a means for working-class people to cope with, and at times escape from a life working under someone else's terms. I find a similar phenomenon at work in the history of rock 'n' roll. The image of cotton picking is one of the primary signifiers in early rock 'n' roll music as it serves to frame a backdrop for the struggle against work and the rebellion against authority within rock culture. Other images of rebellion in rock 'n' roll emerged a decade earlier in the urban, rhythm and blues culture of the war years and the late 1940s.

In 1941, the year that Jordan began his successful recording career, 8.4 percent of the U.S. workforce had been on strike. The overwhelming majority of the strikes were wildcat strikes—strikes that were not authorized by the leadership of the union bureaucracy—conducted by rank-and-file workers who struggled against both their employers and their own union leaders, who had pledged not to strike for the duration of the war, an agreement that FDR was desperate to obtain at the outset of war. In 1941, there were 4,288 strikes involving 2,362,620 workers. As Jordan's career sky-rocketed during the 1940s, so did labor disputes between workers and management. Thousands of work stoppages involving millions of workers occurred in every year during the war, and they continued the year after the end of the war. When Jordan recorded his second crossover hit, "Ration Blues," in 1943, which reached number 11 on the pop charts and stayed at number 1 on the "Harlem Hit Parade" for six weeks, there were 3,752 strikes involving 1,980,000 workers.

The 1940s were also the spike years of the "great migration" of African Americans from the South to the urban centers in the North and South-west. Between the years 1916 and 1960 approximately 6 million blacks left the South and moved to urban areas both in the North in places like Chicago, New York, and Philadelphia, and the West, including Kansas City and St. Louis, as well as further west to Oakland and Los Angeles. The long-term migration of blacks from the South was due in part to the spectacular failure of Reconstruction, but the significant spike in the demand for labor that followed from the entry of the United States into the war also had a huge effect on the structure of demographic change. The push of Jim Crow and the pull of relatively well paying jobs in the manufacturing areas created new opportunities for African Americans. As a result of the relative improvement in their job prospects, African Americans in urban areas became a new class of consumers as well, as they helped to support the increase in record sales of rhythm and blues music in the mid- to late 1940s.

In spite of racial segregation in the music industry, Louis Jordan scored a number 1 hit on the pop charts with "Is You Is or Is You Ain't My Baby" in 1944 when 2,120,000 workers were involved in 4,956 strikes. After the war, the waves of wildcat strikes in the United States continued. The year 1946 marked the most tumultuous year in the history of the American labor movement, when 14.6 percent of the workforce went on strike, setting a record with 4,985 work stoppages. That year Jordan recorded his biggest hit with an interpretation of a country song titled "Choo Choo Ch' Boogie," which sold over 2 million copies. Many of the hits Jordan recorded during the war were directly aimed at problems facing the American working class, including the tunes mentioned above, like "Ration Blues," "Inflation Blues," and "Re-conversion Blues."

In addition to expressing the grievances of workers, however, Jordan's music also embodied the feeling of power and leverage that the working class enjoyed during the labor shortages that prevailed during the war. Songs like "Let the Good Times Roll" and "Saturday Night Fish Fry" are indicative of the phenomenon, where Jordan's lyrics reflect the more Dionysian side of life, as opposed to songs like "Ration Blues" and "Inflation Blues," which emphasize grievances. The main themes of "Saturday Night Fish Fry" and "Let the Good Times Roll" are the rejection of delayed gratification and confrontation with authority figures that attempt to put an end to the "good times." In "Saturday Night Fish Fry," partygoers end up in fisticuffs with the cops who try and break up their party, while in "Let the Good Times Roll," the emphasis is on spending lots of money in pursuit of immediate gratification. As in most of Jordan's songs, both themes are portrayed through humor and irony. Indeed, it was his ability to capture the rebellious and irreverent mood of both the black and white working class through humor that partly explains his significant crossover success during the 1940s.

The example of Louis Jordan points to what Theodor Adorno refers to as the ways in which "music … sketches in the clearest possible lines, the contradictions … which cut through present-day society." My appropriation of Adorno's position on the situation of music in the modern world is not true to the original argument, since Adorno wrote very disparagingly about jazz and popular music, which he viewed as a problem that stemmed from the commodification of music, which in turn leads to standardization and alienation, key features of the totally "administered" society under the rule of capitalist exchange value. In my view Adorno, who was writing about popular culture while in exile in the United States during the war, was mistaken in arguing that "the current musical con-sciousness of the masses can scarcely be called Dionysian." While Adorno did not have popular music in mind when he argued that music revealed certain contradictions at the core of modern capitalist society, it remains the case that popular music during this period was mediated by the pervasiveness of class struggle that enveloped American society during the 1940s, and for this reason Adorno's aesthetic theory remains useful for an analysis that seeks to uncover the class content of rhythm and blues and rock 'n' roll.

To make Adorno's aesthetic theory work for popular music of the time (rhythm and blues in particular), I take his critical Marxist argument that the economic base mediates the cultural superstructure and shift the analysis away from the universal domination of exchange value over use value, or from the analysis of how in everyday life all human products are subjugated to the rule of exchangeability and the universality of the commodity form, to an analysis of how *class struggle* mediates, but in no direct way determines, the cultural superstructure. Contrary to Adorno, commercial and popular music provided the working class of this era a means to express utopian hopes and Dionysian desires.

Rather than see the essential antagonism in the culture industry as that of the struggle between the individual attempt to realize their individuality in musical creation and the structural requirements of capital to realize exchange value—which destroys individuality and allows alienation to reign supreme—I focus on the class struggle as the crucial antagonism that is revealed in the music. The category of *mediation*—how the object (music) is a moment of the totality—is a crucial concept offered by Adorno, and I find it very useful in revealing the class content of popular music in the 1940s, in spite of Adorno's own pessimism about the possibility that anything produced by the culture industry could have any political value for the working class.

In short, while Adorno focused on the relatively hegemonic logic of capital and the struggle of the avant-garde musicians (like Schoenberg and Berg) against that logic, I see rhythm and blues music of the 1940s as a mediated cultural form that expressed a *counterlogic* of labor, which signifies a struggle against work as well as the playful deconstruction of highbrow and lowbrow cultural sensibilities. Both of these elements are present in the rhythm and blues of the 1940s, as well as rock 'n' roll during the early and mid-1950s. Appropriating Adorno's critical Marxist analysis addresses the problem of reification that prevails in most histories of rock 'n' roll that mystify the "danger" and "rebelliousness" of the atmosphere that characterized the early years of rock 'n' roll.

The working-class cultural struggle against work stretches back to the songs of slaves working in the cotton fields. The white working class also has a musical tradition that is oriented around the cultural resistance to work and exploitation which stretches as far back as the eighteenth century. This particular cultural struggle connects the music of the slaves to the Delta Blues of Robert Johnson's generation and all the way through to the jump blues of Louis Jordan and the rock 'n' roll of Chuck Berry and Little Richard. The struggle against work that animates blues music also influenced white honky-tonk musicians like Hank Williams and white rockabilly musicians like Carl Perkins, Johnny Cash, and Elvis Presley.

The epic labor struggles of the 1940s that erupted in the industries which had grown up during the war contributed to the form of a new kind of music which developed out of a unique mixture of diverse cultures as millions of people migrated out of rural areas in search of manufacturing jobs in the southwestern and in the northern areas of the United States when the war jump-started an economy mired in depression. For the people who did not leave the rural South in search of work, the labor question still figured prominently in the popular culture, including the formation of blues and country music, although in a different way, primarily within the context of cotton picking.

These two distinct ways in which the labor question became a focal point in country music, honky-tonk, blues, and rhythm and blues—the desire to escape the sorrows and suffering of field labor and sharecropping in the rural South, and the dramatic collision of capital and labor in the manufacturing industries in urban areas in the North and Southwest—gave substance to much of the music that became rock 'n' roll. It is in the lyrics and in the form of the music as well as the arrangement of the instruments. It is also expressed in the reflections of the musicians themselves, when they situate their music in their everyday lives of that period.

Rock 'n' roll is at least as old as the late 1940s, a unique period of social unrest in the United States. The key issues that triggered this period of turbulence were the spatial and social transformation of the labor process, which led to a popular focus on the labor question and the race question, which in turn found acute expression in the early years of rhythm and blues music. Tight labor markets created by wartime production allowed all workers to enjoy a rising standard, which followed the increasing leverage with which to negotiate with their employers. Increasing demand for labor also provided black workers the opportunity to challenge racial segregation, both in terms of the distribution of jobs and in terms of political and spatial marginalization in society more generally.

Workers during this period were both advancing their right to a larger slice of the pie and openly demonstrating their willingness to spontaneously walk off the job as a means to secure a hold on their stake. The spike in wildcat strike activity combined with the rowdy atmosphere of urban, working-class leisure spaces demonstrated a peculiarly ostentatious lifestyle, which was most visible in styles of clothing and openly sexual dance styles. Sometimes working-class pretensions were made explicit in the lyrics of jump blues tunes, but even when it is not in the lyrics, it is in the music itself: the shuffle rhythms, the heavy backbeat, pounding boogie-woogie piano, walking bass lines, the noisy, growling, and "honking" saxophones, and especially the electric guitars, which together with the saxophones produced so much noise that the singers had to shout to be heard, ushering in a new genre of singers in the late 1940s known collectively as the blues shouters, which included Big Joe Turner, Jimmy "Mr. Five by Five" Rushing, and Wynonie Harris.

Because rock 'n' roll emerges during this period and not in the mid-1950s, some historians call this phenomenon the "secret" history of rock 'n' roll. The secret, however, is presented by historians like Nick Tosches as a "secret" simply because rock 'n' roll is older than Elvis. It may be relatively unknown to the casual fan that rock 'n' roll did not start with Elvis Presley, but Tosches neglects to examine the social content of that largely unknown pre-Presley social history. In his book *Unsung Heroes of Rock 'n' Roll*, Tosches emphasizes the controversial nature of the rhythm and blues artists of the late 1940s, referring to the era as a "forsaken time of relentless excess" and "the wild years before Elvis." While Tosches has adequately captured the rebellious mood of early rock 'n' roll perhaps better than any other writer/critic, it remains the case that in his account, the rebellious spirit of rock 'n' roll seems to hang in the air all by itself, like a rebel without a cause. Tosches is correct to describe the era as a time of "relentless excess" and the attitudes as "forsaken," but there is no adequate analysis of where that rebelliousness or "forsaken time of relentless excess" comes from. Another good example of this phenomenon is Robert Palmer's book *Rock & Roll: An Unruly History*, which like Tosches's book is an excellent *internal* history of rock 'n' roll, but it also fails to adequately capture what is "unruly" about this history. The "unruliness" of rock 'n' roll seems to float in the air, unsupported by any edifice.

The rebellious character of rhythm and blues music was sustained by the increasing political power of the American working class, which benefited significantly from structural changes in the economy. Steep increases in the demand for labor during the war drove the unemployment rate down to an insignificant 1.3 percent of the population by 1943, which was less than a tenth of the unemployment rate in 1937, the most "prosperous" year of the Great Depression. Perhaps the most important indication of the increasing leverage that workers were enjoying in the tight labor market was the reason behind why workers were separated from their jobs. In a stunning reversal of fortune, by 1943 fully 72 percent of job turnovers were accounted for by *voluntary resignation*, whereas in 1937 *layoffs* accounted for 70 percent of job turnover. One-third of the workforce (approximately 15 million workers) was able to move into higher paying jobs with better working conditions. Weekly earnings in manufacturing jumped up 65 percent after 1941, rising from $32.18 to $47.12 by 1943. For most workers who left rural areas for a defense job in the urban factories, the new environment of better wages encouraged rising expectations. When factory workers who were working in the defense plants got a taste for the improved lifestyle that went along with a relatively good paycheck, they developed a desire for more. The issue was how to get the companies that held the defense contracts to share the newfound wealth with their workers.

Just before and during World War II, more than 16 million people joined the armed forces, and in the effort to ramp up production for war, American companies drew upon 15 million new workers from the reserve army of labor, millions of whom were people who migrated from rural areas to urban production centers that were located primarily in the North and Southwest, but also in urban areas in the South like the shipyards in Mobile, Alabama. Among the new wartime workers were 6 million women and over 1 million African Americans. The massive migration of workers was the largest ever seen in America. All told, more than 4 million people had left rural areas from thirty states for production centers in urban areas in eighteen other states from 1940 to 1946. According to the U.S. Census Bureau, the overall increase in population within the cities that served as wartime production centers was around 19 percent, whereas for African Americans the increase in population was close to 50 percent!

The working-class migration to urban centers where factory work was located also included groups of African Americans who formerly worked as domestic workers in white, upper-middle-class suburbs. In his autobiography, Chuck Berry recalls:

> The effects of the war were felt quickly throughout the home front. Materials such as rubber, copper, gasoline, and soap became scarce, and some were even rationed. There was a shortage of goods, but there was an abundance of jobs and everybody worked for the war effort. The suburban rich people were panicking because the maids and domestic workers were all leaving them for higher-paying jobs at the defense plants. ... As a result, maids, gardeners, and garbage technicians got the chance to revisit their former employers in the suburbs where they tooted their Cadillac horns while driving by, "Just coming out to say hello!"

Berry's construction of the image of African Americans cruising white, upper-middle-class suburbs in order for their former employers to see them driving fancy new cars nicely captures the mood of working-class pretensions during that period.

Huge demographic shifts as the result of the steep increase in the demand for labor meant that workers had the upper hand even in the face of a hostile business community, the presidential administration, *and* a union bureaucracy that demanded sacrifice and obedience in the name of patriotism and national "emergency." The years between 1941 and 1946 were unique for American workers because they displayed an unusual willingness to use their main weapon, the wildcat strike. Worker pretensions among the rank-and-file were at an all-time high in the history of the American labor movement. Many of the wildcat strikes were playful and celebratory. In Fairfield, Alabama, in 1944, wildcat strikers held a jitterbug dance in the street just outside of the windows of the management offices at the mill where they were on strike. In 1943 workers in Stamford, Connecticut, conducted a general wildcat strike that shut down the entire city, where a reporter recalled that the atmosphere felt more like a carnival than a strike. The wildcat strike data from the early to mid-1940s are truly remarkable numbers. They reveal significant turmoil within the United States during the war in spite of the efforts by the Roosevelt administration to create a stable climate of production for the war. Mine workers were able to force concessions from both the mine companies and the Roosevelt administration, a truly remarkable feat. Roosevelt threatened to conscript mine workers when they went on strike in 1943, and in response to the president's threat, the United Mine Workers union pulled *more* workers out on strike. They continued to pull workers out of the pits until the Roosevelt administration gave in to their demands and forced the mine companies to capitulate. It was no coincidence that these were also the years that gave birth to rock 'n' roll music in America.

The seed elements of rock 'n' roll, which took root in Louis Jordan and his generation, developed and were nourished within a cultural milieu that I refer to as the working-class pretensions of the 1940s. To appreciate the class dimension that colors the history of rock 'n' roll music is to examine how rhythm and blues musicians took the electricity of the wildcat strike movement of rank-and-file workers during the 1940s and plugged it in through amplified guitars and blew it hard through growling and honking saxophones. While the wildcat strikes reverberated through the structures of power in American politics, rhythm and blues music gave American popular culture a shot in the arm. By pretension I mean both the advancement of a claim on something—a certain material standard of living, a cultural lifestyle, a demand for equal rights, etc.—as well as ostentation in the presentation of self. The period of years between the outbreak of war and the end of the decade is truly remarkable in that workers routinely walked off the job due to many issues that might seem trivial today. For example, in 1944, 300 auto workers at a GM factory in Detroit walked off the job when management attempted to ban smoking, and shortly before the end of the war workers at a Cadillac factory in Detroit walked off the job when they found out that they would not be allowed to play checkers at work! Imagine workers trying something like that today. The wave of wildcat strikes was punctuated by a massive general strike, which occurred in Oakland, California, in 1946.

In short, the increasing power exercised by American workers during the 1940s was the basis for keeping the culture of rhythm and blues aloft during the 1940s and into the 1950s. To focus on these issues is to give a reason for the rebellious attitudes of those intimately connected to the rhythm and blues and rock 'n' roll culture that figure in the historical accounts written by critics like Tosches and Palmer, who have been unable to give a reason for why rhythm and blues and rock 'n' roll took an oppositional stance to the status quo during this period in American history.

Many of Jordan's tunes were performed in storytelling modes in the call-and-response style. In addition to the form of call-and-response, the lyrical content of jump blues also has roots in the work songs of field slaves and the blues music that developed from that context.

The history of country blues is rooted in the experience of suffering endured by slaves and their descendants who endured the oppressive share-cropping system that prevailed between the end of the Civil War and the early twentieth century. These conditions of abject poverty and backbreaking labor are what produced "the blues" in the first place. According to the legendary electric bluesman Howlin' Wolf:

> Well I was broke when I was born, that's why I grew up howlin'. We talk about the life of human beings [in our music], how they live. A lot of people wonder what the blues is, and I'm gonna tell you. When you ain't got no money you got the blues. ... A lot of people holler, "Well, I don't like the blues," but when you ain't got no money to pay the rent and when you can't buy you no food you damn sure got the blues. When you ain't got no money you got the blues cuz you're thinkin' evil. ... If you gettin' everything you need [and more] you don't have no right to worry about nothin. But when you don't got nothin, you got to worry about something, and that's when the blues comes in. You say, "I don't have this and I don't have that." When you look around and you see these other people have this and they have that, and in your heart you feel like you're nobody, then you got the blues.

Blues music was distinct in the way in which the music was intimately bound up with everyday life. Unlike much of the music that was produced by Tin Pan Alley, which was distinctly separated from the everyday life of the producers and consumers of the music, blues music was oriented toward textures of daily life, the problems and the pleasures that individuals directly experienced. Life and art were not separate in the culture that created blues music. The blues is a set of feelings produced by a stark existence, and blues music was developed in order to cope with those bad feelings or even as a means to chase those feelings away. Music critic and historian Albert Murray refers to this as the difference between the blues "as such" and blues music. The function of chasing away the blues in music is referred to by Murray as "Stompin' the Blues." Master bassist and singer/songwriter Willie Dixon claimed blues music "relaxes the mind about bad feelings." Pianist Memphis Slim, another key figure in the development of blues music during this era, put a slightly different spin on the meaning of the blues. For Slim, in addition to being about coping with identity crises that follow from abject poverty and alienating work, blues music is also about resistance and fighting back. "The blues goes back to slavery," according to Slim. "When slaves wanted to say things that they couldn't say, that would get them in trouble, or [when they wanted to] *get back at the boss*, they would sing" [emphasis mine].

Getting back at the boss, as well as getting back at authoritative figures that working-class people face in their everyday lives is a central theme that connects blues, jump blues, and rock 'n' roll. One way that slaves coped with not being able to say what they wanted to say was to use code to fool the slave masters. The use of code and deception became part of African American folklore through the trickster tales, the best known of which is perhaps the Brer Rabbit character. Brer Rabbit stories were typical of slave stories that told of magical animals or lesser gods that were able to use deception to overcome the superior strength and power of their opponent. The stories usually tell of small victories, but the rich tradition of the trickster-hero tales demonstrates how the slaves kept alive their utopian desires to overcome slavery. The key to understanding the figure of the trickster is in how the trickster must make use of cunning and deception, which becomes possible only through a profound fluency in knowing how and what the slave master—or the boss, or other figures of authority—thought about themselves and the Other.

You can see the trickster-hero figure used in Louis Jordan's hit record "Ain't Nobody Here but Us Chickens," which appropriates the lyrics of an old field song that was popular among slaves. The lyrics of the song, which tell a story about a farmer investigating a disturbance in the hen house, are a metaphor for a victory of the powerless over the powerful by fooling the authority figure. In the song, when the farmer asks what is going on in the hen house, he hears the response, "There's nobody here but us chickens." The voice inside the hen house goes on to tell the farmer that laying eggs is serious business, which requires plenty of rest and sleep, and that the farmer should therefore leave them alone so they can get back to sleep. In this way, the thief inside the hen house uses the farmer's knowledge and interests against the farmer. The voice can appeal to the farmer's greed as a way to get the farmer to leave the hen house. Of course, when the farmer leaves, the thief goes about his/her mischievous ways.

Louis Jordan probably did not intend to make a political statement with "Nobody Here but Us Chickens"; however, placed within the social context of the time, the song does take on political meaning. It may seem obvious that Jordan, an African American, would be familiar with and draw upon the figure of the trickster-hero in his music, but "Ain't Nobody Here" was also a huge cross-over hit. As George Lipsitz has argued, Jordan's hit records frequently crossed over to the white pop charts because "white people turned to black culture for guidance, because black culture contains the most sophisticated strategies of signification and the richest grammars of opposition available to aggrieved populations." Jordan's music points to the way in which commercially produced popular culture provided working-class individuals ways to position themselves to resist authority and create novel identities.

Jordan claimed that "when you come to hear Louis Jordan, you hear things that make you forget what you'd had to do the day before and just have a good time, a great time." In the spirit of escaping work, one of Jordan's big hits was "Let the Good Times Roll," a song with obvious connotations for workers enjoying an atmosphere of more leverage in the labor market. "Let the Good Times Roll" was written in 1946, the same year that workers were on general strikes all across America. The first two verses of "Let the Good Times Roll" read: Hey everybody let's have some fun/You only live once/And when you're dead you're done/So don't sit there mumblin' and talkin' trash/If you wanna have a ball you gotta go out and spend some cash. The rejection of delayed gratification is a central theme to the song, and it is repeated in the second to last verse, where Jordan sings: "Hey tell everybody Mr. Jordan's in town/I got a dollar and a quarter just rarin' to clown/But nobody play me cheap/I got fifty cents more that I'm gonna keep/So let the good times roll." The bravado of Jordan's performances and lyrics, where he announces that he's come to town to spend money, have a good time, and make sure everyone else at the club also has a good time, reflects the rejection of delayed gratification and the Protestant work ethic, norms which prevailed among middle-class white society.

Such bravado in rhythm and blues music mirrored the outrageous audacity of bombastic workers who were able to abruptly part ways with employers deemed unacceptable or unfair. In many cases, a better job was literally around the corner. Jordan's emphasis on spending lots of money signified that workers were not embracing the bourgeois norm of delayed gratification and sacrifice. By and large, American workers understood that the war was used as an excuse by the power elite to squeeze excessive amounts of surplus value from their labor, while attempting to impose false austerity on the working class. Rank-and-file workers who led the wildcat strikes saw through the ideology of delayed gratification and sacrifice as still more attempts by the bourgeoisie to impose austerity on workers, while capitalists consumed most of the wealth produced by economic growth. By the 1950s, the cultural staying power of the working-class rejection of delayed gratification and the emphasis on spending money can be seen in records like Little Richard's 1956 hit, "Rip It Up," where Richard exclaims, "Saturday night and I just got paid/I'm a fool about my money, don't try and save!" "Rip it Up" was one of the most important compositions of its era, as it was covered by the likes of Bill Haley, Buddy Holly, Elvis Presley, Wanda Jackson, Gene Vincent, and Pat Boone, demonstrating the widespread cultural resonance of the rejection of delayed gratification in popular culture.

Another key musician from the postwar era who had an important influence on the formation of what I refer to as working-class pretension in rock 'n' roll culture was T-Bone Walker from Texas.

T-Bone Walker was closer to the classic blues than the "shouting" rhythm and blues style, but he is a key figure in the history of rock 'n' roll because of his astonishing guitar work, which emphasized single notes through picking as opposed to the strumming style of rhythm guitar. Walker helped to establish the guitar solo as a key feature in rock 'n' roll music. He also developed unconventional performances that incorporated outrageous bodily contortions into his guitar solos. Years before Chuck Berry was doing his duck walk across the stage, and more than a decade before Jimi Hendrix was playing guitar with his teeth, T-Bone Walker was playing electric guitar behind his head, jumping up in the air with his guitar, landing on the ground in the splits. T-Bone was a close friend of Charlie Christian, the guitarist who played in the Benny Goodman band. Together with Christian, Walker demonstrated the enormous potential of the electric guitar. In the jazz idiom before Christian, guitar was seen as primarily a rhythm instrument, and in the traditional blues, guitar was largely understood as an acoustic instrument. When Les Paul developed the electric guitar, everything changed. After Charlie Christian's and T-Bone Walker's innovations, the guitar rivaled the saxophone as the preferred instrument for the skilled instrumental soloist in rhythm and blues music.

T-Bone Walker's biggest hit was "Call It Stormy Monday," recorded on Black and White Records in 1947 and perhaps the most important blues guitar record ever cut. It became a pop standard virtually overnight, and it has been covered and performed by countless bands since, including Count Basie, Muddy Waters, Isaac Hayes, Albert King, B.B. King, Eric Clapton, and the Allman Brothers, who recorded it for their famous live album that captured their signature performance at the Fillmore East. The virtuoso guitar playing in "Stormy Monday" redefined what was possible on guitar, profoundly influencing younger guitar geniuses like Chuck Berry and Jimi Hendrix.

Apart from the classic guitar licks played masterfully by Walker, the song is famous for its lyrics. The lyrical refrain of the song is about work, or rather the flight from work. The term *stormy* refers to the juxtaposition—via metaphor—of the paradise of the week-end to the bad weather endured during the workweek. Monday is signified as "stormy" because many workers begin the workweek with a hangover from the heavy drinking and partying that took place during the night, if not the entire weekend, before. Walker's record signifies a popular tradition from the nineteenth century when workers would take an extra day off work without the official recognition or permission of the employer. Beginning in the early decades of the nineteenth century, nearly a century before the labor movement achieved the two-day weekend, factory workers referred to Monday as "Saint" Monday, because they often stayed home or came in to work very late due to the fact that they were recovering from a hangover. In short, "Saint" Monday, became an unofficial holiday of sorts. Before the Fair Labor Standards Act of 1938, which instituted the forty-hour workweek, there was no weekend as we now know it, but thanks to nearly a century of fighting for shorter hours of work, the labor movement finally delivered another day for the weekend. Walker's famous tune signifies the history and tradition of "Saint Monday" in the following lyrics:

> They call it stormy Monday,
> But Tuesday's just as bad.
> Yes, they call it stormy Monday,
> But Tuesday's just as bad.
> Wednesday's worse, and Thursday's also sad.
> Yes, the eagle flies on Friday and Saturday I go out to play,
> Yes, the eagle flies on Friday, and Saturday I go out to play …
> They call it stormy Monday.

Although workers won an extra day off each week in the 1930s, it was still the case, as T-Bone Walker signifies, that Monday through Friday remained sheer misery. Friday night, however, the eagle flies! The anti-work/proleisure theme from "Stormy Monday" is the continuation of "stomping the blues," as described by Albert Murray. Walker's record helped keep alive the counterlogic of labor, which animates both rhythm and blues and rock 'n' roll. In fact, this central image in working-class culture was recorded a generation after T-Bone's record, on Fats Domino's smash hit record "Blue Monday," originally cut for Imperial Records in 1956. "Blue Monday" made it to number five on the "pop" charts and number one on the rhythm and blues charts. The lyrical content of the song is virtually the same in "Blue Monday" as it is in "Stormy Monday." In "Blue Monday," Fats Domino declares how much he despises "blue" Monday because he has to "go to work and slave all day." In the middle of the week Domino complains that he is "so tired" that he has "no time to play." And as if to tip his hat to T-Bone Walker, he sings, "Sunday mornin' I'm feeling bad, but it's worth it for the time I've had," and "I've got to get my rest, 'cause Monday is a mess."

Louis Jordan's music made its way into the 1950s generation through the key figure of Chuck Berry.

Berry's music also continued the working-class tradition of singing about the drudgery of work and the profound hollowness of the Protestant work ethic for working-class people. In "Too Much Monkey Business," recorded on Chess Records in 1957, Berry sings about the meaninglessness of low-paying, degrading jobs and other aspects of working-class life that get in the way of the important things, like driving fast cars, listening to rock 'n' roll, dressing up in the sharpest threads, romancing your lover, and pursuing more leisure time in general. The practices inscribed within the major institutions in our society, including work, school, and marriage, are interpreted by Berry as "monkey business" for these reasons. "Monkey business" is something to escape. Chuck Berry's genius was to articulate these experiences of alienation in a way that appealed to large numbers of working people, making him a huge crossover success, much like Louis Jordan a generation earlier. The first lines of "Too Much Monkey Business" proclaim: "Runnin' to-and-fro hard workin' at the mill/Never fail in the mail, yeah, come a rotten bill!/Too much monkey business, too much monkey business for me to be involved in."

At the end of the song Berry sings: "Workin' fill' station—too many tasks/Wipe the windows, check the tires, check the oil dollar gas!/Don't want your botheration, get away leave me!/Too much monkey business for me.

The lyrical content of "Monkey Business" was mirrored, to some extent, a year later in Eddie Cochran's 1958 hit record, "Summertime Blues," recorded on the Liberty label. "Summertime Blues" has had a lasting influence. It was famously covered by the Who in the late 1960s, the Stray Cats in the 1980s, as well as by the country music recording star Alan Jackson in 1994. The first few lines of "Summertime Blues" read: "I'm gonna raise a fuss, I'm gonna raise a holler/About a workin' all summer just to try and earn a dollar/Every time I call my baby, and try and get a date/My boss says, 'No dice son, you gotta work late." Cochran's song expresses what most working-class youth experience. Summertime is supposed to be about relaxation and pleasure, but the need to work makes summertime "blue." Eddie Cochran's career was not as extensive or successful as that of Chuck Berry's (due to his death in a car crash at age twenty-one), but Cochran's popularity in 1958 did rival that of the more popular recording stars of the 1950s.

In the hands of a maestro like Chuck Berry or Eddie Cochran, the electric guitar was a key development in rock 'n' roll and a crucial expression of working-class pretension, because it is impossible to ignore its sound, which is often too noisy for those who don't have an ear for rock 'n' roll. Indeed, the electric guitar is the perfect instrument for expressing cultural resistance, primarily because it's loud, but also because it can be distorted to create a gritty noise that nicely expresses a worker's desire to fight back against the boss, in the sense expressed by Willie Dixon, who argued that blues music is partly about "getting back at the boss."

CHAPTER 11

Labor's Time
Shorter Hours, the UAW,
and the Struggle for American Unionism

Jonathan Cutler

Introduction

On Wednesday, January 8, 1964, only seven weeks after the assassination of John F. Kennedy, Lyndon Johnson stood before a joint session of Congress to deliver his first State of the Union Message since being installed as president. The next morning, a *New York Times* headline dutifully publicized the now-famous White House call for an "unconditional war on poverty in America." Little noticed by the *Times*, but prominently featured in a *Wall Street Journal* head-line, was a second announcement: "Johnson … Spurns a 35-Hour Work-Week." "I believe the enactment of a 35-hour week," said the President, "would sharply increase costs, would invite inflation, would impair our ability to compete, and merely share instead of creating employment."[1]

The president's opposition to the shorter workweek did not come entirely as a surprise. Both the idea of a War on Poverty and the opposition to the shorter workweek were inherited from the Kennedy administration. Indeed, Kennedy, in his 1963 State of the Union address, had declared his opposition to the movement for a shorter workweek. Kennedy stated that he looked forward to "an end to the growing pressures for such restrictive measures as the 35-hour week, which alone could increase hourly labor costs by as much as 14 percent, start a new wage-price spiral of inflation, and undercut our efforts to compete with other nations."[2]

Today, there is almost no memory of shorter hours as a road not taken on the way to Johnson's Great Society. What ever happened to the idea of a shorter workweek? What ever happened to the future in which progress was to be marked by growing abundance and diminished work? What ever happened to organized labor's perennial demand for shorter hours and higher wages?

The juxtaposition of Kennedy and Johnson's repudiation of shorter hours and the simultaneous initiation of a War on Poverty illuminates some of the ways in which social policy discourses in the United States were transformed during these years.

Original publication details: Jonathan Cutler, *Labor's Time*, pp. 1–21. Temple University Press, 2004.

Nobody today remembers what the War on Poverty *was not*; but in the early 1960s Kennedy and Johnson were crystal clear that it was not a shorter workweek. At the start of the Great Society debates, the War on Poverty was a state-sponsored alternative to a labor-led shorter hours initiative. Four decades later, the War on Poverty has many critics and defenders, but no major competitors—least of all the forgotten shorter hours movement. Scholars have argued for forty years about the benefits and liabilities of particular Kennedy and Johnson administration social policy initiatives, but the most enduring influence of the War on Poverty may well be the framing of political discourse itself, including the almost complete displacement of the idea of a shorter workweek as a mechanism for mitigating unemployment and increasing wages.

Comparison of the forgotten discourse of shorter hours with the inherited politics of the War on Poverty also illuminates a surprising and relatively unexplored dimension in the interaction of race and labor in the postwar era. It is commonly asserted that the liberal leadership of the industrial union movement supported civil rights and the War on Poverty, even as these progressive efforts often were undermined by the racial bigotry of the old skilled trade unions. As Jill Quadagno has explained, "the War on Poverty—especially Federal initiatives to pressure craft unions to open apprenticeship programs to minorities—inflamed a long-running conflict between these two Democratic party constituents—trade unionists and African Americans—triggered a backlash among resentful skilled tradesmen ... and [created] a constituency of Reagan Democrats in the 1980s."[3] According to this scenario, the backlash was represented by the leader of the skilled trades unionists, George Meany, "a former plumber who envisioned a narrow role for trade unionism and who ruled the AFL-CIO with an iron fist." By contrast, United Automobile Workers (UAW) president, Walter Reuther, was represented as the progressive alternative to Meany, an advocate for a more expansive vision of organized labor, a union official who ruled his organization with a velvet glove, and "a man deeply committed to civil rights and to organizing the unorganized."[4]

But this common refrain about Reuther and Meany, and about the politics of labor and race, is rendered suspect by the lost history of the shorter hours struggles of the 1950s and 1960s. Walter Reuther *opposed* the movement for a shorter workweek. He did not simply neglect the movement. As president of the UAW, Reuther used every weapon at his disposal to subvert the movement for a shorter workweek throughout the 1950s and early 1960s.[5] When Kennedy and Johnson were compelled to address "growing pressures" for shorter hours during the early 1960s, the source of that pressure came, not from Walter Reuther, but from George Meany and the skilled trades unions of the old American Federation of Labor. It was Meany, with his narrow vision of trade unionism, not Reuther and his allegedly expansive commitments to the unorganized and the unemployed, who led the agitation for a 30-hour workweek in response to the unemployment of the early 1960s.[6] The Kennedy administration—including the president himself–was repeatedly forced to reiterate his opposition to shorter hours in response to Meany's public agitation.[7]

Meany was neither a labor militant nor a vanguard force for interracial solidarity and Quadagno is probably right to assume that Meany's own inclinations were probably hostile toward the demands of black and Hispanic workers. But Meany was not immune to grassroots pressure politics from an emboldened civil rights movement. In the late 1950s and early 1960s, civil rights activists inside and outside the labor movement began to press Meany regarding the growing crisis of black and Hispanic unemployment.[8]

The effectiveness of minority grassroots pressure on Meany was enhanced by conflict among a divided union leadership.[9] Meany would have been largely insulated from grassroots pressures inside and outside the labor federation if not for the fact of an ongoing leadership feud between Meany and Walter Reuther. Meany's position as AFL-CIO president was not secure so long as Walter Reuther repeatedly flirted with the idea of challenging Meany's leadership of the merged labor federations. Furthermore, analysts predicted that any contest could be close, with both sides potentially dependent on the support of African-American trade unionists in a battle for dominance.[10] Meany's shorter hours agitation was completely opportunistic and was carefully aimed to exploit Reuther's major vulnerability as a labor leader: his repudiation of the classic demand for shorter hours. Not surprisingly, Meany's own shorter-hours activism seemed almost perfectly timed, not only to the ebb and flow of the labor market, but also to the periodic flare-ups in his ongoing battle with Reuther.[11]

Within organized labor, the discourse of shorter hours was traditionally used to defuse the social panic that accompanied frantic competition for work during periods of rising unemployment. It was a market strategy that aimed to meet diminished demand for labor with diminished supply. Most other populist gestures toward labor solidarity aimed to mitigate job competition by conjuring imagined communities (of men, of whites, of Americans) for the protection of privileged labor market positions, chiefly through immigration restrictions and race and gender-based limitations on access to skilled trade apprenticeships.[12] But the core logic of these labor supply strategies necessarily generated ferocious market exclusions (of women, of people of color, of "foreigners").[13] By contrast, the logic of shorter hours was unique in its capacity to articulate a vision of diminished job competition on the basis of less work for all rather than protected work for the anointed.[14]

Historically, the movement for shorter hours within the old AFL was by no means sufficient for transcending racist restrictions on union eligibility. Indeed, the historic campaigns for a 10-hour day and an 8-hour day were largely undertaken in order to maintain intra-union solidarity *within* a context of racist exclusion, rather than as part of an effort toward interracial solidarity within the working class.[15] However, when emboldened civil rights activists rebelled against these racial restrictions in the 1960s, vulnerable trade union leaders like Meany embraced the shorter hours demand as a plausible way to respond to the rising call for racial justice within and beyond the house of labor.

Meany was not the only skilled trade unionist to respond to the demands of civil rights groups with appeals to the unifying power of the shorter hours movement. Indeed, beginning in the late 1950s, Harry Van Arsdale, president of Local 3 of the International Brotherhood of Electrical Workers in New York City and head of the Central Trades and Labor Council in the City, responded to pressure from local civil rights activists by arguing for a shorter workweek "as the answer to growing unemployment in the city … particularly among Negroes and Puerto Ricans."[16] In 1962, Local 3 made national headlines when it initiated an unprecedented and ultimately successful strike for a 25-hour workweek. Prodded by civil rights groups and local politicians, the Local agreed to include "a substantial number of Negroes and Puerto Ricans among its apprentices. In the end, more than 200 were admitted."[17] President Kennedy responded to the national headlines by announcing that he was opposed to Local 3's drive for shorter hours.[18]

There was also a popular movement for 30 hours' work at 40 hours' pay in Walter Reuther's UAW during the 1950s and early 1960s. It was based in the largest UAW local, the massive Ford Local 600, with over 15,000 African-American members of a total 1950s membership of approximately 60,000. The 30–40 movement at Local 600 attracted a broad-based movement of African-American militants, along with Irish, Italian, and Polish skilled tradesmen, and a broad array of semi-skilled mass-production workers, all of whom supported the demand as a progressive response to the challenge of automation and the threat of technological unemployment. The fight for shorter hours within the UAW, however, faced the determined opposition not only of the White House and the automobile industry, but also the leadership of the union itself.

It was Reuther, as much as Meany, who insisted on a narrow, even fatalistic conception of the role of collective bargaining, especially in the battle against unemployment. As Nelson Lichtenstein has suggested, Reuther "lectured" his rebellious membership about the limits of collective bargaining. "You can't solve the problems of unemployment at the bargaining table," he said.[19] And it was Reuther, as much as Meany, who sought to rule with an iron fist, even if it meant using repressive tactics to undermine an interracial movement of local union dissidents who championed a shorter workweek throughout the 1950s and early 1960s.[20]

Reuther's suppression of the shorter hours demand during the 1950s and early 1960s had significant consequences for the political discourses of race and labor in the postwar era. As David Roediger has suggested, "Reduction of working hours [can become] ... an explosive demand because of its unique capacity to unify workers across the lines of craft, race, sex, skill, age, and ethnicity."[21] Roediger has also suggested that any framework for understanding the intersection of race and labor must move "beyond explanations based on the labor market" toward investigations of the interactions between cultural discourse and possessive investments in whiteness.[22]

To be sure, the historic shorter hours discourse demonstrated only a limited capacity to alter the investment climate for identity formation and its influence left untouched deep investments in whiteness, masculinity, and heterosexuality. Within the workplace, the movement for shorter hours has never substituted for militant mobilization against racist and sexist divisions of labor.

Nevertheless, there are important ways in which a comparative analysis of the contrast between the discourse of shorter hours and the War on Poverty can contribute to Roediger's demand for explanations that move beyond a simple labor market analysis to an examination of work, desire, and race.

The ultimate aim of the shorter hours movement, as John R. Commons suggested at the start of the twentieth century, was to disarm the "whip of unemployment," and in this regard its aims seemed to accord with the subsequently articulated goals of the War on Poverty. But unlike contemporary anti-poverty crusades, the strategic basis of the shorter hours movement rested on notions of "joint aggrandizement," rather than paternalistic discourses of moral obligation and pity.[23]

Michael Harrington's book *The Other America*, a central text in the construction of the anti-poverty discourse of the 1960s, took no notice of the shorter hours movement.[24] For Harrington, the Other America "cannot really speak for itself."[25] In place of joint aggrandizement, and what George Rawick called "working class self-activity," Harrington's discourse appealed directly to the paternalistic inclinations of his audience. "How long shall we ignore this underdeveloped nation in our midst? How long shall we look the other way while our fellow human beings suffer? How long?"[26] Harrington's anti-poverty discourse depends, ultimately, on an exaggerated distinction between the obligated subject and its passive object. "The poor," Harrington concluded, "are not like everyone else."[27]

One might suggest that Harrington's harangue was an assault on privilege, especially the privileges of whiteness. And, indeed, those who felt most threatened by such an assault took refuge in an illiberal backlash against racial change. As George Lipsitz suggests, this ongoing backlash is championed by "demagogic politicians [who] try to reassure white people that whatever else they lose, they will retain the possessive investment in whiteness."[28]

Harrington's discourse not only reinforced investments in whiteness among the illiberal opponents of his anti-poverty crusade, but also reinforced the possessive investment of whiteness among his most conscientious liberal supporters. As Rawick argued in reference to slavery, "The entire view of ... Victim and Object is related to the matter of guilt. Only those who feel themselves innately superior can feel such guilt about the conditions of others."[29] Harrington explicitly embraced the necessity of promoting a discourse of "shame" and insisted that "the fate of the poor hangs upon the decision of the better-off."[30] Lipsitz is correct when he concludes—against the grain of discourses like that of Harrington—that "liberal social welfare policies" cannot "solve the 'white problem' in the United States" insofar as they "reinforce the possessive investment in whiteness."[31]

Nowhere is this phenomenon more transparent than in the racial politics of work. At the heart of the shorter hours movement, asserted John Commons in 1906, is the allure of "more wages and less work."[32] Half a century later in 1962, the editorial page of the *Wall Street Journal* reached the same conclusion. "The drive for a shorter workweek may have the appearance of a 'more jobs' campaign, but what it comes down to is a plan to get more pay for less work."[33]

But what happens when the desire for less work is obstructed and repressed? Writing about the nineteenth century, Roediger called attention to the ways in which "whites could ... use Blacks as a counterpoint to come to terms with their own acceptance of steady and even regimented labor."[34] As white workers repressed the desire for less work and more wages, compensation could be found in the category of whiteness wherein the desire for less work was first disavowed, then pathologized, and finally projected onto Others. As Rawick explained, "The Englishman met the West African as a reformed sinner meets a comrade of his former debaucheries ... He must suppress even his knowledge that he had acted that way or even that he wanted to act that way. Prompted by his uneasiness at this great act of repression he cannot leave alone those who live as he once did or as he still unconsciously desires to live. He must devote himself to their conversion or repression."[35]

In the twentieth century, the War on Poverty reinforced the inclination to conversion among its liberal supporters and repression among its illiberal opponents, but in both cases, it drew upon and reinforced the nineteenth century valorization of whiteness and work, disavowing pleasure and play among whites; pathologizing it among blacks. The illiberal opponents of the welfare state lashed out at signs of laziness and pleasure. But the liberal defenders did not differ from the illiberal opponents in their disdain for laziness and pleasure. Instead, liberals went to great lengths either to deny that the Victims preferred pleasure to sacrifice and work (as when Harrington confided that "on the surface of Harlem life ... [you] will find faces that are often happy, but always, even at the moment of bursting joy, haunted"[36]) or to insist that those who do parade such preferences were ripe for conversion (as when Harrington lamented that the Other Americans "do not postpone satisfactions ... When pleasure is available, they tend to take it immediately," but conversion remained possible insofar as "their sickness is often a means of relating to a diseased environment"[37]).

Scholars seeking to explain the backlash against the War on Poverty often assume that a coalition of racially sensitive labor elites, liberal politicians, and African-American civil rights activists was undermined by the intractable racism of the entire skilled trade union movement and the white rank and file of the industrial union movement. Kennedy, Johnson, and Walter Reuther come up smelling like roses, while the remainder of the labor movement is dismissed as having been always already destined for Reagan country.

Tom Sugrue argues that the "UAW's record on race relations was mixed ... On the national level, the UAW was on the cutting edge of civil rights activism throughout the 1940s, 1950s, and early 1960s ... On the other hand ... white rank-and-file union members, often abetted by local leaders, worked to protect the color line in many plants. [Because of the] organizational structure of the UAW—especially its localism ... UAW International officials were reluctant to interfere with the internal affairs of union locals."[38] Reuther, according to this view, was a great progressive whose one flaw was that he was either unable or unwilling to impose his progressive will on autonomous union locals.

If Sugrue emphasizes the illiberal culture of racism among white rank-and-file workers, scholars like Judith Stein blame the decline of liberalism on the "narcissism" of civil rights activists who diverted attention from the underlying class interests of all workers.[39] Sugrue has rightly accused Stein of minimizing the grievances of African Americans in an effort to subordinate race politics to an abstract politics of class. Yet, for all the important differences between Sugrue's culturally sensitive assessment of the racism of Detroit's white rank and file and Stein's scandalous attempt to minimize the grievances of African-American workers, Stein and Sugrue—like Quadagno—exonerate Reuther. Stein makes the exoneration explicit, concluding that it was "not Reuther's policies, that doomed labor and liberalism."[40]

Sugrue and Quadagno blame the breakup of progressive politics on the racism of the white rank and file, and Stein pins the blame on the narcissism of civil rights activists, but all three pin their hopes on Walter Reuther. These hopes, however, are entirely misplaced. Although it would certainly be a mistake to underestimate the racism of the white rank and file, Reuther's contribution to the politics of postwar labor and race relations can only be celebrated if one is either unaware of his opposition to the movement for a shorter workweek, or unmoved by the eclipse of a progressive alternative to the path of intense racial polarization that ultimately undermined both the labor and civil rights movements.

Reuther's opposition to the shorter workweek, although perhaps surprising to some, was part of the public record during his tenure as president of the UAW and the CIO, and his repudiation of the demand has been noted, if only in passing, by several scholars, including Reuther's recent biographer, Nelson Lichtenstein.[41] Furthermore, rejection of the shorter hours movement was far from incidental or arbitrary. Rather, it marked a key point of departure for Reuther's more general break with the syndicalist tradition in the American labor movement and the development of his own brand of union corporatism.

According to the syndicalist theories of figures like John Commons, "A trade union is simply a combination to get a larger return."[42] This "pure and simple" notion of a labor union maintained that any authentic labor movement must abandon "the field of production" and focused exclusively on the terms and conditions of the sale of labor-power to employers. By contrast, corporatist unionists seek a far more expansive role for labor, including direct participation in the management of production.

In the classic terms of organized labor, a syndic—a delegate or agent in a business exchange—represents organized combinations of workers in the sale of labor-power.

As George McNeill explained in 1887, the shorter hours movement constituted a centerpiece of syndicalist labor philosophy. According to McNeill, workers "desire to sell the smallest portion of their time for the largest possible price. They are merchants of their time. They feel that, if they flood the market—that is, sell more hours of labor than the market requires—stagnation will follow."[43] The entire bargaining process was to be mediated through market exchange and shop-floor bargaining with the simple aim of winning more wages, less work, and better working conditions.[44]

The leading figures of American corporatism explicitly repudiated the syndicalist worldview, especially the idea that labor should abandon the field of production.[45] Jacob Benjamin Salutsky (J.B.S.) Hardman, the most articulate defender of American corporatism and a great admirer of Walter Reuther, never missed an opportunity to heap scorn on the syndicalist traditions of the American labor movement. In 1928, Hardman protested against the triumph of syndicalism.

> The chieftains of labor were bargainers, shrewd politicians, and, save for rare exceptions, they were totally unrelated to the fundamental processes and problems of industry. The opportunity … lay in a direction more significant than collective bargaining. Labor could, if it would, assume responsibilities for production and ascend to active participation in the control of industry. But leaders of labor stuck to what they thought was their God-ordained job: they would sell labor for as good a price as they could command, but exercise control of industry they would not. They brushed aside the power that lay in their reach. They lacked the will to power.[46]

Commons was, in turn, as critical of Hardman's perspective as Hardman was of Commons. Commons complained that if a union underwent "the changes necessary in the character" required for it to "direct its energies to the production of wealth," it would "cease to be a trade union."[47] Commons was not simply fearful that corporatist experiments might not work. In fact, he was more concerned with the consequences for workers, if corporatist labor leaders *succeeded* in establishing their agenda within organized labor. Any union that concerned itself with "the risks and responsibilities of production … raises up [a leadership] element interested in profits rather than wages … and, sooner or later, [it] goes over to the … employers."[48]

Although the anti-corporatist discourse of syndicalism has often been understood to imply business-friendly labor relations, while the audacious and even revolutionary rhetoric of corporatist discourse seems to point in the direction of labor militancy, these caricatures tend to obscure some of the underlying tendencies of the two labor philosophies. The syndicalists, in fact, were convinced that there was a constitutive antagonism at the core of the relations between the buyers and sellers of labor-power. Commons, for example, spoke of "the irrepressible conflict of capital and labor … The methods of unions cannot be understood except in terms of conflict." [49]

The defenders of corporatism were also keenly aware of these conflicts between labor and capital, but they argued that such employment relations were *needlessly* antagonistic. Clinton Golden and Harold Ruttenberg, two great defenders of corporatist labor relations, described the "almost universal desire of workers to tell the boss 'to go to hell,'" a desire accompanied in practice by workers who possess "the freedom to quit when the boss insulted or humiliated them, or when the work was not to their liking." But Golden and Ruttenberg interpreted this proto-syndicalist rebellion not as "a revolt against the authority of management as such, but against its arbitrary use and abuses."[50]

On the other hand, when management had "the vision and courage to share … responsibility with its workers through their unions, then, and only then, will full production
be achieved."[51]

For corporatists, the syndicalist retreat from responsibility for production was an
understandable but avoidable response to the arbitrary and capricious misuse and abuse
of managerial authority. Enlightened or sophisticated management should meet little or
no resistance from labor once responsibility is shared on a cooperative basis. Corporatists
embraced "a prophetic vision" of industrial relations founded upon "workers' participation in responsibility for the conduct of business."[52] As C. Wright Mills explained,
"Ideally, if all management personnel did not show up for work, the plant could be
effectively operated by the workers and their unions."[53]

In many respects the corporatist vision of full production on the basis of shared
responsibility and industrial democracy is consistent with both middle-class discourses
of anti-market republicanism and socialist visions of worker control. Like the independent, self-employed, yeoman farmer, the industrial worker is called upon to stand apart
from the haggling of the market and participate fully in the self-management of society.
As Mills suggested, "Classic socialism shares its master purpose with classic democracy.
The difference between Thomas Jefferson and Karl Marx is a half century of technological change."[54]

The syndicalist discourses of George McNeill and John R. Commons, however, stand
in stark contrast to these corporatist schemes that aim to transcend the market in the
name of an expansive industrial democracy. McNeill's merchants of time aimed to find
leverage within the market; Hardman and the corporatists envisioned an industrial
democracy able to transcend the market. The shorter hours movement, as both sides
understood, was firmly rooted in the syndicalist tradition of the American labor
movement.[55]

Corporatist ideology tends to assume an underlying social harmony, but should such
harmony fail to appear on cue, the establishment of corporatist labor relations is secured
by structural transformations that establish new mechanisms of authority in the relations
between unions and members.[56] As Golden and Ruttenberg explain, "Police powers or
disciplinary powers are vested in the union in direct proportion with the amount of
responsibilities it assumes … To fulfill these responsibilities the union must have sufficient authority to discipline those workers who, for example, may stop work in violation
of the contract."[57] Similarly, corporatist labor relations also rely on a transformed business and legal environment in which labor unions are provided with the institutional
security that makes union-employer collaboration possible.[58]

The eclipse of the shorter hours movement within the American labor movement was
one of the central manifestations of the triumph of corporatist labor relations in the
United States. Within the UAW, in particular, the victory of the Reuther administration
over the syndicalist movement for a shorter workweek was achieved primarily through
the increasingly pronounced disciplinary powers that were vested in the union as a result
of the historic, structural transformation of organized labor.

For more than two decades, UAW president Walter Reuther managed to resist popular
pressure to put the syndicalist demand for a shorter workweek at the top of the postwar
union bargaining agenda. A biographer might hope to gain some sympathetic insight
into the psychic life of Walter Reuther in order to explain the pattern of his leadership
activity, but for a sociohistorical analysis of the UAW and the shorter hours movement,
the question of Reuther's motivation recedes in importance relative to the *structural* and

historical factors that allowed Reuther to take the positions that he did without losing his leadership position within his own union.[59] As David Brody once suggested, it is not enough for labor history to simply publicize or criticize the intentions of corporatist labor leaders like Reuther. "Who would deny what [the leadership of the CIO] made abundantly clear in the public record? But why did they succeed?"[60]

Within the UAW, the fate of the shorter hours movement functions as a kind of proxy for the corporatist transformation of the union: the more vulnerable the leadership, the more voluble the syndicalist discourse of shorter hours; the more secure the leadership, the less effective the shorter hours agitation. How did Walter Reuther accumulate sufficient institutional power to make *his* corporatist ideology count despite the enthusiastic syndicalism of the union rank and file?

Nothing illustrates the urgency of a structural, rather than a motivational, analysis of Reuther's postwar opposition to the shorter hours movement than the fact that he had once been a leading promoter of the shorter hours demand. In 1938, when Reuther was himself an opponent of the incumbent UAW administration, he served as the chief spokesperson for a dissident insurgent caucus in the UAW and led a campaign for a 32-hour workweek in the automobile industry.[61] One might conclude, from this fact, that the young and militant Reuther understood the importance of the syndicalist shorter hours demand, but that he subsequently lost his nerve and knowingly betrayed the movement. One might just as easily conclude, however, that as a young Socialist, Reuther was deeply committed to corporatist visions of work and self-discipline and that even in the early years, he never actually believed in shorter hours or shared the syndicalism of the rank and file. But as an anti-incumbent insurgent in the UAW of the 1930s, even a would-be corporatist like Reuther was compelled to give lip service to syndicalist schemes in order to win the support of the membership. Only later, when Reuther was the leader of the incumbent administration and had established his authority within the union, could he successfully impose his own corporatist vision on the life of the union. How, then, did he succeed? What changed, structurally and historically, between 1938 and 1958 that allowed Reuther to reverse his public position on the question of shorter hours? In what sense might Reuther have been more insulated from rank-and-file pressures in the late 1950s and early 1960s than he had been in the 1930s?

In some cases, the union bureaucracy became insulated from the rank and file through changes to its own organizational structure. In one such instance, a change in membership rights helped to relieve pressure for a shorter workweek within the UAW. In October 1938, when Walter Reuther proposed that the International Executive Board of the UAW seek a 32-hour workweek throughout the automobile industry, a *Wall Street Journal* article announced, "32-Hour Week Idea May Become Troublesome Issue."[62] In seeking to understand the base of support for the shorter hours movement, the *Journal* pointed to the question of union membership rights and the pressure to reconcile the demands of the employed and the unemployed members. "The actual voting membership of many locals (those members who regularly attend meetings) are in the majority still unemployed. It is the pressure of these," the *Journal* explained, "which is causing presidents of locals to back the 'spread-the-work' plan. At the same time … local leaders are now trying to convince the working membership that 40 hours pay for 32 hours of work will be obtained for them if they agree to the plan."[63] *Ward's Automotive Reports*, an industry newsletter, suggested that "the persistent 32-hour week agitation for a six-hour, five-day week … would undoubtedly be accompanied by a demand for wage raises proportionate to the decreases in working hours."[64]

As a union that was, for the most part, established and led by skilled trade unionists, the UAW allowed members to retain membership rights during periods of unemployment.[65] As one early student of the UAW noted, "The strength of the unemployed in controlling union decisions may be important in the determination of policy … [In] the UAW-CIO [a person who has lost a job] can continue indefinitely as a member in good standing … As a result of this general situation, policies of the UAW-CIO with reference to such questions as seniority and work-sharing will, as time goes on, be influenced more and more by the unemployed members, unless the constitution is changed."[66]

Reuther was already thinking along these same lines. He suggested that, in light of the massive number of unemployed in the auto industry, the union "should be careful not to bring in a large section of these people into the union. If they do, they will be creating a very difficult position for the union because … we can't make more jobs and we should be careful not to organize all of these people in the hope of getting them back in the plant."[67] With little fanfare, the convention adopted a constitutional provision that a union member "must, at the time of application, be an actual worker in and around the plant."[68]

The structure of union membership also influenced the fate of the shorter hours movement in more immediate ways at Ford Local 600, which provided the primary institutional base for shorter hours agitation throughout the 1950s. During the height of World War II, the Ford Local 600 membership swelled to include more than 80,000 Ford employees. After the war, Ford embarked on a massive initiative to reduce its dependence on the militant and centralized workforce at the Rouge through a combination of automation (Ford engineers coined the phrase in the early 1950s) and plant relocation (called "decentralization" at the time). By the end of the 1950s, Local 600 was a mere shadow of its former self. Those older members who managed to hang on to their jobs were either retired or near retirement and they ultimately outnumbered the actively employed element of the membership. Among retirees, the attention shifted from shorter hours to early retirement. Local union officers discovered that they could ignore the shorter hour demands of actively employed workers with impunity so long as they carried the vote of the retirees.

Some of the most consequential changes during these years related to larger transformations within organized labor and within the basic framework of industrial relations in the United States. For example, Reuther's rise to power within the UAW was accompanied by the establishment of the UAW as the legally recognized, sole representative of the autoworkers. In the context of the rivalry between the AFL and the CIO in the late 1930s and early 1940s, however, the authority of the UAW-CIO was directly challenged by the UAW-AFL, a breakaway, rival auto union. It was in the context of this battle that Reuther and his allies had initiated the drive for a shorter workweek.

In January 1940, amidst the union rivalry, *Ward's Automotive Reports* announced with considerable alarm that the industry's worst fears had recently been confirmed "in the announcements from the two UAW camps" regarding "demands for contract revision" in the spring of 1940. "Outstanding in the platforms are 30-hour work-weeks at present 40-hour pay, paid vacations, higher pay levels and others." *Ward's* was quite explicit about the connection between the rival unionism and the demands for less work and more pay. Union competition for the loyalty of the workers "resembles any other election, in which the candidates promise whatever they believe will bring votes their way … The difficulty in this development is that … the men may seek delivery on the promises made them. Should this ensue, trouble will again be visited on the labor front."[69] Any prolonged rivalry might force union leaders to be as militant in delivering on contract demands as they had been in formulating those demands. *Ward's* reported, "The general hope is that one side or the other acquires complete dominance and thereby is enabled to exercise control over the men."[70]

If the UAW-CIO ultimately managed to acquire such dominance—and exercise control over the membership—it did so in the context of a changing legal environment for labor relations. In 1940, the "exclusive representation" provision of the National Labor Relations Act of 1935 was used by the UAW-CIO and the automobile industry to terminate the rivalry between the UAW-AFL and the UAW-CIO.[71] *Ward's* reported that National Labor Relations Board (NLRB) elections might contain a "seed of tranquility in them… insofar as they may go to end the interunion factionalism."[72] Immediately after the UAW-CIO was certified as the exclusive representative at General Motors (GM), *Ward's* confidently predicted, "At this writing it does not appear that disagreements which will develop in the new contract over such issues as larger pay, shorter hours, etc. will eventuate in strike action … the best opinion in both labor and management circles is that a strike, at least one of large dimensions, is improbable now."[73]

On May Day, a holiday historically associated with labor's fight for shorter hours, *Automotive Industries* reported "the union's decisive victory" in the NLRB election, along with a statement by Walter Reuther, then director of the GM department of the UAW-CIO, that the demand for "a 30-hour week with 40-hour pay" would not be pursued in the short term, although it remained a "long range goal of the union." It was the explicit aim of the newly certified CIO union, announced Reuther, to negotiate "in an orderly and constructive spirit."[74] Reuther, already in retreat, was ready to test the limits of his newfound insulation from the challenges of rivals.

The UAW-CIO was, for the most part, unchallenged in its dominance of auto industry unionism after its decisive triumph over the UAW-AFL. The 1950s witnessed a considerable reduction in the amount of union rivalry and raiding, aided not only by the altered legal environment, but also by the 1953 no-raiding pact between the AFL and the CIO, and the 1955 merger of the two federations. The *Wall Street Journal* took note of the merger process and affirmed, in a sub-headline, that the truce "Could Help Businessmen, Too."[75]

The National Labor Relations Board continued to protect the peace pact between the auto industry and the UAW-CIO from those rival union challenges that did arise. The NLRB adopted a so-called contract-bar rule that barred, during the life of a contract, petitions for elections that challenged incumbent unions. During the early 1950s, GM joined with the UAW-CIO to fight off one of the most significant remaining rival challenges to the union. The company and the union contended that their pioneering five-year contract—the famous 1950 "Treaty of Detroit"—should serve as "a bar to the requested election" of a rival union.[76] Mindful of the "salutary and stabilizing effect" of the relationship between GM and the UAW-CIO, the NLRB decided that "the time has arrived when stability of labor relations can better be served … by holding as a bar collective-bargaining agreements even for 5 years' duration" and dismissed the petition for a challenge election.[77] As Christopher Tomlins has argued, the "Board … succeeded in turning contract-bar into a major tool for securing incumbent unions."[78]

Although the institutional security of incumbent unions was certainly enhanced as a result of NLRB limitations on challenges from rival unions, these measures did not completely extinguish all rank-and-file leverage *within* unions. In some cases, however, the incumbent union bureaucrats could depend on employers for institutional security. Confronted with various forms of "dues" protests and individualized defections, for example, union leaders and employers often united in support of responsible unionism.

As Reuther insisted, "if General Motors wants stable labor relations, if they want us to live up to all these responsibilities that they talk about, I think General Motors had better make up its mind that they can get this type of labor relations only by giving our Union ... the type of recognition that makes it possible to carry out that responsibility. We cannot accept responsibility without authority, and you cannot have authority unless you have these other things."[79] GM did make up its mind and provided Reuther with the tools he would need to reinforce his authority.

Notes

1   "Johnson State of the Union Provides Budget of $97.9 Billion, War on Poverty, Atomic Cutback," *New York Times*, January 9, 1964, p. 1; "State of the Union: Johnson Urges a 'War on Poverty,' but Only New Plan Is Overtime Pay Study; Spurns a 35-Hour Work Week," *Wall Street Journal*, January 9, 1964, p. 3.

2   "Text of President Kennedy's Message to Congress on the State of the Union," *New York Times*, January 15, 1963, p. 4.

3   Jill Quadagno, *The Color of Welfare* (New York: Oxford University Press, 1994), pp. 61–62.

4   Ibid., 76. Prior to the merger of the AFL and the CIO, Meany had served as president of the craft-unionist AFL and Reuther as president of the industrial-unionist CIO. For an excellent review of the conflict between the AFL and the CIO, see Morris (1958).

5   Ronald Edsforth, "Why Automation Didn't Shorten the Work Week: The Politics of Work Time in the Automobile Industry," in *Autowork*, edited by R. Ahser and R. Edsforth (Albany: State University of New York Press, 1995).

6   The *Wall Street Journal* closely monitored Meany's campaign for a shorter workweek. See, for example, "AFL–CIO to Seek Law for 35-Hour Work Week," *Wall Street Journal*, February 24, 1959, p. 3; "Kennedy Opposes Work Week Cut To Trim Jobless," *Wall Street Journal*, March 16, 1961, p. 3; "AFL–CIO Urges Unions To Seek Higher Wages, Shorter Hours," *Wall Street Journal*, December 13, 1961, p. 7; "AFL–CIO Drive for Law to Cut Work Week Likely to Be Slated by Leaders Next Week," *Wall Street Journal*, August 7, 1962, p. 5; "AFL–CIO Opens Drive for 35-Hour Week, Calls Level of Unemployment 'Intolerable,'" *Wall Street Journal*, August 14, 1962, p. 4.

7   For Kennedy administration responses to Meany's shorter hours agitation, see "Kennedy Opposes Work Week Cut To Trim Jobless," *Wall Street Journal*, March 16, 1961, p. 3; "AFL–CIO Urges Unions To Seek Higher Wages, Shorter Hours," *Wall Street Journal*, December 13, 1961, p. 7; "35-Hour Slogan," *Wall Street Journal*, March 13, 1963, p. 18; "AFL–CIO President Describes Automation as 'Curse to Society,'" *Wall Street Journal*, November 15, 1963, p. 14.

8   The most prominent instance of civil rights pressure *within* organized labor was A. Philip Randolph's Negro American Labor Council. Randolph began mobilizing African-American trade union officials in the summer of 1959 in order to build pressure on Meany to respond to the crisis of African-American poverty and unemployment. Randolph himself was responding to a larger context of civil rights mobilization outside the labor movement. See Meier (1963) and Pfeffer (1990, 206–39).

    Walter Reuther and Randolph had been Socialist Party comrades in the 1930s and were life-long allies. Reuther was, for the most part, spared the kind of high-profile pressure tactics Randolph used to force Meany's hand. Reuther did, however, face challenges within his own union from an emboldened civil rights consciousness, especially at Ford Local 600. Reuther's battles to contain these challenges constitute one of the major concerns of this book.

9   Anne E. Kornhauser, *Craft Unionism and Racial Equality: The Failed Promise of Local 3 of the International Brotherhood of Electrical Workers in the Civil Rights Era* (M.A. Essay, Department of History, Columbia University, New York, 1952), pp. 444–446.

10 "Restless Reuther: He May Try to Replace Meany This Year, Make AFL-CIO More Militant," *Wall Street Journal*, June 21, 1961, p. 1.

11 For well-publicized rumors of a Reuther challenge to Meany, see "AFL-CIO to Seek Law for 35-Hour Work Week," *Wall Street Journal*, February 24, 1959, p. 3; "Restless Reuther: He May Try to Replace Meany This Year, Make AFL-CIO More Militant," *Wall Street Journal*, June 21, 1961, p. 1.; "Reuther May Bring into the Open His Feud with AFL-CIO Chiefs over Internal Splits," *Wall Street Journal*, November 15, 1961, p. 2; "Reuther, Meany Prepare to Clash," *Wall Street Journal*, December 6, 1961, p. 18; "Merged Labor's Ailments: AFL-CIO Convenes, Strained by Internal Battles, Declining Membership and Assaults on Racial Policies," *Wall Street Journal*, December 7, 1961, p. 30; "Meany, Reuther Clash over Appointment; Old AFL-CIO Enmity Likely to Erupt Again," *Wall Street Journal*, August 16, 1962, p. 2.

12 Michael J. Piore and Charles F. Sabel. *The Second Industrial Divide: Possibilities for Prosperity*. (New York: Basic Books, 1984). p.116.

13 In her account of exclusionary gender politics and the UAW, Ruth Milkman has emphasized the urgency of "strategies that can win broad support (from men as well as women) … especially in the present period of economic contraction and restructuring" (1987, 159). For gender politics and the hours question in unions, see Gabin (1991) and James (1976). For an excellent account of battles between nationalism and dissident demands for a shorter workweek within the UAW, see Frank (1999).

14 Jonathan Cutler and Stanley Aronowitz, After Work (New York: Routledge 1998).

15 W.E.B Du Bois, *Black Reconstruction in America* (New York: Atheneum 1935), p. 354–355. Noel Ignatiev, "The American Blindspot": Reconstruction According to Eric Foner and W.E.B. Du Bois," *Labour/Le Travail* 1993: 31: 243–251.

16 Kornhauser (1993, 22).

17 Kornhauser (1993, 1).

18 "Kennedy Opposes Work-Week Cut Below 40 Hours," *Wall Street Journal*, January 25, 1962, p. 3.

19 Nelson, Lichtenstein, *Walter Reuther: The Most Dangerous Man in Detroit* (Urbana: University of Illinois Press, 1995), pp. 530 fn43.

20 Andrew, Willam D. "Facitonalism and Anti-Communism: Ford Local 600," *Labor History* 1979:20:227–255; Lichtenstein (1995, 314–319).

21 David Roediger, "The Movement for a Shorter Working Day in the United States before 1866" (Ph.D. Dissertation, Department of History, Northwestern, Evanston, IL. 1980), p.5. David Roediger and Philip S. Foner, *Our Own Time: A History of American Labor and the Working Day* (London: Verso, 1989).

22 David Roediger, "Notes on Working Class Racism: A Tribute to George Rawick." *In With the Shell of the Old: Essays on Workers' Self Organization, A Salute to George Rawick*, edited by D. Fitz and D. Roediger (Chicago: Charles H. Kerr Publishing, 1990), p.13; George Lipsitz, *The Possessive Investment in Whiteness: How White People Profit from Identity Politics* (Philadelphia: Temple University Press, 1998).

23 John R. Commons, "Restrictions on Trade Unions." *Outlook* 1906; 84: 470–476.

24 Michael Harrington, *The Other America: Poverty in the United States* (New York: Macmillan Company, 1962), p. 167. For the influence of Harrington's book, and Dwight Macdonald's prominent 1963 review of the book in the *New Yorker*, see Irving Bernstein, *Guns or Butter: The Presidency of Lyndon Johnson* (New York: Oxford University Press, 1960), pp. 91–92.

25 Harrington (1962, 167).

26 Harrington (1962, 167); George Rawick, "Working Class Self-Activity," Radical America, 1969: 3: 23–31.

27 Harrington (1962, 135).

28 Lipsitz (1998, 218).

29 Rawick (1969, 102).

30 Harrington (1962, 156).

31 Lipsitz (1998, 22).

32 Commons (1906, 474).

33 "Mean Mr. Meany," *Wall Street Journal*, August 13, 1962, p. 8.

34 David Roediger, *The Wages of Whiteness: Race and the Making of the American Working Class*. (London: Verso, 1991), p. 180.

35   George Rawick, *From Sundown to Sunup: The Making of the Black Community* (Westport, CT: Greenwood Press, 1972), p. 132.
36   Harrington (1962, 72).
37   Harrington (1962, 126, 131).
38   Thomas J. Sugrue, *The Origins of the Urban Crisis: Race and Inequality in Postwar Detroit* (Princeton, NJ: Princeton University Press, 1996), pp. 100–101.
39   Judith Stein, Running Steel, *Running America: Race, Economic Policy, and the Decline of Liberalism* (Chapel Hill: University of North Carolina Press, 1998), p. 195.
40   Stein (1998, 387 fn12).
41   Lichtenstein (1995, 290, 364); Jack Stieber, *Governing the UAW* (New York: John Wiley & Sons, Inc., 1962), p. 45–53, 143–53. Art Preis, Labor's *Giant Step: The First 20 Years of the CIO: 1936–1955* (New York: Pathfinder, 1964), p. 441; Andrew (1979); Edsforth (1995); Sugrue (1996, 159).
42   Commons (1906, 471).
43   George McNeill, "The Hours of Labor." *The Labor Movement: The Problem of Today*, edited by G. McNeill (Boston, MA: A.M. Bridgman & Co., 1887), p. 470.
44   For a recent discussion of syndicalism, see Howard Kimmeldorf, *Battling for American Labor: Wobblies, Craft Workers, and the Making of the Union Movement* (Berkeley: University of California Press, 1999).
45   For a well-known discussion of "corporate ideology" among American labor leaders, see Ronald Radosh, "The Corporate Ideology of American Labor Leaders from Gompers to Hillman" *Studies on the Left*, 1966; 6: 66–88.
46   J.B.S. Hardman, "Postscripts to Ten Years of Labor Movement." In *American Labor Dynamics: in the Light of Post-War Developments*, edited by J.B.S. Hardman (New York: Harcourt Brace and Company, 1928), p. 8. An almost identical passage can be found in Wright C. Mills, *The New Men of Power: America's Labor Leaders*. (New York: Harcourt Brace and Company, 1948), p. 117. The connection is not arbitrary: Mills dedicated the 1948 book to Hardman, his mentor.
47   Commons (1906, 471).
48   Commons (1906, 472).
49   Commons (1906, 470, 472).
50   Clinton S. Golden and Harold J. Ruttenberg. *The Dynamics of Industrial Democracy* (New York: Harper & Brothers Publishers, 1942), p. 5.
51   Golden and Ruttenberg (1942, 230).
52   The "prophetic vision" quoted is that of Louis Brandeis. See Steven Fraser, *Labor Will Rule: Sidney Hillman and the Rise of American Labor* (Ithaca, NY: Cornell University Press, 1991), p. 150.
53   Mills (1948, 253).
54   Mills (1948, 252).
55   Nelson Lichtenstein correctly argues that Reuther's corporatism "put him at odds" with those in organized labor who "retained much of their pre-New Deal worldview, which saw competition for a limited set of jobs as a fundamental constraint faced by the labor movement … Like Kennedy, Reuther argued that 'there is enough work to do in America to keep us busy,' if only the economy were geared to full production … Reuther therefore rejected a reduction in statutory hours." (1995, 364).
56   Leo Panitch, "Recent Theorizations of Corporatism: Reflections on a Growth Industry." *British Journal of Sociology*, 1980: 31: 159–187.
57   Golden and Ruttenberg (1942, 212).
58   Ruth Berins Collier and David Collier. "Inducements versus Constraints: Disaggregating 'Corporatism'." *American Political Science Review*, 1979:73: 967–986.
59   Mark Leff, "The House that Reuther Built: Assessing 'Labor Liberalism.'" *Labor History*, 1966: 37: 347–352. As Mark Leff has noted, Nelson Lichtenstein's biography of Reuther reads, "as if Lichtenstein's narrative were immersed in Reuther's own consciousness … [The] considerations shaping Reuther's initiatives, alliances, ideological rationales, and compromises get top billing" (1996, 348).
60   David Brody, "Radical Labor History and Rank-and-File Militancy." *Labor History*, 1975: 16: 117–127.

61 "Auto Workers and 32-Hour Week," *Workers Age*, November 12, 1938, p. 6. *Workers Age* was the newspaper of Reuther's factional opponents, followers of Jay Lovestone, a one-time CP leader in the United States who became a leading anti-Communist figure of the Cold War. During the late 1930s, the so-called "Lovestoneites" were aligned with UAW president Homer Martin and were careful students of Reuther's dissident faction. They took note of Reuther's leadership of the shorter hours movement and reckoned with the potential threat the movement posed to the incumbent administration of Homer Martin. See Ted Morgan. *A Covert Life: Jay Lovestone, Communist, Anti-Communist, and Spymaster* (New York: Random House, 1999). Robert J. Alexander, *The Right Opposition: The Lovestoneites and the International Communist Opposition in the 1930s* (Westport, CT: Greenwood Press, 1981).

62 "32-Hour Week Idea May Become Troublesome Issue," *Wall Street Journal*, October 11, 1938, p. 1.

63 "32-Hour Week Idea May Become Troublesome Issue," *Wall Street Journal*, October 11, 1938, p. 1.

64 "The 32-Hour Week and Labor's Demands," *Ward's Automotive Reports*, December 17, 1938.

65 Steve Babson, *Building the Union: Skilled Workers and Anglo-Gaelic Immigrants in the Rise of the UAW* (New Brunswick, NJ: Rutgers University Press, 1991).

66 William Heston McPherson, *Labor Relations in the Automobile Industry* (Washington, DC: The Brookings Institution, 1940), p. 33.

67 Proceedings of the Special Convention of the International Union, United Automobile Workers of America, Cleveland, OH, 1939, p. 505.

68 Proceedings of the Special Convention of the International Union, United Automobile Workers of America, Cleveland, OH, 1939, p. 506.

69 "Labor and General Motors," *Ward's Automotive Reports*, January 27, 1940.

70 "Labor Situation Unchanged," *Ward's Automotive Reports*, February 18, 1939.

71 For the use of the exclusive representation principle in the case of GM and the UAW, see Boyle (1986). Although scholars of American labor have taken little notice of the corporatist dimension of the principle of exclusive representation, the notion is commonplace within the field of political science and the comparative analysis of corporatism. Collier and Collier, for example, argue that legal provision of a "monopoly of representation" to labor organizations can accelerate "the tendency for labor leadership to become an oligarchy less responsive to the needs of the workers" (1979).

    For labor and labor-law scholarship suggesting that rivalry might enhance the vitality and responsiveness of organized labor, see George Brooks, *The Sources of Vitality in the American Labor Movement* (Ithaca, NY: Cornell University Press, 1960). Steward J. Schwab, "Union Raids, Union Democracy, and the Market for Union Control." University of Illinois Law Review, 1992: 25: 367–416.

72 "The Labor Situation," *Ward's Automotive Reports*, August 12, 1939.

73 "CIO Wins Most General Motors Plants," *Ward's Automotive Reports*, April 20, 1940.

74 "Negotiations Between GM and UAW to Start Soon," *Automotive Industries*, May 1, 1940.

75 "Inter-Union Truce? AFL and CIO Chiefs Meet Today, Seek End to Membership Raids," *Wall Street Journal*, June 2, 1953, p. 1. For a positive "labor" interpretation of the merger written by one of its chief architects, see Goldberg (1956).

76 "NLRB Bans Union Representation Elections During 5-Year Contracts," *Wall Street Journal*, February 9, 1953, p. 2.

77 "General Motors Corporation Detroit Transmission Division," in *Decisions and Orders of the National Labor Relations Board* (1953), 1143.

78 Christopher Tomlins, *The State and the Unions: Labor Relations, Law and the Organized Labor Movement in America, 1880–1960* (Cambridge: Cambridge University Press, 1985), p. 233.

79 "Speech by Walter P. Reuther at GM Conference, February 9, 1941," in Box 18, Folder 17, Walter P. Reuther Collection, Wayne State University Labor Archives, Detroit, MI. See also Lichtenstein (1977).

CHAPTER 12

The Unmaking of the English Working Class
Deindustrialization, Reification, and Heavy Metal

Ryan M. Moore

In his monumental work, *The Making of the English Working Class*, E.P. Thompson documented the formation of class consciousness and culture among the English proletariat in response to industrialization in the years roughly between 1780 and 1850. Working-class culture was radicalized by the Jacobins of the French Revolution, Thomas Paine's *Rights of Man*, Robert Owen's vision of socialism, and Luddite destruction of machinery. But English workers' responses to industrialization were not always so political. The same time period saw the dramatic rise of millenarian movements that prophesized apocalypse with reference to the Book of Revelations, the most popular of which was Joanna Southcott's 'cult of the poor.' Although easy to dismiss as paranoid fantasy, Thompson's historical analysis treated those millenarian movements as an important 'sign of how men felt and hoped, loved and hated, and of how they preserved certain values in the very texture of their language.' These prophesies of impending doom took hold among people whose communities and traditions had been uprooted, only to find themselves de-skilled, impoverished, and threatened with sickness and starvation in England's overcrowded industrial cities. Thompson's social history demonstrated that class exploitation can have cultural consequences in which power and chaos are only indirectly confronted through fantasy and metaphor. Even the most bizarre and paranoid visions cannot be written off as mere 'false consciousness.'

Thompson wrote that the Industrial Revolution was 'a time when men's psychic world was filled with violent images from hell-fire and Revelation, and their real world was filled with poverty and oppression,' However, he might just as easily have been referring to the emergence of heavy metal in a time when deindustrialization was decimating many of these same factory towns in the late twentieth century. Some of the self-anointed mystics Thompson described bear a striking resemblance to the heavy

Original publication details: Ryan Moore, "The Unmaking of the English Working Class", from *Heavy Metal Music in Britain*, edited by Gerd Bayer, pp. 201–224. Ashgate, 2013. Reproduced with permission from Ashgate Publishing.

metal doomsayers who surfaced from declining industrial cities like Birmingham and Sheffield. Consider the Unitarian minister Ebenezer Aldred, a 'dreamy and wild' man with 'grey hair flowing down his shoulders' who 'lived in a kind of solitude'; or 'Zion' Ward, a crippled shoemaker who believed he was Christ but that he had once been Satan during his lifetime. Thompson reports that Ward's lectures calling for the overthrow of all clergy 'drew enormous audiences' of up to 2,000 during the summer of 1831, until he was eventually found guilty of blasphemy and imprisoned for two years. His story thus parallels many heavy metal bands whose profane performances achieved massive popularity along with persecution from the powers-that-be. Ward also gained a following among young people with a message of sexual liberation and Antinomianism (the belief that Christians are not obliged to obey moral law), preaching 'If you love one another, go together at any time without any law or ceremony.'

This chapter will draw a parallel between the ways that heavy metal reacted to the social crises of the 1970s and 1980s and the millennial cults and radical social movements during the Industrial Revolution. Heavy metal dwells in a world of demons, monsters, and other forces of evil and destruction, and like millennial cults it has fulfilled its apocalyptic imaginations with Biblical prophesies, from Black Sabbath's 'War Pigs' to Iron Maiden's 'The Number of the Beast' to Venom's 'The Seven Gates of Hell.' Because of a perceived lack of political engagement, as well as its low cultural status, heavy metal has received far less attention from scholars, despite higher album sales and concert attendances that suggest greater popularity than punk. And yet heavy metal may hold the keys to understanding the plight of working-class youth in the 1970s and 1980s, particularly their failure, inability, or refusal to confront the social inequalities and injustices stemming from deindustrialization. I will begin by illuminating the relationship between heavy metal's origins and the restructuring of political economy, and then advance to an analysis of how heavy metal exhibits a reified form of class consciousness.

Deindustrialization, Working-Class Masculinity, and the Origins of Heavy Metal

Deindustrialization refers to the decline of the manufacturing sector in the advanced capitalist economies of Western Europe and the United States beginning in the early 1970s and continuing into the twenty-first century. In Britain, the number of manufacturing jobs declined from 8 million in 1971 to 5.5 million in 1984. The crisis reached its peak in 1976, when the number of unemployed reached 1.5 million, representing 6.4 percent of the workforce, the highest unemployment figure since 1940. Deindustrialization has been inextricably linked to globalization and the emergence of a 'post-Fordist' economy, as manufacturing jobs have often been outsourced to low-wage and non-union regions, particularly in the Third World. It is also part of a process of spatial restructuring whose consequences were especially harsh for large industrial cities: in Britain the cities of London, Manchester, and Liverpool lost a disproportionate number of jobs and experienced a 15 to 20 percent decline in their populations between 1971 and 1981.

Deindustrialization must be seen in the context of a wider strategy in which capital has gone on the offensive against labor since the 1970s by busting unions or demanding givebacks, depressing wages, and cutting benefits. The evisceration of the British welfare state began as the International Monetary Fund called for £1 billion in austerity cuts for 1977–78. As conservatives came to political power after the elections of Margaret Thatcher in 1979 and Ronald Reagan in 1980, they further enabled capital flight through neo-liberal policies of deregulation and exacerbated its consequences with dramatic cuts in social services and the welfare state. Britain's Employment Acts of 1980, 1982, and 1984 were such that 'national unions and the labour movement in general were the object of attack.' Meanwhile, capital has increasingly come to rely on more easily disposable pools of contingent workers, especially temps and part-timers who earn lower wages and are entitled to fewer benefits. In Britain, service employment grew from 11.3 million in 1971 to 13.3 million in 1984. As a result, real wages have declined since the 1970s, the inequalities in the distribution of wealth have become more extreme, and organized labor and its agenda of social democracy are marginalized from mainstream politics.

Deindustrialization has contributed to the polarization of the class structure, but it has also been experienced in gendered terms as a crisis of masculinity. The job losses and downward mobility caused by deindustrialization have emasculated working-class men, and this insecurity has coincided with the increasing numbers of women in the work-force and the overall visibility of the feminist movement, which many men have inter-preted as another threat to their privileged status in society. The transition from a goods-producing to a service-based economy has also redefined work in a way that is threatening to previous conceptions of masculinity. The skills that service work demands and rewards, such as self-presentation, emotional labor, and customer service, have his-torically been defined as 'women's work.' Conversely, the conventional meanings of masculinity, especially among working-class men, have rested on attributes that are asso-ciated with the manufacturing economy, such as production, muscle, and the mastery of heavy machinery. At the same time, the culture of consumerism and media saturation has ushered into men's lives the cycle of objectification and vanity once reserved for women. As consumers and spectators are bombarded with an endless flow of images, celebrities, and brand name commodities, masculinity has been redefined along the lines of the 'new lad,' as British and Australian media have dubbed him. This transformation of working-class masculinity was light-heartedly depicted in *The Full Monty*, where recently unemployed Yorkshire steelworkers find new jobs as male strippers.

The adolescent years are crucial in the formation of working-class masculinity, par-ticularly as it is mediated by schooling, peer groups, and parent culture. In *Learning to Labor*, Paul Willis describes the ways in which non-conformist working-class boys become especially concerned with their performances of masculinity, which is expressed in their rebellion against school authorities and the educational process in general. In an economy where manufacturing jobs were still relatively plentiful, this socialization into working-class masculinity was somewhat functional, as the rebelliousness of working-class boys ensured their failure in the educational system and lack of social mobility, while their investment in masculinity, as Willis argues, prepared them to embrace a future of manual labor. But the consequences of deindustrialization have disrupted this link, and so heavy metal found its audience among the first generation of working-class youth and masculinist rebels who did not have a factory job waiting for them when they left school, and who would therefore constitute a surplus population subject to intensi-fied processes of social control. In the USA, the connections between deindustrializa-tion, downward mobility, and heavy metal subculture have been elucidated in Donna Gaines's ethnography of headbangers growing up in Bergenfield, New Jersey during the 1980s. Tagged as 'losers' by their peers, shuttled between remedial schools, drug and alcohol rehabilitation clinics, and mental institutions, and confronted with a labor market where personal appearance is of paramount importance, these self-described 'burnouts' looked to the future like 'animals before an earthquake.'

The rise of heavy metal coincided not only with the decline of heavy industry but also the decline of the 1960s counterculture. Heavy metal evolved as a hybrid of the hippies and previous working-class youth cultures. Heavy metal subculture appropriated the hippie counterculture's rebellious symbols (long hair, dope, loud music) and attitudes (lessened inhibitions about sex, inherent suspicion of authority, passive indifference to achievement). However, along with punk, it shunned the utopian dreams of Woodstock Nation. Heavy metal merged these with the styles of antecedent working-class subcultures, like the Rockers in England and Hell's Angels in the USA, who were also rebellious yet characterized by hyper-masculinity and patriarchal gender roles, militarism and xenophobia, and fear of racial and sexual difference. The context of deindustrialization and its threats to working-class masculinity further intensified the search for symbolic forms of compensatory power. Although metal-heads take pride in their rebelliousness, they generally adhere to conventional gender identities and reproduce hegemonic relations between and within the sexes. So whereas the more middle-class post-hippie New Age subcultures of the 1970s cultivated an aesthetic of naturalness and authenticity, the culture of heavy metal was replete with images of power, violence, and hedonism.

This is not to say that heavy metal represents a grass-roots or authentic working-class culture, as the connection to its audience is mediated by the corporations of the music industry and other powerful economic interests. However, heavy metal achieved popularity because its dominant themes of power, alienation, and violence resonated with this audience, and in turn heavy metal performers fashioned their music and iconography to meet the expectations of their fans. Indeed, heavy metal has some of the most loyal and intense fans of any form of popular culture, identifying themselves as 'proud pariahs.' Live albums, from Deep Purple's *Made in Japan* (1973) to Led Zeppelin's *The Song Remains the Same* (1976) to Iron Maiden's *Live After Death* (1985), were essential to heavy metal from the beginning, and in time audience participation became an integral element of these live recordings (e.g., Iron Maiden singer Bruce Dickinson repeatedly calling on fans to 'Scream for me, Long Beach' during the recording of *Live After Death*). With the rise of MTV, heavy metal videos also began to use concert footage in which fans were prominently featured, such as the music videos for Ozzy Osbourne's 'Iron Man' (1982), Judas Priest's 'Electric Eye' (1987), or Def Leppard's 'Pour Some Sugar on Me' (1987). In heavy metal, it becomes very difficult to separate text from audience; instead, meaning is created in the reciprocal flows of social interaction between the two. It therefore must be examined both as a cultural practice whose meanings are collectively constructed and, historically, as a cultural practice shaped by working-class encounters with deindustrialization.

Reification and Class Consciousness in Heavy Metal

My argument is that in the imagery of heavy metal music and subculture, working-class consciousness in the context of deindustrialization is mediated by reification. Reification was first conceptualized by Georg Lukács as a metamorphosis in which 'a relation between people takes on the character of a thing and thus acquires a "phantom objectivity".' Under the capitalist mode of production, society's creations appear to have a life of their own independent of human control, as if they are forces of nature and are therefore timeless and immutable. Lukács traced reification back to Marx's notion of commodity fetishism, in which exchange value reshapes social relations among people such that they 'assume, in their eyes, the fantastic form of a relation between things.' Reification is therefore a consequence of capitalist societies in which people lose control over the production process and social relations are determined by economic forces that operate with mysterious objectivity, as suggested by the common metaphor of the 'invisible hand' of the market. The common denominator between alienation, rationalization, and the money economy is the way that people create social forces which then take on an objective form which is beyond their ability to control.

Reification expresses the sense of being at the mercy of processes that are absolute and overwhelming in their consequences yet invisible and impersonal in their origins. In heavy metal, reification is evident in the way that social forces of power and destruction are envisioned as inhuman or supernatural beings that cannot be comprehended, much less resisted, by ordinary human beings. It is an expression of the powerlessness of people in the face of socio-economic forces, 'like the sorcerer, who is no longer able to control the powers of the nether world whom he has called up by his spells,' in the words of Marx and Engels (alluding to Johann Wolfgang von Goethe's poem 'The Sorcerer's Apprentice') that also resemble the lyrics of many heavy metal songs. Consider, for instance, the parallels between this passage from Marx and Engels and the way Black Sabbath depicts humanity as the slaves of supernatural forces in 'Lord Of This World' (1971), which exist in a realm dominated by 'evil ways' and a cruel 'master of the world.' In short, reification describes how people make the things that will become their masters, selling their souls along the way, but come to believe that these masters have actually been created by 'someone above.'

And yet reification is not only apparent in the way that heavy metal subculture represents the powers-that-be as demons and monsters, but also in the instances where it tries to harness supernatural forces as sources of resistance and empowerment. While the extent of heavy metal's associations with Satanism and witchcraft has certainly been overblown into a moral panic, it is also clear that some young metal fans have indeed experimented with the occult in an attempt to gain magical powers or get revenge on authorities or peers. Likewise, while the music of Black Sabbath usually portrays Satan and the supernatural as forces of destruction, in 'The Wizard' (1970) they contrastingly fantasize about magical forms of resistance against demonic evil. The wizard causes the 'demons' to 'worry' and thus brings forth 'joy,' even making people 'happy.'

Aleister Crowley, the notorious English occultist and drug enthusiast, has occupied an analogous role in heavy metal lore, from Jimmy Page's purchase of his estate to Ozzy Osbourne's 'Mr. Crowley' (1981) to Iron Maiden's 'Moonchild' (1988). Heavy metal's search for mystical sources of empowerment also speaks to a profound sense of disempowerment in the social world, for it can only imagine fantastic and otherworldly methods of resistance to power. Reification thus operates in a dual sense, both in the way that heavy metal depicts oppressive authorities as evil spirits and in its fantasies about resistance derive from magical energies. In either case, the imagery of heavy metal expresses a mystification of power relations, a general sense of confusion about how social power subjugates young people and the working-class and how exploited peoples can take power and resist their exploiters.

The notion that heavy metal's devils, monsters, and evil spirits are actually metaphors for social power contradicts the prevailing view of heavy metal as escapist fantasy.

Like the millennial movements of the Industrial Revolution, its apocalyptic imagery is a cultural response to socio-economic disruption and injustice. However, the reification of class consciousness in heavy metal poses the same problem that it did for Lukács and his successors in the Frankfurt School: if capitalism appears to be natural, timeless, and operating with a life of its own, how is it possible to imagine social change? Indeed, the cultural politics of heavy metal are typically anti-authoritarian but libertarian. Its symbolism is ripe with opposition to individuals and institutions that exercise power visibly and directly, but the same ideology of libertarianism is complicit with economic forces that are often more destructive in their consequences but are largely invisible or seem to be inevitable.

Black Sabbath solidified the partnership between heavy metal and demonology. Musically, as Robert Walser observes, they 'took the emphasis on the occult even further, using dissonance, heavy riffs, and the mysterious whine of vocalist Ozzy Osbourne to evoke overtones of gothic horror.' On Black Sabbath's self-titled debut album (1970), Satan appears as a force of destruction to be feared, not a deity to be worshipped. On the terrifying eponymous song, Ozzy Osbourne sings from the perspective of someone being chased by Satan, screaming 'Oh no, no, please God help me,' as bells ring ominously alongside the guitar drone. Everyone is running to escape Satan by the time the song reaches its climax. In 'N.I.B.,' the Devil is a manipulator who steals people's souls and takes psychological control over their whole persona. This song is sung from the devil's perspective as he gains complete power over someone by using the promise of a better life based on 'love.' The enticing invitation 'My name is Lucifer, please take my hand' reveals the devious ways of the devil. These two sides of power – a force of violent annihilation on some occasions, an omnipotent master of personal deception and control in others – characterize Satan's appearances in most other Black Sabbath songs. These are primarily songs about power, whether it is power over an entire community of people or total control over one individual.

The paradigmatic example of how Satan and black magic symbolize the social powers that create war, poverty, and injustice is 'War Pigs,' in which the architects of war are portrayed as witches, sorcerers, and evil minds. 'War Pigs' begins with the sound of air raid sirens and Tony Iommi's distinctive heavy but slow guitar sludge, with Osbourne singing about military leaders 'in their masses' who are likened to 'witches at black masses' who 'plot destruction.' While the music's tempo increases, 'War Pigs' charges that politicians start wars 'just for fun,' but they leave poor people to do the fighting, treating them like 'pawns in a chess game.' As the song comes to a close, it is Judgment Day, God is taking vengeance, and the warmongers are on their knees begging for mercy. Satan appears in the song's last line, laughing and spreading his wings, perhaps knowing that although his minions have been destroyed, he will live on to create more episodes of destruction in the future. 'War Pigs' is a powerful anti-war song, but again it reifies warfare by portraying it as a conflict between supernatural forces in which divine intervention is the only hope for peace.

Satan had made previous appearances in the history of popular music before heavy metal, but his meaning was somewhat different. In the blues, the devil periodically materialized as a 'trickster" with whom someone like Robert Johnson, according to blues legend, could make a deal in exchange for extraordinary powers on the guitar. This image has its roots in West African folklore, as George Lipsitz has written: 'The trickster figure at the crossroads – often interpreted in the romantic tradition as the devil – is really Eshu-Elegbara (Legba, Elebgba, Esu), not the incarnation of evil, but an unpredictable deity with the power to make things happen, a god described … as "the ultimate master of potentiality".' In the blues, Satan is often encountered at the crossroads, a symbolic place where decisions must be made and multiple possibilities arise. He is not a force of unequivocal evil and destruction in the same way that he is in Black Sabbath songs, but rather a spirit with the ability to make things happen and instill people with creative powers.

In 1968, the Rolling Stones' 'Sympathy for the Devil' was recorded in the midst of a worldwide revolt of young people. In this song, the devil 'introduces' himself as a figure who has presided over other revolutionary and apocalyptic moments in history. The devil is to be feared and respected but is not a figure of unambiguous evil, for he also personifies the specter of change which entranced millions of youths all over the world in 1968. In Marshall Berman's readings, the devil in this song is akin to the one Goethe created in *Faust*, in which experimentation and annihilation are irrevocably bound together in modernity's spirit of creative destruction. 'Sympathy for the Devil' urges the 1960s generation to know who they are dealing with – to guess his name and the nature of his game – but it does not caution them to stay away. The Rolling Stones had summoned the devil during the previous year in *Their Satanic Magesties Request*, but the results were notoriously disastrous, as they levitated the devil into a cosmic psychedelic imitation of the Beatles' *Sgt. Pepper's Lonely Hearts Club Band*. Satan was better suited for 1968, the cataclysmic year when the impossible was demanded and the forces of law and order responded, in Vietnam and at home, by laying young souls to waste.

The differences in the meanings of Satan from 'Sympathy for the Devil' to Black Sabbath's songs express an extraordinary loss of confidence in social change among young people in just a few short years. The revolts of the 1960s were fueled by a sense of possibility as well as discontent. Young people had inherited the self-assurance of a society steeped in economic affluence, in which youth was made a symbol of post-war optimism. The young generation maintained that belief in their collective importance even as they came to oppose the dominant social system; perhaps naively or arrogantly, they believed they would make history. So, for instance, in 1967 Abbie Hoffman, Jerry Rubin, and the Yippies organized an anti-war action in which they fantasized that supernatural spirits might be conjured to serve peace, as they costumed themselves as witches and humorously performed a ritual to levitate the Pentagon and exorcise its evil spirits. This sense of possibility had largely evaporated by 1970, as the New Left deteriorated into vulgar sloganeering and violent clashes with the police, while the counterculture watched its music and lifestyle become increasingly commodified and co-opted. Years later, punk captured the despair and nihilism of young people with the battle-cries of 'no future' and 'no values.' But the feeling of impotence was already evident in 'War Pigs,' where it is God, not the anti-war movement, who brings the war machine to justice, and even then Satan just laughs, spreads his wings, and presumably lives on to fight another day.

Iron Maiden also dwelled in demonic imagery but further expanded the scope of images of power borrowed from history and mythology. The band originally formed in London's East End, where working-class subcultures of skinheads and mods had previously emerged from neighborhoods razed by urban redevelopment. Iron Maiden initially cultivated an urban, street-tough image drawn from the punk movement that surrounded them in the late 1970s. Their original singer, Paul Di'Anno, looked and performed more like a punk rocker. Also in a sensibility that was closer to punk than heavy metal, their mascot Eddie was conceived by his creator Derek Riggs to embody 'the idea that the youth of the day was being wasted by society.' Eddie appeared against a background of city streets on the album covers of *Iron Maiden* (1980) and *Killers* (1981), as well as the singles for 'Running Free,' 'Sanctuary,' and 'Women in Uniform.' Despite his undead form, the early version of Eddie was strictly an urban creature. So although Iron Maiden's music was always distinguishable as heavy metal, its imagery of urban decay, political violence, and 'wasted youth' was quite similar to punk's depiction of social chaos.

'Running Free' exemplifies the early Iron Maiden's aesthetic, where power appears in more socially realist forms, if only as something to be escaped. The song introduces a protagonist who resembles so many of Iron Maiden's fans who are young, broke, with bad luck, nothing to do, and 'nowhere to call their own'. The protagonist soon finds himself in jail, though he assures the listener that 'they ain't got a thing on me.' The single's covert art similarly depicts a young longhair trapped in an alley and running from some ghoulish-looking monsters. The song's triumphant moment is certainly its chorus, one of the great heavy metal sing-alongs that prompts its audience to affirm collectively: 'I'm running free, yeah.' 'Running Free' became a staple of Iron Maiden's concerts, and the sound of thousands of young misfits singing along with this chorus, as recorded in *Live After Death* (1985), speaks volumes about heavy metal. This sensibility continued on their next single, 'Sanctuary,' which again narrated a tale of escape from the law. The cover art for 'Sanctuary,' however, depicted Eddie holding a knife over the dead body of Prime Minister Margaret Thatcher, apparently after she had been caught tearing down one of the group's posters.

Iron Maiden's representations of power were thus more direct and realistic in their early years, locating themselves and Eddie in the decaying urban environment of London in the late 1970s, escaping if not resisting authority and the law. But they changed dramatically after 1980 with the release of *The Number of the Beast* and addition of singer Bruce Dickinson. Iron Maiden continued to present images of power and authority, but these became increasingly reified as they drew not only from the supernatural and demonic but also mythology, literature, and history. Various songs were inspired by the Book of Revelations, Greek mythology, Viking conquerors, Egyptian pharaohs, and Japanese samurais, as well as science fiction, Romantic poetry, World War II battles, and various historical figures. For subsequent albums and tours Eddie was costumed as a British soldier, a lobotomized prisoner, an Egyptian pharaoh and a mummy, and a futuristic cyborg. As an eclectic (some would say incongruous) mixture, Iron Maiden's imagery was abstracted from its social and historical context, and abstraction reified those images of power by making them appear to have a life of their own.

Iron Maiden's selectively appropriated histories and mythologies of conquest, slaughter, and slavery depicted the powers-that-be as overwhelming and irresistible. In 1988 they released the concept album *Seventh Son of a Seventh Son*, whose songs fit together in a story of fate, power, and evil. The album plays on the mythology that boys who are the seventh son of a father who is himself a seventh son are born with special powers of clairvoyance. On the album's first song, 'Moonchild,' Satan confronts the expectant mother with news of her son's sealed fate and warnings that he will 'torment' her should she try to escape this prophesy. The final threat is that her 'soul will bleed to death' in solitude.

There is no hope of running free from these powers and prophesies, no sanctuary to be found from these otherworldly authorities. When the child is finally born in 'Seventh Son of a Seventh Son,' he seems to be a pawn in the struggle between the forces of Good and Evil. At the end of the song, the line 'So it shall be done' makes clear he will have no agency in the matter. As he gets a little older, the child foresees the destruction of his community in 'The Prophesy.' But despite his special powers, the child is powerless to intervene in the destruction of his village. Not only do the other villagers ignore him, but when catastrophe finally strikes they actually condemn the seventh son, believing that he has cursed them, even though it is the child who is the truly tormented one. As the album comes to an end we are told that 'only the good die young' and 'all the evil seem to live forever.' In sum, although *Seventh Son of a Seventh Son* dwells in fantasy and magic, it is not difficult to see how this is a story tailor-made for alienated heavy metal youth who feel helplessly doomed by the powers-that-be in the real world. The seventh son can see his community's imminent destruction but he is powerless to do anything about it, and no one is listening to him anyway. When disaster strikes, he is turned into a scapegoat in much the same way that rebellious young people and youth culture have been demonized throughout recent history.

Conclusion: Hell Awaits

In heavy metal as a whole, there are some moments of what might be called 'class consciousness,' like 'Breaking the Law' or Motörhead's 'Eat the Rich.' But otherwise the most noticeable thing about the extent of class politics in heavy metal is its absence. At least to my knowledge, there are no heavy metal songs about deindustrialization or factory closings in the style of Bruce Springsteen or Billy Joel's 'Allentown,' for instance. From the perspective of Althusserian ideology critique, it is precisely this absence or omission – that which is not said and indeed cannot be said – that must be explained as the 'problematic' of heavy metal (see Althusser). Along with punk, heavy metal came of age in a historical moment of social crisis catalyzed by economic restructuring, but unlike punk it only rarely confronted those social conditions directly. In the face of deindustrialization, heavy metal's predominantly working-class performers and audiences became entranced by images of devils, monsters, and supernatural catastrophes, much like the hundreds of thousands of followers of Southcott's 'cult of the poor' and other millennial prophets of doom did during the Industrial Revolution.

I have argued that reification in part explains the relative absence of class consciousness in heavy metal. When reified, socially constructed forms of exploitation and power are represented as otherworldly in their origins and overwhelming in their effects, while on the other hand resistance can only be imagined in mystical or fantastic terms. As Marx and then Lukács originally diagnosed it, reification is a consequence of the capitalist mode of production that seems to operate with mysterious objectivity while transforming social labor into commodities that appear to possess magical properties independent of their producers. On the concrete terrain of everyday life, the reified iconography of heavy metal in 1970s and 1980s Britain corresponded to working-class youth's socio-political experience – they knew they were screwed, but it was hard to articulate why. Alienated youth might admonish power when it is exercised directly, like when schools discipline them, parents abuse them, police bust them, or the government tries to censor their music. But deindustrialization, globalization, outsourcing, and automation are not so easily represented or resisted; they just seem to happen.

Cultural studies originated with the need to theorize resistance at the point of consumption, in the way that young people fashion subversive style from the commodities they consume or audiences contest ideological messages encoded in media texts.

But the events and changes of the past 35 years or so suggest that cultural studies also needs to seek to explain the relative absence of resistance as international capital and neo-liberal ideologies have achieved a kind of broad consensus, even among many of their victims. The challenge is to do this without resorting to disingenuous arguments about the manipulative machinations of the corporate media or dismissing all but the most politicized forms of culture as variations of false consciousness. Heavy metal represents an exemplary case study in how popular culture embodies contradictory tendencies and methods, one which is similar to the alternately recuperative and oppositional elements of working-class culture that E.P. Thompson charted for the early nineteenth century. Overall, however, it is a case study better suited to explaining why there was little or no culture of working-class resistance in the face of deindustrialization. Heavy metal's absence of class consciousness also points to the need for a new labor movement, now growing into a global network of movements, which can expose capitalism as a social rather than supernatural phenomenon that people have the collective power to resist and change.

CHAPTER 13

The Jobless Future
Sci–Tech and the Dogma of Work

Stanley Aronowitz and William DiFazio

Introduction

The nation's economy is staggering out of the recession, say most of the gauges that measure it, but people who are getting jobs tell a sobering story:

> Many good factory jobs and white-collar office jobs with good wages and benefits are giving way to unstable and mediocre jobs. That makes the recovery different from any other.
>
> Trends that started in the 1980s have produced a new look to working America. Part-time jobs, temporary jobs, jobs paying no more than the Federal minimum wage, jobs with no more benefits than a few vacation days are displacing permanent regular jobs that people would lose in past recessions and reclaim when business picked up.

Less than three months after this report appeared in the *New York Times* (in December 1992), there was a variation on this theme: "Employment agencies call them contingent workers, flexible workers or assignment workers. Some labor economists, by contrast, call them disposable and throwaway workers." According to Audrey Freedman, an economist for Manpower, the big temporary-help company, "The labor market today, if you look at it closely, provides almost no long-term secure jobs."

After nearly three years of recession, the painfully slow "recovery" that economists said occurred in late 1992 failed to reduce official joblessness below 7 percent, or 9 million people, throughout 1992 and early 1993. By March 1993 the January figures on industrial production, consumer buying, and other indicators showed a slight dip, leaving in their wake both consternation and doubt that the U.S. economy was finally breaking out of the doldrums. When February payrolls grew by 365,000, Secretary of Labor Robert Reich noted that unemployment was still two percentage points higher than before the recession. Moreover, most employment gains had been part-time jobs, he said. In fact, if part-time employment was calculated as partial unemployment, if the military was excluded from the employed (as it had been until the Reagan Bureau of Labor Statistics revised the basis for computing the number of jobholders), and if discouraged

Original publication details: Aronowitz & DiFazio, 1994. Reproduced with permission from University of Minnesota Press.

workers—those who had stopped looking for work—were factored into the jobless figure, the numbers would be much higher, closer to 12 percent, which corresponds to the rate in most of Western Europe. Since the late 1980s unemployment rates around the globe seem intractable, and not directly influenced by the overall performance of a national economy.

The traditional "smokestack industries" have been in decline. The general decline has not been only in the manufacturing sectors but in the nonmanufacturing sectors as well. This process has been going on for twenty years as U.S. economic dominance has been transformed into the United States as one major player among others in the global economy. Barry Bluestone and Bennett Harrison have traced the transformation:

> During the decade of the 1970's we estimate that between 450,000 and 650,000 jobs in the private sector in both manufacturing and non-manufacturing were wiped out somewhere in the United States of both small and large runaway shops. But it turns out that such physical relocations are a tip of a huge iceberg. When the employment lost as a direct result of plant, store and office shutdowns during the 1970's is added to the job loss associated with runaway shops, it appears that more than 32 million jobs were destroyed. Together, runaways, shutdowns and permanent physical cutbacks short of complete closure may have cost the country as many as 38 million jobs.

In 1982, 1,287,000 jobs were lost as the result of plant closings and layoffs. Between 1977 and 1982, 150,000 jobs were lost in the steel industry. There are millions of unemployed, underemployed, and discouraged workers in the United States. Unemployment in the major industrial sectors seems to be out of control, and employed workers wonder if they are next. Union membership declines, and workers who strike legally are threatened with "replacement workers," a sanitized term for scabs in an antiunion decade. Workers are replaced, and no one knows who is next. Will they go the way of longshoremen replaced by containerization, or auto workers replaced by robots, or steelworkers replaced by disinvestment and a restructured global steel industry? No one knows, but the predictions are ominous. As Wassily Leontief and Faye Duchin report, a 1982 study from Japan "suggests that among the most advanced robots currently in use, displacement rates of 2–4 workers per shift are possible."

All of the contradictory tendencies involved in the restructuring of global capital and computer-mediated work seem to lead to the same conclusion for workers of all collars— that is, unemployment, underemployment, decreasingly skilled work, and relatively lower wages. These sci-tech transformations of the labor process have disrupted the workplace and workers' community and culture. High technology will destroy more jobs than it creates. The new technology has fewer parts and fewer workers and produces more product. This is true not only in traditional production industries but for all workers, including managers and technical workers:

> Forecasts made by the BLS [Bureau of Labor Statistics] and for *Business Week* by Data Resources Incorporated (DRI) in fact show that the number of high-tech jobs created will be less than half the two million jobs lost in manufacturing in the past three years. While high-tech industries as defined by the BLS will generate 10 times the number of jobs expected from the rest of industry, it will still amount to only 730,000 to one million jobs. And most of those will be traditional occupations, not technical ones. Fewer than one-third will be for engineers and technicians, according to DRI, and the remainder will be managers, clerical workers, operators and other factory workers.

Technological progress and capital accumulation seem to disrupt the social fabric in the United States. A weakened position in the international economy demands that American industry increase its productivity and cut its unit labor cost. As Carl G. Thor, president of the American Productivity Center in Houston, says, "The trick is to get more output without a surge in employment." Technological change and competition in the world market guarantee that increasing numbers of workers will be displaced and that these workers will tend to be rehired in jobs that do not pay comparable wages and salaries. Women and minorities will suffer the most as the result of these changes; the increased participation in an occupational sector by women and minorities is often an indicator of falling wages in that occupation.

The problems of plant shutdowns and technological change in production industries are fairly well known, but we lack reliable information concerning the fate of displaced workers, and our social knowledge of the effects of technological change and corporate restructuring in the private service sectors is virtually nonexistent. Until recently, most economists, business analysts, and sociologists assumed that the long-term decline of manufacturing employment was not a serious social issue because of the concomitant expansion of such industries as financial services, insurance, and retail and wholesale trades. The guiding assumption here was that the expansion of jobs in these industries would absorb those who lost their production jobs. For forty years after World War II, this assumption proved more or less valid for large numbers of younger workers. Now, however, contemporary trends in major financial corporations point to mass layoffs among middle managers as well as clerical employees: consolidation of computer services may cause skilled operators and programmers to seek jobs in other sectors; a glut of college graduates has saturated the job market, changing the criteria for employment in sectors that traditionally did not hire the educated; recent M.B.A.s are being hired to replace senior managers and reduce payroll costs; and there has been a dramatic increase in part-time and contract employees replacing permanent staff. These changes have become apparent since the "crash of '87." Wall Street layoffs have become a daily occurrence, spreading to banks and other financial institutions. These layoffs are a result of three factors: corporate mergers that result in reorganization and allow for downsizing, that is, the elimination of workers who duplicate services; the rapid spread of technological innovations such as telecommunication systems; and more advanced computer networks that eliminate workers even as productivity rises. In banking, the combination of these changes has already led to layoffs among some of the country's leading banks, including Chase Manhattan, Bank of America, and Chemical Bank-Manufacturers Hanover Trust.

The paradox is that even when business investors pour substantial portions of their capital into machinery and buildings, these investments do not significantly increase the number of new permanent, full-time jobs. Computerized machines employ very little direct labor; most of it is devoted to setup, repair, and monitoring. The actual production process is almost laborless because control over it is now built into the machines by computer processes such as numerical controls, lasers, and robotics. In short, computer-based technology inherently eliminates labor. The more investment in contemporary technologies, the more labor is destroyed.

Computer-mediated work processes are now worldwide. In the early 1990s, Japan and Germany, whose national economies were second only to that of the United States, began to experience substantial reductions in production and workforces. In stark contrast to the 1980s hype of the invincibility of the Japanese, especially its effective corporatism, the early 1990s witnessed severe changes in the Japanese economic outlook. For the first time since the early postwar years, many of the largest corporations such as Mitsubishi laid off thousands of workers, cut production, and began to transfer work to less-developed countries. Suddenly, Japanese industrial and labor relations policies resembled those of Western Europe and the United States. Germany, whose economic "miracle" cluttered press reports for two decades, found itself in the doldrums; plant closings and layoffs dotted the industrial landscape and, not unexpectedly, the government faced deep budget deficits and debt.

Some of the decline can be attributed to the steep descent of consumption of basic industrial and consumer goods such as steel and autos in the United States, which, despite the relative deterioration of its world position, remains the largest market for both industrial and consumer goods. But we must consider the possibility that capital-intensive production processes that aggravated unemployment, the extensive use of overtime work as an alternative to new hiring, and relative wage and benefit reductions have deepened the recession and made it much harder to produce a vigorous recovery. Since the end of World War II, working people have been encouraged to mortgage everything, including their souls, on the assumption that, economic ups and downs notwithstanding, there was no real barrier to ever higher living standards. The historic demand for shorter hours that accompanied the introduction of labor-replacing technology has been ditched in favor of work without end. But, as Bill Clinton has reiterated as both candidate and president, there is a shortage of "quality" jobs in the restructured economy; we wish to add that there is shortage of quality pay, as well.

Of course, not all investment has been in manufacturing or money instruments. Some of it has fueled the enormous growth of informatics: the production of computer hardware and software; electronic communication equipment and processes; and the vast array of services attached to information, much of it channeled to finance. Informatics facilitates even more rapid money and other market exchanges. The various forms of labor-reducing informatics span a wide range of industries from goods production to retail and wholesale trades and nearly all services, large and small. Supermarkets use electronic devices for inventory control and to register prices on nearly all items. Small businesses use informatics as well. A liquor store, for example, is likely to use a computer to track inventory, eliminating the need to hire a full-time stock clerk. Computers are now part of the pharmacist's tools, and even some independent grocers use them. Although the information and computer "revolution" at first created millions of new jobs, it destroyed many others. Tens of thousands of workers once employed as retail clerks in "mom and pop" stores, albeit at low wages, are no longer needed. In the wake of the growth of the giant supermarket chains and multilocation department store chains that dot the retail landscape, one of the major weapons of survival for owners of small clothing, hardware, and grocery stores is cutting labor costs by working longer hours themselves and using machinery.

Even before the worldwide recession began with the stock market crash of November 1987, hundreds of companies entered into transnational mergers and acquisitions. In some cases, such as the automobile industry, these relationships predated the 1980s, but that decade was marked by several joint ventures between U.S. and Japanese corporations that reduced further the need for many of their respective parts plants. The practice of "outsourcing" meant that many corporations closed their parts plants and used the same contractors to produce everything from windshield wipers to engine parts to sheet metal components. It was the decade not only of the global car, but also of the global sweatshop. Americans were regularly plied with reports of products they used in everyday life being produced by workers in Mexico, Malaysia, and China who earned a small fraction of a U.S. or Western European wage. In many other industries such as machine tools, computer chips, and other hardware components, the idea of a national identity to a commercial product became an advertising fiction used for the purposes of neutralizing protectionism. Sony, Japan's leading electronics corporation, bought substantial portions of the U.S. record industry. Japanese and European capital formed conglomerates through takeovers of U.S. corporations; in turn, U.S. investment grew in countries like China, Mexico, and Taiwan, leaving substantial sectors of the U.S. economy in the hands of foreign companies and, equally important, laying waste to vast stretches of the industrial heartland. Pittsburgh and the Monongahela valley, the Youngstown area, and Buffalo, once booming steel towns, are industrial wastelands; only Pittsburgh managed to remain economically viable by becoming a regional financial center.

The effects of global restructuring are fairly well known by now. Awakened by the near demise of the Chrysler Corporation in 1979, Americans were sternly warned that unless they learned to tighten their belts, the consequences for the American dream would be dire. Indeed, by 1990 the once-proud U.S. lead in wage levels had been wiped out. The Bureau of Labor Statistics reported that U.S. wages eroded from first in 1970 to sixth, behind Germany, Sweden, Austria, Italy, and France. For example, the wages of German workers were nearly 50 percent higher and those of Swedish workers more than 40 percent higher than those of U.S. workers. In that twenty-year period, real wages actually deteriorated, while the wages for all other major industrial countries except the Soviet Union and Great Britain grew in real terms. The concerted assault by government and major corporations on workers' income, begun in 1981 when, in a dramatic gesture, President Reagan fired 11,000 striking air traffic controllers, managed to impose a virtual wage freeze on the overwhelming majority of manufacturing workers. Plant closings, tepid trade union response bordering on the supine, and an intense antiunion ideological environment conspired to weaken workers' resistance so that, by the mid-1980s, the nonunion sector drove labor relations.

This, in brief, is the context within which a severely reduced job "market" began to take shape, not only for U.S. workers, but potentially for all workers. In this book we argue that the progressive destruction of high-quality, well-paid, permanent jobs is produced by three closely related developments.

First, in response to pervasive, long-term economic stagnation and to new scientifically based technologies, we are experiencing massive restructuring of patterns of ownership and investment in the global economy. Fewer companies dominate larger portions of the world market in many sectors, and national boundaries are becoming progressively less relevant to how business is done, investment deployed, and labor employed. As the North American Free Trade Agreement illustrates, there is no reason other than political considerations to value the concept of the nation with respect to the production and distribution of goods and services. As much as machinery, organization at the level of the corporate boardrooms and the workplace is a crucial technology of labor destruction.

Second, the relentless application of technology has destroyed jobs and, at the same time, reduced workers' living standards by enabling transnational corporations to deterritorialize production. Today, plant and office locations are less dependent on geographic proximity to markets, except in the case of some services. Informatics, of which computer-mediated processes are the most common in financial, retail, and wholesale services, permit production and services to be dispersed throughout the globe with impunity. Increasingly, electronically transmitted information is the medium of business, and for the most part it does not depend on place.

Third, National Public Radio recently reported that a number of U.S. corporations were locating their design and development activities in India, where, they claimed, systems analysts, programmers, and engineers were highly competent and much lower paid than their Western (American) counterparts. Similarly, Du Pont is preparing to build a major synthetics fiber and petrochemical facility in Shanghai. In the past, U.S. scientific and technical experts were largely responsible for designing and supervising foreign plant construction, but Du Pont is employing Chinese engineers, chemists, and technicians, many of whom were trained in the United States and other advanced industrial countries and others who were not. These cases illustrate a second theme of this book: informatics not only displaces and recomposes manual labor but also displaces technical and scientific labor—a new and expanding frontier of global restructuring. As we shall see, because these are most of the new "quality" jobs about which economists and political leaders speak, we argue that there is absolutely no prospect, except for a fairly small minority of professional and technical people, to obtain good jobs in the future.

Consequently, whatever validity it had in the past, the neoclassical economic philosophy and the policies it engenders, according to which economic growth leads to relatively full employment and higher living standards, are rendered obsolete by recent developments. If the economy respects no national boundaries, the impact of nationally based fiscal, monetary, and industrial policies are severely limited, just as labor and welfare policies that are not truly international in scope and application are fated to be eroded. Forget the old social-democratic slogan of full employment in a humane welfare state.

The era of "jobs, jobs, jobs" and all that this slogan implies is over. We suggest that if justice depends on employment and the good life depends on the rewards of hard work, there can be no justice, and the good life may be relegated to a dim memory. However, we renounce neither justice nor pleasure. In the final section of this book we propose alternatives to the long wave of the job culture as the substitution for the good life.

Contrary to the ideologically conditioned theory shared by sociologists, psychologists, and policy analysts that "nonwork" produces, and is produced by, social disorganization and is symbolic of irresponsibility and personal dysfunctionality, recipients of guaranteed annual income who are relieved of most obligations to engage in labor do not fall apart. The incidence of alchoholism, divorce, and other social ills associated with conditions of dysfunctionality does not increase among men who are not working. Nor do they tend to experience higher rates of mortality than those of comparable age who are engaged in full-time work. Given the opportunity to engage in active nonwork, they choose this option virtually every time.

For example, East Coast longshoremen who are not working but receive adequate income find many things to occupy their time. Many spend more time with their families, some engage in side businesses, and others take up hobbies or fix up the house. They retain their industrial community and much of its culture. Most important, they are happier because they do not have to labor every day at a hard, often life-threatening job where the dangers associated with loading and unloading cargo are compounded by the need to handle materials that are frequently hazardous to their health. Because of the pleasures of nonwork—work in the specific sense used here, paid labor under a hierarchical management system—the men are not pleased to be called to put in a day's labor.

Most of all, they have regained "free" time. This freedom, perhaps more than the activities in which they become absorbed as an alternative to paid labor, fulfills the premier promise of technological displacement that in its earlier ideological expressions was heralded by the labor movement and intellectuals as the main historical benefit of industrialization. An alarming number of workers, both intellectual and manual, surrender nearly all of their waking and even dreaming time to labor. The by now ancient slogan of the movement for shorter hours—"eight hours work, eight hours sleep, and eight hours to do with what we will"—has been abandoned. The notion of free time is as distant from most people's everyday experience as open space. Labor has been dispersed into all corners of the social world, eating space and time, crowding out any remnants of civil society that remained after the advent of consumer society, and colonizing the life world. We are able neither to work nor to play; unlike the older industrial model where labor was experienced as an imposition from above, the dispersal of work makes the enemy invisible because labor is now experienced as a compulsion dictated by economic anxiety more than by the "need" to work.

Under current economic and social conditions, the major casualties of technological changes on the waterfront and, increasingly, in the auto, electronics, and communications industries, are the children and grandchildren who will never have the chance to work on the docks or in the factories and accumulate enough time to achieve dignified nonwork. The time of the new generations of never-to-be industrial workers is not free even though they are relieved of paid labor. Instead, it is suffused with anxiety that they may never again enter the cycle of labor and consumption that defined working lives in the Fordist era, or they displace the anxiety of nonwork without income in lives of petty crime (in which case they need not apply for public assistance). Whereas before containerization, as late as 1960, sons of longshoremen certainly would have followed their fathers onto the waterfront, in the postwork society, life for the children of dockers is in most respects harder than it was for their parents. Many among the next generation who have been unable to accumulate the requisite cultural capital to qualify for employment in one of the knowledge industries or have not had the luck to find a job in one of them are, lacking guaranteed income, reduced to undignified nonwork—or worse, are driven to seek low-wage dead-end jobs because they are suited neither for unemployment nor for lives as drug dealers or petty thieves.

It may be objected that this argument seems Eurocentric; it applies at best to the fate of work in so-called "advanced" industrial countries. As industrial production moves away from the United States and Europe, especially to Latin America and Asia, some have envisioned the rebirth of the industrial proletariat. And presumably, because of this shift, few of these issues such as joblessness and class decomposition apply. According to this view, the old slogans of labor solidarity have not disappeared; they have merely been deterritorialized. This thesis, however, ignores the fact that industrialization in formerly agricultural regions is occurring at an accelerating rate under the new scientific-technological regimes, which are by no means local. Computer-mediated labor processes are the standard against which global labor is measured, not merely labor in the traditionally industrialized countries. For example, some of the *maquiladoras* on the Mexico-U.S. border are often more technologically developed than older U.S. plants that produce the same products. They make auto parts, computers, and other high-tech commodities as well as furniture and textiles, which, as we have seen, are increasingly produced with computer-mediated and laser technologies. Thus, whereas earlier capital migrations relied on low and intermediate technologies because the advantages of employing low-wage labor outweighed the costs of introducing advanced machine processes, we may now observe new forms of capital migration that tend to make the labor process—if not (yet) wages and working conditions—uniform.

Workers on the Mexican side of the border may earn at most about eighty dollars a week, but they are often paid much less. And even though Mexico has some protective factory and environmental legislation, it is observed more in the breach than by enforcement. Moreover, as workers organize in Mexican factories, employers have not hesitated to steal away in the night to other areas in the country where wages are even lower and workers are less prepared to form independent unions.

The North American Free Trade Agreement (NAFTA) may be viewed as merely the conclusion of the first chapter in a long process of overcoming some aspects of the traditional unequal division of labor between north and south. In the next decade, U.S. wages and living standards are likely to continue to deteriorate. If labor organization emerges in Mexico and other parts of Latin America, wages there will rise, but not by enough to deter migration of U.S. plants, at least during the 1990s. In the near future, Texans and Californians will cross the border in greater numbers every day to work in Mexico and Mexican workers will continue to migrate to certain jobs in the United States, approximating the situation at the already blurred U.S.-Canadian border. At the same time, as in Canada, Mexican industry is increasingly subject to U.S. investment; this will set a pattern for transnational investment in other countries of Latin America, particularly Brazil, which, along with Mexico, had before the current economic crisis succeeded to some extent in developing its own industrial base.

Deterritorialized production applies also to knowledge. By the early 1990s, for example, China and India were offering U.S., Japanese, and European capital access to highly qualified scientific and technical labor. U.S. computer corporations began to let contracts to software corporations in India. Du Pont and other chemical corporations were building petrochemical complexes in Shanghai, employing Chinese engineers and chemists at eighty dollars a month. The fairly well developed Mexican bioengineering sector is actively negotiating with U.S. corporations to "share" discoveries and technical achievements.

Even in science and technology, whose products are situated in their own historical and institutional contexts and as often as not are appropriated for socially dubious purposes, the product never entirely "disappears" into consumption but is incorporated into the common built environment. Yet although the work of some of those engaged in the production of arts and science retains excitement, challenge, and end products that possess genuine durability, few have the good fortune to be custom cabinetmakers, theoretical physicists, literary critics, social scientists, molecular biologists, or computer engineers.

Just as the scientific-technological revolution has utterly transformed the workplace in all categories of labor, we are obliged to examine its consequences for the conception of work that undergirds cultural identity, the self, and our collective understanding of the norms by which the moral order imposes a mode of conduct upon us. In his notebooks, Marx wrote in 1857–58:

> The free development of individualities, and hence not the reduction of necessary labour time so as to posit surplus labor, but rather the general reduction of the necessary labor of society to a minimum, which then corresponds to the artistic, scientific etc. development of the individuals in the time set free, and with the means created, for all of them. Capital itself is the moving contradiction [in] that it presses to reduce labour time to a minimum, while it posits labor time, on the other side, as the sole measure and source of wealth.

It may be argued that the history of capitalism during the last hundred years may be recounted in terms of this contradiction. This transformation in industrial production has stunningly fulfilled the tendencies that were prefigured in Marx's description: once based chiefly on the practical knowledge handed down to succeeding generations by craft traditions, production is now based on abstractions of organization and on science.

The promise of this movement, however, has been subsumed almost entirely under the sign of capital reproduction. Capital fears its own moving spirit. Vast quantities of labor are set free from the labor process, but rather than fostering full individual development, production and reproduction penetrate all corners of the life world, transforming it into a commodity world not merely as consumption but also in the most intimate processes of human interaction. Intellectual labor, its ideology of professional autonomy in tatters as a result of its subordination to technoscience and organization, becomes a form of human capital the components of which are specialized knowledge and differentially accumulated cultural capital determined mainly by hierarchically arranged credentials. Most professionals, let alone "liberated" manual workers, enjoy little free time for artistic and scientific development, either of their individuality or indeed of the productive forces. To the contrary, we live in a time when not only are individuals thwarted, but the political economy of late capitalism appears—at least in one crucial area, research and development—to fetter the new productive force: knowledge.

On June 30, 1993, the *New York Times* reported that U.S. companies are cutting funds for scientific and technological research:

> Scientific research by private industry, the traditional powerhouse of innovation and technological leadership in the United States, is suffering deeper financial woes than previously disclosed, suggesting that America is slipping in the international race for discoveries that form the basis of new goods and services. The National Science Foundation reported in February that industrial research on research and development had begun to shrink after decades of growth.

Of course, much of the previous growth was military, and was therefore driven by and dependent on public funds. But with recession, the tapering off of the cold war, and the enormous deficits accumulated by government and by corporations caught up in the swirl of the leveraged buyout mania of the 1980s, funds have dried up. For example, as we noted earlier, the National Institutes of Health, which formerly funded a third of the research proposals submitted to the agency, supported only 10 percent in 1991. More to the point, the priorities of the federal scientific and technical bureaucracies, which are increasingly tied to the requirements of corporations, have restricted the *kind* of research they are willing to support. Consequently, there is almost no hope that biomedical projects that fall outside the purview of molecular biology and biophysics will be funded. And, as we have seen, research scientists are feeling pressure to make arrangements with private corporations in order to obtain desperately needed research funds. In short, the commodification of basic science, combined with its increasingly technical character and declining funds, may in the future all but seal the fate of the United States as a major economic power.

For the plain truth is that overfunding and "useless" knowledge is the key to discovery. From the discoveries of Galileo to the "idle" ruminations of Frege, Gödel, Einstein, and Bohr, patronage, whether public or private, permitted unbounded dreaming that led to new ways of seeing and ultimately—but only ultimately—new modes of producing.

When government and corporate policy makers insist on "dedicated" research as a condition of support, they announce that they have opted for failure rather than long-range innovation. This blatant act of research shooting itself in the foot is by no means intentional. Rather, it is the result of the logic of technoscience and the human capital paradigm according to which unsubordinated knowledge is perceived to threaten the social order either by draining economic resources or by proposing unpalatable jolts to the imagination. Moreover, it signals a profound failure of nerve, a refusal to take the risk that some knowledge can never be translated into technology and will remain outside the framework of accepted science and that some knowledge might even subvert cherished beliefs within the prevailing social order. For the social sciences and the humanities, cost reductions exacted a steep toll on research, but during the Reagan-Bush era many projects were rejected by conservative leaders of the National Endowment for the Arts and the National Endowment for the Humanities on political grounds, a manifestation of the conservative ideological attack on postmodern cultural expression.

The crisis in research of course has serious consequences for the U.S. national economy, but it augurs equally badly for hope that intellectual work will be possible for more than a tiny fraction of scientists and artists in the future. Its effects are even more far-reaching. For, in a higher education system already incurring severe criticism for the low number of U.S.-born scientific and technical majors and graduates at the undergraduate and graduate levels, the decline in basic research constitutes a disincentive for young people to enter the sciences. At leading universities, many if not most advanced-level physics, mathematics, and chemistry students are foreign born.

The irony of this situation is that the completion of the process by which science is almost entirely subsumed under capital and which, concomitantly, transformed intellectual work into human capital, is by no means in the system's interest. For just as the emergence of knowledge as a productive force "solves" the problem of productivity while at the same time intensifying the problem of how capital valorizes itself, so the subordination of knowledge to the imperative of technical innovation undermines one of the central presuppositions of innovation: *unfettered* free time for knowledge producers.

In recent years this contradiction has been at play in universities, even in first-tier institutions, which place increasing administrative burdens on faculty; the second and third tiers impose, in addition, heavier teaching loads. Under the impact of economic constraints we have entered a new era of academic cost cutting and of surveillance whose intended as well as unintended effects are to discourage independent intellectual work. For a society that trumpets the growth imperative as the key to its survival, and for which knowledge is the acknowledged economic spur, such measures are, of course, self-defeating.

Our proposals are based on the presuppositions of this study: that economic growth grounded in technological innovation does not necessarily increase employment unless there is a sharp reduction in working hours, and even then may not be sufficient to sustain a level approaching full employment; and that since a considerable number of recently created jobs are part-time, poorly paid dead ends, there is a powerful argument that we have reached the moment when less work is entirely justified. In addition, our proposals assume the goal of assuring the *possibility* of the full development of individual and social capacities.

These statements further imply that—if our assertions that the world economy will not sustain full employment in the coming decades and the social safety net will remain full of holes are correct—we need to reconsider the pace of technological change and the effects of corporate reorganizations that have shed tens of thousands of employees in the past several years. Until measures such as a substantial reduction of working hours, a guaranteed income plan, a genuine national health scheme, and the revitalization of the progressive tax system have been introduced into law and union contracts, job-destroying technologies and mergers and acquisitions should be rigorously *evaluated* in terms of their implications for the well-being of communities and workers. In an era of uncontrolled growth amid economic stagnation, corporate efforts to make workers and communities pay the costs of falling profits are exacting heavy tolls and should be stopped.

Needless to say, we do not support technophobic perspectives on technological transformation. As our critique of Hannah Arendt and the earlier discussion of work and skill show, we do not mourn the passing of craft. Given guaranteed income, shorter hours, and work sharing, we welcome the coming of a postwork society and have tried to refute the sociological and psychological "wisdom" that labor is an intrinsic need beyond survival. In fact, we have claimed that, as a mode of life, its historicity has been demonstrated by the nature and the spread of cybernetic technologies.

The Need to Reduce Working Hours

There has been no significant reduction in working hours since the implementation of the eight-hour day through collective bargaining and the 1938 enactment of the federal wage and hour law. Since then, we have witnessed a slow increase of working time despite the most profoundly labor-displacing era of technological change since the industrial revolution. People are laboring their lives away, which, perhaps as much as unemployment and poverty, has resulted in many serious family and health problems. In turn, the lengthening of working hours has contributed to unemployment and poverty among those excluded from the labor system.

Therefore, there is an urgent need for a sharp reduction in the workweek from its current forty hours—a reduction of, *initially*, at least ten hours. The thirty-hour week at *no reduction in pay* would create new jobs only if overtime was eliminated for most categories of labor. And, although some people may prefer flexible working arrangements that are more compatible with child-rearing needs or personal preference, the basic workday should, to begin with, be reduced to six hours, both as a health and safety measure and in order to provide more freedom from labor in everyday life. Finally, we envision a progressive reduction of working hours as technological transformation and the elimination of what might be termed make-work in both private and public employment reduces the amount of labor necessary for the production of goods and services. That is, productivity gains would not necessarily, as in the past, be shared between employers and employees in the form of increased income, but would result first in fewer laboring hours.

Obviously, restricting laboring hours raises some important questions: How do families maintain their living standards if income is substantially reduced by restricting overtime and other work-sharing arrangements? Will people use free time to develop their capacities or will time be absorbed destructively? Who will pay for work-sharing? Is it feasible in a global economy where capital moves freely in search of cheap labor? We will address the last question first because although it is politically agonizing, it poses fewer conceptual problems.

The experience of the German labor movement is instructive in this regard. In 1985, the Metalworkers Union (IG Metal), which represents auto, steel, and metal fabricating workers, struck for reduced hours. After a relatively short walkout involving millions of workers in the most technologically advanced sectors of the economy, employers yielded to the demand for a thirty-five-hour workweek, to be implemented in stages over five years. Gradually, other sectors have adopted the shorter workweek, but there is no federal law because the labor-supported Social Democrats are out of power. The competitive position of German industries is not suffering because of this innovation, in part because of the tremendous productivity of German workers made possible by cutting-edge technologies that have been widely introduced in production. Moreover, in countries such as Germany where the social wage includes substantial government-administered health benefits and guaranteed income and pensions, labor costs to employers may be lower than in the United States, which does not have these state-sponsored provisions, even when wages are higher. In the United States, employers have shouldered much of the burden of the welfare state, spending as much as 40 percent of wages on fringe benefits.

While notions of solidarity have suffered in Europe in the past several decades, particularly in the wake of a major influx of immigrants from the Middle East and Africa, Italian and German labor movements nevertheless retain considerable ideological loyalty to concepts such as class unity. The victory of the German metalworkers—and a parallel struggle by public employees—attests to the power of discursive and ideological influences in determining the shape of the politics of work. Although the German economy has suffered during the recession of the past decade and there is considerable xenophobia throughout German society against immigrants during a period of high joblessness, the discourse of social justice has not disappeared because the labor movement insists that employers share the pain of economic woes. Moreover, the unions have insisted that the promise of pay equity between East and West Germany be fulfilled.

In some countries, capital may not freely export jobs without consultation with unions and the government. Clearly, reducing working hours without simultaneously addressing the issue of capital flight is unthinkable. In 1988 the U.S. Congress passed modest plant-closing legislation requiring employers only to notify employees and the community of their plans to close a facility. This law could be strengthened to compel collective bargaining with unions and local governments over the conditions of capital flight, including the extent of compensation and effects on the community. To discourage plant closings, employers could be required to pay substantial compensation to displaced workers and to communities, and they could be required to offer transfer rights to their employees. Unions have sought to protect jobs by persuading Congress to pass the so-called domestic content bill according to which a percentage of the components of commodities (autos and garments, for example) sold in the United States would have to be produced by U.S. workers. This provision has been incorporated into the North American Free Trade Agreement (NAFTA) for some items; it could be extended to become a basis of plant-closing legislation.

The most important issue raised by our proposals is international coordination of labor demands. It is evident that the purely national framework within which labor movements operate is for many purposes archaic. But although there are some instances of genuine coordination of strikes, bargaining, and even legislation, labor movements are often at loggerheads over their own position in the international division of labor. In the face of global competition, it is nothing short of suicidal for labor to remain in competition with itself. Unless these issues are addressed, discussions of the need for shorter hours can never advance beyond the proposal stage.

The question of living standards strikes at the heart of the cultural dimension of this issue. For millions of Americans, working almost all the time is the only way they can maintain their homes and provide for the care and education of their children. Here we offer suggestions. We need free, publicly provided child care services like those in many European countries. Since mortgage payments or rent plus child care absorb as much as 50 percent of the income of many households, they bear on laboring practices. Second, the United States could adopt the European system of treating post-secondary education as a public resource therefore a public expense.

At the same time, we would propose that higher education be a right rather than a privilege reserved for a minority of the population, as it is in most of Europe and the countries of the Americas. Here we can observe considerable differences between the United States, Western Europe, and developing countries. In most of the world, all education is paid for by the state, but access to education is severely regulated. In Europe, a relatively small percentage of students enter postsecondary programs, including technical institutes. In most of the less developed regions of the world, most people are denied a decent elementary and secondary education, much less opportunities for university degrees.

Since the 1960s, U.S. colleges and universities have been more accessible to students than they used to be. Some 50 percent of high school students enter some kind of post-secondary education program; about half of them go to community colleges and technical schools. Dropout rates, however, are enormous, and sometimes as high as 70 percent. Plainly, if the revolution in scientific and technical knowledge has occurred, fairly high levels of educational achievement are now a necessity for larger numbers of young people. Just as secondary education became a right at the beginning of the twentieth century, so higher education must become a right at the turn of the twenty-first.

CHAPTER 14

Shiftless of the World Unite!

Robin D.G. Kelley

If "conspicuous consumption" was the badge of a rising middle class, "conspicuous loafing" is the hostile gesture of a tired working class.
—DANIEL BELL, *Work and Its Discontents*

All observers spoke of the fact that the slaves were slow and churlish; that they wasted material and malingered at their work. Of course they did. This was not racial but economic. It was the answer of any group of laborers forced down to the last ditch. They might be made to work continuously but no power could make them work well.
—W.E.B. DU BOIS, *Black Reconstruction in America*

Nearly a quarter century ago, a historian named George Rawick published an obscure article in a small left political journal that warned against treating the history of the working class as merely the history of trade unions or other formal labor organizations. If we are to locate working-class resistance, Rawick insisted, we need to know "how many man hours were lost to production because of strikes, the amount of equipment and material destroyed by industrial sabotage and deliberate negligence, the amount of time lost by absenteeism, the hours gained by workers through the slowdown, the limiting of the speed-up of the productive apparatus through the working class's own initiative." Unfortunately, few historians have followed Rawick's advice. Still missing from most examinations of workers are the ways in which unorganized working people resisted the conditions of work, tried to control the pace and amount of work, and carved out a modicum of dignity at the workplace.

Not surprisingly, studies that seriously consider the sloppy, undetermined, everyday nature of workplace resistance have focused on workers who face considerable barriers to traditional trade union organization. Black domestic workers devised a whole array of creative strategies, including slowdowns, theft or "pan-toting" (bringing home leftovers

Original publication details: Robin D.G. Kelley, "Shiftless of the World Unite", from *Race Rebels: Culture, Politics, and the Black Working Class*, pp. 1–5; 7–10; 12–13; 17–22; 32–34. The Free Press, 1994, 1996. Including a portion from W.E.B. Du Bois, *Black Reconstruction in America*. All reproduced with permission from Simon & Schuster.

and other foodstuffs), leaving work early, or quitting, in order to control the pace of work, increase wages, compensate for underpayment, reduce hours, and seize more personal autonomy. These individual acts often had a collective basis that remained hidden from their employers.

Black women household workers in the urban South generally abided by a "code of ethics" or established a sort of blacklist to collectively avoid working for employers who proved unscrupulous, abusive, or unfair. Quitting or threatening to quit just prior to an important social affair to be hosted by one's employer—commonly called an "incipient strike"—was another strategy whose success often depended on a collective refusal on the part of other household workers to fill in. Likewise, in the factories strategies such as feigning illness to get a day off, slowdowns, sometimes even sabotage, often required the collective support of co-workers.

Studies of black North Carolina tobacco workers reveal a wide range of clandestine, yet collective, strategies to control the pace of work or strike out against employers. When black female stemmers had trouble keeping up with the pace, black men responsible for supplying tobacco to the stemmers would pack the baskets more loosely than usual. When a worker was ill, particularly black women who operated stemmer machines, other women would take up the slack rather than call attention to her condition, which could result in lost wages or dismissal. On the factory floor, where stemmers were generally not allowed to sit or talk to one another, it was not uncommon for women to break out in song. Singing in unison not only reinforced a sense of collective identity but the songs themselves—religious hymns, for the most part—ranged from veiled protests against the daily indignities of the factory to utopian visions of a life free of difficult wage work.

Theft at the workplace was among the more common forms of working-class resistance, and yet the relationship between pilfering—whether of commodities or time—and working-class opposition has escaped the attention of most historians of the African American working class. Any attempt to understand the relationship between theft and working-class opposition must begin by interrogating the dominant view of "theft" as deviant, criminal behavior. First of all, what theft is must be placed in historical context. As E. P. Thompson and Peter Linebaugh point out in their studies of English workers, changes in the law in response to workers' actions often turned accepted traditions—what Thompson calls "the moral economy"—into crime. At the center of class conflict in the eighteenth century were dock workers in London who suddenly lost the right to dip into tobacco cargoes for their personal use; farmers who were denied access to "common" lands for grazing and gathering wood; shipwrights, caulkers, and other laborers in the shipbuilding industry who discovered that they could be jailed for continuing the very old practice of taking "chips" of excess wood home with them. For years afterward, workers continued to take things from work, but now they were stealing. For some the consequences were unemployment, jail, deportation to the "New World," or the gallows.

The idea of the moral economy certainly operated in the Jim Crow South, as is evident in the actions of domestic workers. While "pan-toting" was regarded as theft by many employers, household workers believed they had a right to take home leftovers, excess food, and redundant or broken utensils for their home use. Not only was it the moral thing to do, given the excesses and wastefulness of wealthy families and the needs of the less privileged, but pan-toting also grew out of earlier negotiations over the rights and obligations of waged household labor. Insisting that pan-toting was not theft, one Southern domestic worker declared, "We don't steal; we just 'take' things—they are a part of the oral contract, exprest [*sic*] or implied. We understand it, and most of the white folks understand it." The "white folks" who tolerated pan-toting viewed it as either further proof of black women's immorality or justification for low wages. In other words, because pan-toting entailed the loss of food and clothing, low wages were intended to compensate for the *employer's* loss. Others simply treated pan-toting as a form of charity. As one employer put it, "When I give out my meals I bear these little blackberry pickaninnies in mind, and I never wound the feelings of any cook by asking her 'what that is she has under her apron.'" Aside from the more familiar instances of pan-toting, washerwomen throughout the South occasionally kept their patrons' clothes when they were not paid in a timely and adequate fashion.

From the vantage point of workers, as several criminologists have pointed out, theft at the workplace is also strategy to recover unpaid wages and/or compensate for low wages and mistreatment. In the tobacco factories of North Carolina, black workers not only stole cigarettes and chewing tobacco (which they usually sold or bartered at the farmer's market) but, in Durham at least, workers figured out a way to rig the clock in order to steal time. And in the coal mines of Birmingham and Appalachia, miners pilfered large chunks of coke and coal for their home ovens. Black workers sometimes turned to theft as a means of contesting the power public utilities had over their lives. During the Great Depression, for example, jobless and under-employed working people whose essential utilities had been turned off for nonpayment literally stole fuel, water, and electricity: people appropriated coal, drew free electricity by tapping power lines with copper wires, illegally turned on water mains, and destroyed vacant homes for firewood.

Unfortunately, we know very little about black workplace theft in the twentieth-century South and even less about its relationship to working-class resistance. Historians might begin to explore, for example, what philosopher and literary critic Michel de Certeau calls "wigging," a complicated form of workplace resistance in which employees use company time and materials for themselves (e.g., repairing or making a toy for one's child, writing love letters). By using part of the workday in this manner, workers not only take back precious hours from their employers but resist being totally subordinated to the needs of capital. The worker takes some of that labor power and spends it on herself or her family. One might imagine a domestic who seizes time from work to read books from her employer's library. A less creative though more likely scenario is washerwomen who wash and iron their own family's clothes along with their employers' laundry.

Judging from the existing histories, it seems that domestic workers adopted sabotage techniques more frequently than industrial workers. There is ample evidence of household workers scorching or spitting in food, damaging kitchen utensils, and breaking household appliances, but these acts were generally dismissed by employers and white contemporaries as proof of black moral and intellectual inferiority. Testifying on the "servant problem" in the South, a frustrated employer remarked:

> the washerwomen … badly damaged clothes they work on, iron-rusting them, tearing them, breaking off buttons, and burning them brown; and as for starch!—Colored cooks, too, generally abuse stoves, suffering them to get clogged with soot, and to "burn out" in half the time they ought to last.

Although most of the literature is silent on industrial sabotage in the South, especially acts committed by black workers, there is no question that it existed. In his work on tobacco workers in Winston-Salem, Robert Korstad introduces us to black labor organizer Robert Black, who admitted to using sabotage as a strategy against speedups:

> These machines were more delicate, and all I had to do was feed them a little faster and over load it and the belts would break. When it split you had to run the tobacco in reverse to get it out, clean the whole machine out and then the mechanics would have to come and take all the broken links out of the belt. The machine would be down for two or three hours and I would end up running less tobacco than the old machines. We had to use all kind of techniques to protect ourselves and the other workers.

It is surprising to note how little has been written about workplace theft and sabotage in the urban South. Given what we know of the pervasiveness of these strategies in other parts of the world, and the fact that sabotage and theft were common practices among slaves as well as rural African Americans in the postbellum period, the almost universal absence of these sorts of clandestine activities among black industrial workers in historical accounts is surprising. Part of the reason, I think, lies in Southern labor historians' noble quest to redeem the black working class from racist stereotypes. The company personnel records, police reports, mainstream white newspaper accounts, and correspondence have left us with a somewhat serene portrait of folks who, only occasionally, deviate from what I like to call the "Cult of True Sambohood." Southern racist ideology defined pilfering, slowdowns, absenteeism, tool-breaking, and other such acts as ineptitude, laziness, shiftlessness, and immorality. But rather than escape these categories altogether, sympathetic labor historians are often too quick to invert them, remaking the black proletariat into the hardest-working, thriftiest, most efficient labor force around. Part of the problem, I suspect, lies in the tendency of historians to either assume that all black workers lived by the Protestant work ethic or shared the same values usually associated with middle-class and prominent working-class blacks. But if we regard most work as alienating, especially work performed in a context of racist and sexist oppression, then we should expect black working people to minimize labor with as little economic loss as possible.

When we do so, we gain fresh insights into traditional, often very racist documents. Materials that describe "unreliable," "shiftless," or "ignorant" black workers should be read as more than vicious, racist commentary; in many instances these descriptions are the result of employers, foremen, and managers misconstruing the meaning of working-class activity which they were never supposed to understand. Fortunately, many Southern black workers understood the "Cult of True Sambohood" all too well, and at times used the contradictions embedded in racist ideology to their advantage. In certain circumstances, their inefficiency and penchant for not following directions created havoc and chaos for industrial production or the smooth running of a household. And all the while the appropriate grins, shuffles, and "yassums" mitigated potential punishment.

Because black men and women toiled in work spaces in which both bosses and white workers demanded deference, freely hurled insults and epithets at them, and occasionally brutalized their bodies, it becomes even clearer why issues of dignity informed much of black infrapolitics in the urban South. Interracial conflicts between workers were not simply diversions from some idealized definition of class struggle; white working-class racism was sometimes as much a barrier to African American's struggle for dignity and autonomy at the workplace as the corporate-defined racial division of labor. Thus episodes of interracial solidarity among working people, and the fairly consistent opposition by most black labor leaders to Jim Crow locals, are all the more remarkable. More importantly, for our purposes at least, the normative character of interracial conflict opens up another way to think about the function of public and hidden transcripts for *white* workers. For Southern white workers to openly express solidarity with African Americans was a direct challenge to the public transcript of racial difference and domination. Indeed, throughout this period Southern biracial union leaders, with the exception of certain left-wing organizers, tended to apologize for their actions, insisting that the union was driven by economic necessity and/or assuring the public of their opposition to "social equality" or "intermixing." Thus, even the hint of intimate, close relations between workers across the color line had consequences that cut both ways. Except for radicals and other bold individuals willing to accept ostracism, ridicule, and even violence, expressions of friendship and respect for African Americans had to remain part of the "hidden transcript" of white workers. This is an important observation, for it means that acts and gestures of *antiracism* on the part of white workers had to be disguised and choked back; when white workers were exposed as "nigger lovers" or when they took public stands on behalf of African Americans, the consequences could be fatal.

This chapter, and some of the work on which it draws, just begins to explore the realm of workplace infrapolitics. It aims to recover daily acts of resistance by African Americans who, until recently, have been presumed to be silent or inarticulate. Given the incredibly violent and repressive forms of domination in the South, workers' dependence on wages, the benefits white workers derived from Jim Crow, the limited influence black working people exercised over white dominated trade unions, and the complex and contradictory nature of human agency, clandestine forms of resistance should be expected.

Whether or not battles were won or lost, the mere threat of resistance elicited responses from the powerful which, in turn, shaped the nature of struggle. Repression and resistance are inextricably linked and African American resistance did make a difference. We know, for example, that Southern rulers during this era devoted an enormous amount of financial and ideological resources to maintaining order; police departments, vagrancy laws, extralegal terrorist organizations (e.g., the Ku Klux Klan and the White Legion), and the spectacle of mutilated black bodies were part of the landscape of domination surrounding African Americans. Widely publicized accounts of police homicides, beatings, and lynchings, as well as black protest against acts of racist violence, abound in the literature on the Jim Crow South. Yet, while dramatic acts of racial violence and resistance are usually well documented and make good stories, they represent only the tip of a gigantic iceberg.

We need to recognize that infrapolitics and organized resistance are not two distinct realms of opposition to be studied separately and then compared; they are two sides of the same coin that make up the history of working-class resistance. As I have tried to illustrate, the historical relationships between the hidden transcript and organized political movements during the Age of Jim Crow suggest that trade unions and political organizations able to mobilize segments of the black working class were successful because they at least partially articulated the grievances, aspirations, and dreams that remained hidden from public view. On the other hand, we must be careful not to assume that organized movements are merely articulating a full-blown hidden agenda that had been percolating until the proper moment. Such a view underestimates the impact that social movements themselves have on working-class consciousness. Involvement in a movement often radicalizes workers who might have otherwise expressed their grievances silently. Hence, efforts on the part of grass-roots unions to mobilize Southern black workers, from the Knights of Labor and the Brotherhood of Sleeping Car Porters to the Communist Party and the Congress of Industrial Organizations (CIO), clearly played a role in shaping or even transforming the hidden transcript. Successful struggles that depended on mutual support among working people and a clear knowledge of the "enemy," not only strengthen bonds of solidarity but also reveal to workers the vulnerability of the powerful and the potential strength of the weak. Furthermore, at the workplace as in public space, the daily humiliations of racism, sexism, and waged work, combined with the presence of a labor movement, embolden workers to take risks when opportunities arise. And their failures are as important as their victories, for they drive home the point that even the smallest act of resistance has its price. The very power relations that force them to resist covertly also make clear the terrible consequences of failed struggles.

African American workers' actions, thoughts, conversations, and reflections were not always, or even primarily, concerned with work, nor did they fit well with formal working-class institutions, no matter how well these institutions might have articulated *aspects* of the "hidden transcript." In other words, we cannot presume that trade unions and similar labor institutions were the "real" harbingers of black working-class politics; rather, even for organized black workers they were probably a small part of an ensemble of formal and informal avenues through which people struggled to improve or transform daily life. For a worker to accept reformist trade union strategies while stealing from work, to fight streetcar conductors while voting down strike action in one's local, to leave work early in order to participate in religious revival meetings or rendezvous with one's lover, or to choose to attend a dance rather than a CIO mass meeting is not necessarily a sign of an "immature" class consciousness, but reflects the multiple ways working people live, experience, and interpret the world around them.

CHAPTER 15

Occupy the Hammock
The Sign of the Slacker behind Disturbances in the Will to Work

Michael J. Roberts

The philosophers of antiquity taught contempt for work…, the poets [Virgil] sang of idleness, that gift from the Gods: O Melibaeus! A god has granted us this idleness!
 – Paul Lafargue, *The Right To Be Lazy*

The Return of the Repressed in New Working-Class Organizing Efforts

In the fall of 2012 and summer of 2013, something unexpected happened in the US political-economy. Service-sector workers in the fast-food industry and workers at the retail giant Wal-Mart staged several strikes and other workplace protests as part of a sustained organizing drive for union recognition, a significant raise in wages and better working conditions. At Wal-Mart, workers assisted by the United Food and Commercial Workers Union (UFCW) formed the Organization United for Respect at Wal-Mart (OUR Wal-Mart). In addition to several organized strikes across 11 states, OUR Wal-Mart also organized a one-day walkout on "Black Friday," the busiest shopping day of the year.[1] Less than a week after the Black Friday action conducted by OUR Wal-Mart, workers in the fast-food industry organized their own walkouts at several locations in New York City, including Burger King, Kentucky Fried Chicken, Taco Bell and McDonald's, who, according to *Market Watch*, has enjoyed increasing profits amounting to $1.4 billion in 2013.[2] According to the *Huffington Post*, this figure is close to the amount that US taxpayers shell out to cover assistance programs for fast-food workers who cannot make ends meet with the wages they earn in the industry.[3] In 2014, McDonald's worldwide profits were $4.7 billion.[4] After the New York strikes in 2012, fast-food workers backed by the Service Employees International Union (SEIU) and other organizations carried their fight into the summer and fall of 2013 when they launched a nationwide campaign of strikes in seven cities across six states, including an expansive strike-wave conducted on August 29 that included 58 cities.[5] Asking for a "living-wage" ($15-an-hour) in addition to union recognition, it was the largest, most expansive strike

Class: The Anthology, First Edition. Edited by Stanley Aronowitz and Michael J. Roberts.
© 2018 Stanley Aronowitz and Michael J. Roberts. Published 2018 by John Wiley & Sons Ltd.

wave in the history of the industry. As of fall 2014, workers in the fast-food industry continue to organize and conduct strikes across the country.[6] In the following pages, I interpret these new forms of worker militancy, and especially the conservative responses to them, in terms of *disturbances* in what Daromir Rudnyckyj refers to as the "globalization of the will to work."[7]

These strikes and protests are the most recent evidence of a growing trend among workers in the private sector who, in the last few years, have been seeking union representation in greater numbers. According to a 2007 study conducted by Richard Freeman for the Economic Policy Institute, 44% of workers in the United States favor union representation, while 85% desire more of a collective say at the workplace than they currently enjoy.[8] Journalists and social scientists have begun to speculate about whether or not these numbers and the recent strikes represent the beginning of a break from the recent history of declining union membership.[9] During the early 1970s, one-third of workers in the private sector were members of labor unions, but after decades of conducting a losing battle with employers in both the private and public sectors, organized labor represents a mere 11.3 percent of all US workers, and less than 7 percent in the private sector.[10] The question remains whether or not workers will begin joining unions in large numbers like they did in the 1930s. Service-sector workers face hostile employers like Amazon and Wal-Mart, where management has a record of retaliation against organizing efforts through various forms of intimidation and harassment and, in some cases, the firing of militant workers, sending the message that the retail giant is willing to break the law in order to prevent unionization of its workforce.[11] Good news for the workers came in November 2013, however, when the National Labor Relations Board (NLRB) ruled against Wal-Mart, stating that the federal agency will prosecute the illegal firings of 117 workers who were involved in organizing activity.[12] The NLRB ruling is likely to hasten organizing and protest activity among the 1.3 million Wal-Mart workers and perhaps workers throughout the service sector more generally.

The willingness of workers in the service sector to organize and go on strike took both journalists and social scientists by surprise since these workers have long been considered unlikely agents of workplace resistance. Conservative journalists working at Fox News were both surprised *and* irritated by the strikes and protests. First, they interpreted the strikes as a major inconvenience for consumers of fast food. Then they framed the striking workers as an example of the "undeserving poor," a central category in conservative discourse that frames poverty as the result of deviant-individual behavior rather than structural changes in the economy that follow from the struggle between labor and capital. For example, much was made of the advice given to workers at McDonald's when the company provided their employees with a video website tutorial on how to create a sustainable monthly budget. The video claims that workers should be able live on minimum wage, or on wages not much above the minimum, as long as they remain careful and responsible with their money.[13] Right-wing journalists pointed to this as proof that poverty is the result of irresponsible behavior, leading them to the conclusion that the striking workers who ask for higher wages should be condemned on moral grounds for being greedy, since their situation was caused by their carelessness with their money. Indeed, one commentator on the Fox News show "Bulls and Bears" said in no uncertain terms that, "people are not in poverty because they are making minimum wage."[14] What most alarmed conservative pundits was the sudden public attention to the possibility that Congress might raise the minimum wage, because according to conservatives, an increase in the minimum wage would diminish the incentive to work.

In short, the minimum wage and other government interventions in the labor market are said to foster a culture of dependency, which for reactionaries is usually code for the lack of a will to work. Since these events, two signifiers have been consistently circulating among conservative, and to a lesser extent, liberal media outlets: the hammock and its potential occupant, the slacker. Why these discursive markers have become so threatening to the hegemony of neoliberalism needs exploration.[15]

The fact that the median annual wage of fast-food workers (roughly $18,000 dollars according to the Bureau of Labor Statistics) falls below the poverty line for a family of three (roughly $19,000 dollars) is consistently ignored by conservatives in the media and in Congress. This is to say nothing of the empirical problem of how to measure poverty. Many economists have argued for decades that the poverty line is set too low because the economic context within which the metric was first created (the 1960s) is radically different than the economic context of today.[16] Another issue that goes largely unexamined by conservatives is the relationship between the level of the minimum wage and the level of productivity gains achieved by workers over the past few decades. If the amount of the minimum wage had kept pace with productivity gains created and realized by workers since the early 1970s, the minimum wage today would be nearly *22* dollars an hour.[17] Most of the productivity gains in the past few decades have gone to those at the very top end of the wealth distribution in the United States.[18]

Academics turned liberal-left pundits like Paul Krugman and Robert Reich argue that the terrain of the fight over minimum wage and other government welfare programs is empirical, *not* cultural or ideological. The aim for liberals is to demonstrate, empirically, that deviant-individual behavior is not the cause of poverty. In addition, liberal pundits seek to demonstrate that welfare programs have very little effect on work incentives. The right-wing argument that assistance programs create disincentives to work is referred to by Krugman as the "hammock fallacy."[19] In short, Keynesian demand-side policies like the minimum wage, food stamps and other government assistance programs for the poor do not discourage people from working hard. Krugman, in particular, makes the case that a "hammock" *is* necessary, but only for those who are unable to work, and he shows empirically that this is exactly what our government assistance programs for the poor are doing. By demonstrating that these programs do not discourage able-bodied individuals from working hard, Krugman and others on the liberal left agree with those on the political right that it would be immoral to resist work. The goal for liberals is to present poor people as moral citizens worthy of recognition as subjects constituted by the will to work. As a result of this cultural and ideological dynamic, liberals prefer to use the metaphor "social safety-net," rather than "hammock," when referring to government assistance programs that target poor people. A safety-net is for deserving subjects, while the hammock signifies abuse by "bad subjects" in the Althusserian sense: namely, slackers.[20]

In this way, the liberal left participates together with conservatives in what C. Wright Mills refers to, in his "Letter to the New Left," as the "labor metaphysic."[21] This point of view sees "labor itself as a kind of redemption by which spiritual and social needs are fulfilled and without which humanity in its most fundamental sense is impossible."[22] For both sides of the political aisle, to "suggest a campaign to reduce work on social and ideological grounds remains highly suspect."[23] The hammock, then, exists as a metaphor at the center of both conservative and liberal discourses that attend to the object of work. For both, it exists as a potential problem, a signifier that reveals instability in the hegemony currently enjoyed by both Republicans and "new" Democrats.[24] The slacker signifier points to the question of how time is constituted by our cultural practices and it exists as a potential (de)constructor of the notion that unproductive time is something that must be killed. I read the slacker as the figure that embodies the time that must be killed, a figure that embodies the time that has not yet been rationalized by the imperatives of capitalist social relations. What is remarkable about these recent events, then, is *not* that conservatives routinely "get the facts wrong" about poverty and the relationship between government welfare programs and work incentives. Rather, what is remarkable is how swiftly and forcefully reactionaries moved to frame striking workers in terms of the binary that frames the deserving and undeserving poor, a discursive maneuver that leads inevitably to an attack upon the figure of the slacker.[25] As I argue below, what is ultimately at stake in these responses to the threat posed by the sign of the slacker is the neoliberal project of inculcating what Rudnyckyj calls – in a Foucauldian manner – the "regime of self-improvement."[26]

Discourse and Ideology in the Minimum-Wage Debates

To raise the issue of productivity increases within the debate about minimum wage would require reflection upon what share of the wealth produced by labor should go to workers. That kind of reflection is potentially dangerous territory for reactionary political leaders and conservative news pundits, because it ultimately leads one to the recognition that labor creates capital, rather than the other way around. Such a line of reasoning is simply off limits because it undermines the dominant ideology which presents labor as the dependent variable in our political–economy. We tend to think that the well-being of workers is made possible by employers. Conservatives make much of this ideology when they talk about business leaders as "job creators."[27] Upon closer inspection of what happens during the production process, however, we see that the opposite is the case. Measurements of productivity provide us with a glimpse of how it is that capital is made possible by labor, since labor is the only commodity that can create more value than it, itself, is worth. This relationship between labor and capital, which is the foundation of our political–economy, is mediated, obscured and ultimately displaced through ideology. This is precisely why, in his critique of the discourse on economics, Karl Marx refers to the workplace in capitalism as the "hidden abode" of production, an aspect of everyday life that is taken for granted without critical reflection.[28] As Kathi Weeks has argued in her 2011 book, *The Problem with Work*, "political theorists tend to be more interested in our lives as citizens and noncitizens, legal subjects and bearers of rights, consumers and spectators, religious devotees and family members, than in our daily lives as workers."[29]

In order to avoid this kind of conversation in American politics, conservatives in the media, in academia and in Congress prefer to discuss the share of wealth going to workers in terms of "markets." Conservative discourse focuses on how it can *only* be the undisturbed market that determines wage levels for workers.[30] Democratic processes of wealth distribution or workers' demands for a greater share of the wealth that they produce are said to interfere with, and distort, the proper, "natural" functioning of markets. In this way, the discourse of neoliberalism represents the market as an external, objective mechanism – akin to Newton's law of gravity in the discourse of physics. For this reason, it is argued that only the market can be the guarantor of social justice. Thus, to resist the market would be a quixotic enterprise, like trying to resist gravity. This is how the social world gets turned upside down in ideology: social relations (markets) created by human agents are represented (misrecognized) as external and prior to the people that create them.[31] Close examination of the history of capitalism reveals that there has never been any such thing as a "free market." Markets have always been made by historical actors, and the state has always been necessary to create and re-create the conditions for capital accumulation throughout the different phases of capitalist development, from the primitive form of accumulation in the early years of capitalism that were characterized by bloody violence and the expropriation of land from the peasants, to the monopoly form of accumulation today, which is characterized by chronic over-production and enormous waste.[32] Furthermore, recent research has shown that incentives funded by the tax-payer designed to attract businesses to particular locales are a waste of resources.[33]

In addition to moving business operations to new locales in search of cheap labor, capitalists also frequently turn to techniques of automation as a means to increase unemployment, what Marx referred as the creation and maintenance of the "reserve army" of labor.[34] In this way, capitalists always work toward manipulating labor markets by seeking ways to increase the supply of labor and drive down the cost of labor. For example, when workers for the Bay Area Rapid Transit (BART) system went on strike in the summer of 2013, the CEO of User Voice, Richard White, argued, "get 'em back to work, pay them whatever they want, then find a way to automate their jobs so this never happens again."[35] The issue of replacing unruly workers with machines was also discussed by business leaders who considered the possibility that Congress and/or individual states and cities might raise the minimum wage in the wake of the fast-food workers' demands. On the Fox News program "Varney and Co." (July 29, 2013) host Stuart Varney raised the issue when he interviewed a spokesperson from the Employment Policies Institute. Varney leads off the interview by saying, "if you get fifteen bucks-an-hour, in comes the I-Pad to do it [take orders from fast food customers] for nothin?" His guest responds by saying that "technology is racing beyond these demands [pause]...businesses are looking for ways [pause]... there are computer-based applications right now that will show restaurant operators how they can get customers to order by I-Pad and pay by I-Pad." In both of these cases (the workers on strike at BART and the workers on strike in the fast-food industry) we see clearly how business leaders respond to workers that they perceive to be both too expensive and too disobedient by replacing them with computers or robots.[36] This kind of dynamic – where capital seeks automation in an attempt to control labor and increase its supply – has been at work for decades in the US and global political-economy. One only has to look at the particular industries where, historically, workers have had the most political power (auto, steel, mining and shipping) to see the most sophisticated levels of labor-saving technologies. Machines and computers have largely displaced human labor in all of these industries.[37] In this way, capital *responds* to the varying degrees of power exercised by labor.

Rarely do mainstream media outlets capture the issues so clearly, but the words of business leaders like White and commentators like Varney reveal that capital depends upon the reserve army of labor as both a means to control workers and a means to continue accumulating. Indeed, tight labor markets are a political problem for business leaders, which is why throughout the history of the United States representatives of business elites like the US Chamber of Commerce and the National Association of Manufacturers have sought the help of the federal government in their effort to ensure through legal means (for example, the Taft–Hartley Act of 1947) that workers never fully exploit their main source of leverage against capital, namely the withdrawal of their labor-power through strikes, walkouts, slowdowns, soldiering, slacking-off, etc.[38] Relatively high unemployment is the best insurance that capital has against insubordinate workers. Workers, for their part, also seek to change the prevailing conditions in the labor market through the fight for shorter hours of work. But when workers intervene in the labor market, bourgeois ideologues cry foul and insist that markets must not be disturbed by strategies and policies that favor the position of workers relative to capitalists. The problem for the capitalist class is how to conceal their own attempts to manipulate the labor market behind the discourse of "free enterprise." To be more precise, there is no conspiracy at work here. Rather, the problem for conservatives is how to respond to the moments when the text or discourse of neoliberalism becomes unstable, as when particular signifiers like the slacker threaten the reproduction of ideological practices.

In short, class struggle between labor and capital creates and shapes markets, especially labor markets. Markets are not things that exist outside of, or prior to, social relations. The discourse of neoliberalism (re)presents market conditions that favor the capitalist side of the class divide as the so-called "free-market" economy, the way things are supposed to work without the intervention of the state or labor unions. In this way, the particular point of view of capital is misrepresented as the universal, objective perspective of society as a whole. Indeed, as Marx demonstrated, the field of economics *is* the point of view of capital, but in order to maintain its hegemony the ruling class must (re)present its particular interests as if they are objective. In everyday life today, the phrase we use to express this point of view is, "what is good for Wall Street is good for Main Street." In the 1950s, Charles Wilson, the President of General Motors argued that "what was good for our country was good for General Motors and vice versa."[39]

Another argument that conservatives make in their attempt to thwart efforts to raise the minimum wage is to claim that raising it would discourage potential business owners from starting new businesses, the argument being that anyone starting a business would create new jobs, which is assumed, *a priori*, to be a good thing. The *kind* of jobs created is never considered for examination. For example, the reactionary billionaire Charles Koch said in an interview with the *Wichita Eagle* that he wanted Congress to abolish the minimum wage because it creates a "culture of dependency" in addition to making it impossible for business owners with "limited capital" to "start a business."[40] This is an old argument, which has never been supported by empirical evidence.[41] The phrase "culture of dependency" is sometimes code for the relative independence of workers in a context where workers have some leverage to resist the demands made by capitalists. Whenever conditions prevail that allow workers to resist the work imperative thrown down upon them by capital, conservatives turn to the discourse on the culture of dependency.

Koch's position was mocked by television host Stephen Colbert who applied Koch's reasoning to the early years of the US republic, saying, "He's [Koch] right. Having to pay your employees really hurts small business. I mean, look at our nation's forefathers. Many arrived with only the blouse on their back, but thanks to no minimum wage law, they started a booming cotton industry." Examination of the video clip reveals that as Colbert utters the phrase "booming cotton industry," the audience is shown an image of slaves working in cotton fields.[42] Colbert exposed what is really at stake with the fast-food workers' strikes, namely the conditions under which work is imposed by one class onto another. How is one class able to make another work, and work under conditions that favor the master? Under what conditions is the working class able to resist and impose different conditions that favor its own position? While the empirical evidence makes a mockery of the argument that poverty is primarily the result of deviant-individual behavior, there is actually much more at stake with these events, because they reveal a class relation that under normal circumstances remains obscured by the routines of everyday life.

Against the liberal position of Krugman and Reich, what is perhaps most interesting in the conservative response to the fast-food strikes is *not* how they get it wrong, empirically, about what creates the conditions of poverty. Rather, it is how they could not avoid coming down on the side of discipline and repression, unintentionally exposing a *relationship* between rulers and ruled that lurks in the shadows of reactionary discourse, which, under normal circumstances, focuses on the behavior and "freedom" of autonomous individuals. In other words, while commentators at conservative networks like Fox News claim they believe in individualism and the value of individual freedom, their coverage of the fast-food workers' strikes revealed that they actually support one side of a *relationship* (employers) against freedom for those on the other side (employees). This raises a very important issue. Under certain political-economic conditions, the face of freedom mutates into the face of *un*freedom. The labor strike is a significant phenomenon in a capitalist political-economy precisely because it reveals a workplace relationship based upon domination that is, under normal circumstances, concealed by the discourse of neoliberalism, which places an emphasis upon rational individuals who interact as free agents in the marketplace. Conservative discourse struggles to keep the focus upon activity in the marketplace, where free individuals interact as buyers and sellers of goods. Activity in the workplace, which is characterized by unfreedom and asymmetrically structured power relationships, is outside of the gaze of neoliberal discourse. If neoliberal discourse maintains hegemony in the constitution of reality, then conservatives gain the upper hand in the national conversation about freedom and happiness. In the past few decades the political right has largely monopolized the discourse of freedom in American politics, by framing freedom within a right-wing libertarian framework.[43] But when strikes occur such as the fast-food workers' strikes, the political right abruptly flip-flops from advocating freedom to suddenly supporting its opposite, repression. *Alas, the capitalist discursive subject is Janus-faced.*

In an interview on *Democracy Now*, one of the fast-food workers who participated in the strikes – he works 60 hours a week at two jobs, one at Burger King and the other at Pizza Hut – revealed that one of the main reasons why he and his co-workers went on strike was to protest working conditions that he described as "a dictatorship at work." This is precisely the kind of phenomenon obscured by the conservative discourse on neoliberalism, but again, strikes are exceptional social and political moments for they break open a space that reveals the workplace relationship for what it is, namely a confrontation between what Hannah Arendt refers to as rulers and ruled.[44] The workplace occupies an enormous part of our everyday lives. It exists as a universe of unfreedom, the elephant in the room that nobody wants to talk about, but nonetheless sits in the middle of our capitalist democracy. In another portion of the interview, the worker says that it is time for all workers to "*come out of the shadows* and let the public be aware of how we live our day-to-day lives… What have we got to lose by speaking up? We're already dying slowly" (italics mine).[45]

This raises another issue with the striking workers in the service sector, and that concerns how we think of ourselves as human beings, and what it means to have a good life. Closer inspection of the McDonald's employee budget tutorial mentioned above reveals that it assumes the individual in question has *two* jobs, one paying $1100 dollars a month, and the other $900 dollars a month. In addition, there is only $20 allocated for health insurance, $600 dollars for mortgage/rent and *no* money at all for clothes and heat! One cannot help but wonder what kind of home a family of three could rent for that amount, let alone obtain with a mortgage payment of just $600 dollars a month. One of the main items of advice in the McDonald's tutorial was that their workers should not spend a dollar a day on a treat like a candy bar or pack of gum. That way they could save $365 dollars a year. This begs the question: How low should we set the bar on what counts as a reasonable standard of living? Why do we expect some people who work so hard to deny themselves such modest forms of pleasure? What does that say about our society and culture?

For conservatives in the media who covered the strikes, it was impossible to conceal this aspect of the workplace relationship, and this is precisely what makes these strikes and protests so interesting to examine. Indeed, once it became impossible to deny the existence of the unfree relations between rulers and ruled that constitute the workplace, conservatives were compelled to rationalize and justify the repression, unhappiness and suffering endured by these workers by way of twists and turns in their discourse. One of the most interesting of these justifications is the argument that the minimum wage is *supposed* to cause suffering. The argument here is that suffering is good because it motivates people to move up the so-called "economic ladder" to better-paying and more enjoyable kinds of jobs. In short, pain is required to get people to work hard. Fox News analyst Greg Gutfeld explained the argument on the show "The Five," by saying, "the first step on a ladder is not supposed to be comfortable. You're not supposed to be hanging out there. You double the salary, then you turn that rung into a hammock."[46] This argument was echoed by fellow Fox News anchor, Tracy Byrnes, who argued that "the goal in life is not to be on minimum wage forever. The goal in life is to do a great job and get promoted and move out of it. So this notion that we're gonna keep raising the minimum wage in order to share the wealth is ridiculous."[47]

Both Gutfeld and Byrnes attempt to make the case that working a minimum-wage job is supposed to be a temporary phenomenon, implying that most people who play by the rules will soon work their way up the ladder to a better job. The image of the ladder, of course, is simply given in their explanations. Their discourse relies upon the myth that most fast-food workers are teenagers working their way to better jobs when they get older. The other myth that grounds these arguments is the quasi-religious narrative, which claims that the individuals who are wealthy in our society deserve to be so, because they previously suffered through working hard at low-paying jobs before becoming rich. Of course these arguments are misleading, as a cursory analysis of the empirical data reveals. According to a study conducted by the CEPR in 2013, the median age of fast-food workers is now over 28, and over one-third of fast-food workers are college educated.[48] The fact that these arguments do not square with empirical reality reveals that they are code for what is really at stake: the problem of getting *other* people to work, and work hard for the benefit of their rulers. In short, the function of these coded texts is to encourage working people to identify their interests with the interests of those who are in charge. Most interesting for the purposes of this essay is the mention of the term "hammock," by both conservatives and liberals. The hammock has become a crucial signifier in the recent struggle over the formation of willing workers in the new global political-economy.

The Figure of the Slacker and the Cultural Dimension of the Minimum-Wage Debate

What is interesting to notice in both of the arguments above is that the figure of the slacker represents a *threat*. Lurking behind all the talk of economic opportunity and success through hard work is a certain fear, namely that workers with power may seek to change the terms and conditions of employment or, worse yet, re-evaluate the work ethic. The main issue for the capitalist class is how to get *other* people (the working class) to work hard, which is essentially what pundits like Gutfeld are saying when they argue that minimum wage is *supposed* to make people suffer. Work incentives and motivation are the main issue at hand, the will to work. The very low minimum wage, together with relatively high unemployment, works, as in Nathaniel Hawthorne's *Scarlet Letter*, because the suffering of low-wage workers is supposed to set an example for the rest of us about what lies in wait if we do not keep our noses to the grindstone and do whatever our employer asks of us as a means to get ahead.[49] Workers toiling away at minimum-wage jobs compete against one another in an attempt to escape the pain and stigma of living on poverty wages, while unemployed and undocumented workers compete against formally employed workers to bid down wages across the economy more generally. On the other hand, raising the minimum wage and lowering the rate of unemployment makes it more difficult for employers to control workers.

What is at stake for conservatives is the possibility that workers may choose *not* to work so hard, what I am calling a disturbance in the will to work. Herein lies the reason for the fear generated by the sign of the slacker in reactionary discourse: the slacker figure is always present as a *temptation* for working-class subjects to reject the ethos of the Calvinist work ethic.[50] The slacker signifier represents a kind of instability in the text that constitutes the discourse of neoliberalism. Reactionaries rely upon what Freidrich Nietzsche refers to as the feeling of "ressentiment" as a means to keep the slacker figure at bay.[51] Rather than identify with the bohemian slackers, resentful waged workers are encouraged to blame the slacker instead of the capitalist for their economic woes. But the job of policing the terrain that separates the slacker as *other* from the working-class subjects of political economy is always-already threatened with the transgression of the border between the two. *We are drawn to the slacker as we fear it.*

It is never guaranteed in advance that conservative discourse will succeed in whipping up working-class resentment against the figure of the slacker. The constant hammering away at the hammock metaphor is a sign that the relationship between rulers (capitalists) and ruled (workers), which we usually take for granted, is a rather tenuous one. Capitalists can never be sure that their efforts to reproduce relationships of domination will be successful. This phenomenon is not unlike that of the minstrel show as interpreted by Eric Lott in his magnificent book, *Love and Theft: Blackface Minstrelsy and the American Working Class*. According to Lott, "the audiences involved in early minstrelsy were not universally derisive of African Americans or their culture… there was a range of responses to the minstrel show which points to an instability or contradiction in the form itself… in early blackface minstrelsy [there was a] dialectical flickering of racial insult and racial envy, moments of domination and moments of liberation, counterfeit and currency…."[52] The representation of the slacker also presents the readers (audience) with a range of responses. One never knows in advance if workers will embrace or reject the sign of the slacker, because as was the case with the figure of the minstrel, there is simultaneously an attraction to, and fear and loathing of the figure of the slacker, which reveals the combinations of fear, guilt *and* pleasure within our libidinal investments in these texts.[53]

Congressman and former vice-presidential candidate Paul Ryan also used the image of the hammock when he attacked programs that provide a social wage, like unemployment insurance, food stamps, Temporary Assistance for Needy Families (TANF) and social security. During the 2012 presidential campaign he argued, "We don't want to turn the safety net into a hammock that lulls able-bodied people to lives of dependency and complacency that *drains them of their will* and their incentive to make the most of their lives" (italics mine).[54] Conservatives are correct to point out that the key issue is the possibility that workers may lose their will to work. Liberals like Krugman, on the other hand, refuse to consider that possibility, since for them the challenge is to demonstrate that welfare recipients are indeed, good subjects, just like most workers in our political economy who embrace the work ethic. But for Ryan, government assistance programs "drain the will" of workers to "make the most of" themselves. The struggle ultimately is not empirical, but ideological; it is a struggle over the will of workers and control over the sign that marks the slacker.[55]

Ryan's is a classic reactionary discourse that conceals (unconsciously) the reality of workers creating surplus value (which is, metaphorically speaking, a hammock made by workers for capitalists insofar as labor creates capital in the first place) by employing a narrative of lazy welfare recipients who live off of the tax revenues collected from working people. In this way, the worker–capitalist divide is displaced by the divide between all people who "work" and those who do not, namely welfare recipients and bums. Conservative discourse situates capitalists and workers on the same team, against welfare recipients who are on the opposing team. The opposing-team metaphor is usually a racialized concept. "Welfare" is usually code for urban, black and lazy.[56] But again, the racist discourse on lazy welfare recipients is always a tenuous one at best, one that is not always able to interpellate individuals as obedient subjects in a straightforward way.[57]

It is worth examining this metaphor of the hammock at more length, because it reveals what is truly at stake from the capitalist point of view, namely that *there is not room for two (classes) in the hammock*. There is a very interesting contradiction contained within the conservative point of view. This contradiction permeates our culture at large: most people want to be wealthy in order *not* to suffer in poverty and dull, sometimes back-breaking work, whether sitting in a chair in a cubicle or displacing soil with a shovel. We all participate in the fantasy of occupying the hammock. The appeal of a wealthy lifestyle is motivated precisely by the desire for leisure and the rejection of delayed gratification. This desire largely explains the enormous popularity of hit television shows like "Lifestyles of the Rich and Famous," hosted by Robin Leach, or Music Television Network's show, "MTV Cribs," among others. Conservatives and liberals claim that most Americans embrace the work ethic, but that is not why millions of people are watching those shows. The discourse on the moral value of hard work for its own sake is contradicted by many forms of popular culture, including shows like these that enjoy enormous popularity precisely because viewers (most of us) fantasize about what it would be like to live a life of leisure and luxury without having to work. Popular culture reveals that while in everyday life workers may be forced to repress their desire to occupy the hammock, the desire never goes away. Rather, it is displaced onto the forms that constitute certain domains of popular culture.[58]

This way of looking at the contested terrain of popular culture is perhaps best articulated by Ellen Willis, who argues that,

> Mass consumption, advertising, and mass art are a corporate Frankenstein; while they reinforce the system, they also undermine it. By continually pushing the message that we have the right to gratification now, consumerism at its most expansive encouraged a demand for fulfillment that could not so easily be contained by products; it had a way of spilling over into rebellion against the constricting conditions of our lives... the history of the sixties strongly suggests that the impulse to buy a new car and tool down the freeway with the radio blasting rock and roll is not unconnected to the desire to fuck outside marriage, get high, stand up to men or white people or bosses, join dissident movements. In fact, the mass media helped to spread rebellion... On one level the sixties revolt was an impressive illustration of Lenin's remark that the capitalist will sell you the rope to hang him with.[59]

Critics on the left, like Ellen Willis, argue that conservatives have correctly identified the main issues as cultural, not empirical, as liberals like Krugman and Reich insist. Willis' passage above is a radical spin on the point of view presented by conservatives like Daniel Bell, who, in his book the *Cultural Contradictions of Capitalism*, identifies roughly the same ideological and cultural conflicts that Willis points to in the passage above.[60] Conservatives like Bell understood that policing the work ethic would become a central problem in the era of "late capitalism," where scarcity has been overcome, and consumerism promotes "hedonism," in order to reproduce the conditions of capitalist accumulation.[61] Herbert Marcuse, for his part, presented the cultural contradictions of late capitalism in terms of what he called "surplus repression."[62] In late or "monopoly" capitalism, the work ethic is more vigorously enforced and policed by conservatives the more that work itself becomes less necessary as a result of decades of developments in labor-saving technologies that have conquered scarcity.

The television shows that focus upon the extravagant lifestyles of wealthy people co-exist on television with numerous late-night infomercials about how to get rich quick, which indicates another very popular narrative in our culture, one that extols the ability to climb the so-called "economic ladder" with the least amount of energy and in the least amount of time possible. Furthermore, numerous books published every year promise their readers that the secrets to getting rich fast are contained within their covers. This narrative exists in stark contradiction with the religious-conservative narrative that extols the virtues of suffering and endless hard work for its own sake. It is as if our culture is bi-polar. On the one hand we worship the idea of getting wealthy with no effort at all. On the other hand, we worship suffering. How are we able to cope with this cultural bi-polarity? If most of us do not desire work for work's sake (especially for poverty wages), then why do we expect *other* people to work long hours and endure poverty for as long as it takes, with no real expectation of getting rich quick? How can reactionary discourse handle this peculiar contradiction?

In short, there is a double standard at work. Certain individuals in our political-economy are celebrated for finding riches without much effort and for indulging in an excess of pleasure, whereas other (usually racialized) subjects of political-economy are supposed to suffer and delay their gratification indefinitely as a means to prove their moral worth to the rest of us. *A certain kind of person is expected to suffer for our sins.*

In the American experience, this cultural bi-polarity is often handled by displacing class onto race, which in turn allows for the construction of a discourse about "deserving" and "undeserving" poor people.[63] Undeserving people are framed as able-bodied adults who refuse to pull their own weight in the economy, preferring to live off of welfare benefits provided by the taxes paid by people who are waged workers. This is a crucial discursive maneuver that conservatives rely upon in order to accommodate the stark contradictions that exist in our political-economy and our culture. The "undeserving" poor are often framed in racialized terms as the so-called urban "underclass," but there is no underclass per se.[64] Rather, the so-called "underclass" should be considered as a low-waged or unwaged fraction of the working class. In cultural terms, as long as working-class people show deference and a willingness to work hard, even at low wages – the will to work – they are considered worthy, but if low-waged and un-waged working-class people stand up for themselves, they are attacked as lazy dependents who are irresponsible with their money and, as a result, mooch off of the welfare system. Ronald Reagan made good political use of this stereotype in the 1980s when he talked about the so-called "welfare queen" who, allegedly, managed to live a lavish life as a welfare recipient.[65] Indeed, Reagan created the blueprint for contemporary conservative pundits who attack the welfare system in the United States today. Liberals, for their part, attempt to represent the urban underclass as victims of the economy rather than agents who exploit the system. In both liberal and conservative discourse, slacking is a serious offense.

Sometimes the representation of the bohemian "bum" is used in place of the racialized urban dweller to the same effect. The bum stereotype is usually a single, white man, framed as an able-bodied counter-cultural figure eager to boast about living on the public dole. Both liberals and conservatives participate in the discursive attack on the bohemian bum, because it is more difficult to frame this type of bad subject as a victim. For example, in a news segment titled, "When the Safety Net Becomes a Hammock" (*Fox News*, August 9, 2013), Fox News correspondent John Roberts features a young "surfer-bum" in San Diego who receives $200 dollars a month in food stamps. The video shows images of the young man using food stamps to feast upon lobster and sushi while he informs Roberts that he prefers to wake up late most days and then surf all day with his friends. If you look closely at the background images, however, you can see clearly that the young man lives in a working-class neighborhood. It is also important to note that the young man is not receiving any other government subsidy, and lobster cannot be on the menu every day if your budget is a meager $200 dollars a month. Furthermore, we never get to see whether or not the young man works odd jobs with irregular hours to make spending cash. Nevertheless, you can practically see the blood boil in Roberts' veins as he listens to the surfer-bum talk about his lifestyle, while wearing a smirk on his face and displaying a twinkle in his eye that seems to taunt the reporter and the nature of the inquiry. The surfer seems aware that he is participating in a theatrical performance, willing to play the part of the villain. Roberts even says that he was "taken aback" by the young man's refusal to be ashamed of his lifestyle. One wonders if Roberts is really so angry about the fact that the man is on food stamps. Perhaps the source of outrage can be found in the fact that the surfer-bum has found a way to escape the drudgery of full-time work.

In the introduction to Roberts' feature, we are encouraged to believe that President Obama's generous welfare policies are the cause of the increased "abuse" of food stamps in the United States, because it is simply too easy to get assistance. The segment uses a typical bait and switch tactic to draw our attention away from the economic recession and the fact that the overwhelming majority of people on food stamps are not "cheaters." Still, there is something more at stake than cheating. What is most interesting is the unusual willingness for a news reporter to reveal his anger (bias) while in the guise of an objective journalist. A little psychoanalysis goes a long way in explaining why Roberts, who represents both the reactionary bourgeois and the resentful working-class audience of Fox News, is so angry at this surfer and his lifestyle. It is worth quoting George Rawick, the author of the classic book on American slavery and the culture of resistance created by slaves, *From Sundown to Sunup*. In his book Rawick writes,

> The Englishman met the West African as a reformed sinner meets a comrade of his previous debaucheries. The reformed sinner very often creates a pornography of his former life. He must suppress even his knowledge that he had acted that way or even wanted to act that way. Prompted by his uneasiness at this great act of repression, he cannot leave alone those who live as he once did or as he still unconsciously desires to live. He must devote himself to their conversion or repression.[66]

The surfer-bum featured by Roberts reveals that he wants to be a "rock star" in addition to being a surfer, a fantasy shared by many if not most young people living in the United States. The video shows him playing an electric guitar in between parts of the interview. Perhaps Roberts himself once had that same fantasy, but now, like most of his viewers, that fantasy has long since been repressed. Roberts tells his audiences that the young man has "chosen the life of a beach bum in this sea-side paradise." It's interesting to note that Roberts uses the phrase "sea-side paradise," revealing that he too feels the powerful appeal of a leisurely life on the sand and in the sun. Indeed, the audience is interpellated in the same way.

Toward the end of the segment Roberts says to the young man, "Is it safe to say that this notion of holding down a steady job is just something that is not in your wheel house... it's just not something that appeals to you?" Suddenly, the interview turns on what is *really* at stake, as we move from considering the issue of welfare cheats to the issue of choosing *not* to work. It seems that, in the end, what matters more than the possibility that some individual may be able to exploit the food stamp system is the *other* possibility that a person from a working-class background can refuse the life of full-time work. Refusing work is the major offense, because most people do not see that way of life as a possibility, even as they themselves desire it, as the passage above by Rawick suggests. When people who work their fingers to the bone for very little in return see others who have been able to escape that way of life, the common reaction is envy, anger and resentment. When an individual realizes that in spite of the fact that they have played by the rules and yet they still were not able to climb the economic ladder of success, then someone must be to blame. But in ideology, blame can never be placed at the feet of the capitalist system. Enter the figure of the slacker: coded either as surfer-bum or the racialized, urban under-dweller. Within the current context of the neoliberal discourse that glorifies work, the bum plays the role of Hester Prynne. *This phenomenon should be understood for what it is: a ritual in sado-masochism.*

This is what is meant by the metaphorical phrase, "there isn't room for two in the hammock." Ultimately, nobody desires long hours of degrading work at low pay, including most importantly, the master, who occupies the hammock under normal conditions. This explains, finally, why the political right becomes so upset when workers go on strike, or when workers choose to be surfer-bums instead of workers. It upsets what appears to be "the way things are," to borrow a familiar phrase. As Louis Althusser argues, ideology works by making contingent, historically mediated social relations appear as "obvious," and without need of explanation. "Ideology," he says, "has no history." In terms of the metaphor of the hammock, it is understood as obvious that only the master is allowed to occupy and enjoy the hammock, while the servant is expected to embrace their subject position as a worker who serves the master. In ideology, that goes without saying. If the servant ever forgets this arrangement and dares to go on strike for a better life, or chooses the lifestyle of the surfer-bum over that of the factory worker or precarious service-sector worker, then they must be punished so that they, and people like them, remember how things are supposed to be. This ritual of sado-masochism in everyday life is the material that gives rise to the ideology that frames reactionary discourse, which in turn works toward the reproduction of the social relations in our political-economy.[67] In short, individuals *become classed subjects* through these sado-masochistic rituals that govern workplace relations and everyday life.

Gutfeld's discourse of economic ladders is a prime example of this ideology. The master occupies the hammock, while the servant must wait and delay gratification, with the hope of someday joining the master class. In the meantime, the servant may find the opportunity to move up to the next rung of the ladder, assuming another individual is waiting in the wings ready to assume the subject position of worker on the bottom rung. Eventually, we are told, we may be able to climb into the hammock, as long as we play by the rules created by our masters. Alas, sooner or later *never* comes. Stephen Colbert also satirized this form of reasoning when he exposed the absurdity of the McDonald's budget tutorial at the point when the spokeswoman in the video says, "try this [budget] for a month to see that you really will spend less," to which Colbert intervenes, "then try it for a year, then ten years, then 50 years, then ask yourself, 'why am I still working at McDonald's? I'm 85 years old!'"[68]

Conclusion

By way of conclusion, I should like to turn to the Occupy Wall Street movement and the intervention it has made in our public discourse on inequality and the economy. Is it not the case, as Kristin Lawler argues, that the slacker signifier also animates the form and content of that movement?[69] Most of the participants in the actual camps constitute what some have called a new, post-industrial working class, namely the *precariat* (as opposed to the proletariat). Journalists like Paul Mason refer to the Occupy participants – as well as the Arab Spring youth and the youth fighting against austerity in Europe – as "graduates without a future."[70] The precariat is characterized by an advanced degree and a casual attachment to work, as individuals bounce around between one low-skilled, low-paying, service-sector job and the next, in spite of having qualifications for better-paying, more desirable and more intellectually demanding jobs.[71] Today, job security linked to economic growth, one of the defining characteristics of modernization, has become a thing of the past due to decades of advances in labor-saving technologies.[72] But it would be wrong to say that capital has been in the driver's seat all along in the creation of the neo-liberal, post-industrial and postmodern reality. The workers who conducted wildcat strikes in record numbers in the late 1960s and early 1970s refused to continue on with the Keynesian–Fordist compromise between labor and capital that provided workers with steady cost-of-living raises as compensation for giving up control over the labor process and accepting alienating working conditions.[73] Young workers at that time demanded a better life both inside and outside of work; indeed, a main rallying-cry of both worker and student protest movements in 1968 was the demand to change everyday life.[74] According to Mario Tronti and Antonio Negri, it was the "strategy of refusal" among young American and European workers that partly explains why both Keynesianism and Fordism (twin pillars of modernization) failed.[75] What comes next?

The new social formation of global capitalism is forcing us to reconsider time spent outside of work, but under what conditions will we experience this "free" time? If work, job security and endless economic growth provided the content of the discourse that legitimated modernity, what are the *cultural implications* of post-industrial social formations and the unwinding of what Lyotard calls the "meta-narratives" that legitimated modernity?[76] What is left when the meta-narratives of modernity collapse or unwind under the weight of postmodernity? One interpretation of such an "unwinding" of meta-narratives, if you will, is to see it as the condition of "slack," as when a taut rope is suddenly released. This condition of slack upsets both liberal and conservative discourse, for as Stanley Aronowitz has argued, time outside of work (as the result of widespread automation) is the new postmodern reality, but "it's remarkable how unprepared we are to think about it."[77] Today, slackers who consciously lack the will to work are finding ways to create new forms of meaning in the time spent outside of work.[78] The decline and unwinding of the meta-narrative on labor and work (the "labor metaphysic") has opened up space for individuals to no longer be subjected to what it is that they have become. Perhaps, then, slackers can be interpreted as working on undoing the processes that historically have produced and reproduced the classed subjects of the capitalist-political economy and the will to work. This is, in part, what is at stake for Lyotard and Michel Foucault with the end of modernity and the dialectic of the Enlightenment.[79]

Will the neoliberal "regime of self-improvement," as Rudnyckyj defines it, succeed in the instillation of a new will to work among subjects of the global political-economy?[80] Or, will slackers find ways to keep the rope from tightening once again, maintaining the slackness that opens up new spaces of freedom and experimentation within the intervals described by Stephens and Weston? Slack could be read in terms of a potential promise for a new kind of freedom, constituted by an *ethos*, as described by Foucault, "in which the critique of what we are is at one and the same time the historical analysis of the limits that are imposed on us and an experiment with the possibility of going beyond them."[81] This, it seems, is how the Occupy Movement has embraced the figure of the slacker, as an experiment, one which we could take advantage of in these postmodern times. A first step would be to resuscitate the epic struggle for shorter hours of work that once animated the nineteenth-century labor movement. As labor leaders in organizations like the Industrial Workers of the World (IWW) understood, shorter hours of labor decrease unemployment, and thereby increase the leverage that workers enjoy relative to capitalists.[82] Such leverage could be used to make radical changes in the routines of everyday life, because the fight for shorter hours of work is both a means and an end. It is a means to increase the power of workers relative to capitalists and an end in itself: leisure time. Before those steps can be taken, however, there first needs to be an ideological shift that reinterprets the value of work for work's sake, something that the IWW consistently argued in pamphlets and in songs, including Harry McClintock's iconic tunes, "Hallelujah I'm a Bum" and "The Big Rock Candy Mountain." Perhaps it is no coincidence that the IWW has had the best success so far of any labor organization in organizing the precariat at places like Starbucks Coffee Company.[83]

Another alternative worth consideration is reviving the idea of a universal, guaranteed annual income.[84] But this idea should be separated from the original context from which it emerged. In the 1970s, conservatives like Milton Friedman proposed the guaranteed income as a *technical* issue, designed to solve economic problems. The cultural and ideological dimension of work was not a topic for conversation, and it is still not up for reflection among those on the left who are currently talking about the idea. A guaranteed income is considered by both left and right as an economic issue, with little or no relation to cultural problems, because the concept is framed within a context that addresses economic inequality. Thus, it is understood as a "how to" issue rather than a "why" issue (why work?). Most importantly, liberals and conservatives continue to wring their hands over the possibility that a guaranteed income would discourage people from working.[85]

In ideology it appears as if only the master deserves access to the hammock, but when the figure of the slacker upsets the ideological rituals of sado-masochism in everyday life, we get a glimpse of how it is that workers fight for their chance to occupy the hammock. At last we have reached what is truly at stake with the fast-food workers' strikes and the discourse on hammocks among the right and left that has framed these recent events. Perhaps there is, after all, room for more in the hammock. It may be that a return to the ancient Greek attitude towards work is what we need: a trip back to the future. As the dramaturge Gotthold Ephraim Lessing once said, "Let us be lazy in everything, except in loving and drinking, except in being lazy."[86]

Notes

1 http://www.salon.com/2012/11/23/1000_walmart_protests_across_the_us/
2 http://www.marketwatch.com/story/mcdonalds-profit-up-14-on-us-same-store-sales-2013-01-23
3 http://www.huffingtonpost.com/2013/10/21/mcdonalds-profit-taxpayers_n_4136336.html
4 http://america.aljazeera.com/articles/2015/6/5/workers-minimum-wage.html
5 http://www.salon.com/2013/08/29/largest_fast_food_strike_ever_today_50_cities_will_be_affected/
6 http://www.salon.com/2014/09/04/get_a_clue_mcdonalds_why_im_walking_off_my_fast_food_job_today/
7 Daromir Rudnyckyj, "Regimes of Self-Improvement: Globalization and the Will to Work," in *Social Text 120*, Volume 32, Number 3, Fall 2014, p. 119.
8 "Do Workers Still Want Unions? More Than Ever," Economic Policy Institute, February 22, 2007.
9 http://www.dissentmagazine.org/article/can-the-one-day-strike-revive-the-labor-movement
10 See Nelson Lichentstein, *State of the Union: A Century of American Labor* (Princeton, NJ: Princeton University Press, 2002).
11 http://www.alternet.org/how-amazon-continues-get-away-abusing-its-workers
12 http://www.thenation.com/article/177254/labor-board-sides-workers-walmart-cant-silence-employees-any-longer
13 http://www.forbes.com/sites/laurashin/2013/07/18/why-mcdonalds-employee-budget-has-everyone-up-in-arms/
14 http://video.foxnews.com/v/2569747360001/do-minimum-wage-hikes-help-or-hurt-workers/?#sp=show-clips
15 I use the terms conservative and reactionary in much the same way as Corey Robin, in his recent book, *The Reactionary Mind: Conservatism From Edmund Burke to Sarah Palin* (New York: Oxford University Press, 2011). For Robin, "conservatism is… a meditation on – and theoretical rendition of – the felt experience of having power, seeing it threatened, and trying to win it back… Conservatism is the theoretical voice of this animus against the agency of subordinate classes" (pp. 4 and 7). I read the sign of the slacker as a provocation that excites and disturbs conservatives insofar as its presence threatens to undermine a certain feeling of power among reactionaries. Robin, in his analysis of power relations between employers and employees writes, "in the employment contract… workers consent to be hired by their employers, but until the twentieth century that consent was interpreted by judges to contain implicit and irrevocable provisions of servitude; meanwhile, the *exit option of quitting* was not nearly as available, legally or practically, as many might think" (italics mine, p. 5). My focus on the sign of the slacker places an emphasis on the

exit option as the most serious threat posed to conservatives in the arena of the labor relations within the current global-capitalist context. The slacker figure, in short, exists as a temptation for workers to exit their relationships with employers.

16 http://billmoyers.com/2013/09/18/why-is-the-federal-poverty-line-so-low/

17 "The Minimum Wage is Too Low," John Schmitt, Center for Economic and Policy Research (CEPR), March, 2012.

18 http://www.epi.org/publication/ib330-productivity-vs-compensation/

19 http://www.nytimes.com/2014/03/07/opinion/krugman-the-hammock-fallacy.html?module= Search&mabReward=relbias%3Aw%2C%7B%222%22%3A%22RI%3A16%22%7D

20 A representation of the figure of the slacker that I like can be found in Richard Linklater's 1991 film, *Slacker*. In the movie there are no main characters and no linear plot or narrative. Instead, the camera follows seemingly random characters (none of whom are working) from one scene to the next, characters that mimic a chain of sliding signifiers, endlessly circulating through the film. I discuss this issue in terms of the decline of meta-narratives at the end of this essay. For Althusser, the "bad subject" is the one who fails to be interpellated by ideology. Briefly, interpellation is the process whereby individuals are positioned as subjects by institutions like education and the news media, which for Althusser are two of the key institutions inside the ideological state apparatus within the capitalist social formation. Interpellation works by way of recognition, where the individual recognizes him or herself as an addressee of discursive hailing on the part of authoritative figures. See Louis Althusser, "Ideology and Ideological State Apparatuses," in *Lenin and Philosophy* (New York: Monthly Review Press, 2001). I do not take a strictly Althusserian approach, however, as Althusser's Lacanian perspective closes off the possibility for examining resistance and the failures of interpellation that occur during extraordinary moments, like protest activity and social movements. These moments create gaps in the interpellation process.

21 https://www.jacobinmag.com/2011/03/letter-to-the-next-left/

22 See Stanley Aronowitz, "Why Work?" in *Social Text*, Number 12, Autumn 1985, p. 21.

23 Stanley Aronowitz, "Why Work?" in *Social Text*, Number 12, Autumn 1985, p. 19.

24 "New" Democrats refers to the change in direction inside the Democratic Party after the election of Bill Clinton. After Clinton, Democrats and Republicans embraced neoliberalism and the power of Wall Street over the formation of global capitalism that followed the collapse of the Soviet Union.

25 I will argue that the signifier "slacker" acts as a marginal figure that returns to the center, in terms of how Jacques Derrida understands the relationship between center and margin within a given text. Conservative discourse, by focusing so much attention upon the metaphor of the hammock and figure of the slacker, reveals an instability in the discourse, which in turn uncovers instability in the social relations that marginalize the slacker. See Derrida, *Margins of Philosophy*, translated by Alan Bass (Chicago: University of Chicago Press, 1984). Briefly, I appropriate the practice of deconstruction insofaras I consider how the subject of the Calvinist work ethic (workers broadly defined, but especially subjects that constitute the petite bourgeois class) *depends* upon the slacker as Other. In my appropriation, I attempt to show that while the slacker is construed as the opposite of the subject of the Calvinist work ethic, the attempt to assign a negative value to the slacker requires a certain policing of the boundary between worker and slacker that is always porous. The subject at the center of the text, so to speak, is the Calvinist worker-subject, who must constantly marginalize and repress the slacker, but the very being of the Calvinist worker-subject is *parasitic* upon the slacker. The frontier between the two is constantly policed because it can always be transgressed, indeed is always-already transgressed. What is on the outside, the slacker, is also on the inside. In addition to Derrida's post-structuralism, I make use of the theoretical perspective of V.N. Volosinov's *Marxism and the Philosophy of Language* (Cambridge, MA: Harvard University Press, 1986). I discuss this in more detail in the second half of the essay.

26 Rudnckyj looks at recent attempts within new management practices to increase worker productivity and self-discipline as a more contemporary version of the phenomenon that Michel Foucault refers to as "governmentality," the ability of figures of authority to produce subjects that will their own subjection. See Foucault, *Government of Self and Others: Lectures at the College de France, 1982–1983*, translated by Graham Burchell (New York: Palgrave, 2010), and *Discipline and Punish*, translated by Alan Sheridan (New York: Vintage, 1995).

27   Business leaders in several state-level chambers of commerce together with national associations like the National Restaurant Association and the CEO of Home Depot have founded the "job creators" network as a means to intervene in the public discourse about the role of the private sector in promoting economic well-being for US citizens. See their website at: http://www.jobcreatorsnetwork.com/about/.On their website they claim, "government policies are breaking the backs of business owners and killing job creation."

28   See Karl Marx, "The Sale and Purchase of Labour-Power," in *Capital: A Critique of Political Economy, Volume 1* (Penguin Books, 1990), p. 279.

29   Kathi Weeks, *The Problem With Work: Feminism, Marxism, Antiwork Politics, and Postwork Imaginaries* (Durham, NC: Duke University Press, 2011).

30   See David Harvey, *A Brief History of Neoliberalism* (New York: Oxford University Press, 2007). See also Milton Friedman, *Capitalism and Freedom* (University of Chicago Press, 2002).

31   See Georg Lukacs, "*Reification and the Consciousness of the Proletariat*," in *History and Class Consciousness*, translated by Rodney Livingstone (Cambridge, MA: MIT Press, 1972).

32   See Karl Polyani, *The Great Transformation* (Boston: Beacon Press, 2001), Alfred Chandler Jr., *The Visible Hand* (Belknap Press, 1993) and Paul Baran and Paul Sweezy, *Monopoly Capital* (New York: Monthly Review Press, 1966). It should be noted that new forms of primitive accumulation have emerged in many areas of the global economy including China.

33   http://www.latimes.com/opinion/op-ed/la-oe-florida-government-incentives-to-businesses-20140916-story.html. Thus, not only is it the case labour creates capital, but when the state intervenes on the side of capital to allegedly "create" jobs in the private sector, these schemes turn out to be a way for capital to force local governments to compete against each other in order to create substantial subsidies for businesses they hope will settle in their location.

34   Karl Marx, *Capital: A Critique of Political Economy, Volume 1* (Penguin Books, 1990), Chapter 25.

35   http://www.salon.com/2013/07/08/silicon_valley_is_stoking_the_wrong_kind_of_revolution/

36   There is a tradition in Marxist social theory that embraces the replacement of labor by machines, because the argument is that no human being should be wasting their life at degrading and dangerous jobs. Indeed, the argument is that only when workers refuse work and successfully fight for shorter hours do capitalists have an incentive to automate. Marx himself makes this case, but his son-in-law Paul Lafargue is perhaps better with the pen when he argues that, "O idiots, it is because you work too much that the industrial equipment develops slowly…listen to an economist, no other than M. L. Reybaud, whom we were fortunate enough to lose a few months ago. 'It is in general by the conditions of hand-work that the revolution in methods of labor is regulated. As long as hand-work furnishes its services at a low price, it is lavished, while efforts are made to economize it when its services become more costly'" (*The Right to be Lazy*, translated by Charles H. Kerr, Chicago: Charles H. Kerr Publishing, 1989, p. 59).

37   See David Noble, *Forces of Production* (Oxford University Press, 1986), and Stanley Aronowitz and William DiFazio, *The Jobless Future: Sci-Tech and the Dogma of Work* (Minneapolis, MN: University of Minnesota Press, 1993). The second edition was published in 2010.

38   See also Frances Fox Piven's book, *Challenging Authority: How Ordinary People Change America* (New York: Roman Littlefield, 2006). According to Piven, "Networks of cooperation and interdependence inevitably give rise to contention, to conflict, as people bound together by social life try to use each other to further their often distinctive interests and outlooks…the leverage inherent in interdependence is potentially widespread, especially in a densely interconnected society where the division of labor is far advanced. This leverage… can be activated from below, by the withdrawal of contributions to social cooperation by people at the lower end of hierarchical social relations" (p. 20). The figure of the slacker is defined in this paper as the agent of the withdrawal of social cooperation in terms of workplace relations.

39   It is important to note that this phenomenon is not an example of conspiracy on the part of the representatives of capital. Rather, as an ideology, the discourse of neoliberalism interpellates subjects across class lines, so that rulers and ruled participate in the rituals of everyday life as believers, so to speak.

40   *Wichita Eagle*, July 9, 2013.

41   For a recent study see John Schmitt's paper, "Why Does the Minimum Wage Have No Discernible Effect on Employment? CEPR, Feb. 2013.

42   http://thecolbertreport.cc.com/videos/8fg72p/minimum-wage---mcdonald-s-spending-journal

43   See Stanley Aronowitz, *The Death and Rebirth of American Radicalism* (Routledge, 1996).

44   See Hannah Arendt, *The Human Condition* (University of Chicago Press, 1998).

45   *Democracy Now*, August 2, 2013.

46   Gutfeld's argument was lampooned by John Oliver on the *Daily Show*. http://thedailyshow.cc.com/videos/wj3t4a/pay-mas---fast-food---minimum-wage

47   http://video.foxnews.com/v/2569747360001/do-minimum-wage-hikes-help-or-hurt-workers/?#sp=show-clips

48   http://www.cepr.net/index.php/blogs/cepr-blog/slow-progress-for-fast-food-workers

49   For a similar analysis of this dynamic at work in the welfare system in the US, see Fox Piven and Richard Cloward, *Regulating the Poor: the Functions of Public Welfare* (New York: Vintage, 1993).

50   See footnote 24.

51   See Friedrich Nietzsche, *The Genealogy of Morality*, translated by Maudemarie Clark (New York: Hackett Publishing 1998).

52   See Eric Lott, *Love and Theft: Blackface Minstrelsy and the American Working Class* (New York: Oxford University Press, 2013) pp. 15 and 18. Lott also argues that "although minstrelsy was indeed in the business of staging and producing 'race,' that very enterprise also involved it in a carnivalizing of race, as the range of critical response has begun to suggest, such that the minstrel show's ideological production became more contradictory, its consumption more indeterminate, its political effects more plural than many have assumed" (p. 21).

53   Eric Lott, *Love and Theft: Blackface Minstrelsy and the American Working Class* (New York: Oxford University Press, 2013), p. 7 and p. 242. I return to this issue below where I discuss the work of George Rawick.

54   http://krugman.blogs.nytimes.com/2012/04/21/about-that-hammock/?module=Search&mabReward=relbias%3Aw%2C%7B%222%22%3A%22RI%3A16%22%7D&_r=0

55   On class struggle over the terrain of the sign, see V.N. Volosinov, *Marxism and the Philosophy of Language* (Cambridge, MA: Harvard University Press, 1986).

56   See Martin Gilens, *Why Americans Hate Welfare: Race, Media and the Politics of Antipoverty Policy* (University of Chicago Press, 2000).

57   See footnotes 18 and 24.

58   I make this argument in more detail in my book, *Tell Tchaikovsky the News: Rock'n'Roll, the Labor Question and the Musicians' Union 1942–1968* (Durham, NC: Duke University Press 2014). I examine the content of rock and roll music in terms of the desire for free time and the rejection of delayed gratification and the Calvinist work ethic. Popular culture, as Stuart Hall has argued, should be seen as a site of contestation rather than simply a form of domination as argued by the theorists of the culture industry like Max Horkheimer and Theodor Adorno, in their book, *Dialectic of Enlightenment*. Translated by Edmund Jephcott (Stanford University Press, 2002). See Stuart Hall, "Notes on Deconstructing the Popular," in *People's History and Socialist Theory*, ed. Raphael Samuels (New York; Routledge, 1981).

59   Ellen Willis, *Beginning to See the Light: Sex, Hope and Rock and Roll* (Hanover, NH: Wesleyan University Press, 1992), p. xvi.

60   See Daniel Bell, *Cultural Contradictions of Capitalism* (New York: Basic Books, 1996).

61   See Ernst Mandel, *Late Capitalism* (New York: Verso 1999).

62   See Herbert Marcuse, *Eros and Civilization* (Boston: Beacon Press 1955). According to Marcuse, "repressiveness is perhaps the more vigorously maintained the more unnecessary it becomes... the struggle for existence takes place in a world too poor for the satisfaction of human needs without constant restraint, renunciation, delay... whatever satisfaction is possible necessitates work, more or less painful arrangements... The prevalent scarcity has, throughout civilization... been organized in such a way that it has not been distributed collectively in accordance with individual needs... Instead, the *distribution* of scarcity, as well as the effort to overcome it, the mode of work, have been *imposed* upon individuals – first by mere violence, subsequently by a more rational utilization of power... the gradual conquest of scarcity was inextricably bound up with and shaped by the

interest of domination. Domination differs from rational exercise of authority. The latter, which is inherent in any social division… is confined to the administration of functions… necessary for the advancement of the whole. In contrast, domination is exercised by a particular group or individual in order to sustain and enhance itself in a privileged position" (pp. 4 and 35–6).

63 For more on the history of the relationship between race and class in the US political-economy see W.E.B. Du Bois, *Black Reconstruction in America: 1860–1880* (New York: The Free Press, 1992).

64 See Michael Katz, *The Undeserving Poor: America's Enduring Confrontation with Poverty* (New York: Oxford University Press, 2013).

65 http://www.npr.org/blogs/codeswitch/2013/12/20/255819681/the-truth-behind-the-lies-of-the-original-welfare-queen

66 George Rawick, *From Sundown to Sunup: The Making of the Black Community* (Westport, CT: Greenwood Publishing Company, 1972).

67 See Lynn Chancer, *Sadomasochism in Everyday Life: The Dynamics of Power and Powerlessness* (Rutgers University Press, 1992).

68 http://thecolbertreport.cc.com/videos/8fg72p/minimum-wage---mcdonald-s-spending-journal

69 http://www.possible-futures.org/2011/12/01/fear-slacker-revolution-occupy-wall-street-cultural-politics-class-struggle/

70 See Paul Mason, *Why It's Still Kicking Off Everywhere* (New York: Verso, 2013).

71 See Guy Standing, *The Precariat: The New Dangerous Class* (New York: Bloomsbury Academic, 2014).

72 See Aronowitz and DiFazio, *The Jobless Future: Sci-Tech and the Dogma of Work* (Minneapolis, MN: University of Minnesota Press, 1993). The second edition was published in 2010.

73 See Stanley Aronowitz, *False Promises* (Durham, NC: Duke University Press 1992) and Aaron Brenner et al., *Rank and File Rebellion: Labor Militancy and Revolt From Below During the Long 1970s* (New York: Verso, 2010).

74 http://www.blackstudies.ucsb.edu/1968/scope.html

75 See Mario Tronti, "Workers and Capital" in *Telos*, Number 14, Winter 1972.

76 See Jean-Francois Lyotard, *The Postmodern Condition*, translated by Geoff Bennington and Brian Massumi (Minneapolis, MN: University of Minnesota Press, 1984).

77 "Why Work?" p. 29.

78 http://www.washingtonpost.com/wp-dyn/content/article/2010/04/02/AR2010040201452.html

79 I realize that the phrase belongs to Horkheimer and Adorno, but I see Foucault's reflections on the Enlightenment as part of the same project. See Michel Foucault, "What is Enlightenment," in *Interpretive Social Science: A Second Look*, edited by Paul Rabinow and William M. Sullivan (Berkeley, CA: University of California Press, 1987), pp. 157–174. Foucault argues that "the critical ontology of ourselves… has to be conceived as an attitude, an *ethos*, a philosophical life in which the critique of what we are is at one and the same time the historical analysis of the limits that are imposed on us and an experiment with the possibility of going beyond them." (p. 174).

80 Daromir Rudnyckyj, "Regimes of Self-Improvement: Globalization and the Will to Work," in *Social Text 120*, Volume 32, Number 3, Fall 2014, p. 119.

81 Michel Foucault, "What is Enlightenment," in *Interpretive Social Science*, edited by Paul Rabinow and William M. Sullivan (Berkeley: University of California Press, 1979), p. 174.

82 For a more extensive analysis of the history of the shorter-hours of work movements, see Jonathan Cutler, *Labor's Time* (Temple University Press, 2004).

83 https://iww.org/content/iww-starbucks-workers-union-declares-global-week-action-against-starbucks-union-busting-soli

84 http://www.pbs.org/newshour/making-sense/why-americas-favorite-anarchist-thinks-most-american-workers-are-slaves/

85 http://www.pbs.org/newshour/making-sense/why-americas-favorite-anarchist-thinks-most-american-workers-are-slaves/

86 See Paul Lafargue, *The Right to Be Lazy* (Chicago: Charles H. Kerr Publishing, 1989), p. 21.

PART TWO
The Middle Class

CHAPTER 16

The Vanishing Middle

Stanley Aronowitz

What Is the Middle Class?

The "middle class" is located at the apex of the American imagination. Rather than simply being a descriptive category that refers to a social group or formation, the term hovers near the leading edge of American politics and ideology. Candidates for public office never cease to evoke the middle class as the object of their discourse. Every economic topic, including taxes, jobs, and housing, contains references to the plight of – or the interests of – the "middle class." And the middle-class ideal, whatever it might be, is said to mark American history and culture and set the United States off from Europe and the rest of the world. The economist and sociologist Werner Sombart tells us that America is the exception to the European rule that society is divided into antagonistic social classes, because America has no feudal tradition. Feudalism was a social structure marked by pervasive economic and social inequality and constituted the origin of traditional classes in Europe and Asia. The United States, in contrast, is said to be a nation of considerable social mobility, because its social structure is fluid. Later historians, including Richard Hofstadter, Daniel Boorstin, and Louis Hartz, have added to this thesis, arguing that US history is marked by consensus rather than conflict. There may be little room at the top, but anyone of humble origins can, with hard work and a considerable bit of luck, rise to middle-class status. Although many young people dream of riches or fame, most Americans believe themselves to be middle class and would gladly settle for a secure middle-class niche. Of course, what defines this niche is hotly disputed: does it mean ownership of a small business, including an independent profession such as law or medicine? Does it mean home ownership? Does it consist of having a steady job with a predictable salary? Its cousins and competitors are the doctrines of individualism, entrepreneurship, the work ethic, parsimony, and, of course, the American Dream.

The American Dream is a myth of many parts. For some it represents the aspiration to be "my own boss." For many more it is identified with home ownership, a rather modest scaling down of hope. And middle-class morality typically substitutes for genuine politics. As C. Wright Mills notes, Americans tend to see political actors in terms of good guys and bad guys; we ascribe such phenomena as widening income gaps, white-collar crime, and corporate misfeasance not to the ordinary functions of capitalism and class disparities but to evil, self-serving motives. Motives and intentions are even inscribed into laws as interpreted by the courts. For example, during the economic meltdown

Class: The Anthology, First Edition. Edited by Stanley Aronowitz and Michael J. Roberts.
© 2018 Stanley Aronowitz and Michael J. Roberts. Published 2018 by John Wiley & Sons Ltd.

beginning in 2007, common middle-class sense ascribed the problem to "corporate greed" rather than undertaking a sober analysis of capitalist dynamics. Since the early 1970s, the US economy has survived on the fiction that our money has a solid material foundation rather than it sitting on vast debt of all sorts, a myth that escaped both economists and the general public until the roof fell in – and even then, proposals abounded about how to restore the debtor economy. Or if debt is publicly acknowledged, its intrinsic role in the formation of fictitious capital is ignored or denied. Otherwise, it would be hard to explain why, after December 2007, the official date, according to the National Bureau of Economic Research, of the first major twenty-first-century economic crash, federal government decision makers sought to ease the path to further debt accumulation through consumption as a major component of the road to recovery. As the economist Richard Wolff has pointed out, "stimulus" means renewing debt as the motive force of economic activity, a program likely to result in the same deep decline that marked the years after 2006. The middle class, no less than expert opinion, seems unable to grasp the structural roots of the crisis.

For most of us, therefore, a good job is one that brings an income that enables a household to secure some of the good things in life, such as home ownership and, increasingly important, our kids' college attendance, because higher education seems to many to be the road to economic well-being. When these aspirations are threatened, especially in economic terms, the middle class becomes, for a brief moment, a political actor. For when its status is threatened, in social and cultural terms, the myths that sustain America's claim to domestic tranquility and global leadership are jeopardized, because its collective imagination is inextricably bound to the middle-class ideal.

In 2008, presidential candidate Barack Obama, whose successful nomination was attributable, in the main, to his early opposition to the Iraq war, ran in the general election on a platform of helping the "middle class" claw its way out of mounting debt, sidestep the imminent threat of joblessness, avoid the home foreclosures that were multiplying exponentially after late 2006, and dodge the other symptoms of the emerging economic crisis. During the campaign, the Iraq war faded as an issue, because the Bush White House promised a gradual withdrawal of US troops and conducted an apparently successful "surge" of additional troops to quell the anti-US insurgency that had plagued the post-Saddam military situation. More to the point, the looming depression overshadowed all other issues. Obama effectively employed his middle-class mantra because the Republican White House had lost its credibility during the later years of the Iraq war, especially for its indecisive response to the gathering financial storms.

In the United States, the phrase "working class" has almost no currency. The reluctance to embrace working-class identity might be ascribed to the dominance of the link between the concept of middle class with certain income levels, implying forms of consumption that allegedly blur the lines between the owners of productive or commercial property and those who own personal property such as homes and cars and are creditworthy. Factory, construction, and other wage workers are likely to hold mortgages on their own homes, typically have cars, and, in many instances, send their kids to college or have themselves attended some institution of post-secondary education. That one possesses a credit card, a mortgage, may even own a modest vacation home or a boat, and go on holiday may qualify as a badge of middle-class status, regardless of occupation. Thus, according to the prevailing political and media wisdom, during much of the post-World War II era the American middle class included most of those who, in Europe and almost everywhere else in the world, are described as working class.

The prevailing historical wisdom is, and has been for most of the twentieth century, that the United States is a middle-class nation. This conviction is grounded in the nation's history. From the sixteenth century to the turn of the twentieth century, America was, largely, a land of independent farmers, small merchants, artisans, and relatively small manufacturing firms, and, after the seventeenth century, self-employed professionals like lawyers, physicians, and engineers. The slave South was the great exception, and, indeed, slavery was termed a "peculiar institution," although it is arguable that the revenues produced from the labor of slaves contributed significantly to the capital formation needed for bringing the country into the industrial era. That the postbellum years witnessed the flowering of "robber barons" and an era of vast wealth accumulation arising from industrial concentration, rail, real estate, and stock speculation failed to deter the fervent advocates of the concept of America as a middle-class oasis. And with the assistance of the US Army, the 1870s and 1880s witnessed a colossal land grab mainly at the expense of Native Americans as much as it saw intense industrial, scientific, and technological development. These decades were what became known as the Gilded Age, a time of the industrial tycoon who controlled an increasing portion of the national wealth and exercised inordinate influence over the federal, state, and local governments. Yet these developments failed to persuade expert and political perception that concentrated wealth did not alter the political and social landscape.

Perhaps only the denizens of the so-called "Progressive Era" – journalists, socialists, social reformers – recognized the impact of the new class divide between large-scale capital and labor on an increasingly embattled middle class and on the political economy and culture of the nation. However, that era was relatively short lived, lasting, according to some historians, from the 1890s until World War II. After the war, amid European devastation, America experienced unparalleled expansion, a rising standard of living that affected the majority of the population, and, equally important, a dramatic increase in the number and variety of salaried employees.

One of the corollaries of large-scale manufacturing and the consequent rise of the large corporations was the rapid growth of administrative employees. As Mills demonstrates in *White Collar*, the "new" salaried middle class was highly stratified, ranging in status and income from managers at the pinnacle, followed by qualified professionals (no longer able to hang out their shingle and become small entrepreneurs but instead obliged to work for salaries), to clerks, mostly women, who performed routine and repetitive tasks. At the turn of the twentieth century and not only in the United States, the new middle class was on the road to outstripping, in size and social importance, the old, entrepreneurial, self-employed middle class, which was being cut down to size by large-scale corporate capital. By the 1960s, this new middle class also outnumbered industrial workers.

One of the earliest examples of scholarly attention to white-collar employees appeared in 1912. Emil Lederer, a German sociologist, was one of the first observers of the "middle position" of *salaried* employees, those between owners and wage workers. He identified this stratum as a "new" middle class, new because it differed from the "old" middle class of owners of small productive and commercial property. Members of the new middle class worked for salaries and were generally employed by large corporations and the state. Lederer was among the more influential theorists of the middle class, and his work became a standard reference for subsequent writers on the new middle class. Among those who read his work was Siegfried Kracauer, the eminent German cultural critic whose writing on popular culture was among the most influential sources for the Frankfurt School and later for cultural studies.

Lederer was chiefly interested in the class and economic position of the new salaried employees, although he also addressed issues of status and prestige. While Kracauer locates the vast increase of salaried employees in the "structural changes in the economy towards the modern large-scale enterprise," his work *The Salaried Masses* focuses on the ideological and cultural programs of firms aimed at winning over the salaried employees "to their side" in their eternal conflict with wage labor. *The Salaried Masses* is a deft integration of the political and economic aspects of the emergence of the new middle class with an examination of the acutely significant culture of the "office." He finds that among the attractions of white-collar jobs is that they are "not manual" but that the work offered few intrinsic satisfactions, despite strenuous managerial efforts to persuade employees otherwise. Kracauer observes that the hollowness of administrative labor opens the way to the consumption of cultural and other goods as a "counterweight to desolation."

Walter Benjamin called Kracauer "a ragpicker at daybreak," and it is true that Kracauer's study offers no systematic economic treatment of the structural position of the new middle class. Instead, he gathers together fragments of the lives of salaried employees at play, in the neighborhood, and at work in order to provide a more complete picture of their experience. He stipulates what for others such as Lederer and his collaborator Jacob Marschak are the main points: to situate salaried employees in the economic and social structure and principally the class system. Kracauer is mostly concerned with the more-or-less complete recruitment of salaried employees to capital's side by means of "the ideologies that fetter them." These ideologies appealed to the salaried masses' feeling of superiority based on their schooling, which awards them a degree of status but no concrete material rewards. On the contrary, far from the individuality promised by high capitalism, Kracauer shows that the salaried employee has become the crucial element of the increasing massification of contemporary society exemplified in the "standard character." These characters "adapt themselves more or less easily to the firm," continuously aware of the distinction between themselves and the proletariat, and their adoption of "bourgeois ideology" masks the gap between their self-conception and their actual living and working conditions. These salaried employees, in the main, were not radically different from industrial workers.

Despite Kracauer's work, it was not until the 1930s that some novelists and sociologists noticed a "crisis" in the middle class in the aftermath of the Depression. Hans Fallada's best-selling novel of German middle-class life, *Little Man, What Now?*, became a standard reference for those, such as Wilhelm Reich and Max Horkheimer, who tried to understand the appeal of fascism. They traced the middle-class attraction to the Nazis to the extreme social and political isolation and fragmentation of the middle class and its lack of organizational and ideological independence. Perhaps the most notable of the social scientific accounts was Lewis Corey's economic and historical survey of the emergence of the new middle class in the United States. Published in 1935, only a year after his major work, *The Decline of American Capitalism*, a Marxist analysis of the causes of the Depression, *The Crisis of the Middle Class* rose, briefly, to the best-seller lists but quickly vanished into the library stacks. The popularity of his book on the middle class may be attributable to his attempt to show that the economic crisis had not only crushed industrial and service workers but was also a crisis for a salaried middle class that had once felt privileged and even inured from the vicissitudes of the economy. But, unlike Kracauer, whose emphasis was on the power of ideology on middle-class social life, Corey's treatise shows that from professionals and managers to clerical labor, the conditions of economic privation had moved across the class spectrum. His conclusion was that the new middle class was faced with the stark alternatives of remaining mired in the assumptions of the existing system in either its liberal or fascist varieties or choosing to ally with the working class in a struggle for socialism.

Corey, whose original name was Louis Fraina, had been an important figure in socialist literary circles before World War I and a major force during the founding years of the American Communist Party. He harbored few illusions about the chance for rapid systemic transformation. But his book appeared during a period of rising working-class insurgency and a dramatic revival of American radical thought and action. That his hopes were overtaken by the New Deal's adroit, if incomplete, measures to alleviate the effects of the crisis on both wage and salaried workers did not diminish the economic and historical argument that capitalism was inherently incapable of sustaining economic well-being for a substantial length of time.

But Corey's almost exclusive focus on material conditions ignored what may have been the most decisive triumph of the New Deal: its effective deployment of what might be termed "symbolic" capital to thwart tendencies toward more radical solutions to the economic crisis. For what the New Deal lacked in substantive solutions – after all, only World War II yanked the United States out of the Depression – it compensated for in forms of mass mobilization around rather modest reforms, at least in comparison to the gravity of the situation. Corey shared, along with most of the Left, a serious underestimation of the power of discourse when combined with an array of highly visible state-sponsored palliatives in allaying discontent. A year after the appearance of his book, the labor movement, by now an important political as well as economic force, gladly joined the Roosevelt coalition for its promise of more substantial economic and social reforms and for the hope that it would become a bulwark against advancing fascism.

A Class Without Events

"The white collar people ... slipped quietly into modern society. Whatever history they have had is a history without events, whatever common interests they have do not lead to unity; whatever future they have will not be of their own making." These are the first sentences of what may be Mills's greatest book, *White Collar*, the second volume in Mills's social-structure trilogy. The book was published three years after *The New Men of Power*. Despite its numbers, the new salaried middle class had, in its six decades of growth, failed to constitute an independent political force, let alone achieve economic independence.

For Mills, the "old" middle class, which included craftsmen and independent professionals like physicians, lawyers, and engineers, should not be relegated to history. A year after the publication of *White Collar*, he wrote the first version of his now famous essay "On Intellectual Craftsmanship," a plea for a new conception of the professoriate as a social formation that could overcome the alienation of white-collar work by reuniting work and life. In the wake of the almost complete domination of social life by the large corporation and corporate media, hopes for the independent carpenter, for example, might be viewed with not a small measure of skepticism. But Mills plainly believed that the intellectual might, in many ways, be a vehicle for the revival of a key practice of the old middle class, "spontaneity in work" and, perhaps more to the point, the almost vanished integrated life where work and private life are not viewed by subjects as separate but are part of the same totality. Here one can see a bit of romanticism in Mills's adulation of the craftsman. He himself adopted crafts as an avocation. He took apart and rebuilt his BMW motorcycle and performed much of the work building a house in West Nyack, New York. Thus his description in the first section of *White Collar* of the veritable demise of the old middle class of farmers, still the bulk of small entrepreneurs in 1950, feels like a dirge rather than a dispassionate assessment.

But Mills is no celebrant of the middle class as such. He harbors little sympathy for the small retailer and other small merchants. They are, indeed, the repositories of what is often referred to as the "American Way." Their position as the exemplars of American ideology – individualism, competition, free enterprise, and so on – far outweighs their economic importance. While many Americans have become reconciled to the dominance of large corporations over key aspects of life, a considerable fraction of them still define the American Dream in terms of the chance to own a small business.

White Collar stands, after 60 years, as the most comprehensive work that American social science has produced in the study of the new middle class. Mills does nothing less than to formulate a detailed stratification system of the new middle class, from state and corporate bureaucracies embodied in the "managerial demiurge" at the top of the status hierarchy, to intellectuals in intermediate positions, to what he describes as the "enormous file" of clerical labor.

In writing about clerical labor, he deftly combines straightforward sociological description and analysis interspersed with examples of the pre-World War II "folklore of the white collar girl." This mythical figure hails from a small town and comes to the big city, where she "settles down" only after holding several jobs. There she may fall in love, but life is never easy. She is likely to experience uncertainty in work and love. "The love story of the white-collar office girl often involves frustrating experiences with some boy-friend."

Referring to popular novels of the interwar period, particularly Christopher Morley's *Kitty Foyle*, Mills demonstrates that the common belief, buttressed by the media, of the inevitability of marriage and happiness ever after is merely one of our sustaining middle-class myths. Kitty chooses a career rather than falling into a problematic marriage and succeeds in her work, but she feels incomplete without a family, a testament to the enduring power of the middle-class ideal (p. 203).

Mills's description of the "modern office" points to the replacement of manual labor by machines and the increasingly factory-like character of the work: "As office machinery is introduced, the number of routine jobs is increased, and consequently the proportion of 'positions requiring initiative' is decreased. Mechanization is resulting in a much clearer distinction between the managing staff and the operating staff." While the typewriter was the typical office machine of the secretary and was not as factory-like as the bookkeeping machine, we may bring his analysis up to date by adding the computer as the characteristic office machine. Although the computer is a more complicated device, it confirms the generality of the industrial model that has taken over the large office. That is, the modern office's occupational structure corresponds to the mechanization and division of labor of office work since the early twentieth century.

In recent years, aided by the computer's versatility and the tremendous advances in communications that render the office somewhat archaic, some large firms have reintroduced an old industrial practice: homework. Some clerical workers, just like some salaried professionals – social workers, journalists, programmers, and systems analysts – work from home. They may go into the office occasionally, but computer technology avoids the need for the modern office in which hundreds or even thousands of women were concentrated in an enormous workspace directed by a male office manager who was able to keep close watch on their every move, except, of course, in the ladies room and after-work meeting places.

Mills reserves some of his most biting observations for the section on work in the modern workplace. In contrast to craftsmanship, intellectual or manual:

> Underneath virtually all experience of work today, there is a fatalistic feeling that work per se is unpleasant. One type of work, or one particular job, is contrasted with another type, experienced or imagined, within the present world of work; judgments are rarely made about the world of work as presently organized as against some other way of organizing it, so also, satisfaction from work is felt in comparison with the satisfactions of other jobs.
>
> (Mills, *White Collar*, p. 229)

White-collar employees are deprived of "work as purposive human activity" (p. 217) and for this reason seek other satisfactions to compensate for the decline of work as the heart of meaning in life (pp. 218–219). Mills's discourse on work remarkably parallels Karl Marx's famous essay in the *Economic and Philosophical Manuscripts* on alienated labor. For Marx, labor is equated not with work as an instrumental activity, organized to produce specific products or yield income for other purposes, but with purposive human activity that mediates our relationship to nature. Labor is transformative of both nature and human nature, and just as labor changes nature, so nature changes us. Capitalism modifies that relationship because it separates humans from nature, or, rather, nature becomes pure instrumental object and we "forget" that we are part of natural history. Some own the means of material production and appropriate the labor of others. Alienation is the result of the concentration of ownership in few hands, the division of labor between mental and manual work, and work rationalization in which routine replaces the worker's initiative.

Alienation remains, for Mills, the basis for the popular acceptance of mass culture and mass consumption as the real purposes of life. The implication of Mills's analysis is that the demise of the "gospel of work" as meaningful activity and its replacement by instrumentalism in which income is its only "meaning" constitutes the foundation of his judgment that leisure reigns supreme as the object of human activity in the modern world. But Mills also calls attention to the decline of the family and the community as the principal sites of human relationships.

> As the work sphere declines in meaning and gives no inner direction and rhythm to life, so have community and kinship circles declined as ways of "fixing man into society." In the old craft model, work sphere and family coincided; before the Industrial Revolution, the home and the workshop were one. Today, this is so only in certain smaller-bourgeois families, and there it is often seen by the young as repression.
>
> (Mills, *White Collar*, p. 237)

In these ruminations we can see Mills's nostalgia for a bygone time. Marx, no critic of industrialism, believed that, however onerous, the introduction of mass production would resolve the scourge of human existence: chronic scarcity that led to work without end. Mills finds no occasion to praise the achievements of modern capitalism. Instead, even though the young rankle under the authority of the household in which work and life were unified, the alternative is radically worse.

Where are the institutions capable of providing meaning to working life? The short answer has frequently been a socially conscious labor movement that goes beyond seeking to raise wages and secure dignified working conditions. While industrial unions in the 1930s and 1940s helped to raise living standards in monetary terms, they turned away from the objective of addressing the labor process itself. White-collar unions, no more than their much more powerful industrial counterparts, have patterned themselves on the tendency of the rest of organized labor to focus rather narrowly on the employment contract – wages, working conditions, and benefits. They do not deal with "work and life." In short, despite the dramatic success of public-sector white-collar unionism from the late 1950s to the mid-1970s, the unions have refused the task of addressing the unique position of the new middle class in society.

A little more than a decade after the appearance of Mills's study, the American labor movement, after 30 years of consolidation of its Depression-era gains in the industrial workplace, experienced a second coming: the 1960s and early 1970s was an era of intense white-collar organizing, first in health care and then among the millions of government employees at federal, state, and local levels. Some of the most dramatic gains were made among teachers, whose two major unions, taken together, are now America's largest, with a combined membership of almost four million. But, chiefly at the municipal and state governments, unions made huge strides among clerical workers, including in universities. By the mid-1970s, more than a third of public employees were in unions, and the proportion was much higher in education. Unionism sank roots among the professoriate as well. But it did not take long before these organizations fitted themselves into the already established union models forged in production and transportation: the point of work was now to enable the worker to consume more on the basis of a labor contract that secured her job from the ups and downs of the economy and the arbitrary whims of the managers and that provided steady raises and a measure of health and pension benefits. Their chief goal was job and retirement security, and only occasionally did they concern themselves with the totality of their members' lives, let alone the lives of working people in general. Where unions concerned themselves with the work world per se rather than merely its monetary rewards or issues facing their members such as housing, education, and recreation, these were the exceptions to the rule.

At the same time, organized labor recorded few gains among white-collar workers in private-sector institutions such as banks and insurance companies, head offices of large and medium-sized corporations, and among the vast sales force that worked in department stores and for firms that sold material goods, insurance, and other services. Most labor leaders believed these employees were beyond the scope of collective bargaining because they identified with their employers and, in fact, were understood as being part of management. While this perspective was usually tacitly rather than explicitly held, after the 1940s – which witnessed a significant Left-led union effort to organize New York Bank employees – unions made only sporadic efforts to organize private-sector white-collar and professional employees.

The *failure* of organized labor to build unions among private-sector white-collar workers and employed professionals meant that these categories were raw meat for the media and the sales effort that promoted consumerism with a vengeance. Mills:

> No longer is the framework within which a man lives fixed by traditional institutions. Mass communications replace tradition as a framework of life. Being thus afloat, the metropolitan man finds a new anchorage in the spectator sports, the idols of mass media, and other machineries of amusement.

So, the leisure sphere—and the machinery of amusement in terms of which it is now organized—becomes the center of character-forming influences, of identification models; it is what one man has in common with another; it is a continuous interest. ...

The amusement of hollow people rests on their own hollowness and does not fill it up; it does not calm or relax them, as old middle-class frolics and jollification may have done; it does not re-create their spontaneity in work, as in the craftsman model. Their leisure diverts them from the restless grind of their work by the absorbing grind of passive enjoyment of glamour and thrills. To modern man leisure is the way to spend money, work is the way to make it. When the two compete, leisure wins hands down.

(Mills, *White Collar*, p. 238)

The Routinization of the Intellect

We recall Karl Mannheim's statement that only the intellectuals are truly capable of detachment from the limits on thought and action imposed by classes in contemporary society. Without their dispassion and incessant criticism of the status quo in science, culture, and politics, society would surely degenerate into a morass of squabbling and stagnation. But if intellectuals are the seat of critical thinking and new ideas with which to confront the new conditions of life, Mills finds them wanting, mainly because they have lost their freedom to think against the grain. The chapter titled "Brains, Inc." begins with Mannheim's perspective of intellectuals' "relatively classless" position, which qualifies them for a degree of freedom not available to other social formations, but it concludes with a grim reminder that they have been thoroughly incorporated as part of the bureaucracies of the media and other corporate organizations:

> Bureaucracy increasingly sets the conditions of intellectual life and controls the major market for its products. The new bureaucracies of state and business, of party and voluntary association, become the major employers of intellectuals and the main customers for their work. So strong has the demand for technical and ideological intelligentsia of all sorts become that it might even be said that a new patronage system of a complicated and sometimes indirect kind has arisen. Not only the New Deal, Hollywood, and the Luce enterprises, but business concerns of the most varied types, as well that curious set of institutions clustering around Stalinism, have come to play an important role in the cultural and marketing life of the intellectual.

(Mills, *White Collar*, p. 149)

Mills writes, "Although the large universities are still relatively free places in which to work, the trends that limit the independence of intellect are not absent there. The professor is, after all, an employee, subject to what this fact involves." One of the entailments of this fact is the "vague general fear, sometimes called discretion and good judgment—which leads to self-intimidation and finally becomes so habitual that the scholar is unaware of it" (p. 151). Science, like communications and technical machinery, is mobilized for "the creation and diffusion of new symbolic fortifications for the new and largely private powers these bureaucracies represent" and incorporated in a "research cartel to which researchers must turn out elaborate studies and accurately timed releases, buttressing" the established powers (pp. 153–154). Indeed, in the wake of the decline of any sort of effective political opposition – save for a handful of marginal groups – the intellectual is no longer a political agent either. "The recoil from detachment and the falling into line seem more organized, more solidly rooted in the centralization of power and its rationalization of modern society as a whole" (p. 155).

The passing of the free intellectual has given rise to the "technician" of existing powers. "Intellectual activity that does not have relevance to established money is not likely to be highly valued" (p. 156). The intellectual cum administrator, "idea man," and publicist has been made solidly middle class, part of the apparatuses of power rather than their independent critic. Even Hollywood takes note of this phenomenon. At about the same time as *White Collar*'s publication, films such as *All the King's Men*, Robert Penn Warren's fictional biography of the Louisiana politician Huey Long, may be read as a tale of power's demand that the intellectual be a technician or face oblivion. And *Born Yesterday*, a hilarious 1950 comedy about Washington political corruption in the interest of business, also features a subplot of an intellectual hired to keep the business-man's girlfriend busy by teaching her literature and philosophy, ironically a pastime that turns into a reversal of their relationship as she is exposed to the Enlightenment ideal of critical thinking. She turns against her boyfriend and the congressman in his pocket and becomes the intellectual her paid mentor can no longer be.

Back to the Future

In the 1960s and 1970s, public employees, an important fraction of the new salaried middle class, finally achieved their historic event. A third of federal, state and local workers joined the unions and negotiated better income: wages, health and pension benefits, and improved working conditions. For 30 years they made steady gains. Among the most significant effects of unionization was the emergence of women, blacks and Latino work-ers into union leadership and, equally important, traditional middle-class consumer lifestyles. They were able to become home mortgage holders, send their children to college, and at the top levels even purchase foreign vacations and vacation homes. Among the public employees, teachers did the best. Their unions, the National Education Association and the American Federation of Teachers, organized a clear majority of professional teachers. In 2013, their combined membership was four million. More important than sheer numbers, almost all major cities had teacher unions that bargained with school districts for collective bargaining agreements.

But the new century proved to be a bitter time for public employees. Even before the economic meltdown of 2007–2008, mired in chronic fiscal crises, school districts reduced salary increases and froze other benefits. After 2008, collective bargaining in the public sector became a fiscal bloodbath for most of its workers. State and local governments laid off tens of thousands and demanded steep concessions, not the least of which were wage freezes and pension reductions. The Federal Postmaster General proposed to shut more than 3000 post offices, discontinue Saturday service, and lay off tens of thousands of workers. The postal unions waged an aggressive campaign to save the postal service which had been already crippled by privatization. They mobilized politicians, commu-nity organizations and the general public and were able to stay the hand of the Postmaster General. And, when Republican Wisconsin governor Scott Walker and the Republican controlled legislature repealed collective bargaining for state workers, the labor move-ment did not lay down and roll over. Instead they rallied more than 100,000 of their members, their family members and activists to occupy the state legislature's chambers and demonstrate in the state capitol's Madison streets. In the end, they did not succeed in overturning Walker's bold maneuver, but a new movement was born in the state that presaged the emergence of a new period of struggle. In Chicago, the 40,000 member Teachers Union struck against austerity and won a partial victory. However, in the main the forward march of public employees' labor had come to a crashing halt. Unions, locked into the electoral process rather than direct action, managed to win some victories in City Hall, but the outcome was still murky.

The "vanishing middle class" became a widely embraced evaluation during the early years of the twenty-first century. Many corporations, especially small and middle sizes, sharply reduced their pension and health insurance programs, and laid off workers. The banks, insurance companies, and headquarters managements cut large slices of managerial and sales staffs, swelling middle-class unemployment to a degree unknown since the Great Depression of the 1930s. As the middle class faced an uncertain future, among its ranks, older workers in particular despaired of being able to reenter the labor force. Yet the middle class ideal survives and continues to mystify our national consciousness.

CHAPTER 17

The Struggle Over the Saloon

Roy Rosenzweig

Introduction

On December 2, 1889, hundreds of trade unionists paraded through the streets of Worcester in a show of strength and determination. "Eight Hours for Work, Eight Hours for Rest, Eight Hours for What We Will" declared a banner held high by local carpenters. The banner drew upon the chorus line of "Eight Hours," the official song of the eight-hour movement and probably the most popular labor song of that period. Twenty-three years later Worcester's labor newspaper still used the first two stanzas of "Eight Hours" to express the goals of the city's machinists:

> We mean to make things over;
> We're tired of toil for naught;
> We may have enough to live on,
> But never an hour for thought.
>
> We want to feel the sunshine,
> We want to smell the flowers;
> We are sure that God has willed it,
> And we mean to have eight hours.[1]

Like the words to "Eight Hours," the actual quest for "eight hours for what we will" reverberated through the labor struggles of the late nineteenth and early twentieth centuries. As a compositor told the U.S. Senate Committee on Relations Between Labor and Capital in 1883: "A workingman wants something besides food and clothes in this country … He wants recreation. Why should not a workingman have it as well as other people?"[2] And in industrial communities across America workers fought not only for the right to time and space for leisure but also for control over the time and space in which that leisure was to be enjoyed. This study examines how workers struggled to maintain "eight hours for what we will" and what that "eight hours" meant to them.

Original publication details: Roy Rosenzweig, "The Struggle Over the Saloon", from *Eight Hours for what we will: Workers and leisure in an industrial city, 1870–1920*, pp. 1; 230; 57–59; 61; 93–104; 116–117; 119–123; 126; 247–248; 255–258; 263–265. Cambridge University Press, 1983. Reproduced with permission from Cambridge University Press and R. Rosenzweig.

Class: The Anthology, First Edition. Edited by Stanley Aronowitz and Michael J. Roberts.
© 2018 Stanley Aronowitz and Michael J. Roberts. Published 2018 by John Wiley & Sons Ltd.

The Rise of The Saloon

For many Worcester workers the saloon offered a variety of attractive activities from social services to informal socializing to singing and gambling. But did the late nineteenth century saloon hold any significance beyond its role as a social service and recreational center? Does the nature of the late nineteenth century saloon suggest anything about the central values and beliefs of Worcester workers?

Worcester saloons of the late nineteenth century reflected and reinforced a value system very much different from that which governed the dominant industrial, market, and social relations of that era.

Many observers trumpeted the saloon as "the rooster-crow of the spirit of democracy." It was, proclaimed the Reverend George L. McNutt, "the one democratic club in American life," the "great democratic social settlement." Of course, the saloon was much less open and democratic in fact than these commentators would have us believe. Most saloons at least informally barred members of the "wrong" sex, ethnic group, race, neighborhood, or occupation. Still, the commentators were partially right; the saloon was actually a "democracy" of sorts – an *internal* democracy where all who could safely enter received equal treatment and respect. An ethic of mutuality and reciprocity that differed from the market exchange mentality of the dominant society prevailed within the barroom.[63] Although collective and cooperative social relations were not the exclusive property of the immigrant working class, the saloon was one of the few late nineteenth century institutions that publicly and symbolically celebrated these alternative values.

Some understanding of the potential role of drink and the saloon in fostering this ethic of reciprocity and mutuality can be gained by looking at rural Ireland, the birthplace of many Worcester saloon patrons. "Drinking together," notes anthropologist Conrad Arensberg, "is the traditional reaffirmation of solidarity and equality among males" in Ireland. The most important drink custom for fostering such sentiments was "treating" – "a social law in Catholic Ireland enforced with all the vigour of a Coercion Act," according to one commentator. "If a man happens to be in an inn or public-house alone, and if any of his acquaintances come in, no matter how many, it is his duty to 'stand,' that is, to invite them to drink and pay for all they take. ... It is a deadly insult to refuse to take a drink from a man, unless an elaborate explanation and apology be given and accepted."[64] Treating thus provided the nineteenth-century Irishman with a crucial means of declaring his solidarity and equality with his kin and neighbors.

These drink rituals were not an isolated sphere of Irish life; they were firmly embedded in a reciprocal life-style that governed at least some social relationships in the Irish countryside. Although the Irish rural economy was subject to external, exploitative, colonial rule, local social and economic relations were often based on a system of mutual rights and obligations rather than a rationalized market of monetary exchange. Helping a neighbor with a house-raising, for example, was often part of that local system of mutual obligation, which existed outside of the realm of direct cash exchange. The liberal provision of liquor at such an event offered a means of reciprocating, of symbolizing one's acceptance of the mutuality, friendliness, and communality on which it was based.

As "a norm of equality and solidarity," treating rituals implied resistance to individualism as well as acquisitiveness. Indeed, the whole saloongoing experience affirmed communal over individualistic and privatistic values. After 1800, historian W. J. Rorabaugh notes, "drinking in groups ... became a symbol of egalitarianism. All men were equal before the bottle." Inebriation further encouraged the breaking down of social barriers.[69]

For some, to be sure, saloongoing was a solitary experience, but for most it was a group activity. It was a way of carousing with friends, neighbors, and fellow workers whom one could not (or should not) bring into the home. And because such socializing took place outside the home, it was more of a public occasion, and therefore open to a much wider group than the kinfolk that one might normally bring into the home. More than just the size of the gathering, the nature of the event – the drinking, singing, talking, card playing, billiard shooting – brought workers together for a collective public sharing of their recreation. As such, the saloon rejected the developing individualistic, privatistic, and family-centered values of the dominant society.

The saloon clashed with the values of industrial America not just in its communality and mutuality but also in the unwillingness of some patrons to endorse fully the work ethic of that society. Critics of drinking frequently lumped together the very rich and the very poor as unproductive classes "most exposed to the temptation of intemperate drinking." Employers, beginning in Ichabod Washburn's day, depicted drinking as a major threat to steady work habits. Thus, the Washburn and Moen Wire Manufacturing Company petitioned against saloons in the vicinity of their North Works because "the opportunities for slipping into a dram shop either on the way to work or from work, make it so much easier for the men to squander their wages which means a lessening of their efficiency for us."[70]

The Struggle Over the Saloon, 1870–1910

In December 1881 Worcesterites debated whether to vote "yes" (and sanction the sale of liquor under a licensing system) or "no" (and close all liquor dealers and saloons) in the first annual local option election mandated by a new state law. Prominent among the leaders of the anti-drink or "no-license" forces was Philip L. Moen, the head of the Washburn and Moen Wire Manufacturing Company as well as the son-in-law of the man who had founded the company and promoted the temperance cause a half century earlier. During the hotly contested 1881 temperance campaign Moen and forty-one other leading Worcesterites – three-quarters of them were either manufacturers or Protestant ministers – issued a broadside attack on "open drinking saloons" for "impoverishing multitudes, causing measureless misery and crime, [and] crippling our industries."[1]

The other side in the local battle over the saloon was acutely aware of the economic power and cultural prominence of the temperance forces. *Worcester Daily Times* editor James H. Mellen charged that the temperance campaign was really a vendetta against the Irish and other blue-collar workers, who lacked spacious homes and thus drank only in public saloons. According to Mellen, the "better element" behind the no-license crusade included many drinkers "who believe in drink as a luxury, and that the plebians should not be allowed to degrade the habit by participation." "Many people will vote 'no' whose cellars are stocked with liquors," he complained on another occasion, adding that this practice "savors of class legislation."[2]

The actual vote – in which the pro-license forces triumphed narrowly – confirmed Mellen's perception of temperance as a class issue. On the Irish and working-class East Side the votes ran about 2.5 to 1 in favor of licensing saloons, whereas in the elite pre-cincts on the West Side the proportions were roughly reversed.[3] Like the movements for parks, playgrounds, and a Safe and Sane July Fourth, which also flourished in Worcester in the late nineteenth century and the early twentieth, the temperance crusade was, in part, an effort by the city's middle and upper classes to reform, reshape, and restrict working-class recreational practices. The resulting conflicts made leisure time and space into arenas where workers and industrialists struggled over the values, world view, and culture that would dominate working-class life.

Campaigns against Working-Class Drink Places

In March 1890 Alfred S. Roe, the principal of Worcester High School, reflected on the recent license election for the readers of *Light*, a local "society" journal. No-license voters, he pointed out, held a variety of opinions about the propriety of alcohol consumption, but what united them was their "thorough agreement ... that the saloon is here and everywhere an unmitigated evil, and that it must go." Opponents of liquor licensing repeatedly reminded voters that they sought to eliminate the *saloon*, not drinking per se. "Prohibition is not at issue," one no-license advertisement assured voters: "The Saloon is the enemy we are fighting."[5]

In focusing their movement on the saloon, middle- and upper-class temperance supporters like Roe responded to the rapid development of the saloon by the working class as its own social institution. During the last third of the nineteenth century the number of saloons in the United States had tripled.[6] That temperance crusades concentrated on this emerging "workingman's club" rather than on the individual drinker meant that the battle over the saloon often took on aspects of a "class war" over the recreational world of the industrial working class. In Worcester, at least, the generals of that class war were the city's Protestant ministers, its manufacturers, and their wives. Of course, more diverse groups enlisted in the various campaigns: to limit the total number of liquor licenses and to restrict licenses to specific areas (the springtime license petition movement); to close all drink places through the annual December local option elections (the no-license movement); and to use regulations and police enforcement to make the saloon a more orderly place. And some groups – particularly the Swedes – gradually moved into leadership postions. However, throughout the late nineteenth and early twentieth centuries the native Protestant elite staffed the command post of the war on the saloon.

After Massachusetts legalized sales in 1875 the annual springtime petition battle over license restriction, over *who* would receive a license from the city, became a major arena for conflict on the drink question. The licensing decisions of the Board of Aldermen (and after 1893 the License Commission) were the number one topic of conversation around the city for days before and after the licenses were issued. Speculation was so intense that in some factories workers formed betting pools based on predicting the winners of the licensing sweepstakes.[7]

Much of the earliest agitation for the restriction of liquor licenses came from the Protestant clergy. Hardly a year went by without petitions, sermons, and speeches by the Protestant clergy urging some general or specific license limitation. Closely allied with the Protestant clergy in license-restriction efforts were some of the city's leading industrialists. On one typical license-restriction petition from 1878, manufacturers and ministers made up the two largest occupational groups. Typically, Henry C. Graton, a manufacturer of leather belting and a member and benefactor of Grace Methodist Church, signed along with his minister.[8]

The exemplar of this clerical–industrial alliance on temperance and other major questions was Ichabod Washburn, wire manufacturer, builder of the city's first "temperance house," and secretary of a Worcester temperance society. Known locally as "Deacon Washburn" because of his position in the orthodox Union Congregational Church, he actively supported the key institutional pillars of his twin faiths in "mechanics and evangelical Christianity." He not only presided over the Evangelical Missionary Society and financed the building of its Mission Chapel but also helped found the Worcester County Mechanics Association and donated $25,000 toward the building of its magnificent Mechanics Hall. For Deacon Washburn, piety and profits went hand in hand. "If your mill owners want to make good dividends," he advised, "let them see to it that they have plenty of good orthodox preaching, a good minister well housed … and it will prove to be the best part of their investment; for goodliness is profitable to all things."[9]

Washburn's son-in-law, Philip L. Moen, followed him as both head of the million-dollar wire corporation and deacon of the Union Congregational Church. Although the pre-Civil War unity of Christians and capitalists could not be wholly sustained in the 1870s and 1880s, the alliance remained firm on the issue of temperance. The 1878 license-restriction petition included not only Philip L. Moen but also the Reverend George Gould, the minister of the Union Congregational Church, the Reverend William T. Sleeper, the co-founder with Washburn of the Mission Chapel and its current pastor, and the Reverend Henry T. Cheever, Washburn's brother-in-law and the former minister of the Mission Chapel.[10]

There was a remarkable continuity with the temperance movement of earlier in the century. In the 1830s the founders of Worcester's industrial economy – the mechanics and manufacturers – had led the temperance forces; now forty or fifty years later the heirs to a mature industrial economy carried the battle forward. In addition, the evangelical Protestant churches and the Mechanics Association joined together and ideologically molded both generations. Temperance men had started Worcester's Mechanics Association in the early nineteenth century, and it remained a hotbed of temperance support in the last quarter of the century: the signers of the 1878 petition included at least nine past or future presidents of the Mechanics Association.[11] The most important change in the personnel of the temperance movement actually reinforced its elite status. The wives of the manufacturers and ministers now took an increasingly active role. The signers of an 1881 license-restriction petition, for example, included the wives of Philip L. Moen, Henry Graton (the leather belting manufacturer), and the superintendents of both the wire works and the Crompton Loom Works.[12]

This petition, like many early petitions, sought to persuade the board to issue no licenses at all. But manufacturers increasingly recognized the futility of this strategy and instead sought simply to prevent the issuance of licenses in the vicinity of their factories. Beginning in 1891 Washburn and Moen annually opposed the granting of any liquor licenses south of Cambridge Street, about one mile from the company's massive South Works, and in 1895 it petitioned against "the tremendous evil" of saloons in the vicinity of their North Works. Numerous other Worcester companies followed the lead of Washburn and Moen. In 1893, for example, Crompton Loom Works, Ames Plow Company, and S. R. Heywood Boot and Shoe Manufacturing petitioned against saloons seeking to locate near their factories.[13]

Just as licensing split the working class along ethnic and religious lines, it also may have divided the native middle and upper classes according to their place in the city's economy. Whereas Worcester's industrialists unanimously condemned the saloon, some merchants and small-business men appear to have been much friendlier. At the same time that Moen and his employees challenged the liquor license of Elijah Kennan's Exchange Hotel, nearby grocers, men's clothiers, and tobacconists came to his defense. Two other downtown saloonkeepers, who were also threatened by anti-license petitioners in 1883, mobilized even more impressive support from more than twenty-five neighboring merchants and their clerks. Downtown merchants, however, usually confined their support to the more affluent and established drink sellers like hotel owner Kennan or George Hewitt, the city's leading wholesale liquor dealer.[17] And some even denounced the drink trade as vigorously as any manufacturer or minister. Nevertheless, as was true earlier in the nineteenth century, many merchants – perhaps out of solidarity with other Main Street businessmen or out of a greater concern with consumption than with production – appear to have shied away from the temperance movement that won the allegiance of so many other members of the middle and upper classes.

Many of the same class, ethnic, and occupational lines of division on the drink question can be found in the other annual battle over the saloon: the local option vote each December over whether Worcester would license any saloons at all that year. Although a no-license victory in local option elections required the votes of the native-American middle class as well as some segments of the native and immigrant working class, the leadership of the no-license forces remained largely with the city's manufacturers and ministers. Broadsides urging "no" votes carried the signatures of these men as well as those of other prominent Worcesterites: judges, bank presidents, and leading politicians like Senator George Frisbie Hoar. Rank-and-file no-license activists included only a slightly more diverse constituency. Almost half the members of the twenty-two no-license committees organized through the Protestant churches for the 1886 election came from the upper levels of the city's white-collar work force. Only one-fifth held blue-collar jobs, and many of these belonged to the committees formed at the black Baptist and Swedish Methodist churches.[18]

Local option elections, which began in 1881 and continued until national prohibition in 1920, followed class and ethnic lines fairly closely in the 1880s. The immigrant and working-class precincts of the East Side voted "yes" by 2 or 3 to 1 margins; the native middle and upper classes voted "no" in similar proportions. In the 1890 election, for example, ethnicity and licensing sentiment correlate perfectly. Ward 5, with 67.2 percent of its adult males of foreign birth, voted 70.8 percent for liquor licensing, whereas Ward 8, with 87.5 percent of its adult males of native birth, voted 61.7 percent against licensing. These sharp ethnic and class divisions kept most license contests close and hotly contested, with victory often hinging on the degree of organization of the opposing sides or the level of voter turnout. License supporters lost only five of the forty local option votes, but their margin of victory averaged less than 5 percent annually.[19]

When no-license campaigns failed, saloon opponents sought instead stricter regulations or tighter enforcement of existing rules. They advocated and won passage of rules barring Sunday sales, side- or back-door entrances, screens blocking public view into the saloon, sales after 11 P.M., and "public bars" selling drink without food. Women played a particularly active role in the struggle to enforce existing regulations. Most dramatically, in 1874, when Worcester saloons were openly violating statewide prohibition, bands of women (following the example of the Women's Crusades, which had begun in Ohio a few months earlier) marched on the city's saloons to pray, sing hymns, ask patrons to take the "pledge," and beseech proprietors to abandon their illegal and immoral business. Whether through moral example or public pressure, they also seem to have persuaded state constables to increase their seizures of illegal liquors. The "praying bands" of women apparently came from the same elite Protestant circles that championed license restriction and no-license. The members of one major committee included Elizabeth Cheever Washburn (Ichabod's widow) and the wives of at least three other manufacturers.[24]

Upper-class men spearheaded other efforts to win tighter enforcement of Worcester's liquor laws. In 1883 one hundred manufacturers, ministers, lawyers, and bankers – a virtual who's who of elite Worcester – formed the Citizens' Law and Order League to insist upon "the enforcement of the restrictive features of existing laws for the regulation of the liquor traffic and attendant vices." Three years later the Worcester Christian Temperance Union sponsored the Reverend Hugh Montgomery in a one-man vigilante crusade against liquor law violations.[25]

The Ideology of the Middle- and Upper-Class Temperance Movement

Worcester's manufacturers, ministers, and mothers thus commanded an anti-saloon army, whose foot soldiers included members of the native working and middle classes (with the partial exception of downtown merchants) as well as large numbers of Swedish immigrant workers. Most often, Worcester's French-Canadian and Irish communities stood on the other side of the temperance barricade. What does this social and cultural division tell us about temperance ideology in late nineteenth century Worcester? What sort of meanings did Worcesterites of different social classes and ethnic backgrounds attach to their temperance sentiments?

For the ambitious, self-improving mechanics of Ichabod Washburn's generation, temperance and evangelical Christianity were directed as much inward as outward, as much at self-control as at social control. Thus, temperance and religion both responded to and hastened an emerging industrial capitalist society; they offered optimistic solutions to both the personal anxieties and the problems of industrial discipline and social disorder brought about by such a rapidly changing society.[26] By the time of Philip L. Moen's generation, temperance ideology was gradually shifting away from its internal focus on personal reform and improvement toward a more exclusive concern with the external threat posed by working-class drinking and particularly by the working-class saloon. Washburn, after all, had begun building his wire business in a relatively homogenous town of 5,000, many of whom worked in small workshops. Fifty years later Moen presided over an established million-dollar wire corporation in a city twelve times as big with an immense immigrant working-class population that toiled in giant factories. In the intervening years this immigrant working class had developed the saloon as one of its central social and cultural institutions. To attack drinking – and especially the saloon – now became a statement with much more direct class implications.

The offensive against the saloon and its values was equally a defense of a set of bourgeois values that the saloon seemed to threaten. The urban-industrial saloon, Norman H. Clark has observed in his recent reinterpretation of American temperance, challenged "the moral values so recently articulated as the bourgeois tradition: self-confidence, conscience, sexual discipline, ambition, measurable accomplishment, loyalty, reverence, responsibility, respect." These values, rooted in what has been called the emerging "bourgeois interior" of American life, were, as Clark argues, profoundly individualistic and supported a "developing consciousness of individual, rather than communal, dignity." Just as the saloon symbolized the rejection of this middle-class world view, the middle-class home stood as its affirmation and bastion. The addition of new saloons to Webster Square, the Reverend L. W. Staples told the Worcester Board of Aldermen in 1887, menaced a "neighborhood of homes, peaceful, happy, prosperous homes." Three years later the society paper *Light* used similar language to celebrate the results of a year without liquor licenses: "Homes are today made happy by the presence of a sober father, where in times gone by tears and oaths were constant reminders of unnatural actions on the part of this same man."[27]

The middle-class home, which temperance advocates all over America sought to protect, did not exist in an economic vacuum; it rested on the economic base of industrial capitalism. Thus, the temperance movement of the late nineteenth century and the early twentieth defended not just the culture of the Protestant middle class but also the economic interests of Protestant manufacturers. The Reverend Mr. Staples, for example, appealed to both his parishioners' sentimental attachment to home and family and their rational self-interest in a disciplined work force. The elimination of the saloon, he claimed in November 1886 after Worcester's first six months under no-license, had benefited the city financially by "greatly increasing the efficiency of the city laborers, and all wage earners in the great industries of Worcester." In 1893 a temperance group similarly argued "that the men earn better wages, lose less time, do better work under no-license, while the relations between employers and workmen are more harmonious." Fifteen years later O. W. Norcross, a longtime temperance crusader and a prominent Worcester builder, echoed the same theme: "Manufacturers and employers with rare exceptions favor no-license. They report that under no-license their employees are steadier and more industrious; men are not so often absent from their work."[28]

It is difficult to untangle the degree to which middle-class and elite temperance arguments responded to actual, rather than just perceived, threats to family or factory. To be sure, alcoholism could be devastating for both middle- and working-class families. And in the context of inadequate working-class incomes, even moderate drinking could drain family finances, subvert saving for house purchases, and strain family bonds. Finally, there is ample evidence that drinking impaired work safety, discipline, efficiency, and productivity. At the same time, however, temperance ideology, as historian Harry Gene Levine has pointed out, "contained a powerful strand of fantasy" and "scapegoating." It presented abstinence as a "total solution" and alcohol as a "total cause" for much more fundamental economic and social problems rooted in the unequal distribution of power and wealth and the organization of work under industrial capitalism.[29] Indeed, even from the standpoint of pure self-interest (a concern, for example, with maintaining social order, hierarchy, and discipline) rather than altruism (a concern, for example, with poverty or alcohol-related diseases), the temperance movement was possibly misdirected. At least in Worcester, as we have seen, the saloon – the central focus of temperance venom – nurtured a working-class culture that rejected, but did not challenge, the dominant cultural and economic order.

Workers and Temperance

Accurately or not, Worcester's elite perceived temperance as a defense of the industrial discipline of the factory and the cultural discipline of the middle-class home. But what about the large number of working people who shared their antipathy to alcohol?

The most obvious explanation would be that these workers had absorbed the complete package of native middle-class values. Temperance, one historian argues, was "a symbol of middle-class membership" and, as another historian adds, appealed to "the aspiring working-man."[30] Some working-class temperance supporters, who might be termed "middle-class mobiles," did see sobriety as a strategy for individual advancement. But for a much larger group, which might be called "working-class respectables" or "settled livers," temperance was more of a strategy for maintaining a secure and stable way of life centered on the church and traditional ethnic institutions. And for still a third (and in Worcester quite small) group, which might be labeled "temperance radicals," anti-drink sentiment was a means for attacking the dominant power structures in the society and winning group advancement of some kind. Such analytical categories usefully recall some of the divisions in styles of July Fourth celebrations and also help to illuminate the range of working-class temperance positions. But they can distort individual experiences and values. Working-class temperance advocates could simultaneously embrace dreams of self-advancement, attachments to traditional institutions, and visions of class solidarity, just as they could fall off the wagon and rejoin their less temperate brethren in the saloon. And to complicate matters further, working-class temperance sentiment in Worcester was organized primarily through the city's ethnic communities rather than through commitments to any particular set of views on the drink question.

The drink question thus spawned a bewildering array of positions in late nineteenth century Worcester. The Protestant industrial elite and their native middle-class allies attacked the saloon for a combination of cultural and economic reasons. Some workers – particularly native skilled workers and Swedish immigrants – joined these crusades, although their actions often grew out of distinct ethnic, religious, and class perspectives. Few Catholic immigrants joined in this assault on the saloon, but some of their number did attack drinking as a problem that faced their communities. In addition, the Catholic temperance movement actually incorporated a variety of motives: a search for middle-class respectability, an interest in a stable and settled ethnic community, and a desire for social change. The saloon and the temperance movement thus became intense battlegrounds buffeted by the powerful and complex forces of class, gender, and ethnicity. But what was the impact of these clashes both on the saloon and on social and political life in Worcester?

The Struggle Over the Saloon and its Consequences

"The question is often asked," Worcester City Marshal James Drennan noted in his 1870 Annual Report, "why don't the police officers put a stop to these beer nuisances and prevent the sale and drinking of beer Sundays?" But Drennan scoffed at such bothersome complaints, equating them with the question "why don't the officers stop the rivers from descending on their course to the sea?"[64] Such fatalistic reminders of the irrepressibility of working-class drinking habits did not, of course, stop a generation of opponents of the saloon from fighting to limit the number of liquor licenses, to close all drink places through local option, or to use regulations or police powers to make the saloon a more orderly place.

In a city with a strong industrial elite and a weak working-class labor and radical movement one might assume that these class-based attacks on the saloon would prove quickly successful. In fact, they quickly failed. For the most part, Worcester working-class saloongoers simply ignored or evaded the regulations so carefully wrought by their antagonists. Through such evasions, workers frustrated the efforts of Worcester industrialists to extend their hegemony to recreation as well as work. Worcester workers generally succeeded in preserving their right to use their leisure time for "what we will," even if that meant drunkenness.

Efforts to enforce liquor laws and create more orderly saloons also had mixed effects. Yet what is most surprising, given the political and economic power of those advocating stricter enforcement, is, again, the widespread evasion of the regulations. To evangelical Protestants, the prohibition against Sunday liquor sales was obviously one of the most cherished provisions of the liquor law. But this regulation clashed with even more deeply ingrained working-class patterns. For many workers, Sunday was both their only day of leisure and the day after payday. Consequently, despite regulations to the contrary, Sunday was "the great business day" for saloonkeepers. Indeed, according to City Marshal Washburn, some proprietors apparently even left "the city during the six working days, and returned to their homes and business only on the Sabbath." Illegal Sunday sales accounted for about one-quarter of all liquor complaints between 1875 and 1879. Even more commonly violated than the Sunday ban was the law against "public bars" or drink places dispensing only liquor. Most saloonkeepers made only token compliance with the 1878 law, which required that they have "the necessary implements and facilities for cooking, preparing, and serving food." One saloonkeeper purchased an elegant range and good quality crockery, but told a reporter that "he had not had a fire in his stove and at the end of the year it would be sold for what it cost; as it would not be second-hand." Ultimately, the police gave up on enforcing the prohibition against "drink-only" establishments. "No attempt has been made to close the open bar on account of public opinion," Marshal Washburn admitted in 1879.[71]

The working-class leisure patterns that defeated the Sunday drink prohibitions and the "public opinion" Washburn cited as preventing enforcement of the public bar regulations provide the key to understanding why Worcester elites were never able to dominate effectively the nonwork lives of the immigrant working class. Drinking and the saloon were too much an integral part of Worcester's ethnic working-class world to be easily repressed by legal means. Police officials cited community opposition as the primary explanation for their failure to enforce the liquor laws. Reflecting on the difficulties of enforcing the 1886 no-license law, City Marshal Washburn wrote: "As the law is now recognized, the officers have not only to fight the liquor dealers, but a large share of the community." Two years earlier City Marshal Amos Atkinson had similarly blamed the lack of "moral support of the community at large" for his failure to eliminate unlicensed liquor establishments.[72]

Community residents subverted the enforcement of liquor laws by alerting liquor sellers to possible police raids, by helping dealers hide the illegal goods, and especially by directing popular pressure at police officers. "An officer taking the stand to testify in an ordinary liquor case," grumbled City Marshal Washburn in 1883, "goes there knowing that all the suspicions ever leveled at any mortal are to be directed at him, and it is not to be wondered at that many of them shrink from too much prominence in this business." According to Washburn, other forms of detective work were not considered "dishonorable," but "the minute war is waged upon illegal rum-selling, gambling, and kindred evils, that minute, officers become 'spotters,' 'informers,' 'peelers' and their social degradation is sure and rapid."[73]

Worcester police feared ostracism because so many of them belonged to the same Irish working-class community as did the liquor sellers and their customers. By the mid-1880s first- and second-generation Irish, primarily from blue-collar backgrounds, made up about one-half of the police force. Despite efforts to create a "temperance" police force, many officers drank. In 1874, for example, Michael McNamara was almost dismissed from the police force for getting drunk during the Father Mathew Total Abstinence Society's trip to Boston.[74]

Community pressure and police sympathy did not, however, protect all liquor law violators from apprehension and prosecution. Nevertheless, even those arrested usually escaped any immediate fine or imprisonment; jail sentences were extremely rare even for repeat offenders.[75] Such light sentences partially reflect the expert legal assistance of some of the city's smartest lawyers. "No class of offenders," wrote City Marshal Washburn of liquor law violators, "are so ... ably defended." Local Democratic politicians like John R. Thayer and M. J. McCafferty devoted a good deal of their law practices to representing Worcester drink sellers. "All the eloquence that the 'Bar' can procure," Washburn noted bitterly, "is brought to *condemn the officer* and *condole the offender*." Where eloquence failed, time-consuming appeals did the trick. Between 1880 and 1881 almost three-quarters of those convicted in the lower Central District Court appealed to the Worcester County Superior Court. And, according to Washburn, "not over twenty percent of the appealed cases have ever been heard of since, or ever will be." The sympathetic views of the judges and juries in the superior court further benefited saloonkeepers.[76]

Legal restrictions on searches of private dwellings (where most illegal drink traffic centered) and requirements that police actually witness an illegal sale also protected liquor sellers. In 1879, for example, one policeman related how he and a fellow officer spent Sunday afternoon watching forty people come and go from a particular home. When they actually approached the house, "they heard the price of drinks for a party asked and stated; and heard money drop upon the floor." When they entered the house, they "found sixteen persons within. There were beer mugs with beer in them, tumblers with the remnants of whiskey and sugar in them, wet places on the floor where the beer had foamed over, and other evidences of the illegal traffic." However, when the violators were brought to court, "the prisoner and friends swore that it was only the visit of a few friends and the beer and liquor was given away." Since the police officers had not actually witnessed a sale, the judge dismissed the case. "There are hundreds of complaints made ... that amount to nothing because of the requirements of the law," complained City Marshal Edward Raymond in a "Statement to Business Men."[77]

Thus, the law provided protection for boisterous and collective recreational styles that were vehemently opposed by the dominant economic group in Worcester. Even saloonkeepers, as property holders, or at least tenants, enjoyed the safeguard of the law's regard for private property. Through evasion, group pressure, and use of the legal system, saloongoers and saloonkeepers were able to defend one of the central institutions of working-class life from the attacks of some of the most powerful people in Worcester. But to conclude on this note would be to overstate both the strength of working-class culture and the impotence of elite attacks on that culture. Evaluated in another way, the struggle over the saloon suggests some of the important weaknesses of Worcester's ethnic working-class culture.

To state the obvious, the defense of the saloon involved no explicit challenge to power relations in Worcester. For the most part, workers overcame the law by ignoring it, not by confronting it in a formal or "political" way. In the annual no-license votes, the saloon was rarely defended as a working-class "right." Instead, supporters of liquor licensing usually argued their position on the grounds that no-license simply did not work.[78] Even the maneuvering over legal protections rarely raised broader issues of popular rights. Resistance to the attacks on the saloon was, like ethnic working-class culture, defensive and inward looking. Although saloongoers did not accept the dominant individualistic and competitive ethos of the industrial elite, neither did they mount an explicit challenge to that ethos. They simply ignored it. The unwillingness or inability of the police to use substantial force to ensure compliance with the liquor laws made it less likely that the alternative culture of the saloon would be transformed into an oppositional culture that directly attacked the larger system of class inequality. The likelihood of a class-wide mobilization growing out of the conflict over the saloon was further lessened by the cross-class alliances that the actual struggle created.

The defense of the saloon – both against license-restriction petitions and no-license crusades – involved workers in collaboration with those outside their class. Whereas most proprietors of small saloons had close ties to surrounding ethnic working-class communities, many of the larger liquor dealers and brewers did not. George Hewitt, the city's leading liquor dealer, was a wealthy businessman who belonged to the Masons, an organization that Catholics suspected of nativism. Many of the lawyers and politicians who defended the liquor interests also participated in a social world very different from that of saloongoers. Liquor lawyer and Democratic politician John R. Thayer hunted foxes with members of the West Side social elite, represented East Side workers on the Board of Aldermen, and defended their saloonkeepers in court.[79]

On the surface such alliances had no particular political significance. When examined more closely, however, it becomes evident that they tended to work against the development of working-class politics in Worcester. For the saloonkeepers in general and the large liquor dealers and brewers in particular, the defense of their economic interests was their overriding political goal. They sought, therefore, the defeat of no-license campaigns and the election of a sympathetic Board of Aldermen, which would freely issue liquor licenses, and a friendly city government, which would not enforce the liquor laws too rigidly. Since the liquor dealers were the financial mainstay of the city's Democratic party, they usually tried to manipulate party politics in service of these particular goals rather than of any larger social interests.[80] To this end they often – particularly in the 1870s and 1880s – backed coalition "Citizens'" candidates rather than straight Democratic tickets in the mayoralty elections. In effect, they helped to elect men tied to the city's social and economic elite who were also willing to tolerate the liquor interests. In 1883 and 1884, for example, they strongly backed mayoralty candidate Charles C. Reed, a carriage-wheel manufacturer, a member of the Mechanics Association and the Board of Trade, and a Republican in state and national politics. Even when the liquor dealers backed regular Democratic candidates, they often supported members of "the aristocratic element" of the party.[81]

Whereas Worcester workers usually preserved their control over their non-work lives – whether they wanted to drink at the corner saloon, shoot billiards at the Father Mathew Hall, or sew with the Swedish Ladies Aid Society – they less often triumphed at the ballot box or on the picket line. The resilience of the saloon in the face of the temperance crusade was an important victory, but given the compromises it involved and the internal divisions it exacerbated, it could not be translated into increased power in other realms.[88]

Notes

Introduction

1   *Worcester Telegram*, Dec. 3, 1889; Oct. 28, 1915; *Labor News*, June 7, 1913. On "Eight Hours," see Philip S. Foner, *American Labor Songs of the Nineteenth Century* (Urbana, Ill., 1975), 222–4; William Brooks, "Liner Notes," *The Hand That Holds the Bread: Progress and Protest in the Gilded Age* (New World Records, NW 267, 1978).

2   U.S. Congress, Senate, *Committee of the Senate Upon the Relations Between Labor and Capital, Hearings*, 4 vols. (Washington, D.C., 1885), 3:386.

The Rise of the Saloon

63   Royal L. Melendy, "Saloon in Chicago," "The Saloon in Chicago," *American Journal of Sociology* 1990: 6: 291; George L. Nutt, "Why Workingmen Drink," *Outlook* 1901: 69: 115–18. Even the national field secretary of the Church Temperance Society called the saloon the "most democratic institution in America"; Clipping and Minutes, Jan. 11, 1920, Scrapbook, Twentieth Century Club of Worcester, Worcester Public Library. On reciprocity, see David Harvey, *Social Justice and the City* (Baltimore, 1972), 206–7, 209, 282; Karl Polanyi, Conrad M. Arensberg, and Harry W. Pearson, eds., *Trade and Market in the Early Empires* (1957; rpt. Chicago, 1971).

64   Robert F. Bales, "Attitudes toward Drinking in the Irish Culture," in D. J. Pittman and C.R. Snyder, eds., *Society, Culture and Drinking Patterns* (New York, 1962), p. 157–87.

69   Richard Stivers, *A Hair of the Dog: Irish Drinking and American Stereotype* (University Park, Pa., 1976), p.140; Rorabaugh, *Alcoholic Republic*, 151; Cavan, *Liquor License*, 43.

70   Bureau of Statistics of Labor, Mass. *Report, 1871*, 543; *WT*, Apr. 16, 1895. Significantly, the Knights of Labor with its emphasis on the dignity of labor and its producerist ideology was the labor organization most hostile to drinking and the saloon; see David Brundage, "The Producing Classes and the Saloon: Denver in the 1880's" (paper presented at the Knights of Labor Centennial Symposium, Chicago, Ill., May 17–19, 1979); Ronald M. Benson, "American Workers and Temperance Reform, 1866–1923," (Ph.D. thesis, Univ. of Notre Dame, 1974), p. 150–86.

The Struggle Over the Saloon

1   "Citizens of Worcester," Dec. 1881, Broadside Collection, WHM. I identified the signers of the broadside in the *Worcester Directory, 1882* (Worcester, 1882).

2   *Worcester Daily Times (WDT)*, Dec. 5, 6, 1881.

3   *WDT*, Dec. 12, 1881. The West Side vote was actually around 2.1 to 1 against license. The wards do not precisely reflect ethnic and class divisions, because they were pie-shaped and radiated out from downtown.

5   Alfred S. Roe, "Temperate Worcester," *Light* 1 (Mar. 8, 1890):8; *WT*, Dec. 13, 1909. See similarly "Editorial," *Light* 4 (Nov. 7, 1891):219; "Citizens of Worcester"; *LN*, Sept. 26, 1914.

6   Norman H. Clark, *Deliver Us from Evil: An Interpretation of American Prohibition* (New York, 1976), 50.

7   *WT*, Apr. 17, 1893.

8   *Worcester Evening Gazette (WEG)*, Apr. 26, 1878. Based on the occupational scheme developed in Stephan Thernstrom's *The Other Bostonians: Poverty and Progress in the American Metropolis, 1880–1970* (Cambridge, Mass., 1973), about three-quarters of the signers could be classified as "high white collar." There were twelve ministers and twenty-eight manufacturers but no blue-collar workers. I identified signers in the *Worcester Directory;* Charles A. Nutt, *History of Worcester and Its People*, 4 vols. (New York, 1919), vols. 3 and 4; and Franklin P. Rice, ed., *The Worcester of Eighteen Hundred and Ninety-Eight* (Worcester, 1899). For other clerical-led protests, see *WEG*, Apr. 26,

May 1, 1875, and the annual protests recorded in the Board of Aldermen Minutes and the Board of Aldermen Petitions, Board of Aldermen MSS, Worcester City Hall; hereafter cited as Board of Ald. Minutes, Petitions. Unitarian and Episcopal ministers were, perhaps, less active than their evangelical counterparts. They were not, however, absent from the temperance campaigns, as one might expect, based on the arguments of some historians about the "pietist" and "liturgical" divide over the drink question. For a summary of this argument, see Clark, *Deliver Us from Evil*, 89–91. For the presence of Unitarians on both sides of the temperance question in early nineteenth century Worcester, see Ian R. Tyrell, *Sobering Up: From Temperance to Prohibition in Antebellum America, 1800–1860* (Westport, Conn., 1979), 110.

9   Joshua Chasan, "Civilizing Worcester: The Creation of Industrial and Cultural Order, Worcester, Massachusetts, 1848–1876" (Ph.D. thesis, Univ. of Pittsburgh, 1974), vi, 146–62; Ian R. Tyrell, *Sobering Up: From Temperance to Prohibition in Antebellum America 1800–1860*, (Westport, Conn., 1979).

10   See relevant biographies in Charles A. Nutt, *History of Worcester and Its People*, 4 vols. (New York, 1919), 2: 596 for these interconnections.

11   According to Tyrell, *Sobering Up*, 102, nine of the sixteen founders of the Mechanics Association supported prohibition and only two opposed it. I checked the signers of the 1878 petition against a list of Mechanics Association presidents in Nutt, *History of Worcester*, 2:1058.

12   Board of Ald. Petitions, Apr. 20, 1881. I identified the signers in the *Worcester Directory*; Nutt, *History of Worcester;* Franklin P. Rice, ed., *The Worcester of Eighteen Hundred and Ninety-Eight.* (Worcester, 1899). On women and temperance, see Harry Gene Levine, "Temperance and Women in 19th Century America," in Oriana Kalant, ed., *Research Advances in Drug and Alcohol Problems, Vol. 5: Alcohol and Drug Problems in Women* (New York, 1980), 25–67; Barbara Leslie Epstein, *The Politics of Domesticity: Women, Evangelism, and Temperance in Nineteenth-Century America* (Middletown, Conn., 1981), 89–146; Ruth Bordin, *Woman and Temperance: The Quest for Power and Liberty, 1873–1900* (Philadelphia, 1981).

13   *WT*, Apr. 21, 1891, Apr. 16, 1895; Board of Ald. Minutes, Mar. 16, 1891; *WT*, Apr. 18, 1893; Board of Ald. Minutes, Apr. 10, 1893. See also *WT*, Mar. 30, Apr. 9, 1901.

17   Petition in favor of E. L. Kennan, May 7, 1883, Board of Ald. Petitions (at least half the signers were proprietors of Main Street stores or their employees); Petition in favor of liquor license for John McGuire and John L. Truax, Apr. 18, 1883, Board of Ald. Petitions; *WT*, May 7, 1889. I identified the signers of these petitions in the *Worcester Directory*.

18   "Citizens of Worcester"; "Appeal to Voters," Dec. 1886, Politics and Propaganda file, WHM; committee members were listed in the *No-License Advocate*, Dec. 3, 1886 (copy available at AAS), and traced in *Worcester Directory*. Except for the representatives from the black Baptist Church, all the blue-collar workers were skilled. Blacks averaged less than 1% of Worcester's population between 1870 and 1920. For an excellent study of this community, see Ella L. Vinal, "The Status of the Worcester Negro" (M.A. thesis, Clark Univ., 1929).

19   *WT*, Dec. 10, 1890. I used the published U.S. Census figures to correlate the ethnic basis of the voting. For a more detailed discussion of these correlations, see Roy Rosenzweig, "'Eight Hours for What We Will': Workers and Leisure in Worcester, Massachusetts, 1870–1930" (Ph.D. thesis, Harvard Univ., 1978), 219–20. The victory margin was calculated from the annual licensing votes provided in the local newspapers.

24   *WT*, Apr. 12, 1895, Mar. 13, 1901; *WEG*, Mar. 18, 20, 21, 23–5, 1874. On the elite profile of women's crusades elsewhere, see Charles A. Isetts, "A Social Profile of the Women's Temperance Crusade: Hillsboro, Ohio," in Jack S. Blocker, Jr., ed., *Alcohol, Reform and Society: The Liquor Issue in Social Context* (Westport, Conn., 1979), 101–10; Ruth Bordin, *Women and Temperance: the Quest for Power and Liberty*, 1873–1900, (Philadelphia, 1981).

25   "Worcester Citizens' Law and Order League," Broadside, Jan., 1883, Temperance Society Pamphlets, AAS; I identified signers in the *Worcester Directory*. *WST*, Apr. 18, 1886.

26   On early nineteenth-century temperance ideology and evangelical religion, see W. J. Rorabaugh, *The Alcoholic Republic* (New York, 1978), 205–13; Tyrell, *Sobering Up*, 110–13.

27   Clark, *Deliver Us from Evil*, 53, 12; Letter to Mayor from L. W. Staples, Apr. 23, 1887, Board of Ald. Petitions; *Light* 2 (Dec. 13, 1890):3. On the "home protection" theme, see Levine, "Temperance and Women," 55–7; Epstein, *Politics of Domesticity*, 89–113.

28   "Six Months of No-License in Worcester," Nov. 5, 1886, Broadside Collection, WHM; Committee of Five, "A Statement to Businessmen," Nov. 17, 1893, copy of broadside found in Worcester Room, Worcester Public Library; O. W. Norcross, "No-License the Better Business Policy," *Worcester Magazine* 11 (Dec. 1908):319. See also *Solid Facts for Thinking Men*, Dec. 7, 1889 (a temperance newspaper, copy available at WHM); *Light* 3 (May 30, 1891):303; *No-License Advocate*, Dec. 3, 1886; *WT*, July 5, 1886, Dec. 13, 1909.

29   Harry Gene Levine, "Temperance and Prohibition in America" (forthcoming in a book on alcohol and drug problems edited by Griffith Edwards and Jerome Jaffe), and Harry Gene Levine, "The Birth of Demon Rum: Changing Attitudes about Alcohol in America" (paper presented at the Annual Meeting of the American Association for Public Opinion Research, Buck Hill Falls, Pa., May 1981).

30   Joseph R. Gusfield, *Symbolic Crusade: Status Politics and the American Temperance Movement* (Urbana, Ill., 1963), 5; Jay Dolan, *Catholic Revivalism: The American Experience* (Notre Dame, Ind., 1978), 155.

64   *Annual Report of the City Marshal, Year Ending December 31, 1870*, (Worcester, 1871), 12; hereafter cited as *City Marshal*.

71   *City Marshal, 1875*, 51; *City Marshal, 1875–1879; WEG*, Apr. 22, 1879, May 13, 27, 1878.

72   *City Marshal, 1886*, 218–19; *City Marshal, 1884*, 251. See also *City Marshal, 1889*, 154; *WDT*, July 6, 1887.

73   *City Marshal, 1884*, 251; *City Marshal, 1883*, 315–16. See also *WDT*, June 11, 1886; *City Marshal, 1892*, 171.

74   *WDT*, Feb. 2, 1885; Folio 2, 232, Richard O'Flynn MSS.

75   *WEG*, Apr. 22, 1879; *City Marshal, 1875*, 49; Arrest Lists, James Drennan MSS. According to the lists in the Drennan MSS, only six of eighty-five people convicted in 1882 received jail sentences, and most of them appealed their cases.

76   *City Marshal, 1883*, 315; Arrest Lists, James Drennan MSS; *WEG*, Apr. 22, 1879. For complaints about the Superior Court, see *City Marshal, 1875*, 50; *City Marshal, 1876*, 24; *WDT*, Dec. 13, 1880. It appears that lawyers for the drink sellers tried to keep temperance advocates from sitting as jurors on their clients' cases; see Massachusetts Supreme Judicial Court, *Massachusetts Reports* (Boston, 1888), 145:282.

77   *WEG*, Apr. 22, 1879; "Statement to Businessmen," Nov. 17, 1893. See also *WDT*, Dec. 13, 1880, Apr. 27, 1885; *WEG*, Oct. 20, 1886; *City Marshal, 1881*, 205; *City Marshal, 1884*, 251; Arrest Cards, James Drennan MSS.

78   Occasionally, a defense was developed on the grounds of "popular right." See, for example, *WDT*, Dec. 6, 1884.

79   *WDT*, Apr. 17, June 6, 1885; RGD, 99:204, 101:72, 104:633, 911; Nutt, *History of Worcester*, 3:48–9; R. M. Washburn, *Smith's Barn: "A Child's History" of the West Side Worcester, 1880–1923* (Worcester, 1923), 127–8; *WST*, Jan. 11, 1885; *WDT*, May 9, Dec. 11, 1882. On nativism and the Masons, see Roy Rosenzweig, "Boston Masons, 1900–1935: The Lower Middle Class in a Divided Society," *Journal of Voluntary Action Research* 6 (July–Oct. 1977):119–26.

80   See *WST*, Nov. 30, 1884; *WDT*, June 3, 1886.

81   *WST*, Nov. 30, 1884; *WDT*, Dec. 6, 1879. On Reed, see Rice, *Worcester of Eighteen Hundred and Ninety-Eight*, 727–8. On the tendency of Democrats to nominate "aristocratic" candidates, see also *WST*, Nov. 28, 1886.

88   For a discussion of "worker politicians" elsewhere, see Alan Dawley, *Class and Community: The Industrial Revolution in Lynn* (Cambridge, Mass., 1976), 194–219; Daniel Walkowitz, *Worker City, Company Town* (Urbana, Ill., 1978), 253–7. This is not to argue a direct cause and effect between a strong saloon culture and a weak labor movement. Cities like New York and Milwaukee, for example, combined vibrant saloons with active trade unions. Even in those cities, however, it seems likely that conflict over the saloon weakened the working class politically and economically. In industrial communities generally but in Worcester particularly – with its large Swedish pietist population – the drink question subverted working-class political, economic, and cultural solidarity.

CHAPTER 18

The Salaried Masses
Duty and Distraction in Weimar Germany

Siegfried Kracauer

Selection

'Why do you want to be a commercial employee?' 'Because I like that sort of job.' 'Which line of business?' 'Soft furnishings.' 'Why precisely that?' 'Because I find the work light and clean.'

Another answer to the first question: 'Because I prefer a job that's not manual.'

Another answer again: 'I'd like to be in sales.' 'Why don't you go for a craft?' 'I wouldn't like to work in a factory.'

With answers like this, boys and girls leaving school fill out questionnaires obtained from the career guidance department of the Zentralver-band der Angestellten. The spelling is not always flawless, and the unruly grammar of colloquial speech often overlays the learned rules of written German. A year or two later and apprentices with their literary spurs will write confidently in their business letters: 'Most respectfully yours …'.

A non-manual job, preferably in sales, work that's light and clean – the rosy dreams do not all come to fruition. At any rate, it is not enough to feel the call, you must also be chosen – chosen by the authorities driving forward the economic process that drives them.

In Dresden, shoemakers are said to have decided recently to employ only apprentices who have completed two years of secondary school. So a person may not even patch and sole just from an inner inclination. Such folly shows how ingrained the certification system is in our nature, as was observed with some resignation at the last trade union congress. And if not in our nature, then still in the basis of our contemporary social system. We all know (or probably do not know) the various certificates whose magic influence alone opens certain spheres in the civil service hierarchy. An advanced certificate is sought nowadays as a qualification for upper-middle civil servants – a requirement that big banks and many other commercial and industrial concerns restrict entry into the bliss of their clerical departments to young people with a certificate of secondary education, and they prefer those who have the advanced level. In Berlin, according to reliable information, out of a hundred commercial trainees, fifty might have gone on to complete the final year of secondary education. Of the fortunate certificate-holders, many remain

Original publication details: Siegfried Kracauer, *The Salaried Masses*, tr. Quintin Hoare, pp. 30; 33–34; 40-41; 81–82; 88–94 . Verso, 1998. Reproduced with permission from Verso.

confined throughout their lives to an activity that every ambitious former elementary-school pupil could perform just as well; a higher level of education by no means always ensures a higher salary; retrenchment measures, and other evils termed strokes of fate, hit qualified and unqualified alike. But since the powers-that-be view qualification certificates as talismans, everyone materially able to do so chases after them and seeks to enhance his own monopoly value as much as possible. The rush for further education surpasses the desire for knowledge, and technical employees turned out by vocational schools are now establishing graduate associations. Before long everyone will have a certificate for something. One member of the Deutsche Bankbeamtenverein, who in conversation with me could not hide his satisfaction at the thought that all bank employees were qualified, made the following comment with direct reference to this circumstance: 'Some of them come from good middle-class families. Their level is definitely not proletarian.' The comment is instructive in two respects. It expresses not merely an important aim of the qualification system, but also the fact that this aim is being achieved. If certain certificates may really be necessary, while others are to be explained by the shortage of lebensraum, the fact is that most people with either certificate of secondary schooling are of medium- or petit-bourgeois origin. Proletarian children must be very gifted to push beyond the eight years of elementary school, and once they have climbed sufficiently high, they often disappear from view like Indian fakirs. And since society mainly gives privileges to members of the middle class, who know from birth what is right, it creates for itself a kind of bodyguard in the enterprise. This is all the more reliable when it gets its hands on handsome weapons in the form of certificates and diplomas, with which it can cut a dash and grow rich.

Ever since capitalism has existed, of course, within its defined boundaries rationalization has always occurred. Yet the rationalization period from 1925 to 1928 represents a particularly important chapter, which has produced the irruption of the machine and 'assembly-line' methods into the clerical departments of big firms. Thanks to this reorganization carried out on the American pattern – and which is still far from complete – large sections of the new salaried masses have a lesser function in the labour process than they had before. There are a great many unskilled and semi-skilled employees today performing mechanical tasks. (For instance, in the one-price stores that have sprung up recently, salesgirls' duties are mechanized.) The former 'NCOs of capital' have become an imposing army whose ranks contain a growing number of mutually interchangeable private soldiers.

No less a person than Emil Lederer calls it 'an objective fact, if one maintains that salaried employees share the fate of the proletariat'. He even hazards the assertion that 'today ... the social space in which we still find modern slavery ... is no longer the plant in which the great mass of workers work; that social space is instead the office.'[1] There is room for argument about his apportionment of slavery, but the proletarianization of employees is beyond dispute. At all events, similar social conditions prevail for broad layers of salary-earners as for the proletariat itself. An industrial reserve army of salaried employees has come into being. The view that this is a temporary phenomenon is countered by the alternative view that it could be dismantled only along with the system that has conjured it up – a discussion about which we shall have more to say. The existential insecurity of salaried staff has increased, moreover, and their prospect of independence has almost entirely disappeared. In view of this, can the belief be sustained that they constitute some kind of a 'new middle class'? We shall see that illusions produced for salary-earners encounter a sizeable demand.

Short Break for Ventilation

The commercial director of a modern factory explains the business to me before my tour of inspection. 'The commercial operation of the work process', he says, 'is rationalized down to the last detail.' He points to diagrams whose colourful networks of lines illustrate the whole operation. The plans hang in frames on the walls of his room. On the other wall there are two peculiar cases that look a bit like children's abacuses. Within them little brightly coloured balls, arranged on vertical cords, rise in close formation to varying heights. One glance at them, and the director at once knows all about the firm's current situation. Every couple of days the little balls are repositioned by a statistics clerk. 'Do you know what tour tickets look like?' the commercial director asked me. I nodded in astonishment. 'I'll show you our own tour tickets.' We enter a room whose iron shelves hold countless booklets that really do look just like tour tickets. They contain, folded together, all the dockets needed for carrying out the work process. The work process: i.e. the sum of functions to be performed from the arrival of the order to the dispatch of the commissioned goods. Once the order begins its journey, the route it has to follow is determined by means of the dockets. The equipment in the office of the manager, who has to supervise the entire tourist traffic, bears about the same resemblance to the freely invented office equipment in Fritz Lang's spy film as a fantastic sunset does to a genuine oleograph. A cupboard-like centrepiece studded with coloured light-bulbs forms the principal ornament of the real office. In general, the sole purpose today of red, yellow and green tints is to organize an enterprise more rationally. From the flashing and dimming of the tiny bulbs, the manager can at all times deduce the state of work in the individual departments. In the course of the tour through the offices that the commercial director makes with me, we gradually pace out the network of lines on the wall of his room. The marvellous thing is that the operation of the plan is set in motion by real people. A number of girls are evenly distributed about the room at Powers machines, punching cards and writing. The Powers (or Hollerich) machinery, used for bookkeeping and every kind of statistical purpose, performs by mechanical means feats whose accomplishment had previously required a never wholly reliable intellectual labour, as well as incomparably more time. The chosen instrument of machine processing is the punch-card covered with rows of figures, upon which operationally important items can be represented in numbers. Each card is perforated with the help of the punching machine and then contains the record file in perforation code. Once the cards are ready, they travel to the sorting and tabulating machines in the adjoining room. In a trice the former arrange the material according to the various items, while the latter write down the perforated numbers in the desired tabular form and add up the columns automatically. Gentlemen tend the heavy monsters, whose racket vastly surpasses the monotonous clatter of the punching girls. I ask the office manager about the machine-girls' work routine.

'The girls', he replies, 'punch for only six hours and during the remaining two hours are employed as office clerks. In this way we avoid overtaxing them. All this takes place in a predetermined cycle, so that each employee encounters all tasks. For hygienic reasons, moreover, from time to time we slip in short breaks for ventilation.'

What a scheme – even ventilation outlets are not forgotten.

'We worked for nine months on the whole system', the commercial director comments. The office manager holds a thick folio under my nose, in which the work plan applicable to the machine room is entered accurately to the minute.

'If ever, Heaven forbid, you suddenly fall ill', I said to the office manager, 'can someone else take your place at once and assume control with the help of this book?'

'Yes, of course.'

Among Neighbours

'A uniform stratum of employees is in the process of formation. The grouping of the population according to class viewpoint has made big advances since the pre-war period.' What Emil Lederer and Jacob Marschak maintain in their excellent study 'The New Middle Class' (*Grundriss der Sozialökonomik*, Section IX, Part 1), which in 1926 directed attention for the first time to the altered condition of salaried employees, Lederer himself has just recently had to qualify anew. 'Even if the capitalist intermediate strata today already share the destiny of the proletariat', he writes in his study 'The Restructuring of the Proletariat' (included in the August 1929 issue of the *Neue Rundschau*), 'the majority of them have nevertheless not yet abandoned their bourgeois ideology.' His judgement is shared by Richard Woldt, who in a treatise on German trade unions in the post-war period (incorporated in the collective work *Strukturwandlungen der Deutschen Volkswirtschaft* ['Structural changes in the German national economy']) characterizes as follows the attitude of the middle strata in decline: 'A certain professional ideology still stands in a relationship of tension with the actual facts.' Large sections of the population today do indeed base their bourgeois existence, which is no longer bourgeois at all, on monthly salaries, so-called intellectual labour and a few other similarly trivial characteristics. In total harmony with the experience articulated by Marx: that the superstructure adapts itself only slowly to the development of the base provoked by the forces of production. The position of these strata in the economic process has changed, their middle-class conception of life has remained. They nurture a false consciousness. They would like to defend differences, the acknowledgement of which obscures their situation; they devote themselves to an individualism that would be justified only if they could still shape their fate as individuals. Even where they struggle as wage-earners in and with the unions for better conditions of existence, their real existence is often conditioned by the better one which they once had. A vanished bourgeois way of life haunts them. Perhaps it contains forces with a legitimate demand to endure. But they survive today only inertly, without getting involved in a dialectic with the prevailing conditions, and so themselves undermine the legitimacy of their continued existence.

Shelter for the Homeless

The average worker, upon whom so many lowly salaried employees like to look down, often enjoys not merely a material but also an existential superiority over them. His life as a class-conscious proletarian is roofed over with vulgar-Marxist concepts that do at least tell him what his intended role is. Admittedly the whole roof is nowadays riddled with holes.

The mass of salaried employees differ from the worker proletariat in that they are spiritually homeless. For the time being they cannot find their way to their comrades, and the house of bourgeois ideas and feelings in which they used to live has collapsed, its foundations eroded by economic development. They are living at present without a doctrine to look up at or a goal they might ascertain. So they live in fear of looking up and asking their way to the destination.

Nothing is more characteristic of this life, which only in a restricted sense can be called a life, than its view of higher things. Not as substance but as glamour. Yielded not through concentration, but in distraction. 'Why do people spend so much time in bars?' asks one employee I know. 'Probably because things are so miserable at home and they want to get a bit of glamour.' 'Home', by the way, should be taken to mean not just a lodging, but an everyday existence outlined by the advertisements in magazines for employees. These mainly concern: pens; Kohinoor pencils; haemorrhoids; hair loss; beds; crêpe soles; white teeth; rejuvenation elixirs; selling coffee to friends; dictaphones; writer's cramp; trembling, especially in the presence of others; quality pianos on weekly instalments; and so on. A shorthand-typist prone to reflection expresses herself in similar vein to the aforementioned employee: 'The girls mainly come from a modest milieu and are attracted by the glamour.' Then she gives an extremely odd reason for the fact that the girls generally avoid serious conversations. 'Serious conversations', she said, 'only distract and divert you from surroundings that you'd like to enjoy.' If distracting effects are ascribed to serious talk, distraction must be a deadly serious matter.

Things could be different. From results he obtained by investigating the household budget of salaried employees (as elaborated in his study *Die Lebenshaltung der Angestellten* ['The standard of living of salaried employees'], Freier Volksverlag, Berlin 1928), the Afa-Bund's economic policy adviser Otto Suhr draws the conclusion that employees do indeed devote less money to food than the average worker, but they rate so-called cultural needs more highly. The employee, according to Suhr, spends more on cultural requirements than on lodging (inclusive of heating and lighting), clothes and laundry combined. Along with health, transport, gifts, donations, etc., the category of 'cultural needs' covers, among other things, tobacco products, restaurants, and intellectual or social events. And society consciously – or even more, no doubt, unconsciously – sees to it that this demand for cultural needs does not lead to reflection on the roots of real culture, hence to criticism of the conditions underpinning its own power. Society does not stop the urge to live amid glamour and distraction, but encourages it wherever and however it can. As remains to be shown, society by no means drives the system of its own life to the decisive point, but on the contrary avoids decision and prefers the charms of life to its reality. Society too is dependent upon diversions. Since it sets the tone, it finds it all the easier to maintain employees in the belief that a life of distraction is at the same time a higher one. It posits itself as what is higher and, if the bulk of its dependants take it as a model, they are already almost where it wants them to be. The siren songs of which it is capable are demonstrated by the following excerpt from the department-store publicity brochure repeatedly cited above, which belongs in a model collection of classic ideologies:

> One further influence is worthy of mention, which derives from the layout and furnishing of the store. Many of the employees are from quite modest backgrounds. Perhaps their homes consist of cramped, poorly lit rooms; perhaps the people with whom they come into contact in their private lives are not very educated. In the store, however, the employees for the most part spend their time in cheerful rooms flooded with light. Contact with refined and well-educated customers is a constant source of fresh stimuli. The often quite awkward and self-conscious girl trainees more quickly accustom themselves to good behaviour and manners, they take care about their speech and also their appearance. The varied nature of their work broadens the sphere of their knowledge and improves their education. This facilitates their ascent to higher social strata.

If we leave aside the customers' education and the improvement – as may be done with a clear conscience – we are left with the cheerful rooms flooded with light and the higher social strata. The beneficent influence exercised by the flood of light, not just upon the urge to buy but also upon the staff, might at most consist in the staff being sufficiently duped to put up with their mean, poorly lit homes. The light blinds more than it illuminates – and perhaps the abundance of light pouring out lately over our large towns serves not least to increase the darkness. But do the higher strata not beckon? As it has turned out, they beckon from afar without commitment. The glamour they provide is indeed supposed to bind the mass of employees to society – but to raise them only just so far that they will remain more certainly in their appointed place. Instructive in this connection is a 'Ramble through fifteen account-books' that was published not long ago in *Uhu*. A few of the headings run: 'How come the Müllers can afford a sailing-boat?'; 'How come the Schulzes can pay 10 Marks for board and lodging on their summer holi-day?'; 'However do the Wagners manage to go in for such expensive clothes?' Well, they simply can. Herr Schulze explains that his old lady is good at economizing, and Frau Wagner reports that her husband presses his own trousers. 'That's how you keep up appearances', she adds philosophically. Let us hope the trousers are not too shiny. Although many of the pleasures cut down on are undoubtedly real, the deeper moral of the *Uhu* expedition is obviously to inculcate in the so-called middle class the conviction that even with a modest income they can maintain the appearance of belonging to bourgeois society, so they have every reason to be content as the middle class.

At the same moment at which firms are rationalized, these establishments rationalize the pleasures of the salary-earning armies. My question as to why they treat the masses as a mere mass is met by one salaried employee with the bitter reply: 'Because people's lives are bled far too dry for them to have the least idea what to do with themselves.' No matter whether this is the case or no: in the establishments in question, the masses are their own guests; and, what is more, not just from any consideration for the commercial needs of the employer, but also for the sake of their own unavowed impotence. People warm each other, people console each other for the fact that they can no longer escape from the herd. Being part of it is made easier by the palatial surroundings. These are par-ticularly plush in the Haus Vaterland, which embodies most completely the type roughly adhered to also in picture palaces and the establishments of the lower intermediate strata. Its nucleus is formed by a kind of immense hotel lobby, across whose carpets even the Adlon's guests would be able to walk without feeling demeaned.[13] Since only the most modern is good enough for our masses, this exaggerates *die neue Sachlichkeit* style.[14] The mystery of *die neue Sachlichkeit* could not be more conclusively exposed than here. From behind the pseudo-austerity of the lobby architecture, Grinzing grins out.[15] Just one step down and you are lapped in the most luxuriant sentimentality. But this is what character-izes *die neue Sachlichkeit* in general, that it is a façade concealing nothing; that it does not derive from profundity, but simulates it. Like denial of old age, it arises from dread of confronting death. The room in which the new vintage is sampled presents a splendid view of Vienna by night. The Stephans-turm stands out faintly against the star-spangled sky, and an electric tram lit from within glides across the Danube Bridge. In other rooms adjoining *die neue Sachlichkeit* the Rhine flows past, the Golden Horn glows, lovely Spain extends far away in the south. All the more unnecessary to describe the sights, in that no word can be added to, or removed from, the matchless claims of the Haus Vaterland prospectus. This, for instance, is what it says about the Löwenbräu Bar: 'Bavarian landscape: Zugspitze with Eibsee – alpenglow – entry and dance of the Bavarian

Schuhplattler lads';[16] and about the Wild West Bar: 'Prairie landscapes near the Great Lakes – Arizona – ranch – dancing – cowboy songs and dances – Negro and cowboy jazz band – well sprung dance-floor.' The Vaterland encompasses the entire globe. The fact that nineteenth-century panoramas are coming back into such high regard in all these establishments is related to the monotony in the sphere of work.

All events relating to the unorganized salaried masses, and equally all movements of these masses themselves, are today of an ambivalent nature. Inherent in them is a secondary significance that often distances them from their original determination. Under pressure from the prevailing society they become, in a metaphorical sense, shelters for the homeless. Apart from their primary purpose, they acquire the further one of binding employees by enchantment to the place the ruling stratum desires, and diverting them from critical questions – for which they anyway feel little inclination. So far as contemporary film production is concerned, I have demonstrated in two essays published in the *Frankfurter Zeitung* – 'The Little Shopgirls Go to the Movies' and 'Contemporary Film and its Audience'[17] – that almost all the industry's products serve to legitimize the existing order, by concealing both its abuses and its foundations. They, too, drug the populace with the pseudo-glamour of counterfeit social heights, just as hypnotists use glittering objects to put their subjects to sleep. The same applies to the illustrated papers and the majority of magazines. A closer analysis would presumably show that the image-motifs constantly recurring in them like magical incantations are intended to cast certain contents once and for all into the abyss of imageless oblivion: those contents that are not embraced by the construction of our social existence, but that bracket this existence itself. The flight of images is a flight from revolution and from death.

Notes

1   'Die Umschichtung des Proletariats' ['The restructuring of the proletariat'], included in the volume *Angestellte und Arbeiter* ['Salaried employee and worker'] published by the Afa-Bund, Freier Volksverlag, Berlin 1928.

13   The Hotel Adlon: one of the most luxurious Berlin hotels in the early years of this century, recently restored.

14   *Die neue Sachlichkeit*: 'New Objectivity' – or 'New Sobriety', as the Weimar cultural critic and historian John Willett prefers. This was an aesthetic movement taking its name from a 1925 exhibition of pictures of 'tangible reality' put on in Mannheim by the gallery owner G. F. Hartlaub. Influencing a wide range of arts, it was consciously counterposed to expressionism.

15   Grinzing is a Viennese suburb associated with schmaltzy music and romantic nights out.

16   *Schuhplattler*: folk dance involving slapping of the thighs and shoe-soles.

17   *The Mass Ornament. Weimar Essays*, translated and edited by Thomas Levin, Harvard University Press. Cambridge Mass. and London 1995, pp. 291–304 and 307–20.

CHAPTER 19

The Twilight of the Middle Class
Post-World War II American Fiction and White-Collar Work

Andrew Hoberek

Introduction

The Twilight of the Middle Class

> "...privileged and deprived, an American sort of thing."
> —Don DeLillo, *Underworld* (1997)

Morris Dickstein poses his recent study of post-World War II American fiction *Leopards in the Temple* (2002) as a corrective to the by now standard tendency to emphasize the cold war in accounts of this period.[1] But while Dickstein takes the critics of cold war culture to task for what he sees as their oversimplification of both art and politics, he concurs with them on at least one major point. "If social suffering, poverty, and exploitation topped the agenda of the arts in the 1930s," Dickstein writes "neurosis, poverty, and alienation played the same role in the forties and fifties when economic fears were largely put to rest."[2] The idea that postwar culture abandoned the economic for the psychological has likewise been central to studies of cold war culture, where it underwrites the argument that postwar culture was characterized by a (deeply political) rejection of the more overtly political concerns of the thirties. Thus Thomas Hill Schaub argues in *American Fiction in the Cold War* (1991) that postwar authors, participating in "the anti-Stalinist discourse of the new liberalism," prioritized "psychological terms of social analysis ... over economics and class consciousness as the dominant discourse of change."[3] While they differ on how to interpret the shift from economics to psychology—from capitalism and class struggle to "psychological nuance and linguistic complexity" (Dickstein 20)—Dickstein and critics like Schaub agree that this shift is the defining characteristic of postwar fiction.

Original publication details: Andrew Hoberek, *The Twilight of the Middle Class*, pp. 1–17; 33; 35–44; 47–52; 131–136; 139–141. Princeton University Press, 2005. Reproduced with permission from Princeton University Press.

It is perhaps for this reason that critics of cold war culture themselves downplay the very questions of "economics and class consciousness" for whose omission they take postwar writers to task. We might expect these critics to see Dickstein's more neutral, and at times even celebratory, account of this shift as continuous with cold war triumphalism—a latter day version of Richard Nixon's economic boosterism in his 1959 "kitchen debate" with Nikita Kruschev.[4] Yet when they mention the postwar economy, it is often in similar terms. In his account of the postwar vogue of wide-screen movies like Cecil B. DeMille's 1956 *The Ten Commandments*, for instance, Alan Nadel reads these films as visual analogues of "the expansive economic and technological growth of America in the 1950s."[5] Nadel's brief mention of the economy is rare, moreover. Often critics of cold war culture simply bracket the economy, restricting their analyses to the political and cultural realms. Even the Marxist critic Barbara Foley succumbs to this tendency, arguing that Ralph Ellison's *Invisible Man* (1952) engages in the red-baiting endemic to postwar anticommunism but nowhere addressing the economic framework within which—we might expect a Marxist to believe—the novel's politics are embedded.[6] "If Ellison's own experiences with the left during the years represented in the Harlem section of *Invisible Man* was not one of unremitting bitterness and betrayal," she asks, "what then might have been the source of the novel's overwhelmingly negative portrayal of the Brotherhood?" (541). Foley's answer is political bad faith and careerism. While Ellison's successive revisions of the draft certainly support this contention,[7] Foley does not consider that Ellison might also be responding (as I will argue in my own chapter on *Invisible Man*) to economic issues relevant to the world of the fifties rather than the thirties. Her essay on Herman Melville's "Bartleby the Scrivener," by contrast, exhaustively describes the economic and class issues that rove New York City during the period of the story's composition.[8] The implication is that such issues mattered during the antebellum period but were less important, or even unimportant, in the 1950s. Despite their helpful attention to the political backsliding of the cold war era, accounts like Nadel's and Foley's either explicitly or implicitly accept Dickstein's assertion that following World War II "economic fears were largely put to rest."[9]

This book argues, by contrast, that economics and class remained central to postwar writing, belying our standard assumptions about the irrelevance of such matters in the postwar period. Of course, there is good evidence for these assumptions. Statistics compiled by the business historian Jeffrey Madrick make it clear that the postwar years were indeed prosperous ones, and not just in comparison with the lean years of the Depression. Along with the fact that "family incomes doubled ... between 1947 and 1973,"

> By 1970 four out of five American families owned at least one car, two out of three had a washing machine, and almost all families had a refrigerator. About 65 percent of American families owned their own homes, and almost all had flush toilets and running water. The proportion of white males who had graduated from college rose from 6 percent in 1947 to 11 percent in 1959 and to about 25 percent in the 1980s. More than half of working Americans had a private pension, compared with only about 15 percent after World War II, supplementing Social Security benefits, which themselves were only a generation old.[10]

As Paul Krugman and others have noted, moreover, the postwar economy not only grew at a remarkable rate, but its fruits were—by the standards of either pre-Depression America or our own time—remarkably evenly distributed.[11]

Given such real and relatively widespread prosperity, the elision of economic matters in accounts of postwar writing seems understandable. As early as 1962, to be sure,

Michael Harrington had called into question the assumption that "the basic grinding economic problems had been solved in the United States."[12] In *The Other America* Harrington argued that postwar social criticism's focus on "the emotional suffering taking place in the suburbs" (1) belied the existence of an "invisible land" (1) inhabited by "the dispossessed workers, the minorities, the farm poor, and the aged" (17). But Harrington's objection to such criticism was that it disregarded those who remained on the margins, not that it misrepresented the mainstream. Similarly, recent accounts of the postwar period, such as George Lipsitz's *Rainbow at Midnight* (1994), Alan Wald's *Writing from the Left* (1994), and *The Other Fifties* (1997), edited by Joel Foreman, have turned from the mainstream to the various class and racial subcultures that existed during this period.[13] But while such revisionist accounts usefully remind us that not everyone in the fifties had equal access to the fruits of the economic boom, they leave untouched our sense that those who did have such access somehow transcended the economic realm.

This assumption is reinforced by the fact that while postwar prosperity is generally associated with a particular class, it is one that is traditionally understood in the United States as classless. This idea of American "middle-classlessness" has proven especially compatible with our understanding of the postwar boom,[14] as Jack Beatty's account of the boom suggests:

> The expanding middle class had in it two distinct kinds of workers: white-collar and blue-collar. Back then, thanks to the wages won for him by his union, the blue-collar man (the gender specification is unavoidable) could live next door to the white-collar man—not to the doctor, perhaps, but to the accountant, the teacher, the middle manager. This rough economic equality was a political fact of the first importance. It meant that, in a break with the drift of things in pre-war America, postwar America had no working class and no working-class politics. It had instead a middle-class politics for an expanding middle class bigger in aspiration and self-identification than it was in fact— more people wanted to be seen as middle-class than had yet arrived at that state of felicity. Socialism in America, the German political economist Werner Sombart wrote in 1906, foundered upon "roast beef and apple pie," a metaphor for American plenty. The expanding middle class of the postwar era—property-owning, bourgeois in outlook, centrist in politics—hardly proved him wrong.[15]

The myth of America as a classless—because universally or at least potentially universally middle-class—nation has a long history, as Beatty's reference to Sombart suggests. But in its current incarnation it is inseparable from what Krugman calls the "middle-class interregnum" that lasted from the New Deal thirties through the late seventies, and has been succeeded by a "new Gilded Age" characterized by a vast and growing gap between rich and poor.[16] The postwar middle class, Beatty argues, "muted the class conflict that Marx had prophesied would one day destroy capitalism" by providing "a reproof to the very idea of class (65)."[17]

We might expect accounts of the middle-class dimensions of postwar literature and culture to undermine this conception of the middle-class as a nonclass. Yet these accounts, while usefully skeptical about what Dickstein calls the "deep discomfort at the core of American affluence and power" (16), tend—by reading the middle class solely in the light of privilege—to affirm its putative transcendence of the economic. "This was a time," Barbara Ehrenreich writes in her 1983 study *The Hearts of Men*, "when the educated middle class worried about being *too* affluent."[18] Jackson Lears, reading some of the same texts as Ehrenreich, argues that " 'a new class' of salaried managers, administrators, academics, technicians, and journalists" achieved cultural hegemony in the postwar period by identifying its "problems and interests with those of society and indeed humanity at large."[19] Through frequently popular works of social and cultural criticism, Lears argues, this class falsely universalized its own concerns about "the bureaucratization of bourgeois individualism in America" (46–47), in the process rendering others' concerns "marginal or even invisible to the wider public culture" (50). Catherine Jurca, finally, imputes a similar disingenuousness to postwar accounts of middle-class "suffering" and "discontent," which she views as self-interested counterfeits designed both to ratify middle-class affluence vis-à-vis less fortunate groups, and to allow individual members of the middle class a sense of distinction vis-à-vis their less self-aware counterparts.[20] While properly chary toward "exaggerated claims about postwar affluence" (139), Jurca is not chary about such claims as they relate to the middle class.[21]

To a certain extent, these accounts all continue—from a perspective more sophisticated about race, gender, and, less decisively, class—the project of the social criticism they describe, which in the words of one intellectual historian was preoccupied with "the problems of prosperity."[22] Thus William H. Whyte writes in *The Organization Man* (1956)—a locus classicus of postwar social criticism cited by Ehrenreich, Lears, and Jurca—that "it is not the evils of organization life that puzzle [the organization man], *but its very beneficence*."[23] More concretely, Whyte argues that the comfort and security enjoyed by the members of the middle class blunt their ambitions and render them all the more susceptible to the pressures toward conformity that characterize the organizations in which they work and, increasingly, do almost everything else. While some critics continue to see the problems of prosperity as authentic, and others have redescribed them as strategies for achieving or maintaining cultural dominance, most concur that they were not "material."[24]

Richard Ohmann's 1983 essay "The Shaping of a Canon: U. S. Fiction, 1960–1975" at first glance seems to belong in this category, although Ohmann departs from the consensus about the middle class's transcendence of the economic in a crucial way. Ohmann argues that middle-class gatekeepers in the publishing industry, the media, and the academy awarded "precanonical" status to fiction that translated middle-class insecurity into the narrative of individual breakdown that he calls the "illness story."[25] He thus concurs with Lears that the middle class exercised cultural hegemony by falsely universalizing its specific concerns, which for Ohmann, too, have to do with the pressures exerted by society on the individual. But Ohmann understands the resulting cultural products not simply as an expression of privilege, but also as symptomatic registers of the middle class's less than fully dominant role in the postwar economy. The postwar middle class, in Ohmann's account, was a "subordinate but influential class" (397) that exercised control over the content of postwar culture at the discretion of the "ruling class" that actually "own[ed] the media and control[led] them formally" (386). Ohmann, to be sure, emphasizes the novel authority of the middle class—or what he calls, following Barbara and John Ehrenreich, the "Professional-Managerial Class" or "PMC"—at this juncture. In the Ehrenreichs' influential description, the PMC is the class of "salaried mental workers" that "emerged with dramatic suddeness [*sic*] in the years between 1890 and 1920" and that constitutes an authentically new class with interests opposed to those of both owners and workers.[26] Drawing on the Ehrenreichs' essay, Ohmann insists that his account "turns upon class but not just upon the two great traditional classes" (387), though his own reference to ruling-class media-owners suggests that at least one of the two traditional classes was alive and well.

Moreover, with the demise of the postwar boom (which began faltering shortly before the mid-seventies end date Ohmann selects for his study), the members of the middle class have increasingly entered the other great traditional class of those who sell their labor. Beatty and Krugman both extol the postwar middle class in contributions to the crisis-of-the-middle-class genre that has been a journalistic staple (with the exception of a brief hiatus during the late nineties tech boom) for several decades. As such accounts suggest, this crisis has taken the form not simply of the disappearance of median incomes, but also of white-collar workers' new vulnerability to the sorts of workplace exploitation traditionally associated with those who work for a living. As Robert Seguin succinctly puts it, "with the recent downsizing of middle management, the increasing technological displacements of engineers and architects, and the sessionalization/detenuring of university departments, positions and locations once regarded as concrete evidence of Marx's errors are today under an intense pressure of proletarianization" (13). To say this is not, as Seguin hastens to add, by any means to deny the differences between the members of what is still called the middle class and the members of either the traditional working class or the new service class. To assert this would be absurd: it's still far better to work in an office than to clean it, and some people who work in middle-class occupations—lawyers, brokers, executives—still do quite well in the so-called New Economy.[27] But even a New Economy booster like Robert Reich admits that the well-paid, nonhierarchical, creative jobs he ascribes to "symbolic analysts" coexist with the far less appealing kinds of work he categorizes under the headings "routine production services" and "in-person services."[28] In addition to software engineers and cinematographers, the global economy employs (far more) data-entry clerks and phone-service representatives (and, as Andrew Ross points out, the hype over the former jobs helps to inculcate an ethos of overwork within the high-tech workforce more generally).[29] There is, in this regard, a kind of false pastoralism in accounts of the postwar middle class as the embodied refutation of Marxism. If subsequent events have contradicted the circumstances that presumably proved Marx wrong, then perhaps we shelved our copies of *Capital* too early. The fate of the middle class in recent years if anything seems to confirm Marx and Engels' assertion that "society as a whole is more and more splitting ... into two great classes directly facing each other": those who own capital and those who must sell their labor at the former group's terms.[30] The postwar middle class did well, but the fate of the middle class since the seventies suggests that this had more to do with the postwar boom and the redistributive policies of the mid-century welfare state than with the inherent nature of the postwar economy.

Of course, it is one thing to worry about contemporary white-collar workers subject to downsizing, or the assault on the forty-hour week, or capital's perpetual flight to cheaper labor pools, and quite another to worry about postwar white-collar workers whose comfortable jobs putatively threatened their individuality. But while the well-off members of the postwar middle class seem like the antithesis of their successors in terms of income, security, and other factors, their situations share an important element if we consider the rise of the postwar middle class in structural terms. In the first half of the twentieth century "the rise of corporate and bureaucratic structures" triggered a process of "remarkable growth and metamorphosis" through which "managers and white-collar workers" replaced "independent entrepreneurs" as the prototypical members of the American middle class.[31] Historically the basis of middle-class status in the United States had been the ownership of small property. Of course, the American middle-class ideal mutually embodied in the otherwise very different figures of the Jeffersonian freeholder and the Franklinian entrepreneur was from the start mostly limited to white men, and even for them this ideal began to break down early on.[32] But it was the changes brought about by industrialization—the growth of corporations, the elaboration of their managerial strata through vertical integration, the expansion of finance capital and the professions—that really accelerated the shift from entrepreneurship to white-collar employment.[33] The PMC emerged in the final decade of the nineteenth century as the first middle-class generation not to define itself through (the increasingly limited possibility of) property ownership, instead attempting to shift the basis of social authority onto management.[34]

The advent of the PMC, however, did not immediately or completely reconfigure the structure of the middle class as a whole. Throughout the first half of the twentieth century, the PMC coexisted with the small-property-owning middle class whose national political role had climaxed with Populism but which remained significant—albeit increasingly on a regional rather than a national scale—at least through the 1930s.[35] The PMC was, however, on the side of history, growing alongside the increasingly more complicated managerial structure of early twentieth-century monopoly capitalism as its scale received successive boosts from the rise of industrial trusts, the economic impetus of the World War I, and the merger movement of the 1920s.[36] During this period, the PMC relied upon the ideology of professionalism to bolster its members' agency within "large bureaucratic entities."[37] The thirties, and the New Deal, initiated a significant transition for the middle class, as for capitalism more generally. On one hand, PMC ambitions reached a high point with the New Deal implementation of limited forms of centralized planning: here at last managerial oversight was deployed to save capitalism from its own obvious failures, for the good of all. At the same time, however, the New Deal represented much more of an accommodation with big business than Progressive-era policies ever had. It was "managerial," but less in the sense of articulating an overall vision of society than of attempting to balance various conflicting interests, and marked a shift from "moralism" to "opportunism" on the part of Progressivism's increasingly technocratic heirs.[38] Concurrently with this shift in attitude at the highest levels of the PMC, at least some white-collar employees in the education system, the culture industry, and the new state bureaucracies began to conceive of their work not in professional-managerial terms but as a form of routinized mental labor.[39] These two shifts taken together—the decline of PMC faith in the managerial ideal, and an increasingly negative understanding of mental labor within large organizations—anticipate the new middle-class consciousness that would assume its definitive shape following World War II.

The war itself provided another huge boost—the largest yet—to the processes of corporate expansion and centralization. The hundred largest American corporations' share of manufacturing grew from 30 percent to 70 percent between 1940 and 1943 alone.[40] By the end of the war, there were over 500,000 fewer small businesses than at its start,[41] and over 1,600 mergers had taken place, "nearly one-third of which involved corporations with assets of $50 million or more taking over smaller enterprises."[42] By "1948, the corporate sector held almost 60 percent of national income-producing wealth."[43] The governmental sector, and the corporate-government nexus, also expanded in this period, as World War II defense spending gave way to the even more feverish outlays of the cold war and the federal government pursued a Keynesian program of spending and regulation designed to promote permanent growth.[44] The white-collar workforce grew apace, and in a frequently cited statistic white-collar workers surpassed blue-collar workers as the largest segment of the nonfarm workforce in 1956.[45] By this point, moreover, even the remaining small-property owners could not avoid "constant interaction with corporate and bureaucratic America."[46]

Postwar descriptions of the middle class forged in this context largely abandon the PMC's more positive understanding of organizations and the sense of agency—both individually and as a class—that this understanding enabled. For figures as diverse as Edward Bellamy, Charlotte Perkins Gilman, and Thorstein Veblen, the overall organization of society had seemed like the cure for the poor management of specific institutions.[47] For Whyte—who sees Progressivism as the enemy because it replaced the Protestant Ethic with a "Social Ethic" that "ma[de] morally legitimate the pressures of society against the individual" (6–7)—the problem is not so much specific organizations as the all-encompassing abstraction that he calls "The Organization." As Timothy Melley argues in his study of late twentieth-century fiction and social criticism *Empire of Conspiracy* (2000), Whyte and his contemporaries engaged in a discourse of "agency panic" that posed a reified, "all-or-nothing conception of agency" against an equally "monolithic conception of 'society' (or 'system,' or 'organization')."[48] Taking my cue from Lears' and Ohmann's arguments about the universalization of middle-class concerns, I argue that this discourse of constrained agency is best understood as a product of the transition from small-property ownership to white-collar employment as the basis of middle-class status. In brief, the postwar period constitutes a tipping point in the history of the middle class, when PMC efforts to rewrite individual and class agency in managerial terms give way to skepticism about organization as such and nostalgia for the putative autonomy of the property-owning old middle class.

This understanding of what it means to be middle class poses dispossession in abstractly individualized terms. Nonetheless, it reconfigures middle-class status around employment in ways that not only depart from the PMC's activist self-conception but also point toward the more concrete forms of dispossession experienced by the contemporary middle class. Descriptions of the organization man's threatened individuality, this book argues, simultaneously obscure and reveal concerns about downward class mobility. This occurs, for instance, in Whyte's discussion of "the use of psychological tests" as "symptomatic" of the organization man's situation:

> Originally, they were introduced by the managers as a tool for weeding out unqualified workers. As time went on, and personality tests were added to aptitude tests, the managers began using them on other managers, present and prospective, and today most personality testing is directed not at the worker, but at the organization man. If he is being hoist, it is by his own philosophy. (42)

Beneath this passage's ironic deflation of the PMC project of managing workers lies a submerged parable of the managers' own fate: if they are now subjecting themselves to the personality tests once reserved for workers, the unacknowledged implication is that they themselves have become workers.

What the *Fortune* editor Whyte only alludes to, C. Wright Mills makes explicit in his still influential 1951 study *White Collar*.[49] For Mills white-collar work exhibits the same sort of rationalization that had been central to the Fordist transformation of the factory in the early twentieth century:

> Even on the professional levels of white-collar work, not to speak of wage-work and the lower white-collar tasks, the chance to develop and use individual rationality is often destroyed by the centralization of decision and the formal rationality that bureaucracy entails....

The introduction of office machinery and sales devices has been mechanizing the office and the salesroom, the two big locales of white-collar work. Since the 'twenties it has increased the division of white-collar labor, recomposed personnel, and lowered skill levels. Routine operations in minutely subdivided organizations have replaced the bustling interest of work in well-known groups. Even on managerial and professional levels, the growth of rational bureaucracies has made work more like factory production. The managerial demiurge is constantly furthering all these trends: mechanization, more minute division of labor, the use of less skilled and less expensive workers. (226–27)

Here Mills understands the threat to agency not as some generalized specter of conformity but rather as the concrete loss of control in the workplace that, as it earlier had for factory workers, precedes and underwrites other kinds of proletarianization (one can be replaced with less expensive workers).

Thus while Mills acknowledges the variations in income, status, and workplace power within what he calls white-collar pyramids (70–76), his overarching historical narrative stresses "the centralization of small properties" (xiv) that has structurally proletarianized the middle class by placing its members "in exactly the same property-class position as the wage-workers" (71):

In the early nineteenth century, although there are no exact figures, probably four-fifths of the occupied population were self-employed enterprisers; by 1870, only about one-third, and in 1940, only about one-fifth, were still in this old middle class. Many of the remaining four-fifths of the people who now earn a living do so by working for the 2 or 3 per cent of the population who now own 40 or 50 per cent of the private property in the United States. Among these workers are the members of the new middle class, white-collar people on salary. For them, as for wage-workers, America has become a nation of employees for whom independent property is out of range. Labor markets, not control of property, determine their chances to receive income, exercise power, enjoy prestige, learn and use skills. (63)

To make this point is not to deny the real prosperity enjoyed by the postwar middle class and the upper levels of the unionized working class. Nor is it to confuse white-collar workers with the members of the traditional working class, or to obviate the (ongoing) differences between those at different levels of white- collar pyramids. But it is to impute a structural priority to the middle class's loss of its historical control over property, which in a capitalist economy rendered it vulnerable *as a class* to future losses of income and job security.

While it is a staple of discussions of Mills to cite his alleged transcendence of Marxism, this is a fundamentally Marxist argument. In this case Mills owes an insufficiently acknowledged debt to a book he mentions only briefly in a long list of sources, Lewis Corey's 1935 *The Crisis of the Middle Class* (Mills, *White* 357). Corey, too, had argued that economic concentration had transformed "the old middle class of small producers" into a "'new' middle class of salaried employees."[50] No doubt one reason that Corey's argument has traveled less well than Mills's is his Depression-era claim—made with an eye to contemporary events in Germany—that the members of the dispossessed middle class should be encouraged to identify with and as workers lest they become recruits to Fascism. But if the postwar boom (thankfully) invalidated this thesis, Mills's appropriation of Corey suggests that it did not invalidate Corey's underlying claim that the transformation of the middle class symptomatized the increasing binarization of the U.S. class system.[51] While this seems to contradict our standard understanding of the postwar period as an era of redistribution, Adolf Belle's preface to the 1968 edition of his and Gardiner Means's classic 1932 study of economic concentration, *The Modern Corporation and Private Property*, suggests that it need not do so. Berle points out that the commonplace understanding of redistribution in fact conflates two separate meanings of "wealth." While "individually owned wealth has enormously increased" in the postwar era, he acknowledges, "relatively little of it is 'productive' property—land or things employed by its owners in production or commerce." Instead, the largest amount is invested in "owner-occupied homes" and the next largest in "consumer durables" such as "automobiles and home equipment."[52] On one hand, then, a relatively equal distribution of *income* during the postwar period created a large class of people, white-collar workers and otherwise, who enjoyed a middle-class standard of living. On the other hand, however, this process concealed an ongoing concentration of *capital* continuous with the current unequal distribution of wealth.

Good middle-class incomes and an active welfare state, not to mention cold war strictures against anything smacking of Marxism, rendered the concentration of capital difficult to see in the postwar period. But postwar representations of the middle class nonetheless found a substitute narrative of declension in the story of the middle class's fall from its golden age of property-owning autonomy. Lipsitz argues the concentration of property during World War II undermined "the ideal of small-business ownership [that] constituted a popular symbol of freedom in the United States,"[53] although this is only partly true. Following Melley's account of agency panic—which he argues conserved individualism discursively by continually describing it as threatened—we can argue that the postwar decline of property ownership as a material reality in fact led to its ascendancy as "ideal" and "symbol." Mills, for instance, invokes the classic terms of property-owning liberal individualism alongside his more Marxist narrative of structural proletarianization.[54] In the past, he writes,

> since few men owned more property than they could work, differences between men were due in large part to personal strength and ingenuity. The type of man presupposed and strengthened by this society was willingly economic, possessing the "reasonable self-interest" needed to build and operate the market economy. He was, of course, more than an economic man, but the techniques and the economics of production shaped much of what he was and what he looked forward to becoming. He was an "absolute individual," linked into a system with no authoritarian center, but held together by countless, free, shrewd transactions. (9)

Eschewing his skepticism elsewhere in *White Collar* about "sentimental versions of historical types that no longer exist, if indeed they ever did" (xiii), Mills here reproduces the classic terms of American (white, male, middle-class) self-making. In contrast with this golden age, he writes, "The decline of the free entrepreneur and the rise of the dependent employee on the American scene has paralleled the decline of the independent individual and the rise of the little man in the American mind" (xii).

Despite the obvious difficulties with such liberal nostalgia, however, it still provides a way of thinking about the pervasive anxieties of the postwar middle class in class terms rather than individual ones, and historically rather than existentially. Even in works lacking Mills's Marxist perspective, like Whyte's *Organization Man* and David Riesman's *The Lonely Crowd* (1950), this narrative of decline provides a sedimentation of class history usefully at odds with the countervailing pressure toward an existential narrative of conflict between individual and society.[55] Whyte's invocation of the Protestant Ethic

to describe a lost era of middle-class ambition and creative endeavor, for instance, functions in this manner. Less obviously, Riesman postulates an emergent shift within contemporary society from "inner-direction" (in which guidance comes from goals implanted
early in life by parents and other adult authorities) to "other-direction" (in which it
comes from the continuously changing signals sent by peers and the media).[56] While
Riesman subtitles *The Lonely Crowd* "The Changing *American* Character" (my emphasis),
he notes that

> if we wanted to cast our social character types into social class molds, we could say that
> inner-direction is the typical character of the "old" middle class—the banker, the tradesman,
> the small entrepreneur, the technically oriented engineer, etc.—while other-direction is
> becoming the typical character of the "new" middle class—the bureaucrat, the salaried
> employee in business, etc. (20)

Riesman sees the rise of other-direction, that is, at least in part as a class phenomenon,
one conditioned by the loss of the private property that served, during an earlier "era of
private competitive capitalism," as "a kind of exoskeleton" separating "the individual
self" from "other people" (114).

Riesman and Whyte are typical postwar authors, then, not insofar as they understand the crisis of individualism in terms that verge on the existential, but rather insofar as they deploy such terms in ways that simultaneously mask and reveal the historical
transformation of the American middle class. It is worth noting, however, that not all
postwar texts need to be teased into giving up their economic engagements; as Ohmann's
essay on postwar fiction makes clear, middle-class dissatisfaction does not so much
determine the production of this fiction as guide what gets canonized. The classic realist account of the dismantling of the American middle class is Ira Wolfert's largely
neglected 1943 novel *Tucker's People*. Here I mean classic realism in the sense theorized
by Georg Lukács, in his discussion of "the classic form of the historical novel," which
for him "portray[s] the struggles and antagonisms of history by means of characters
who, in their psychology and destiny, always represent social trends and historical
forces."[57] Such fiction, neither "romantically monumentalizing the important figures
of history [nor] dragging them down to the level of private, psychological trivia" (47),
instead offers types of "the inter-relationships between the psychology of people and
the economic and moral circumstances of their lives" (40). This sort of fiction, epito-
mized for Lukács by Walter Scott's historical novels, arises with "the class struggles
between nobility and bourgeoisie... whose last decisive stage was the ... French
Revolution" (27–28), and comes to an end with the bourgeois reaction to the failed but
nonetheless threatening revolutions of 1848. Fredric Jameson has observed that this
chronology, which lays the groundwork for Lukács' well-known critique of modernism
as inherently apolitical, leaves out "writers and whole cultures which lay outside
Lukács' personal interests and background."[58] While Jameson is concerned to recover
various versions of politically progressive modernism, we might also apply his argument, in the American context, to writing that remained outside the canons of experimental modernism. *Tucker's People*, later filmed as the Abraham Polonsky noir *Force of
Evil* (1948), starring John Garfield, tells the story of a gangster's efforts to consolidate
the numbers rackets in New York City. But the novel can also be read as an allegory of
the traditional middle class's disappearance in the face of an increasingly large-scale
capitalism. *Tucker's People*, we might say, continues to operate as Lukácsian classic

realism, although coming at the opposite end of the historical trajectory initiated in Great Britain by Scott, it records not the triumphant emergence but the ignominious decline of the small bourgeoisie.

As the novel opens the small businessman Leo Minch is reluctantly entertaining a proposal from another character named Samson Candee to go into the numbers business in Harlem. Minch has just lost his garage business because his landlords have turned him in for allowing his brother Joe to store liquor trucks owned by his bootlegger boss Ben Tucker. In fact, they had merely used Leo's indiscretion as a pretext to recover the property, whose value "Leo's success with his business had increased."[59] This is not the first, nor will it be the last, time that Leo loses his business to larger operators. Leo's story, Wolfert makes clear at the end of book 1, is an historically typical one:

> He had been born in the time of Rockefeller. He had spent his business life being hounded from the woolen business to butter-and-egg routes to real estate to the garage business to policy. He had run from place to place, looking for one place where he could hole up and be overlooked and at peace in a world of expanding big business. But all his running had done was advance him towards the time of Hitler, when big business and its creatures, when trusts and monopolies and their methods, having grown powerful and hungry in the hunt, were foraging even among the rabbit holes. (71)

Repeatedly driven from businesses whose very growth attracts bigger players and makes it impossible for him to compete, Leo accepts Candee's proposition, and builds a successful policy operation in Harlem. Unbeknownst to Leo, however, Ben Tucker is planning to take over and consolidate the New York numbers business. He does this by arranging for a certain popular number to hit so that Leo and his colleagues will have to pay out all their assets and he can buy them out, a "method," Wolfert writes, that "was simple and had a long tradition among monopolists" (74). Leo finally surrenders his organization to Tucker in exchange for a top managerial position, in a deal that has been brokered by Leo's brother. When Joe asks Leo if he "begin[s] to see the possibilities" in this arrangement, Leo replies—in words that might serve as the epitaph of the small-property-owning old middle class—"I see that I had a business when I came up here and now I'm working for Tucker for salary" (143).

Wolfert reinforces this point with another story of middle-class expropriation, the family history of Tucker's lawyer, Henry Wheelock. In a chapter whose title ("An American Hero's Son") invokes the national heritage of liberal individualism, we learn that Wheelock's father was a hotel manager in a small town built by the "big lumber companies" in "western timber country" (147). Like Leo Minch, Roger Wheelock lies at the end of the line for the old middle class, in a world shaped by big capital. When the lumber companies had "plundered the forests and got theirs out of it" (147) they moved on, precipitating a general economic collapse: "The sawmills nearest town started closing and the branch of the furniture company that advertised 'From Forest To You' moved away and the railroad cut its passenger train schedules in half" (149). The elder Wheelock, who "had known what the big lumber people were up to" and had paid off the mortgages on the hotel in the hopes that "if he owned [it] all free and clear, then he would be safe" (148), finds himself stuck with a useless business. Eventually the bank repossesses the hotel and asks Roger Wheelock "to stay on as manager" (155), thereby completing his transition from old middle-class independence to white-collar employment. Henry, who at the time is struggling to find work as a lawyer in New York City, meditates on his father's life:

> Roger knew the end, his son thought, the minute the big lumber companies started working on the forests. He saw the day and he tried to prepare for it. He got his hotel all paid off and he thought that would be the rock he would stand on. Then the rock began to sink and he had to fight to hold the rock up. It was a hopeless fight. He was a man holding up something that was holding up him. The old man must have known it would be hopeless and must have known it was hopeless, but he kept right on with it. It was heroic. It was a life to which music should be played. (153)

The experience of seeing his father ruined by men who "had no thought of people as people or as anything but tools or opponents" (147), the novel suggests, drives Henry to his position as Tucker's amoral, cynical lawyer. *Tucker's People* analogizes crime and business, not simply because "Tucker's organization [is] like that of any many-sided management corporation geared to absorb new businesses" (175), but more importantly because "business—without thought of anything but money—could destroy the lives of great numbers of people.... The murderer was the same kind of personality in either case, whether he was a big man and sat in a corporation's office ... or whether he was a small man and had to supervise everything himself" (174).

Although he thus treats business as no better than gangsterism, Wolfert's politics have less to do with Marxism than with the politics of small property that, Mills notes, have generally taken the place of class politics in the United States (55). Leo, for instance, loses his first business when the expanding woolens industry attracts speculators who drive "prices ... up and down violently without regard to value," causing "a steeply falling market" that catches Leo "with shelves loaded" (9). He uses what's left of his credit to pursue "an opening...in butter-and-egg routes in the suburbs" (9), but this leaves him dissatisfied because "had been a merchant all his life, providing goods—not merely service. To sell service, somehow, seemed false" (10). Later, he becomes a successful real estate speculator himself, but the methods he must employ—"loss leaders and premiums, doing things for good will that a man who was there to make a living out of running the store itself could not have afforded to do"—only make him feel more "dissatisfied and insecure" (10). Retrenching, he buys two apartment houses with the goal of "pay[ing] off the mortgages and own[ing] them outright," as well as leasing the garage that he is "determined to run as a business, not as a mere squeeze-box for squeezing out profits" (11). Leo's victimization at the hands of speculators and his desire to run his businesses for their own sake rather than for the sake of profit echo the agrarian-producer ethos of the Populist-Progressive era.[60] One would not be surprised, in this regard, to see Frank Norris's farmer-turned-businessman Charles Cressler take the stage and assert, as he does in Norris's 1903 *The Pit*, that "the Chicago speculator ... raises or lowers the price out of all reason, for the benefit of his pocket," "gambling" on its eventual price to the detriment of farmers because, unlike them, he "don't care in the least about the grain."[61] But the novel's politics are not simply anachronistic. Leo's preference for goods over services also resonates with the postwar understanding of white-collar work as a field where members of the middle class no longer "manipulate *things*" but instead "handle *people* and *symbols*" (Mills, *White* 65; Mills's emphases), where "the 'softness' of men rather than the 'hardness' of material ... calls on talent and opens new channels of social mobility" (Riesman, *Lonely* 127). In this respect, *Tucker's People* provides a bridge between the small-property-owning politics of Populism and its descendants on the contemporary left[62] and right.[63]

Wolfert's main investment in old-middle-class ideals lies, however, in his idealization of the relationship between Leo and his employees. By no means perfect—he cuts Candee out of their numbers business before it becomes successful, for instance—Leo nonetheless knows and treats each of his employees as an individual, in explicit contrast to big business's tendency to treat people as "tools" or "opponents":

> Leo admired the placid way in which Mr. Middleton took his hard luck and used to give him a cigar once in a while. He listened to Juice's story sympathetically several times and once had Edgar take the door off his car to see if that would help Juice stay in it. It didn't. He was sorry for Delilah and secretly proud to have a college graduate working for him. He found her some pupils to tutor on Saturday mornings when she did not go to school and told her that if she got enough pupils, she would not have to work for him. (92)

The novel reinforces this point formally by providing detailed back-stories for each of Leo's employees, something that we only get in the case of Tucker's big organization for his inner circle. In classic old-middle-class terms, Leo's treatment of his employees epitomizes the coincidence of decency and profitability. On one hand these employees, many of them former "domestic servants or charwomen in offices and hotels" (87), are "grateful for their jobs and happy in them" (92): "He felt they all loved him ... and, actually, they did" (92). On the other hand, Leo's practices are "copied by other bankers because the methods were profitable" (65). Self-consciously collapsing two different definitions of "good," the novel notes that "Leo, who was a 'good' man, could make it a 'good' business" (65). Despite its seemingly evenhanded exposure of Leo's character flaws, *Tucker's People* ultimately romanticizes the small employer; indeed, its attention to these flaws only reinforces the idea that small business is inherently ethical despite the motivations of any particular businessman.[64] It is thus not a proletarian novel, since it views events not from a working-class but from an old-middle-class perspective. Its working-class characters never become collective historical agents in their own rights, but remain the objects of a history told from the perspective of people like Leo Minch and Roger Wheelock.[65]

Nonetheless, Wolfert's invocation of old-middle-class ideals transcends nostalgia insofar as he understands these ideals as casualties of the historical process of middle-class expropriation. Wolfert makes this point clear in the scene where Leo negotiates with Wheelock and Tucker the terms under which he will transfer his business to Tucker. Wheelock questions, for instance, why Leo pays much more for one of the apartments he uses as a drop-off station for policy slips, and learns that the renter is "a boy who worked with [Leo] to put himself through college" and now "can't find what's fit for him to do." Leo "pay[s] half his rent" because "a college boy with a wife has to have a place that's nice to live" (130). Wheelock thinks, "There were a lot of things like that, ... sloppy things, where expenses could be cut when the business would be managed properly" (130). When Tucker arrives for the meeting he continues this line of inquiry, insisting that "things is going to be run up there on a businesslike"—by which he means profitably standardized—"basis": no more covering collectors' shortages, a lower commission for everyone, a lower payoff for customers who hit (139). Systematizing Leo's operations in this manner, Tucker trims away Leo's ability to treat employees on an individual basis, what Wheelock thinks of as Leo's inability "to get used to paying people their wages and letting them alone" (130). This produces tragic results for both Leo and his employees:

Leo's bookkeeper, Frederick Bauer, unable to quit because Leo's brother Joe thinks it would be a bad example for Leo's other workers, becomes embroiled in a kidnapping scheme that leads to his shooting and Leo's fatal stroke. Leo's ability to shelter his employees from the exploitative logic of capitalism has been contingent, the novel insists, upon his control over his own capital. Thus it is no coincidence that, as the final stage in their negotiations, Tucker barely lets Leo retain his $31,000 cash reserve, letting Leo know that he knows about it and making it clear that he allows him to keep it only to bind Leo more closely to him (142). Granted the return of what was previously his own capital at his new employer's sufferance, Leo—and by extension the American middle class he represents—loses the autonomy that property grants, bringing an era of history to a close.

From the perspective of postwar literary history, the realism of *Tucker's People* was a dead end. But the transformation of the middle class that Wolfert's novel takes as its explicit historical backdrop shapes all postwar fiction in one way or another. The middlebrow novels of middle-class life popular in the fifties, for instance, translate the shift from entrepreneurship to employment into generational conflicts whose successful resolution phantasmatically negates this shift's worst effects. Elizabeth Long has argued that Sloan Wilson's 1955 *The Man in the Gray Flannel* Suit enacts a shift "from entrepreneurial adventure to corporate-suburban compromise," in which the protagonist Tom Rath rejects his employer Ralph Hopkins's single-minded devotion to business, "in favor of a balance between work and privatized familial happiness."[66] But the contrast between Hopkins and Rath is not simply a contrast between workplace and domestic forms of satisfaction: it is also a contrast between a founder of a company and one of his employees, played out in the form of an Oedipal relationship. As Jurca's reading of the novel suggests, its true fantasy is not a retreat into the family but Rath's unexpected recovery of entrepreneurial status thanks to his grandmother's bequest of valuable Connecticut real estate (139–42). Rath repudiates Hopkins and still gets to have what he has; what Hopkins has, crucially, is not income but capital. Cameron Hawley's 1952 *Executive Suite* similarly fantasizes reversing the middle class's historical trajectory through the medium of a successfully resolved generational conflict, although Hawley, unlike Wilson, attempts to do so within the corporate context. *Executive Suite*, whose epigraph is "the king is dead ..." (Hawley's ellipsis), begins with Avery Bullard, the owner of a furniture company, collapsing on a New York sidewalk in the midst of reluctantly searching for the executive vice-president demanded by his investors. It concludes with the succession of a young engineer named Don Walling to Bullard's position. Walling thus takes Bullard's place as King, reassuring the novel's readers that upward mobility still exists. But this is not the whole story, since the novel also suggests that Walling brings to his job an emphasis on personnel matters that marks him, in Whyte's reading, as a typical organization man (Whyte, *Organization* 83–84).[67] In the terms that we earlier saw employed by Mills and Riesman, Walling exemplifies the white-collar middle class in that he is less interested in making furniture than in managing furniture-makers. At the same time Walling, who has come up through the firm as an actual designer of furniture, epitomizes old-middle-class values. In a climactic speech he even suggests that it was Bullard who first abandoned these values by okaying a training film emphasizing profit over workmanship and greenlighting an inferior line of furniture.[68] *Executive Suite* thus transposes the transformation of the middle class from the economic to the moral realm, insisting that as long as men like Walling exist this transformation remains reversible. Like *The Man in the Gray Flannel Suit*—and unlike *Tucker's People*—Hawley's novel incorporates the transformation of the middle class only to offer a fantasy of its reversal.

Chapter One

Ayn Rand and the Politics of Property

It wasn't too long ago that Ayn Rand, despite her enormous and ongoing popularity, was all but invisible in the criticism and history of twentieth-century American fiction, although that has begun to change. Sharon Stockton and Michael Szalay have recently demonstrated the centrality of Rand's conception of brain work to the Depression Era in which she wrote her first bestselling novel, *The Fountainhead* (1943).[1] In what follows I make a case for her ongoing relevance in the postwar era, focusing primarily on her 1957 novel, *Atlas Shrugged*. Unlike many of the authors I deal with in this study, Rand writes books whose engagement with the questions of mental labor central to the postwar reorganization of the middle class is self-evident, if not as simple as her reputation might suggest. Rand's conception of mental labor, and the politics to which it gives rise, are much more complicated (if in many ways no less conservative) than we usually give them credit for being. Rand's absence from the critical canon is, in this respect, continuous with the evasion of the economic that continues to structure our readings of postwar fiction.

The crisis of the middle class described by Whyte receives its fullest exposition—albeit not as such—in *Atlas Shrugged*. In Rand's novel, a group of industrialists, inventors, and sympathetic artists goes on strike—the working title of the novel was "The Strike"[6]—to demonstrate to the world what happens when they withdraw the productive energies that politicians, intellectuals, and ungrateful employees simultaneously denounce and exploit. The symbol of this band of renegades, stamped on their own personal brand of cigarettes and cast in a three-foot gold statue suspended on a granite column in their Rocky Mountain hideaway, is the dollar sign. As one of the strikers explains to Dagny Taggart, the railroad executive who shares their values but who resists joining them until the final pages of the novel, they have adopted the dollar sign as their ensign in defiance of its common use as "the one sure-fire brand of evil," preferring instead to understand it as a badge of "achievement, … success, … ability, [and] man's creative power."[7] Like Trilling and Whyte, Rand understands money as the symbol of a productive energy belonging to an idealized past. Informing her that the dollar sign "stands for the initials of the United States," one striker tells Taggart that the United States "was the only country in history where wealth was not acquired by looting, but by production, not by force, but by trade, the only country whose money was the symbol of man's right to his own mind, to his work, to his life, to his happiness, to himself," but has lost its way because it has turned "its own monogram [into] a symbol of depravity" (630).

The strikers' regard for what another of them calls the "one magnificent century" in which the United States "redeemed the world" (711) presumably finds a sympathetic audience in Dagny, who shares their nostalgia for nineteenth-century American capitalism. In Dagny's case, this nostalgia finds its focus in her ancestor Nat Taggart, the founder of the family company for which she now works. Nat Taggart's career stands in salutary opposition to his descendant's work as Taggart Transcontinental's Vice-President of Operations. Where Dagny must continually deal with a company whose executives—exemplified by Taggart's president, her brother Jim—are timid, hyperconscious of bureaucratic restraints, and more interested in engineering profitable government regulations than in running trains, her forebear worked blessedly alone:

He was a man who had never accepted the creed that others had the right to stop him. He set his goal and moved toward it, his way as straight as one of his rails. He never sought any loans, bonds, subsidies, land grants or legislative favors from the government. He obtained money from the men who owned it, going from door to door—from the mahogany doors of bankers to the clapboard doors of lonely farmhouses. He never talked about the public good. He merely told people that they would make big profits on his railroad, he told them why he expected the profits and he gave his reasons. He had good reasons. Through all the generations that followed, Taggart Transcontinental was one of the few railroads that never went bankrupt and the only one whose controlling stock remained in the hands of the founder's descendants. (62)

Rumored to have murdered a state legislator who tried to use regulatory chicanery to make a profit on his failure, Nat Taggart is his successor's antisocial *beau ideal*. Passing his statue in the concourse of the Taggart station she feels "a moment's rest... as if a burden she could not name were lightened and as if a faint current of air were touching her forehead" (63). John Galt, the organizer of the strike, makes clear the connection between Dagny's reverence for her ancestor and the strikers' ideals when he tells her that she can signal her willingness to join them by "chalk[ing] a dollar sign on the pedestal of Nat Taggart's statue—where it belongs" (884–85).

Rand notes of Galt's home in the strikers' refuge of Atlantis that it has "the primitive simplicity of a frontiersman's cabin, reduced to essential necessities ... with a super-modern skill" (655); likewise, one of his lieutenants lives in a home "like a frontiersman's shanty thrown together to serve as a mere springboard for a long flight into the future" (710). Nor is it an accident that she situates Atlantis itself in the Mountain West. As a product of the postwar period, *Atlas Shrugged* participates in the celebration of frontier individualism that likewise animates works of American studies scholarship like Henry Nash Smith's *Virgin Land* (1950), R.W.B. Lewis's *The American Adam* (1955), and Leslie Fiedler's *Love and Death in the American Novel* (1960). At the same time, one of the novel's last scenes consists of a nightmarish depiction of stranded rail passengers rescued by a wagon train. For Rand, the pioneer only serves as a metaphor for her true hero, the robber baron. The moment of declension in her mythos is not the closing of the frontier that preoccupied Frederick Jackson Turner's heirs, but rather the moment when, say, Andrew Carnegie sells out to U.S. Steel or Thomas Edison's workshops institute team research—the moment, that is, when the individual owner or inventor cedes control to the collaborative organization of management and mental labor characteristic of the modern corporation. This explains *Atlas Shrugged*'s characteristic investment in such anachronisms, from the perspective of business history, as a family-owned railroad system or the head of a steel company who personally invents a revolutionary new alloy.

But although *Atlas Shrugged*'s plot focuses on the eventual conversion of Dagny Taggart and mill owner Hank Rearden, and spends a lot of time theorizing the natural aristocracy that links heirs like Taggart and copper magnate Francisco D'Anconia to self-made men like Galt and Rearden, its actual historical referent is not the American ruling class. Rather, I will argue in what follows, its ahistorical fantasies of owner-operators serve as a site for the conservation of *middle-class* agency in a period when the traditional basis of such agency—private property—had given way to a new definition of middle-class status based on white-collar employment. If Rand's heroes proudly define themselves as producers and traders, her villains reproduce the picture of white-collar self-abdication central to *The Organization Man*. Mr. Thompson, the head of state in the totalitarian government that coalesces as the strikers withdraw, is no jackbooted führer, but on the contrary "a man who possessed the quality of never being noticed":

> In any group of three, his person became indistinguishable, and when seen alone it seemed to evoke a group of its own, composed of the countless persons he resembled. The country had no clear image of what he looked like: his photographs had appeared on the covers of magazines as frequently as those of his predecessors in office, but people could never be quite certain which photographs were his and which were pictures of "*a* mail clerk" or "*a* white-collar worker," accompanying articles about the daily life of the undifferentiated— except that Mr. Thompson's collars were usually wilted. (494; Rand's emphases)

Literally embodying the triumph of the group over the individual central to Whyte's analysis of postwar business, the "undifferentiated" and explicitly white-collar Thompson likewise shares the organization man's lack of ambition: "Holding enormous official powers, he schemed ceaselessly to expand them, because it was expected of him by those who had pushed him into office.... The sole secret of his rise in life was the fact that he was a product of chance and knew it and aspired to nothing else" (494). Whereas Galt and his crew are self-contained, self-starting prime movers symbolized by Galt's invention of a motor that runs on atmospheric electricity, their opponents are mere conduits for an impersonal and purely reactive evil. Rand's villains, she insists, do not reveal their true natures when they stop casting their motives in terms of altruistic service and instead profess a will to power or profit. Rather, both forms of self-description serve as screens for the true horror behind their actions, a thanatopic "lust to destroy whatever was living, for the sake of whatever was not" (1052). By means of this contrast, Rand's novel allegorizes the transformation of middle-class identity central to the work of Whyte and other postwar social critics. Rand's particular value lies in her commitment to property relations, which will allow her to function for us in much the same way that Adam Smith and David Ricardo function for Marx: as a misguided but nonetheless useful register of the relations of production subtending social and cultural phenomena.

Among postwar social critics, as I argued in the introduction, Mills most forcefully and directly links middle-class malaise to the transformation of property relations. If, for Mills, the new middle-class white-collar worker is the deindividuated "cog and ... beltline of the bureaucratic machinery" (80), this is because he lacks the old middle class's defining relationship to small capital. The possession of such capital made the middle-class entrepreneur, in Mills's most hyperbolic formulation, into "an 'absolute individual,' linked into a system with no authoritarian center, but held together by countless, free, shrewd transactions" (9). It is of course the case that this account of American economic history obscures significant disparities in who could own property, not to mention the fact that for much of this period some Americans were owned *as* property. Mills's investment in this version of the American past might, moreover, seem even more suspect when placed alongside Rand's strikingly similar sense of the market as matrix for the ideal social system. Consider, for instance, the following passage from *Atlas Shrugged,* another of the strikers' rhetorical set-pieces about money:

> Money rests on the axiom that every man is the owner of his mind and his effort. Money allows no power to prescribe the value of your effort except the voluntary choice of the man who is willing to trade you his effort in return.... Money permits no deals except those to mutual benefit by the unforced judgment of the traders. Money demands of you the recognition that men must work for their own benefit, not for their own injury, for their gain, not

their loss—the recognition that they are not beasts of burden, born to carry the weight of your misery—that you must offer them values, not wounds—that the common bond among men is not the exchange of suffering, but the exchange *of goods*.... And when men live by trade—with reason, not force, as their final arbiter—it is the best product that wins, the best performance, the man of best judgement and highest ability—and the degree of a man's productiveness is the degree of his reward. (383; Rand's emphasis)

For Rand, the market is not the source of social inequality but the mechanism for eliminating hierarchical relationships, the basis for what is in effect a functioning anarchy. In the strikers' haven, there are "no laws ..., no rules, no formal organization of any kind," other than the "custom[]" that forbids "the word '*give*' " (659). On this basis, the strikers erect a perfectly functioning social system that for the first time fulfills man's nature as "a social being" (690). Despite the vast gulf separating their politics, then, Rand shares Mills's vision of a society structured not around an "authoritarian center" but through a multiplicity of "free, shrewd" exchanges.

Whereas Rand sees this system as the ideal and heretofore unrealized fulfillment of human history, however, Mills sees it as a moment now irretrievably lost to the "centralization of small properties" (xiv) and the resulting concentration of economic control. The process of middle-class expropriation that culminated in the mid-twentieth-century United States, as a factor in the ongoing centralization of property, helps to explain *Atlas Shrugged's* anachronistic investment in the managerial revolution that began in the mid-nineteenth century, and was more or less a fait accompli by World War II. The idea of a railroad still owned and managed by its founder's descendants completely belies the railroad industry's historical participation in this revolution, as those familiar with Alfred Chandler's *The Visible Hand* (1977) will recognize. Railroads, Chandler argues, played a central role in the shift from "small, personally owned and managed enterprises...coordinated and monitored by market price mechanisms" to large, vertically integrated organizations "monitored and coordinated by salaried employees" because they were, along with telegraph companies, the first businesses "to require a large number of full-time managers to coordinate, control, and evaluate the activities of a number of widely scattered operating units."[8] The extent and complexity of railroads' operations, that is, drove the development of precisely the forms of bureaucratic administration by professional managers that rendered owner-managers like Nat Taggart obsolete. Dagny Taggart thus fights a battle that, in a more historically accurate account, Nat Taggart would already have lost. Or perhaps even more accurately, she fights a battle against forces that Nat Taggart would himself have set in motion.

Rand's celebration of owner-managers like Taggart and Rearden might make sense, however, if we see them not as a belated generation of robber barons but rather as outsized representatives of the middle-class entrepreneur whose historical twilight had occurred more recently. And in fact, the novel itself suggests this connection insofar as the strikers give up the giant industries they are unable to run in the modern world for the life of middle-class proprietors. Dagny, having stumbled prematurely on their mountain hideaway, finds the oilman Ellis Wyatt, for instance, supervising just two workers (665), while "Calvin Atwood of the Atwood Light and Power Company of New York is making the shoes" (668) and others have opened small shops on "the valley's single street" (670), among them a former automaker whom Dagny spies "weighing a chunk of butter" at his new grocery store (670). This transformation of captains of industry into shopkeepers, while meant to highlight the dignity of free trade, suggests the historical dilemma behind Rand's simultaneous love and fear of the nineteenth-century past. Recognizing that her traders' utopia is unfeasible in the contemporary world, and able to realize it only in the terms of a nostalgic regression, Rand cannot depict the new world of large industry *and* individual trade that the strikers promise to build after the old system's failure. The novel ends with Galt announcing, "We are going back to the world" (1074), unable actually to show what happens when they do.

In its form, then, *Atlas Shrugged* reveals the problem inherent in its own celebration of the capitalist producer and trader: the way in which capitalism itself, by continually concentrating property in larger and more complex forms, leads to the disenfranchisement of individuals that Rand abhors. Ever more centralized property, and not external controls, undermines the market of free individuals that can only be restored through an artificial return to smaller-scale capitalism. This is not, however, to suggest that Rand's investment in a (by mid-century) largely residual mode of property ownership likewise marks her politics as residual. On the contrary, Mills for one stressed the durability of "the ideology suitable for the nation of small capitalists" in a United States "transformed from a nation of small capitalists into a nation of hired employees" (34). For Mills, the persistence of the politics of small capital, "as if that small-propertied world were still a going concern" (34), ironically served the big business interests responsible for small capital's difficulties:

> at the same time that small firms are being driven to the wall, they are being used by the big firms with which they publicly identify themselves. This fact underlies the ideology and the frustration of the small urban capitalist; it is the reason why his aggression is directed at labor and government. (51)

Big business, Mills argued, uses "small businessmen [as] shock troops in the battle against labor unions and government controls," thereby "exploit[ing] in its own interests the very anxieties it has created for small business" (53). *Atlas Shrugged* exemplifies this process, blurring the distinction between small and large capital by stressing what Rand sees as their shared conflict with government.[9]

Rand's decision to make Dagny Taggart a railroad executive makes sense insofar as by 1957 the railroad industry exemplified the industrial decline that *Atlas Shrugged* imputes to the economy as a whole. Here, too, though, Rand fails to get her business history exactly right. At one point during a press conference held to discuss the opening of a new rail line, Dagny tells the assembled reporters that "the average profit of railroads has been two percent of the capital invested" (220). Assuming that *Atlas Shrugged* does in fact take place in the late fifties, this statistic slightly undershoots the actual figure, even for what had been lean years for the industry. According to John F. Stover's 1961 *American Railroads*, "the four largest railroads had a net income of only 2.9 percent" in 1957, although the figure for the industry as a whole since 1945 had "ranged from 2.76 per cent to 4.31 per cent" and "averaged ... 3.64 per cent."[10] More important than the actual figure, however, is the way in which Rand implicitly poses this particular industry as a representative of the postwar economy more generally. There is no doubt that the railroads were in trouble in the late fifties, and in fact had been in decline since rail mileage had peaked in 1916.[11] In *Atlas Shrugged*, however, the progressive decline of Taggart Transcontinental emblematizes an economy more like that of the Depression thirties than the boom fifties. The reader's introduction to Dagny, riding a Taggart train diverted by a broken switch and halted by a faulty signal light, anticipates a world in which—even before the total collapse that sets wagon trains in motion—goods are scarce, machines are breaking down and cannot be fixed, and streets are filled with empty storefronts.[12] But of course the railroad industry's difficulties were not typical of the postwar economy. In the same year, for instance, airlines posted a 7.75 percent return on their investments,[13] and much of the railroads' troubles in these years was the result of competition from both the airlines and the equally well-off trucking industry.

This is not to endorse the market-based analysis of the railroads' vicissitudes that have governed the most recent round of attacks on what is left of U.S. rail service, however. As Amtrak's proponents have pointed out in response to attacks on its inefficiency, the carrier receives only a small percentage of the government funding devoted to highways and the infrastructure of the aviation industry.[14] This pattern was already established by the late fifties, belying Rand's sense—which, of course, remains central to conservative rhetoric—of government as the purely negative enemy of business. In the postwar period railroads were, to some degree, victims of aggressive government regulation left over from their glory days in the late nineteenth century.[15] At the same time, however, the industry's competitors benefited not only from the absence of similar regulation but also from positive government action, including massive direct funding for highways, airports, and other facilities.[16] As Kim McQuaid has pointed out, World War II and the cold war led to a new symbiosis between government and big business, with the state more and more exerting its financial, regulatory, and even diplomatic and military powers in the interests of business.[17]

On one hand, *Atlas Shrugged* fully acknowledges this new corporate-state intimacy through its depiction of executives like Jim Taggart and the steel maker Orren Boyle, who devote their time to engineering government regulations that allow them to ruin their competitors and steal their products. Indeed, Rand's description of Boyle reads, in the post-Enron world, like a left indictment of corporate welfare and the CEO star culture:

> Orren Boyle had appeared from nowhere, five years ago, and had since made the cover of every national news magazine. He had started out with a hundred thousand dollars of his own and a two-hundred-million-dollar loan from the government. Now he headed an enormous concern which had swallowed many smaller companies. This proved, he liked to say, that individual ability still had a chance to succeed in the world. (49)

Here Rand's novel seems to dramatize Mills's sardonic comment six years earlier that "nobody talks more of free enterprise and competition and of the best man winning than the man who inherited his father's store or farm" (36). *Atlas Shrugged* is filled with similar critiques of businessmen who spend their time "running to Washington" rather than "running ... mills" (283). Such depictions at times make it seem as though the novel is as opposed to big business as to Rand's more expected government and union targets.

But this is not the case, insofar as Rand sees men like Taggart and Boyle as abberations from capitalist business practice rather than its norm. Rand's insistence, driven home by Taggart's final breakdown, that such men act out of a perverse death-drive rather than self-interest highlights her flawed picture of postwar capitalism. In her world, as we have seen, steel companies prosper because their owners invent new metals, not because Taft-Hartley and other legislation weakens the labor movement or because the Korean War generates sharp demand for steel while accelerated depreciation encourages steel companies to expand.[18] Likewise, oil companies succeed because the young "prodig[ies]" who run them discover "rich new oil field[s], at a time when the pumps were stopping in one famous field after another" (16–17), not because the U.S. government exerts its power to open up Middle Eastern oil fields to American companies.[19] This is not to say that the federal government, after World War II, became simply the tool of big business. In fact, both big oil and big steel endured regulatory incursions from antimonopolist legislators from the South and West. Even these legislators were operating, however, not in the interests of public service but rather in those of small producers in the same field who briefly managed to swing the ideology of small capital in their favor.[20] In *Atlas Shrugged*, by contrast, government action is only inimical to business, and companies thrive best in an atmosphere where, as one character says of the temporarily booming state of Colorado, government "does nothing … outside of keeping law courts and a police department" (254).

Rand's own brief history of the railroads, first published two years after *Atlas Shrugged*, makes clear how her understanding of government as purely antagonistic to business requires her to blur the distinction between small and large capital. In "Notes on the History of American Free Enterprise" (1959), Rand reduces the early history of the railroads to a battle between individualistic capitalists and coercive government regulations, arguing that "the evils, popularly ascribed to big industrialists, were not the result of an unregulated industry, but of government power over industry."[21] This argument is most convincing when she contends that Cornelius Vanderbilt only engaged in stock market manipulation because city and state politicians reneged on promises of favorable action, hoping to make a profit by selling Vanderbilt stock short (105–6). Elsewhere, however, the lines between business and government get blurrier, and can only be maintained by the same problematic distinction that she makes in *Atlas Shrugged* between proper and improper businessmen—or, as she calls them in "Notes on the History of American Free Enterprise," "free enterprisers" and those who "achieve[] power by legislative intervention in business" (104). As in the novel, Rand's investment in the free market leads her to claim not just the moral but the strategic high ground for businesses that go it alone, arguing that "the degree of government help received by any one railroad, stood in direct proportion to that railroad's troubles and failures. The railroads with the worst histories of scandal, double-dealing, and bankruptcy were the ones that had received the greatest amount of help from the government" (103). Yet Rand's own description of the eminently successful Central Pacific on the subsequent page belies her claim not to have discovered any "exceptions to this rule" (103):

> The Central Pacific—which was built by the "Big Four" of California, on federal subsidies— was the railroad which was guilty of all the evils popularly held against railroads. For almost thirty years, the Central Pacific controlled California, held a monopoly, and permitted no competitor to enter the state. It charged disastrous rates, changed them every year, and took virtually the entire profit of the California farmers or shippers, who had no other railroad to turn to. What made this possible? It was done through the power of the California legislature. The Big Four controlled the legislature and held the state closed to competitors by legal restrictions—such as, for instance, a legislative act which gave the Big Four exclusive control of the entire coastline of California and forbade any other railroad to enter any port. During these thirty years, many attempts were made by private interests to build competing railroads in California and break the monopoly of the Central Pacific. These attempts were defeated—not by methods of free trade and free competition, but by *legislative action*. (104; Rand's emphasis)

What is most interesting here is not that Rand contradicts her assertion that recourse to government leads inevitably to business failure, although that is certainly the case. Rather, it is the way in which she is enabled to do this by the implication that the Central Pacific's manipulation of the legislature originates not with the railroad but with the legislature itself—that it is legislative and not corporate "action" that is at issue here. This sleight of hand enables Rand to transform what might otherwise be described as a conflict between small and large capital—with the latter employing legislative action among its weapons against "competing railroads"—into a conflict between business per se and government per se. Lining up the sides in this way obscures the distinction between big and small capital.

If there is no distinction between big and small capital, then the conflict "between holders of small property … and holders of larger property" (Mills, *White* 55) that those like Corey and Mills saw as central to pre-twentieth-century U.S. history likewise disappears. The ills of small business, many of them caused in both the long and short term by big business, become the imagined ills of big business; the defense of big business against the very state that it just as often employs to its own ends becomes small business's duty. No longer anchored in actual socioeconomic conditions as they had been through the Progressive Era, the politics of small capital became more powerful than ever following the war, when they were pressed into the service of the large capital that had been small capital's historic enemy. It makes sense that the politics of small capital would continue to appeal to the remants of the petit bourgeoisie, even if they were being manipulated in the interests of another class. Less logical is why they would appeal to the structurally proletarianized—*and therefore no longer really middle class*—mass of white-collar workers for whom a more traditional class politics might make more sense.

One obvious answer is the enormous political pressure deployed against class politics throughout U.S. history, particularly during the cold war. Another is the fear of downward mobility through being identified with the working classes that Mills notes in his discussion of why white-collar workers do not unionize (301–23). In Mills's time, many white-collar workers enjoyed remuneration for their labor far superior to that of their small-capitalist parents. Their inheritors, as we have already noted, continue to enjoy significant advantages in pay, status, and authority that depend upon their distinction, however phantasmatic from a structural point of view, from others who must sell their labor in the contemporary economy. Finally, less obviously, capital continues to seduce the "disappearing middle" with things like home and stock ownership that blur the distinction between property and capital,[22] or between capital and capital that matters, thereby keeping white-collar workers invested in the ideology of property as such.[23]

While Rand means to reorient our understanding of what counts as productive labor—giving us a world in which owners supply both capital and labor, and workers at best offer little more than loyalty—the redefinition of labor caused by the expansion of the white-collar workforce continually takes her project in unintended directions. For at the same time that the expansion of white-collar labor was transforming the middle class from owners to workers, it was also transforming labor itself from hand work to brain work. The number of mental laborers in the American economy surpassed the number of manual laborers for the first time in 1956, the year before *Atlas Shrugged* was published.[27] This shift was most deeply felt, according to Mills, in the professions, where old ideologies of autonomy and self-direction came up against the increasing prominence of salaried work for organizations (113), and Atlantis's doctor exemplifies this moment of transition. Telling Dagny that he "quit when medicine was placed under State control," he goes on to say that he could not work for politicians who wanted to "dictate the purpose for which my years of study had been spent, or the conditions of my work, or my choice of patients, or the amount of my reward" (687). Here Rand's antigovernment ideology, like that of the opponents of the Clinton health care plan, provides the thinnest of glosses over what is in essence a complaint about one's exile from the means of production—one's transformation, that is, into a worker. As recent years have made clear, capital is just as likely as the state to effect this transformation among medical professionals.[28]

If the strikers continually threaten to devolve from property owners to mental laborers—thereby replicating the fate of the contemporary middle class—Rand's solution is to reconfigure mental labor as itself a form of property ownership. Another effect of depicting Hank Rearden and Ellis Wyatt as inventors as well as industrialists is to suggest that even if they leave behind their physical property, what they have withdrawn from the world is not their labor but rather the even more valuable property embodied in their ideas. For Rand, artists practicing what Szalay has called the "politics of textual integrity"—the privileging of artistic products over the processes that generate them[29]—exemplify the recondensation of mental labor more generally into property. The artists who live in Atlantis are there not simply to offer aesthetic representations of the strikers' worldview—symphonies that "embody every human act and thought that had ascent as its motive" (20); plays about "human greatness" (723)—but because they ultimately perform the same activity as the inventors and businessmen. All three groups exchange (or refuse to exchange, where the outside world is concerned) the products of their mind. Thus the other activity, besides shopkeeping, in which the strikers most frequently and fervently participate is performance: not the performance-as-process opposed by Szalay's late-modernist proponents of textual integrity, but discrete performances for pay that reaffirm the ability of ideas to serve as alienable property. When Dagny is shocked to discover that Galt has been spending his evenings in Atlantis lecturing on physics, he tells her that the strikers, committed to denying the outside world the fruits of their intellects by working only menial jobs, spend their time together "trad[ing] the achievements of our real professions. Richard Halley is to give concerts, Kay Ludlow is to appear in two plays written by authors who do not write for the outside world—and I give lectures, reporting on the work I've done during the year [at] ten dollars per person for the course" (714). Here it is not their minds that the strikers take off the market, but the products of their minds—a crucial distinction, since it reverses the historical trajectory of the middle class by transforming them from mental laborers to owners and sellers of intangible but nonetheless real property.

Rand makes the logic behind this move explicit in her 1964 essay "Patents and Copyrights," arguing that

> every type of productive work involves a combination of mental and physical effort: of thought and of physical action to translate that thought into a material form. The proportion of these two elements varies in different types of work. At the lowest end of the scale, the mental effort required to perform unskilled manual labor is minimal. At the other end, what the patent and copyright laws acknowledge is the paramount role of mental effort in the production of material values; these laws protect the mind's contribution in its purest form: the origination of an *idea*. The subject of patents and copyrights is *intellectual property*. (*Capitalism* 130; Rand's emphases)

Rand here affirms the superiority of mental labor, which lies in its counterintuitively greater productivity. By preventing the "unauthorized reproduction of the object," she goes on to note, intellectual property "law declares, in effect, that the physical labor of copying is not the source of the object's value" (*Capitalism* 130). Physical labor does not create, but only reproduces; only mental labor, contra Mills and other theorists of white-collar work, actually makes things. Rearden, refusing the government's offer of "an impressive profit, an immediate profit, much larger than you could hope to realize from the sale of the metal for the next twenty years" (171) in exchange for not producing it, tells his puzzled interlocutor, "Because it's *mine*. Do you understand that word?" (172; Rand's emphasis). Because it is his—because, that is, its formula is his—he and he alone can make and sell the metal whose status as property lies not in its physical instantiations but in his ownership of an idea.

Rand's reconfiguration of property as ideas rather than things reveals how main-stream—if not in fact prescient—her economic thinking was. In particular, this move anticipates the key concept of Gary Becker's influential 1964 study *Human Capital*. Citing "a realization that the growth of physical capital, at least as conventionally meas-ured, [now] explains a relatively small part of the growth of income in most countries," Becker focuses his study on "activities that influence future monetary and physical income by increasing the resources in people," especially education.[30] Becker's argu-ment quite legitimately attempts to take into account the shift from industrial capitalism to the new form—variously called, among other things, "postindustrialism," "post-Fordism," "network capitalism," and "informatization"—"in which providing services and manipulating information are at the heart of economic production."[31] But Becker's model of human capital also implicitly elides the difference between this change in the relations of production and the less tenable assertion that the binary class system no longer applies to capitalism. It does so by fudging the definition of "capital." Insofar as he focuses on "monetary and physical income," Becker ignores the distinction—funda-mental to the Marxist understanding of class—between those who own capital and those who must sell their labor to its owners. The concept of human capital thus fails to distinguish between intellectual property (an idea that one can sell for profit) and skills (that one can use to bargain for a better income from one's employer). It is no doubt true, as Becker's successor Pierre Bourdieu argued in 1984, that "a growing proportion of the ruling fraction derives, if not its power, at least the legitimacy of its power from educational capital acquired in formally pure and perfect academic competition, rather than directly from economic capital."[32] Of course, the Bush administration has reminded us that old-fashioned economic capital still goes a long way, just as Bush's Yale degree suggests the limits of Daniel Bell's 1973 assertion that "the university, which once reflected the status system of the society, has now become the arbiter of class position."[33] But more importantly, concepts such as human capital and Bourdieu's cultural capital are problematic in that—precisely through their focus on education—they make it possible to understand employed mental laborers as entrepreneurs. They do, that is, precisely what Rand's novels do.

Bourdieu himself suggests the limits of the concept of cultural capital when he notes that

> although executives and engineers have the monopoly of the means of symbolic appropria-tion of the cultural capital objectified in the form of instruments, machines and so forth which are essential to the exercise of the power of economic capital over this equipment, and derive from their monopoly a real managerial power and relative privileges within the firm, the profits accruing from their cultural capital are at least partially appropriated by those who have power over this capital, i.e., those who possess the economic capital needed to ensure the concentration and utilization of cultural capital.[34]

The possessors of even high-level cultural capital, that is, remain beholden as employees to those who own economic capital. If this is a problem for those at the top of white-collar pyramids, it is even more so for those lower down, for whom curtailed autonomy can translate directly into the loss of money and job security. The recent trend among downsizing companies of firing experienced white-collar workers in favor of younger, cheaper ones, for instance,[35] provides a sharp rebuke to the more celebratory accounts of human capital. Such downsized workers are free to trade their human capital precisely as workers are free to trade their labor: largely at the will of those who can purchase it. In this respect, the idea of the mental laborer as entrepreneur—which arose at a time when stable jobs were equated with ennui—now provides a fantasy of agency within an economy in which job security is increasingly tenuous. Witness, for instance, the *Wall Street Journal's* CareerJournal.com article "Should You Stay Energized by Changing Your Job Frequently?"[36]

Such romanticized—and deeply Randian—notions of craftsmanship and liberal exchange prevent contemporary white-collar workers from understanding themselves as workers. Harney and Moten provide an example close to home when they suggest that one reason tenure-track academics are so willing to participate in the exploitation of casual adjunct labor is that they view their work through the lens of "liberal individualism and market exchanges" rather than paid employment.[37] Academics' sense that some kinds of intellectual labor (research) are superior to others because, in Randian terms, they are solitary and thus creative forestalls more collective (if less glamorous) ways of conceiving the labor done in universities. In this respect some tenure-track academics' resistance to academic unions no doubt bears out Mills's argument that the "status psychology of white-collar employees" is a major impediment to white-collar unionism (312, 301–23 passim). Academics thus prove themselves to be prototypical white-collar workers at precisely the moment when, Ross argues, white-collar workers are becoming more like academics, translating the characteristically academic-artistic investment in "nonmonetary rewards—mental or creative gratification—as compensation for work" into things like the dot-comers' heroic cult of overwork.[38] Rand's characters would be totally at home in this structure of feeling, which they would recognize depends not so much upon the Romantic conception that *"the artist cannot afford to be rewarded well"* as upon the more characteristically American notion that the artist cannot afford to be rewarded well *except by the market.*[39]

Rand's relatively novel understanding of mental labor as entrepreneurship depends upon the same free market fundamentalism, and the same shift of focus from big capital to big government, as her nostalgia for nineteenth-century small property. She has her villains, for instance, include the following language outlawing intellectual property as part of Directive 10–289:

> Point Three. All patents and copyrights, pertaining to any devices, inventions, formulas, processes and works of any nature whatsoever, shall be turned over to the nation as a patriotic emergency gift....The Unification Board shall then license the use of such patents and copyrights to all applicants, equally and without discrimination, for the purpose of eliminating monopolistic practices, discarding obsolete products and making the best available to the whole nation. No trademarks, brand names or copyrighted titles shall be used.... All private trademarks and brand names are hereby abolished. (499–500)

Here, predictably, it is the regulative state that seeks to undermine by fiat the property rights—in this case, intellectual property rights—of individuals.

The more recent history of intellectual property suggests, however, that Rand once again misses how capitalism itself undermines these rights in its relentless drive toward centralization. For Rand, as we have seen, property becomes property through the process whereby an individual realizes his or her productivity. Hence she asserts, elsewhere in her essay on patents and copyrights, that "a *discovery* cannot be patented, only an *invention*" (*Capitalism* 130; Rand's emphases). As anyone familiar with debates over the property status of the human genome will recognize, however, it is precisely the transformation of "discoveries" into property to which capitalism has turned in its latest phase. Global capital is currently reorganizing itself around what Caren Irr calls a "virtual land grab," a return to the stage of primitive accumulation whose object this time around is "the sudden and immensely profitable treatment of a vast array of existing relations as property relations":

> In this enclosure of the global textual commons, Disney has seized monopolistic hold over the folk and fairy tales of a Brothers Grimm-type European heritage; Time-Warner aims to acquire exclusive access to recent history in the form of the Zapruder tapes; pharmaceuticals companies lay claim to the biological commons of the rainforests; and corporate-funded geneticists race to see who will decode and patent the information contained in the human genome. By converting existing natural and cultural resources into certain kinds of texts, corporations are now able to claim monopolistic ownership in a range of potentially supervaluable intellectual commodities.[40]

Just as the original phase of primitive accumulation freed the lower classes from feudalism by rendering them landless laborers, so this new phase transforms knowledge and information previously held in common into the site of corporate employees' mental labor. The profits from this labor accrue not to the individual creator claiming his "right to the product of his mind" (Rand, *Capitalism* 130), but rather to the large corporations that manipulate the law to transform found materials into their property.

Within this framework, the notion that mental laborers are entrepreneurs encourages white-collar employees to identify with the corporate owners of intellectual property, just as home ownership encourages the members of the middle class to identify with the owners of property as such. In both cases, big capital benefits from a confusion between what it owns, the means of production, and what the members of the middle class own, their labor and (if they are lucky) nonproductive personal property. Just because capital has been severed from individual producers and vested in corporate entities does not mean, of course, that it has ceased to exist, or that individuals no longer benefit from it. On the contrary, as Mills argued in 1951, the fact "that the power of property has been bureaucratized in the corporation does not diminish that power; indeed, bureaucracy increases the use and the protection of property power" (111). In this regard, Rand's mistake—which I have been arguing is her failure to distinguish between an earlier model of middle-class small property and property as such—has been an enormously productive one for the last half-century of capitalism. Intellectual property law as it has been codified in recent decisions, Irr argues, promotes corporate ownership of texts not only "over public interest in the distribution of knowledge" but also over against a largely residual notion of authorship: "in the late twentieth century, the author can be construed as an almost entirely anonymous creature—faceless, factual, dispersed into the events in which he was an integral but somehow also impersonal player."[41] If the author now sounds like a classic postwar organization man, this suggests the extent to which Corey and Mills's accounts of white-collar expropriation have been fulfilled in the new era of intellectual property, in which ideas rather than things have become the characteristic object of production. The academic Left has been talking for some time now about how universities are becoming more like businesses, although for the purposes of critiquing contemporary capitalism the larger and more pressing problem may be the fact that businesses are becoming more like universities. As Ross argues, the university which during the cold war abetted capital by serving as "a medium for subsidizing or socializing capital's cost of training, research, and development" has now "become a site of capital accumulation in its own right, where the profitability of research and teaching programs and the marketability of learning products is fast coming to the fore as the primary driving force behind academic policy."[42]

Within this rapidly coalescing regime, academics' understanding of their research work as both craft labor and personal property does not just reflect a general white-collar worldview with its origins in the postwar era and authors like Rand. It also limits the shape of much more profitable sectors of the economy. Take, for instance, the recent debates over music piracy, in which the members of Metallica and other celebrity musicians argued that file sharing abrogated their property rights. At the same time, some artists lower down the record-label food chain argued that they actually profited from file sharing, insofar as most of their income came not from publishing but from touring, for which the dissemination of their music provided publicity.[43] In Corey's terms, we might see artists like Metallica as well-paid employees taking on the mantle of small-property owners for the benefit of big corporations, and to the detriment of other artists who are either more exploited employees of the labels or actual small businesspeople. In this case, the nostalgia for the market that we have tracked through Rand's work becomes the basis for the extraction of surplus value from mental laborers carrying on their backs the corpse of what we used to call "the middle class."

Notes

Introduction: The Twilight of the Middle Class

1 For an overview of criticism of cold war culture see my "Cold War Culture to Fifties Culture," *Minnesota Review* n.s. 55–57 (2002): 143–52.
2 Morris Dickstein, *Leopards in the Temple: The Transformation of American Fiction 1945–1970* (Cambridge: Harvard University Press, 2002), 6; hereafter cited parenthetically.
3 Thomas Hill Schaub, *American Fiction in the Cold War* (Madison: University of Wisconsin Press, 1991), 91, passim.
4 On the kitchen debate see Elaine Tyler May, *Homeward Bound: American Families in the Cold War Era* (New York: Basic, 1988), 16–20.
5 Alan Nadel, *Containment Culture: American Narratives, Postmodernism, and the Atomic Age* (Durham: Duke University Press, 1995), 91, 90–116 passim.
6 Barbara Foley, "The Rhetoric of Anticommunism in Invisible Man," *College English* 59.5 (September 1997): 530–45; hereafter cited parenthetically.
7 Barbara Foley, "From Communism to Brotherhood: The Drafts of *Invisible Man*," *Left of the Color Line: Race, Radicalism, and Twentieth-Century Literature of the United States*, ed. Bill V. Mullen and James Smethurst (Chapel Hill: University of North Carolina Press, 2003), 163–82.
8 Barbara Foley, "From Wall Street to Astor Place: Historicizing Melville's 'Bartleby,'" *American Literature* 72.1 (March 2000): 87–116.

9 An important exception to this generalization is Lary May's essay "Movie Star Politics: The Screen Actors' Guild, Cultural Conversion, and the Hollywood Red Scare," *Recasting America: Culture and Politics in the Age of Cold War*, ed. Lary May (Chicago: University of Chicago Press, 1989), 125–53. Using the movie industry as an example, May argues that postwar anticommunism was deployed by "corporate leaders" (127), against the dual backdrop of "widespread prosperity" (136) and "the greatest strike wave in the country's history" (126), to quell labor radicalism and "convert national values and popular imagery away from doctrines hostile to modern capitalism" (127).

10 Jeffrey Madrick, *The End of Affluence: The Causes and Consequences of America's Economic Dilemma* (New York: Random House, 1995), 125. See also James T. Patterson, *Grand Expectations: The United States, 1945–1974* (New York: Oxford University Press, 1996), 61–62, and Alan Brinkley, "World War II and American Liberalism," *The War in American Culture: Society and Consciousness during World War II*, ed. Lewis A. Erenberg and Susan E. Hirsch (Chicago: University of Chicago Press, 1996), 317.

11 Paul Krugman, "For Richer," *The New York Times Magazine* (20 October 2002): 62–67, 76–78, 141–42. See also Claudia Goldin and Robert A. Margo, "The Great Compression: The Wage Structure in the United States at Mid-Century," *The Quarterly Journal of Economics* 107.1 (February 1992): 1–34, whose argument Krugman mentions.

12 Michael Harrington, *The Other America: Poverty in the United States* (New York: Macmillan, 1962), 1; hereafter cited parenthetically.

13 George Lipsitz, *Rainbow at Midnight: Labor and Culture in the 1940s* (Urbana: University of Illinois Press, 1994); Alan Wald, *Writing from the Left: New Essays on Radical Culture and Politics* (New York: Verso, 1994); Joel Foreman, ed., *The Other Fifties: Interrogating Midcentury American Icons* (Urbana: University of Illinois Press, 1997). This approach is also taken by a number of the essays in May, *Recasting America*, especially part 4.

14 Robert Seguin, *Around Quitting Time: Work and Middle-Class Fantasy in American Fiction* (Durham: Duke University Press, 2001), 4, 1–5 passim; hereafter cited parenthetically.

15 Jack Beatty, "Who Speaks for the Middle Class," *Atlantic Monthly* May 1994: 65; hereafter cited parenthetically.

16 Krugman, "For Richer" 76, 62.

17 For a readable critique of the doctrine of middle-classlessness, with an emphasis on its contemporary variations but with a chapter on the history of this idea since the Revolutionary Period ("History: The Fate of Autonomy"), see Benjamin DeMott, *The Imperial Middle: Why Americans Can't Think Straight about Class* (New Haven: Yale University Press, 1990).

18 Barbara Ehrenreich, *The Hearts of Men: American Dreams and the Flight from Commitment* (Garden City: Anchor, 1983), 29; Ehrenreich's emphasis. Ehrenreich does note the sometimes devastating economic consequences for women cast outside middle-class prosperity by the converging breakdowns, since the mid-seventies, of "the family wage and the breadwinner ethic" (175, 172–80 passim).

19 Jackson Lears, "A Matter of Taste: Corporate Cultural Hegemony in a Mass-Consumption Society," in May, *Recasting America* 50; hereafter cited parenthetically.

20 Catherine Jurca, *White Diaspora: The Suburb and the Twentieth-Century American Novel* (Princeton: Princeton University Press, 2001), 140; hereafter cited parenthetically.

21 These accounts are clearly related to what Robert D. Johnston describes as the "demonization model" employed by historians of the middle class. See Johnston, *The Radical Middle Class: Populist Democracy and the Question of Capitalism in Progressive Era Portland, Oregon* (Princeton: Princeton University Press, 2003), 3–6.

22 Richard H. Pells, *The Liberal Mind in a Conservative Age: American Intellectuals in the 1940s and 1950s* (New York: Harper, 1985), 188–216.

23 William H. Whyte, *The Organization Man* (1956; Garden City: Anchor, 1957), 13; Whyte's emphasis. Hereafter cited parenthetically.

24 Ehrenreich, *Hearts* 29.

25 Richard Ohmann, "The Shaping of a Canon: U.S. Fiction, 1960–1975," *Canons*, ed. Robert von Hallberg (Chicago: University of Chicago Press, 1984), 386, 390, 377–401 passim; hereafter cited parenthetically.

26   Barbara and John Ehrenreich, "The Professional–Managerial Class," *Between Labor and Capital*, ed. Pat Walker (Boston: South End, 1979), 12, 18, 5–45 passim.

27   For a skeptical discussion of this term see Doug Henwood, *After the New Economy* (New York: New Press, 2003).

28   Robert B. Reich, *The Work of Nations: Preparing Ourselves for 21st-Century Capitalism* (New York: Knopf, 1991), 173–80.

29   Andrew Ross, "The Mental Labor Problem," *Social Text* 18.2 (2000): 1–31.

30   Karl Marx and Friedrich Engels, *The Communist Manifesto* (1848; New York: Monthly Review Press, 1998), 3.

31   Olivier Zunz, "Class," *Encyclopedia of the United States in the Twentieth Century*, ed. Stanley Kutler, Vol. I (New York: Scribner's, 1996), 195, 198.

32   Stuart Blumin argues in *The Emergence of the Middle Class: Social Experience in the American City, 1760–1900* (New York: Cambridge University Press, 1989) that a self-conscious middle class first takes shape in the Jacksonian period around the emergent distinction between manual and non-manual labor. Taking a self-consciously culturalist approach that is as much concerned with where people live and what they consume as with how they earn their living, he conflates "entrepreneurship and salaried (as opposed to wage-earning) employment" (68). But his partly anachronistic use of the term "white-collar" suggests how the entrepreneurial ideal was already losing ground to a world in which "experienced clerks" claimed similar status with "small nonmanual businessmen" in the emergent hierarchy of head work over hand work. At the same time, his account makes clear that white-collar workers were not entirely separate from entrepreneurs, as they would later come to be. Antebellum clerks not only, like owners, "made more money than skilled workers and hardworking masters," but also "seem to have moved much more frequently into income- and wealth-enhancing business proprietorships" (121).

33   Olivier Zunz, *Making America Corporate 1870–1930* (Chicago: University of Chicago Press, 1990), 13–14, passim.

34   Ohmann's *Selling Culture: Magazines, Markets, and Class at the Turn of the Century* (New York: Verso, 1996) provides a richly researched account of the formative years of the PMC, which Ohmann credits with the birth of national mass culture. Jeffrey Sklansky's intellectual history *The Soul's Economy: Market Society and Selfhood in American Thought, 1820–1920* (Chapel Hill: University of North Carolina Press, 2002) provides a deep history of the PMC's managerial ethos as it evolves out of republican ideals of property-owning independence over the course of the nineteenth century.

35   On Populism in its classic form see Alan Trachtenberg, *The Incorporation of America: Culture & Society in the Gilded Age* (New York: Hill and Wang, 1982), 173–81. In *The Age of Reform: From Bryan to F. D. R.* (New York: Vintage, 1955), Richard Hofstadter writes that "by the turn of the century, it is possible to distinguish two chief strains of feeling in the Populist-Progressive tradition. The first, more Populist than Progressive, more rural and sectional than nationwide in its appeal, represents, in a sense, the roots of modern American isolationism" (273). Zunz describes these two strains in terms of a split within the middle class between "those who contributed to the building of corporate capitalism" and a residual but still influential group of small-property owners "who clung to proven, and presumably more fulfilling, ways of doing business" (*Making* 12–13). Johnston provides a less teleological account of this conflict. For an account of Depression-era Populism as more an outgrowth of traditional old middle-class ideals than the sort of protofascism it is sometimes depicted as, see Alan Brinkley, *Voices of Protest: Huey Long, Father Coughlin, and the Great Depression* (New York: Knopf, 1982).

36   John Blair et al., *Economic Concentration and World War II*, Report of the Smaller War Plants Corporation of the U.S. Senate Special Committee to Study Problems of American Small Business (Washington, DC: GPO, 1946), 4–20.

37   Edwin Layton, *The Revolt of the Engineers: Social Responsibility and the American Engineering Profession* (1971; Baltimore: Johns Hopkins University Press, 1986), ix. Layton describes how engineers—who had no choice but to work for corporations—prevented themselves "from becoming mere cogs in a vast industrial machine" (7) by giving their loyalty not to employers but to a professional ethos grounded in "esoteric knowledge" and dedicated to the good of society (4–5).

Cecelia Tichi covers some of the same ground in her account of the engineer as culture hero in *Shifting Gears: Technology, Literature, Culture in Modernist America* (Chapel Hill: University of North Carolina Press, 1987). For an example of the engineer's symbolic power, and the deployment of this power against fears of middle-class banality, one need only recall George Babbitt's excitement, at the conclusion of Sinclair Lewis's 1922 novel, *Babbitt*, at his son's decision to pursue an engineering career.

38 Hofstadter, *Age* 312–14, 319, 316. Hofstadter argues that "by 1933 the American public had lived with the great corporation so long that it was felt to be domesticated," with the result that the antimonopoly sentiments of the Progressives were "subordinated in the New Deal era to that restless groping for a means to bring recovery that was so characteristic of Roosevelt's efforts" (312). Thus what "Antitrust enforcement" there was "became a hunt for offenders instead of an effort to test the validity of organized power by its performance in aiding or preventing the flow of goods in commerce" (314).

39 Michael Denning, *The Cultural Front: The Laboring of American Culture in the Twentieth Century* (New York: Verso, 1996), 96–104, passim. In *New Deal Modernism: American Literature and the Invention of the Welfare State* (Durham: Duke University Press, 2000), Michael Szalay rightfully takes Denning to task for his overemphasis of the radical political dimensions of this shift (19–21). But Szalay's own account of writers worried about the transformation of their creative endeavors into routinized salaried employment within federal arts bureaucracies reinforces Denning's argument that this period saw a new stress on the "labor" in mental labor.

40 Marty Jezer, *The Dark Ages: Life in the United States 1945–1960* (Boston: South End, 1982), 25.

41 Jezer, *Dark* 25–26; Lipsitz, *Rainbow* 61.

42 Lipsitz, *Rainbow* 61.

43 Zunz, "Class" 197.

44 Brinkley, "World War II" 319–20; Robert M. Collins, *More: The Politics of Economic Growth in Postwar America* (New York: Oxford University Press, 2000).

45 Carol A. Barry, "White-Collar Employment: I—Trends and Structures," *Monthly Labor Review* (Jan. 1961): 11.

46 Zunz, "Class" 197–98.

47 Edward Bellamy, *Looking Backward, 2000–1887* (1888; Boston: Bedford, 1995); Charlotte Perkins Gilman, *Women and Economics: A Study of the Economic Relation between Men and Women as a Factor in Social Evolution* (1898; New York: Harper & Row, 1966); Thorstein Veblen, *The Engineers and the Price System* (New York: B. W. Huebsch, 1921).

48 Timothy Melley, *Empire of Conspiracy: The Culture of Paranoia in Postwar America* (Ithaca: Cornell University Press, 2000), 48, 10, passim; hereafter cited parenthetically.

49 C. Wright Mills, *White Collar: The American Middle Classes* (1951; New York: Oxford University Press, 2002); hereafter cited parenthetically. In his survey of histories of the middle class Johnston claims that *White Collar* is "still after half a century the most important book we have about the American middle classes" (4).

50 Lewis Corey, *The Crisis of the Middle Class* (New York: Covici-Friede, 1935), 146, 164; second quote italicized in the original.

51 "The change," Corey writes, "is all the more significant as salaried employees were clearly members of the middle class in 1870, while only a minority are now. Add that minority—the 1,800,000 higher salaried employees and professionals—to the surviving independent enterprisers, and the middle class becomes 4,500,000, *or only 9% of the gainfully occupied compared with 18% in 1870, a decrease of 50%*. Include the masses of lower salaried employees and professionals, who are *not* middle class economically, and the working class becomes an overwhelming majority: 38,750,000 persons, or 75% of the gainfully occupied" (274–75; Corey's emphasis).

52 Berle makes this argument in the new preface he wrote for a reissue of the classic early thirties study of economic concentration, *The Modern Corporation and Private Property*, that he coauthored with Means. See Adolf A. Berle, "Property, Production and Revolution: A Preface to the Revised Edition" (1967), Adolf A. Berle and Gardiner C. Means, *The Modern Corporation and Private Property*, rev. ed. (1932; New York: Harcourt, 1968), ix.

53 Lipsitz, *Rainbow* 62.

54 For these terms see Sklansky, *Soul's Economy*, for the philosophical arguments underlying them, see C. B. Macpherson, *The Political Theory of Possessive Individualism: Hobbes to Locke* (Oxford: Clarendon Press, 1962).

55 For a reading that stresses this latter narrative see Melley, *Empire* 47–79.

56 David Riesman, with Nathan Glazer and Reuel Denney, *The Lonely Crowd: A Study of the Changing American Character* (1950; New Haven: Yale University Press, 1969); hereafter cited parenthetically.

57 Georg Lukács, *The Historical Novel*, trans. Hannah and Stanley Mitchell (Lincoln: University of Nebraska Press, 1983), 34, 19–88 passim; hereafter cited parenthetically.

58 Fredric Jameson, Introduction, Lukács, *Historical* 3–4.

59 Ira Wolfert, *Tucker's People* (1943; Urbana: University of Illinois Press, 1997), 3; hereafter cited parenthetically.

60 For a more complicated version of these politics see Walter Benn Michaels, *The Gold Standard and the Logic of Naturalism* (Berkeley: University of California Press, 1987).

61 Frank Norris, *The Pit* (1903; New York: Penguin, 1994), 115.

62 A prominent strand of the antiglobalization movement, for instance, criticizes giant retailers like Wal-Mart and Amazon not only for the way they treat their workers but also for "drastically undermin[ing] the traditional concepts of value and individual service that small business is known for offering." See Naomi Klein, *NO SPACE NO CHOICE NO JOBS NO LOGO: Taking Aim at the Brand Bullies* (New York: Picador, 1999), 158. Likewise, Eric Schlosser's *Fast Food Nation: The Dark Side of the All-American Meal* (2001; New York: Perennial, 2002), takes the fast food industry and agribusiness to task not only for their labor practices but also for the threat they pose to independent restaurateurs and small farmers. Schlosser's paean to In-N-Out Burger is a classic American salute to the virtues of small business. This family-owned chain, modest by the standards of McDonald's and Burger King, "has followed its own path": not only does it provide "the highest wages in the fast food industry" but "the ground beef is fresh, potatoes are peeled every day to make the fries, and the milk shakes are made from ice cream, not syrup" (259–60). Finally, Ruth Ozeki's novel *My Year of Meats* (New York: Penguin, 1998), which mounts a fascinating (and frequently very funny) attempt to revive old–middle-class values in the face of globalization (particularly global agribusiness) criticizes Wal-Mart for participating in the "demise of regional American culture" to the specific detriment of small property owners: "Main Street is dead, which is no news to the families whose families ran family businesses on Main Street" (56).

63 See chapter 1.

64 Mills, by contrast, provides a completely deromanticized description of what he calls "the lumpen-bourgeoisie," owners of marginal, failure-prone businesses and struggling farms whose reliance on family labor in particular finds Mills at his most dialectical:

> Behind the colorless census category "unpaid family worker," there lie much misery and defeat in youth. That too was and is part of the old middle-class way. Perhaps in the nineteenth century it paid off: the sons, or at least one of the sons, would take over his equipped station, and the daughter might better find a husband who would thus be set up. But the average life of these old middle-class, especially urban, units in the twentieth century is short; the coincidence of family-unit and work-situation among the old middle class is a pre-industrial fact. So even as the centralization of property contracts their "independence," it liberates the children of the old middle class's smaller entrepreneurs. (*White* 31)

65 See Brinkley's account of the communitarian as well as simply individualist aspects of Depression-Era Populism as articulated—in ways that reverberate through *Tucker's People* all the way to the current fight against Wal-Mart—around criticism of retail chains (*Voices* 144–48).

66 Elizabeth Long, *The American Dream and the Popular Novel* (Boston: Routledge & Kegan Paul, 1985), 89, 63–90 passim.

67 See also Whyte's readings of *The Man in the Gray Flannel Suit* and other popular fiction in the section of *The Organization Man* entitled "The Organization Man in Fiction" (*Organization* 267–91).

68 Cameron Hawley, *Executive Suite* (Cambridge: Riverside, 1952), 331, 333; hereafter cited parenthetically.

Chapter One: Ayn Rand and the Politics of Property

1   Sharon Stockton, "Engineering Power: Hoover, Rand, Pound, and the Heroic Architect," *American Literature* 72.4 (December 2000): 813–41; Szalay, *New Deal* 75–119.

6   Leonard Peikoff, "Introduction to the 35th Anniversary Edition," Ayn Rand, *Atlas Shrugged* (1957; New York: Signet, 1992), 1.

7   Rand, *Atlas Shrugged* 630; hereafter cited parenthetically.

8   Alfred Chandler, *The Visible Hand: The Managerial Revolution in American Business* (Cambridge: Harvard University Press, 1977), 3, 79.

9   Jennifer Burns is currently writing a groundbreaking dissertation in the Berkeley history department on the complexities of Rand's reception, including her appeal among small businessmen. See Burns's essay "Godless Capitalism: Ayn Rand and the Conservative Movement," *Modern Intellectual History* 1.3 (November 2004): 1–27.

10 John F. Stover, *American Railroads* (Chicago: University of Chicago Press, 1961), 211.

11 Stover, *American* 210.

12 This is in New York City. Things are even worse in the countryside:

> They drove through small towns, through obscure side roads, through the kind of places they had not seen for years. She felt uneasiness at the sight of the towns. Days passed before she realized what it was that she missed most: a glimpse of fresh paint. The houses stood like men in unpressed suits, who had lost the desire to stand straight: the cornices were like sagging shoulders, the crooked porch steps like torn hem lines, the broken windows like patches, mended with clapboard. The people in the streets stared at the new car, not as one stares at a rare sight, but as if the glittering black shape were an impossible vision from another world. There were few vehicles in the streets and too many of them were horsedrawn. She had forgotten the literal shape and usage of horse-power; she did not like to see its return. (263)

13 Stover, *American* 210.

14 Sylvia de Leon, "No Way to Run a Railroad: A Bailout Won't Solve Amtrak's Fundamental Problem," *Washington Post*, 24 June 2002, *http://web.lexis-nexis.com/universe* (accessed August 28, 2004).

15 Stover, *American* 252–53.

16 Ibid., 217.

17 Kim McQuaid, *Uneasy Partners: Big Business in American Politics, 1945–1990* (Baltimore: Johns Hopkins University Press, 1994).

18 Judith Stein, *Running Steel, Running America: Race, Economic Policy, and the Decline of Liberalism* (Chapel Hill: University of North Carolina Press, 1998), 17, 14.

19 McQuaid, *Uneasy* 48–58; David S. Painter, *Oil and the American Century: The Political Economy of U.S. Foreign Oil Policy, 1941–1945* (Baltimore: Johns Hopkins University Press, 1986).

20 McQuaid 52–54; Stein, *Running* 21.

21 Ayn Rand, *Capitalism: The Unknown Ideal* (New York: Signet, 1967), 102; hereafter cited parenthetically.

22 Krugman, "For Richer" 62.

23 See Randy Martin, *On Your Marx: Relinking Socialism and the Left* (Minneapolis: University of Minnesota Press, 2002), 159–83.

27 Barry, "White-Collar" 1:11.

28 As Mills notes, however, what has recently happened for doctors was already happening in the late forties among the proletarianized nurses at the medical profession's feminized base. Mills describes "'training schools' ... owned and operated by hospitals [whose] primary purpose is not so much 'education' as simply a means for getting cheap labor, for they find it less expensive to train students than to hire graduate nurses" (*White* 117–18).

29 Szalay, *New Deal* 6, 75–119.

30 Gary S. Becker, *Human Capital: A Theoretical and Empirical Analysis with Special Reference to Education* (New York: National Bureau of Economic Research, 1964), 1.

31 Alain Touraine, *The Post-Industrial Society; Tomorrow's Social History: Classes, Conflicts and Culture in the Programmed Society*, trans. Leonard F. X. Mayhew (1969; New York: Random House, 1971); Daniel Bell, *The Coming of Post-Industrial Society: A Venture in Social Forecasting* (1973; New York: Basic, 1976); David Harvey, *The Condition of Post-modernity: An Inquiry into the Origins of Cultural Change* (Cambridge; Blackwell, 1989); Manuel Castells, *The Rise of the Network Society* (Cambridge; Blackwell, 1996); Michael Hardt and Antonio Negri, *Empire* (Cambridge: Harvard University Press, 2000). The quote is from Hardt and Negri, *Empire* 280.

32 Pierre Bourdieu, *Distinction: A Social Critique of the Judgement of Taste*, trans. Richard Nice (1979; Cambridge: Harvard University Press, 1984), 315.

33 Bell, *Post-Industrial* 410.

34 Bourdieu, *Distinction* 301–3.

35 Stephanie Armour, "Higher Pay May Be Layoff Target," *USA Today*, 23 June 2003, Money, 1B.

36 Tony Lee, "Should You Stay Energized by Changing Your Job Frequently?" Career-Journal.com, *http://www.careerjournal.com/jobhunting/strategies/19980111-reisberg.html*.

37 Harney and Moten, "Doing" 171, 154–80 passim.

38 Ross, "Mental Labor" 22.

39 Ibid., 15; Ross's emphasis.

40 Caren Irr, "Literature as Proleptic Globalization, or a Prehistory of the New Intellectual Property," *South Atlantic Quarterly* 100.3 (Summer 2001): 797–98.

41 Ibid., 795.

42 Ross, "Mental Labor" 25.

43 Brian Mansfield, "When Free Is Profitable," *USA Today*, 21 May 2004, *http://web.lexis-nexis. com/universe* (accessed August 28, 2004).

CHAPTER 20

The Rise of Professionalism
A Sociological Analysis

Magali Sarfatti Larson

The Rise of Corporate Capitalism
and the Consolidation of Professionalism

The classic, older professions sought to control their markets and to gain a privileged position in the occupational and social hierarchies. Modern professionalization is, thus, an attempt to translate one order of scarce resources into another: the possession of scarce knowledge and skills is, indeed, the principal basis on which modern professions claim social recognition and economic rewards. As used in the professional project, the notion of expertise incorporates contradictory principles. On the one hand, it embodies the rationalizing and universalistic legitimation of market monopoly, insofar as it is *standardized* expertise, accessible to all who care to be adequately trained and qualified. On the other hand, expertise is also used to claim superior rewards and to establish social distance from other occupational groups—a claim which is as much supported by the structural limitations on access to training as it is by the professions' deliberate efforts to achieve corporate exclusiveness.

The rise of modern educational systems brings an ideological resolution to the tension between universalistic principles and exclusive privilege embodied in the notion of expertise. Mass access to the lower echelons of the public school system allows the higher levels of the educational hierarchy to claim meritocratic legitimations for their selection of entrants. The inegalitarian uses of acquired expertise are thus concealed by the alleged universalism of the schools' criteria of selection.

The unification of training and research in the modern university is a particularly significant development. As graduate and professional schools emerged at the top of the educational hierarchy, the professions acquired not only an institutional basis on which to develop and standardize knowledge and technologies; they also received, in university training, a most powerful legitimation for their claims to cognitive and technical superiority and to social and economic benefits.

Original publication details: Magali Safatti Larson, *The Rise Of Professionalism: A sociological analysis.* Reproduced with permission from University of California Press, 1979.

The rise of a new type of institution of higher education in the United States depended, in turn, on the massive availability of surplus capital, especially after the depression of 1893. While the university represents a major factor in the advance of professionalization, it is only one development in the twentieth-century maturation of industrial capitalism. Remarkable economic growth—interrupted, it is true, by numerous downturns and recessions before the cataclysm of 1929—is the background for the reorganization of American society after the Civil War. The growing importance of the great industrial corporations and the transformation of production under their influence; the motor role of new industries, especially mass-consumption industries, in our century; the centralization of power and decision-making in the political system; the emergence and consolidation of functional groups which speak directly to the state for their constituencies; growing governmental intervention in the economy, accelerated by the First World War and by the response to the Great Depression—these are some of the epochal developments that mark the waning of competitive capitalism.[1]

The transformation is accompanied by the predominance of a new type of capitalist firm and new modes of competition. Large productive units, characterized by high ratios of fixed capital per worker and high productivity, need to plan and regulate production, distribution, and employment in order to insure profits in expanding markets. Their new administrative structures emphasize expert decision-making as applied science and technology become increasingly integrated with production and with management.[2]

Associated with the expansion of the monopoly and state sectors of the economy, we find long-term trends toward the transformation of the occupational structure: the decline of small entrepreneurs and independent workers and the corollary bureaucratization of most work-settings are among the most significant. An expression of these developments is the steady increase of nonmanual occupations which service the public or private bureaucracies, create or handle new technologies, provide consumer services in the "affluent society," and fill the increasingly specialized slots of the division of labor. From the last decades of the nineteenth century on, the growth of a public system of higher education attempted to respond to these new demands of the labor market.

To structural changes corresponds a shift in ideology toward new forms of legitimation of power. At the core, the emergent conception of authority appeals to the rationality of science—science as a method and as a world view, more than as a body of knowledge—and to the rationality of scientifically oriented experts who act in the bureaucratized institutions of the new social order.[4]

The New Context of Professionalization

Some urban sectors of progressivism—in particular, those associated with the women's movement and the settlement movement—may have unwittingly transferred to the industrial city an individualistic fundamentalism of rural stamp.[10] But progressivism, in fact, symbolizes the point of no return for reform movements which had framed their protest in terms of the modes and values of a passing order. From there on, efficiency in the service of "moral uplift" becomes more and more the predominant theme, opening an area of reconciliation between leading sectors of progressivism and the large industrial corporation.

The emergence of a *national* ruling class was one of the core structural developments to which progressivism reacted and which, in turn, made possible the shift in dominant ideology. For many contemporary historians, the Progressive Era is, in fact, one act in the process by which this new and relatively coherent ruling class came to preside over the reorganization of both civil and political society.[11] In the Age of Jackson, a new kind of entrepreneur had "struggled to free business enterprise of the outmoded restrictions of special incorporation and banking laws and to end what was an overcentralized control of credit."[12] The rapid industrial expansion after the Civil War, the completion of the railroad network, and therefore the rise of national markets of commodities and labor, spawned a new breed of capitalists.[13] The downturns of the seventies and the eighties, capped by the major economic crisis of 1893, accelerated the merger movement and the drive for industrial rationalization in terms of efficiency and economies of scale. However, the strongest stimulus behind the rapid "combination movement" of the years 1897–1904 was not the desire for efficient production but the fear of anarchy and the risks of competition.[14] As the rising corporations expanded their capacity for self-financing, investment bankers also broadened their role. By the early 1890s the United States no longer needed to depend on foreign capital; finance capitalism emerged from the depression of the 1890s as the principal allocator of investment funds and an important coordinator of further growth. As investment bankers assumed a role of comparable importance to that of national political leaders and industrial magnates, a joint financial-industrial leadership came into being. Its rise both depended on and called forth a new, active role of the state.

Fearful of antibusiness regulation, business leaders had at first tried to prevent it by getting increasingly involved in politics. But the exacerbation of class conflict in the 1880s and the depression of the early 1890s showed to the most advanced sector of business that regulation and coordination of economic activity depended largely on "political capitalism"—that is, "the utilization of political outlets to attain conditions of stability, predictability, and security—to attain rationalization in the economy."[15] Government regulation was welcomed by the enlightened sectors of corporate business, so long as they could maintain a decisive influence over it. In the first decades of the twentieth century, organizations such as the National Civic Federation, while paving the road towards an entente with business unionism, influenced regulatory and legislative commissions, insuring that industry would be allowed a voice and a veto in the areas that concerned it.[16]

Adapting the system to the new needs of corporate capitalism required a close partnership between top-level economic leaders and the state. Political centralization, placing decision-making in the hands of "responsible" leaders, capable of reconciling sectional differences in a broad, "national" view, was thus an axis of the institutional order envisaged by at least some sectors of the national ruling class. In private as well as in public affairs, decision-making was to flow from the center to the periphery. Political leadership in the Progressive Era found the vision needed to unify the disjointed society under an ideology adapted to the phase of corporate capitalism.

Except in age and political experience, the Progressive Party cadres were not strikingly different from the Taft Republicans to whom they left the Grand Old Party in 1912. Both groups were overwhelmingly urban, upper middle class, Anglo-Saxon, Protestant, and highly educated: more than half of the Progressives were professional men, while 63 percent of the Old Guard Republicans had attended college.[17] The issue that divided them most clearly was the tactics of popular democracy: the Progressives endorsed the initiative, the referendum, the direct primary, and the recall of judicial decisions, which, to the Old Guard, spelled a threat to the Constitution and, more concretely, an attack upon the very structure of the party.

An analysis of municipal reform—a major battleground of the reformers after 1890—reveals, in fact, that "the ideology of democratization of decision-making was negative rather than positive.... It was used to destroy the political institutions of the lower and middle classes and the political power which those institutions gave rise to, rather than to provide a guide for alternative action."[18] Citywide elections—together with the promotion of strong mayors and the city manager form of executive—displaced the ward politician, close to his working-class and ethnic constituency. Municipal reform maximized instead the influence of "cosmopolitan" businessmen and professionals who could derive citywide recognition from their involvement with broad issues and their national connections.[19]

Samuel P. Hays observes an upward shift—analogous to that from the ward to the whole city—between township (or county) and the state level:

> The focal points of this transition were schools and roads.... In each case professionals with cosmopolitan rather than local perspectives were extremely influential in shifting the scope of interest and level of decision-making. The state highway commission supplanted the township trustee in road affairs and the state superintendent in public instruction became an increasingly influential figure. A similar upward shift in decision-making took place between the state and federal government. The most dramatic aspect of this process was the change in regulatory legislation.... In each case nationally organized businesses with markets and other interests beyond the confines of a single state actively promoted national regulation.[20]

A general process of political centralization thus appears to underlie the rhetoric and the tactics of "direct democracy." The New England town-meeting was not, in fact, the model of decision-making pursued by the reformers. Their inspiration came from the efficient business enterprise: as one of the truly national institutions of the period, the corporation, with its centralized control of functional components, provided a focal model for progressivism, for Teddy Roosevelt's New Nationalism and, in general, for the new concept of the state.

Leaders in the established professions, and in the new applied specialties that were emerging within the expanded structure of government and public services, actively promoted rationalization on the corporate model. This new type of professional welcomed the corporate systems of decision-making "not only because of their scope of coverage but because of their coercive potential. The professional sought to carry standards of life generated by a few to the population at large. His task was to persuade the yet unconvinced."[21] For many of these men, the application of the corporate model to public affairs was a means of establishing the independence of their professions from the private corporations and their "predatory wealth." The paradox is only apparent. The new style of expert leadership which they sought to establish could not exist without its corporate moorings; but the ubiquitous affirmation of the expert in distinct corporate systems—an affirmation which sometimes led to open conflict—reinforced scientific expertise as a transcendent principle and as a potential basis of professional autonomy.

The tendency appears clearly in the scientific management wing of mechanical engineering and, most particularly, in the new concept of professionalism advocated by Morris Cooke, the favorite disciple of Frederick W. Taylor, the founder of scientific management. Cooke, in fact, succeeded in steering the mechanical engineering profession toward reform, where Taylor himself had failed.[22] "The fundamental consideration in the work of an engineer—if he is ever to pull himself out of his present status of being a hired servant—is that he shall make public interest the master test of his work," wrote Cooke in 1921.[23]

As Director of Public Works for the city of Philadelphia from 1914 to 1919, Cooke put the principle into practice and advanced the concept of the professional engineer as expert leader in rational government. He used his battle against the utilities companies to denounce the engineering consultants associated with the companies' interests and to demonstrate the futility of a code of ethics in a professional association controlled by business.

Although Cooke's influence was undoubtedly profound with the rank-and-file of the profession, his faith in public service to solve the inherent subordination of the engineer was not widely shared. Cooke's solution presupposed, indeed, that the principles of scientific management would triumph and bring about "a massive restructuring of industrial bureaucracies and a reorganization of the utilities. If these things had come to pass, then Cooke's proposals would have made good sense."[24]

The corporate business leadership, while it was sympathetic to Taylor's rationalization and strict control of labor, was not about to share control of the enterprise with an independent group, no matter how expert and how scientific in its orientations. In the first decades of our century, scientific management, in fact, was more attuned to progressivism in public affairs than to the practical needs of big business, to whom Taylor had originally addressed his program. Reinhard Bendix has shown, however, that the social philosophy of scientific management—reinterpreted in the 1920s and 1930s and transformed by Elton Mayo's approach—was gradually incorporated by the top levels of corporate industry.[25] The intervening factor was the general shift in the dominant ideology which began with progressivism. As Samuel Haber convincingly argues in his study of Taylorism, scientific management provides a key to the emergent ideology of corporate capitalism.

Haber shows that Taylor's formulations integrated all the essential meanings that the core notion of efficiency took in the public mind of the time: the personal virtues of hard and disciplined work (and, therefore, the Yankee heritage and the Mugwump tradition); the "energy output-input ratio of a machine"; the relation between costs and profit in a commercial enterprise; and finally, social efficiency, that is, the "leadership of the competent" in a state of social harmony.[26]

For a time, the more simplistic and moralistic versions of the gospel of efficiency captured the popular imagination.[27] In the early part of the twentieth century, the language of efficiency appeared to unify the various reform campaigns into a "reform syncretism" centered on the new concept of the state: "Conservation, scientific management, and Americanization expressed cognate sentiments ... the leaders of all three suggested measures which involved a rejection of laissez faire and the acceptance of social guidance and control."[28]

The impact of the ideology of efficiency was profound.[29] The most general and abstract dimension which it incorporates is the appeal to science—or, broadly speaking, to rational and systematized knowledge: science appears not only as the chief instrument for mastery and control over the physical and even the social environment, but also as the ultimate legitimation for practical choices and everyday courses of action. In this sense, scientific management and its popular versions accurately reflect—or anticipate—the transformation of the productive forces by the integration of applied science and technology at all levels of the production process.

In the concrete setting of industry, the ideology of scientific management expresses the demise of the self-made man or captain of industry as the central self-justifying myth of the capitalist class. The common submission of *both* workers and employers to the "objective" laws of science heralds, indeed, a later ideological development: that which sees in corporate capitalism and in the depersonalization of capitalist property a "managerial revolution" and the waning of class. As Haber observes of Louis Brandeis' conception of industrial democracy: "Those aspects of management to which the laws of science did not as yet apply were to be subject to collective bargaining. Where science did apply, a union representative might serve as a watchdog to make sure that it was the laws of science and not class interest which was obeyed. *That the laws of science might serve class interest did not seem to be a possibility.*"[30]

In scientific management, science appears as the transcendent norm which will eliminate the arbitrariness of class power. In Taylor's own words: "The man at the head of the business under scientific management is governed by rules and laws which have been developed through hundreds of experiments *just as much as the workman is,* and the standards which have been developed are equitable."[31] Candidly emphasizing the *ideological* character of the transformation, Taylor adds: "In its essence scientific management involves a complete mental revolution on the part of the workingmen.... And it involves an equally complete mental revolution on the part of those on the management's side."[32]

At a more concrete level, scientific management is an expression of the core legitimation of mature capitalism: because technology and applied science promise a quasi-unlimited expansion of output and resources, they eliminate the cause for "zero-sum-game" conflict. Continuous economic growth and continuous increases in productivity are thus the mediators through which science resolves, or at least dilutes, class conflict.[33]

In the appeal to science, therefore, we find the overall cognitive and normative legitimation for the rise of the manager and the rise of the expert: ideologically, the "carriers of embodied science"—that is to say, trained and credentialed experts—are assigned a crucial and directive role, while the ideology also emancipates them from class allegiances and class interests.

In the context of the factory, scientific management projects the technocratic ambitions of the rising profession of engineering. But the contradictions and functions of the ideology are also revealed in this context. If, indeed, efficiency can be accurately and directly measured in the production of real commodities, this measurement is not unequivocal. As Haber points out, "Mechanical efficiency is an output–input ratio of matter or energy, whereas commercial efficiency is the relation between price and cost. Occasionally, these efficiencies are opposed."[34]

The glorification of technological ingenuity had justified, much before Taylor, the exalted position of the engineer, next to the master, in the hierarchical division of labor of the early factory system. It may be that this traditional belief concealed the essential subordination of the engineering profession from even such acute observers of the later industrial system as Thornstein Veblen.[35] But the practical engineers themselves, despite some misgivings, had less illusions about the ultimate determination of efficiency: "It was with a certain grimness that the engineers who seemed to believe that engineering could be practiced without regard to money values were condemned. 'These men may be ingenious inventors or designers, they may be great mathematicians, they may even be eminent as scientists, but they are not engineers,'" wrote the president of the Stevens Institute of Technology in 1907.[36]

The extension of notions of efficiency to organizations which produce only services or fictitious commodities maximizes the ideological implications. The extension discloses, first of all, an analogy between factory and society which symbolizes the bringing of the whole social order under the imperative creed of limitless economic growth. Efficiency in service industries cannot be gauged, however, by the direct mechanical measurement of input-output ratios of energy; its measurement is therefore necessarily reduced to cost-benefit evaluations. But when efficiency criteria are applied to the management of agencies outside the marketplace (such as the government, its administrative arms, nonprofit organizations such as schools, hospitals, philanthropies, and the like), evaluation of input and output becomes increasingly indirect. Above all, the attempt to measure efficiency in the production of services or fictitious commodities implies a necessary reduction of quality to quantity.[37] The tendency shows even with an apparently qualitative indicator of productivity or efficiency—that is, the proportion of "qualified" personnel at the various levels of an organization. The upgrading of qualifications is, indeed, equated with growing proportions of *credentialed* employees, with improvements in the personnel's average years of formal schooling or in the average scores obtained in a variety of aptitude tests.[38]

All these attempts to measure and increase efficiency in the production of services involve an extension of the role of the "experts." Scientific management ideologies attempted to bestow upon the engineer—and, later, upon the trained business administrator—the crown of the entrepreneur. In the same manner, the extension of the ideology of efficiency beyond the realm of real commodity production gave a decisive impetus to professionalizing occupations such as bureaucratic social workers, city planners, or school superintendents.

The possibility of claiming special "scientific" and organizational expertise comes to most of these occupations by virtue of their position in organizations which are increasingly bureaucratic. Centralization, hierarchical ordering, and delegation of administrative and managerial functions give those in planning or coordinating positions the possibility of defining the meaning of efficiency and the parameters for its measurement. Obviously, they do not perform this task of definition to their own disadvantage.

Two central structural changes underlie the ideological shift symbolized by scientific management and, in politics, by the Progressives: namely, the reorganization of production by the giant corporation and the quasi-simultaneous extension of state power and functions. Progressive reform took the corporate model of organization from the economy and transferred it to the polity, thus making political centralization concomitant to the centralization of economic production. It could be argued that the initial locus of bureaucratization in the United States is not the state, but large-scale industry.[39] From the Progressive Era on, bureaucratization advanced simultaneously in both political and civil society, providing a structural support for the diffusion of the ideology of efficiency.

The chief legitimizing principle of bureaucracy is, for Max Weber, its superior efficiency in the handling of large-scale problems. Bureaucracy appears to be the structural form under which the reorganization of commodity production by monopoly capital is "relayed" ideologically throughout the body social. In the particular historical development of the United States, central institutions of truly national scope were established almost contemporaneously in the economic and political spheres and, if we count the national universities, in the sphere of higher education as well. This parallel reorganization is reflected at the level of ideology in the unifying themes of efficiency, regulation, and expertise. It is during this phase of transition toward corporate capitalism that American professions consolidated their position in the occupational and social hierarchies. The success of professionalization movements in this phase therefore illuminates the organic relationship of professionalism—as an affirmation of expertise—with the two central structures of the new social order: namely, the large business corporation and the state.

In the light of the new ideology, the state acquires connotations of "objectivity" which are implicit in the appeal to science as an instrument of legitimation. The three main principles of progressive political reform, "non-partisanship, the strong executive, and the separation of politics from the administration"[40] all converge toward the notion of a transpolitical and ultimately technocratic state. Non-partisan, the state is severed from the visible class dimensions of political strife and debate. This "strong executive" administers, in fact, a social reality in which all interests can be reconciled by the magic of science applied to the limitless expansion of output. This emergent conception of the state foretells, thus, the not-so-unrealistic utopia of depoliticized conformity in a mass consumption society.

The emergence of the modern university completes the institutional framework within which experts can become organically tied to the reformed apparatus of the state. The "Wisconsin idea" of the university hopefully proposes a symbiotic relationship between the new national institutions of higher learning and the transpolitical state. In this conception, the professional expert can achieve—at least ideologically—emancipation from "predatory wealth" and thus assert his altruistic autonomy. The connotations of classlessness attached by the ideology of scientific management to experts in private organizations are reinforced by the conception of a "neutral" state and by the rise of the national university.

With its emphasis on running the state as an industrial corporation, the ideology of efficiency resolves the particularly American conflict between the ideology of egalitarian democracy and the claims of expertise. Concretely, the notion of a transpolitical state run by "classless" experts reconciled the class interests of at least part of the Progressive leadership with the movement's clamor for democratic revival: "Efficiency provided a standpoint from which progressives who had declared their allegiance to democracy could resist the leveling tendencies of the principle of equality. They could advance reform and at the same time provide a safeguard to the 'college-bred.'"[42]

Progressivism combined the directive power of privately managed corporations with an appearance of neutral regulation. Regulatory legislation contributed in the long run to the legitimacy of the large business corporation: apparently under control, it could be regarded as one more responsible member of the industrial community. Responsible membership is implicitly defined as involving acceptance of two cardinal principles of the social order: the private appropriation of social surplus and the private direction of social production. But the appeal to science and to "classless" expertise appear to subordinate the new social system to objective and transcendent laws. Not surprisingly, the movements that shaped the emergent order could enlist the support and participation of cosmopolitan urban professionals: in a sense, these movements incorporated the characteristic fusion which professional ideology seeks to effect between the goal of monopolistic market control and antimarket themes of public service and social usefulness.

In sum, the emergence of a national ruling class and of a new system of social stratification in the period of transition toward monopoly capitalism is structurally supported by large organizations: in the private as well as in the public sector, organizations administered in the bureaucratic mode are the new foundations of power and property, as well as the generators of "new middle-class" occupations and careers. Their size and their mode of administration appear to insulate these large organizations from the direct influence of class interests. Guided—at least ideally—by principles of functional rationality and applied science, these apparently classless organizations transmute power into authority by invoking the legitimacy of expertise. Thus, the reorganization of American society after the Civil War not only established a new system of social stratification but also, logically, created a new set of ideological legitimations for inequality.

The corporation, the state, and the modern university—all three organized on the bureaucratic model—are the central status-giving institutions which the United States lacked in the age of laissez faire. A national educational system and, in particular, the national institutions of higher education, function in the new order as the central reproducers and legitimators of the class structure. Appeals to science and to limitless growth merge as a mainstay of the new dominant ideology. Mediated by organizations, the class structure of monopoly capitalism is ultimately legitimized as a functional emanation of the social division of labor and, therefore, as the mirror of differential abilities and motivations.[43]

The monopoly, state, and academic sectors (the academic sector being both the producer and the employer of credentialed experts) define the organizational contexts within which professions find new instruments for self-organization and self-assertion. Large-scale bureaucratic organizations transform, therefore, the social matrix of professionalization: they provide the climate of ideological legitimation for both old and new professions; they also provide models, sponsorship, equipment, and resources. Far from being in conflict with the model of profession, the "bureaucratic phenomenon" creates the structural context of successful professionalization. Outside of the central bureaucratic apparatus of the new social order lies professional marginality, in both the collective and the individual sense.[44]

Generalization of the Professional Project; The Structural Background

After the Civil War, the westward move, the massive rates of immigration and urbanization, together with economic growth and the long-term increase of agricultural and industrial productivity, brought about the gradual restructuring of the labor force. The principal changes are well-known: the first, the most significant, was the decline of agricultural employment. Agriculture remained the predominant field of employment until 1910, although it attracted a smaller and smaller proportion of all workers. From 53 percent of the whole in 1870, gainful workers in agriculture declined to 31 percent in 1910 and 27 percent in 1920; in this last year, employment in manufacturing and mechanical industries reached 30.3 percent of the labor force and began, in turn, its proportional decline. The second major trend is, therefore, the gradual decrease of workers engaged in the production of physical goods and the growing movement toward distribution— transportation, trade, and communications—as well as toward services of all kinds, after 1870.[45] The third most obvious change is the rise of the public sector, which overlaps in part the enormous increases in the clerical and professional occupations.[46]

In the rise of the cities, in the emergence of national labor markets and in the growing tendency toward concentrated employment in the large industrial corporation and in the state sector, it is possible to discern the structural bases of a national class system. Everyday reality, however, was different. Robert Wiebe remarks that even in the 1880s and 1890s,

> The concept of a middle class crumbled at the touch. Small business appeared and disappeared at a frightening rate. The so-called professions meant little as long as anyone with a bag of pills and bottle of syrup could pass for a doctor, a few books and a corrupt judge made a man a lawyer, and an unemployed literate qualified as a teacher. Nor did the growing number of clerks, salesmen, and secretaries of the city share much more than a common sense of drift as they fell into jobs that attached them to nothing in particular, beyond a salary, a set of clean clothes, and a hope that somehow they would rise in the world.[47]

In the rapidly growing urban centers, the massive presence of foreign-born whites exaggerated the estrangement from the city of a native population which, in 1890, was still predominantly rural and concentrated in small towns.[48] Americanization and the melting pot seemed hardly credible ideologies. The industrial proletariat was profoundly divided by the diversity of its origins and work situations. The relative concentration of foreign-born workers and, to a lesser extent, their children, in certain occupations and industries aggravated the fragmentation of the class. Unionization was minimal.[49] At the level of the community, ethnic and cultural issues were much more vital than the national questions addressed by the platforms and ideologies of the major political parties.[50]

A class system had to come out of these bits and pieces. At least some sections of the industrial proletariat had shown their capacity for cohesive action in the intense class struggles that followed the great railroad strike of 1877. During the 1880s and 1890s, the "threat from below" appears to have brought some reactive unity to the divided middle strata; it blurred, at least temporarily, the bitter divisions between old and new wealth: both to "gentlemanly reformers" and to urban middle strata, the arrogance of the plutocracy seemed decidedly preferable to the rise of the "uncivilized" masses. But in the early twentieth century the memories of Populism and of urban and industrial class struggle were attenuated, while the fear of Bolshevism had not yet taken hold: a change in attitude toward the working class and the urban poor was possible.

From the 1880s on, the social justice movement—in which women's organizations and settlement workers, besides the organized church, played an increasingly prominent role—had been outlining a new role for the educated urban strata. From the settlements, in particular, came a more radical approach to urban problems than the moral solutions of the Social Gospelers and other Protestant humanitarians. Focusing on the environmental roots of poverty and personal degradation, the new secular brand of urban reformers actively organized campaigns for protective labor legislation and minimum living standards. They were still inspired, however, by a Christian ideal of universal brotherhood and individual uplift. Although sympathetic to the broader demands of the labor movement, they refused to recognize the necessity of class conflict or to accept the reality of class struggle.[52]

A reform movement which appeared to confront the power of the new ruling class without denouncing the class system—a movement which, furthermore, implicitly gave a badge of moral superiority to middle class reformers with regard to *both* the "plutocracy" and the lower classes—could indeed, attract a wide array of social forces. At the local level, progressivism appears to have been at least as much a movement of new aggressive business elites, represented by local chambers of commerce, as an expression of the bitterness of bypassed notables and old-fashioned entrepreneurs.[53] The constant rise in the cost of living was a possible unifying factor among otherwise disparate groups. Inflation affected, besides the working masses, "middle class and professional families…for their incomes were least responsive to general price changes."[54]

Another important factor is the very diversity and ambiguity of the progressive ideology: it projected, at one level, a quasi-Populist image but asserted more and more clearly as time went by the superiority of the competent and the role of the expert in efficient, "scientific" reform.

In fact, the central themes of progressivism—"moral uplift" for the masses, based on the formal expansion of political participation and on economic growth—are typical of an optimistic ideology, seeking the conciliation of irreconcilable interests. In a phase of transition, reformers who stressed individual effort and individual mobility could genuinely see more social fluidity and openness than the class system actually permitted. Espousing the promise of economic growth and efficient management, significant fractions of the intermediate class could promote, in the service of reform, the interests of the new industrial and financial magnates. For many reformers, the collusion may have been unwitting and their hopes of democratic reform sincere. As a hypothesis, I would argue that "new middle-class" reformers occupied, at best, ancillary positions with regard to the new ruling class. Yet their ideological convergence around the goals of rationalization and economic expansion was structurally based: there is evidence to suggest that the most significant fraction of the intermediate class—composed of professionals and managerial specialists with a "cosmopolitan" and national outlook— was rising and asserting itself in intimate connection with the central institutions of the new social order.

First among these was the bureaucratic apparatus of the state, including the system of public education.[55] The public sector was important not only as the fastest growing employer and as a privileged arena of action for the new "experts" in public affairs; public service and politics were also vehicles for the sense of identity and unity of the cosmopolitan sectors of the intermediate class. The emergent ideology assigned to the "transpolitical" state a central role of arbitration and social cohesion. The passage to corporate capitalism structurally required an expansion of the public sector. Consistent with these trends, the professional reformers addressed their demands for recognition and support to the state, as did the social reformers (who came frequently from the former group) in the fields of labor legislation, consumer protection, public health, school reform, and slum clearance. As the reform activists increased their leverage, their own self-assertion as experts tended to merge with their promotional efforts on behalf of the organizations where they worked.[56] In electoral as well as in social and professional reforms, the "expert" leaders defined the form that institutions, policies, or services were to take, reserving for themselves, at least in principle, the role at the helm.

In the dominant centers of the economy—the large business corporations—"new middle-class" occupations were more clearly subordinate to a heteronomous hierarchy than in the public sector. Yet, there too, new specializations or new articulations of the bureaucratic mode of organization spawned new claims to expertise.[57] Bureaucratization defined the typical pattern of middle-class career and a typical source of middle-class authority. For many professions, the corporation directly or indirectly provided a new context of organizational and ideological resources. The new approach to professionalization is typically illustrated by engineering, the largest of the new expert occupations called forth by large-scale industrialization.[58]

Edwin Layton observes that engineers, "like the progressives...saw themselves as a middle group between capital and labor."[59] This perception led them, on the one hand, to seek governmental recognition for their profession. At the Conservation Congress of 1908, the leaders of the four major engineering associations successfully proposed a series of resolutions, calling for the creation of a department of public works and "of a cabinet post for an engineer, thus according to the profession national recognition."[60] Engineers obviously welcomed the role that the predominant tendency within progressivism assigned to the expert: "Since engineering was the profession that applied scientific laws to practical problems, scientific solutions to social problems meant putting engineers in positions of leadership."[61]

But, on the other hand, engineers rejected the faith in democracy and the mistrust of the corporation that was voiced, at least rhetorically, by national progressivism. As corporation employees, the engineers could not oppose big business without renouncing the very base of power and social mobility of their profession: "where progressives favored regulation by government, engineers looked for reform coming from within the business community and through the agency of the engineer."[62]

What Layton calls the engineers' "obsessive concern for social status" fits with the image of an upwardly mobile group, largely drawn from a declining social category— small commercial or farm entrepreneurs—that was dependent on the large business corporation for its own advance.[63] By the end of World War I, this concern with status had fused with the conception of independent professionalism advocated at first by only a small elite. It had been, however, a contradictory conception: at the same time that engineering leaders attempted to exclude businessmen from their societies by raising the membership requirements, they continued to glorify the typical mobility path that led the corporate engineer from technical to managerial positions. Efficient management meant, moreover, that business would be run according to physical laws—embodied in technology—and to the "laws" of economics and social evolution—embodied in the corporation. Professionalism could thus be reconciled with business loyalty and with the public defense of corporate industry.

Not surprisingly, there was practically no opposition to this brand of professionalism until the 1920s. At this time, men such as Morris Cooke and his successors, moving away from elitist status concerns, sought to channel the economic discontent of average engineers into a direct relation with the state and into a broader technocratic conception of the engineer's social role. Engineering thus illustrates the alternative sources of support sought by a subordinate occupation in its professionalization efforts. In the context of the industrial corporation, professionalism was in large part a reaction to bureaucratic subordination; it nevertheless borrowed from the corporation a legitimizing ideology (scientifically based efficiency) and a model of individual advancement (promotion through the bureaucratic hierarchy). The public sector appeared, thus, as an independent or countervailing source of power and public recognition. Another such source was the modern university. The educational system was the third institutional area of major importance for the rising sectors of the intermediate class. The direct relevance of the national university to the success of professionalization justifies a brief account of its emergence on the American scene.

The decade of the 1880s marked a turning point in American higher education. Despite the high rate of population growth, enrollments had remained static since the

Age of Jackson.[64] From 1885 on, attendance picked up steadily at the major colleges and universities. By the early 1890s, Edward Ross, returning from Berlin, could marvel at the "boom in educational lines"; in the ten years from 1885 to 1895, the student bodies had grown by 20 percent at the private Eastern colleges and by 32 percent in the state universities.[65] Industrial and financial leaders may still have believed, like Andrew Carnegie, that bookish knowledge was "fatal to success" in business and that the "school of experience" was the best for American youth.[66] Yet, like Carnegie himself, they were insuring a steady flow of money for the institutions of higher learning or founding new private universities, like John D. Rockefeller at Chicago or Leland Stanford in California. Following on the promise of the 1862 Morrill Act, legislative funding was becoming a reality in the 1890s. The university had attained an unquestioned position among American institutions.

Lawrence Veysey suggests that one major underlying reason for this change was the concern of self-made men for the social status of their children. For the new and affluent America of the Midwest and the West, the college degree was acquiring a new meaning: not only because it was a distinction that could be achieved with relative ease, in imitation of the traditional Eastern elites; but also, more importantly, because it established social distance between an older and largely Anglo-Saxon immigration and the mass of newly arrived Central and Southern Europeans.[67] The function that middle-class aspirations increasingly assigned to the university had a powerful effect on its structure and later evolution. The emergent model of the American university, however, had been in gestation since the 1860s.

A first act in this process was the demise of the small sectarian college, which had proliferated in the Jacksonian period as the typical "unfree" unit in a "free market" of education. By 1860, says Richard Hofstadter, financial insolvency was eliminating the more marginal of these institutions, while internal disorder was being resolved by a more secular turn and a more autonomous role of the faculties.[68] In both established Eastern colleges and outlying denominational schools, the proportional decline in the number of students preparing for the ministry reflected the advance of secularization.[69] The Jacksonian emphasis on "practicality" and, after 1840, the spread of didactic scientific instruction prefigured in a primitive way the educational models that were to compete after the Civil War.

The early conception of the college had relied on religion and, almost secondarily, on the classics, to emphasize strict "mental discipline." Its lingering effects may be traced in the rhetorical piety and conservative Christianity surprisingly voiced by presidents and demanded of faculties at new institutions like Johns Hopkins or the University of Chicago. Greatly transformed, the classical emphasis may have subsisted in the ideal of well-rounded cultivation of mind that came to be chiefly associated, in our century, with the private liberal arts college and with the Ivy League.[70] Yet, as an institutional model, "mental discipline" was on its way out by 1865.

In the decade that followed, the major trend of reform was undoubtedly utilitarian, in the sense of a voluntary adaptation by academic sectors to what they perceived to be the demands of "real life" in an industrial and democratic society.[71] What is generally seen as the typical American contribution to the modern university model derives from this tradition. If, as Veysey believes, unpopularity and public indifference explain the freedom of institutional experimentation enjoyed by the university until the 1890s, then we should consider the utilitarian model of reform as a deliberate effort to integrate the college into the mainstream of American life. Not surprisingly, the model found its chief advocates among the new faculty in the applied and social sciences and among administrators—especially the strong presidents who, in the manner of captains of industry, were fashioning the institutions of the future.[72]

The utilitarian desire for an "adaptation to reality" was concretely expressed in a number of "democratic" beliefs and programmatic changes. First of all, a broadened notion of "calling" contributed to dignify a great number of technical and specialized pursuits, which were henceforth able to claim a place in the American university, while the European institutions almost uniformly relegated them to vocational schools. The Morrill Acts—establishing land grants for colleges that would provide agricultural and mechanical instruction—deliberately promoted the vocational orientation of the university. This typical emphasis explains in part the wide diffusion of professionalization as a model for the collective improvement of social status. It also merges with the central role that the American university would come to play as an agency of individual social mobility, democratically dispensing its badges of status superiority to broad segments of the public.

The openness to multiple vocations is intimately linked, on the one hand, with the democratic belief in the equality of all fields of learning—a belief which guided the founding of Cornell in 1868, and directly inspired the elective curriculum.[73] On the other hand, vocational openness merges with the hope for a "classless" institution: a university, that is, in which all students should be treated equally, and, going one step further, one that should admit all students regardless of sex, race, religion, and even previous educational attainments. As President Andrew Draper of Illinois declared in 1907: "The universities that would thrive must put away all exclusiveness and dedicate themselves to universal public service. They must not try to keep people out; they must help all who are worthy to get in."[74]

From the 1890s on, the fact that the national university had become an integral part of the new social order manifested itself in the tendency toward increasing standardization of its basic features. Undoubtedly, regional and institutional differences persisted, fusing with differences in social environment, class image, and preferred educational orientation.[82] Around 1910, the differences between the Ivy League and the Big Ten or, more broadly, between private and public universities, had crystallized. Yet, for all the differences, institutional competition for place in the national hierarchy of higher education spurred imitation and increased uniformity. Reputation was concretely expressed in size: size of the student bodies, size and "completeness" of the faculty, size of the installations, size of the endowments. As Walter Metzger has put it, "in a vast society strewn across a vast continent," Big Education was bound to rise alongside Big Business, Big Government and, later, Big Labor.[83]

The increase in size promoted the alignment of the university with the bureaucratic managerial model taken chiefly from the industrial corporation. In the period 1880–1910, business leaders became almost everywhere the predominant group on university boards of trustees.[84] More directly important, the foundations that emerged in the first years of the twentieth century—in particular the Rockefeller Institute and the Carnegie Foundation for the Advancement of Teaching—played pivotal roles in the modernization of higher education and professional training along lines that replicated concentration and centralization in the economy. Critics such as Thornstein Veblen or John Jay Chapman bitterly denounced the subordination of higher learning to big business: "The men who stand for education and scholarship have the ideals of business men," declared Chapman in 1909. "The men who control Harvard today are very little else than business men, running a large department store which dispenses education to the millions. Their endeavor is to make it the *largest* establishment of the kind in America."[85]

Chapman exaggerated. Bureaucratization was largely an inevitable consequence of the increase in size, but it was also fostered by the desire for security of the average faculty member, who could not avail himself of the competitive advantages the academic marketplace was bringing to a minority of his colleagues.[86] On the other hand, the university appeared to offer to a rapidly growing number of teachers a refuge, and an alternative to the business world, increase in numbers meant an increase in autonomy and independence, and business pressures for conformity responded in part to the new measure of power acquired by faculties.[87] The notion that the university was "different" persisted, despite the relative convergence of the institutional model with the corporation and the state apparatus.

To the elites of the new middle class, the university provided a common socialization, which preceded, in fact, their rise and assertion in the new social order. As Wiebe remarks, "since the emergence of the modern graduate school in the seventies, the best universities had been serving as outposts of professional self-consciousness, frankly preparing young men for professions that as yet did not exist."[89] The model of university that emerged in the nineties was characterized, among other things, by its openness to new fields of learning and to "professional training…in fields that had a genuine but still only potential and undeveloped scientific or scholarly content."[90] The early institutionalization of research careers merged, in America, with the pragmatic and utilitarian orientations imposed upon even the most traditional universities by outside financing; both factors helped the rapid development of applied sciences or "quasi-disciplines." The American university acquired, therefore, centralized and quasi-monopolistic power to sanction many different specialties as legitimate forms of knowledge and expertise.

More concretely, the links that professions, old and new, could establish with the university in time gave all of them an academic wing. Teachers in professional schools, relatively insulated from the pressures of the client or the marketplace, could promote a "purer" brand of professionalism than their practicing colleagues, while working at the same time to develop the cognitive and technical basis of their disciplines. It was in the academic sectors of medicine and, in particular, the law, that not only professionalism but also progressivism found their leading advocates. Since academics normally publish more than practitioners, the academics' views also tended to color the literature of reform and the literature of professionalization, projecting a misleading image of the mood and orientations of the professional rank-and-file. But, despite this discrepancy, the vocational openness of the American university reinforced the tendency toward professionalization. First, this was true because aspiring occupations or less "genteel" professions could realistically strive for university affiliation and hope to emulate the successful path followed by medicine and the law. Second, it was true because "academicization" rapidly increased the influence of university graduates in a field; and, simultaneously, because it gave academic professionals an increasing influence over growing numbers of professional aspirants.[91]

At the beginning of the twentieth century, only a minority of the professional and managerial middle class had passed through the university; but it was a particularly active, cohesive, and significant minority. Concerned with the present, while asserting their confidence in a future of which they had no total image, these men and women formed in the cities nuclei of "cosmopolitanism"—and from these sprang the cadres of modernization.[92] Journalists and editors of newspapers and periodicals played an important role in spreading and unifying their views.[93] Taking advantage of a system of communications which now physically integrated the country, these modern representatives of the intermediate class sought links in other cities and regions with peers of like mind. Indeed, their support for progressive reform carried on, at different levels of the society, the ordering function that state and corporation were performing at the center: the reformers' sectional organizing, as well as the modernization of local institutions which they undertook, were powerful forces of national integration, for they spread the central ideological themes of the new corporate order and established organizational relays between the local and national levels.

In the Progressive Era, sectors of the intermediate class whose self-definition and self-esteem were increasingly based on occupation, and increasingly oriented toward national frames of reference, acquired something akin to class consciousness. Professionalism was one expression of this consciousness.

The strategies of professionalization had been clear for a long time. National professional associations, and often training schools, had been in existence in dentistry, pharmacy, school teaching, and architecture since the 1840s and 1850s—that is, before the revival of organization efforts in the older professions toward the last decades of the century. What is interesting is the generalization of these strategies in the 1880s and 1890s, and their use by specialized occupations which in no way shared the market situation of the old "free" professions.

Professions concerned with the administration of the business corporations—such as engineers, accountants, market analysts, and the like—emerged in subordinate markets, subsumed de jure or de facto under bureaucratic and hierarchical organizations. The *ideology* of independent practice, "fee-for-service" consultation, and professional autonomy (as a substitute for the former two) played an important role in the professionalization of these occupations. Yet market control—in the sense of an autonomous monopoly in the provision of expert services—was clearly beyond their reach. This was even more so in "public-service" occupations such as social work, school and college teaching, or school administration: these occupations do not *exchange* services at all with their users, but instead find themselves in situations of preestablished monopoly, entirely determined by the monopolistic expansion of the state into new functional areas.

Market organization and control was therefore a weak dimension of these "new style" professional projects. By the logic of my theoretical interpretation, then, *the dominant, and almost the unique, meaning of these professional movements was the conquest and assertion of social status*. The emergence of an occupation-and-education-centered middle class meant that comparisons tended to be made "upwards" rather than "downwards" by less prestigious or less fortunate occupations: the prizes won by medicine and the law (or by their elites) inspired others. As Wiebe observes, "the exceptional vitality of the new middle class derived in large measure from the very personal benefits its membership bestowed."[94] Not all sectors of the intermediate class could take these benefits for granted. This was the turning point, however, at which the material and moral benefits included in profession status became a "normal" part of the professions' image and of the expectations surrounding professional careers. Adopting—and adapting—the strategies of professionalization fruitfully used by medicine and the law, occupations in structurally different situations sought the rewards of professional status: prestige, as public recognition of collective worth; income, to be translated into respectable middle-class styles of life; and, to defend these rewards, monopolistic closure of access.

The quest for professional status spread as a typical concern of educated middle-class occupations, promising individual advancement through collective efforts. Bureaucratization and educational mobility extended this individualistic promise to the middle class as a whole and even beyond it, to the working class. Progressive reform, indeed, often assumed that the foundation for the moral and economic "uplift" of the masses, as well as for the Americanization of the immigrant, lay in some form of education. This emphasis on education as a social panacea reflects the persistent strength of individualism, stated now in terms of maximizing individual abilities—and individual gains—through collective efforts. At another level, this belief ideologically denies the effect of class and ethnic barriers, and thus plays a cohesive role for the heterogeneous middle class itself: access to education, or rather the hope of individual mobility through education, appears as one common characteristic shared by large sectors of the intermediate class. At a time when middle strata, old and new, were being clearly divided into "central" and "marginal" sectors by their differential access to national centers of power and resources, they maintained certain common elements of consciousness. A composite ideology, combining old and new components of bourgeois and petty bourgeois status, old and new legitimations, contributed for a time to conceal the structural fractures within the intermediate class.

In capitalist society, the central function of ideology is to conceal the existence of class and the basic structure of exploitation. In the United States, the bourgeois society par excellence, the concealment of class emphasizes individualism and individual solutions; it typically takes one sector of the intermediate class as exemplar and as propagator.[95] In the Progressive Era, a new sector or stratum became the focus of the ideology of classlessness, as a relay to the bypassed farmers and small entrepreneurs: not coincidentally, this stratum found its main opportunities of advancement in apparently classless organizations, in an apparently neutral State, and in apparently classless knowledge.

The "quantitative ethic" typical of a capitalist society both expresses and reinforces the role of money as the central indicator of success and social status. The inflationary period that followed the depression of 1893 exacerbated the concern with money among wage-earners and status-conscious middle strata. The low level of emoluments constituted, thus, a major spur to organize, not only among industrial workers or salaried occupations such as social work and school teaching, but for the "learned professions" as well. The choice of professionalization over unionization as a strategy of collective mobility, at least in this early phase, is of general significance: professionalism, indeed, makes an important contribution to the ideological denial of structural inequality.

The tactics of organization adopted by would-be professionals are in many respects similar to those of the craft union. The overall strategy, however, reveals the professionals' distinctive approach to social stratification. Discussing the contemporary differences between unionization and professionalization, two sociologists remark:

> Instead of engaging in a power contest between haves and have-nots, the [professional] association undertakes to protect and expand the knowledge base, enforce standards of learning, entry, and performance, and engage in similar activities designed to enhance the position of the practitioner while simultaneously purporting to protect the welfare of the public in the person of the client. Indeed, professional claims concerning the primacy of the public good over the practitioner's own private benefit might be viewed as a critical difference between the professionalizing and the unionizing modes of mobility, were it not for the considerable evidence that the claims are watered down with rhetoric.[96]

The union perspective approaches the determination of the price of labor as a conflict between antagonistic and opposing class interests; this, indeed, is one of the dimensions of class consciousness. The institutionalization of business unionism depoliticizes this conflict approach and narrows it down to limited goals and limited institutional settings.[97] The ideological connotations, however, remain different from those involved in the professional project.[98] Appeals to the public interest can be used by unions as well as professional associations; business unionism can justify internal stratification by emphasizing collective identity and solidarity, as much as or more than professional organizations. On the job, however, goals *and* strategies focus exclusively on collective benefits, even if the union members may translate economic incentives into purely individualistic terms. When the ideology that links individual worth to individual "merit" expressed in "badges of competence" becomes *dominant*—when the dominated classes to some extent accept it, consciously and unconsciously—collective gains do not bring a sense of personal empowerment to the individual worker. If, in bourgeois ideology, "the consciousness of human worth is a consciousness *of self as individual, standing out from a mass who seem pretty much the same,*"[99] collective victories do not satisfy the individualistic compulsion to prove oneself "worthy" by one's own means.

As professionalizing occupations move to create and affirm collective worth, one of the incentives for participation, as well as one of the major goals of the movement, is to secure the supports for *individual* dignity and *individual* careers. Income and other indicators of status are important not only in themselves but also in comparison to the status indicators possessed by other social groups and individuals. Likewise, for most professionals, the coveted autonomy over the conditions and the technical content of work is *also* an element of qualitative distinction between professional work and subordinate or proletarian occupations. The expertise in terms of which all this is claimed is *also* a basis on which to exact deference and compliance in personal interaction. Individual differentiation, even though it must be attained within a collectivity and by collective means, is therefore a major promise of the professional project.

Moreover, although professionalization may be seen as "a power struggle, on a societal level," it is a struggle waged within the same class, against rival occupations, rather than across class lines.[100] The struggle on the societal level is largely an ideological battle for recognition, for only through social recognition can personal superiority be securely affirmed. Professionalization, as a movement for status advancement, *must* appeal to general values of the dominant ideology if it is to make its own values acceptable; unions, in their hours of glory, asserted the moral and functional superiority of the working class in terms that necessarily implied the rejection of the social hierarchy and basic values of capitalist society. The socialist movement explicitly asserted collective class identity in terms of the totality of a superior social order; but professions derive an ideology of neutrality from their generalized, "societal" appeal—that is, an ideology which implicitly stresses the classlessness of professionals and, explicitly, the service of the public as a whole.

It has been shown many times, however, that professions and professionalizing occupations address the "public as a whole" only in ideology: traditional professions sought sponsorship from the upper class, and emerging professions seek it today from particular groups in the legislative or executive branches of government. The claims of expertise and altruism made by professions do not have to be substantiated for an "undifferentiated mass," but for "segmental publics ... such as clients utilizing services or colleagues employed in related tasks and fields, [who] are in a position to recognize the skills of the professional and grant the necessary autonomy."[101] Needless to say, these publics vary from each profession or segment of profession, and are themselves stratified in terms of class, race, gender, and culture.

Notes

1 For an account of this passage in the Marxist tradition, see Paul Baran and Paul M. Sweezy, *Monopoly Capital* (New York: Monthly Review Press, 1968). For a different, non-Marxist approach to structural changes in contemporary capitalism, see John K. Galbraith, *The New Industrial State* (New York: Signet, 1967).

2 For a historical account of the formation of these firms, see Alfred D. Chandler, Jr., *Strategy and Structure*, (Cambridge, Mass.: MIT Press, 1962). For productivity trends in the American economy, see Lance E. Davis *et al., American Growth; An Economist's History of the United States* (New York: Harper & Row, 1972), pp. 33–54 and 205–211.

4 See Jürgen Habermas, "Technology and Science as 'Ideology'," in *Toward a Rational Society*, pp. 81–122 (Boston: Beacon Press, 1971); see also Magali Sarfatti-Larson, "Notes on Technocracy: Some Problems of Theory, Ideology and Power," *Berkeley Journal of Sociology*, 17 (1972–1973): 1–34.

10 See Samuel P. Hays' discussion in *Response*, chap. 4. See also Davis, *Spearheads*.

11 See, in particular, Kolko Gabriel, *The Triumph of Conservatism* (New York: Free Press, 1968); James Weinstein, *The Corporate Ideal in the Liberal State: 1900–1918* (Boston, Beacon Press, 1968); and Williams, *Contours*.

12 Weinstein, *Corporate Ideal*, p. xii.

13 On the railroads, see Robert W. Fogel, *Railroads in American Economic Growth* (Baltimore: johns Hopkins Univ. Press, 1964).

14 Richard Hofstadter points out that "almost three-quarters of the trusts and almost six-sevenths of the capital in trusts" came into existence in the short period 1898–1904 (Richard Hofstadter, *The Age of Reform*. New York: Vintage, 1955, p.160). The following table documents the consolidation process:

Giant Consolidations and Market Control (1894–1904)

Percent of industry controlled	Consolidations & parent company		Firm disappearances		Capitalization in million U.S.$	
	N	*% of total*	*N*	*% of total*	*Value*	*% of total*
42.5–62.5	21	6.7	291	9.7	613,5	10.3
62.5–82.5	24	7.7	529	17.6	2130,6	35.7
82.5 & over	16	5.1	343	11.4	998,0	16.7
"Large"	25	8.0	302	10.0	455,5	7.6
Total	86	27.5	1,465	48.7	4197,6	70.3

Source: Louis M. Hacker, *The Course of American Growth and Development* (New York: John Wiley & Sons, 1970), p. 248. It is interesting to read the above data together with the following series (from Hacker, *Course*, p. 275):

Growth in Real GNP and Productivity (1889–1929)
Average Annual Percentual Rates of Change

Period	Real net national productivity	Total factor input	Total factor productivity
1889–99	4.5	2.9	1.5
1899–1909	4.3	3.1	1.1
1909–19	3.8	2.3	1.5
1919–29	3.1	1.6	1.4

15 Kolko, *Triumph*, p. 3.

16 See Weinstein, *Corporate Ideal*, for an analysis of the National Civic Federation.

17 On the Progressive leadership, see Alfred D. Chandler, Jr., "The Origins of Progressive Leadership," in *The Letters of Theodore Roosevelt*, Elting E. Morrisson, ed. (Cambridge, Mass.: Harvard Univ. Press, 1951–1954), VIII, Appendix III, pp. 1462–1464; Samuel P. Hays, "The

Politics of Reform in Municipal Government in the Progressive Era," *Pacific Northwest Quart.*, 55 (1964): 157–169; George Mowry, *The California Progressives* (Berkeley: Univ. of California Press, 1951); Norman Wilensky, *Conservatives in the Progressive Era: The Taft Republicans of 1912*, (Gainesville, Fla.: Univ. of Florida Press, 1965), chap. 3.

18   Hays, "Politics of Reform," p. 168.

19   See *ibid.*

20   Samuel P. Hays, "Political Parties and the Community-Society Continuum," in *The American Party Systems*, William N. Chambers and Walter Dean Burnham (New York: Oxford Univ. Press, 1967), p. 171.

21   *Ibid.*, p. 170.

22   Monte Calvert suggests that Taylorism may be seen as an attempt to create a new role for the old entrepreneurial elite, as the machine shop was displaced by modern industry. The American Society of Mechanical Engineers welcomed, at first, the favorable publicity that management engineering was creating for the profession. But scientific management, in fact, was wedded to bureaucratization and rationalization of production; it would only have precipitated the death of the machine shop, which Taylor himself loved so well. When Taylor assumed the presidency of A.S.M.E. in 1906, the reforms he attempted were bitterly resisted by the membership, and not only by the old-style entrepreneurs, who had already lost control of the association to the elite of corporate engineers. See Calvert, *The Mechanical Engineer in America, 1830–1910* (Baltimore, 1967), pp. 235–243, and Edwin Layton, *The Revolt of the Engineers* (Cleveland: Case Western Reserve University, 1971), chaps. 6 and 7.

23   Quoted by Layton, *Revolt*, p. 159.

24   *Ibid.*, p. 172.

25   See Reinhard Bendix, *Work and Authortity in Industry* (New York,1956), chap. 5.

26   Samuel Haber, *Efficiency and Uplift* (Chicago: Univ. of Chicago Press, 1964), pp. ix and x.

27   Louis Brandeis' appeal for efficiency in the Eastern Rate case of 1910–1911 appears to have triggered in the press—and with the public—a real "efficiency craze," which had "both its explicitly moral and its apparently technical aspects." (Haber, *Efficiency*, p. 55.)

28   *Ibid.*, p. 62.

29   The ideology of efficiency is quite clear in Abraham Flexner's *Medical Education in Europe* (New York: Carnegie Foundation for the Advancement of Teaching, Bull. No. 6, 1912). Scientific management ideas were also influential on the management of universities, see Lawrence R. Veysey, *The Emergence of the American University* (Chicago: Univ. of Chicago Press, 1965), p. 353.

30   Haber, *Efficiency*, p. 96, italics mine.

31   Quoted by Bendix, *Work*, p. 278, italics mine.

32   Quoted by *ibid.*, p. 276.

33   Taylor thought that scientific management would result in such increases in productivity that large increases in both wages and profits would become possible; see quotation from Taylor in Bendix, *Work*, p. 276. Productivity played the same role in Herbert Croly's thought, which influenced Roosevelt. See Hays, *Response*, pp. 88 ff.

34   Haber, *Efficiency*, p. 11.

35   See Thornstein Veblen, *The Engineers and the Price System* (New York: Harcourt, Brace and World, 1963 ed.).

36   Haber, *Efficiency*, p. 12.

37   Education illustrates the difficulty of assessing productivity in the services, both in terms of input factors (an attempt now almost abandoned) and of output factors, in which last case "output" may be measured either through numbers of pupils-hours of teaching per day, or by the students' achievement on standardized tests. The implications of the reduction of quality to quantity are evident. On the difficulties of measuring productivity in education, see Mark Blaugh, *An Introduction to the Economics of Education* (Baltimore: Penguin, 1970), chaps. 6, 7, 9.

38   The attempt to find "objective" standards for the selection of personnel is obviously not limited to service organizations or service workers. It was, in fact, pioneered by vocational psychologists in the Army during World War I, and continued by industrial psychologists, despite the initial reservations of management. See Bendix, *Work*, pp. 291–293.

39   Max Weber commented that the United States in the first decades of the twentieth century still bore "the character of a polity which, at least in the technical sense, is not fully bureaucratized."

from Max Weber, "Essay on Bureaucracy," in *From Max Weber: Essays in Sociology*, trans. and ed. Hans Gerth and C.W. Mills (New York: Oxford University Press, 1959), p. 211. See pp. 209–211.

40   Haber, *Efficiency*, p. 101.

42   *Ibid.*, p. 116.

43   The article by Kingsley Davis and Wilbert E. Moore, "Some Principles of Stratification," in *Class, Status and Power*, Reinhard Bendix and Seymour Martin Lipset, eds., *Class, Status and Power* (Routledge & Kegan Paul PLC, 1967), pp. 47–53, is still one of the most coherent expositions of this ideological view, presented as social science.

44   Peter Drucker observes: "Knowledge opportunities exist primarily in large organizations. Although the shift to knowledge work has made possible large modern organizations, it is the emergence of these organizations—business enterprises, government agency, large university, research laboratory, hospital—that in turn has created the job opportunities for the knowledge worker. … The knowledge opportunities of yesterday were largely for independent professionals working on their own. Today's knowledge opportunities are largely for people working within an organization as members of a team or by themselves." Peter Drucker, *The Age of Discontinuity* (New York: Harper and Row, 1968), pp. 274–275.

45   The broad changes in the occupational structure appear clearly in the following table:

Percent distribution of gainful workers, older than 10 years, by broad occupational categories

Category	1870	1900	1910	1920	1930
Physical goods	74.9	65.4	62.7	60.5	50.8
Transport, communications, trade	11.0	17.3	16.8	17.3	20.4
Clerical Occupations	0.6	2.5	4.6	7.3	8.2
Professional service	2.6	4.1	4.6	5.1	6.7
Public service[a]	0.7	1.0	1.2	1.7	1.8
Domestic & personal services	9.7	9.7	10.1	8.0	10.1
Total gainful workers	100.0	100.0	100.0	100.0	100.0

[a]Not elsewhere classified: Omits, therefore, professionals, and, in particular, the large body of public-school teachers; clerical assistants; postal workers; and personnel employed in the construction and maintenance of roads, streets, sewers, and bridges, in government printing offices, in navy yards, etc.

Source: Alba M. Edwards, *Population: Comparative Occupational Statistics for the United States, 1870–1940* (Washington: U.S. Government Printing Office, 1943), p. 101.

46   As explained in note 45, the available figures for public service do not adequately reflect the enormous growth of the sector; the few categories covered by the census definition (public protection, armed forces, custodial personnel, public officials, and personnel involved at all levels in public works) show, nevertheless, the largest percentage increase of all occupational categories in the period 1870–1930. Here are some percentage increases for selected occupational categories:

Year	Total pop.	All gainful workers	All prof. workers	Teachers Profess.	Public service	Clerical workers
1870 } 1880 }	... 30.1	... 39.1	... 63.6	...	... 52.4	... 70.3
1890	24.8	30.7	62.2	252	72.7	56.3
1900	21.4	27.9	30.2		40.6	36.7
1910	21.0	31.3	40.6		47.6	43.7
				152		
1920	14.9	9.0	23.9		39.1	80.8
1930	16.1	17.3	46.4		35.8	29.7
1930 } 1870 }	218.4	290.5	781.3	787	1631.3	1127.7

Source: H. Dewey Anderson and Percy E. Davidson, *Occupational Trends in the United States* (Stanford Univ. Press, 1940).

47 Robert H. Wiebe, *The Search for Order, 1877–1920* (Hill and Wang; unknown edition, 1966), pp. 13–14.

48 Only 8 percent of the native white stock lived in cities of 100,000 or more, compared to 33 percent of the foreign-born; 58 percent of the latter were urban. See Davis *et al., Economic Growth*, pp. 135–136.

49 For the relative concentration of immigrants and their descendants in different occupational categories, see Edward P. Hutchinson, *Immigrants and their Children, 1850–1950* (New York: John Wiley and Sons, 1956). The percentage of the work force that unionized varied as follows: 1880, .3 percent; 1890, 1.4 percent; 1900, 2.7 percent; 1910, 5.6 percent; 1920, 12.1 percent. From 7.4 percent in 1930, the proportion of unionized workers jumped to 16.6 percent in 1935 and then attained its present level (22 to 25 percent) in 1945. See Davis *et al., Economic Growth*, p. 220.

50 See Hays, "Political Parties."

52 See Davis, *Spearheads*, and Roy Lubove, *The Professional Altruist: The Emergence of Social Work as a Career: 1880–1930* (Harvard University Press, 1965).

53 Extrapolating from the political visibility of the "gentlemanly" elites, Hofstadter offers a general explanation of Progressivism as a reaction to "status deprivation" (Hofstadter, *Reform*). The evidence available is often contradictory: the characteristics of the progressives at the state and national levels are not substantially different from those of the Old Guard Republicans; their characteristics appear to be reversed, moreover, at the precinct and local levels. See Hays, "Politics of Reform," and "Political Parties," pp. 163–164.

54 Haber, *Efficiency*, p. 21. The cost of living rose about 35 percent in the years 1897–1913 (Hofstadter, *Reform*, p. 168).

55 For data on the growth of government expenditures, see Davis *et al., Economic Growth*, pp. 653 and 661. For expenditures on education, see p. 651. In the period 1900–1930, the number of elementary schoolteachers increased by 63 percent, that of secondary schoolteachers by 671 percent, and that of college professors by 388 percent. The number of teachers in professional schools proper increased by 96 percent. See Anderson and Davidson, Percy E. Davidson and H. Dewey Anderson, *Occupational Trends in an American Community* (Stanford: Stanford University Press, 1937).

56 In social work, this tendency deepened the gap between settlement workers, acting "from below" and social work professionals, who were asserting themselves as experts on the basis of the casework method and individual therapy in bureaucratized institutions of health and charity. See Davis, *Spearheads;* Roy Lubove, *The Professional Altruist* (Cambridge, Mass.: Harvard Univ. Press, 1965).

57 For instance, accountants and auditors are included by the census in the category "clerical occupations." The occupation (including "bookkeepers and cashiers") increased by 1407 percent in the period 1870–1930. See Anderson and Davidson, *Trends*, p. 584. The financial group in the occupations included under trade also grew very rapidly (by 126.9 percent in the period 1910–1930). See pp. 436 and 440.

58 In 1930, the category "technical engineers" was second largest (7.7 percent) to that of "teachers and professors" (38.4 percent) among professional and technical workers. The category had increased from 7,374 (or 2.2 percent of all professional workers) in 1870 to 226,249 in 1930. The percentage increases in the number of engineers and other technical or professional workers typically employed by industry are among the highest of all occupational categories:

	1870–1900	*1900–1930*	*1870–1930*
Technical engineers	486%	423%	2968%
Chemists, assayers, metallurgists	1046	432	5997
Designers, draftsmen	1373	442	7888

At the end of the period, 26.5 percent of all engineers were still in private practice, teaching, and research. The percentages employed by the public sector (12.2 percent) and other industries were growing: building and road construction employed 15.7 percent of all engineers; telephone and telegraph, non-bituminous mining, electric light and power plants, electrical machinery, and iron and steel machinery other than railways employed about 6 percent each. See Anderson and Davidson, *Trends*, pp. 497 and 549.

59 Layton, *Revolt*, p. 64. I follow his account in this section, in particular his chaps. 3 and 4.

60   *Ibid.*, p. 63.

61   *Ibid.*, p. 66.

62   *Ibid.*, p. 67.

63   In 1924 the Society for the Promotion of Engineering Education surveyed a representative cross-section of engineering freshmen: the parents of 42.5 percent of the sample were owners or proprietors of businesses, most of them small commercial or agricultural units. Another 28.2 percent were employed in executive or supervisory positions; 5.6 percent were engineers or teachers; and 13 percent were skilled workers. Only 13 percent of the fathers had a college degree; 61.3 percent lived in rural areas or towns under 25,000. Quoted by Layton, *Revolt*, p. 9.

64   Attendance at twenty of the oldest and leading colleges rose 3.5 percent during the 1870s, while population grew by 23 percent. Veysey, *Emergence*, pp. 4–5.

65   Willis Rudy, John S. Brubacher, *Higher Education in Transition: A History of American Colleges and Universities* (History of Ideas. Transaction Publisher, 4th ed. 1997), p. 161. Ross is quoted by Veysey, *Emergence*, p. 263.

66   Quoted by Veysey, *Emergence*, pp. 13–14. See also his pp. 266 ff.

67   See *ibid.*, pp. 265–266.

68   See Richard Hofstadter and Walter P. Metzger, *The Development of Academic Freedom in the United States* (Columbia University Press; 1st ed. 1955), chap. 6.

69   Separate theological schools developed after 1865. By that date, ministerial candidates had dropped to one-fifth of the student body in sectarian colleges, from one-third in 1840. At Harvard, Yale, and Princeton, they declined from one in three in 1830 to one in thirteen in 1876. Hofstadter and Metzger, *Academic Freedom*, p. 350.

70   See Christopher Jencks, David Riesman, *The Academic Revolution* (Higher Education Series, Transaction Publishers, 2001), chap. 6, on the "bifurcation of higher education."

71   In this discussion, I follow mainly Veysey, *Emergence*, especially Part I.

72   On the role of presidents, see Veysey's discussion of Harvard and Cornell, pp. 81–98 and of Western Universities, pp. 100–109. See also pp. 17–18, 61–62, and 360–380 on the new breed of administrators. See, as well, Hofstadter and Metzger, *Academic Freedom*, pp. 233ff and 305ff; and Jencks and Reisman, *Academic Revolution*, pp. 25–26.

73   The elective system was the chief reform that Charles W. Eliot had in mind when he began his forty-year reign at Harvard in 1869. Electives gave a decisive impulse to curricular expansion and to the influence of professional schools on undergraduate curricula. The elective system reached its peak around 1903; after that, it increasingly appeared to be incompatible with the maintenance of quality in heterogeneous and highly stratified urban environments. See Veysey, *Emergence*, pp. 81–100 and 118–119. See also Brubacher and Rudy, *Higher Education*, pp. 112ff; and Hofstadter and Metzger, *Academic Freedom*, pp. 360 and 397.

74   Quoted by Veysey, *Emergence*, p. 64.

82   For the interplay of these factors and the major types of institutions at the end of the nineteenth century.

83   Hofstadter and Metzger, *Academic Freedom*, p. 454.

84   Their rise was parallel to the decline of clergymen. At 15 private institutions, the proportion of clergymen on the board of trustees declined as follows: 1860–1861, 39.1 percent; 1900–1901, 23 percent; 1930–1931, 7.2 percent. At Harvard, 7 trustees out of 36 were clergymen in 1874–1875, against only one in 1894–1895. Hofstadter and Metzger, *Academic Freedom*, p. 352.

85   Quoted by Veysey, *Emergence*, p. 346.

86   See Hofstadter and Metzger, chap. 9, in particular pp. 454 ff. See also Richard Shryock, "The Academic Profession in the United States," *Bulletin of the American Association of University Professors*, 38 (1952):32–70.

87   For the increase in the numbers of college professors, see Anderson and Davidson, *Trends*, pp. 502–503 and note 55 above.

89   Wiebe, *Search*, p. 121.

90   Joseph Ben-David, *Scientist*, p. 165. See his discussion of the American model of university, pp. 142ff; and Joseph Ben-David and Abraham Zloczower, "Universities and academic systems in modern societies," *European Journal of Sociology*, 1962: 3: 45-84.

91 The percentage of students in the corresponding age groups increased as follows in the United States:

Academic Year	Students as % of 18–21 yrs. old	Students as % of 18–24 yrs. old
1869–70	1.68	1.14
1889–90	3.04	1.78
1909–10	5.12	2.89
1929–30	12.42	7.20
1949–50	29.58	16.50
1959–60	34.86	20.49

From Daniel Bell, *The Coming of Postindustrial Society* (New York: Basic Books, 1973), p. 219.

92 Stinchcombe offers the following definition of cosmopolitanism: "First, cosmopolitans are likely to regard the social world as orderly and predictable, capable of being understood and manipulated. Second, they are likely to collect information about the world outside their interpersonal experience by entering into written communication about it. … Third, we will expect their orientation toward their immediate interpersonal environment … to be affected by their attachments to temporally and spatially distant considerations. … In general, cosmopolitans' actions will be oriented to an orderly system above their personal expertise; they will find out about that order through written communication; and the constraints of action in that order will reduce their responsiveness to concrete interpersonal milieux." Arthur L. Stinchcombe, "Political Socialization in the Latin American Middle Class," *Harvard Educ. Rev.*, 38 (1968), p. 512.

93 The Progressives included over 20 percent newspaper editors and journalists (Norma Wilensky, *Conservatives in the Progressive Era Taft Republic* [University Pr of Florida, 1st ed, 1965], chap 3.) From 1900 to 1929, the circulation of newspapers and periodicals grew considerably: the percentage increase for the aggregate circulation of all newspapers, including those in foreign language, was 184.2 percent for the period; the total circulation of periodiacls grew by 129.0 percent, and the *number* of news and opinion periodials increased by 417.5 percent. See Anderson and Davidson, *Trends*, pp. 523–524.

94 Wiebe, *Search*, p. 113.

95 The intermediate class actually does function as a sociological "relay," and is relatively permeable. Although, actually, upward mobility rates do not differ substantially in most industrialized countries for the movement from "manual into non-manual," the United States has a relatively higher rate of access to elite categories for sons of working-class or "manual" fathers. See S. M. Miller, "Comparative Social Mobility," in *Structured Social Inequality*, Celia S. Heller, ed. (New York: Macmillan, 1969), pp. 325–340.

96 Marie R. Haug and Marvin B. Sussman, "Professionalization and Unionism," in *Professions in Contemporary Society*, Special Issue of *American Behavioral Scientist*, 14 (1971), pp. 525–540. See also the penetrating analysis by Jean-Michel Chapoulie, "Sur l'analyse sociologique des groupes professionnels," *Revue Franç. de Sociol.*, 14 (1973): 86–114.

97 It should be recalled that scientific management, by insisting on the common goal of productivity, instituted an objective that appeared to transcend class conflict. At its 1925 convention, the A. F. of L. endorsed the goal of increased productivity, as the condition for achieving its demands (personal communication by James O'Connor).

98 For an enlightening empirical study of factors affecting the choice between unionism and professionalization among employed engineers and scientists, see Kenneth Prandy, *Professional Employees: a Study of Scientists and Engineers* (London: Faber & Faber, 1965).

99 Richard Sennett and Jonathan Cobb, *The Hidden Injuries of Class* (New York: Vintage, 1973), p. 65, italics mine.

100 Marie R. Haug and Marvin B. Sussman, "Professionalization," p. 527.

101 Marie R. Haug and Marvin B. Sussman, "Professional Autonomy and the Revolt of the Client," *Social Problems*, 17: (1969): 153–161.

CHAPTER 21

The New Working Class

Serge Mallet
Translated by Andrée and Bob Shepherd

The Differentiations Within the Working Class

Whoever wants to elaborate a strategy and a tactic for the working class movement needs to take into account the concrete character, the real face of the social groups which confront each other in the social struggle. Marx elaborated the philosophical concept of the proletariat as the universal agent of history. But in his political works, in those which deal with precise situations, he was always careful to analyse schematically the societies he reduced to the two big classes of *Capital*: he listed seven subclasses in *La Lutte des classes en France* (The Class Struggle in France). F. Engels distinguished eight in *Révolution et contre-révolution en Allemagne* (Revolution and Counter-revolution in Germany).

If all the Marxist theorists have admitted without reserve these distinctions within the bourgeoisie or the peasant world, there has always been a certain embarrassment associated with their positions on the differentiations within the working class. Pierre-Joseph Proudhon talked about 'the working classes',[9] but he included in his analysis groups of semi-craftsmen who maintained ownership of their means of production. Intent on defining the specific role of the working class, the Marxists were often drawn to deduce from the philosophical concept of the proletariat a sociological unit which had never existed in reality. This tendency was particularly affirmed in the development of Leninist ideas and the influence that Russian Marxism had after the October revolution. The Russian working class during the period when Lenin was writing *Le Développement du capitalisme en Russie* (The development of capitalism in Russia)[10] seemed singularly homogeneous in comparison with the diversity which already characterised the western proletariat. It reflected at once the very primitive nature of Russian industrial capitalism and the semifeudal traits of tzarist Russia, where the maintenance of servile institutions in the middle of the nineteenth century, institutions in the heart of which industry itself had been born, had delayed the development of a class of industrial workers who were economically, technologically and sociologically distinct from the servile peasantry.

Original publication details: Mallet, 1975. *The New Working Class*. Reproduced with permission from Spokesman Books, The Russell Foundation.

Growing consciously from the still-developing working-class and taking power in its name, the party quite naturally tended to magnify the concept of working-class, progressively freed from all relationship with the sociological truth of industrial workers. The Stalinist period saw this situation spread to the parties of the western world. In certain countries such as England and Belgium, where the communist party has never taken root in the working class, this assimilation of the party to a mythical working class, the real working class remaining outside the influence of the Communist Party, resulted often in caricature. In fact, the autonomous working class movement developed in those countries without the party taking any part in it. In a country such as France, where the Communist Party had the advantage of a working class audience which it did develop on several occasions, in particular in 1936, the situation was more complex. The reality of its insertion into the working class protected it from the most flagrant excesses of subjectivism. In the practice of class struggles, the French communists have never fallen into the adventurism which the disregard of the concrete conditions of the working class inevitably engenders. But they have always experienced serious difficulties in analysing correctly these conditions and drawing the lessons from them for the elaboration of an offensive strategy.

In the official theory of the French Communist Party, the only concession made to the complexity of the internal structure of the working class has remained the recognition of the existence of a certain 'workers' aristocracy' which, according to Lenin, was considered to be necessarily committed to reformism. This situation was all the more paradoxical because it is in exactly this fringe of the working class that from 1936 onwards most of the working-class communist *cadres* were recruited.

> In the only work that the communist theoreticians have published on social stratification in France (*Les Classes sociales en France*: Social Classes in France[11]), Maurice Mouvier-Ajam and Gilbert Mury (whose personal work is infinitely more subtle than this dogmatic assertion, and who left the French Communist Party in 1966 to join the 'Marxist-Leninist' (Maoist) Party which was in the process of being formed, only to be obliged to resign very quickly in the face of the attacks which were mounted against him) criticised the formula of 'worker's poujadism' used by certain authors—amongst whom myself—to characterise certain forms of the workers' action which resulted in practice in defending the economic position of the most backward of the capitalist groups.

Thus we can observe the clarification of the absolutely original situation of the working class within the capitalist world. Unlike the traditional middle classes, it has nothing to defend which are its chattels, its estate, its property; it does not have the choice between an essentially poujadist action, that is to say the illusory demand for a return to an earlier, better situation, and really revolutionary action, which takes into account the necessities of the future. One single way has opened up before it, the way of progress.

Any Marxist cannot but agree with the general argument used by the authors to define the particular role played by the working class as a whole in the history of society. But one can notice that this argument leads the authors quite simply to conclude that there can be neither error nor deviation in any fraction of the workers' movement during the development of the class struggle. The class struggle continually shows us examples however, of struggles undertaken by social groups for interests which are not directly theirs. One finishes here by concluding that the working class, even a fraction of the working class can, at certain moments and under certain conditions undertake an action which is contrary to their general interests.

For a Marxist Sociology of Work

The dissolution of the social-democratic theoretical tradition which became final after the destruction of the German and Austrian social-democracies by Nazism, the triumph of Stalinist subjectivism in the Soviet Union and in a large section of the western workers' movements, left Marxism disarmed to react to the evolution of industrial society in the west. Just as Marxism had ceased to be used as a means of understanding society, wherever 'it had become the official ideology', so it ceased to be used for the study of the class on which it based its will to liberate.

Marx and Engels had nevertheless always insisted on the fact that 'the essence of the bourgeois mode of production was ceaselessly to renew the instruments of production, thus the conditions of production, thus all social relationships',[12] and that the modifications in the organisation of work, as in those of the technical relations of production, made their repercussions felt on the behaviour and characteristics of the working class itself. Notwithstanding this warning, notwithstanding the fact that Marx had, notably in *Capital,* granted the greatest importance to the structures of the organisation of industrial work, and that he in some way affirmed himself as the 'first sociologist of work', Marxist theory between the wars almost entirely ignored the internal evolution of the world of work.

The texts of Antonio Gramsci, little known at the time, on 'Americanism and Fordism'[13] only serve to confirm by their uniqueness the general neglect. And the ostracism from which the work not only of Georges Friedman, but of a Marxist such as Pierre Naville suffered at the hands of the French labour movement marks an injurious rupture between the sociology of work, and the working class and trade union movements.

If the empirical and positivist conceptions of American origin imposed themselves on Western Europe in spite of the deep theoretical influence of Marxism on the emerging social sciences, then it is to a large extent because of this defect of 'official' Marxism; its incapacity to integrate the mutations in the technical processes of production and the new forms of the organisation of work into the conflicts inherent in the capitalist mode of production.

The positivist conception of the sociology of work, which accords to technology the primacy over the relations of production and dissolves social class into multiple groups with 'differentiated status', between which it swears itself incapable of establishing structural links, thus appeared to many western researchers as the only method capable of understanding 'the facts'.

During a period when profound changes were shaking French society, the reaction of many young sociologists against 'rhetorical sociology' seemed justified. Drawn along by their static methodology, they eliminated from the field of sociology the contradiction and concept of 'possible consciousness' which the statistical interview could never uncover. Real social history brings these concepts into the light in a way that complacent questionnaires could never do.

Alain Touraine, in his now classic work *Sociologie de l'action* (The Sociology of Action), in fact remarked that 'the working class movement demands all the rigour of an historical study of industrial society. Trade union action is a dynamic part of the general process of changing class relations, and consequently contributes to the emergence of a type of society in which in theory the creative consciousness becomes manifest together with its insistence that all social reality should be interpreted as being the product of work.'[14]

This universal historic dimension of the working class movement has been at times, and on the basis of superficial observations, called into question and reduced to the role of the regulating mechanism of a society whose essential structures it accepts. In accordance with these theories, the working class, far from being the 'historic subject of industrial civilisation' to use the expression of Alain Touraine, would in fact abandon the control of its own destiny to a group of technocrats having as much negotiating power as that of the industrial and financial leaders, and presenting almost identical sociological characteristics. This theory of the evolution of the trade union movement into an institution fulfilling a specific function in industrial society and contributing to its capacity to integrate all tensions and contradictions, has clearly dominated American industrial sociology and has become widespread in Europe.

Much the same can be said of these theories as was written of the famous thesis of Selig Perlmann (*A Theory of the Labour Movement*) which largely influenced them. They seemed to be the 'descriptive rationalisation of a trade union model in a particular situation',[15] but 'they proved themselves to be useless for the explanation of variations in the "density" of union action.'

In spite of their wish to escape from the positivism of concrete industrial sociology, the functional theorists explicitly share its essential motivation. Functionalist sociology, although not clearly expressing an apologia of today's dominant system in industrial society, nevertheless shows itself to be a conservative sociology in the stress it puts on factors for 'change' which 'are only considered by it to be deviant.'

One can no more say that functionalist analysis *is* sociology, than one can say that phrenology is psychology.

Social stratification, for Talcott Parsons and his disciples[16] is the sum of all relations between individuals according to the norms of 'efficiency' and of competence, which are those of the American society of his day. In this sense, more faithful to the American 'liberal' mythology than Perlmann, who at least knew the American working class and the social reality with which it was confronted, Parsons and the 'functionalists' who claim to be part of his school, established an absolute relationship between the state of equilibrium provisionally achieved by American organized capitalism and the pressures of individual personality, of which sociability is, and can only be translated as, the adaptation of individual tendencies to the existing structure. This reasoning leads Parsons to reject as part of the same 'deviance' both the pre-capitalist ideologies and also those which call the *status quo* into question in the name of the future of society. The notions of function and dysfunction, which Robert K. Merton[17] admits can explain the adaptive mechanisms of society only in relatively open structures which allow mobility, express as technical facts the naive belief of the greatest American sociologists in the durability of their social system.

We are certainly not concerned to refute systematically the accumulated facts of functionalist methods, but to challenge—and this was Talcott Parson's role in particular—the elevation of a useful research method into a dogmatic science, into an integrating ideological truth.

Herbert Marcuse,[18] like C. W. Mills on this point, described perfectly, in *One Dimensional Man*, the 'shift' by which a methodology which wishes to be essentially empirical becomes transformed into an ideology of acceptance of the given reality. 'Because of its limitation—which lies in the fact that its method refuses to use transitive concepts ... the analysis which describes facts understands them in a limited fashion and becomes an element in the ideology which underlies the facts. This sociology which asserts that it finds its norm in the existing social reality fortifies in individuals this 'faith without faith' in the reality of which they are the victims.'

The contempt for history and for totality, the refusal of the concept of social class as a central concept in the conflicts of social history, in a word the positivism manifested by American sociology, does not derive from the reality of American society as certain people, who wanted to organise the 'peaceful coexistence' of functionalist and pseudo-historical sociology, thought until recently. But the 'reality' that American sociology hoped to be, a sociology of 'wishful thinking', had such success in masking the social reality of the American ruling classes from themselves that functionalist sociology collapsed, together with the American dream, in the explosion of grenades at the Chicago convention and the conflagrations of the black ghettoes.

It is curiously true that in the Soviet Union and the eastern countries functionalism is in the process of conquering incipient sociology, while at Columbia, at Berkeley and elsewhere, the best methodologists are discovering that their 'objective science' could conceal ideology, and assimilate, in the light of their newly-found political experience, the traps of 'false consciousness'.

Does Technological Alienation Exist?

Marx considered the development of the division of labour to be one of the essential characteristics of capitalist production. He condemned the material and moral consequences of the loss of working class professional autonomy in large-scale industry, but he considered that as manual craftsmanship was liberated from the rites and the mysteries by which the 'savoir-faire' of the guilds were transmitted in the Middle Ages, the condition of the working class became more clear. To his mind, the image of the proletarian who 'has nothing to lose but his chains' is tied not simply to the loss of his economic initiative, but also precisely to the loss of this professional autonomy. Marx wrote in *Capital*: 'The veil of professional secrets which hide from man's view the material basis of their life, social production, began to be lifted during the era of manufactures, and was entirely torn apart at the advent of large-scale industry. Its principle, which is to consider each process by itself and to analyse it in its constituent movements, independently of their execution by muscular force or manual aptitude, created the new science of technology...'[19]

Indeed, with the disappearance of professional autonomy, the producer saw himself dispossessed of the only property which the capitalist system had left him, the ownership of his own trade. The disappearance of the old group of workers with many skills will be slow; in the Latin countries in particular the resistance of the old urban structures, already highly developed in the Middle Ages, and the maintenance of the economic and political pre-eminence of the small bourgeoisie, retard the process of concentration. These forces will slow down by several decades the general application of the technological processes already highly developed in the anglo-saxon countries and in the United States. Marx was not wrong in considering that the archaic category of professional workers, despite being involved in the first forms of working class organisation, were not so far removed from the *petit-bourgeois* forms of production. According to Marx it was necessary that the lost links which maintained the individual character of production be shattered, for the working class to constitute itself into an autonomous class.

However the formation of great masses of semi-skilled workers exercising an activity in which creative work is reduced not simply on the economic level to a commodity, but what is more, to an object in the technical process itself, produced other consequences on the evolution of the working class movement which Marx did not at first envisage. Certainly, the brutal initial homogenisation of the working class, the disappearance of professional initiative and the individualisation of work, contributed to a large extent to the formation of a working class consciousness which tended fundamentally to modify the characteristics of the relations of production. But the very resistance of the proletariat, the political and union organisation of the working class and also increased competition, including technological competition, between capitalists, led the system through a whole series of arrangements which avoided this 'accumulation of misery at one pole' which the author of *Capital* foresaw. Today the most dogmatic of the working class theoreticians are more or less agreed that there is not, in advanced capitalist countries, the absolute pauperisation of the working class. Wanting at all costs to prevent the working class asking itself questions concerning the organisation of the whole of society's productive processes, capitalism has more or less consciously turned workers' demands from the productive sphere towards the private sphere, towards the world of consumption. At the same time as the generalisation of the mechanisms of the division of labour which separated the producer from his production, there was also created the separation between the man at work and the family man. One must recognise that there is a close dialectical connection between the organisation of work, based on the loss of workers' initiative, and the tendency of the big unions in the West to lose interest in the organisation of the system of production itself, and to satisfy themselves with winning wage increases usable only in the sphere of consumption. During the era of the mechanisation of work the worker does not simply cease to feel himself to be an individual producer as Marx foresaw. He ends by no longer feeling himself to be a producer at all. There is a tendency to abandon demands based on the nature and content of production, and to be content with demands in the sphere of consumption, which is itself determined and oriented by the capitalist mode of production. This is not unconnected with the development of reformist tendencies in the whole of the western working class movement, whether the predominant influence is that of social-democratic or communist organisations. In fact, from this point of view, the practice of social conflict during the second quarter of the twentieth century was broadly the same in England and in France. This has been 'the struggle for bread-and-butter', the struggle for greater powers of consumption, integrated into the framework of needs created by capitalist industry itself. Together with the reduction of political action to parliamentarist and electoralist practice, it was as widespread across the channel as in France. Certainly, in the organisations claiming allegiance to Lenin, the reference to total revolution has never ceased to be maintained. 'One day there will be bread and roses for all'. But this reference tended to be more and more formal. It would be dangerous to consider that the development of dogmatism and opportunism within the western working class is simply due to the bureaucratic practices of this or that leadership, the sad heritage of 'the social-democratic betrayal', or 'the negative consequences of a personality cult'. In fact, the bureaucratisation of the working class movement in the West was the consequence and not the cause of the structure of the working class, itself determined by the technical organisation of capitalist production. It is remarkable that Marxist authors never related the phenomena of economic concentration and bureaucratisation specific to capitalism, to the technical organisation of labour. In 1923 Lenin, for example, considered that the Soviet Union had everything to gain from introducing the Taylor system into its industries. He saw the future of industry in the creation of large industrial units organised on the production-line method, and believed it possible to reconcile this dehumanising method of production with the fulfilment of socialist man. In fact, it seemed to him that from the moment the ownership of the means of production had been returned to the producers, the organisational aspect of labour could remain what it had been in the most advanced capitalist organisations. Certainly Lenin was at that moment preoccupied with the problem of the creation of large-scale industry in the Soviet Union, the material basis of socialism, and it was legitimate that he should look at the most profitable modes of production, which could release Russian capitalism from its proverbial unproductiveness and archaic routines. But it is not without interest to note that it was almost at the same moment, in the countries which were the most advanced in terms of the generalisation of the mechanisation of work, that sociologists and psychologists were demonstrating the frailty, even from the point of view of capitalist profitability, of Taylor's and Henry Ford's conceptions. The celebrated Hawthorne experiment, directed by Elton Mayo, and later the experiments in group dynamics, demonstrated that production workers deprived of creative initiative tended to produce less than the worker to whom this initiative had been restored. Certainly, and it is curious that few Marxists have been tempted to reflect on this contradiction, the warnings of American industrial sociologists have not fundamentally modified the organisation of the technical relations of production in large-scale American industry. For nearly forty years, all the large American businesses have maintained permanent research teams of sociologists and psychologists, whose work they have completely ignored, apart from making certain innovations of detail about which a lot of fuss has been made, but which do not differ fundamentally from the procedures used in modern agriculture to increase the milk yield of cows or the laying of eggs.

One may wonder in view of this whether the resistance of the controllers of capitalism to the restitution of workers' initiatives, whether strictly in the technical organisation of production, or at the expense of productivity, is not due to a confused understanding that the mechanisation and division of labour are in fact the best system for preventing the development of open resistance to the system of capitalist production. In a word, capitalism, in order to safeguard the famous power of decision of the *entrepreneurs*, needs a system of production in which the producer is reduced to the state of an object, and it will maintain this system even if, from the point of view of productivity, it seems today not to be the best.

Is the New Working Class Revolutionary?

Organisational capitalism has achieved the maximum degree of that fundamental contradiction which Marx had analysed: the contradiction between the ever-increasing socialisation of productive forces and the private nature of the ownership of the means of production and exchange. In this sense, the recourse of organisational capitalism to socialist techniques seems less like a reinforcement of its internal structures as the result of the compromise which it is obliged to make because of the need to develop productive forces. The balance of organisational capitalism can thus not be guaranteed except to the extent that it manages to win the assistance of the classes which contribute to production. In a word, the objective contradictions of the structure are such that they render much more dangerous than in the past the existence of oppositional forces contesting the nature of the relations of production.

It is, as we know, on an analogous appreciation that Herbert Marcuse based his analysis of the 'One Dimensional Man'. But as to the objective need felt by capitalism, he concluded that 'the political imprisonment' is achieved here and now by the brilliant but rather summary formula he used during a debate with André Gorz and myself at the University of Mexico in 1966; 'the cop is nowadays in the very head of the worker-consumer.'

Quoting in *One Dimensional Man* the investigation on Caltex reproduced in this volume[20] he came to the conclusion, the opposite of my own, that 'in the new technological world, of work, the negative attitude of the working class becomes weaker.'

In the same way his pessimism leads him to accept as an obvious truth that 'the fact that human effort is less and less used in the productive processes indicates that the political force of the opposition declines. Given the increasing proportion of white-collar workers, then if there was a political radicalisation it is in the groups of white-collar workers that an independent political consciousness would appear, which is a very unlikely development'.[21]

In the light of the insults which have been thrown at him by the most responsible leaders of all the communist parties, it is curious that the pessimism of Marcuse is matched on this point by the leaders of the Communist Party. For if they obviously refuse, and violently, the Marcusian idea according to which the working class could no longer be the bearer of the revolutionary ideal, a simple study of the texts would prove that it is simply because Marcuse and the communists do not refer to the same historical period. Marcuse, like all men blessed with common sense, admits, working from the reality of America, that there has been a qualitative decline in the importance of the traditional proletariat, and thus bases himself above all on the new groups of workers, white-collars amongst others, to express his radical pessimism. The communist leaders continue, and will continue no doubt for a long time, to take account only of the traditional groups of the working class which they further tend to define according to the very unmarxist criteria used by the I.N.S.E.E. (The National Institute of Statistics and Economic Studies). They neglect the fact that the same socio-professional categories have widely-varying significance according to the degree of sophistication of each particular industry. But as far as the 'new social groups' are concerned, in the manufacturing and service industries, their distrust is at least equal to that of Marcuse. Certainly, after having denied for a long time the existence of these new groups within the working class or having excluded them from the ranks of the traditional working class 'aristocracy', the communist leaders of Western Europe eventually conceded the possibility of giving these groups a certain role to play in the working class movement. However, the latest articles on this question in the sphere of so-called 'orthodox Marxism' show that it persists in refusing to consider them as completely developed and integrated within the working class. 'One can argue forever about the problems of these famous "new social groups": whatever their intrinsic importance, these problems could never form the backbone of socialist policy. So as not to go too far off track, let us bring to the fore what is the essence of the discussion: the struggle between the owners of the means of production and the production workers, the wage-earners who own nothing but their working capacity.'[22] In this text, the last before his death, Maurice Thorez arbitrarily assimilated the new working class into a 'new middle class strata' which, he correctly observed, display some elements related to the process of production, thus objectively linking them to the fate of the working class, and also parasitic elements, objectively linking them to the exploiting classes. But one is inclined to ask oneself why he reintroduces into the discussion the fundamentally anti-scientific notion of 'middle class' that Marxism has always challenged. In reality, the reticence manifested over the new groups within the working class—technicians, research workers and qualified workers of automated concerns—only reflects the incapacity of traditional workers' organisations to adapt their action to the new forms of capitalist organisation and to elaborate an offensive strategy for the transition to socialism in the economically-developed countries.

Is the new working class revolutionary? If one means by this question a revolutionary consciousness in the traditional sense of the term, finding its expression in the determination firstly to seize political power by any means and at any price, and only then to go on to the next phase of organising society in a new way, then the working class is without question not revolutionary. It is not revolutionary because it imposes two conditions preliminary to the transformation of existing structures. The first is that the transformation of the economic, social and political structures cannot be had at the price of the destruction of the existing means of production, or even of its serious weakening—'the machine is too valuable to smash'. Secondly, it has taken note of the negative consequences of the achievement of political power which is *not* immediately accompanied by the transformation of the structures of the social hierarchy. Furthermore, it does not consider itself capable of conquering here and now the elements needed for the realisation of these new social relations. It therefore has a tendency to place before the cry 'we must take power' the question 'What shall we do with it?'

But if one understands by 'revolutionary' the wish to modify the existing social relations fundamentally, then the objective conditions within which the new working class acts and works makes it the perfect avant-garde of the revolutionary socialist movement. In fact, the more important research, invention and quality control become, the more human work becomes concentrated in the preparation and the organisation of production, the more the sense of initiative and responsibility increase; to put it briefly, the more the modern worker reconquers *on the collective level* the professional autonomy which he had lost during the period of the mechanisation of work, and the more will demands for control develop. Today's conditions of production offer objective possibilities for the development of generalised self-management of production and the economy by those who carry the weight. But these possibilities are confronted simultaneously by the capitalist structures of the relations of production, its criteria of profitability based on the short-term profit of the owners, and the technocratic structure of the firms which seem more to inhibit the harmonious development of their own productive possibilities. The recent social conflicts, which have developed during the last few years in the West, and the strike of May 1968 which crowned this series of movements, have shown that the advanced sectors of the working class are no longer content to make wage demands. Instead they challenged the techno-bureaucratic centres which direct the economy, to such an extent that they no longer seemed to be justified by developing technical and economic needs. On the contrary they appeared to be a survival from the past, protecting the privileged status of the existing hierarchies.

The evolution of the trade union movement in Western Europe reflects the new characteristics of this growing consciousness: just about everywhere it is the evolution of industrial sectors where the new working class predominates which tends to shift union organisations which have until now been characterised by purely reformist actions, towards a fundamental questioning of the system of capitalist production. This is true of technical and chemical unions, and new unions of industrial draughtsmen, the evolution of which pushed the British trade union movement to the left. The same is true of the German chemical and car unions, and the Belgian gas, electricity, chemical and petrochemical unions. Finally in France the unions most affected by this development are the federations of chemical industries, technicians, oil, and steel. These were all purely reformist organisations just as the C.F.D.T.† once was, and most of F.O.† still is.

Precisely because it is placed in the centre of the most complex mechanisms of organisational capitalism, the new working class is brought to realise more quickly than the other sectors the contradictions inherent in the system. Precisely because its elementary demands are largely satisfied, the new working class is led to ask itself other questions whose solutions cannot be found in the sphere of consumption. Its objective situation places it in the position of seeing the deficiencies in modern capitalist organisation, and to arrive at a consciousness of a new way of organising productive relationships, as the only way of satisfying the human needs which cannot be expressed within the present structures. Its action tends to be fundamentally challenging not simply of capitalism but, what is more, of all technocratic ways of controlling the economy. It is the hierarchical status of industry which is called into question each time there is a demand for some sort of control. It is true that so far, such demands have not been coordinated, and do not constitute a general plan of action which could modify the balance of political forces within western society. But this situation is more particularly due to the incapacity of the organised trade unions to formulate an offensive strategy based on systematically putting forward structural reforms of an anti-capitalist nature, rather than the temptation of the new working class to let itself be 'integrated' into the neo-capitalist system. In fact this temptation, if it existed, would not have resisted the deepening contradictions of neo-capitalism itself. It is in the immediate interests of the modern working class that technical development continues, together with its consequences; substantial reduction in working hours, job revaluation, mobility, and more varied activities within the productive sphere.

Capitalism on the contrary has a tendency to slow the development of productive forces when their principal result has been consistently to reduce the rate of profit, and when it includes more and more economic instruments of a socialist nature, the effects of which capitalism cannot be sure of controlling. One of the problems which has to be faced in the elaboration of an offensive strategy of the most advanced section of the working class based on objective possibilities for action, obviously lies in the difficulty of coordinating struggles in this sector with those in other, more traditional sectors. Even though the new working class sees its numbers increase every year, and its place in the productive process gives it a logistic power much stronger than is measured simply by its numerical strength, it still only constitutes a minority of the working class and *a fortiori* of the whole of the working classes. However, the different sectors of society are not isolated by the great wall of China! Just as the most advanced form of capitalist industry has a tendency to influence the most retarded forms, so the behavior of the new working class influences the other sectors. The demands for control of the organisation of production, for the guarantee of security of employment, against bureaucratic methods of running the economy, have now become generalised in the same way as they emerged in the advanced sectors of industry.

May 1968 moreover, gave a first reply to this question. By drawing into the united movement, despite misgivings and resistance, at least nine or ten million workers, the advanced sectors of manufacturing and servicing industries showed that it was possible, at least in terms of action, to get the working masses in the traditional industries to go beyond the narrowly defensive and corporatist vision of their own interests which they hold. Undoubtedly, the inhibiting elements inherited from the old working class consciousness, an amalgam of resignation to industrial capitalism and a religious attachment to a 'revolutionary' party which refuses revolution on the grounds that to do so would be to make an absolute value of despair, once again largely held sway in 1968, although only by the force of attrition.

The problem is that at the moment the *avant-garde* of the workers' movement do not yet control their own ideology. They are pulled in one direction by the fervour of the students, whose actions they understood, but not the language. (The action was real, whereas the language was loaded down with all the old skins abandoned by the workers' movement during its successive moults, from Bakunin to Trotsky.) The corporatist demagogy of the traditional workers' movement pulls in another direction. Thus the *avant-garde* had, day after day, to invent its own forms of action, its own demands, even its own language. This was without doubt a factor which reduced the effectiveness of their struggle, above all when repression ceased to be exercised and ceased at the same time to be the simplified focal point which united heterogeneous forces. But 'it's only a beginning'. The historical problem posed brutally in May by the young workers and students, by the sectors which were the most associated with new economic and technical developments, will be more and more clearly defined. The students, these producers-to-be, will soon learn that it is because science today is a factor of production that they will have to conquer the technocratic university and put it to the service of society—and thus of themselves.

It is not on the basis of this diffuse awareness of the role that science and the university play that the young technicians and workers have reacted to students' movements. Living permanently within the process of modern production, they live without being conscious of the prodigious anticipation of Marx, who traced, in one of his most striking expressions, the fundamental contradiction between the mode of production brought into being by large-scale industry and the system of production which it persist in maintaining.

'With this upheaval [automation, which he described a century before, and as well as, Mr. Diebold] it is neither the time spent working, nor the immediate work achieved by man, which seem to be the principal foundation of the production of wealth; it is the appropriation of his productive force in general, his understanding of nature and his capacity for dominating it, seeing that he is part of a social structure; in a word the development of the social individual represents the essential basis of production and wealth.

The theft from another person of the time spent at work on which present wealth is based, seems a miserable basis when compared to the new one, created and developed by large-scale industry itself.'[23]

The technicians and workers of the advanced industries will cease to regard the students, those 'sons of the bourgeois' condemned to the modern forms of proletarianisation as foreign. And the latter will stop repeating the satisfied and grossly paternalistic phrase 'we do not want to be your future exploiters'. As if the semi-skilled workers-to-be of scientific research, the economist-clerks of the computers and the sociologist-note-takers of 5-minute interviews were to exploit anything but their own moral and material misery! The student-worker alliance will not be established, as Marcuse thinks—or I should say thought before 1968—between the proletariat of *Germinal* and the students of 1848, but rather between the different professional groups in modern production work, the producers of sciences and techniques more than products, who will build the true industrial society, purged of its capitalist and technocratic archaisms.

10 February 1969.

Notes

9 *De la capacité politique des classes ouvrières* (Of the Political Capacities of the Working Classes) Posthumous works, Paris (1865).

10 Foreign language edition, Moscow (1963).

11 Editions Sociales, Paris (1964), p. 99.

12 *Manifest Communiste*. Editions Costes, Paris (1934), p. 60.

13 Gramsci: Complete Works. Editions Einaudi, Turin (1952) Book One, pp. 311–342: *Notes sur Machiavel, la politique et l'Etat moderne* (Notes on Machiavelli, politics and the modern state) (written in prison in 1929).

14 *The Sociology of Action*. Editions du Seuil (1966), p. 345.

15 L. M. Tremblay. *The Theory of S. Perlmann*. University of Laval-Quebec (1965), p. 45.

16 *The Social System*. New York (1951).

17 *Eléments de théorie et de méthode sociologique*. (Elements of Sociological Theory and Method) Editions Plon, Paris (1965).

18 Herbert Marcuse, *One-Dimensional Man; Studies In The Ideology Of Industrial Society* (Boston, Ma: Beacon Press, 1964), p. 144.

19 *Capital*. Book One, Chapter XV T. II, p. 164. E.S., Paris (1949).

20 H. Marcuse: *op. cit.*, pp. 56–57.

21 *Ibid*. p. 63.

22 Maurice Thorez: *Notion de classe et rôle historique de la classe ouvrière* (The Idea of Class, and the Historical Role of the Working Class), a paper presented at the week of Marxist thought on 13:03: 1963.

23 Marx: *Fondements de la critique de l'économie politique* (The Gundrisse …) Editions Anthropos, Paris (1968) T.11, pp. 220–222.

CHAPTER 22

How the University Works
Higher Education and the Low-Wage Nation

Marc Bousquet

The Rhetoric of "Job Market" and the Reality
of the Academic Labor System

The overall balance between supply and demand in academic labor markets will shift markedly, we believe, over the next few decades. The most dramatic changes will occur in the 1997–2002 period, when we project a *substantial* excess demand for faculty in the arts and sciences. If present trends persist, we would expect that there would be roughly four candidates for every five positions—a condition that could continue in subsequent years unless significant adjustments occur or policy changes occur. Although we project no comparable imbalance during the 1987–1992 period, we do expect some appreciable tightening of the academic labor markets to begin as early as 1992–1997.

—William G. Bowen and Julie Ann Sosa,
Prospects for Faculty, 1989 (emphasis in the original)

One way of describing the recent movement of thought about the academic labor system is as a series of waves. A "first wave" of labor consciousness emerged before 1970, propelling the self-organization of the academic workforce, especially in public institutions, where more than half the faculty are unionized. This labor awareness was contested by the administratively oriented second wave (of which Bowen's job-market study is emblematic), generally informed by a neoliberal ideology that idealizes market epistemology and naturalizes market relationships. Sweeping to dominance about 1980, this wave has the virtue of focusing on the connection of graduate education to the larger system of academic work (which the unions have been slow to do). In characterizing that connection primarily as a market relationship, administrative knowledge has been strongly contested by a third wave of knowledge produced by what is in North America a fifty-campus movement of graduate-employee unionists, or GEU (Coalition of Graduate Employee Unions). While far from dominant, the knowledge of the GEU

Original publication details: Marc Bousquet, *How the University Works*, pp. 186–209. New York University Press, 2008. Reproduced with permission from New York University Press.

movement is sharply ascendant in recent years, to the point where one *Chronicle of Higher Education* article on the graduate-employee coalition dubbed 2001 the year of the graduate student employee (Smallwood).

The rhetorical richness of this market language has had a profound effect on how we think about graduate education. In particular, the rhetoric elaborating the market-crisis point of view sustains a general consensus that the system of graduate education is producing more degree holders than necessary and that this "overproduction" can be controlled "from the supply side" by reducing admissions to graduate programs.

This common sense is deeply flawed, to the point where I think we have to acknowledge that "market knowledge" is a rhetoric of the labor system and not a description of it. Because the incoming flow of graduate students is generally tightly controlled to produce "just enough" labor, graduate departments really can't reduce admissions without making other arrangements for the work that the graduate students would have done. Since the restoration of tenure-stream lines is rarely a department-level prerogative, a department with the power to reduce graduate-student admissions will generally be driven to substitute other casual appointments (postdocs, term lectureships, single-course piece workers). In terms of casualization, there is clearly no net improvement from this "supply-side" fix. Indeed, these other modes of casualized work are filled by persons who are themselves enmeshed in the system of graduate study. The system will continue to require "just enough" of these other term workers, all of whom will have had some experience of graduate education.

This supply-side fantasy supports the most pernicious armchair activism of them all, persistently circulating the notion that graduate faculty can balance "the market" from the conference table at which they discuss the dossiers of applicants to their programs. On the one hand, of course, it is reasonable to imagine that reversing thirty years of casualization (i.e., by recovering jobs) will result in a reduced need for graduate students to do flexible labor. This could eventually reduce the graduate student population. On the other hand, however, it simply does not follow that reducing the graduate student population will alter the labor system. (This is like arguing that blowing smoke up a tailpipe makes a car run backward.) To a certain extent, the fantasy of supply-side control reflects the depoliticization and privatization of the professoriate: the desire to "be ethical" without having to enact a politics, to solve the problem with better management rather than struggle in solidarity with other persons who work.

Ultimately, the notion that the employment system can be controlled by the administration of graduate programs (i.e., by reducing Ph.D. "production") has to be seen as profoundly ideological. Even where there is a vigorous effort to diagnose the nature of the labor system, the ideology of the market returns to frame the solution, blocking the transformative potential of analysis that otherwise demonstrates the necessity of nonmarket responses. Encapsulating his own arguments on "Literary Study in the Transnational University," J. Hillis Miller enumerates "worldwide changes" that frame the material base of casualization, including the end of the cold war, the globalization of economies and media, and the conversion of the research university to a technological service mission, as well as the "concrete, material changes" of corporatization: defunding, growing class size, threats to tenure, the conversion to part-time faculty, underemployment of degree holders, and the commercialization of knowledge.

Miller sees—he *knows*—that the problem is casualization, that graduate students and former grad students are flex labor, and that there are always "just enough" of them. And yet he retreats from the standpoint of globalization studies to speak in the folksy tones of the foreman at the plant when framing his solution: Well, I guess we better hold up the line and slow the production, boys; "demand" for our "product" is down. There is a steep-walled canyon between the analysis and the action plan that is not specific to Miller but, instead, is nearly uniform across the profession, which is reluctant to see the political nature of the struggle with casualization.[3] Insofar as the Fordist ideology of production and the neoliberal ideology of "markets in balance" provide false solutions to the post-Fordist academic economy, they help that post-Fordism along.

The Fordism of the discourse surrounding graduate education is a nearly unchanged survival of the dominant interpretive frame established between 1968 and 1970, when a freight train of scholarship decrying a cold-war "shortage" of degree holders suddenly reversed itself in attempting to account for a Vietnam-era "surplus." In what follows, I focus primarily on the development over time of the state-of-the-profession discourse of one organization, the Modern Language Association. MLA-centered communication does not fully encompass the discourse even of its "own" discipline, but there is remarkably little difference in the analytical frames employed by the various fields of study across disciplines: most appear to employ the market heuristic.[4] (If anything, the "hard sciences" appear more addicted to the ideological introjection of market values, perhaps because they are often less inclined to address casualization as a structural issue.) In addition, the MLA discourse appears to have influenced other humanities scholarship on employment issues and has been widely acknowledged by the mainstream press as authoritative on these questions. Featuring labor-intensive classes that often serve as university-wide requirements (writing, second-language acquisition, introductory cultural surveys), language departments have long been at the leading edge of casualization, together with mathematics and other humanities disciplines that provide general education. It is probably as a result of this early and extended experience of casualization that language and cultural-studies faculty are among the most visible authorities on the question. (Or, perhaps it is only because so many journalists have studied in English departments.) While there is unevenness in academic casualization, there are systematic consistencies across disciplines as well: in science and engineering, casual postdoctoral employment can last ten years before a full-time appointment is secured (Regets). In any event, the MLA discourse does appear to fairly emblematize the general state of disciplinary discourse on higher ed workplace issues.

Even at the time, this Fordist language was not adequate to the task of describing the structural transformation of the university, which was already beginning to disarticulate from the nation-state and retool itself into the transnational bureaucratic corporation described by Bill Readings. (Continuing the process observed by Clyde Barrow of the university's adopting a "corporate ideal" in the first decades of the twentieth century.) But Fordism provided an exceptionally powerful set of heuristics, values, and legitimations for the cold war expansion of what the era's ideologues were proud to call the "knowledge industry." Many more "plants" were built, a lot more doctoral product was moved, and "knowledge production" was enormously enlarged.

In other words, as long as demand for the doctoral product remained apparently limitless, Fordism was good knowledge, or at least it made sense. But between 1968 and 1970, the good knowledge of the cold war rapidly became the bad knowledge of retrenchment and casualization.

Initially, the term "job market" described an annual face-to-face event at the MLA convention, and not an ongoing systemic reality (as in "the market is really bad this year"). Inaugurated in 1955, the "Job Mart" (formally named the "Faculty Exchange") represented a modernization and rationalization of the hiring process that up to then had been conducted by the old-boy network. This was a two-room system. In one room, the association collected the dossiers of all job seekers for department chairs to peruse. In another room, job seekers waited for messages from chairpersons requesting interviews. This Job Mart operated a great deal like a face-to-face labor market in which persons certified to do higher education faculty work actually gathered in a room (somewhere between a marketplace and a shape-up hall) to "sell their labor." The system was not replaced until after 1969, when it "broke down" because the problem "was now one of locating jobs rather than candidates." At this point, the association dismantled the Job Mart and initiated the Job Information Service, which ceased to collect candidate dossiers and began to publish job listings (Association of Departments of English, i-ii).

To this moment, the 1971 inauguration of the Job Information Service, we can trace the first stroke of what I think we can accurately call the informationalization of the MLA. The job market was no longer the humble "mart," an event arranged by the association. Instead, it had become an external system or force that the association was obliged to provide information about: "The one thing needful—the one thing the profession has never had but which MLA is uniquely qualified to provide—is complete and detailed information on the job market at regular intervals throughout the year" (association officer William Schaefer, quoted in Association of Departments of English, ii). Not incidental to the emergence of this new "informational" mission is the pressure exerted by members of the association affiliated with the antiwar and other social movements for the association to figure as an instrument of social agency (which had resulted in, among other things, a successful effort by Paul Lauter and others to elect Louis Kampf to the presidency of the association in 1968).[5] Implicit in the informational mission was the disavowal of responsibility for making things happen; instead, the task is to describe, forecast, and advise—ideally, in exchange for a fee.

A key component of the informationalization process was the literalization of the market analogy, so that the market became something that needed to be reported on continuously (at "regular intervals throughout the year") and that such reporting could be construed as a useful contribution. At the 1969 meeting, the MLA voted to create a job Market Study Commission, charged primarily with two responsibilities: "(1) examining the procedures of the Association as they have historically affected the market" and "(2) studying the operation of the market itself within the larger economic context" (Orr, 1185). The framing of these tasks clearly identifies "the market" as something external to the profession (and its association), something with an internal essence ("the market itself") unfolding in continuous and uniform time, embedded in an impersonal "larger economic context." No longer merely an analogy, the concept of job market now has empirical reality for humanities faculty and evidently borrows some of the aura and aspirations—the realpolitik and econometrics—of labor-market analysis, such as the 1969 Cartter study, "Academic Labor Market Projections and the Draft," designed to assure the wartime Congress that it could expect a comfortable "oversupply" of higher education faculty despite the prospect of expanded compulsory military service. The 1970 Orr report, "The Job Market in English and Foreign Languages," crystallized the terms of analysis that would be applied to what was then called retrenchment and which we now understand as casualization: the one-year drop in job availability was "but the first massive indication that supply and demand in these fields are seriously out of balance" (Orr, 1186). By 1971, a major "labor market" study in the sciences was in print, followed by Cartter's 1976 book. The notions of "Ph.D. oversupply," the fantasy of supply-side control, and the application of a "labor market" heuristic to professional work appeared to be instrsically related. While the market analogy made the most sense from the perspective of the "buyer" in a "buyer's market"—that is, from the perspective of employers, such as industry, the state, and professional academic management—it made less sense from the point of view of the professional worker, who traditionally seeks collegial participation in determining the size, compensation, and composition of the workforce, including control of the terms under which apprentice professionals can be expected to serve. Rather than leave these considerations to a "market," professionals have tended to exert influence on at least a national scale by way of professional associations (which explains in part the degree to which many faculty seek the leadership of organizations like the MLA in these matters, perhaps even more than their union locals). In this context, the adoption by various disciplinary associations of the new "informational" mission needs to be seen as intrinsic to a neoliberal transformation, specifically underwriting knowledge of "the market" *against* the labor knowledge of structure and labor's consciousness of itself as a collective agent in the workplace and in the arenas of law, politics, and "the economy."

The Orr report, for instance, cites "a number of economic and cultural trends [that] are finally reaching a dangerous convergence" (1185); "pressures upon us ...national if not global in scope," the "limit to what the public will pay for [our] product," (1186), and so forth. The past thirty years of official "analysis" from disciplinary associations and foundations has for the most part simply replayed these chords—of trends, pressures, limits, and forces—all evidently transpiring in a field of titans, beyond the possibility of faculty contestation. The field of titans point of view leads to the dissemination of discursive constructions like the "lifeboat" analogy that is frequent in autobiographical and historiographic narratives of the profession. In lifeboat narratives, the era of "well-paid and secure" academic jobs figures as a historical accident (a peculiarity, brought about as a by-product of military-industrial expansion, or an unexpected historical gift dropped in the lap of a single cohort of the professoriate). From this perspective, succeeding generations are represented as, more naturally, drowning in the tide of history. Of course, the young "very much want, often desperately, to be let in, to climb aboard" (Tave, 7), but who can stem the tide?

The ideological content of the Orr report and its successors is exactly its tendency to represent limits and forces as beyond contestation. But in foreclosing the possibility of action at the level of structure, the market analogy also offers new fantasies of action, especially in relation to the concept of supply. One of the key contributions of the market heuristic to the Orr report and its successors is the problematization of the concept of supply, as in the now-familiar formulation that graduate programs are "turning out too many Ph.D.'s and M.A.'s for the market," that there is a state of "Ph.D. overproduction," leading to a Ph.D. "oversupply" (1190). For Orr, the problematizing of the concept of supply is a real intellectual convenience, because it both (a) offers the fantasy of doing something to "the market" (i.e., balancing it) by "controlling" or "regulating" supply (1186, 1191), and (b) diverts attention from the real problems of "demand" (i.e., the willingness of administrations to use nondegreed flexible labor instead of degreed persons in jobs). Orr and his successors need "the market" to legitimate the fantasy of a supply-side fix, a fantasy that averts the consciousness of political struggle that would quickly transpire if the concept of "demand" were problematized.

Job-Market Theory as Second-Wave Knowledge

One might expect that from the perspective of forty years we would have a clearer view of casualization—that our understanding has gotten better and better, and that we are smarter than a naïve earlier generation. Unfortunately, this does not appear to be the case. Orr's 1970 report, while it does enthusiastically embrace the market heuristic and the new fantasy of supply-side influence, also provides a trenchant description of managerialism and casualization. Orr is perfectly aware that increased education work does not translate directly into increased professorial jobs, because "American society" is willing to accept colleges "staffed largely by persons trained differently from traditional professors" (1188). He is equally aware that the university has "welcomed new Ph.D. candidates with eagerness," not only to meet the "national emergency" of the cold war, "but also for another reason." This other reason? It doesn't seem to make any difference to them

> whether most freshmen and many sophomore courses in many areas, particularly English and foreign languages, are taught by experienced Ph.D.'s, by new M.A.'s, or by those even less qualified. Since B.A. graduate students or M.A.'s working toward the Ph.D. can be had at a lower cost per class than established professors, administrations have not overlooked the opportunity that presented itself.... Somewhat the same forces operated ... in the many institutions which suddenly began to offer the M.A. (1:1:90)

None of Orr's numerous suggestions for professional action actually address this process of substituting student labor for teacher labor, blaming impersonal "economic factors" and "certain forces" that "have caused" universities "to rely more heavily than before on Ph.D. candidates" to teach lower-division classes (1191), nor does he seem to care about lower-division teaching ("perhaps it really doesn't matter," he says). Nonetheless, he is very much aware of the extent and urgency of the casualization process, observing that an unnamed midwestern school, completely without doctoral instruction in 1955, by 1970 employed five graduate student teachers for each full-time teacher. He goes on to observe, complete with exclamation point, that at one "established school," the ratio of graduate employees to full-time faculty was 30 to 1. However appealing it found the market heuristic, Orr's report took it for granted that "the market" was merely one of many lenses for approaching graduate education.

Throughout the 1970s, there is a first wave of knowledge about the profession, supported in large part by active faculty unionism and movement politics, that struggled with the new ideological formation of the job market. In 1971, the young activist elected to the presidency of the MLA, Louis Kampf, elaborated the collective understanding that "unionization is a necessity" in his presidential address to the annual convention:

> We are workers under industrial capitalism. If we understand that, we can understand our alienation, our sense of powerlessness. For teaching, we collect wages: that is our basic connection to educational institutions, not the claims of humanist rhetoric. We are, in short, an intellectual proletariat. Consciousness of this condition can lead to self-hatred or cynical careerism. It can also lead to our uniting around the oppression we share with other alienated workers, the better to rid ourselves of the oppressors.
>
> ("'It's Alright,'" 383)

It is hard to see that any subsequent awareness has improved upon Kampf's formulation, and insofar as the structures of feeling dominating the academy from the 1970s forward can be described as "self-hatred or cynical careerism," it has been a temptation for too many to see this unionist, intellectual workerism informed by commitments to a broad movement politics as the "lost cause" of the 1960s. In fact, graduate-employee unionism retained much of the movement commitments aired by Kampf. In contrast, although faculty unionism has rarely reached out to movements beyond the campus (or even to other workers on campus, including adjuncts and graduate employees), there was nonetheless a widespread labor consciousness. High points in this first-wave discourse include, especially, articles in 1974 and 1978 by Paul Lauter and others in *Radical Teacher* and *Universitas,* the journal of the SUNY union, later republished as "Retrenchment: What the Managers Are Doing" and "A Scandalous Misuse of Faculty: Adjuncts" (Lauter, *Canons and Contexts,* 175–197, 198–209). At this stage, buoyed by a militant labor movement on the national scene, even the discourse of department chairs was frequently pro-union: Marilyn Williamson's 1973 piece is fairly typical in arguing that "the union agreement holds many advantages," even for department administrators, and observing tartly that "to me as a chairman, the word 'flexibility' has come to have one meaning: the ability to reduce my staff or my funds" (3–4). During the early 1970s, at least one anti-union article in the MLA newsletter for department chairs represented itself as an "alternative perspective" in the context of the general enthusiasm for collective bargaining (Alderman).

So, before 1975, it was common even for department chairs to recognize that the Fordist "production" analogy and neoliberal market analogies were "absurd" or "crude" and to insist that "concretely we are dealing with live human beings" (Adams, 7). In 1979, Paul Hunter understood that the replacement of full-time lines by graduate student labor constituted a virtual war on young people: "There is no youth in our profession any more," he wrote; "we face an immediate prospect of being in a profession that gets older every year, that fails to admit the young to its permanent numbers at all, that systematically excludes beginners from its ranks despite taunting them in graduate schools that foster both dreams and expectations" (7). He goes on:

> Once the MLA encompassed a variety of languages in its meeting halls. Now there are only two: the language spoken by the tenured and secure, a language of rationalized compla-cency; and the language of the unemployed, the underemployed, the temporarily employed, the part-time, the untenured, the uncertain, the paranoid, the disillusioned—a language of desperation, fury, and despair. It would be easy to be sentimental about their plight, but it would be trivial to treat the issue sentimentally and thus make it easy to comfort ourselves by the usual cynical reply, "But at least they are young, and their options are still open." (8)

Hunter has no quick solutions to offer, but his piece is in part an attempt to revive a generational frame of analysis, one that is inevitably significant for understanding how the transformation of higher education represents an increased exploitation of the young (which helps to explain why it is commonly students who are the most visible opponents of the corporate university).

By 1980, there was a fully developed second wave of response to casualization, one that no longer knew any exterior to market ideology. Second-wave knowledge takes "the market" as empirical reality and as the practical horizon of study: the question is no longer to understand or alter the structural forces shaping demand for degreed labor but simply to project and accommodate that demand. The practical consequence of second-wave thought was to generally contain and silence the interventionist labor knowledge of the 1970s and, more specifically, to enrobe the processes of casualization with an aura of market rationality and natural inevitability. Throughout the 1980s, the question of degree-holder "supply" remained highly problematized, with the primary discursive effect of rendering the structural transformation of "demand" relatively unproblematic. By naturalizing the notion of tidal or cyclic "fluctuations in demand," second-wave knowledge throughout the 1980s repeatedly concealed wholesale casualization beneath a circular and self-authenticating market rhetoric: because the system is a market, it naturally fluctuates; because the system fluctuates, it must be a market.

In this period, the annual publication by the MLA of charts showing hills and valleys in the number of jobs available from year to year bolstered this new common sense. The charts suggested that there was a kind of "business cycle" to academic job opportunities, from which tidal and cyclic rhythm would inevitably proceed both good times and bad. Accompanying staff essays explained how "outside economic forces" buoyed the occasional bull years and artifically extended the natural bearish periods. The profession was meant to understand that, although it was frequently a source of disappointment, "the market" operated according to perfectly understandable and rational principles. This new epistemology radically transformed disciplinary communication in the early part of the decade: whereas the 1981 official "working paper" on employment issues reiterated the 1970s call for "collective activism" in order to protect the workplace circumstances of young people, J. Hillis Miller in 1986 was able to brush aside the concerns of youth with the forecast of a better future, claiming that "demographic and actuarial changes [would] mean many new positions" in the mid 1990s (281). (Even at the time, it cannot have been clear that the appearance of jobs ten years in the future would address the circumstances of a typical forty-year-old degree holder visiting the convention as a jobseeker for the fifth year in a row.) What is important about this informatic futurology, however, is the exclusion during the early 1980s of structural knowledge from the professional discourse. Informationalization doesn't unfold only by installing the flexible work regime; it sustains the flex system continuously by interfering with the consciousness of flex workers. While the evidence and labor knowledge of casualization occasionally intruded on the flow of disciplinary information (e.g., Lauter, "Society and the Profession"), these emergent alarms were quickly muffled and explained away by the dominant heuristic of market.

The 1989 Bowen report is in many respects the fullest development of this mode of thinking, and one that appears to vigorously impose the ideology of "market" on data that virtually trumpets the structural reality of casualization. Subtitled "A Study of Factors Affecting Demand and Supply, 1987 to 2012," the Bowen project elaborates its view of the "roller-coaster pattern" of the business cycle in academic jobs in the first lines of its introduction: "periods of rapid expansion and retrenchment" after 1945, "swings that have been sharp and sometimes destabilizing" (3). (The cyclic long view over forty-five years is meant to lend credence to the report's projections of a quarter-century into the future.) Offering what it describes as a "highly quantitative analysis" aimed to enable university administrations to assure themselves of a smooth flow of "outstanding faculty," the project views its task as best accomplished by understanding the cycle of academic business: "We hope to provide a clearer sense of whether the 'boom' and 'bust' pattern of faculty staffing is likely to repeat itself and an improved understanding of how to avoid such disruptive and inefficient cycles" (4). While Bowen goes to a great deal of trouble to distinguish between "projections" and "predictions" (predictions describe what will happen; projections describe what will happen if specific assumptions are met), this distinction only highlights the counterfactual nature of the Bowen assumptions. It is only by actively excluding the evidence of structural transformation (the replacement of tenured faculty with managed labor, expanding reliance on graduate employees and other nondegreed teachers) that Bowen is able to impose this Platonic vision of the business cycle on the data, leading him to project that fantastic "massive upsurge" in "demand for faculty."

The most dramatic stroke in this regard was Bowen's decision, as he put it, "to define 'faculty' quite carefully." The universe of Bowen faculty included only the ladder ranks and full-time instructors, virtually excluding part-timers and faculty without the doctoral degree. The blundering represented by this decision is obvious in hindsight, though it's not been commented upon. Most observers have been content to accept Bowen's explanation that he couldn't have "predicted" what he called "massive cutbacks" in the 1990s (Magner, "Job Market Blues") —as if retrenchment and casualization were a phenomenon of that decade and not well established twenty years earlier. As previously noted, there was already a well-developed understanding of the exploitation of part-timers and graduate students, and plenty of hard quantitative data, too: the 1988 National Study of the Postsecondary Faculty counted hundreds of thousands of part-time faculty, a massive segment of the workforce that represents the near doubling of the ratio of part-time to full-time faculty in less than two decades, from about 20 percent in 1970 to nearly 40 percent in 1987. The fact that Lynne Cheney—of all people— was essentially alone in attempting to debunk the Bowen projections shows the staying power of the positivist market fantasy even in the most well meaning and politically committed quarters of the academy.

Bowen's error is in his attempt to understand the employment system *as* a system while excluding the largest categories of its working parts.

Equally problematic are Bowen's suppositions regarding institutional decision-making. Despite enormous evidence to the contrary, Bowen starts his calculation with the assumption that retiring and other departing faculty will be replaced by degree holders "on a one-for-one basis" (25). Indeed, the reality for many departments since 1968 has been very different from Bowen's assumption. Even in those circumstances where the raw number of full-time faculty remains stable, there has commonly been a substantial increase in the number of students; in other circumstances, the one-to-one replacement of full-time faculty has meant the substitution of non-tenure-track instructors for professorial labor. Overall, for most of the past thirty-five years, many departments have slowly given up professorial lines or else counted themselves lucky when they were able to hire one to one, despite a radically increased workload.

Bowen goes on to estimate various scenarios leading to a "net new-position demand," based on the even more ahistorical assumption that "institutions always *want* to have more faculty and will add faculty positions *when they can afford to do* so" (153). The emphasis is Bowen's and probably reflects his moral certitude. Doubtless Bowen is right that institutions should "want to have more faculty," but was there any basis in fact for this claim? The evidence clearly shows that the sort of "faculty" that institutions have been "adding" has consistently been term workers and graduate students. While there may well be occasional instances where administrations have chosen to increase the professorial faculty at the expense of other funding priorities (buildings and sports facilities, information technology, etc.), these cases would run against the general trend of administrative decision-making, and it seems that the most successful pressure to increase tenure-track hiring has come from academic unions. Bowen's ideas about what "institutions want" reflect the collegial common sense of Dink Stover at Yale ("Gosh, fellas, if the old u. could afford it, they'd keep you on for sure!"), but it's not clear that they bear any documented relation to the reality they purport to describe. Faced with the evidence of casualization advancing unevenly in the disciplines (i.e., a greater aging of tenurable faculty in the humanities), Bowen reads this datum exactly against the trajectory of its meaning (i.e, that full-time positions for humanities teachers have been more quickly converted to part-time slots, and therefore there will be fewer full-time positions to fill). Bowen instead manages to read this data as evidence that there will be *more* full-time hiring in the humanities— essentially saying that the slowed entry of young people into the ladder ranks "means" that there will soon be more young people in the ladder ranks (which is the same as saying that "because people have been eating less red meat lately, they'll soon need to eat more red meat"). The closer one looks at Bowen's study, one has to feel that Bowen sees more or less what he wants to see. Where nearly every other observer saw steadily growing reliance on part-time faculty —the ratio near doubling in twenty years—Bowen claims to see "no evidence of a significant trend in the part-time ratio" and, quite eccentrically, assumes "no change" in that ratio while projecting the "demand" for tenurable faculty over a quarter century (77 n.8).

One further example. With a similar commonsensicality, Bowen suggests that talent-rich doctoral "labor markets" lead to a more accomplished faculty, asserting that institutions are able "to raise hiring standards when there is a plentiful supply of talented young faculty." If Bowen had looked more carefully, he might have seen what the 1992 NSOPF study was able to conclusively demonstrate: despite the "oversupply" of degree holders, "new entrants" to the ranks of full-time faculty after 1985 were markedly less (not more!) likely to hold the Ph.D. than previous cohorts. Analysis of the "new entrants" data was completed some time after Bowen's study, but it's particularly helpful because it confounds cherished assumptions about the nature of the employment system. Startlingly, the group of junior faculty hired between 1985 and 1992 were almost 30 percent more likely to claim the B.A. or M.A. as their highest degree than were faculty hired any time earlier. This means that, under conditions of Ph.D. "oversupply," roughly 40 percent of the "new entrants" do not hold the doctorate. (By contrast, about 70 percent of the senior group of faculty, including many persons hired under the 1960s expansion cohort, hold the doctorate.) This pattern is consistent across institution type: research universities and other doctorate-granting institutions, as well as comprehensive and private liberal arts institutions, all show a substantial slide in the percentage of junior faculty holding the doctorate. The increase in nondoctoral faculty is stratified by discipline rather than by institution type: humanities and the fine arts show the most dramatic decline in doctorally degreed junior faculty, with a mere 55 percent of junior faculty in the humanities holding the Ph.D. (by contrast, 73 percent of senior faculty in the same fields hold the Ph.D.). But all program areas showed a substantial slide, with the exception of natural sciences, which showed a slight increase in doctorates among the new entrants (National Center for Education Statistics, "New Entrants," table 4.1).

Under the current system of academic work, the university clearly does not prefer the best or most experienced teachers; it prefers the cheapest teachers. Increasingly, that means the creation of nontenurable full-time instructorships and other casual appointments, a casualization that has unfolded unevenly by discipline and is especially pronounced in English and writing instruction. In this instance, Bowen has again simply applied the dominant logic and assumed that, even within the context of a general assault on the tenure system, "of course" the managers would hire the best "doctoral product" available. From the posture of common sense, it seems reasonable to assume—as many people have—that the replacement of tenured positions with "full-time" term contract positions means that persons holding doctorates will be awarded those jobs. The fashionable notion that we have an "oversupply" of degree holders sustains this assumption: many graduate faculty imagine that their students who don't get tenurable work will be leading contenders for contract positions, in which, it is further assumed, they will pursue the scholarship, teaching, and service that they would have done in a tenurable position, albeit on a more sped-up basis, less well paid, and without the protections of tenure. While it is true that numerous degree holders seek and would gladly accept these positions, the facts are quite clear: holders of doctorates have not enjoyed a preferential status for those jobs. Non-tenure-track positions have been awarded to persons without the doctorate in numbers large enough to substantially reduce the overall percentage of Ph.D. holders in the full-time workforce.

Taken as a whole, including trends in the use of graduate employees, part-time lecturers, and the number of non-Ph.D.'s hired into full-time instructor positions, the academic labor system increasingly prefers teachers *without* the Ph.D.—even when, as in the languages, desperate and deeply indebted holders of the Ph.D. are willing to work without tenure and for salaries below $30,000. Bernard Berelson's 1960 study of graduate education was able to demonstrate, by survey of department chairs, an empirical preference for the doctoral degree holder as an undergraduate teacher (52–53). By contrast, thirty years later, Bowen can only offer an impressionistic assumption that the same holds true. (If he'd surveyed the literature, he would have found that academic management was busy developing a large discourse advertising the "quality of instruction'" delivered with ever-fewer numbers of degreed faculty.) And in the circulation of this "bad information" through Bowen, despite what are certainly Bowen's individual good intentions and earnest scholarship, we begin to understand the real nature of an informationalized higher education: not the classic liberal and enlightenment fantasy of information that "wants to be free" for everyone, but the power of capital and the corporate university to make neoliberal ideology count as reality. When we think about it, of course, the information university doesn't "want" doctoral degree holders as faculty: as a general rule, the holders of doctoral degrees are disinclined to view students as information deficits or themselves as information-delivery devices. In believing that "education," "knowing," "research," and "study" are embodied human practices, dialectical or dialogic and not reducible to information transfer, the typical doctoral degree holder represents an obstacle to the fantasy of dollars for credits driving the managerial revolution toward a fully informationalized higher ed.

Through the 1980s and early 1990s, second-wave fantasies of the "job market," such as Bowen's, were all but unchallenged as they proceeded to do the corporate university the enormous service of covering up the processes of corporatization, managerialism, and casualization. It is important to understand that this supply-side second-wave knowledge does the same disservice even when it projects the opposite of Bowen's conclusions, as when the 1995 Massy-Goldman paper found "oversupply" and "overproduction" in the fields of science and engineering. (Though it is instructive to see the corporate university's swift response to small errors in that paper: the methodology of Massy and Goldman's study or "simulation" was carefully and promptly critiqued by staff employees at the Council of Graduate Schools [Syverson], in stark contrast to the uncritical celebration surrounding Bowen's projections.)

In acknowledging that Bowen's projections were flawed, the managers of university business have carefully conserved the neoliberal assumptions that created his projections in the first place, leaving their own agenda not only undisturbed but actually advanced, having given the clear impression that this "market" was volatile ("markets" always are) and difficult to predict, even by venerable experts, leading to an even larger interest in expert information. Through this period and to the present, the notion of a job market continues to provide the dominant narrative of academic work in the liberal and corporate media. Newspaper and Internet headlines scream the intelligible tale of second-wave knowledge: "Study Says U.S. Universities Produce Too Many Doctorates" (Magner); "A Surplus of Scholars Fight for Jobs in Academia" (Hodges); "Tenure Gridlock: When Professors Choose Not to Retire" (Wyatt); "Slaves to Science: For Post-docs, Finding a Supernova Is Easier Than Finding a Job" (Weed); "Oh, the Humanities! Pros Use Prose in Job-Hunting: Post-Tweed Breed of Professor Knows Marketing" (Argetsinger). At the present time, in the full ripening and apogee of second-wave knowledge, the system of graduate education is no longer understood as being "like" a market; it is generally understood, simply and self-evidently, that graduate education *is* a market.

By 1997, the dominance of market ideology had fully bloomed into a resplendently laissez-faire structure of feeling. In November of that year, Jules Lapidus, then president of the Council of Graduate Schools, took to the pages of the *Chronicle of Higher Education* to endorse a strong, free-market theory of graduate education, bolstered by a vigorously neoliberal ideology of the graduate student as consumer. Conceding that pursuing the Ph.D. is a "risky business" for many students, Lapidus agreed that it had "always" been so and vigorously opposed any regulation of the system: "The idea of developing some method to relate enrollments in graduate programs to projections of supply and demand in the job market runs counter to the American value of free choice." Concluding that "students have to decide for themselves if they believe that doctoral education is a good investment of their funds and their time," Lapidus seemed to feel that the ideology of choice ends the matter: "As far as I know, no one is being forced to study for the Ph.D."

The market epistemology is perhaps most distressing when it is adopted by those who are hurt most by it: graduate employees, term faculty, and junior members of the professoriate. As a historian in his early thirties and unable to find a permanent job despite having published three monographs, Robert E. Wright argued in his April 2002 *Chronicle* editorial, "A Market Solution to the Oversupply of Historians," that "the solution is clear. The salaries for new assistant professors [then about $40,000] should be lowered until the number of qualified job applicants…and the number of job openings become more equal." Being of a literary bent, and reading quickly, naturally I sought in Wright's proposal some satirical intent. I even heard an echo of "A Modest Proposal" in "A Market Solution." But on careful reading, Wright turns out to be in deadly earnest. An economic historian with a book published by Cambridge University Press, Wright sincerely means to propose that academic employers get together to fix the woes of the "market," not by intervening rationally (say, by restricting the use of graduate student labor and regulating the overuse of term faculty) but, rather, by further degrading the conditions of academic work. On the one hand, of course, the absurdities of what Wright calls his "market-oriented approach" are obvious: his plan would simply sort not for the best faculty but for the faculty that can afford to teach for smaller wages (by virtue of moonlighting, a pension, or other source of independent income); nor does it acknowledge the empirical, historical fact that the wage savings of the university's vast expansion of term labor have not so far been dedicated to creating new professorial jobs. What guarantee does he have that the university would dedicate these new wage savings to a larger pool of tenure-track faculty? And if we could find a mechanism to enforce such a guarantee, why not develop that enforcement mechanism without lowering wages in the first place?

Perhaps we should acknowledge the degree to which Wright's "proposal" simply realizes the absurd assumptions driving our own ideas about "the market" and academic work, especially our understandable but exaggerated sense of helplessness before its demands. What if, instead of constantly adjusting ourselves (and our compensation) to "meet the needs of the market," we started to adjust or regulate the "market" to meet *our* needs? This would mean, as a matter of course, that faculty would have to take more control of their workplaces and, rather than lowering faculty wages to the level of graduate employees and adjunct instructors (as Wright distressingly proposes), raise the wages of graduate employees and adjunct instructors to the level of the faculty (or even higher, in order to eliminate the motivation for replacing faculty workers with discounted labor). There is nothing utopian about this proposal: as true apprentice teacher-scholars and not cheap labor, most observers will agree that graduate employees should (a) teach no more than one course a year and (b) receive a living wage, currently in many major education centers ranging from $18,000 to $24,000.

One can easily argue that it should be more expensive to have a graduate program than not to have a graduate program (as it is in some of the less-exploitive circumstances at present and in many cases in the past). One might argue, likewise, that it should be more expensive to use flex labor than to use faculty labor (in the same way that it is more expensive to buy groceries at the convenience store). The base calculations for the salary of a part-time lecturer could begin at around $7,000 per class (one-eighth of a 4/4 load, with a starting salary near $50,000), and end up—after calculating fair health coverage, a retirement contribution, other benefits, a premium for "convenience," and a multiplier for years of experience—in the range of $9,000 to $11,000 per class, possibly quite a bit more for the term worker with many years of service.

Of course, at reasonable wages, the university has little motivation to admit "too many" graduate employees or rely unduly on term faculty. All of these calculations are perfectly rational—they can even be represented, if one wishes, as a "correction to the market" (à la Wright's pro-market plan to lower wages)—and have the advantage of being ethical. Furthermore, all of the problems of "the market" would vanish when fair wages were instituted across job descriptions. At the moment when everyone doing teacher work nonprofessorially is paid fairly, and far more expensively than heretofore, the assistant professor will become the cheapest labor available (relative to the fair wages of graduate employees and term faculty), and "demand" for assistant professors will cease to be a problem. Not coincidentally, in an environment of reasonable wages for everyone, Bowen's projections would in all likelihood have been more or less accurate.

At the forefront of this nonmarket or market-regulation approach to the "job crisis" are the union movements of graduate employees and adjunct academic labor. It is commonly remarked by members of the faculty that organized term faculty "are organizing themselves out of a job," as if by eliminating the university's motivation to hire them on exploitive terms, there will suddenly be no work for them. The same sentiments are commonly expressed in other workplaces, as in the railroads and in steel plants when white workers derided the efforts of African American workers to organize. It is, after all, the work of the proletariat to abolish itself. In actual fact, of course, the work of the academy will remain to be done: students will still need to taught, advised, and inspired. (Furthermore, in practical terms, since the turnover rate even of full-time term faculty is 30 percent a year, it is hard to imagine the need to "fire adjuncts" in order to create professorial jobs faster than the already existing attrition.) Even if it were true on some abstract or collective level that graduate employees and the former graduate employees working on a term basis were indeed organizing themselves out of a job, it is only to organize themselves collectively into better ones.

Certainly, not all graduate employees and term workers reject the "market-oriented" approach to their present and future work prospects. The *Chronicle of Higher Education* has been able to report on small groups of graduate employees who oppose unionization. Unionization votes by graduate employees have failed in a small minority of cases. And both graduate employees and term workers inevitably feel the pressure of having to "sell themselves" in a cruel, irrational, and exploitive workplace so that for many it feels, just as the *Washington Post* contends, that "job-hunting" in some sense equals "marketing." But an estimated 20 percent of graduate employees in the United States are now covered by union contracts (a figure that Gordon Lafer considers "comparable to the most highly organized states in the country and 50 percent above the national norm"). And there appear to be more contracts on the way. It is at least possible that soon enough the majority feeling among graduate employees (who eventually become all of the labor in the system, term faculty and tenure stream alike) will become the concerted will to make the "market" responsive to their needs, and not the other way around.

Notes

3   Reminding us that "markets" are social formations, Evan Watkins calls academic-disciplinary responses of which Miller's is typical, "an interesting notion of 'ethical'" that "folds neatly" into marketization processes more generally: "Thus 'economic realities' don't intrude from the outside to set a limit on how many Ph.D.'s we should 'ethically' produce; economic practices are part of the training from the beginning" (164).

4   For example, see the mathematician Geoff Davis, whose model and recommendations are widely quoted by university administrations (University of Washington, for example). Claiming that the "history of mathematics Ph.D. production" is one of "perpetual instability" and "continual alternation" between shortage and surplus, Davis models a "10-year boom-bust cycle" in the job market. The positive "knowledge" represented by this model leads Davis to claim that "there are straightforward ways to remedy the situation," primarily better modeling and the "rationalizing" of "Ph.D. production."

5   Richard Ohmann discusses these events in chapter 2 of *English in America*, "MLA: Professors of Literature in a Group" (27–50). See also Kampf, "It's Alright, Ma" and interviews with Lauter and Kampf by student activists (Pannapacker and Parascondola, 1998), together with Kampf's letter of resignation from the Job Market Study Commission, appended to the Orr report (1198).

Works Cited

Adams, Richard P. "Nobody Wins the Numbers Game." *ADE (Association of Departments of English) Bulletin* 43 (1974): 6–8.

Alderman, Taylor. "Collective Bargaining: Another Viewpoint." *ADE (Association of Departments of English) Bulletin* 42 (September 1974): 34–36.

Argetsinger, Amy. "Oh, the Humanities! Pros Use Prose in Job-Hunting: Post-Tweed Breed of Professor Knows Marketing." *Washington Post*, December 30, 2000, C1.

Barrow, Clyde W. *Universities and the Capitalist State: Corporate Liberalism and the Reconstruction of American Higher Education, 1894–1928.* Madison: University of Wisconsin Press, 1990.

Berelson, Bernard. *Graduate Education in the United States.* New York: McGraw-Hill, 1960.

Bowen, William G., and Julie Ann Sosa. *Prospects for the Faculty in the Arts and Sciences: A Study of Factors Affecting Demand and Supply, 1987 to 2012.* Princeton, N.J.: Princeton University Press, 1989.

Cartter, Allan M. *Ph.D.'s and the Academic Labor Market.* New York: McGraw-Hill, 1976.

Cartter, Allan M., and R. L. Farrell. "Academic Labor Market Projections and the Draft." In *The Economics and Financing of Higher Education in the United States.* Washington, D.C.: Joint Economic Committee of the Congress, 1969, 357–374.

Cheney, Lynne V. "The Phantom Ph.D. Gap." *New York Times,* September 28, 1989, A27.

Davis, Geoff. "Employment Picture for New Ph.D.s: Rationalizing Ph.D. Production." *Science's Next Wave* (American Association for the Advancement of Science). March 7, 1997. Available at: www.nextwave.sciencemag.org/cgi/content/full/1998/03/29/73.

Hodges, Jane. "A Surplus of Scholars Fight for Jobs in Academia." *New York Times,* January 16, 2000, sec. 3, p. 15.

Hunter, J. Paul. "Facing the Eighties." *ADE (Association of Departments of English) Bulletin* 62 (September/November 1979): 1–9.

Kampf, Louis. "'It's Alright, Ma (I'm Only Bleeding)': Literature and Language in the Academy." MLA Presidential Address: Chicago, December 27, 1971. *PMLA* 87.3 (May 1972): 377–383.

——. "I Want to Resign." Letter dated July 6, 1970. Reprinted in David Orr, "The Job Market in English and Foreign Languages." *PMLA* 85.5 (October 1970): 1198.

Lafer, Gordon. "Graduate Student Unions Fight the Corporate University." *Dissent.* Fall 2001. Available at: www.dissentmagazine.org/archive/fao1/lafer.shtml.

Lapidus, Jules. "Why Pursuing a Ph.D. Is a Risky Business." *Chronicle of Higher Education,* November 14, 1997, A60.

Lauter, Paul. *Canons and Contexts.* New York: Oxford University Press, 1991.

——. "Content, Culture, Character." *Works and Days* 21.1–2 (2003): 51–56.

——. "Society and the Profession, 1958–1983." *PMLA* 99.3 (May 1984): 414–426.

Magner, Denise. "Job Market Blues: Instead of the Anticipated Demand, New Ph.D.'s Are Finding Few Openings." *Chronicle of Higher Education,* April 27, 1994, A17.

——. "Study Says U.S. Universities Produce Too Many Doctorates." *Chronicle of Higher Education,* June 30, 1995, A16.

Massy, William, and Charles Goldman. *The Production and Utilization of Science and Engineering Doctorates in the U.S.* Palo Alto, Calif.: Stanford, 1995.

Miller, J. Hillis. "Reply." In *Profession 1997.* New York: Modern Language Association, 1997, 233–235.

——. "The Triumph of Theory, the Resistance to Reading, and the Question of the Material Base." MLA Presidential Address 1986. *PMLA* 102.3 (May 1987): 281–291.

Modern Language Association. *Final Report of the MLA Committee on Professional Employment.* December 1997.

——. "Working Paper of the Commission on the Future of the Profession, May 1981." *PMLA* 96.4 (September 1981): 525–540.

National Center for Education Statistics, U.S. Department of Education. "The Condition of Education 2000." Summary document of various NCES publications, html version. 2000. Available at: www.NCES.ed.gov.

——. "New Entrants to the Full-Time Faculty of Higher Education Institutions." Analysis of NSOPF-93 and NSOPF-88. NCES Publication 98–252. 1998. Available at: www.NCES.ed.gov.

Ohmann, Richard. *English in America: A Radical View of the Profession.* New York: Oxford University Press, 1976.

Orr, David. "The Job Market in English and Foreign Languages." *PMLA* 85.5 (October 1970): 1185–1198.

Parascondola, Leo. "Interview with Paul Lauter." *Workplace* 1.2, December 1998. Available at: www.cust.ubc.ca/workplace/workplace2/lauter.html (accessed January 15, 2001).

Readings, Bill. *The University in Ruins.* Cambridge: Harvard University Press, 1996.

Regets, Mark. "Employment Picture for Ph.D.s: 1995 NSF Data on Labor-Market Conditions for New Ph.D. Recipients." *Science's Next Wave* (American Association for the Advancement of Science). March 7, 1997. Available at: nextwave.sciencemag.org/cgi/content/full/1998/03/29/76.

Smallwood, Scott. "Success and New Hurdles for T.A. Unions." *Chronicle of Higher Education*, July 6, 2001, A10.

Syverson, Peter D. *When Simulation Becomes Reality: Press Reaction to Massy/Goldman Study Creates Erroneous Message*. Council of Graduate Schools Research Center, 1997. Available at: www.cgsnet. org/vcr/cctr508.htm.

Tave, Stuart. "The Guilt of the Professor." *ADE (Association of Departments of English) Bulletin* 59 (1978): 6–12.

University of Washington Graduate School. "Ph.D. Career Paths." May 1998. Available at: www.grad. washington.edu/stats/phd_survey/phd_survey.htm.

Watkins, Evan. "The Educational Politics of Human Resources: Humanities Teachers as Resource Managers." *minnesota review* 45/46 (Fall 1995/Spring 1996): 147–166.

Weed, William Speed. "Slaves to Science: For Post-docs, Finding a Supernova Is Easier Than Finding a Job." *Salon.com*. February 28, 2000. Available at: www.salon.com/books/it/2000/02/28/postdoc/index.html (accessed March 10, 2001).

Williamson, Marilyn L. "An English Chairman Looks at Unionization." *ADE (Association of Departments of English) Bulletin* 39 (December 1973): 3–6.

Wright, Robert E. "A Market Solution to the Oversupply of Historians," Editorial. *Chronicle of Higher Education*, April 12 2002, B20.

Wyatt, Edward. "Tenure Gridlock: When Professors Choose Not to Retire." *New York Times*, February 16, 2000, sec. 3, p. 15.

CHAPTER 23

The Mental Labor Problem

Andrew Ross

In the winter months of 1998–99, Local 802 of the American Federation of Musicians (AFM) succeeded in organizing, and securing a contract for, the part-time Jazz Program faculty in the Mannes College of Music at the New School University. Among the seventy adjunct teachers represented by the union were some venerable musicians from the world of jazz, including Chico Hamilton, leader of the famous quintet, and seasoned virtuosos, like Benny Powell and Jimmy Owens, who have played with the Count Basie and Duke Ellington orchestras.[1] Hired from year to year, often for chronically low compensation, and without any benefits or pension plan, these faculty looked to the oldest of the craft unions in the arts (founded in 1896) to muster support from community leaders and elected public officials and to win recognition from their employer through the National Labor Relations Board (NLRB). The day the musicians' contract was signed, the New School also offered pensions and benefits to three thousand other nonunion adjunct faculty. While this offer was clearly aimed at forestalling any further unionization, it also exemplified the old labor maxim that "justice for one is justice for all."

This campaign, named Justice for Jazz Artists (with its echo of the Service Employees International Union's legendary Justice for Janitors campaign of the early 1990s), may have been a microscopic landmark on the busy landscape of academic labor, but its significance radiates in many directions. In the AFM's first bid to represent musicians as teachers, the local ran what its chief organizer described to me as a "real, large-scale corporate campaign" by using the arena of public opinion. His comment conveyed pride in the newfound strength of the organizing department, which was only three years old and therefore dated from the 1996 election of the Sweeney-Trumka-Chavez-Thompson directorate of the American Federation of Labor and Congress of Industrial Organizations (AFL-CIO). In the course of the campaign, organizers appealed to the public perception that jazz greats had been denied their due desserts, historically and to this day.

Among all arts workers, jazz musicians arguably have the most visible profile as artists whose work has been most lionized by all classes of audience, and whose personal compensation has been most blatantly discounted. Indeed, the contract helped to remedy the local's own long neglect of jazz musicians in New York City. The New School's own

Original publication details: Andrew Ross, "The Mental Labor Problem", from *Social Text*, 63, Vol 18, No 2, Summer 2000. Duke University Press, 2000. Reproduced with permission from Duke University Press.

credibility, as an institution with a progressive pedigree, most recently soiled by head-line-making student protests over the paltry minority representation on its faculty, was put to the test by this bargaining unit of primarily African American musicians. The seasoned profile of these working teachers also refuted the more typical image of underpaid adjunct faculty as fresh-faced Ph.D.'s facing the first, albeit prolonged, obstacles to their professional ambitions for secure employment. Most striking of all, the campaign yoked together artists and academics in ways that gave rise to some friction over whether a musicians or a teachers union ought to be representing the adjuncts.

While sectors of the performing arts have been unionized for several decades, and faculty sectors of the academy since the 1960s, both professions have been resistant, historically, to industrial-style organization, retaining a craft culture of flexible bargaining, each in its own distinctive ways. However disparate their solo career traditions, the artisan-jazzman here shares the same position and predicament as the professional academic whose labor has been degraded and deprofessionalized in recent years. What are the economic circumstances that have accelerated this degradation? As this essay seeks to argue, artistic and academic traditions extol sacrificial concepts of mental or cultural labor that are increasingly vital to newly important sectors of the knowledge industries. No longer on the margins of society, in Bohemia or the Ivory Tower, they are providing a rationale for the latest model of labor exploitation in core sectors of the new industrial order, and pioneering the workplace of tomorrow.

The Cost of Idle Curiosity

The original founders of the New School in 1919, among whom were Progressive titans like Charles Beard, Herbert Croly, Wesley Clair Mitchell, James Harvey Robinson, Thorstein Veblen, and John Dewey…certainly supported the extension of education to trade union members, and indeed, the new institution was associated with the Workers Education Bureau of America. But the prospect of industrial-scale union organization among faculty would have been as distasteful to these scholars as the growth, now all but entrenched, of an expansive administrative bureaucracy with the managerial clout to dictate every root and branch of academic policy. They conceived the New School in large part because the wartime policies adopted by their own university administrators had demanded a fealty to college and state that offended their fierce devotion to intellectual independence. Indeed, the Columbia University administration went so far as to reorganize its departments into military corps (the Medical Corps, the Legal Corps, the Language Corps, the Economic and Social Service Corps, etc.), and dismissed two faculty for their "antiwar" sentiments, prompting Beard, and later Robinson, to resign in a blaze of publicity.[2] Launched as a clear alternative to the elite condominium of service to God, country, and capital, the fledgling New School (disastrously, as it happens) would have no president, trustees, or bureaucratic cohort to constrain the free exercise of the intellect.

The most meticulous rendition of the scholarly ideal of self-governance appears in Veblen's own "memorandum on the conduct of universities by businessmen," *The Higher Learning in America*. In this 1919 volume, the Progressive aversion to corporate trusts and capitalist waste merges with the customary repugnance of the scholar-gentleman for a narrowly vocational approach to learning and for the utilitarian application of knowledge for financial gain.

The university ideal, according to Veblen, should be the pursuit of "Idle Curiosity," and any treatment of knowledge as a "merchantable commodity" is a desecration of an exalted calling.[4] Neither is Veblen's university a fit environment for training students to pursue legal or business careers. Above all, Veblen's book spotlights his withering opposition to the penetration of academe by the techniques of business salesmanship and advertising—all too familiar today as the corporatization of higher education in an advanced stage, with its sharp market orientation and its managerial premium on cost-effective delivery of risk-free educational product. By way of compensation, his passion for Idle Curiosity is the direct scholarly equivalent of "art for art's sake," so quarantined from the world of "wont and use" as to render its devotees ineffectual as economic or social actors outside of their professional sphere. It is a cult whose devotions still flourish today, but it is increasingly attended only by the securely tenured or tenurable, who are, even as we speak, about to become a minority in their workplaces. In its heyday, this cult was most assiduously observed in colleges patterned after the model of elite East Coast institutions living off their legacy of pre-Jacksonian colonial hierarchies. Western universities, church-affiliated and other special-interest colleges, and land-grant institutions were more inclined to honor a community service ethos that ran counter to the self-marginalizing spirit of Idle Curiosity.

Unlike fellow Progressives (the influential engineer Morris Cooke unflinchingly recommended tenure abolition and academic Taylorism in his 1910 report, *Academic and Industrial Efficiency*[5]), Veblen railed against the advent of cost-effectiveness in his dreamy precincts of academe *at the same time* as he called for more efficiency in industry. In the world of factories, he argued, it is the financial captains and the Vested Interests who are wasteful and who sabotage the potential of productive manufacturing. But industrial democracy, in the shape of labor power-sharing, is not the answer for Veblen. The caste of practical intellectuals that he lionizes—the engineers—promises to deliver a more rational system of production, pre-empting, among other things, the need for industrial workers to organize their interests against the wasteful exploitation of labor for profit.[6] The scholar holds a similar position within the academy. Like the engineer, the scholar would be loyal to science and not beholden to business interests, and if only the customs of Idle Curiosity were properly observed, the management model of productivity quotas, so redolent of industry, could be kept safely at bay. If Veblen's faith in the pure and generous spirit of the scholar was anachronistic even in his day, and at odds with the Midwestern traditions of his own educational background, it would not become an actual *liability* to the material well-being of the academic workforce until much later in the century. In our day, the legacy of this "impecunious" credo has not only failed miserably to stave off the worst incursions of corporate mentality. Through its informal neglect of money matters, this ideal may also have actively contributed to the proletarianization of large sectors of Veblen's profession, a sizeable percentage of whom now earn compensation at or near the poverty line.

A Great Divide

Before I expand on this claim, let us consider the lot of musicians in the year when Veblen's book was published, for it is the common conditions of academic and artistic labor that I am pursuing here. By the end of World War I, the AFM had already accomplished a great deal. The union had set the first wage scales for orchestras traveling with grand operas, comic operas, musical comedies, and similar attractions. It had lobbied for congressional reform of copyright law and, in its first wave of protectionist ardor, for curtailing the unregulated admission to the United States of foreign musicians working for lower wages. Its members had been hard hit by the wartime Cabaret Tax and then by Prohibition, but a much bigger threat lay in the application of recording technology on an industrial scale, which was rapidly changing how music was produced, heard, and sold. Radio broadcasting of musical performances had already reduced the number of job opportunities for live performers, and, very soon, the canned music of talking pictures put thousands of movie theater accompanists out of work. The forward march of cultural industrialization had begun, and the musicians, actors, singers, dancers and others who had crisscrossed the postbellum landscape in hundreds of small performing companies now faced an uncertain future in the age of Vitaphone and Movietone. Traditional commercial forms of theater, vaudeville, and the circus would take a beating, and their larger, and hence lucrative, audiences would be poached away by the millions.

Jobs for artists of all categories did not decline, however, at least not until the meltdown of the Great Depression. Nonetheless, the conditions of artistic expression would be decisively altered by industrialization in the 1910s and 1920s. Practitioners of the high culture genres, cut off from a popular consumer base and catering more and more to an educated and well-heeled cognoscenti, would eventually drift into the quarantine zone of the nonprofit sector. There, a full-blown cult of artistic license would flourish, sponsored, in the postwar years, by a Cold War policy establishment that lavishly promoted the superior civic liberties of the West. The nonprofit enclave proved an ideal hothouse for the psychopathology of the late Romantic artist, living hand to mouth and visibly chafing at the comforts, however scant and short-lived, provided by a medley of corporate, government, and bourgeois patrons. By contrast, in the commercial sectors of film, radio, advertising, TV, journalism, and recording, arts workers, beginning in the early 1930s, would accept a more stable and increasingly union wage in exchange for the virtual surrender of artistic autonomy.

The great divide between the high arts and popular culture has, of course, been discussed to death (including by this author) as a measure of changes in the aesthetic life and mass social organization of modern times. The corresponding change in the nature of cultural labor has received much less attention. Even within the literature that could be grouped together under the heading of cultural policy, the lion's share is given over to the "funding problem" of the arts, such as changes in the sources and traditions of patronage and institutional money supply. By contrast, there is relatively little focus on the "labor problem" of the arts.[7] Among the exceptions to this rule are two quite different, but not untypical, approaches to this topic of cultural labor—the cultural discount and the cost disease.

The Cultural Discount

In the first approach, the cultural labor problem figures primarily as the challenge of maintaining a steady supply of workers willing to discount the price of their labor for love of their craft. This might be characterized as a version of "how difficult it is to find good help these days." The most incisive version of this thesis can be found in San Francisco Foundation executive William Kreidler's useful account of the rise and decline of the nonprofit arts foundation. Central to Kreidler's analysis is the principle of the cultural discount, by which artists and other arts workers accept non-monetary rewards—the gratification of producing art—as compensation for their work, thereby discounting the cash price of their labor.[8]

Kreidler points out that, in the nineteenth century, it was the model of individual proprietorship that characterized most theaters, orchestras, opera companies, performing arts impresarios, and many museums, both high and low (though the separation between elite and popular, as Lawrence Levine and others have shown, was much less distinct at that time).[9] While these for-profit proprietorships had to meet the test of the marketplace to survive, they were still heavily subsidized and sustained by the willingness of cultural workers to accept deeply discounted compensation for their labor. Indeed, it is fair to say that the largest subsidy to the arts has always come from workers themselves. To this day, all such workers, even those employed on market-driven contracts, tend to earn compensation well below that commensurate with their skills and levels of educational attainment. The cruel indifference of the marketplace does not seem to deter the chronically discounted. Indeed, and largely because of artists' traditions of sacrifice, it often appears to spur them on in ways that would be regarded as self-destructive in any other economic sector.

Kreidler observes that, lately, arts organizations have begun to worry about the depletion of this discount labor supply. Today's youth, he suggests, are less attracted to the ethos of public service or service to the arts that equates to personal sacrifice, an ethos that was more appealing to relatively affluent, white baby boomers in the post-Kennedy period at the height of nonprofit funding of the arts. As the pipeline of nonprofit funding has sharply reduced its flow, and as leisure time has declined radically for most people in the United States in the last two decades, the arts economy faces an uncertain future in which the older proprietary models have all been subsumed by the commercial culture industries, and in which its traditional dependence on volunteer, discounted labor can no longer be taken for granted. Subtle improvements in the money supply, he concludes, are not likely to offset the long-term impact of labor attrition.

Since Kreidler assumes that the status and levels of comparative compensation enjoyed by artists have not changed significantly since the entrepreneurial heyday of the nineteenth-century arts proprietor, the root of the current arts crisis must therefore lie in the "selfish gene" pool of the boomer parent. Although he does not identify the problem in quite this candid way, it is not unfair to see his conclusion as akin to parental indictments of Gen X apathy. The labor crisis of the arts can thus be laid at the door of youngsters who will not commit to an ideal higher than their own self-absorbed, material interests. Presumably the moral calling of the arts is not well served by a generation distinguished by its cultivation of types like the world-class slacker or the Internet IPO highflyer. If we flesh out this line of argument, we can almost hear the grouchy tones of the parental scold, chiding the listless offspring with mawkish tales about his own hardships of yore, nobly borne in cold-water apartments and fixtureless lofts. Reasoning that appeals to the moral fiber of generational temperament may be consoling, especially to those above the boomer waterline, but it will not provide a cogent assessment of the state of cultural labor. Not when the percentage of employees identified as artists, in national labor statistics, is higher than ever. Not when the principle of the cultural discount is more and more utilized on a semi-industrial scale in sectors of the knowledge industries.

The Cost Disease

A second kind of explanation of the labor crisis, with proven historical impact on arts funding, has been advanced by arts economists. Professionally challenged by evidence of productive activity that does not observe the all-powerful laws of market supply and demand, the liberal economist is drawn to offer a persuasive structural explanation for the "income gap" between the arts and other professions. One influential example was offered by William Baumol in a 1966 study of the performing arts coauthored with fellow Princeton economist William Bowen. With the help of their faculty spouses, who did much of the empirical research, Baumol and Bowen set out to reveal how and why the performing arts have failed to keep up with the impressive productivity gains, measured in outputs per man hour, that have been recorded by other sectors of American industry in the course of the century. For their purposes, they propose to assess the labor cost per unit of the arts as if the arts functioned like any other service-sector industry: "It is helpful to treat the arts, not as an intangible manifestation of the human spirit, but as a productive activity which provides services to the community: one which, in this respect, does not differ from the manufacture of electricity or the supply of transportation or house-cleaning services."[10] In this respect, of course, Baumol and Bowen find that the performing arts do not behave at all like other sectors of the service economy, primarily because they cannot, by their nature, exploit the productivity gains that come with advances in technology. In terms of its technological conditions of production, a contemporary performance of *Macbeth* is not substantially different from its Elizabethan equivalent. "It will be seen," Baumol and Bowen continue, "that the tendency for costs to rise and for prices to lag behind is neither a matter of bad luck nor mismanagement. Rather, it is an inescapable result of the technology of live performance, which will continue to contribute to the widening of the income gaps of the performing organizations."

While the costs of performing will continue to rise without an increase in productivity, Baumol and Bowen conclude, more auspiciously, that productivity in other sectors of the economy will provide workers with more leisure time to consume and participate in the arts, and thereby alleviate some of the economic pressure. This cheerful rider, so indicative of the mid-1960s American climate of chipper expectations, would have a much more consequential echo in Bowen's infamous report on a different service profession, twenty-three years later. His 1989 study of graduate education forecast widespread tenure-track job openings in the professoriat by the middle of the 1990s and may have bootlessly lured thousands into doctoral programs with its assurances of a buoyant future in college teaching.[11]

Baumol and Bowen's 1966 forecast foundered almost as quickly as the one offered by Bowen in 1989. A decline in the leisure time available to the general U.S. workforce set in with a vengeance in the early 1970s and has not been stemmed, not even by the finance capital bonanza of the 1990s bull market, which seems to have triggered even higher levels of performance anxiety. Overwork, as opposed to joblessness, is now the most chronic feature of the labor landscape. Nonetheless, the results of the 1966 study helped to fuel the clamor for increased state funding for the arts, revived that same year, after a hiatus of almost three decades, with the creation of the National Endowment for the Arts (NEA). Baumol's "cost disease" model, as it came to be known (the cost disease condemns the cost per live performance to rise at a rate persistently faster than that of a typically manufactured good), provided empirical support for state intervention in the arts, and subsequently became a staple principle of welfare economics.

But his cost disease does not apply solely to the arts. It is shared, he points out, by other "stagnant sectors" like health and education, whose capacity to provide services is impaired by increasing relative costs.[12] Handicapped from the outset by the cost disease, the arts, in Baumol's opinion, can either join the productive sector—by emulating the culture industries in their adaptation of advanced technologies—or hew more and more to the model of social services, like health or education, or national defense for that matter, which produce a subsidized public good under the heavy hand of bureaucratic supervision.

In some respects, both of these outcomes have come to pass. The institutional divide between the high and low arts has continued to blur, and more and more live performance has come to serve a merely promotional function for cultural product available to remote consumers in some other technologically mediated format. So, too, as George Yúdice has analyzed, the new profile of the artist as a social-service worker is coming to supplant the autonomous avant-garde innovator as a fundable type, increasingly sponsored through local arts agencies. The all-purpose artist-citizen, whose work can help to preserve rural and inner-city communities at risk and stimulate efforts to revive their economies, is increasingly viewed as a means to create jobs through cultural tourism, to promote urban renewal through the competitive siting of museums and arts centers, to save teenagers from substance abuse, or generally to enhance public education through an infusion of communicative skills.[13]

New Model Workers

In the steady withdrawal of federal support for the arts, Yúdice sees a new phase of governmentality. Released from its lingering Cold War obligations, the state is now forging and brokering model partnerships within civil society, between government, corporations, and nonprofit foundations and groups. Akin in some ways to the liberalization of health and education services, this new profile for the arts as the poster child for civic activity extends not just to new kinds of application—"from youth programs and crime prevention to job training and race relations," in the words of "American Canvas," a recent (1997) NEA report by Gary Larson. It also includes the new kinds of sponsors or "partners that arts organizations have taken on in recent years, with school districts, parks and recreation departments, convention and visitor bureaus, chambers of commerce, and a host of social welfare agencies all serving to highlight the utilitarian aspects of the arts in contemporary society."[14] Everyone is potentially a partner in this newly fluid civic sphere where private and public can no longer clearly be distinguished. One of the political outcomes that Yúdice discerns is the soft management of dissent—the traditionally adversarial artist is accommodated through the offering, and voluntary embrace of, partner status. Under this arrangement, time-honored traditions like *épater la bourgeoisie* and bash-the-bureaucrat will be retired, since this new profile does not *require* artists to bite the hand that feeds them as proof of their "free" will in a liberal society.

If this profile does indeed herald a new kind of arrangement of public authority that triangulates state, corporate, and nonprofit sectors, the serviceability of the artist's flexible labor is even more indicative of the moment. Since flexible specialization was introduced as a leading industrial principle, the number of artists employed in the general labor force (defined in decennial Census data and annual Bureau of Labor Statistics reports as eleven occupations: artists who work with their hands, authors, actors and directors, designers, dancers, architects, photographers, arts teachers, musicians/composers, etc.) has swelled from year to year. According to the NEA's annual summaries of Bureau of Labour Statistics (BLS) tabulations, this number more than doubled from 1970 to 1990, showing an 81 percent increase in the course of the 1970s (while artists' real earnings declined by 37 percent), a 54 percent increase in the 1980s, a slight decline in the depression of the early 1990s, and a renewal of growth ever since, reaching a peak of 2 million in 1998. In 1997, artists were enjoying a growth rate in employment (at 2.7 percent) that far outstrips the general workforce (1.3 percent) and even that of other professional specialists (2.4 percent).[15]

These are impressive numbers, but they do not tell a simple story. To figure in the BLS survey, "one must be working during the survey week and have described that job/work as one of eleven artist occupations." Respondents are asked to describe the job at which "they worked the most number of hours in the survey week." Artists working more hours in other jobs outside the arts are classified as employed in those other occupations. By 1998, these amounted to an additional 330,000, for a total of 2,280,000 artists employed in the workforce.[16] Randy Martin points out that these requirements gloss over the verifiable existence of full-time jobs within that occupational sector: "One works in an occupation, a sector, but has the flexibility to remain unattached. The artist can secure an identity for a day's wage, but the rest of the week remains unsecuritized."[17] Because of the high degree of self-employment, and because they are most likely to have other jobs to support a creative trade that habitually employs them for only a portion of a workweek, employment and earnings data on cultural workers have always been unreliable. Even in the most highly unionized entertainment guilds, where the majority of members cannot find work on any given day, the dominant employment model is casual employment on a project-by-project basis. Loyalty is to the guild or craft or union, rather than to a single employer.[18]

There is clearly more going on here than the sleight-of-hand interpretation of statistics to paint a rosy picture of job creation in the arts. Whether or not we can verify a proliferation of new jobs, it is clear that the "mentality" of artists' work is more and more in demand. In respect both to their function and the use of this work mentality, it looks as if artists are steadily being relocated from their traditional position at the social margins of the productive economy and recruited into roles closer to the economic centers of production. Indeed, the traditional profile of the artist as unattached and adaptable to circumstance is surely now coming into its own as the ideal definition of the postindustrial knowledge worker: comfortable in an ever-changing environment that demands creative shifts in communication with different kinds of clients and partners; attitudinally geared toward production that requires long, and often unsocial, hours; and accustomed, in the sundry exercise of their mental labor, to a contingent, rather than a fixed, routine of self-application.

The example of employment patterns in the New Media industries of New York City is a case in point. The backbone of the Silicon Alley workforce in the pioneer start-up phase of this new urban industry was staffed by employees—"creative content-providers," or digital manipulators in Web site and software development—who had been trained primarily as artists. In the entirely nonunionized Webshop workplaces, over half of the jobs are filled by contract employees or perma-temps, with no employer-supported health care. Deeply caffeinated eighty-five-hour workweeks without overtime pay are a way of life for Webshop workers on flexible contracts, who invest a massive share of "sweat equity" in the mostly futile hope that their stock options will pay off. The rate of growth for part-time employment far exceeds that for full-time job creation, and the average 1997 full-time salary (at $37,000) is well below the equivalent in old media industries, like advertising (at $71,000) and television broadcasting (at $86,000).[19] Evolving patterns of subcontracting in Silicon Alley are not so far removed from those that created offshore back offices for data processing in the Caribbean, Ireland, and Bangalore, or semiconductor factories in countries that also host the worst sweatshops in the global garment industry.

For the most part, the Webshops physically occupy spaces filled by manufacturing sweatshops a century ago. Artists who took over these manufacturing lofts beginning in the 1950s enjoyed wide-open floors where work space doubled as living space. This live/work ethos was embraced, to some degree, by the upscale cultural elites who later consolidated "loft living" as a real estate attraction, and it has been extended now into the funky milieu of the Webshops, where work looks almost exactly like play. All in all, the New Media workplace is a prescient indicator of the near future of labor, which combines mental skills with new technologies in alternative environments. Customized workplaces where the lines between labor and leisure have dissolved; horizontal networking among heroic teams of self-directed workers; the proto-hipster appeal of bohemian dress codes, personal growth, and nonhierarchical surroundings; the vague promise of bounteous rewards from stock options; and employees so complicit with the culture of overwork and burnout that they have developed their own insider brand of sick humor about being "net slaves," that is, it's actually cool to be exploited so badly. Industrial capitalists used to dream about such a workforce, but their managerial techniques were too rigid to foster it. These days, the new-wave management wing of the New Economy worships exactly this kind of decentralized environment, which "empowers" workers, banishes bureaucratic constraints on their creativity, and delivers meaningful and nonalienated labor for a grateful and independently minded workforce.

Labor history is full of vicious little time warps, where archaic or long foresworn practices and conceptions of work are reinvented in a fresh context to suit some new economic arrangement. The "sweating" system of farming out work to competing contractors in the nineteenth-century garment industry was once considered an outdated exception to the rule of the integrated factory system. Disdained as a preindustrial relic by the apostles of scientific management, this form of subcontracting is now a basic principle of almost every sector of the postindustrial economy and has emerged as the number one weapon in capital's arsenal of labor cost-cutting and union-busting. Where once the runaway shops were in New Jersey, now they are in Haiti, China, and Vietnam. So, too, the ethos of the autonomous artist, once so fiercely removed from industry's dark satanic mills and from the soiled hand of commerce, has been recouped and revamped as a convenient, even alluring, esprit de corps for contingent work in today's decentralized knowledge factories. Indeed, the "voluntary poverty" of the déclassé bohemian artist—an ex-bourgeois descendant, more often than not, of the self-exiled Romantic poet—may turn out to be an inadvertent forerunner of the discounted labor of the new industrial landscape.

Artists Cannot Afford to Be Rewarded Well?

Ever since the name of the artist was attached to art works, patrons have been extracting prestige and profit from their purchase of some association with the labor of art. In part to maintain and inflate this prestige, artistic labor was elevated to a rank above and beyond the mere workmanship of craft and trade. It was the royal, papal, and noble patrons of the Renaissance who, for their own gain, invented the concept of the artist-genius in emulation of the alchemist who, through his craft, might turn the dross of mere custom into the gold of lavish repute. Traces of this precapitalist prestige survive in those successive phases of patronage characterized by the bourgeois public, the mass market, and the state subsidy (entire nation states claim status on the global landscape on the basis of the great artists they have produced). As for the work of art itself, Marx's distinction between the value of labor and labor power—the value added to a product, in this case, primarily the artist's name—is potentially colossal. The autonomous artist, who emerges in the nineteenth century as a solo entrepreneur working for a largely anonymous public audience, can benefit, in principle, from the surplus value that the name adds to his or her labor. But the name's value tends to increase with the formal estrangement of the artistic soul from the bargaining and haggling of the marketplace. Any taint of mercenary involvement with market supply and demand can diminish the worth of that name.

For the most part, then, this surplus value accrues in reality to the publisher, dealer, promoter, producer, or owner-manager. To say the least, it is in their pecuniary interest to endorse their clients' removal from matters of commerce. The personal agent emerges as the artist's best shot at recouping some of this value. When literary agents first sought to strengthen writers' bargaining power in the literary marketplace of the late nineteenth century, publishers complained that this "philistine" intervention disrupted the sacred bond between writer and publisher.[22] Yet these agents were realizing their clients' labor power in much the same way as trade unionists of the time. (In bargaining for hours and wages, the unionists were also accused of "intruding" on the benevolent capitalist's relationship with his workers.) Did the result amount, as publishers predicted, to any cheapening or commercialization of culture? To some degree, yes, but nowhere nearly as much as the behavior of publishers themselves, already covetous of the popular market, and well primed to pattern the book trade in the mold of the mass media industries that would dominate the twentieth century.

The noble ethos of the unattached artist was conceived in the struggle to break free from aristocratic patronage and was clearly compromised by the simultaneous emergence of a mass commercial audience from the womb of the bourgeois public. Most fatefully, from the perspective of the artist wage, this ethos was soaked in the full torrent of Romantic thought about the separation of art and culture from the commodity production of industrialization. As the industrial division of labor everywhere sought to convert artisans into machine operatives, artists recoiled from being treated like any other trade producer. At the very least, the artist would be an independent skilled worker producing a marginal commodity of taste, but the higher calling of the Romantic imagination demanded something more. The artist was called on to represent, if not wholly embody, those imaginative qualities, skills, and virtues that industrial civilization was systematically destroying.

Ironically, then, the artistic sensibility that was so opposed to utility could not afford to be directly rewarded by trade, yet the commodity value of the artwork rose in direct relation to the artist's remoteness from trade. In time, the very highest value could be attached to the work of those—Van Gogh is the quintessential example—who were most detached, reclusive, ignored, or pauperized by bourgeois society. To some degree, this value could appreciate in inverse proportion to the depression of their labor value while alive. As the moving legacy of Romantic ideas collided and meshed with the evolving arts economy, a curious, and perhaps unique, condition of labor emerged. *The artist cannot afford to be rewarded well.* High-caliber compensation proves fatal to the peer appraisal of an artist's achievement; pecuniary neglect, by that same token, translates into cultural credit.

With the subsequent development of urban, bohemian quarters in low-income districts, this formula would have a geographical basis in the rent economy of the industrializing city and would endure several decades of suburban flight and urban renewal until the waves of gentrification finally washed over its center-city habitat. The special condition of artistic labor, however, persists in all sorts of vestigial ways. Aside from its increasing use as a rationale for flexible labor in the new postindustrial workplace, in its traditional form it may well serve a general function in a capitalist society as an alleviator of liberal guilt for living in an exchange economy that puts a market price on everything. This social sanctioning of discounted arts labor is quite distinct from the pro bono work built into the pricing system of other, more highly paid professions like the law. Alpha professionals, like lawyers, occasionally work for free because they can afford to do so, or because their complicity with structural injustice would otherwise be too obtrusive. This is no less the case for the highest paid arts workers in the commercial sector, like pop musicians, whose continued popularity often depends on high profile appearances at benefit concerts where their fees are seen to be waived for a higher cause. But artists in general are expected, and are therefore inclined, to put in time gratis for love of their art in contexts that would require overtime pay for most other workers.

To compound matters, there persists an ingrained prejudice on the Left against being well paid occupationally, whether in the arts or in the academy. According to this reasoning, an underpaid intelligentsia can identify more readily with those living in low-wage conditions or real poverty. Material self-denial and voluntary poverty are the monkish markers of conscience and left-wing integrity in a reward economy. Compassion and commitment may well flow from this posture, but they are hardly dependent on it. Ultimately, there is something quite patronizing about this belief, redolent, as it is, of middle-class fantasies about the lives and aspirations of working people. This ascetic credo is quite at odds, for example, with the postscarcity thrust of ameliorative laborism, typified by Wobbly chieftain Big Bill Haywood's pronouncement (when asked about the fat cigars he smoked) that "nothing's too good for the proletariat."

For a modern version of Haywood's bravura, consider the priority placed on "getting paid in full," which pervades so much of the culture of hip hop and which is so distasteful to the white rock bohemian critic or indie musician. The ready pursuit of wealth through fame, celebrated so earthily by rappers, is oftentimes infused with the claim for reparations for the music industry's theft of decades of black labor, copyrights, and profits, at the same time as it is shaped by the media world's crass worship of materialism. The tenacious career of hip hop (whose top billers tend to be commercial champions for only a short period of time before they fall to fresh contenders) demonstrates that the choice of preserving one's artistic integrity was never an option equal to "selling out," and was only really adopted as a litmus test of integrity by members of the white rock counterculture who elevated it to an unlikely criterion of faith for most working musicians, let alone African American ones. Deprived, since the "discovery" of the Delta bluesmen, of a supply of domestic primitives, well-meaning liberal rockists (Paul Simon, Sting, David Byrne, Ry Cooder) have patronized Third World musicians hitherto remote from any direct contact with the dollar economy. The Buena Vista Social Club of Cuba's aging, "forgotten" legends is the most recent, and perhaps the best, example of this search for purity of performance unsullied by high exchange rates.

Indeed, the elevation of the rock performer of the 1960s and 1970s saw perhaps the most vibrant revival, in recent times, of the persona of the Romantic poet-artist, untouched by the rule of lucre and ostensibly heedless to market demands. When rockists got around to challenging their long-term servitude to record company contracts and to exploitative managers, they stood to lose cultural credit among fans for negotiating so visibly and brazenly with the industry suits. By contrast, the hip hop "rebel without a pause" of the 1980s, while imbued with multiple Romantic traits, was fully expected to contest the terms under which his music and work were contracted. Public Enemy, among the most visible then, have recently seized the new Internet technology of MP3 (digital compression of audio) in a bid by their self-owned company to outfox the majors by bypassing traditional distribution routes. Gangsta rappers, recruited into the bicoastal wars between the black-owned Death Row and Bad Boy recording empires, became larger-than-life figments of the casino capitalist imagination—burlesque cartoons of the neighborhood bully or player who got lucky—and in so doing called attention to the sheer mercantile substance of their raunchy product. A performer like "Prince," with primarily rockist (albeit glam rock/funk) credentials, confused the genre distinctions altogether when he changed his name (and inscribed "Slave" on his face) to get out of his Warner Brothers contract.

While the pedigree and tenor of the rock troubadours evolved out of folk singer–songwriter traditions that had a heyday in the 1930s, the trappings were borrowed as much from déclassé bohemian velvet as from populist sharecropper denim redolent of the Great Depression. One aims at the cosmopolitan stance as fiercely as the other is determined to be parochial. The former (David Bowie, Jimi Hendrix, Patti Smith, Jim Morrison) glorifies personal deliverance from the social constraints of class consciousness and morality. The latter (Bob Dylan, Bob Marley, Tracy Chapman, Bruce Springsteen) gives voice to generic anthems that register the shared yearnings of the multitude. Virtuoso expression vies with genre interpretation. But these are not simply choices among modes of performance, although they have become very effective commercial marketing profiles. They are also profiles of labor, symbolizing the kind of work that artists are expected, or imagined, to do in society, and so they borrow accordingly from history's wardrobe. For another related example, consider the traditional garb of the Anglo-American intelligentsia, which conveys its studied distance from the worldly uniforms of commerce. The long-suffering tweed jacket of the academic and the high-brow writer evolves directly from the attire of the English country gentleman who does not dirty his hands with city trade. While many alternative forms of sartorial affiliation have flourished in recent years, university intellectuals will generally not wear business suits unless they hold higher administrative positions, and, when they are not aping faded gentility, they will opt, like most other arts professionals, for downwardly mobile apparel.

In the United States, the point of origin for many of the new modes of mental labor remains the New Deal, and the short-lived, but iconoclastic, series of federal programs that directly employed jobless artists and writers. What was the consequence, if any, of the formerly outlandish idea that artists would be targeted by poor relief programs in much the same way as unemployed welders and construction workers?

The Service Ideal

By the mid-1930s, the Depression landscape of breadlines, soup kitchens, and shantytowns had flattened out the élan of bohemia and closed off patronage routes and avenues of income. The proverbial "starving artist" was suddenly no different from the man in the street, struggling to survive. Their social and economic predicament were one and the same. Both needed a living wage. Although its programs barely survived through the end of the decade, Project Number One of the Works Progress Administration (WPA), begun in 1935, organized relief for tens of thousands of artists, writers, actors, and musicians, and parlayed a legacy of semipublic support into the nonprofit infrastructure of foundations, museums, and universities into the years following the war. While its primary aim was simply to put food on the table, this New Deal for the arts was conceived in the ferment of intellectuals' allegiance to the cause of organized labor. The opportunity it offered to promote radical causes inevitably stirred up a hornet's nest among grandstanding members of Congress who oversaw the demise of the programs in a spasm of premature McCarthyism, beginning with The House Un-American Activities Committee's liquidation of the Federal Theater Project in 1939. Unlike the *proletkult* aesthetic adopted by artists and writers who leaned toward Comintern policy, there was no single aesthetic unity to the work produced in the programs. In many respects, then, they were a social-democratic alternative to the bureaucratic cultural policies administered under state Communism and promoted overseas by the Comintern. Insofar as they may have resulted in partial accommodation with the state, they were a relatively inexpensive way of appeasing the political opposition of influential voices.

For some critics, especially those, like Harold Rosenberg, in the *Partisan Review* circle, the WPA programs ruinously emptied out the bohemian ideal, drawing artists in from the more radical margins of society and placing them on a domesticated path toward professionalization.[23] This first step in the bureaucratizing of the arts threatened to compromise the ideal of the autonomous artist. Even worse, the academic ghetto lay ahead. For those, like Rosenberg, who hewed fiercely to the credo of the unattached radical, the independent mind would be a fatal casualty of the transition from the WPA's weekly government wage to the state college's tenure-track salary.

But it was the inexorable rise of the culture industries that had a much greater impact on the profile of cultural labor, while posing an equally grave threat to the value system of key intellectuals like Rosenberg, Irving Howe, Clement Greenberg, and Dwight McDonald. Michael Denning argues that the coalescence of Popular Front activities within the heart of the commercial culture industries gave rise to something new and significant—the "emergence of modern mental labor."[24] With highly successful unionization drives in radio, film, recording, and journalism, performers, writers, and artists could not help but further their sense of common cause with workers organized, after the CIO model, in the great industrial unions of the day. Reinforcing that common cause was a spate of cultural production influenced by Popular Front values and politics.

One result of this arts unionism, Denning observes, is that the classic division between mental and manual labor began to erode decisively. Older ideas about artistic and intellectual work began to dissolve in the face of the new white-collar cultural trades, while a congeries of new corporate forces came to the fore, competing and collaborating at the same time with state agencies to manage mental production, distribution, and consumption on a mass scale. C. Wright Mills would later describe this as the "cultural apparatus," a vast semiorganized network of institutions, where

> arts, science, and learning, entertainment, malarkey, and information are distributed and produced. It contains an elaborate set of institutions; of schools and theaters, newspapers and census bureaus, studios, laboratories, museums, little magazines, radio networks. It contains truly fabulous agencies of exact information and of trivial distraction, exciting objects, lazy escapes, strident advice.

Mills saw this "cultural apparatus" as a direct result of the "overlap between culture and authority," and its raison d'être depended on the use of "cultural workmen for the legitimation of power."[25]

Unlike those in the *Partisan Review* circle, Mills had little nostalgia for the demise of the bohemian ideal of the unattached artist, nor did he share their sniffy contempt for the commercial products of mass and middlebrow culture, but he more or less shared their views about the use of commercial culture to legitimate power. For all the differences between the major schools of leftist commentary about commercial popular culture—whether the Frankfurt school, the New York Intellectuals, or other tendencies represented by Gramsci, Mills, the New Left, and the Birmingham school—their critiques all rested upon a common view of the culture industries as instruments of mass consent and/or social control.

What is striking about Denning's shift of emphasis is that he reminds us that the rise of this new cultural apparatus was *also an opportunity for labor*. Culture, in its new industrial context, was now a product of mass labor, and the politics of labor to which it gave birth bore many similarities to the conditions of industrial unionism. Just as important, however, the workers whose labor was involved—screenwriters, actors, musicians—could exert a direct influence on the shape and content of the product. (Teachers, journalists, and healthcare workers would follow in this mold.) Cultural workers could seek to politicize the product of their labor in a way that autoworkers could not. This was something relatively new in the annals of labor. As a result, the history of commercial culture is one of perpetual compromise, concession, truce, and arbitration both on the side of labor bargaining and also in the business of content bargaining. The reputation of "liberal Hollywood" (not entirely a right-wing invention) stems from both angles of this new politics of labor. In Baumol's analysis of the arts economy, he cites the high level of unionization as an obstacle to efficiency in a sector where independent craft functions are "carefully protected" by each union local. On the other side, we are all too well aware of the ceaseless efforts of many cultural workers to give their artistic product a liberal or progressive slant in the face of systemic pressure to reinforce the capitalist value system.

Intellectuals in the Cold War period devoted a good deal of time to declaiming on the stultifying impact of "mass culture." For critics who had been weaned on workers' causes in the 1930s, it is astonishing how little attention they paid to labor's involvement in the culture industries. Virtually none saw this development as a fit topic for extended commentary. Even C. L. R. James, who keenly followed the record and progress of labor, and who, in *American Civilization*, saw the American entertainment industry as part of the most advanced industrial state of popular civilization, did not necessarily see the culture industry's workplaces as "labor's workplaces." The closest he came was in drawing an analogy between the bargaining process of capital and labor and the process of negotiation hashed out between the industry's owners and the mass audiences of popular culture over the politics of content. Uncomfortable with the view of the Frankfurt and *Partisan Review* critics that moguls and bankers frankly use popular culture's content to affirm capitalist values, James believed the bosses would not dare to impose their political views. Indeed, part of their compact with audiences is the unwritten agreement not to do so.

> The general public accepts, or to be more precise, appears to accept the general political ideas, standards, social ethics, etc. of the society which is the natural framework of the films as they are produced today. Whenever possible a piece of direct propaganda is injected, but the C.I.O., the great strikes, capital and labor, war and peace, these are left out by mutual

understanding, a sort of armed neutrality. If those who control films dared in ordinary times, to give their view of these problems in films, for instance, they would empty the movie houses. The large masses of the people would not stand for any employer view of unions in films. In totalitarian states, the state does exactly the opposite. It uses the film, the popular film, to the limit. In fact the film is merely an arm of the government.[26]

Echoing the Cold War climate that was coming into being in 1950, James depicts the state of affairs as a "sort of armed neutrality." The accord he describes in film is not unlike the recent postwar compact between capital and labor. In return for capital's recognition of basic bargaining rights, labor, by 1950, has accepted the general framework of capitalist society.

The Cold War added a new, international dimension to the uneasy truce to which James was alluding. For almost forty years, the cultural policy that accompanied Cold War "armed neutrality" was tied to a massive exercise in state propaganda (some of it covert). For the purpose of this policy, artists were no longer federal workers, they were now ambassadors of freedom, exported on cultural exchange programs by the United States Information Agency (USIA) to put the best face on liberal, capitalist values. In contrast to the proletarianization of the artist in the WPA of the 1930s, the credo of the autonomous artist was revived by the Cold War. This time around, the autonomy in question was not from trade, as in the Romantic version, but from the state censorship more prevalent in the socialist states. As for cultural workers in the commercial industries, they could be seen to belong to "free" trade unions at least, after the Communist presence in the labor movement had been purged. All of this was presented as a counterpoint to the unfree mental labor of the socialist bloc and its Third World client states.

But by far the most extensive development on this front, and of the welfare state in general, was the massive expansion of the national higher education system in this period. The state thereby bought itself a dependable research arm, especially through defense-related funding in the sciences: corporations were able to have basic research funded and future employees trained at public expense; and the "herd of independent minds," as Rosenberg once described the intelligentsia, was brought under the purview of academic deans and other responsible institutional shepherds. Again, these developments dealt the United States immense advantages in the public relations game of the Cold War. However expedient to the corporate liberal state, these advantages were won in the name of academic freedom and the democratic extension of education to the lower middle class and portions of the working class.

When the American labor market became flexible in the 1980s, and union organizing eroded as a fundamental right, blue-collar unions took a direct hit, but white-collar and professional organizing was still on the rise. The new knowledge industries, either comprising the higher education sector or built around a university research complex, provided a natural union base for salaried employees with less and less control over their own workplace. In the 1990s, the corporatization of higher education set in for real, and the post-Fordist principles of outsourcing, downsizing, deskilling, reengineering, and flexible, temporary contracting began to take a heavy toll on institutions nominally built on tenure, academic freedom, and faculty governance. The tenure-track appointment, hitherto a staple contract in the profession, rapidly became a privileged exception to the rule. Professional academics, long accustomed to regarding their workplace as a nonworldly realm, beholden to different rules and standards from those observed in more "secular" employment sectors, had a rude awakening. In no time at all, it seemed, higher education had became one of the more advanced forms, among the professions, of the adjunct contract workplace, where a large percentage of its part-time labor force were soon struggling to earn any kind of living wage.

A Volunteer Low-Wage Army?

The rapidity with which the low-wage revolution swept through higher education was clearly hastened along by conditions amenable to discounting mental labor. For one thing, the "willingness" of scholars (whether as graduate students or postdoctoral employees) to accept a discounted wage out of "love for their subject" has helped not only to sustain the cheap labor supply but also to magnify its strength and volume. Like artists and performers, academics are inclined by training to sacrifice earnings for the opportunity to exercise their craft. While other traditional professional industries, like law or medicine, depend to some degree on intern labor, none rely economically on the self-sacrifice of their accredited members to anything like the same degree.

Employers have long relied on maintaining a reserve army of unemployed to keep wages down in any labor market. Higher education is now in this business with a vengeance. In addition—and this is the significant element—its managers increasingly draw on a volunteer low-wage army. By this I do not mean to suggest that adjunct and part-timer educators eagerly invite their underpayment and lack of benefits or job security. Nor are they inactive in protesting and organizing for their interests. Like the musicians at the New School, they are beginning to form bargaining units and win contracts, though a contingent workforce is notoriously difficult to organize. Rather, I choose the phrase to describe the natural outcome of a training in the habit of embracing nonmonetary rewards—mental or creative gratification—as compensation for work. As a result, low compensation for a high workload becomes a rationalized feature of the job. In the most perverse extension of this logic, underpayment can even be regarded as proof of the worth of the academic vocation—the ultimate measure of the selfless and disinterested pursuit of knowledge.

No doubt, one of the contributing elements here is a vestige of the amateur ideal of the scholar (even the scholar-gypsy, if you want to talk about flexibility *avant la lettre*). Indeed, one of the "privileges" enjoyed by academic scholars was the right to pursue their work in full ignorance of its economic underpinnings. According to this custom, money matters were too vulgar and trivial to be understood, let alone handled, by faculty. Such pecuniary concerns befouled the sacred quest for knowledge and truth. Again, this customary feature of the scholar's profile has made it easy for power to shift rapidly to managers and administrators, whose ready grasp of fiscal affairs renders their decisions uncontested by faculty entirely ignorant of budgetary priorities set elsewhere. In addition, the comfort offered by job security in the form of tenure was a recipe for complacency on the part of those who should have resisted the corporate measures much earlier and more vigorously. Submission to the selfless, disinterested devotions of the scholar's calling inevitably led to the sacrifice of younger "apprentices" on the altar of an anachronistic faith.[27]

In the restructured, corporate environment of the modern American education system, the net result of this amateur ethos has been deprofessionalization, not the revival of Veblen's virtuous ideal of Idle Curiosity with its canons of faculty governance. We have seen a whole generation of scholars form an underclass of independent contractors, offering their skills hither and thither, on one freeway exit after another, often for what adds up to a subminimum wage. In some respect, this peripatetic regimen is germane to the eccentric work schedule of the traditional academic, who commonly observes no clear boundaries between being on and off the job, and for whom there is often little distinction between paid work and free labor. For the professionally active full-timer, this habitual schedule means that she can take on a range of tasks and obligations that will easily fill out a sixty-hour workweek.[28] For the part-timer, desperate to retain the prestige of being a college teacher, the identity of being a switched-on, round-the-clock thinker, eager to impart knowledge, and in a position to freely extend her mental labor, feeds into the psychology of casualized work and underpayment. The industrial worker, by comparison, is not beset by such occupational hazards.

Again, what we see is the fabrication of a model "flexible employee" out of the cloth of capricious protocols and habits, a worker whose customary training in the service ideals and irregular routines of mental labor can be roundly exploited by cost-cutting managers. Certain characteristic features of the academic work style, like those of artists, whom I earlier depicted, conform to the demands of a contingent labor profile. Most portentous of all, perhaps, is the elective component of this situation. Again, I do not mean to suggest that any single individual is drawn toward this predicament, nor indeed that they are directly implicated in their own exploitation. I am proposing that labor is being casualized in ways that complement the habits and compulsions of the academic mentality. It is in this respect that we can speak, objectively, of a volunteer army, whether of unemployed or of contracted low-wage labor. (Is love of one's disciplinary art so remote, in this respect, from the love of country that drives volunteers into the sacrificial arms of military service?)

As part of its ceaseless search for ways to induct workers in their own exploitation, capital, it might be said, may have found the makings of a *self-justifying*, low-wage workforce, at the very heart of the knowledge industries so crucial to its growth and development. It is no small irony that artists and academics, who would have been borderline, even oddball, features of an older labor landscape, are now more like exemplary, even avant-garde, figures, heralding the next plateau of uneven development. Continuing the process by which capital broke its Fordist compact with core manufacturing labor by moving production to the periphery (offshore, the nonunion South, the service sector), now the once peripheral domains of mental labor are becoming new centers of corporate attention.

Education Enterpreneurs

It's no surprise that the cloistered precincts of the former Ivory Towers have already become a battleground for labor. Too many bullish forces in the corporate sector see higher education as a huge, untapped market for selling goods and services on the basis of the prestigious brand names of universities. At the primary and secondary levels, the spoils of the public school system have long been coveted by "education entrepreneurs," touting the "discipline" of the marketplace over the "inefficiency" of the public realm, and normalizing the rhetoric of corporate management—the public as customer, education as competitive product, learning as efficiency tool. Remember Lamar Alexander's declaration, shortly before becoming secretary of education, that Burger King and Federal Express should set up schools to show how the private sector would run things?[29]

School-business partnerships opened the door not just to Total Quality Management but to every corporate huckster looking for ways to promote and build brand loyalty in the "K-12 marketplace." Tax-supported school vouchers and union-free charter schools were introduced, respectively, as the fast and the slow track toward privatization. While your local high school hasn't yet been bought out by McDonalds, many educators already use teaching aids and packets of materials, "donated" by companies, that are crammed with industry propaganda designed to instill product awareness among young consumers: lessons about the history of the potato chip, sponsored by the Snack Food Association, or literacy programs that reward students who reach monthly reading goals with Pizza Hut slices.[30]

In addition to serving as magnets for corporate sponsorship, the economy of scale and the fiscal autonomy enjoyed by institutions of higher education allow them to function like corporations in their own right. On the labor front, they have adopted many of the same tactics of union busting, downsizing, and outsourcing, and they hire the same antiunion law firms (NYU and Yale both retained the notorious Proskauer, Rose, who openly advertise their antiunion advocacy on their Web site, in their respective NLRB hearings about graduate student unions) to represent their interests in the legal arena. In addition, the modern, corporate university is no longer simply a medium for subsidizing or socializing capital's costs of training, research, and development as it was in the Cold War period. It has become a site of capital accumulation in its own right, where the profitability of research and teaching programs and the marketability of learning products is fast coming to the fore as the primary driving force behind academic policy at many institutions. Corporate sponsorship increasingly buys faculty and entire research programs, while the patenting and selling of on-line courses promises a bonanza of low-cost yields.

In many cases, cost-cutting labor policies are also vehicles for establishing ideological control over curricular content. Recent advances in distance learning, for example, are eagerly championed by administrators and state legislators itching to switch their fixed investment in temperamental bodies and impetuous minds over to the sleek machinery of digital pipes with mega bandwidth. When education is viewed as a product to be delivered without risk, then the most compelling corporate vision is that of the wired, tenureless university, where hired hands prepare or administer on-line courses pumped out to a remote, disaggregated student body. Faculty attempts to establish control over on-line instruction are not simply struggles to stave off the automation of jobs; they are also frontline battles in the Culture Wars over the right to determine and influence curriculum.

While the economic payoffs of digitized instruction appear to be self-evident, these technology-assisted developments have less to do with increased efficiency or cost-effectiveness than with control over the workforce and, potentially, the curriculum. The elimination of the social and cultural services ministered by full-time, flesh-and-blood faculty inevitably results in a sharp drop in the quality of education. Any cost-benefit analysis of on-line instruction should have to assess the challenge of delivering a product of comparable quality. Based on this criterion, no one has ever been able to identify clear gains in productivity or cost-effectiveness from the introduction of computers into the workplace. I am referring here to the phenomenon of the productivity paradox, an IT update of the technology trap first identified by business economists in the fledgling years of automation forty years ago.[31] "Downstream benefits" have not exactly flowed from the habit of throwing "upstream" money into IT systems, applications, upgrades, management, and maintenance that do not serve the practical needs of businesses or other employee organizations. Promotional hype, technological obsolescence, communication overload, and widespread downtime outages caused by worker sabotage are only some of the factors that inhibit productivity.

Second Thoughts

With or without its virtual arm, how efficient will the newly restructured academic sectors prove to be in servicing the labor markets of industrialized knowledge? Higher education is in a pivotal position in this regard. Not only is it now a massive anchorage for discounted labor among its own workforce, it is also a training site, responsible for reproducing the discounted labor force among the next generation of knowledge workers. Are we contributing involuntarily to the problem when, as educators, we urge students, in pursuing their career goals, to place principles of public interest or collective political agency or creative expression above the pursuit of material security? In a labor environment heavily under the sway of neoliberal business models, is it fair to say that this service ideal invites, if it does not vindicate, the manipulation of inexpensive labor?

Fifteen years ago, this suggestion would have seemed ludicrous. Labor freely offered in the service of some common benefit or mental ideal has always been the informal economic backbone that supports political, cultural, and educational activities in the nonprofit or public interest sectors. Selfless labor of this sort is also a source of great pleasure. The world that we value most—the world that is not in thrall to market dictates—would not exist without this kind of volunteer discounted labor. But what happens when some version of this disinterested labor moves, as I have suggested here, from the social margins to core sectors of capital accumulation? When the opportunity to pursue mentally gratifying work becomes a rationale for discounted labor at the heart of the key knowledge industries, is it not time to rethink some of our bedrock pedagogical values? Does the new landscape of mental labor demand more than the usual call for modernizing the politics of labor? What is to be done with the anxiety generated by such questions?

First and foremost, we must remember that the problem lies not in how people operate within an economy, but rather in how that economy is structured, in this case an economy that is still undergoing restructuring and resegmenting into ever more polarized shapes. Education is surely playing its role in mediating the gulf between the deskilled lower tiers, destined for the secondary labor market, and those upper strata ruled by credentials, tracked into fractions of mental labor. Currently, managers of national and global economies tell us that education is the only passport to economic mobility or security in a knowledge society. And yet people with advanced degrees are working in restaurants and taxicabs, or as Microserf temps, and most service jobs in the secondary labor market (with no prospect of advancement) require little more than basic literacy accompanied by a modest facility in pleasing customers. In the Fordist era of the two-tier labor system, it was the simple presence of trade unions, and not gaps in skills, that separated high-wage primary from low-wage secondary labor markets.

Accordingly, the education system (both at the high school and collegiate levels) is overdeveloped in relation to the needs of an economy that will only provide so many meaningful jobs that pay a living wage. So there exists a cruel disconnect between the managerial promises and the opportunities on the ground. While this disparity generates its share of social discontent, the expectations raised by these promises play a crucial role in regulating labor markets. In the sectors of mental work I have looked at here, the prospect of meaningful work provides a rationale for deprofessionalizing while helping to maintain a degraded labor market that disciplines and sets the wage floors of those precariously positioned in the core segments immediately above. In addition, and at a time (quite distinct from the Fordist era) when creative gratification is more and more pursued in the realm of work, the collective educational capital that once stimulated and supported consumption and leisure time is more and more invested in gray areas of unwaged work that the new cultural economy is creating. For example, in an article in this issue of *Social Text*, Tiziana Terranova outlines the role that free labor has played in building much of the Web site infrastructure of digital capitalism. Education is not, then, wasted, as it appears at first sight. Rather, it is systematically being converted into un- or undercompensated labor in ways that need to be adequately charted (just as the hidden costs of unwaged domestic labor of women have sustained the economy for much longer).

Insofar as we participate in this economy as scholars, writers, artists, or digital artisans, there is a responsibility to recognize the cost of our cherished beliefs in aesthetic or educational ideals. These ideals come at a price, and managers of the New Economy are taking full advantage of the opportunities that exist for capitalizing on our neglect of that price. Our traditions of indifference to the world of trade and waged labor are no longer charming eccentricities to be deemed objects of tourist interest in Bohemia or the Ivory Tower, not when they are more and more central to a cultural economy that relies on them to further degrade the cost of labor.

Historically, noncommercial mental workers have found it too challenging, and professionally limiting, to see themselves as workers. Academics have often viewed their daily teaching and service obligations as a menial chore or necessary evil that allows them to pursue the life of the mind in their research—their "real" work—on sabbatical or in summer breaks. Artists contracted by federal or local government programs such as the Comprehensive Employment and Training Act (CETA) (in the 1970s, the biggest public commitment to job subsidies since the WPA) routinely have made a distinction between what they do for a living in the realm of public and community arts, and their own after-hours work as expressive individuals.[32] Even in the WPA years, many artists who qualified for poor relief refused federal assistance through the artists programs because they were averse to being classed as laborers (while others saw the program as a conspiracy to shut them up by offering full-time work). Writers of all stripes continue to regard part-time commercial work as a vile meal ticket that expedites their true calling.

There are sound reasons for abiding by such distinctions. Unpopular forms of intellectual, artistic, and political expression cannot and will not thrive unless they are independent of commercial or bureaucratic dictates. But these conditions of independence can no longer be "defended" stubbornly and solely as a matter of humanistic principle, or as a freestanding right of a civilized society. When capital-intensive industry is concentrated around vast culture trading sectors, when media Goliaths feed off their control of intellectual property, and when the new Vested Interests routinely barter discount wages for creative satisfaction on the job, the expressive traditions of mental labor are no longer "ours" simply to claim, not when informal versions of them are daily being bought off and refined into high-octane fuel for the next generation of knowledge factories.

Pioneer or avant-garde sectors of the new labor landscape must now play host to efforts to organize those whose professional identity has been based on a sharp indifference to being organized. Our common petitions can draw on an intimate and shared experience of the traditions of sacrificial labor. Those still in denial (usually the most secure) will swear off any and every affinity. It will take more than a leap of faith to establish any kind of solidarity among mental labor fractions divided by the legacy of (under-the-table or above-the-salt) privileges passed down over centuries. Nevertheless, while the chief blight of these centuries had been chattel slavery, serfdom, and indentured labor (and we are not done with these), we must now respond to that moment in the soulful lullaby of "Redemption Song" where Bob Marley soberly advises us: "Emancipate yourself from mental slavery."

Because we cannot afford to believe that mental slavery has any less to do with labor than physical slavery did, some part of the task of modernizing labor politics in the age of dot-com and dot-edu (the age of the Yale Corporation, the Microserf, and the consolidated push of Time Warner–Bertelsmann–Disney–CNN–Hachette–Paramount–News Corp) lies in recognizing the special conditions that apply to pricing wages for thought. We have always known that aesthetics comes at a price, especially for those who do not benefit from the prestige it confers. Now we must learn to recognize that aesthetics is part of a price system, to use a pet phrase of Thorstein Veblen's. No one has really thought this out properly. If we don't, others, with less to lose and a world of lucrative copyrights to gain, will do it for us.

Notes

1 The faculty also includes jazz luminaries such as bassist Reggie Workman, saxophonist Billy Harper, pianist Joanne Brackeen, drummer Joe Chambers, trumpeter Cecil Bridgewater, and pianist Junior Mance.

2 See Thomas Bender's account in *New York Intellect* (Baltimore, Md.: Johns Hopkins University Press, 1987), 296–300.

4 Thorstein Veblen, *The Higher Learning in America: A Memorandum on the Conduct of Universities by Business Men* (New York: B. W. Huebsch, 1918).

5 Morris Llewellyn Cooke, *Academic and Industrial Efficiency: A Report to the Carnegie Foundation for the Advancement of Teaching* (New York : The Carnegie Foundation for the Advancement of Teaching, 1910).

6 Thorstein Veblen, *The Engineers and the Price System* (New York: Viking, 1921).

7 Some titles, predominantly relating to the for-profit sector, include: Lois Gray and Ronald Seeber, eds., *Under the Stars: Essays on Labor Relations in Arts and Entertainment* (Ithaca, N.Y.: ILR/Cornell University Press, 1996); Michael Storper, "The Transition to Flexible Specialization in the U.S. Film Industry," *Cambridge Journal of Economics* 13 (1989): 273–305; Toby Miller, *Technologies of Truth* (Minneapolis: University of Minnesota Press, 1998) and "Television and Citizenship: A New International Division of Cultural Labor," in *Communication, Citizenship, and Social Policy*, ed. Andrew Calabrese and Jean-Claude Burgelman (Boulder, Colo.: Rowman and Littlefield, 1999), 279–92.

8 John Kreidler, "Leverage Lost: The Nonprofit Arts in the Post-Ford Era," *In Motion Magazine*, on-line at www.inmotionmagazine.com/lost.html.

9 Lawrence Levine, *Highbrow/Lowbrow: The Emergence of Cultural Hierarchy in America* (New York: Oxford University Press, 1988).

10 William Baumol and William Bowen, *Performing Arts—The Economic Dilemma: A Study of Problems Common to Theater, Opera, Music, and Dance* (New York: Twentieth-Century Fund, 1966), 162.

11 William Bowen and Julie Ann Sosa, *Prospects for Faculty in the Arts and Sciences: A Study of Factors Affecting Supply and Demand, 1987 to 2012* (Princeton, N.J.: Princeton University Press, 1989); and the later study, William Bowen and Neil Rudenstine, *In Pursuit of the Ph.D.* (Princeton, N.J.: Princeton University Press, 1992). It has been argued that Bowen's forecast of abundant jobs would have been realized if universities had not embarked, in the 1990s, on a full-scale program of casualizing its faculty workforce. If colleges were still hiring full-time tenure-track professors, instead of part-timers and adjuncts, today's labor supply would more closely approximate employer demand.

12 Ruth Towse, ed., *Baumol's Cost Disease: The Arts and Other Victims* (Northampton, Mass.: Edward Elgar, 1997).

13 George Yúdice, "The Privatization of Culture," *Social Text*, no. 59 (spring 1999): 17–34.

14 Gary Larson, *American Canvas: An Arts Legacy for Our Communities* (Washington, D.C.: National Endowment for the Arts, 1999), 127–28; cited in Yúdice, "The Privatization of Culture," 25.

15 See the NEA Research Division Notes on "Artist Employment in America," on-line at www.arts.endow.gov.pub.

16 NEA Research Division Note no. 73, April 1999.

17 Randy Martin, "Beyond Privatization: The Art and Society of Labor, Citizenship, and Consumerism," *Social Text*, no. 59 (spring 1999): 38–39.

18 Gray and Seeber, *Under the Stars*, 6.

19 See Andrew Ross, "Jobs in Cyberspace," in *Real Love: In Pursuit of Cultural Justice* (New York: New York University Press, 1998), 7–34; and "Sweated Labor in Cyberspace," *New Labor Forum* 4 (spring 1999): 47–56. For an active Web site, see NetSlaves (Horror Stories of Working on the Web) at www.dis-obey.com/netslaves.

22 Linda Marie Fritschner, "Literary Agents and Literary Traditions: The Role of the Philistine," in *Paying the Piper: Cause and Consequences of Art Patronage*, ed. Judith Higgins Balfe (Urbana: University of Illinois Press, 1993), 54–72. Also James Hepburn, *The Author's Empty Purse and the Rise of the Literary Agent* (London: Oxford University Press, 1968).

23 Harold Rosenberg, "The Profession of Art: The WPA Art Project," *Art on the Edge: Creators and Situations* (New York: Macmillan, 1975), 195–205.

24 Michael Denning, *The Cultural Front: The Laboring of American Culture in the American Century* (New York: Verso, 1996).

25 C. Wright Mills, "The Cultural Apparatus," in *Power, Politics, and People*, ed. Irving Horowitz (New York: Oxford University Press, 1963), 405–22.

26 C. L. R. James, *American Civilization*, edited and introduced by Anna Grimshaw and Keith Hart, with an afterword by Robert A. Hill (Oxford: Black-well, 1993), 123.

27 For analysis in general of these developments, see Cary Nelson, ed., *Will Teach for Food* (Minneapolis: University of Minnesota Press, 1997); Randy Martin, ed., *Chalk Lines: The Politics of Work in the Managed University* (Durham, N.C.: Duke University Press, 1998); and Cary Nelson and Stephen Watt, *Academic Keywords: A Devil's Dictionary for Higher Education* (New York: Routledge, 1999).

28 A recent study of full-time faculty at sixteen midsized colleges and universities found faculty members worked an average of 53.6 hours per week. "Nota Bene," *Academe* (July–August 1999): 11.

29 Alex Molnar, *Giving Kids the Business: The Commercialization of America's Schools* (Boulder, Colo.: Westview, 1996), 3.

30 Ibid., chap. 2.

31 Henry C. Lucas Jr., *Information Technology and the Productivity Paradox: The Search for Value* (New York: Oxford University Press, 1999); John Thorp, *The Information Paradox: Realizing the Business Benefits of Information Technology* (New York: McGraw-Hill, 1999); Leslie Willcocks and Stephanie Lester, eds., *Beyond the IT Productivity Paradox: Assessment Issues* (New York: John Wiley, 1999); Jessica Keyes, *Solving the Productivity Paradox: TQM for Computer Professionals* (New York: McGraw-Hill, 1994).

32 See Steven Dubin's study of Chicago's artists-in-residence programs funded by the Comprehensive Employment and Training Act (CETA) in the late 1970s, *Bureaucratizing the Muse: Public Funds and the Cultural Worker* (Chicago: University of Chicago Press, 1987).

CHAPTER 24

Neoliberalism, Debt and Class Power

Justin Sean Myers

Introduction: Debt, Crisis and Everyday Life

Think about the life of your friends and family. How many of you are able to pay all your bills with money you actually have? Clothing bills. Rent. Tuition. Automobile payments. Medical bills. Utility payments. Odds are, you can't. In this you and those you know are not alone. Millions of Americans earn salaries that cannot pay the cost of rent, food, clothing and education. This pushes people towards credit to manage day-to-day expenses. Be it a credit card bill of $2,000, a car loan of $8,500, a student loan of $15,000 or a mortgage of $300,000, debt is now a part of everyday life. But debt is not merely a piece of paper or plastic. It does not naturally appear when money is tight or expand to cover cost-of-living increases when wages stagnate. It does not exist in a vacuum outside of social power. It is not simply a monetary relation. Debt is a class relation. Those in power have long utilized debt to maintain relations of dependency between classes, from Ancient Greece to pre-colonial India, from eighteenth-century England to nineteenth-century South America (Brass 1999, 2003; Dore 2006; Ford 1926; Graeber 2011; Prakash 1990; Woodfine 2006).

This essay contends that the past 40 years of ever-escalating mortgage and student debt within the United States is not entirely different. Since the 1970s Wall Street has been a major advocate for the liberalization of credit and the creation of a business climate where profits are high, fast and loose (Brenner 2002; Harvey 2005). Recentering class relations around the debt-relation of creditor and debtor became a crucial strategy within the larger movement away from the New Deal, Keynesian economics and industrial capitalism towards Reaganomics, free markets and financial capitalism (Harvey 2005). Within this strategy the financial and corporate elite utilized debt as a weapon of social power to maintain and reinforce the class relationship of capital and labor, bourgeoisie and proletariat. In doing so, neoliberals and Wall Street sought a transformative reorganization of all social relations, away from a society of discipline founded on the factory and the wage-relation toward a society of control organized around the stock market and the debt-relation (Deleuze 1992). The move from discipline to control and wage to debt is consequently understood as a strategic shift in the priorities and accumulation dynamics of the capitalist class. The attempt to accumulate capital by expanding the production of commodities (the manufacturing base) is decentered in favor of the transfer of wealth from the middling classes to Wall Street—a practice of "accumulation by dispossession" (Harvey 2003, 2005). This strategy takes two major forms. One, producing and controlling an "asset" bubble in housing by lending mortgage debt to people who were not eligible for the traditional post-war mortgage of a 30-year fixed rate with 20% down and verification of employment, income and assets (Barth 2009; Blackburn 2008; O'Hara 2009). Two, defunding public higher education, privatizing the costs of higher education through student loans and obtaining the power to deny students the ability to declare bankruptcy on their student loans (Fossey and Bateman 1998; Newfield 2008; Williams 2006a, 2006b, 2006c).

Mortgage and Student Debt: From the 1950s through 2009

In 2007, right before the housing crash, total mortgage debt was valued at $10.5 trillion. This figure is salient considering mortgage debt was a mere $285.9 billion in 1970. The massive increase from 1970 to 2009 reflects a doubling of mortgage debt about every decade: $285.9B in 1970, $926.5B in 1980, $2488.8B in 1990, $4798.4B in 2000 and $10335.2B in 2009 (Federal Reserve 2010a). Coinciding with this dramatic growth in mortgage debt was an ever-increasing debt-to-disposable-income (DTDI) ratio, from 62.3 percent in 1970 to 123.3 percent in 2009 (see Figure 24.1). DTDI is the ratio of the household's monthly disposable income—personal income minus taxes (income, estate, gift, personal property)—that goes towards paying all debts. Not only did DTDI nearly double over these four decades but at 123.3 percent it means that most households pay out more in debt than comes in as income. The majority of this increase in DTDI is attributable to escalating mortgage debt. As a percentage of disposable income, mortgage debt stood at only 43 percent in 1984, but had ballooned to 93.7 percent by 2009 (see Figure 24.1).

Moreover, during this time period household debt increased at a much faster rate than the total economic growth of the United States. This relationship is apparent through the escalating ratio of household debt to gross domestic product (GDP). From 49.4 percent in 1984 to 62.9 percent in 1991, household debt to GDP had risen to 96.4 percent at the end of 2009 (see Figure 24.2).

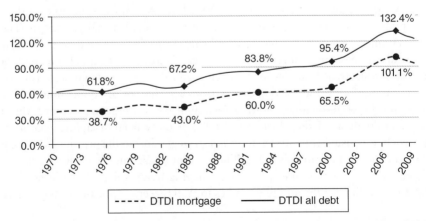

Figure 24.1 Household debt as a percentage of disposable income. Note: Courtesy of Federal Reserve Board, 2010a, table F.100 and D.3.

Alongside the increase of household debt to GDP, homeowner's equity as a percentage of home value begins a steadily decline from the mid 1980s through 2007. Standing at 67.3 percent in 1970, homeowners' equity slipped to 57.8 percent in 1997 before declining sharply after 2003 to rest at 39.2 percent at the end of 2009 (see Figure 24.3). Overall, 51 percent of homeowners have less than 25 percent equity in their home, making the home theirs in belief only (First American CoreLogic 2010).

Student debt at all institutions of higher education (public, private nonprofit, private for profit) mirrors this upward trajectory. However, because 80% of all higher education students are enrolled at public institutions I will focus on student debt at public universities. Today around 80% of financial aid from the government is in the form of loans. Only 20% consists of grants and scholarships. As a result, 55% of the 2010 graduating class at public four-year colleges had debt averaging $22,000 (Baum and Payea 2011:4). This represents a strong increase since the 1970s and 1980s and even the 1990s. The average debt amount for students graduating from public 4-year colleges was $8,800 in

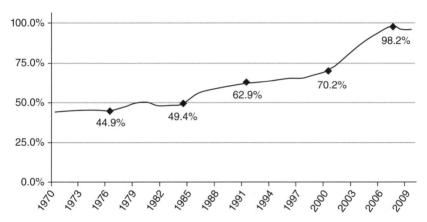

Figure 24.2 Household debt as percentage of gross domestic product (GDP). Note: Courtesy of Federal Reserve Board, 2010a, table F.100 and D.3; U.S. Bureau of Economic Analysis, 2010, Gross Domestic Product.

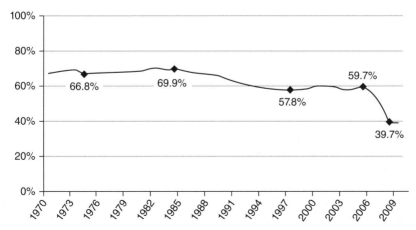

Figure 24.3 Homeowner's equity as percentage of home value. Note: Courtesy of Federal Reserve Board, 2010a, table B.100.

1992–3, \$12,000 in 1995–6 and \$17,700 by 1999–2000 (College Board 2006). The increase in total debt is a reflection of the higher yearly loan amounts of university students. At public four-year institutions for the academic year 1995–6, students who borrowed averaged \$3,800 in loans; by 2007–8 this had increased to \$6,600 (NCES 2011). Accordingly, student debt has become a booming market-space for the accumulation of capital. Student loans have had phenomenal growth over the past two decades, doubling nearly every decade, from \$23B in 1987–8 to \$42B in 1998–9 to \$84B in 2008–9 (Baum et al. 2009:6; Gladieux et al. 1998:7).

Mortgage Debt, Neoliberalism and Accumulation by Dispossession

How is the reader to interpret this data? Are these increases in debt a natural outcome of economic development, population growth or a postindustrial society? No. Debt emerges as a capitalist class strategy to regain declining rates of profit during the 1960s and 1970s. One must look back to the social movements of the 1960s and 1970s to understand the rise of mortgage and student debt because their emergence is rooted in Wall Street's and corporate America's attempt to break the back of the "Great Refusal" (Breines 1989).

Encompassing a multitude of social movements spanning the 1960s and the 1970s—welfare rights, feminism, civil rights, black power, student, environmental, and labor—the "Great Refusal" reflected an era that challenged the major tenants of the Keynesian capital-relation and sought to force capital and the state to internalize the costs of social and ecological reproduction (Breines 1989; Dowie 1996; Katsiaficas 1999; Midnight Notes 1992; Zerowork Collective 1972). Workers were striking for higher wages, more control over the shop floor, and shorter hours (Midnight Notes 1992; Zerowork Collective 1972). Many of their demands attacked the productivity wage of the post-war period—the central mechanism regulating economic growth (Negri 1988). The productivity wage reflected the win–win capital-labor logic of the New Deal state and Keynesian economics by tying wage increases to productivity increases. This coupling allowed wages and the purchasing power of American workers to increase but at a rate that did not infringe upon the profit rates of corporations because expanding production meant increasing market sales for companies in oligopolistic market positions, which enabled corporations with their higher profits to pay higher wages. It should also be noted that this productivity wage was a family wage, one provided to the male breadwinner of the household to cover the costs of his unwaged dependents—housewife and children. However, in the 1960s workers in many industries went on strike and rejected the premise of the productivity wage and therefore the work regulation structuring the post-war boom. These workers demanded wage increases far and above any productivity increases in their work output. They demanded that more and more of the wealth produced go primarily to the workers rather than being shared between workers and the company—management and shareholders. Alongside this, radical groups of the women's movement and the welfare rights movement began to demand a universal basic income for mothers because motherhood was work (Federici 1975; Nadasen, Premilla 2004). Rather than forcing women to rely on their husband or the labor market as an intermediary to income, these groups demanded that the state provide a monthly income to mothers to pay them for all the social reproduction they performed. Cooking, cleaning and child rearing is necessary in order for the production and circulation of commodities to occur but it was a labor that was taken free of charge because it was framed as a biological or natural capacity of women rather than a social division of labor. At the same time university students were demanding free universal higher education or a "fully-funded" university that would educate people for democracy rather than the labor market, and environmental movements were forcing capital and the state to internalize the costs of ecological dislocation brought on by industrial society (Cohen and Zelnik 2002; Dowie 1996; Rogers 2012). Coterminous with these movements urban blacks were demanding investment in their communities, the end of redlining and restrictive covenants, a quality public education and a jobs program, which would require that the United States invest billions in Black communities rather than military weapons research and the war in Vietnam (Georgakas and Surkin 1998).

As a result, during the 1960s and 1970s the cost of reproducing the population and the landbase was becoming too expensive in the eyes of capitalists. The state and corporations increasingly had to factor into their costs of production reproducing people before, outside of, and after they worked, and they could no longer freely use the air, land and water as a waste dump. By the 1970s the New Deal social welfare programs and the Keynesian compromise with industrial unions were deepened by President Kennedy's New Frontier and President Johnson's Great Society Programs, which increased funding for jobless benefits, higher education, Medicare, Medicaid, housing, transportation, community development, the minimum wage, social security, welfare, and food stamps (Piven and Cloward [1971] 1993). Nixon's presidency extended this internalization of the social reproduction of the population to include the ecological reproduction of the landbase, as his presidency witnessed the passing of windfall legislation, including the National Environmental Policy Act, which created the Environmental Protection Agency (EPA: 1970), the Clean Water Act (1970), the Water Pollution Control Act (1972), the Marine Protection, Research, and Sanctuaries Act (1972), the Endangered Species Act (1973) and the Safe Drinking Water Act (1974). The long 1970s also ushered in the passage of the Resource Conservation and Recovery Act (1976), the Toxic Substances Control Act (1976), the Water Pollution Control Act, known as the Clean Water Act (1977), and the Comprehensive Environmental Response, Compensation, and Liability Act, known as the Superfund Act (1980). In all, Nixon the non-environmentalist appears on paper as the greenest president the country has ever seen (Dowie 1996).

Yet these movements went against the dominant tendency within capitalist logic, which is to externalize all costs of production, be they social or ecological (Marx [1867] 1990). If a worker is injured on the job then they should pay for their health care bills. If a company needs a new type of educated worker to perform a particularly skilled job, make the worker pay for their own job education. If a company dumps toxic sludge into the waterway and it contributes to reproductive problems for the women who drink from the surrounding wells, then those women and that community must absorb the economic burden of caring for those children. Companies do this because having to pay for the upkeep and health of the landbase, the community and the workers is an added cost that reduces and in fact can eliminate profits entirely.

Accordingly, corporations and Wall Street did not take too kindly to the attempts to place the health of people and the landbase before the sanctity of private profits and responded with their own social movement known as neoliberalism, whose central goal is to increase the rate of profit by reducing corporate responsibility for reproducing people and the environment (Harvey 2005). As a political project neoliberalism is best understood as the logic of moneylenders, not material producers. It expresses the desires of Goldman Sachs, Bear Stearns and Barclays rather than General Motors or U.S. Steel, the aspirations of Donald Trump instead of Henry Ford; one where the "institutional framework of free markets and free trade is regarded as a fundamental good [and] private enterprise and entrepreneurial initiative are seen as the keys to innovation and wealth creation" (Harvey 2005:64). These beliefs link economic growth, personal freedom and markets into a utopian imaginary that manifests in four major action items for neoliberal advocates who seek to realize this promised land (Harvey 2005). The first is privatization and commodification. This entails the end of services provided or subsidized by the state and their conversion into commodities one buys from various corporations, such as social security, medical care, education, parks, energy and transit. The second is financialization. Everything is expected to be liquid, creditized and bought and sold through financial markets. This includes your house, car, home, retirement accounts as well as the foundations of life: water, seed, land and air. Third is the management and manipulation of crises. A lot of money can be made through speculating on the price of corn in five years, the value of the peso next year, the price of Apple stock tomorrow or restructuring higher education around student loans instead of federal grants and scholarships. As a result, there are attempts to shape political and economic crises, such as the 1960s and 1970s, to produce outcomes in favor of moneylenders and financial speculators. The fourth is state redistributions from the lower to upper classes. This occurs through lowering income and capital gains taxes for the wealthy under the rhetoric of "spurring investment" and "creating jobs." In reality, these tax cuts are implemented to starve the federal and state treasuries and force cuts to social services and infrastructure for the lower classes, including public education, health care, childcare, park access, jobs and pensions. Not only do these actions lower the quality of life for millions of Americans but they also create economic opportunities for capitalists because the lower classes now have to buy services on the market. By starving the state, capitalists are able to force open new areas of profit generation for themselves; this is the central reason capitalists struggle against public services.

However, in order to achieve this political project, the capitalist class had to decompose the power of the existing workforce, the future workforce (students), those marginalized to the reserve army of the under- and un-employed (nonwhites) as well as the reproducers of that workforce (women)—all those who were involved in the Great Refusal. This occurred through planned austerity, deindustrialization, economic restructuring and a policy of free markets, low taxes and financial expansion (Harvey 2005). These movements were personified in Ronald Reagan, the face of the New Right, who removed solar panels from the White House roof, sought to defund and eliminate the existence of the EPA, drastically reduced federal funding for the poor and working classes (Medicaid, food stamps, federal education programs, homeless shelters, etc.), attacked the power of unions, advocated for state's rights—code for the ability of white communities to maintain segregation and racial supremacy—and pushed neoliberal economic policies (Marable [1983] 2000).

Production-based companies sought to reduce their costs of production by relocating overseas to areas where land and natural resources were cheap and plentiful and environmental regulations were few or far between, a practice that enabled companies to pollute at will and avoid the costs of cleanup (Gould et al. 2008). Corporations sought to reduce their labor costs by automating labor processes to deskill and shed jobs in blue and white collar sectors, restructuring or eliminating defined benefit pension plans and relocating production from the high-wage and pro-union Rustbelt to the low-wage and right-to-work Sunbelt or overseas altogether (Bluestone and Harrison 1982; Massey 2007).

Coterminous with this desire to reduce labor costs was the mass migration of women into the workforce, especially within the service sector. This "feminization" of wage work incentivized the individualization of wages and alongside of the de-unionization of the United States weakened the productivity/family wage structure of the post-war era (Eisenstein 2009). Overall, labor markets were restructured around a small number of core workers (full-time with job security, high wages, high benefits, and upward mobility) and a larger number of peripheral workers (part-time, precarious, low wage, low benefit, and no mobility) (Massey 2007; Peck 1996).

Cumulatively, these tactics realized a strategy of forcing down the social wage bill below the existing social consumption norm, one rooted in the New Deal welfare state and Keynesian economics. For the middling classes the outcome has been real wage stagnation or decline, a smaller percentage share of total income and wealth, ballooning CEO to worker pay, declining savings rates and escalating debt levels (Massey 2007; Zweig [2000] 2011).

From Wage Discipline to Debt Control: Neoliberalism and Finance Capital

Many capitalists sought to relocate production practices to lower-cost areas but this was not the only option available. Another tactic was to leave the sector of goods production altogether and seek out alternative avenues to accumulate capital, notably through financial speculation and debt-backed accumulation strategies (Harvey [1982] 2006; 2005). Subsequently, there is a turn away from commodity production towards the practice of "accumulation by dispossession," which aims to "redistribute, rather than generate, wealth and income" not merely through cutting back taxes and state services but by engaging in speculative and predatory capital flows that sought to "orchestrate, manage and control" debt in order to "redistribute assets" from the middling classes to the financial elite (Harvey 2005:159–63). This strategic maneuver occurred within the capitalist class because material goods production was seen as too risky and not profitable enough an investment—unruly workers and increasingly competitive market conditions drove down the rate of profit—compared to merely investing in money itself. For this reason, since the 1970s there has been a structural move within US capital away from industrial capitalism (M-C-M') to financial capitalism (M-M') with the strategy of accumulation by dispossession emerging as the central pillar for the accumulation of capital, the class strategy par excellence of neoliberals.

This move is important because as the dominant faction of the capitalist class, financial capitalists often have different interests than industrial capitalists on taxes, tariffs, interest rates and so on, which makes for different domestic and international policies. Since the 1970s, outside of energy companies, Wall Street has the strongest connections with the Federal Reserve, Congress and the White House and has been the central actor pushing for the expansion of housing and education debt. Housing and education debt, therefore, is not some anomaly or a sign of capitalism run amuck; it expresses the underlying logic of financial capitalism and is an intended outcome of practices that seek the accumulation of capital through a strategy of debt-based consumption.

In decomposing the "high wage" model of Keynesianism, neoliberalism decoupled the dominant production-consumption circuit of the New Deal era—the productivity/family wage—and gutted the existing method for regulating effective demand and the accumulation of capital. One solution was the cheap goods coming in from Asia and Latin America but this was not enough. Merely forcing down the social wage was insufficient; while it could reduce labor costs for capitalists it did nothing to jump start consumer spending, as people living on a future of diminished earnings began to pinch pennies. New mechanisms coupling capital and labor would need to be created to reenergize accumulation dynamics. The solution was a cheap money and credit policy that focused on maintaining a "consumer led" boom via increasing asset inflation (Brenner 2002). The massive financialization of daily life since the 1970s—home, education, medical care, clothing, food, car—signaled the movement of credit from the background to the foreground, from a supplement of wage-income to the primary mechanism maintaining accumulation. Neoliberalism reconfigured the capital relation in a manner that suited financial institutions and a politics of debt-based consumption rather than industrial capital and a politics of wage-based production. The hallmark of this transition is the move from the productivity/family wage to the liberalization of credit, from the one-time commodity sale towards endless returns— simple and compound interest. This shift from General Motors to the General Motors Acceptance Corporation (GMAC), from U.S. Steel to Goldman Sachs, from industrial to financial capitalism, reflects the larger movement from a society of discipline modeled on the wage to a society of control organized through debt, from the backbreaking monotonous pace of the factory assembly line to the instability of the stock market, from the fixedness of material production to the fluidity of satellite signals (Deleuze 1992).

Mortgage and Student Debt: Producing and Regulating Indebtedness

It is quite clear now, in hindsight, that neoliberalization pursued a low-wage high-debt accumulation dynamic. Debt became the ever-elusive money tree, an elixir of life where money begot money. Consequently, the last 40 years witnessed a continual liberalization of debt to fuel the accumulation of capital by drawing more and more consumers into the circuit of financial capitalism and the production of money-interest (Kotz 2008, 2009; O'Hara 2009). Central to this strategy within the mortgage industry was the movement away from the traditional post-war mortgage: a 20-percent down, 30-year fixed-rate mortgage with verification of employment, income and assets (Barth 2009; O'Hara 2009). Given wage stagnation, declining savings levels, crumbling upward mobility and price inflation of the home the 20-percent down, fixed-rate, full-documentation mortgage was no longer viable for millions of Americans. The mortgage industry responded to these changing economic conditions, conditions its own economic policies were creating, with adjustable-rate instead of fixed-rate mortgages, interest-only mortgages instead of principal and interest, and stated and no–documentation mortgages instead of full verification of employment, income and assets. Yet these tactics only pushed the unaffordability of home ownership to the future, as it postponed the bulk of the mortgage payment till later in life, presuming that the family would have moved up the job ladder and be able to afford the increased payments; obviously this was not the case.

In turn, neoliberalism's vast value production became primarily dependent on accumulating the future potentiality of people to become wage-labor. What emerged was a fictitious accumulation circuit based on future wages (debt) that had the possibility of never materializing, and with the 2008 crisis it did not, vaporizing trillions of dollars of fictitious capital. From the 1970s through today an entire financial apparatus developed to produce, organize and regulate value not merely through the accumulation of fictitious labor time (debt) but the inability to realize this fictitious labor time—delinquencies, defaults, foreclosures and bankruptcies. Within such an apparatus of value it became lucrative to extend debt to precisely those individuals and social groups who could not afford to pay off the debt because high interest rates and fees are the foundation of profits for credit lenders (Warren and Warren Tyagi 2003).

At the end of the fourth quarter of 2009, 11.3 million, or 24 percent, of all residential mortgages were in negative equity (First American CoreLogic 2010). Including mortgages approaching negative equity, those with less than 5 percent equity would add another 2.3 million mortgages (First American CoreLogic 2010). Overall, 27.1 percent of all residential mortgages were either in negative or near-negative equity. And of all negative equity mortgages the largest group was those with negative equity of −25 percent or more, constituting over 10 percent of all residential mortgages. During the same time period the delinquency rate (loans that are at least one payment past due) was 10.44 percent and the foreclosure rate was 4.58 percent for residential mortgages (Mortgage Bankers Association 2010). The cumulative delinquency/foreclosure rate of 15.02 percent was the highest ever recorded since the MBA started collecting figures in 1972. By the end of 2009 over 42 percent of all US mortgages were either in negative equity, near-negative equity, delinquency or foreclosure. It can be claimed that the mortgage industry knew this was coming and was a major instigating factor in its push to make it harder for people to declare bankruptcy, principally Chapter 7 bankruptcy where debts are discharged. Lending companies were targeting populations that were less and less likely to be able to pay back debts and as a result companies sought to reduce their risk of financial loss and secure their (potential) profits by denying debtors the ability to walk away from these predatory loans. First proposed in 1997, banks and credit card companies won their battle against debtors, consumer protection organizations and legal scholars in 2005 with passage of the Bankruptcy Abuse Prevention and Consumer Protection Act (BAPCPA). The act was legitimated by the banking and credit card industries as necessary to counter widespread bankruptcy fraud and that the cost savings from fewer people filing for bankruptcy would lead to lower costs for consumers; both claims are untrue (Simkovic 2009).

While household debt exemplifies the liberalization of credit as an artifact of the low-wage high-debt model of neoliberal accumulation, where an ever-expanding debt apparatus was produced to integrate more and more people into the production of money-interest, student debt most clearly embodies the four aspects of neoliberalism outlined earlier: privatization and commodification, financialization, management and manipulation of crises, and state redistributions from the lower to upper classes. During the 1950s and 1960s federal and state governments sunk billions of dollars into the formation of public higher education systems under the logic of human capital planning and Cold War politics. The former legitimated public funding as necessary for up-skilling workers to fuel the development of technological and economic growth. The latter required higher education as a device to prove that representative democracy and capitalism were superior to communism. The outcome for students was low-cost access to the Keynesian university, a university where public funding ensured low tuition costs, low levels of student debt and high grant-to-loan ratios (Williams 2006c).

During the 1960s, public universities in California, Connecticut, Kentucky, Idaho and New York City did not charge tuition and the average tuition charged nationally was in the hundreds of dollars, fees that could easily be paid off with a part-time minimum-wage job (Bousquet 2008; Kepple 2007). In 1964 the cost of public education—tuition, fees, food, clothing and housing—could be covered by working a minimum-wage job 22 hours a week for the entire year (Bosquet 2008:152). My parents were byproducts of the post-war boom in low-cost higher education. When they went to the University of California Santa Barbara in the mid-1970s tuition was less than $700 dollars a year—that would be about $2,800 a year today—and as a result they worked part-time during school to afford living expenses and emerged with no debt whatsoever.

The underpinnings of the Keynesian university did not last long though and began to erode during the 1960s and 1970s as they suffered the multiple shocks of local, regional and national student movements (Newfield 2008; Schrecker 2010; Washburn 2006). The corporate elite did not respond favorably to the campus protests griping the nation, protests encompassing free speech, the marginalization of labor, women's, third world, Black and Latino and gay and lesbian studies, and the university's relationship to the corporate and military industrial complex, amongst many others. Following the wave of campus unrest in the late 1960s, Lewis F. Powell, a corporate lawyer and future Associate Justice of the Supreme Court, penned a letter to a friend, Eugene Sydnor, Jr., who happened to be the Director of the US Chamber of Commerce. In the letter Powell wrote that "the campus is the single most dynamic source" of the "assault on the enterprise system" and outlined a plan of how to regain control over higher education, which included a program to place pro-corporate and pro-capitalist departments, programs, professors, curriculum, textbooks and campus groups on universities while also repressing liberals and leftists by a campaign that required universities to provide "balance" and "equal time," which would appeal to democratic notions of reasoned debate to build up conservatism on campus (Powell 1971). The letter also contended that shifting power within the university away from faculty and students towards administration and boards of trustees was central to regaining control over the university, a practice that has been well documented since the 1970s with the rise of a "managerial class" and the "administrative university" (Aronowitz 2000; Ginsberg 2011). Hewlett-Packard's David Packard echoed Powell's sentiments when he characterized universities as "havens for radicals who want to destroy the free enterprise system" and "are to a large degree, responsible for the anti-business bias of many of our young people today" (Schrecker 2010:100). Powell's and Packard's statements embody the class-consciousness of the capitalist class during this time and its perceived need to restructure the university in response to the power of the student movement, which they felt could bring down the entire capitalist system.

Powell and Packard achieved their goal. The resurgence of conservatism, the Republican Party and corporate power since the crisis of the 1960s and 1970s has meant federal and state defunding of higher education along with an emphasis on the privatization of costs, flexibilization of the workforce, commercialization of knowledge and the creation of an entrepreneurial climate that rewards innovation and market-centric technological development—practices that underpin the rise of the neoliberal university (Aronowitz 2000; Ginsberg 2011; Newfield 2008). While many attribute this transformation to the economic and fiscal crisis of the 1970s in fact it is born of "twenty five years of conservative attacks on the university" (Newfield 2008:5). The attack on the university sought to "reduce the economic claims of their target group—the growing college-educated majority—by discrediting the cultural framework that had been empowering that group" (Newfield 2008:6). The massive defunding of the university was therefore part of neoliberalism's "economic" or class war that sought to erode "the social and cultural foundations of a growing, politically powerful, economically entitled, and racially diversifying middle class, while leaving its technical capacities intact" (Newfield 2008:6). The economic crisis was merely utilized by the capitalist class and those aligned with it to legitimate their attack on student power and the restructuring of a university around profit and debt rather than education and democracy.

The class war from above sought to prevent the transformation of the middle class from a class-in-itself to a class-for-itself. If the university was not going to produce "depoliticized" docile bodies then the power elite no longer wanted to fund these institutions. Within the neoliberal university higher education was no longer allowed to be a "tax drain" on capital accumulation; instead a huge market for the accumulation of capital was produced through massive defunding of higher education by federal and state governments, the escalation of tuition costs to fill the gaps left by public budget cuts and the consequent expansion of a privatized credit apparatus to enable students to pay for the tuition increases. This privatization of access shifted the costs of education from corporations, the wealthy and the public onto the lower classes and individual families, reversing the 80/20 grant/loan model of the Keynesian university to create the 20/80 grant/loan model of the neoliberal university. In doing so, the economic and political autonomy of students to engage in social change would be restricted, as they would have less free time for political organizing and activism (Williams 2006a, 2006b, 2006c). The privatized funding model simultaneously sought to reduce the autonomy of the student from the labor market and ensure that the university was a space for job training, as debt would incentivize students to keep their nose to their grindstone so they could get a job after college to pay back their student loans (Williams 2006a, 2006b, 2006c).

Additionally, bankruptcy regulations surrounding student loans are even more onerous than home, credit card or auto debt. Student loans are the only type of debt that is generally unable to be discharged in Chapter 7 bankruptcy. As a result, the government can garnish your wages, pensions, social security and retirement accounts to pay back Wall Street. Student loans are therefore a close to a guaranteed payment for student loan companies. Why are student loans exempt from the basic premise of democratic capitalist society where corporations and individuals can declare bankruptcy and start again? Because in the 1970s Wall Street essentially claimed that there was an organized debt strike by students who were taking out millions in student loans with no intention of paying them back (Fossey and Bateman 1998). Once again, this scenario was a fictitious creation of banks and student loan companies to create a guaranteed profit stream with no risk, a profit stream created by their defunding of public education in the first place (Fossey and Bateman 1998).

Conclusion: The Society of Control is a Society in Debt, which is the Neoliberal Utopia

As was becoming clear before the economic crisis of 2008 and is plainly apparent afterwards, neoliberalism and its debt-based accumulation dynamics is really a form of parasitism, plain and simple. It utilized the 1960s and 1970s crisis—a crisis of power relations between and within classes—to legitimate a new wave of accumulation premised on a low-wage high-debt model aptly named "accumulation by dispossession." Neoliberalism did not create a middle class, quality jobs with living wages, a stable job structure or sound retirement plans. It did not bring to life the manufacturing cities of the Midwest or the Northeast. It did not make housing or education or medical care more affordable. But what it did, and was very successful at doing, was to drain billions of dollars from the accumulated wealth of the lower classes—wealth built up during the previous post-war boom—and transfer it into the hands of Wall Street in order to prop up their sagging economic portfolios. As a result, the neoliberal utopia clearly exemplifies Karl Marx's famous quote that "capital is dead labor which, vampire-like, lives only by sucking living labor, and lives the more, the more labor it sucks" (Marx [1867] 1990:257). Yet, unlike industrial capitalism, whose vampire-like existence was based on sucking the labor from its disciplined worker in the factory, the financial capitalism of today is omnipresent and sucks the future potentiality of labor from people anywhere and everywhere. Within the United States neoliberalism exemplifies control at a distance. No matter what job you have, what school you go to, what home you own, what hospital procedure you have or the clothes you wear, all these purchases will circulate through the pockets of finance capital, depositing a few cents here and a few dollars there, practices that when multiplied by billions and billions of transactions daily turn into trillions of dollars in no time at all.

A slow trickle in the 1970s, by the 2000s this tsunami of worker savings was being appropriated by Wall Street to batter down the doors of public education, public housing, social security, welfare, food stamps, unions, minimum wage laws and clean air and water regulations. When the debt bubble burst it only got worse. The joblessness and homelessness that neoliberalism produced during the deindustrialization of the Rustbelt in the 1960s, 1970s, and 1980s was quickly reproduced in the supposedly booming Sunbelt. In both locals, people have been forced out of their homes, the lifetime earnings of families have been destroyed and bottoming out property taxes have decimated local and state government's ability to provide basic services. Both regions are now left to face the repercussions of an economic policy that put corporate profits before the health of the people and the planet and legitimized such wanton destruction with claims of freedom and liberty.

Bibliography

Adamson, Morgan. 2009a. "The Financialization of Student Life: Five Propositions on Student Debt." *Polygraph* 21:97–110.

Aronowitz, Stanley. 2000. *The Knowledge Factory: Dismantling the Corporate University and Creating True Higher Learning*. Boston: Beacon Press.

Barth, James R. 2009. *The Rise and Fall of the U.S. Mortgage and Credit Markets*. New York: John Wiley and Sons.

Baum, Sandy and Kathleen Payea. 2011. *Trends in Student Aid 2011*. Washington, D.C.: The College Board.

Baum, Sandy, Kathleen Payea and Patricia Steele. 2009. *Trends in Student Aid 2009*. Washington, D.C: The College Board.

Blackburn, Robin. 2008. "The Subprime Crisis." *New Left Review* 50:63–106.

Bluestone, Barry and Bennett Harrison. 1982. *The Deindustrialization of America*. New York: Basic Books.

Bousquet, Marc. 2008. *How The University Works*. New York: New York University Press.

Brass, Tom. 1999. *Toward A Comparative Economy of Unfree Labor*. Portland: Frank Cass Publishers.

Brass, Tom, ed. 2003. *Latin American Peasants*. New York: Routledge.

Breines, W. 1989. *Community and Organization in the New Left, 1962−1968: The Great Refusal*. New Brunswick: Rutgers University Press.

Brenner, Robert. 2002. *The Boom and the Bubble: The US in the World Economy*. New York: W. W. Norton & Company.

Cohen, Lizabeth. [2003] 2004. *A Consumer's Republic: The Politics of Mass Consumption in Postwar America*. New York: Vintage Books.

Cohen, Robert and Reginald Zelnik, eds. 2002. *The Free Speech Movement: Reflections on Berkeley in the 1960s*. Berkeley: University of California Press.

College Board. Sandy Baum, Saul Schwartz, *How Much Debt is Too Much? Defining Bench Marks for Manageable Student Debt* (New York: The College Board, 2006).

Deleuze, Gilles. 1992. "Postscript on the Societies of Control." *October* 59:3−7.

Dore, Elizabeth. 2006. *Myths of Modernity: Peonage and Patriarchy in Nicaragua*. Durham: Duke University Press.

Dowie, Mark. 1996. *Losing Ground: American Environmentalism at the Close of the Twentieth Century*. Cambridge, MA: MIT Press.

Eisenstein, Hester. 2009. *Feminism Seduced: How Global Elites Use Women's Labor and Ideas to Exploit the World*. Boulder, CO: Paradigm Publishers.

Federal Reserve Board. 2010. "Flow of Funds Accounts of the United States: Flows and Outstandings." Retrieved October 29, 2010 (http://www.federalreserve.gov/releases/z1/default.htm)

Federici, S. 1975. *Wages Against Housework*. London: Falling Wall Press.

First American CoreLogic. 2010. "Media Alert: Underwater Mortgages On the Rise According to First American CoreLogic Q4 2009 Negative Equity Data." First American CoreLogic. Retrieved February 28.2010. (http://www.loanperformance.com/infocenter/library/Q4_2009_Negative_Equity_Final.pdf)

Ford, Richard. 1926. "Imprisonment for Debt." *Michigan Law Review* 25(1):24–49

Fossey, Richard and Mark Bateman, eds. 1988. *Condemning Students to Debt*. New York: Teachers College Press.

Georgakas, Dan and Marvin Surkin. 1998. *Detroit: I Do Mind Dying*. Cambridge, MA: South End Press.

Ginsberg, Benjamin. 2011. *The Fall of the Faculty: The Rise of the All-Administrative University and Why It Matters*. Oxford: Oxford University Press.

Gladieux, Lawrence, Watson Scott Swail and Ermelinda Carvajal. 1998. *Trends in Student Aid 1998*. Washington: College Board.

Gould, Kenneth A., David N. Pellow and Allan Schnaiberg. 2008. *The Treadmill of Production: Injustice and Unsustainability in the Global Economy*. New Jersey: Paradigm Publishers.

Graeber, David. 2011. *Debt: The First 5,000 Years*. Brooklyn: Melville House.

Harvey, David. [1982] 2006. *Limits to Capital*. New York: Verso.

Harvey, David. 2003. *The New Imperialism*. New York: Oxford University Press.

Harvey, David. 2005. *A Brief History of Neoliberalism*. New York: Oxford University Press.

Jackson, Kenneth. 1985. *Crabgrass Frontier: The Suburbanization of the United States*. New York: Oxford University Press.

Katsiaficas, George. 1999. *The Imagination of the New Left: A Global Analysis of 1968*. Cambridge: South End Press.

Kepple, Thomas. 2007. "Tuition and Student Debt Levels Reflect National Priorities." Retrieved May 10. 2010. (http://www.universitybusiness.com/article/tuition-and-student-debt-levels-reflect-national-priorities).

Kotz, David M. 2008. "Contradictions of Economic Growth in the Neoliberal Era: Accumulation and Crisis in the Contemporary U.S. Economy." *Review of Radical Political Economics* 40:2 (Spring):174–188.

Kotz, David M. 2009. "The Financial and Economic Crisis of 2008: A Systemic Crisis of Neoliberal Capitalism." *Review of Radical Political Economics* 41:3 (Summer):305–317.

Lucas, Christopher. 1994. *American Higher Education: A History*. New York: St. Martin's Press.

Marable, Manning. 1983 [2000]. *How Capitalism Underdeveloped Black America: Problems in Race, Political Economy, and Society*. Cambridge, MA: South End Press.

Marx, Karl. [1867] 1990. *Capital*. New York: Penguin Books.

Massey, Douglas. 2007. *Categorically Unequal: The American Stratification System*. New York: Russell Sage Foundation.

Midnight Notes. 1992. *Midnight Oil: Work, Energy, War, 1973–1992*. Brooklyn: Autonomedia.

Mortgage Bankers Association. 2010. *National Delinquency Survey: Fourth Quarter 2009*. Washington, D.C.: Mortgage Bankers Association.

Nadasen, Premilla. 2004. *Welfare Warriors: The Welfare Rights Movement in the United States*. New York: Routledge.

National Center for Education Statistics. 2011. "*Trends in Student Financing of Undergraduate Education: Selected Years, 1995–96 to 2007–08*." Washington, D.C.: U.S. Department of Education.

Negri, Antonio. 1988. *Revolution Retrieved: Writings on Marx. Keynes, Capitalist Crisis and New Social Subjects (1967–1983)*. London: Red Notes.

Newfield, Christopher. 2008. *Unmaking the Public University: The Forty-Year Assault on the Middle Class*. Harvard: Harvard University Press.

O'Hara, Philip Anthony. 2009. "The Global Securitized Subprime Market Crisis." *Review of Radical Political Economics* 41:3 (Summer):318–334.

Peck, Jamie. 1996. *Work-place: The Social Regulation of Labor Markets*. New York: The Guilford Press.

Piven, Frances and Richard Cloward. [1971] 1993. *Regulating the Poor: The Functions of Public Welfare*. New York: Vintage Books.

Powell, Lewis. 1971. "Attack on the American Free Enterprise System." Personal memo.

Prakash, Gyan. 1990. *Bonded Histories: Genealogies of Labor Servitude in Colonial India*. Cambridge: University of Cambridge.

Rogers, Ibram. 2012. *The Black Campus Movement: Black Students and the Racial Reconstruction of Higher Education, 1965–1972*. New York: Palgrave Macmillan.

Schrecker, Ellen. 2010. *The Lost Soul of Higher Education: Corporatization, the Assault on Academic Freedom and the End of the American University*. New York: The New Press.

Simkovic, Michael. 2009. "The Effect of BAPCPA on Credit Card Industry Profits and Prices." *American Bankruptcy Law Journal* 83(1).

Sullivan, Teresa A., Elizabeth Warren, and Jay Lawrence Westbrook. 2000. *The Fragile Middle Class: Americans in Debt*. New Haven: Yale University Press.

U.S. Bureau of Economic Analysis. 2010. "Gross Domestic Product." Retrieved October 29. 2010 (http://research.stlouisfed.org/fred2/).

Warren, Elizabeth and Tyagi Amelia Warren. 2003. *The Two Income Trap: Why Middle-Class Mothers and Fathers Are Going Broke*. New York: Basic Books.

Washburn, Jennifer. 2006. *University. Inc.: The Corporate Corruption of Higher Education*. New York: Basic Books.

Williams, Jeffry. 2006a. "The Pedagogy of Debt." *College Literature* 33:4, 155–169.

Williams, Jeffrey. 2006b. "Debt Education: Bad for the Young, Bad for America." *Dissent* Summer: 55–61.

Williams, Jeffrey. 2006c. "The Post-Welfare State University." *American Literary History* 18:1, 190–216.

Woodfine P (2006) "Debtors, Prisons, and Petitions in Eighteenth-Century England." *Eighteenth-Century Life* 30(2): 1–31.

Zerowork Collective. 1972. *Zerowork: Volume I*. Brooklyn.

Zweig, Michael. [2000] 2011. *The Working Class Majority*. Ithaca: Cornell University Press.

PART THREE
The Capitalist Class

CHAPTER 25

The Capitalist Class
Accumulation, Crisis and Discipline

Michael J. Roberts

Attention to a resurgent power elite in the United States and abroad has spiked in recent years, due in part to the global Occupy Wall Street (OWS) protest movement, but also due to years of increasing coverage of economic inequality among mainstream media outlets, including the *New York Times*, which published a series of articles in 2005 titled "Class in America." More to the point, the *Atlantic Magazine* published an article in 2011 on the rise of a "new global elite" that transcends national boundaries, forming an *über*-class of wealthy people. This class is no longer tied down to nation states, which have increasingly become too parochial to satisfy their political-economic and cultural interests (January, 2011).[1] The so-called "new" global elite, which derives much of its political-economic power from control over the world's financial markets, is what the OWS movement has referred to as the top "one percent" of the population, culturally and economically distinct from, and frequently at political odds with, the bottom 99%. Ironically, it was the giant banking conglomerate Citigroup that helped ignite the global conversation about the rise of a transnational "plutocratic" class when someone leaked an internal document in 2005 titled "Plutonomy [sic]: Buying Luxury, Explaining Global Imbalances." The document states bluntly that "the world is dividing into two blocs – the Plutonomy and the rest."[2]

Another article on the emergence of "plutocracy" in America appeared in *Mother Jones Magazine*, which revealed that the richest one percent owns 40 percent of the entire nation's wealth, while the top ten percent own over two-thirds of the wealth in the United States. The bottom 80 percent of Americans control just 26 percent of the wealth in the United States, while according to Edward Wolff at New York University, the bottom 40 percent own just 0.2 percent of the privately held wealth in the United States.[3] The majority of wealth that so-called "middle-class" Americans own is wrapped up in their home equity, which plunged dramatically after the housing bubble burst in 2008. If you consider only financial wealth, the distribution is even more severe: the bottom 80 percent of the population owns a mere *five* percent of the financial wealth in the United States (*Mother Jones*, "Plutocracy Now," April, 2011). At the global level the statistics are staggering. A 2014 study by Oxfam revealed that the wealthiest 85 individuals in the world have more wealth than the bottom 3.5 *billion* combined, roughly half of the world's population (*The Guardian*, Monday, January 20, 2014). Related issues like the increasing

Class: The Anthology, First Edition. Edited by Stanley Aronowitz and Michael J. Roberts.
© 2018 Stanley Aronowitz and Michael J. Roberts. Published 2018 by John Wiley & Sons Ltd.

power that all kinds of corporations exercise over Congress as well as the decline of the so-called "middle" class, have also garnered more public attention, although interpretation of the issues varies widely across the political spectrum.

Increasing coverage of and changing attitudes toward economic inequality culminated in the Bernie Sanders campaign for President in 2016. While Sanders eventually lost to Clinton in the bid to be the Democratic Party's candidate, his campaign took the country by surprise, just as the Occupy Wall Street Movement had five years prior. The widespread popularity of Bernie Sanders – a self-described "democratic socialist" – among younger people, who are acutely aware that the current and future job market has little to offer, demonstrates that economic inequality and class struggle have returned to center stage in both American and global politics. It seems as if the prognostications of the "end of history," touted by apologists for capitalism after the fall of the Berlin Wall, were profoundly mistaken. Capitalism has, instead, thrown the world into a series of political crises. For many young actors within the global regime of neoliberalism, the time seems ripe for the return of socialism, although a democratic socialism shorn of the curse of Stalinism.

Of course the history of capitalism has always been marked by the relationship between a ruling capitalist class (which in various eras of history breaks into distinct fractions) that exists in antagonism with a working class and its sometimes diverse fractions. Nevertheless, in recent years new developments have emerged that demand analysis. Indeed, four important, interrelated issues that have emerged with the further globalization of capitalism in recent years are: (1) the growing power of finance capital relative to both other powerful factions of capitalists in the global economy *and* entire nation states; (2) the changing form of the relationship between capital and labor within nation states in the West, where the capitalist class is less and less dependent on the domestic working class both in terms of manufacturing consumer durable goods *and* eventually in terms of consuming those goods; (3) the use of government austerity measures to discipline the global working class and impose working conditions that reproduce social relations of production favorable to capitalist class interests; and (4) the emergence of a new system of debt peonage, which mediates the dynamic of the industrial-class relation between capital and labor. (For more on debt peonage see the selection by Justin Sean Myers in Chapter 24.)

I

Developments like these raise the question of the relationship between the government and political-economic elites, a group that C. Wright Mills referred to collectively as the "power elite." Writing in the 1950s, Mills sought to demonstrate that the relationship of interwoven interests between corporate, military and political elites ultimately placed democracy in jeopardy within the geographic boundaries of sovereign nation states.[4] Today, however, the increasing power of global-finance capitalists throws the question of state sovereignty, *as such*, into question. The political-economic situation of undemocratically imposed austerity measures in Greece, Ireland, Portugal and Spain in recent years is evidence of the growing power of multinational banking conglomerates over entire nation states. Today, we may talk of a *financial*-power elite, which has surpassed the industrial fraction of the corporate elite as both the primary driving force of economic growth (also referred to as capital accumulation) on a global scale and as the most powerful political presence in global politics.[5] It is not only the case that financiers on Wall Street provide the lion's share of campaign donations to both the Republican and Democratic parties in the United Sates as a means to change federal laws to suit their pecuniary interests, including the deregulation of financial markets made possible by the repeal of the Glass–Steagall Act of 1932, and its replacement by the Gramm–Leach–Bliley Act in 1999, which was signed into law by a Democrat, Bill Clinton. The financial-power elite also have the power to drive economic policy-making throughout multiple nation states simultaneously, indeed across entire regions of the globe.[6] The large invest-ment banks, together with the managers and investors in charge of the vast hedge funds and powerful private equity firms, constitute the new face of the power elite.

The power and influence enjoyed by corporate business elites over American foreign policy is, of course, not a new phenomenon. In the twentieth century, large corporations based in the United States like the United Fruit Company (today known as Chiquita) had the power to influence American foreign policy to such an extent that the US government sponsored and organized the overthrow of several democratically elected governments that challenged the power of American companies doing business inside their sovereign borders. One such example was the democratically elected government of President Jacobo Arbenz in Guatemala where United Fruit had a substantial base of operations. Land reform policies enacted in 1952 by the Arbenz government that were designed to redistribute vacant, unused, arable land from very large land-owners to small farmers in Guatemala were seen by company executives at United Fruit (as well as American busi-ness leaders represented by the US Chamber of Commerce) as a peril to the operations of United Fruit, which controlled huge swathes of unused, arable land in Guatemala at that time. Political organizations that represent the interests of business owners, like the US Chamber of Commerce, coded the land redistribution policies as a threat to democ-racy and freedom in the western hemisphere, and spoke out frequently in public venues against the Arbenz government (CBS Reports, "Guatemala," September 1, 1982).

Discursive maneuvers like these limit the meaning of the concept "freedom" so that it signifies "free-enterprise," or "free markets" exclusively, and at the expense of other pos-sible meanings like free time (leisure) or the freedom of all people to participate in institu-tions that attempt to exclude individuals on the basis of class, race, sexual preference and/or gender. In other words, the concept freedom is defined from the perspective of capitalists over and against citizens who do not have ownership or control over the means of production (which would be access to land in the Guatemalan case described above). The problem for the capitalist class is how to present its own particular interests as if they were the universal interests of all people. The necessary if not sufficient condition to achieve this kind of hegemony within the sphere of political discourse is control of the economy. This is what Marx (*German Ideology*) meant by the phrase, "the ruling ideas of society are the ideas of the ruling class." Command over the conditions of material pro-duction has a strong relationship to command over the conditions of mental or discursive production. In short, control over material resources matters in global politics.

Thus in 1954, after declaring that the Arbenz government was a "communist threat" in the western hemisphere, the United States, working through its Central Intelligence Agency (CIA), funded and organized a coup d'état, which replaced the democratically elected Arbenz with a military junta led by Carlos Castillo. There are several other cases like this including the overthrow of the democratically elected Salvador Allende in Chile in 1973, after Allende moved to nationalize several large industries inside Chile. As Stephen Kinzer of the *New York Times* has recently documented in his book *Overthrow*, the United States has toppled the governments of 14 sovereign states. This history has been referred to by the historian William Appleman Williams as the "tragedy of American diplomacy."[7]

Corporate interests continue to drive US foreign policy today, whether in cases like the US invasion of Iraq in 2003, or the American political corruption scandal that ended the careers of both the infamous lobbyist Jack Abramoff and his major collaborator inside Congress, the former Speaker of the House, Tom DeLay, in 2006. In the latter case, Abramoff was the go-between for garment manufacturing companies in Saipan, part of the Commonwealth of the Northern Mariana Islands (CNMI) and DeLay, who controlled crucial committees in the US Congress that had authority over the legal status of the CNMI. What the company owners sought, and what both Abramoff and DeLay wanted to deliver to them, was a zone where no labor or environmental regulations could interfere with so-called "free enterprise." In all, 80 US Congressmen were eager to create and maintain an unincorporated territory of the United States without interference from labor unions, workers' rights legislation and restrictions on the environmental impacts of doing business that existed in the mainland United States. Because the CNMI is an unincorporated territory, none of the US immigration or labor laws apply there. DeLay and his backers argued that their pro-business, "laissez-faire" policies were improving the conditions of working-class people living in the CNMI as well as the lives of workers imported from other countries to work there. The claim was that free enterprise benefits all actors in the economy.

In reality, workers toiled under exploitative conditions that resembled the horrors of Dickensian England, with seven-day work weeks and 18-hour workdays. Some women workers were chained to their sewing machines, other women who were pregnant were pressured into having abortions, and many workers had their passports confiscated.[8] The garment companies in Saipan were looking to import workers from other areas like Nepal and the Philippines, pay them a little over one dollar an hour and deny them safe working conditions. Workers recruited from places like Bangladesh were forced to pay thousands of dollars (in some cases close to 6,000) to get the "opportunity" to travel to and work in Saipan, an exorbitant amount by any standard. Since most of the workers could not pay the finder's fee up-front, the fee was taken out of their paychecks by their employers in Saipan in order to pay the labor recruiters for finding them. Many of the workers were purposely not informed about the amount of the fee, or how they would be legally obliged to remain in Saipan until the debt was paid off. The arrangement was carefully constructed so that the garment company owners did not contribute any money towards helping workers travel to Saipan, and once the workers arrived, wages were purposely kept very low to bind the workers to the factories for extended periods working for zero compensation. It typically took workers more than three months of working round-the-clock seven days a week to pay off the finder fees. Worst of all was the emergence of human trafficking in sex slaves, as many of the people who came seeking work were unable to find jobs in the garment factories.

The arrangement crafted by Abramoff and DeLay had a particular catch, however, as the garments displayed tags that read "Made in the USA." While certain Republican Congressmen argued that their policies were a "win-win" for everyone involved, the former Governor of CNMI, Juan Babauta, referred to the situation as an environment of rampant exploitation.[9] For his services, the manufacturing companies in the CNMI paid Abramoff over $200,000. The Congressmen who traveled to the CNMI in order to praise the virtues of "free enterprise," all received campaign contributions from the manufacturing companies there, including Tom DeLay.

Here, then, is another example of how the concept of freedom is significantly trans-figured. The irony should not be lost: an environment of human trafficking and inden-tured servitude in the CNMI was labeled "free-enterprise" by the representatives of the power elite. In an Orwellian manner, things come to signify their opposite. Servitude is freedom. While political-economic elites pursue their economic interests in a rational manner, and at the expense of workers, ideology creates a situation where they interpret their activities as helping others. In other words, we are not talking about an elaborate, secret conspiracy, but rather particular historical conditions that create contexts where individuals interpret their world in a manner that inverts their actual relationships. Ideology allows subjects (individuals who respond to the authorities who address them) positioned by it to claim that servitude equals freedom. Here again, like the situation of US foreign policy in Guatemala described above, the point of view of the capitalist class is imposed on the rest of society. The perspective of the working class is the "Other," so to speak, of the capitalist class, and it remains a problem for the capitalist class to con-tinually attempt to push alternative perspectives and discourses to the margins of society where they remain relatively absent from view. These are questions for politics and his-tory. As we have seen with the OWS movement, the capitalist class is not always success-ful in imposing its perspective on the rest of society. Indeed, the OWS has helped draw attention to what is new in the ways that the capitalist class rules over society at the expensive of citizens "Othered" by the capitalist class.

II

The situation with the power exercised by financial capitalists through the state in the twenty-first century is somewhat different from the role that industrial capital played during the twentieth century. Of course powerful financiers have always played a key role in the various phases of capitalist development, from merchants who financed the very first factories in the early nineteenth century to the giants of finance during the Gilded Age, including figures like J.P. Morgan. But, as Rudolf Hilferding outlined in his book *Finance Capital* (first published in 1910), financiers played a key role in *organizing* and stabilizing capitalist development beginning in the twentieth century through the seizure of the state, and using the state to intervene on behalf of the capitalist class during times of economic crisis. Hilferding's argument was that finance capitalists understood the inherent instability of truly competitive, "free" market capitalism, which is prone to crises that follow from chronic overproduction. To solve the problem of recurring instability and the tendency toward economic crisis in unregulated capitalist formations, finance capital led the way to a new phase of capitalism, namely monopoly capitalism, which is characterized by oligopoly (more on this later), state planning on behalf of the capitalist class, and imperialism.

Indeed, imperialism is a key feature of modern capitalism beginning with the period immediately following the economic depression caused by the Panic of 1893. The eco-nomic crisis of 1893 was understood by both the political right and the political left to be caused by the dramatic rise in the economic surplus, a situation where the durable goods produced by the economy cannot be absorbed by the given aggregate of consumer demand: too many goods for sale, not enough consumers. In order to solve the problem, the power elite, led by President McKinley, opted for finding new markets in countries abroad to absorb the surplus. For the leaders of industry, the problem of the economic surplus was framed in terms of over-*production*, which is why they pushed for finding new markets. On the other side, socialists, trade unionists and middle-class reformers framed the issue as under-*consumption*, and their solution to the crisis was to increase wages for working people to boost their capacity to consume the surplus. The labor movement sought to achieve this through a strategy of working shorter hours to decrease unemployment, boost demand for labor and drive up wages in order to consume the economic surplus. This alternative to imperialism still exists today, and it remains to be seen if the Left will be successful in implementing this agenda.

While during the twentieth century the class struggle produced a mixture of sorts, between the two options, it remains the case that imperialism became a key feature of US policy regarding the economic surplus. Key figures within the power elite at the time were strikingly candid about the relationship between imperialism and the economic surplus. One of the best examples was Major General Smedley Butler, who participated in military actions in Cuba, China, the Philippines and Central America. In his pamphlet, *War is a Racket*, first published in 1935, Butler described his role in the military as "a high class muscle-man for Big Business, for Wall Street and for the Bankers. In short, I was a racketeer, a gangster for capitalism."[10] The kind of imperialism described by Butler is no longer the norm, the 2003 invasion of Iraq notwithstanding. Finance capitalists have changed the rules of engagement.

The size and scope of finance capital today is significantly greater than that of industrial capital in the 1950s, which partly explains how and why the form of imperialism has also changed. The ability of large industrial corporations like United Fruit to engineer regime change in relatively small countries like Guatemala pales in comparison to the power finance capitalists exercise all over the globe today. This is especially the case regarding the economic crises in Greece, Ireland, Portugal and Spain in recent years, where the European Union (EU), led by German and French financial-capitalist interests, has pressured those governments to impose draconian austerity measures – as a means, ostensibly, to show foreign investors that their governments would remain solvent and not default on their debt – in spite of widespread democratic resistance to such measures by the citizens of those states. From the point of view of the political leaders of the EU, the interests of the transnational financial elite outweigh the interests of citizens in sovereign nations. In these cases, imperialism is delivered through toxic interest-rate swaps and manipulated derivatives markets rather than the barrel of a gun. So while reporters like Matt Taibbi[11] at *Rolling Stone Magazine* have revealed that risky, sometimes fraudulent speculation by investment banks like Goldman Sachs, Lehman Brothers, JP Morgan-Chase, UBS and others was responsible for the global economic crisis, the burden of the crisis has been shifted to tax-payers who bailed out the big investment banks, and in turn nation states have imposed austerity measures upon their own citizens by eliminating needed government services and slashing the pay and benefits of public sector workers as a way to cope with rising debts and declining revenues.[12]

Problematically, the news media focus on the politics of austerity has shifted our attention away from what originally plunged the world into this particular economic crisis in 2008. It was deregulation of the financial services industry that made the destructive speculation possible in the first place. The speculation involved the creation of a housing bubble (what Marx refers to as "fictitious capital") where the investment banks encouraged pools of investors like large pension funds to put money into mortgage-backed securities, while the banks themselves planned on selling short in order to exit the bubble before it popped. Congressional hearings in 2010 revealed that in many infamous cases, the banks advised their clients to invest in financial "products" they themselves considered worthless, or "shit" (*The Guardian*, April 27, 2010).

In short, the practices of the new global financial elite created the global economic crisis, but it is working-class people in multiple countries that so far have suffered the consequences.[13] The financial power elite has been able to displace the crisis they caused onto others but, again, the intervention of the OWS movement has made it difficult for finance capitalists to control how people interpret the crisis, even as most of the largest media outlets like Fox News take the point of view of the finance capitalists. Right-wing media have attempted to persuade the public that state spending caused the economic crisis, but the pressure from below coming from OWS has forced other media outlets like the *New York Times* to occasionally challenge the discursive hegemony of the investment banks and the US Treasury. Writing as a columnist for the *NYT*, the economist Paul Krugman revealed that reckless speculation led to the economic crisis in Europe, *not* irresponsible spending by nation states, as conservative pundits have claimed (see Krugman, *End This Depression Now!*). These practices taken together – deregulation of the financial services industry and the austerity measures imposed by nation states in Western Europe and the United States – are the principal causes of the massive, upward redistribution of wealth across the globe in recent years, and it is this issue which has been successfully brought to public attention by the OWS movement.

According to journalist Matt Taibbi, in some situations it is much worse than a case where governments pay for the economic damage caused by reckless speculation among the financial power elite. Much attention has been given to the tax-payer bailouts that allow the big banks to borrow money from the federal government at rates *much* lower than the rates at which the banks lend to the rest of the actors in the economy (a practice that is essentially a form of welfare for the financial elite). Other forms of tax-payer bailouts involve removing toxic assets from the bank holdings and placing them onto the balances sheets of the government. In both these cases, tax-payers fund the infusion of free money into the large banks (see Taibbi's book, *Griftopia*). While these arrangements have caused considerable concern among some pundits and politicians on the left, the relationship between the giant investment banks and all levels of government goes beyond the practices of the federal government giving free money to the big banks.

In the more egregious scenarios, investment bankers cajole local governments to finance public investment projects with very risky deals involving what are called "toxic interest-rate swaps," which end up placing these governments in a situation where they are overwhelmed and incapacitated by debt piled upon them by the investment banks. In places like Jefferson County, Alabama, for example, large investment banks – JP Morgan-Chase in this case – bribe corrupt politicians to fund needed infrastructure improvement projects like sewer system repairs by entering toxic-swap deals with the banks. In these arrangements, governments borrow money on the basis of *variable* interest rates, based upon the vagaries of volatile derivatives markets. While the local governments borrow money at a *variable* rate – set by the London Interbank Offered Rate or LIBOR – they have to pay back the banks at a *fixed* rate. Initially, local governments may be able to borrow at relatively low rates, but in the volatile derivatives market, things can go very bad, very fast, like they did for Jefferson County, which according to Taibbi could have funded their sewer system repairs for 250 million dollars in a traditional financing arrangement of selling government bonds. Instead, the county went into debt for 3 *billion* dollars

(*Rolling Stone*, April 7, 2012). Wall Street traders, who understand the machinations of huge institutional actors like Goldman Sachs, JP Morgan and others, know that these are bad deals for their "customers," but the financial incentives for corrupt financiers are strong enough to risk breaking the law by perpetrating fraud on a very large scale. Eventually criminal charges were brought against both the politicians from Jefferson County and individuals from JP Morgan-Chase who arranged those toxic deals.

As the journalist and lawyer Glenn Greenwald has revealed, many of these kinds of crimes go unpunished, demonstrating that the financial power elite are able to break the law with relative impunity (Greenwald, *With Liberty and Justice for Some*[14]). Meanwhile these crimes create havoc across the US. Deals like the one arranged between JP Morgan-Chase and Jefferson County were created with local governments all across the country, costing local tax-payers an extra 1.25 billion dollars a year to service these toxic loan deals. Cities like Detroit, Chicago and Denver paid banks like Goldman Sachs, JP Morgan-Chase and Citigroup tens of millions of dollars a year as part of these swap arrangements, which translated into an inability on the part of these municipalities to pay their workers who provide much needed services to the public. The irony is that conservative politicians and right-wing media outlets blamed public sector unions for the budget woes of local governments rather than the bankers who commit fraud and politicians who are cajoled into creating these toxic-rate-swap arrangements that cripple local governments (*Mother Jones*, March 23, 2010). A similar situation has developed with regard to the European crisis, where blame has been framed in moral terms: conservatives and mainstream media alike claim that irresponsible spending by governments is to blame for the economic crisis. Framing the crisis in this way helps to shift the analysis in a way that serves the interests of the financial-power elite, demonstrating again the power of discourse in the shaping of class struggle and public policy (see Chapter 34 by Lawler).

III

Social scientists have been studying the phenomenon of increasing economic inequality for decades, but discussion of the growing power of a global elite or a ruling class remained on the margins of American academic and political discourse as long as the United States experienced relative economic growth, that purportedly prevented the possibility of plutocratic rule. After all, Americans have a long tradition of denying that ours is a class-divided society. So, while economic inequality first began to show a significant pattern of expansion in the late 1970s, a phenomenon that Bluestone and Harrison refer to as the "Great U-Turn" in the American political economy, it was said by conservatives to have been mitigated by the relative sustained economic growth in the decades that followed.[15] During the Reagan years, as the federal government began to experiment in earnest with supply-side or "trickle-down" economic policies (which included significant reductions in the tax burdens for corporations and wealthy individuals as well as deregulation of key industries like the airline, trucking and communications industries) conservatives made good use of the phrase, "a rising tide lifts all boats." The fact that some boats rose much higher and faster than others, and that many other boats were in fact sinking, was largely unexamined by the major news media institutions.

If topics like poverty were covered by the media in the 1980s, the issue was framed in terms of the cultural defects of poor people themselves. For example, the journalist Ken

Auletta coined the term "underclass" in the 1980s in order to claim that poverty in the United States was largely the result of dysfunctional cultural norms among the urban poor. In short, he argued that it was the bad behavior of the poor that caused their poverty. For journalists like Auletta, the political-economic system was not to blame for the existence of poverty in America. For the rest of America not trapped in the "under" class, it was believed that economic growth mitigated the possibility of class conflict, or "class warfare," a phrase used frequently by the political right when defending the political-economic status quo from critiques made by the left.

The hegemonic argument that an expanding gross domestic product (GDP) benefits everyone allowed conservative politicians and policy wonks to draw attention away from how they changed the tax structure that reduced the share of federal tax revenues contributed by corporations from over 30 percent in 1950 to under 10 percent by 2007, and the top tax rate for individual millionaires and billionaires from 66 percent in 1945 to 32 percent in 2010 (*Mother Jones Magazine*, April 2011). The political justification for supply-side economics is the argument that, in order to improve the United States economy, the government must first help those at the top of the economic pyramid by reducing both tax burdens and so-called "regulatory burdens" in order to allow the "market" to organize private sector economic activity free from government interference. Then, so the argument goes, the captains of industry would be able to help those below them in the economic pyramid by "creating jobs" with the money saved through tax cuts and decreasing liabilities.

Supply-side economics is also referred to as neoliberalism, because the intellectual underpinnings go back to Adam Smith's 1776 book, *The Wealth of Nations*[16], where Smith made a case for economic "liberalism," an economic strategy which advocated the free reign of impersonal markets without government intervention. Smith argued that so-called "free" markets organize the economy in a way that efficiently distributes scarce resources in a fair and efficient manner, rewarding those at the top for their hard work and intellectual superiority, while those on the bottom of the economic ladder receive less of the economic spoils due to their lack of sufficient effort and/or their intellectual deficiencies. In this way, neoliberalism has been and continues to be legitimated by the ideology of meritocracy.

Conservatives assiduously deny the role played by tax cuts in contributing to the federal debt, preferring instead to place the blame upon government spending on social welfare programs supported by the Democrats in Congress. Indeed, the severe reduction in tax revenues that followed the lowering of tax rates for corporations and wealthy individuals has significantly crippled the ability of governments to provide needed public services. In some cases, wealthy individuals and giant corporations do not pay any taxes at all by moving their money to offshore tax havens, or through the exploitation of tax loopholes. This phenomenon has led to a situation referred to by economist James Henry as "representation without taxation." For instance, according to Ezra Klein at the *Washington Post* (March 25, 2011), General Electric, a company ranked number 6 on *Fortune Magazine's* Fortune 500 list, paid *no* income taxes in 2010. The financial power elite have been able to hoard between 22 and 32 *trillion* dollars by using these tactics.[17]

In the 1980s and 1990s, conservatives who pushed for supply-side economics and the neoliberal political-economic agenda were also able to control the academic discourse of economics beginning in the mid-1970s, by discrediting the demand-side, or Keynesian, position that deficit spending is necessary in times of economic downturn. Demand-side economic policies are designed to help working people spend money in order to stimulate economic growth. This can be achieved by supporting labor unions, promoting tight labor markets through full employment policies, as well as indirectly through social insurance programs like Social Security and Unemployment Insurance, both put into law by Congress during the New Deal era. This position is referred to as "Keynesian," because it is rooted in arguments made by John Maynard Keynes in his influential book, *The General Theory of Employment, Interest and Money*, first published in 1936.[18] Keynes had argued that the Great Depression was caused by a collapse in aggregate demand and that, in order to prevent another depression, governments must run deficits during periods of slow or zero economic growth in order to prevent a system-wide collapse in demand. As Rhonda Levine has demonstrated in her book *Class Struggle and the New Deal*, monopoly capital (big business) turned to Keynesian policies in order to save capitalism (see Chapter 28 by Levine).[19] From the Great Depression until the 1970s, Keynesianism was the norm in academic economics and among economic policy makers in Washington DC, until working-class rebellion in the late 1960s threatened the political-economic foundations of the post-War status quo. From the end of the Carter administration and into the Obama administration, however, neoliberal economics has held the day, as Keynesian ideas have been marginalized. The hegemony of neoliberal discourse also marginalized empirical analyses that challenged the argument that tax cuts for both corporations and wealthy individuals lead to sustainable economic growth in the first place.

In short, there are two issues at hand. One issue is whether or not economic growth is widely distributed. The second issue is how economic growth is possible in the first place, or, to use different words, how wealth is produced in the first place. One way in which neoliberal discourse marginalizes alternatives is through the presentation of political-economic problems as *technical* problems, not political problems.

For much of the nineteenth century – as well as earlier eras – the field of economics was referred to as "political economy," rather than "economics." But toward the end of the nineteenth century, bourgeois intellectuals attempted to remove politics from the study of the economy, which is partly why the field has become so reliant on statistical methodologies like econometrics. The attempt to remove politics assumes that the given capitalist social relations of production are the *norm*, as history and politics are removed from the analysis of the economy. Neoliberal discourse situates subjects in a way that they are positioned to take the given economy as simply "the way it is." The assumption is that the given economic system is, if not the only possible system, then the best possible system, and that means in turn that all economic problems are technical in nature. Because politics (the relations of class forces at work in everyday life) is not allowed to enter the discourse, the "given" is simply accepted. This phenomenon draws attention to the relationship described by Michel Foucault as the power-knowledge nexus. The discourse of academic economics driven by neoliberal ideology presents itself as "neutral" and "objective" social science, but economics is not neutral, it is rooted in perspective of capital, as it attempts to perpetuate the interests of the capitalist class by framing those interests as universal interests rather than particular ones. In short, economics is the point of view of capital.

It would be wrong, however, to argue that bourgeois intellectuals have been able to achieve this level of political hegemony over the discourse on economics. The success of the OWS movement has been its ability to bring politics back into the discourse of economics by challenging the power of professional economists to set the terms for the national conversation about our economy. In short, the OWS movement has helped bring back the "political" into political-economic analysis. The global revolt from below has led left-leaning academics, media pundits and politicians to think outside the box of neoliberal ideology in order to understand and explain the financial crisis of 2007 that led to the so-called "Great Recession." The recent documentary film, *Inside Job*, has exposed how economists who held academic positions on faculties at universities like Columbia, Harvard and the University of Chicago, were paid by investment banks to write academic papers (published in peer-reviewed journals) that legitimated the deregulation of the derivatives industry. This kind of conflict of interest is widespread in the field of economics.

Empirical evidence now reveals that supply-side economics has failed to deliver the goods. According to the economists Paul Krugman and Joseph Stiglitz, the nations that have gone furthest toward implementing supply-side, neoliberal economic policies are the same countries that now have the worst domestic economies in terms of general economic stagnation and high unemployment (Krugman, *End This Depression Now!*). Stiglitz has revealed that for working men in the US economy, median real wages have gone *down* over the past four decades (Stiglitz, *The Price of Inequality*[20]). Much of the worsening economic conditions for men under the median wage can be explained by the decline in power of labor unions in the past four decades. If you shift the emphasis to race, things get much worse. African-Americans have been losing ground much faster than white Americans. Recent years were particularly bad, as African-Americans lost 53 percent of their household wealth between 2005 and 2009. The assets of African-Americans are a mere 5 percent of the national average among whites (Stiglitz, *The Price of Inequality*, p. 13). For young people between the ages of 18 and 35 the situation is also quite bleak. According to Paul Buchheit, the median wealth of this group has dropped by 68 percent since 1984, to just under $4,000 (*Nation of Change*, July 9, 2012).

In short, it is no longer the case that growth in GDP is widely distributed across the population. It has not been true for decades, unlike the years between the end of World War II and the early 1970s, when workers received increases in compensation (wages and benefits) that matched increases in productivity. Roughly one-third of workers in the private sector were, during this era, members of labor unions. It was understood by many economic policy experts who were influenced by the ideas of Keynes, that labor unions had a *positive* effect on the economy through increasing aggregate demand. Thus, while apologists for neoliberalism point to the explosion of productivity and rates of economic growth in the United States in the past few decades, the issue of the distribution of that wealth remains absent from their discourse.

It is a basic tenet of Keynesian economic policy that high wages are necessary to drive economic expansion, as is government spending, otherwise aggregate demand throughout the economy has a tendency to drop off significantly over time, as rising productivity levels increase the size of the economic surplus, which in turn creates what economists call "overproduction" or "overcapacity," a situation where there are too few consumers to absorb the economic surplus. Indeed, rising economic surplus is a chronic structural problem in a capitalist economy. In recurring episodes of American history, economic surplus has led to severe economic downturns like the Panic of 1893 and the Great Depression. During the New Deal, government programs like the Works Progress Administration (WPA), Social Security, Unemployment Insurance and Aid to Dependent Children (which is now known as Temporary Aid to Needy Families) were created as a means to prop up aggregate demand throughout the economy in order to lift the nation out of economic depression and help prevent future recessions and depressions.

These programs became known collectively as the "Keynesian Welfare State." Of course, we now know that the United States did not come out of the economic depression until entry into World War II, as government spending on armaments for the war finally created enough spending to boost aggregate demand across the economy as a whole. Nevertheless, the Keynesian logic still holds: namely, the private sector alone cannot prevent severe economic downturns. Never in the history of capitalism has the private sector been able to prevent serious economic crises. The same logic lies behind President Obama's stimulus plan passed by Congress in 2009 called the "American Recovery and Reinvestment Act," although Keynesian economists like Krugman and Joseph Stiglitz argued that Obama's stimulus plan did not do nearly enough to lift the nation out of recession. Indeed, from the Keynesian perspective, more economic stimulus is needed.

In the 1930s and 1940s, capitalists who were influenced by demand-side economic ideas sought to solve the crisis of capital accumulation created by the Great Depression through arranging contracts with labor unions that pegged the rise in workers' wages to increases in worker productivity. This arrangement in the private sector between union workers and large corporations was termed "Fordism," by the social theorist Antonio Gramsci, in part because the founder of the Ford Motor Company, Henry Ford, understood that workers required relatively high wages in order to stimulate economic growth.[21] It was Ford who instituted the celebrated "five-dollar day," in 1914, which more than doubled the previous wage of $2.34. Although Ford never achieved the $5 mark until World War I, the plan proved to be very profitable for Ford, in part because it created a stable workforce for the company, where previously high turnover had plagued the company. Other large companies followed suit soon thereafter, leading social scientists to refer to this period in American industrial relations as the era of "welfare capitalism," because many large companies sought to increase both wages and benefits for their workers. For Gramsci, "Fordism" was a strategy developed by the capitalist class in order to overcome structural contradictions from earlier periods of capitalist development sometimes referred to as "competitive" or "laissez-faire" capitalism that spanned most of the nineteenth century. The Fordist stage in capitalist development spanned the first three-quarters of the twentieth century.

By the end of the 1960s, however, things began to fall apart. As rank and file discontent among young American union workers during the late 1960s and early 1970s led to a nationwide wave of wildcat strikes, Keynesianism and Fordism revealed their limitations.[22] The American working class was no longer willing to be folded into the Fordist compromise that linked wage increases to productivity increases. Young workers wanted more leisure time and better, less alienating working conditions on the job. In short, wage increases were no longer sufficient to appease working-class demands for a better life. In *response* to a young, militant working class, capitalists launched an attack on labor unions in the early 1970s that was partly waged through campaigns to bust unions altogether, either through manipulation of US labor law, control over appointments to the National Labor Relations Board (NLRB), or extracting far-reaching concessions from union workers during contract negotiations.[23] The Nixon, Carter and Reagan administrations all emboldened capital's attack on labor. Reagan's firing of all air traffic controllers in the United States during the 1981 Professional Air Traffic Controllers Organization (PATCO) strike was a signal to the labor movement that the state was taking sides with capital against labor.

The other tactic for bringing down the American working class involved the dismantling of the Keynesian welfare state, including welfare "reform," and massive cuts in social service programs.[24] Off-shoring of union jobs, together with automation that increases unemployment, has also contributed to creating economic conditions favorable to the capitalist class. The combination of these three strategies has been the primary means of waging class struggle from the capitalist side since the 1970s. In recent years, we have seen how class conflict has again been mediated through the state. The attack on public-sector labor unions in states like Indiana, Wisconsin and Ohio, where Republican governors have attempted to take away the collective bargaining rights of public sector workers, is part of a much longer process that began in the 1970s when big business went on the attack against labor unions in the private sector. *Business Week* magazine stated it very bluntly in an editorial from October 12, 1974, when they said, "Some people will obviously have to do with less….it will be a bitter pill for many Americans to swallow, the idea of doing with less so that big business can have more."

The triumph of neoliberalism and supply-side economics was not achieved until the Reagan years, but in spite of the infamous statement by Richard Nixon that "I am now a Keynesian in economics," the demise of the Keynesian regime of capital accumulation began in the 1970s as influential economists like Milton Friedman at the University of Chicago designed the economic policy architecture that eventually took down both the Keynesian welfare state and the American labor movement. Friedman successfully persuaded key economic advisors in the federal government to replace the Keynesian structure of tax and spend with monetarism, the policy still practiced by the Fed today. Thus, while worker productivity has risen steadily over the past few decades and continues to rise, income compensation in the form of wages for the working class has been stagnant, if not falling, for decades. Remnants of Keynesianism survive in the form of military spending, what President Eisenhower dubbed the "military-industrial complex," and Social Security payments, but by and large the Keynesian welfare state that was built up between the 1930s and 1960s has been destroyed. Today, however, after the meltdown of the financial services industry, some economists are claiming that neoliberalism has been a failure. Economists like Krugman and Stiglitz are arguing for a return to traditional Keynesian economic policy as a means to end the current economic crisis. These Keynesian positions overlap with chapters in this part of the reader by economists associated with the journal *Monthly Review*, which give a broader, more comprehensive analysis of the financial crisis than either Krugman or Stiglitz (see Chapter 32 by Foster and McChesney).

Providing this kind of historical context, which situates the relations between capital and labor within the state over time, provides a way to reinterpret the current economic crisis. Indeed, many of our economic problems attributed to the crash of the financial services industry can be traced much further back in time to the collapse of Keynesianism and Fordism in the mid-1970s, but much of the current analysis of inequality has instead focused on the global economic situation after the financial crisis in 2007. During the so-called "economic recovery" of 2009–2010, 93 percent of all income growth in the US economy went to the top one percent (Stiglitz, *Price of Inequality*). While economic inequality is worse than it has ever been, and while wealth and income inequality now increases faster under periods of economic *growth*, patterns of inequality and the resurgence of a ruling class preceded the financial crisis of 2007–2008 by three decades or more.

Historical examination of the collapse of Keynesianism involves not only an examination of the changing relations between capital and labor, but also the changing conditions of capital accumulation (economic growth). Today, capital accumulates largely through speculation in financial markets, as finance capital has overtaken industrial capital as the dominant class fraction within the power elite. Economists like Bluestone and Harrison refer to this development as the emergence of the "casino society." It is both the changing relations between capital and labor and the new regime of accumulation that have created the conditions for the massive redistribution of wealth upwards to the very top tiers in the global political economy.

IV

The OWS movement also had an impact on the 2012 presidential campaign in the United States by drawing attention to the presence of finance capital in funding both the Democratic and Republican campaigns through large donations, as well as by focusing on one candidate, Mitt Romney, as the personification of Wall Street. Both presidential campaigns in the 2012 race championed the cause of getting people back to work in an effort to convince voters that their candidate had what it takes to lift the country out of recession. The refrain the Republican Party used in their campaign was the phrase "job creators." The phrase may have had a ring of newness to it for some, but the Republican argument is more or less the same as it was in the 1980s: get the government off the backs of the very wealthy individuals who have the putative ability and desire to create jobs for those unemployed people deemed worthy, or deserving of help. As Madeline Bunting has revealed, willingness to work very long hours is the key indicator of "deserving" workers.[25]

But as the economist Dean Baker has demonstrated, corporations do not "create" jobs as a result of tax cuts. There is, in Baker's words, "zero evidence" in support of that argument. Rather, jobs get created only after demand for consumer products goes up. Indeed, the so-called "Great Recession" developed because the bursting of the housing bubble caused a severe drop-off of aggregate demand, over one trillion dollars' worth (*The Guardian*, June 4, 2012). One example of how tax cuts do not create jobs can be found in the Congressional experiment to cut taxes on repatriated corporate profits in 2004. Supply-side economists working at policy think tanks and Republicans in Congress argued that if Congress allowed a "tax holiday" for corporations repatriating their overseas profits, then the result would be job growth. In fact, that did not happen. Congress dropped the tax rate from roughly 35 percent to just over 5 percent, but there was no evidence of job creation afterwards. Instead, the money went to shareholders, increasing their wealth and the stock piles of cash that corporations were refusing to invest back into the economy (Democracynow.org, July 31, 2012).

According to economist James Henry from the Tax Justice Network, it is not only the case that corporations park their profits offshore in order to avoid paying taxes, but wealthy individuals do it as well. A recent study produced by the Tax Justice Network called, "The Price of Offshore Revisited," revealed that between 21 and 32 *trillion* dollars exist in offshore bank accounts worldwide that exist as tax havens for the global political and economic elite (*The Guardian*, July 21, 2012). The conservative estimate of 21 trillion dollars is more than the economic output of the United States and Japan *combined*. This situation is referred to by Henry as "representation without taxation." Again, the issue of state legitimacy is thrown into question as very wealthy individuals and corporations are able to dramatically reduce their share of taxes or avoid paying taxes altogether, thereby forcing the state to exist on very regressive tax structures that chronically underfund the crucial operations of all levels of government.

The 2012 presidential campaign in the United States also drew public attention to the issue of tax evasion by the wealthy when media pundits claimed Mitt Romney was the first presidential candidate to have extensive holdings in offshore bank accounts. The existence of Romney's offshore accounts complicated his claim that his record established during his time working at the private equity firm, Bain Capital, made him most qualified to lead the United States government. In addition to hiding assets in offshore accounts, Romney paid an income tax rate of just 13.9 percent, well below the top tax rate for the average wage-earning American, which is 35 percent (*Reuters*, January 24, 2012). In 2010, Romney paid three million dollars in taxes on revenue of 21.7 million. When asked to disclose tax returns for previous years, Romney refused, raising questions about how much he has paid in taxes over the previous decade. These matters forced Romney to walk a political tightrope as he struggled with the changing national discourse around economic inequality. After the OWS intervention in both American and global politics, Romney's campaign had to cope with the problem of their candidate being tagged as a member of the plutocratic class, as part of the so-called "one percent" that no longer lives in same world as the "99 percent."

Before Romney won the Republican Party nomination, opponents within the party like Newt Gingrich ran attack ads that appropriated the OWS discourse, describing Romney as an aloof financier with a record of *eliminating* well-paying jobs while he was at Bain Capital. Earlier on during the Republican primary process, Texas Governor Rick Perry referred to Romney as a "vulture capitalist." Reporting by the *Wall Street Journal* and the *Washington Post* revealed that Bain's ability to create jobs had been a very mixed bag at best. Romney claimed that while he was at Bain, he and his colleagues helped create over 100,000 jobs, but in that calculation Romney did not include the number of jobs destroyed when companies went bankrupt after being taken over by Bain.[26] Part of the takeover strategy by private equity firms includes increasing the debt load of the companies that are acquired by private equity firms. The justification for increasing the debt of these companies turns on the argument that the extra debt is part of an investment strategy to upgrade a given company's technological infrastructure to make it more productive and efficient. In many cases, companies saddled with debt after being acquired by a private equity firm like Bain end up going bankrupt due to the inability to service the debt. The private equity firms, however, do not suffer the consequences. On the contrary, firms like Bain actually make a profit on takeover deals even if the company they acquire fails and goes bankrupt.

One of the most infamous cases of job elimination and business failures at the hands of Romney's private equity firm occurred when GS Industries, a mini steel mill employing 1,500 workers in Kansas City, was purchased by Bain Capital in 1993. While the Romney campaign blamed the overall decline of the steel industry for the bankruptcy of GS Industries in 2001, reporter Glenn Kessler revealed that it remains the case that Bain made a profit of at least 12 million dollars on their investment in GS Industries (*Washington Post*, May 15, 2012). Bain also added substantial debt to the company. During the years that Bain Capital managed GS Industries, company debt soared to 500 million dollars, and by 2001 the company was making interest payments of 40 million dollars a year. The most egregious issue in the case of GS Industries involved the destruction of the pension and health insurance plans for the union workers at the plant. In 1997, GS Industries settled a strike at the company by promising guarantees on worker pension and health insurance plans. But records now show that while GS Industries was under management by Bain, the pensions were underfunded by 44 million dollars. The managers at Bain then used the bankruptcy process to break the promises made to the workers resulting in over 700 workers losing their pension and insurance plans (*Washington Post*, May 15, 2012). According to the *New York Times*, "Bain structured deals so that it was difficult for the firm and its executives to ever really lose, even if practically everyone else involved with the company that Bain owned did, including its employees, creditors and even, at times, investors in Bain's funds... In four of the seven Bain-owned companies that went bankrupt, Bain investors also profited, amassing more than $400 million in gains before the companies ran aground. All four, however, later became mired in debt incurred, at least in part, to repay Bain investors or to carry out a Bain-led acquisition strategy" (June 12, 2012). There are many other cases like this, including the situation at the company Sensata Technologies, which operates a factory in Illinois that employs 170 people. Bain owns the company, and as of fall 2012, Bain had plans to move the operations to China. During the presidential campaign, workers from the Illinois plant pestered Romney by protesting at the Republican convention, asking him to pressure Bain to keep the jobs in the United States.

In addition to investigating the job-creation claims made by Romney, political commentators on the left insisted that more scrutiny was needed regarding the *kinds* of jobs created by private equity firms like Bain Capital. Of those over 100,000 jobs touted by the Romney campaign, most were low-wage service-sector jobs: 89,000 were from Staples, 15,000 from Sports Authority, and 7,900 were from Domino's. These are not the kinds of jobs people think about when they talk about the so-called "American Dream" and the opportunity for upward mobility. Destroying union jobs and creating low-paying, dead-end jobs is not exactly a record of success. Furthermore, not only did some of the firms that were taken over by Bain go under after being burdened with debt that made their business unsustainable, but Bain Capital also acquired firms that specialized in offshoring jobs to China. In short, it is not simply a case, as the Romney campaign argued, that some companies succeed while others fail (the ups and downs of capitalist business cycles). Rather, the issue is that Bain was involved in the very profitable business of providing offshoring services for American companies looking to move substantial portions of their assets overseas. More to the point, private equity firms like Bain Capital are not in the business of "creating jobs" or of making tangible goods. Instead, private equity firms look for opportunities to *flip* existing companies for profit.

The political justification for taxing wealthy investors at a much lower rate than working- and middle-class wage-earners is grounded upon the assertion that investors take more "risk" in their work than do the average folk. But in reality, private equity firms do not take risks with their own money. Rather, they take risks with *other* investors' money, including capital provided by pension funds. The private equity strategy is to find a struggling company (or one that has potential to become more profitable than it is), buy it for relatively little, then make it more profitable and turn around and sell it for more than the original purchase price. A company like Bain finds outside investors to fund the initial purchase of a company they seek to flip. As Robert Reich has demonstrated, the most common way to make a company more profitable is to fire a portion of the employees, then force the remaining ones to take significant pay cuts and reductions in health care and pension benefits.[27] The other way firms like Bain make profits in these arrangements is through tax write-offs on debt. Typically private equity firms use the company they purchase as collateral to borrow more money from banks, and because the interest on these bank loans is deductible from company income, it appears as if the companies purchased by Bain are even *more* profitable. Then Bain gets the company to issue a special dividend to the original investors (who funded the initial purchase) in order to pay them off before Bain sells the company. When Bain sells the company for much more than it was purchased, Bain pockets, typically, 20 percent from such a sale. This income is treated by the federal government as capital gains, so it is taxed at a top rate of 15 percent.

The costs of whatever "externalities" result from this kind of activity of flipping existing companies (like the loss of jobs) are covered by tax-payers who fund unemployment insurance or Medicaid for workers who get fired by the practices of company flipping by private equity firms. These kinds of business practices add to the burden placed upon governments struggling to ease the pain of unemployment during periods of economic stagnation. In short, tax-payers subsidize this kind of private equity activity. But, as we argue below, it would be a mistake to reduce this phenomenon to simply a question of greed among private equity firms. There are many firms like Bain Capital, and their existence reflects much larger structural changes in the economy that involve the transition from a capitalist economy grounded in industrial production to one grounded in financial speculation.

We must also go beyond examining the kinds of jobs created by the financial power elite and look closely at the ideology that underpins the phrase "job creators." The very phrase is a process that positions individuals to see the issue from the capitalist point of view: namely, that the capitalist provides the possibility of livelihood for workers by "giving" them jobs. This perspective assumes that capital creates labor. But the opposite is the case. Labor makes capital possible, because labor-power is the only commodity that can create more value than it, itself, is worth. As Abraham Lincoln once said, "labor is prior to, and independent of, capital. Capital is the fruit of labor, and could never have existed if labor had not first existed" ("State of the Union Address," December 3, 1861). This is also the core argument of Marx in *Capital, Vol. 1*[28], which must be read as a critique of economic discourse as the perspective of the capitalist. Capital depends upon the labor-power of workers in order to exist, but in the political discourse of "job creation" this phenomenon is obscured. Again, ideology situates us to see the world upside down. In an effort to legitimize the existence of private equity firms, financial power elites like Mitt Romney use the language of *job* creation, but never *wealth* creation. The issue of wealth creation is kept out of sight by the dominant political discourse, which situates us to have our backs to the production process, so that all we see is the marketplace. If we were to turn ourselves around, so to speak, and focus on wealth creation, which takes place during the process of production, then we would be forced to view the social relations of production under capitalist conditions right-side-up, and see that labor creates capital.

When the Obama campaign criticized Romney's track record for outsourcing and offshoring jobs, the Romney campaign responded that offshoring businesses and jobs was ultimately the fault of the Obama administration, because the US government had supposedly made it "too expensive" to do business in the states. The Romney campaign made this claim in spite of the fact that the Obama administration continued to pursue neoliberalism with gusto, including the appointment of people like Larry Summers as a primary economic advisor to the administration, as well as naming Timothy Geithner, who was an executive at Goldman Sachs, the Secretary of the Department of Treasury. In short, the economic policy pursued by Democratic administrations in the past few decades has *not* significantly diverged from that of the Republicans. The Obama administration took its playbook for the economy from the Clinton administration, which oversaw implementation of key neoliberal government policies like NAFTA, welfare reform and the deregulation of the financial services industry. The American media establishment has more or less allowed business groups like the US Chamber of Commerce to set the terms of the national conversation by refusing to scrutinize the belief that leveling down – lower wages, fewer benefits, and longer working hours – is the only option for American workers who need jobs.[29] It is largely accepted that the global race to the bottom has left US workers behind, and that if they want to compete for jobs then they must accept the new norm of longer hours of work for lower wages and fewer benefits than previous generations of workers in the United States.

Widespread disenchantment with the Clinton–Obama political machine drove the Left, and young people, to the campaign of Bernie Sanders, which was very critical of the relationship between Wall Street and the Clinton–Obama machine that continued to dominate the Democratic party as Hillary Clinton sought to win the 2016 presidential election. It remains to be seen whether Sanders' supporters will be able to influence the future direction of the Democratic Party.

V

In spite of rhetorical moves by the Romney campaign to blame Obama for the economic crisis in the United States, the impact of the OWS protest movement created problems for Republicans that did not exist in the 2008 campaign. Romney's attempt to distance himself and his campaign supporters from being labeled members of the "one percent" class was made even more difficult when Edward Conard, a former colleague of his at Bain, and one of the largest donors to his presidential campaign, told the *New York Times Magazine* (May 1, 2012) that the steep and severe increase in economic inequality experienced in the United States in recent decades is a *good* sign that the economy is working as it should. According to Conard, extreme economic inequality in our social structure is necessary because talented people need pecuniary incentives in order to work towards solving the most challenging problems that exist in our society. In other words, from Conard's perspective, we must have extraordinary pay-offs for those who do succeed in the economy in order to motivate talented people who may choose to stay on the sidelines of the economy, doing just enough to get by, preferring to spend their time doing other things besides working. The issue, for Conard, is to get all those talented people idling away on the sidelines to compete in the marketplace, so that, presumably, more competition will lead to more innovation.

During the interview with the reporter from the *New York Times Magazine*, Conard drew attention to a small group of young people sitting nearby in the coffee shop as a way to illustrate his point about potentially gifted slackers who choose not to compete. The reporter describes them as hipsters, "three young people with plaid shirts and floppy hair." Referring to them derisively as "art history majors" (because he was convinced they were college educated), Conard went on to argue that young, educated people refuse to work hard unless the potential rewards are enormous. The slacker norm is for people to work the least amount necessary to enjoy life, which is of course relative to given individuals. In Conard's interpretation of the issue, "art history majors" realize the odds of striking it rich in this economy are stacked against them. Why work harder than necessary if the pay-off is not worth the extra effort? It is understood by people like Conard to be obvious that the pursuit of art history for its own sake is ultimately a waste of time.

The idea that anyone may choose to hang out in coffee shops and talk about art for cultural reasons seems lost on Conard, when he asks the reporter, "What are they doing, sitting here, having a coffee at 2:30?" It seems outrageous and scandalous to Conard that people choose *not* to work. Conard's question reveals a class perspective that is rooted in a contemporary version of the Calvinist work ethic: any activity that is not somehow "productive" (like drinking coffee in the afternoon while discussing art) is not only a waste of time, but immoral precisely because it is a "waste" of time.

In a number of places in the interview Conard appears as largely unsympathetic to working-class people. When asked about the billionaire investor Warren Buffett pledging millions of dollars to charity, Conard replies that such practices are a waste of money, because they drain resources away from "productive" investment. In the Calvinist mindset, work has replaced leisure as the way in which people find meaning and purpose in their lives. This is largely how the financial power elite understand themselves and reproduce themselves as a *class*, even if they see themselves as largely secular, or from a cultural background markedly different from traditional Calvinism. Nonetheless, religious undertones remain, as many among the financial power elite understand themselves as productive individuals contributing not only to society but to God. Indeed, in 2009 this perspective was revealed by the *Wall Street Journal* when Lloyd Blankfein, CEO of the investment bank Goldman Sachs, told a reporter that he and his peers on Wall Street were "doing God's work."[30] This shared cultural connection is the necessary if not sufficient condition for the individuals who control the means of production in the financial services industry to form themselves into a class.

A similar dynamic can be seen in comments made by Paul Ryan, Romney's running mate during the 2012 presidential campaign, although the individuals attacked by Ryan were recipients of government assistance, rather than the figure of the bohemian slacker attacked by Conard. The issue, however, is the same: capitalists have an interest in making it difficult for workers and potential workers to resist work under capitalist social conditions. Ryan made a splash during his public response to President Obama's state of the union address (January, 2011) when he said that the social "safety net" provided by the federal government had become a "hammock that lulls able-bodied people into lives of complacency and dependency." While bohemian slackers pose a *cultural* threat to the capitalist work ethic and the moral discipline necessary for the working class to succumb to capitalist working conditions, the social safety net poses a *structural* threat to the ability of capitalists to command workers. The so-called "safety" net poses a threat to capitalist power because it offers an exit strategy for workers to leave the labor market, even if only on a temporary basis.

As Piven and Cloward (1993) have demonstrated in the book *Regulating the Poor*, when individuals leave the labor market it creates the possibility for workers to gain leverage in relation to capitalists, because a smaller number of people in the labor market means fewer workers are competing for jobs, which in turn drives up demand for labor. Fewer workers in the labor market also translates into an increased feeling of power among workers in relation to capital. Conservatives understand this very well, which is why they are constantly on the attack against any form of government assistance for workers, whether it be Temporary Assistance to Needy Families (TANF), social security, Medicaid, Medicare or unemployment insurance. In short, the ruling capitalist class strives to use the state to keep pushing more workers into the labor market, by a number of means: (1) raising the retirement age for all, (2) making it impossible for others to retire at all by abolishing pensions, (3) setting welfare benefits below minimum wage while attaching work requirements to the benefits, (4) cutting back on the amount of time workers can be on unemployment insurance, (5) cutting Medicaid, and (6) privatizing social security so that investment banks can gamble away working people's retirement funds on the stock market.[31]

Any sign, whether cultural or structural, that workers may choose to exit work and the labor market poses a serious threat to capitalists, because capital depends on workers in order for capital to reproduce itself and the social relations of production that make capitalism possible in the first place. In order to maintain power over workers, the capitalist class must reproduce conditions that force workers to compete among themselves for jobs that are in relatively scarce supply. Control over government spending on social services is one way capitalists can create those conditions, and they pursue those strategies simultaneously with other strategies like automation and offshoring of jobs to other parts of the world. In short, it is a three-pronged strategy to always enlarge the number of people who are unemployed, what Marx called the "reserve army of labor" (see Chapter 32 by Foster and McChesney).

At the cultural level, Paul Ryan made use of Ayn Rand's right-wing libertarian discourse of "takers" and "makers," as a way to frame "class" not in terms of capitalist/worker, but in terms of those who work, and those who mooch off of workers through the redistribution of wealth via taxes collected by the government. Following Ayn Rand, Ryan encourages a framework that interprets the social relations of production as a situation where some people work, while others do not. But the ones who do not work are not the capitalists living off the labor of workers but rather welfare recipients who live off the taxes of waged workers. "Class," then, is defined by the difference between those who are supposedly "productive" versus those who are said to be "unproductive." The effect of the widespread appropriation of this perspective is that working-class individuals act against their class interests by taking sides with the capitalist class *against* other workers who are unemployed (see Chapter 15 by Roberts). The Republican Party was fairly successful in energizing its base around this distinction that exploits the resentment of white, working-class men, an approach that goes back to the 1970s when Richard Nixon first developed the so-called "Southern Strategy," which was a plan to steal white votes from Democrats in the South by whipping up racial resentment among white workers. The 2016 presidential campaign of Donald Trump made good use of this type of resentment.

As a result of the hegemony of the ruling-class perspective in political discourse, what goes unnoticed in these kinds of Tea Party attacks on working-class citizens who occasionally receive aid from the government is that politicians like Congressman Ryan actually support programs that provide "hammocks" for the financial power elite including the hedge fund Elliot Management, the largest contributor to Ryan's super-PAC, "Prosperity Pac." The director of Elliot Management hedge fund, Paul Singer, led the charge to have the federal government bail out the auto industry, which eventually made his firm a handsome sum of 1.28 billion dollars in profits ("Mr. Singer and Mr. Ryan," *The Nation*, October 17, 2012). Singer was also a key player in the effort to put Ryan on the 2012 presidential ticket. In spite of his public persona as a follower of Ayn Rand, and a leader of the Tea Party, Paul Ryan was one of only 23 Republicans in Congress to vote for the federal government's bailout of the auto industry in December of 2008. Ryan essentially cast his vote for Elliot Management, which took over Delphi Automotive Group, the main parts supplier for General Motors. When the auto industry was suffering, Elliot Management purchased Delphi for 67 cents a share, but when news came that the federal government was going to bail out the auto industry (which included giving Delphi 12 billion dollars), shares for Delphi soared to 22 dollars a share, making a staggering 3000 percent profit for Elliot Management. Singer's firm also scuttled a plan to keep Delphi operations in the United Statesthrough outbidding other investors (including a group which involved the United Auto Workers pension fund) in the takeover of Delphi. There was another plan to keep Delphi jobs in the United States, but the group led by Elliot Management killed it. Today only 5,000 Delphi jobs remain in the United States, while 100,000 exist overseas. Thus, in the case of the government bailout for Delphi, tax-payers subsidized the profit for Elliot Management through both a cash gift of more than 12 billion dollars and the leverage necessary to create the inflation of its stock value. To add insult to injury, tax-payers also subsidized the offshoring of jobs to China.

Mitt Romney was also in on the bailout deal. While he infamously argued in an editorial that the US government should "let Detroit go bankrupt," he personally made 15.3 million dollars in profit from the bailout ("Mitt Romney's Bailout Bonanza," *The Nation*, October 17, 2012). Thus, while some workers lost their jobs and others took major concessions as part of the bailout package to save the auto industry, financiers like Romney and Singer walked away with millions. Conservatives in the Republican Party never draw attention to government policies that subsidize hedge funds and investment banks (or corporate welfare in general), but if any scrutiny of such policies makes it into the political discourse, the ruling class relies on supply-side economics to legitimate those programs. Once again, ideology is at work: corporate welfare is coded as "productive" via the discourse of supply-side economics, while welfare for the working class is coded as unproductive and "bad" for the economy.

VI

The reporter who interviewed Ed Conard for the *New York Times Magazine*, Adam Davidson, framed his story as a chance to find out what the one percent really believes about economic inequality when the "cameras aren't there." In public, the leaders of the large investment banks and private equity funds want to keep the conversation limited to discussions that make claims that investors really do play an important role in generating economic growth. What they do not want to talk about, according to Davidson, is their views on inequality, because those views would be a liability especially when the news media is covering a presidential campaign. Uncovering the "truth" about what the economic and political elites really believe tends to frame economic problems in terms of corrupt behavior, or in terms of mean-spiritedness among those who are disconnected from the bottom 99 percent. The conclusion from this way of framing things is that problems in our economy tend to be reduced to the actions and beliefs of a few bad actors. This framework is sometimes referred to as the "some bad apples" theory, where it is understood that the system generally works well, but on occasion some dysfunctional individuals (in relation to social norms, not psychological ones) cause problems. Indeed, we have seen this kind of media framing before, from the corporate scandals of the 1990s involving companies like Enron and Tyco, to the more current political-economic controversies having to do with investment banks like Goldman Sachs, Barclays and JP Morgan-Chase. In all of these cases, the issues have been framed in terms of immoral behavior, corruption, greed among wealthy people and lack of sympathy for less fortunate people. This perspective was bolstered when the *New York Times* published an op-ed by a former Goldman Sachs executive, Greg Smith, who wrote that he left the firm due to its corrupt culture. Smith revealed that the firm was conducting fraud when it advised its clients to invest in products that it knew were relatively worthless. "Call me old-fashioned," Smith wrote "but I don't like selling my clients a product that is wrong for them" ("Why I Am Leaving Goldman Sachs," *NYT*, March 14, 2012).

There are obvious problems with this way of framing the issues, including the ideological reluctance to examine *structural* contradictions in our economic system, as well as an inability to view economic actors as embedded in antagonistic class relations. The conflict, in short, cannot be reduced to bad apples (rule breakers) and good apples, or between immoral behavior and moral behavior. On the contrary, an examination of conflicting interests that are shaped by structural relations is necessary to understand the problem at hand.

First, a close reading of Conard's interview for the *New York Times Magazine* reveals that the capitalist class indeed has a very real problem as a *class*: namely, coercing people to work under conditions favorable to the capitalist class. It is not only a question of getting a few slackers (art history majors) with their "floppy hair" to get off their asses and out of the coffee shops in order to ruthlessly compete against each other in the marketplace. Rather, there is a much larger problem for the capitalist class, and that is the creation of an environment where *all* workers in the global economy are in a constant state of cut-throat competition for jobs. It is in the interests of capitalists as a class to create an environment of severe competition in the labor market, because such conditions allow the capitalist class to have leverage and power over workers as competition in the labor market drives down wages and increases the willingness among workers to work harder, longer and for less recompense. Framing the issue in these terms means that rather than focusing on the behavior of *individuals* within the power elite, we must look much more broadly at the capitalist class in a structural *relation* to the working class. In other words, the object of analysis must be the capital-labor relation, not the immoral bad apples roaming around in the circles of the political-economic elite.

Then the more important question arises: under what conditions does it become possible for the capitalist class to coerce working people to compete among one another for a declining share of jobs, income and wealth in the global economy? The rise of the so-called "global elite" cannot be understood apart from both the *response* of the capitalist class to the labor movement and the Keynesian welfare state on the one hand, and the divergent interests of the industrial and finance fractions within the capitalist class on the other.

In short, it is crucial to see the present formation of capital accumulation not as a simple case of greedy individuals manipulating the system, but rather as a class response to historically specific conditions that create a barrier to the advancement of capitalist-class interests. As the selections in Part Three of the reader reveal, the capitalist class has faced particular barriers to their class interests at specific periods in the history of the accumulation process. During these periods, capital responds in certain ways, depending on the relative strength or weakness of the working class. The present form of globalization, for example, must be understood, in part, as the response of capital to the particular history of the American labor movement.

This is not to suggest, however, that a conspiracy is at work. On the contrary, not only are there competing fractions *within* the capitalist class that prevent the possibility of a sophisticated conspiracy – for example, the conflict between industrial, financial, agricultural and commercial interests – but furthermore, many of the important developments and transformations in the history of capitalist accumulation happen, as it were, behind the backs of actors in the system. Individuals in one corner of the social system understand their own interests in a particular way, as they shape and are shaped by history, but on the other side of the social system individuals may be thinking and acting in ways very disparate from the others, creating complexity in the way the social system unfolds over time. This phenomenon creates a certain amount of contingency in history – "accidents" as it were.

Within historically unique periods, however, certain collections of individuals (classes) are able to have a relatively larger degree of influence over the direction and shape of social change. To paraphrase Marx, people make history, but never as they choose. This means that while the system operates by slippages between structural relationships that are contingent, individuals are nonetheless able to sometimes coalesce into classes, as opposed to mere "interest groups." Classes are distinct from interest groups, because classes only exist in opposition to other classes within a context of unequal power relations. An "interest group," on the other hand, is a concept that assumes the social context is a relatively level playing field where a variety of somewhat disconnected groups of individuals compete on an equal basis for scarce resources. Class, however, is a concept that indicates an awareness of a context characterized by a specific relationship of relative domination and exploitation, rather than a political context characterized by a host of various groups with ambiguous relations.

In order for an "interest group" to become a class, there must not only be a structural relation of antagonism against another class, but there must also be a common culture within the class that links up individuals in a certain way that makes it possible for them to understand themselves as members of a class, rather than disconnected individuals who interact on a relatively random basis. If there is no awareness of class, as the historian E.P. Thompson argued, then class does not fully exist (see Thompson's *The Making of the English Working Class*[32]). This phenomenon is the difference between a class-in-itself (the structural location in the social system) and a class-for-itself (the cultural expression of the class). The issue is to examine the historical conditions in which a class-in-itself becomes a class-for-itself, that is, when individuals create a class *culture* and situate their interests as *class* interests. Several chapters in Part Three look at the historical development of "class consciousness" among the capitalists during particular eras of American history. In these historical periods, the capitalist class develops a class consciousness by way of *opposition to the labor movement* (see Chapter 27 by Sven Beckert for an analysis of how the US capitalist class developed a sense of class consciousness toward the close of the nineteenth century).

Second, the current economic crisis facing the global economy is rooted in structural contradictions that emerged out of the transition from a system of capital accumulation driven largely by industrial capital (i.e. making things) to our current system dominated by finance capital, where accumulation occurs on the basis of speculation in derivatives markets that turn over trillions of dollars on a daily basis. This is an example of how the historical development of capitalism happens behind the backs of its actors. The emergence of an economic system dominated by financial capital was not planned in advance by capitalist individuals within the system. There is no determinism at work here: the rise of finance capital is not the work of the metaphysical force fate or destiny. We can, however, trace the history of how and why this transformation has occurred. The formation of a new political framework of economic growth (sometimes referred to as a regime of capital accumulation) has restructured the global economy along new forms of production and distribution, and the primary feature of *speculation* that exists within the system today was generated as one possible response to structural contradictions within the previous stage of capitalist development. Specifically, the current economic context of financial speculation can be traced back to the problem of chronic stagflation (stagnation plus inflation) that reached a critical stage in the 1970s, throwing the system into crisis, whereby accumulation slowed down to an unacceptable pace from the point of view of the capitalist class. In other words, the transition to accumulation through financial speculation signaled a structural change in the economy that created the conditions for a renewed burst of accumulation, although in a different and markedly wasteful way.

If we turn the clock of history even further back, we see that the crisis of stagflation in the 1970s was, in turn, made possible by the problem of economic surplus that was generated by massive increases in productivity that occurred under previous decades of industrial capitalism, a problem that Paul Baran and Paul Sweezy identified in the 1960s with their important book, *Monopoly Capital*[33]. Economic surplus is the difference between what a society produces and the cost of producing it. In highly developed capitalist economies, there exists a tendency for this surplus to rise, and this in turn creates the conditions for economic crisis. For Baran and Sweezy, capitalism is no longer based upon competition between firms in the marketplace in the sense that it was during the nineteenth century. The economic context of market-based competition between large numbers of relatively equal sized firms came to an end by the twentieth century. Today, a relatively small number of "giant" corporations dominate the world economy, and this has profoundly changed the dynamic of capitalist expansion across the globe. The giant firms no longer compete with each other, as technology and the pricing of commodities is shared and planned together in a relatively cooperative manner between the giant firms that have created oligopoly as the new economic norm. Indeed, it is with the emergence of the giant corporation in the twentieth century that Baran and Sweezy target the beginning of the stage of monopoly capitalism. While the problem of destructive economic competition (from the point of view of large individual firms) was overcome during the development of new, oligopolistic economic arrangements in the twentieth century, new contradictions arose.

According to Baran and Sweezy, under monopoly capitalism the central problem for the capitalist class is that of the economic *surplus*. In other words, the economic system has become so powerful in terms of producing goods and services that "too much" wealth is produced from the point of view of the capitalist class, because as the supply of a commodity goes up relative to demand, then the price tends to go down, which obviously is a problem from the point of view of the seller of that commodity. With the reorganization of the factory shop-floor along the lines of the application of revolutionary labor-saving technologies during the twentieth century, capitalism entered into a new, chronic phase characterized by what Marx called the "epidemic of overproduction." Individual corporations seek to increase efficiency and productivity by introducing new forms of labor-saving technology (which displaces large amounts of workers) in order to increase their output and sales and, in turn, revenues. From the standpoint of the individual corporation, this makes rational sense, but something irrational happens at the level of the system as a whole: namely, as all giant corporations follow their own self-interest in producing more durable goods, the system as a whole goes into crisis because the economic surplus cannot be absorbed across the economy due to lack of aggregate demand. This is the accidental outcome of the systematic imperative toward accumulation on a mass scale.

Professional economists refer to this chronic structural problem as "overcapacity," a situation where companies produce "too many" goods for the market, creating a market glut where there are too few consumers to absorb all the output. For example, journalist David Welch reported that in 2008 the US automobile industry reached the capacity to produce 94 million vehicles a year, which amounted to about 34 million "too many" automobiles, based upon current sales for that year ("Automakers' Overcapacity Problem," *Bloomberg BusinessWeek*, December 30, 2008). Another way to understand this phenomenon is to consider how much capacity goes to waste, or is unused under these particular economic conditions. The technical capacity exists to produce more, but factories stay idle and investment lags because opportunities for profit in these sectors of the economy do not exist. There simply are not enough investment opportunities to soak up all the actual and potential profits generated by the giant corporations that make things. There are now *trillions* of dollars on the sidelines of the economy because there is no place to invest at or greater than the average rate of profit. The irony is that the phenomenon of "overcapacity" exists in simultaneity with severe economic hardship and suffering in many parts of the world, where abject poverty devastates the lives of millions of people (see Chapter 32 by Foster and McChesney). In the example above, we see that the unused capacity in the auto industry totals nearly one-third of overall output. This problem is not unique to the auto industry. When these conditions penetrate the entire economy, economic stagnation follows, because corporations are unwilling to invest capital back into the areas where consumer demand is sluggish. In the real economy of producing durable goods, virtually all areas fit these conditions of lagging consumer demand relative to supply and capacity to produce.

Furthermore, the extraordinary rise in productivity that follows from the introduction of labor-saving technology (which in turn creates a vast economic surplus) is accompanied by declining demand for flesh-and-blood human beings on the factory floor. As *New York Times* reporter John Markoff recently revealed, robots are now able to "make any consumer device in the world" ("Skilled Work, Without the Worker," *NYT*, August 18, 2012). In other words, it is not only the case that capitalists seek to boost productivity with machines. They also seek to get rid of workers, especially relatively expensive unionized workers. While this makes rational sense from the point of view of the individual firm seeking to increase revenues, at the macro scale of the economy it leads to crisis if and when millions of workers are replaced by robots and have nowhere to go but down in the economy, leading to a collapse in aggregate demand. Lots of attention has gone toward the problem of sweat-shop labor on a massive scale in China, and rightly so, but the economic tendency is going in the direction of eliminating labor altogether, even by companies who seek out cheap labor in places like China. In the same article mentioned above, Markoff reveals that the Phillips Electronics company has one factory in China and one in the Netherlands that both make the same model of electric shavers that require specialized tools to construct. The difference between the two factories is that in China the shavers are made by human beings, whereas in the Netherlands they are made by robots. More to the point, the robots do it better. "Robot arms do the same work with yoga-like flexibility," according to Markoff. "Video cameras guide them through feats well beyond the capability of the most dexterous hand." Phillips plans to automate the factory in China soon.

The tendency in capitalist production is to shift towards automation only when it makes financial sense to do so, when robots are more cost effective than human workers. It is obvious that companies move their assets and operations to take advantage of cheap and obedient human workers, but as the *New York Times* article reveals, companies are moving to replace Chinese workers as well, especially as recent evidence shows that Chinese workers are beginning to fight back against deplorable working conditions and starvation wages. Robots, on the other hand, ultimately become more cost effective than human beings because they neither go on strike nor resist work. As Markoff writes, robots in the Phillips factory work "three shifts a day, 365 days a year."

In short, it is a matter of if and when workers refuse to work under conditions set by the capitalists that you see the capitalist response, which is to automate production and eliminate intractable workers. As we discuss in Part One of this reader, eliminating work does not have to translate into disaster for the working class. On the contrary, if the working class can successfully fight for shorter hours of work, and thereby push up wages while working less, then automation need not translate into increasing unemployment and misery among the reserve army of the proletariat. In Part Three, however, we examine the formation, practices and problems of the capitalist class in relation to the practices of the working class.

According to Baran and Sweezy, economic stagnation is the *norm* under conditions of monopoly capitalism. Chapter 32 by Foster and McChesney includes data that reveal that the rate of economic growth has been in decline for decades. In the 1970s, the economy grew at a rate 27 percent lower than the during the 1960s. In the years between 2000 and 2009 the rate of economic growth was 63 percent less than it had been in the 1960s (Foster and McChesney, "Endless Crisis"[34]). Stagnation persists despite the ups and downs of the capitalist business cycle. It is only during unusual episodes, like war, that economic growth is robust within the context of monopoly capitalism. But under normal conditions, when companies are forced to cut back on output, the result is a situation where large corporations have nowhere to invest their excess capital, which after several decades following World War II now approaching 2 trillion dollars, as reported by the *Wall Street Journal*. According to the *WSJ*, the amount of cash and liquid assets controlled by nonfinancial companies is the largest in over 50 years, as companies prefer to build up cash buffers rather than invest in new plants and create new jobs. In short, the common practice of multinational corporations today is to "shun investment" and "hoard cash," rather than reinvest profits back into production ("Companies Shun Investment," *WSJ*, September 17, 2011). The issue for these nonfinancial corporations is where to invest all this excess money, or how to put their capital to work and continue moving the accumulation process along. In short, the problem of the economic surplus creates a particular structural barrier to economic growth and continued accumulation of capital. How then does capital (i.e. the capitalist class) *respond* to these structural barriers that slow down economic growth?

In spite of sluggish economic growth, corporations still managed to set records for profits in 2010, and they continued to be robust through 2014. According to the *New York Times*, corporations have done very well in recent years, setting all-time records for profits in spite of an economy showing little growth and relatively high unemployment. Corporate profits for American companies in the third quarter of 2010 alone soared to over 1.65 trillion dollars ("Profits Are Booming, Why Aren't Jobs?" *NYT*, January 8, 2011).[35] The record profits enjoyed by the largest firms in the economy have emerged together with a declining share of GDP for wages and income for American workers. According to the *WSJ*, "Corporate profits now account for the largest share of gross domestic product since 1950 – 12.6%. Wages and salaries account for the smallest share of GDP since 1955 – 54.9%" ("Corporate Profits' Share of Pie Most in 60 Years," *WSJ*,

July 29, 2011). The largest of these companies, the "Fortune 500," collectively garnered 824 billion dollars in profit for 2011, another all-time record since statistics for these data began being collected over 60 years ago. These numbers reveal that capital has indeed been able to overcome the structural barriers to accumulation presented by the creation of "too much" surplus. The response by capital to structural barriers that limit economic growth has taken on two forms.

The first response has been the displacement of accumulation to various areas of the globe that had previously remained relatively underdeveloped. In short, this means that companies find new markets to sell their goods if domestic markets are oversaturated. It also means transferring assets and production to areas of the planet where labor is very cheap. These two developments together constitute what we mean by the term "globalization" of the economy. Globalization is a spatial strategy whereby capital maintains a very high degree of mobility, moving to areas that are conducive to capital accumulation. Labor, by contrast, is relatively less mobile across the globe. This phenomenon was revealed by the former CEO of General Electric, Jack Welch, when he said "ideally, you'd have every plant you own on a barge to move with currencies and changes in the economy" ("Business is Booming," *American Prospect*, January 28, 2011). In recent years, as economic growth has stagnated in the United States, American corporations moved more of their operations overseas, so that now they earn half of their revenues abroad. American corporations have been increasingly decoupled from the US economy. In 2001, 32 percent of income for the 500 largest publically-traded corporations came from doing business overseas. By 2008, the percentage of income from abroad rose to 48 percent. According to a survey of 1600 companies conducted by Duke University's Fuqua School of Business, fully 53 percent had an offshoring strategy in 2008, up from 22 percent in 2005.[36] The survey concluded that very few companies plan to return to the United States. This phenomenon is nothing new, of course, as capitalism has always been a global system, expanding into new areas of the globe every generation whenever there was the opportunity to do so. The fall of the Berlin Wall in 1989 and the opening up of the Chinese economy to western business interests during the Nixon administration did, however, help to accelerate the process in recent decades.

The second way in which capital has been able to overcome structural barriers to accumulation created by the problem of overcapacity has occurred through shifting the means of accumulation from producing things to speculation in financial markets. Empirically we can see this in the share of GDP accounted for in the areas of the economy referred to as "FIRE": finance, insurance and real estate. In recent decades, the segments of the economy devoted to FIRE have risen, while the share of GDP accounted for by manufacturing has declined. The share of total domestic profits going to the financial services industry has risen from roughly 15 percent in 1965 to 40 percent by 2005. Following the lead of Baran and Sweezy, Harry Magdoff and John Bellamy Foster refer to this phenomenon as the "financialization" of capital. Where Baran and Sweezy analyzed the development of monopoly capitalism and the tendency of surplus to rise, Magdoff and Foster look at the transition to monopoly finance capital, as the giant corporations move their economic surplus into speculation in the derivatives markets as a means to find ways to discharge the surplus and continue to accumulate on a mass scale as before.[37] What this entails is a reversal of the relationship between production and finance. During both the industrialization phase and, to a lesser extent, the monopoly phase of capitalist development, finance was more or less a servant to production. Today, the relationship is reversed as finance now dominates production. This means that speculation, not investment in the manufacture of goods, is the major driving force of economic growth. There have been a few ways in which nonfinancial corporations have moved into finance as a means to reinvigorate accumulation and escape stagnation. First, large corporations invest in the stock market like other investors do, and gamble. The other ways in which nonfinancial corporations move into finance and speculation is through leveraged buyout activities (buying and selling other companies) and banking. For example, the General Motors corporation developed a substantial banking arm under the umbrella of companies it manages called GMAC. In this case, the auto company actually creates a bank. It was not simply an auto financing entity, where customers finance the purchase of their car through GMAC. On the contrary, customers were also able to get a home loan when they bought a car from GM, when GMAC moved aggressively into the mortgage market before the financial crash contributed to the near failure of the company as a whole.

VII

This raises a very important question. The existence of 2 trillion dollars sitting idle in the coffers of the Fortune 500 companies, and the 22–32 trillion dollars in the offshore bank accounts of the wealthiest individuals in the world, combined with the widespread condition of overcapacity in many of the global, goods-producing industries forces us to rethink the issue of scarcity, especially as it has been imposed on the working class via the austerity policies that now characterize all governments in the industrialized world. It is a remarkable contradiction in our global political economy that government-imposed austerity programs ask ordinary citizens to get by on less, while for the global corporate conglomerates the main problem is that their firms have created "too much" wealth relative to the aggregate demand in the global economy. The dominant political discourse, however, frames the issue of "too much" very differently. The rationalization of government cutbacks in the conservative discourse that seeks to legitimate government austerity programs is based upon the premise that governments have spent "too much," creating huge deficits that threaten the "confidence" of investors who hold the debt, which in turn slows down the economy due to rising interest rates allegedly caused by "too much" government spending. It should be noted that bond traders on Wall Street do not share this view, as they continue to buy government bonds. Investors are not concerned that the federal debt is going to plunge the economy into a nosedive.

In short, the dominant discourse shifts our attention away from the tendency of the economic surplus to rise under monopoly capitalism, and towards so-called "excessive" government spending. There is a moral dimension to this argument as well as a "scientific" one. The moral argument is quite simplistic: irresponsible politicians allow the government to live beyond its means, spending more money than it takes in via tax revenues. In the attempt to legitimate austerity programs in social "scientific" terms, conservatives claim that austerity will actually create the conditions for economic growth, which counters the Keynesian argument that during recessions and depressions governments need to spend *more*, not less, to lift the economy out of recession. Economists like Krugman and Stiglitz have already demonstrated that empirical evidence is lacking for the argument that austerity creates economic growth. Indeed, the opposite is true. So why do world political leaders insist on austerity for the working class? Indeed, why austerity at all when the power elite themselves depend upon corporate welfare?

There are glaring contradictions here as well, as publicly visible business leaders speak out against the Keynesian welfare state while they themselves take advantage of it. On the one hand, conservative finance capitalists like Ed Conard rail against "slacker" culture and the welfare state in the United States for helping create an indolent "underclass." On the other hand, their private equity firms like Bain Capital move the companies they own to China, where the state subsidizes their business operations by building factories for them. So while finance capitalists like Conard fulminate against Keynesianism and "welfare" programs designed to aid the working class in the United States, they themselves take advantage of the same kinds of policies both at home and abroad in China. When it makes financial sense for private equity companies and large corporations to take advantage of state-subsidized corporate welfare programs they will do so, all in the name of boosting the stock value of their shareholders. This they call "good" business practice. On the other side, they realize that similar opportunities for the working class pose a threat to their power over workers. Political leaders in the capitalist class like Conard realize that the state is the terrain of class struggle.

It remains the case that the capitalist class has a very real problem in maintaining conditions where workers cannot avoid or resist work and the terms and conditions of work created by the capitalist class. Indeed, the comments made by Paul Ryan echo those made by Ed Conard. The issue for the capitalist class is how to create the conditions that keep them in a position of power over workers. Here, at last, we have the answer to the question, "why austerity?" Austerity is a key component in the capitalist project, which is designed to make it impossible for workers to refuse working under conditions imposed upon them by the capitalist class. Austerity was made possible in the first place by the explosion of debt. The issue of debt is not, of course, limited to nation states, as more and more individuals who are faced with declining wages turn to credit cards to finance everyday items like groceries. But what connects these two kinds of debt is the power relation that develops as a result. As David Graeber argues in his book *Debt: The First 5,000 Years*[38], debt is used by the ruling class to achieve two main goals: (1) the creation of new markets, and (2) the ability to make others work. Increasing debt loads among all workers across industrialized nations, whether through increased credit card debt or student loans, have created a situation where it is much more difficult for individuals to exit the labor market and resist working under conditions set by the capitalist. In short, as Chapter 24 by Justin Sean Myers argues, we must view the creditor/debtor relation as a *class* relation. It is too soon to tell how the class struggle will unfold in the near future. But the OWS movement and the social movement against austerity in Europe are signs that the working class is fighting back. The question for the future is: how much longer will the capitalist class have its way?

Notes

1   Chrystia Freeland. See "Rise of the New Global Elite," in the *Atlantic* magazine, http://www.theatlantic.com/magazine/archive/2011/01/the-rise-of-the-new-global-elite/308343/

2   Chrystia Freeland. "Rise of the New Global Elite," in the *Atlantic* magazine, http://www.theatlantic.com/magazine/archive/2011/01/the-rise-of-the-new-global-elite/308343/

3   See Edward Wolff's report at: http://www.levyinstitute.org/pubs/wp_589.pdf

4   See the widely influential book by C. Wright Mills, *The Power Elite* (Oxford University Press, 2000 [1959]).

5   For more analysis of the financial power elite see the article in *Monthly Review* magazine at: http://monthlyreview.org/2010/05/01/the-financial-power-elite/

6 See Paul Krugman, *End This Depression Now!* (New York: W.W. Norton, 2013).

7 See William Appleman Williams, *The Tragedy of American Diplomacy* (New York: W.W. Norton, 2009).

8 See the documentary *Casino Jack and the United States of Money*, directed by Alex Gibney, Magnolia Home Entertainment.

9 *Casino Jack and the United States of Money*, directed by Alex Gibney, Magnolia Home Entertainment.

10 The quote appears in Howard Zinn's and Anthony Arnove's *Voices of a People's History of the United States*, 2nd ed. (New York: Seven Stories Press, 2009), pp. 251–252.

11 Matt Taibbi, *Griftopia*. (Spiegal and Grau, 2011).

12 For more on the myth that public spending caused the economic crisis in Greece and Spain, see Conn Hallinan's article, "Turning the European Debt Myth Upside Down," in Foreign Policy in Focus, February 27, 2015. You can find it here: http://fpif.org/turning-european-debt-myth-upside/

13 See the video documentary *Inside Job* for a detailed explanation of how the investment banks caused the Great Recession of 2008.

14 Glenn Greenwald, *With Liberty and Justice for Some* (Picador, 2011).

15 See Bluestone and Harrison, *The Great U Turn: Corporate Restructuring and the Polarizing of America* (New York: Basic Books, 1988). They refer to the "Great U Turn" as the process where workers began working longer hours for less pay beginning in the early 1970s, whereas between the end of the Civil War and the early 70s the average working American was working fewer and fewer hours for more and more pay. See also the 2014 video documentary, *Inequality for All*, which features former Labor Secretary of the US, Robert Reich.

16 Adam Smith, *The Wealth of Nations* (Bamtam Classics, 2003).

17 For more on this issue, see the 2012 video documentary, *We're Not Broke*.

18 John Maynard Keynes, *The General Theory of Employment, Interest and Money* (Stellar Classics, 2016).

19 Rhonda Levine, *Class Struggle and the New Deal* (University Press of Kansas, 1988).

20 Joseph Stiglitz, *The Price of Inequality* (W.W. Norton & Company, 2012).

21 See Antonio Gramsci, *Prison Notebooks* (New York: International Publishers, 1971).

22 See *Rebel Rank and File* by Aaron Brenner and Cal Winslow (New York: Verso, 2010).

23 See Thomas Geoghegan, *Which Side Are You On?* (New York: The New Press, 2004).

24 See Frances Fox Piven and Richard Cloward, *Regulating the Poor* (New York: Vintage Books, 1993).

25 See Madeline Bunting, *Willing Slaves: How the Overwork Culture is Ruining Our Lives* (New York: Harper Perennial, 2005).

26 http://www.washingtonpost.com/blogs/fact-checker/post/mitt-romney-and-100000-jobs-an-untenable-figure/2012/01/09/gIQAIoihmP_blog.html

27 https://www.youtube.com/watch?v=rodifJlis2c

28 Karl Marx, *Capital*, vol. 1 (London: Penguin, 1976).

29 See Christopher Martin, *Framed: Labor and the Corporate Media* (Ithaca, NY: Cornell University Press, 2003).

30 See the article in the *Wall Street Journal*: "Goldman Sachs Blankfein on Banking, 'Doing God's Work,'" *WSJ*, November 9, 2009.

31 See *Social InSecurity: 401(k)s and the Retirement Crisis* by James Russell (Boston: Beacon Press, 2015).

32 EP Thompson, *The Making of the English Working Class* (Vintage, 1963).

33 Paul Baran and Paul Sweezy, *Monopoly Capital* (Monthly Review Press, 1964).

34 John Bellamy Foster and Robert W. McChesney, *The Endless Crisis: How Monopoly-Finance Capital Produces Stagnation and Upheaval from the U.S.A. to China* (New York: Monthly Review Press, 2012).

35 See also this coverage in the New York Times: https://www.nytimes.com/2014/04/05/business/economy/corporate-profits-grow-ever-larger-as-slice-of-economy-as-wages-slide.html

36 http://www.iese.edu/es/files/Documento%206_tcm5-28441.pdf

37 See Foster and Magdoff, *The Great Financial Crisis* (New York: Monthly Review Press, 2009).

38 David Graeber, *Debt: The First 5,000 Years* (Melville House, 2012).

CHAPTER 26

The Secret of Primitive Accumulation

Karl Marx

Primitive accumulation plays approximately the same role in political economy as original sin does in theology. Adam bit the apple, and thereupon sin fell on the human race. Its origin is supposed to be explained when it is told as an anecdote about the past. Long, long ago there were two sorts of people; one, the diligent, intelligent and above all frugal élite; the other, lazy rascals, spending their substance, and more, in riotous living. The legend of theological original sin tells us certainly how man came to be condemned to eat his bread in the sweat of his brow; but the history of economic original sin reveals to us that there are people to whom this is by no means essential. Never mind! Thus it came to pass that the former sort accumulated wealth, and the latter sort finally had nothing to sell except their own skins. And from this original sin dates the poverty of the great majority who, despite all their labour, have up to now nothing to sell but themselves, and the wealth of the few that increases constantly, although they have long ceased to work. Such insipid childishness is every day preached to us in the defence of property. M. Thiers, for example, still repeats it with all the solemnity of a statesman to the French people, who were once so full of wit and ingenuity. But as soon as the question of property is at stake, it becomes a sacred duty to proclaim the standpoint of the nursery tale as the one thing fit for all age-groups and all stages of development. In actual history, it is a notorious fact that conquest, enslavement, robbery, murder, in short, force, play the greatest part. In the tender annals of political economy, the idyllic reigns from time immemorial. Right and 'labour' were from the beginning of time the sole means of enrichment, 'this year' of course always excepted. As a matter of fact, the methods of primitive accumulation are anything but idyllic.

In themselves, money and commodities are no more capital than the means of production and subsistence are. They need to be transformed into capital. But this transformation can itself only take place under particular circumstances, which meet together at this point: the confrontation of, and the contact between, two very different kinds of commodity owners; on the one hand, the owners of money, means of production,

Original publication details: Karl Marx, "The Secret of Primitive Accumulation," and "The Hidden Abode of Production", from *Capital, a Critique of Political Economy*, Vol 1, tr. by Ben Fowkes, pp. 873–879; 881–889; 278–280. Penguin Books, in association with New Left Review, 1976. Reproduced with permission from New Left Review.

means of subsistence, who are eager to valorize the sum of values they have appropriated by buying the labour-power of others; on the other hand, free workers, the sellers of their own labour-power, and therefore the sellers of labour. Free workers, in the double sense that they neither form part of the means of production themselves, as would be the case with slaves, serfs, etc., nor do they own the means of production, as would be the case with self-employed, peasant proprietors. The free workers are therefore free from, unencumbered by, any means of production of their own. With the polarization of the commodity-market into these two classes, the fundamental conditions of capitalist production are present. The capital-relation presupposes a complete separation between the workers and the ownership of the conditions for the realization of their labour. As soon as capitalist production stands on its own feet, it not only maintains this separation, but reproduces it on a constantly extending scale. The process, therefore, which creates the capital-relation can be nothing other than the process which divorces the worker from the ownership of the conditions of his own labour; it is a process which operates two transformations, whereby the social means of subsistence and production are turned into capital, and the immediate producers are turned into wage-labourers. So-called primitive accumulation, therefore, is nothing else than the historical process of divorcing the producer from the means of production. It appears as 'primitive' because it forms the pre-history of capital, and of the mode of production corresponding to capital.

The economic structure of capitalist society has grown out of the economic structure of feudal society. The dissolution of the latter set free the elements of the former.

The immediate producer, the worker, could dispose of his own person only after he had ceased to be bound to the soil, and ceased to be the slave or serf of another person. To become a free seller of labour-power, who carries his commodity wherever he can find a market for it, he must further have escaped from the regime of the guilds, their rules for apprentices and journeymen, and their restrictive labour regulations. Hence the historical movement which changes the producers into wage-labourers appears, on the one hand, as their emancipation from serfdom and from the fetters of the guilds, and it is this aspect of the movement which alone exists for our bourgeois historians. But, on the other hand, these newly freed men became sellers of themselves only after they had been robbed of all their own means of production, and all the guarantees of existence afforded by the old feudal arrangements. And this history, the history of their expropriation, is written in the annals of mankind in letters of blood and fire.

The industrial capitalists, these new potentates, had on their part not only to displace the guild masters of handicrafts, but also the feudal lords, who were in possession of the sources of wealth. In this respect, the rise of the industrial capitalists appears as the fruit of a victorious struggle both against feudal power and its disgusting prerogatives, and against the guilds, and the fetters by which the latter restricted the free development of production and the free exploitation of man by man. The knights of industry, however, only succeeded in supplanting the knights of the sword by making use of events in which they had played no part whatsoever. They rose by means as base as those once used by the Roman freedman to make himself the master of his *patronus*.

The starting-point of the development that gave rise both to the wage-labourer and to the capitalist was the enslavement of the worker. The advance made consisted in a change in the form of this servitude, in the transformation of feudal exploitation into capitalist exploitation. To understand the course taken by this change, we do not need to go back very far at all. Although we come across the first sporadic traces of capitalist production as early as the fourteenth or fifteenth centuries in certain towns of the

Mediterranean, the capitalist era dates from the sixteenth century. Wherever it appears, the abolition of serfdom has long since been completed, and the most brilliant achievement of the Middle Ages, the existence of independent city-states, has already been on the wane for a considerable length of time.

In the history of primitive accumulation, all revolutions are epoch-making that act as levers for the capitalist class in the course of its formation; but this is true above all for those moments when great masses of men are suddenly and forcibly torn from their means of subsistence, and hurled onto the labour-market as free, unprotected and rightless proletarians. The expropriation of the agricultural producer, of the peasant, from the soil is the basis of the whole process. The history of this expropriation assumes different aspects in different countries, and runs through its various phases in different orders of succession, and at different historical epochs. Only in England, which we therefore take as our example, has it the classic form.[1]

Chapter 27: The Expropriation of the Agricultural Population from the Land

In England, serfdom had disappeared in practice by the last part of the fourteenth century. The immense majority of the population[2] consisted then, and to a still larger extent in the fifteenth century, of free peasant proprietors, however much the feudal trappings might disguise their absolute ownership. In the larger seigniorial domains, the old bailiff, himself a serf, was displaced by the free farmer. The wage-labourers of agriculture were partly peasants, who made use of their leisure time by working on the large estates, and partly an independent, special class of wage-labourer, relatively and absolutely few in numbers. The latter were also in practice peasants, farming independently for themselves, since, in addition to their wages, they were provided with arable land to the extent of four or more acres, together with their cottages. Moreover, like the other peasants, they enjoyed the right to exploit the common land, which gave pasture to their cattle, and furnished them with timber, fire-wood, turf, etc.[3] In all countries of Europe, feudal production is characterized by division of the soil amongst the greatest possible number of sub-feudatories. The might of the feudal lord, like that of the sovereign, depended not on the length of his rent-roll, but on the number of his subjects, and the latter depended on the number of peasant proprietors.[4] Thus although the soil of England, after the Norman conquest, was divided up into gigantic baronies, one of which often included some 900 of the old Anglo-Saxon lordships, it was strewn with small peasant properties, only interspersed here and there with great seigniorial domains. Such conditions, together with the urban prosperity so characteristic of the fifteenth century, permitted the development of that popular wealth Chancellor Fortescue depicted so eloquently in his *De laudibus legum Angliae*, but they ruled out wealth in the form of capital.

The prelude to the revolution that laid the foundation of the capitalist mode of production was played out in the last third of the fifteenth century and the first few decades of the sixteenth. A mass of 'free' and unattached proletarians was hurled onto the labour-market by the dissolution of the bands of feudal retainers, who, as Sir James Steuart correctly remarked, 'everywhere uselessly filled house and castle'.[*] Although the royal power, itself a product of bourgeois development, forcibly hastened the dissolution of these bands of retainers in its striving for absolute sovereignty, it was by no means the sole cause of it. It was rather that the great feudal lords, in their defiant opposition to the king and Parliament, created an incomparably larger proletariat by forcibly driving the peasantry from the land, to which the latter had the same feudal title as the lords themselves, and by usurpation of the common lands. The rapid expansion of wool manufacture in Flanders and the corresponding rise in the price of wool in England provided the direct impulse for these evictions. The old nobility had been devoured by the great feudal wars. The new nobility was the child of its time, for which money was the power of all powers. Transformation of arable land into sheep-walks was therefore its slogan. Harrison, in his *Description of England*, prefixed to *Holinshed's Chronicles*, describes how the expropriation of small peasants is ruining the country. 'What care our great incroachers?' The dwellings of the peasants and the cottages of the labourers were razed to the ground or doomed to decay. 'If,' says Harrison, 'the old records of euerie manour be sought...it will soon appear that in some manour seuenteene, eighteene, or twentie houses are shrunk...that England was neuer less furnished with people than at the present...Of cities and townes either utterly decaied or more than a quarter or half diminished, though some one be a little increased here or there; of townes pulled downe for sheepe-walks, and no more but the lordships now standing in them...I could saie somewhat.'* The complaints of these old chroniclers are always exaggerated, but they faithfully reflect the impression made on contemporaries by the revolution in the relations of production.

The process of forcible expropriation of the people received a new and terrible impulse in the sixteenth century from the Reformation, and the consequent colossal spoliation of church property. The Catholic church was, at the time of the Reformation, the feudal proprietor of a great part of the soil of England. The dissolution of the monasteries, etc., hurled their inmates into the proletariat. The estates of the church were to a large extent given away to rapacious royal favourites, or sold at a nominal price to speculating farmers and townsmen, who drove out the old-established hereditary sub-tenants in great numbers, and threw their holdings together. The legally guaranteed property of the poorer folk in a part of the church's tithes was quietly confiscated. '*Pauper ubique jacet*' cried Queen Elizabeth, after a journey through England. In the forty-third year of her reign it finally proved necessary to recognize pauperism officially by the introduction of the poor-rate. 'The authors of this law seem to have been ashamed to state the grounds of it, for' (contrary to traditional usage) 'it has no preamble whatever.' The poor-rate was declared perpetual by 16 Charles I, c. 4, and in fact only in 1834 did it take a new and severer form. These immediate results of the Reformation were not its most lasting ones. The property of the church formed the religious bulwark of the old conditions of landed property. With its fall, these conditions could no longer maintain their existence.

Even in the last few decades of the seventeenth century, the yeomanry, the class of independent peasants, were more numerous than the class of farmers. They had formed the backbone of Cromwell's strength, and, on the admission of Macaulay himself, stood in favourable contrast to the drunken squires and their servants, the country clergy, who had to marry their masters' cast-off mistresses. By about 1750 the yeomanry had disappeared, and so, by the last decade of the eighteenth century, had the last trace of the common land of the agricultural labourer. We leave on one side here the purely economic driving forces behind the agricultural revolution. We deal only with the violent means employed.

After the restoration of the Stuarts, the landed proprietors carried out, by legal means, an act of usurpation which was effected everywhere on the Continent without any legal formality. They abolished the feudal tenure of land, i.e. they got rid of all its obligations to the state, 'indemnified' the state by imposing taxes on the peasantry and the rest of the people, established for themselves the rights of modern private property in estates to which they had only a feudal title, and, finally, passed those laws of settlement which had the same effect on the English agricultural labourer, *mutatis mutandis*, as the edict of the Tartar Boris Godunov had on the Russian peasantry.**

The 'glorious Revolution' brought into power, along with William of Orange,[5] the landed and capitalist profit-grubbers. They inaugurated the new era by practising on a colossal scale the thefts of state lands which had hitherto been managed more modestly. These estates were given away, sold at ridiculous prices, or even annexed to private estates by direct seizure.[6] All this happened without the slightest observance of legal etiquette. The Crown lands thus fraudulently appropriated, together with the stolen Church estates, in so far as these were not lost again during the republican revolution, form the basis of the present princely domains of the English oligarchy.[7] The bourgeois capitalists favoured the operation, with the intention, among other things, of converting the land into a merely commercial commodity, extending the area of large-scale agricultural production, and increasing the supply of free and rightless proletarians driven from their land. Apart from this, the new landed aristocracy was the natural ally of the new bankocracy, of newly hatched high finance, and of the large manufacturers, at that time dependent on protective duties. The English bourgeoisie acted quite as wisely in its own interest as the Swedish burghers, who did the opposite: hand in hand with the bulwark of their economic strength, the peasantry, they helped the kings in their forcible resumption of crown lands from the oligarchy, in the years after 1604 and later on under Charles X and Charles XI.

Communal property – which is entirely distinct from the state property we have just been considering – was an old Teutonic institution which lived on under the cover of feudalism. We have seen how its forcible usurpation, generally accompanied by the turning of arable into pasture land, begins at the end of the fifteenth century and extends into the sixteenth. But at that time the process was carried on by means of individual acts of violence against which legislation, for a hundred and fifty years, fought in vain. The advance made by the eighteenth century shows itself in this, that the law itself now becomes the instrument by which the people's land is stolen, although the big farmers made use of their little independent methods as well.[8] The Parliamentary form of the robbery is that of 'Bills for Inclosure of Commons', in other words decrees by which the landowners grant themselves the people's land as private property, decrees of expropriation of the people. Sir F. M. Eden refutes his own crafty special pleading, in which he tries to represent communal property as the private property of the great landlords who have taken the place of the feudal lords, when he himself demands a 'general Act of Parliament for the enclosure of Commons' (thereby admitting that a parliamentary *coup d'état* is necessary for their transformation into private property), and moreover calls on the legislature to indemnify the expropriated poor.[9]

While the place of the independent yeoman was taken by tenants at will, small farmers on yearly leases, a servile rabble dependent on the arbitrary will of the landlords, the systematic theft of communal property was of great assistance, alongside the theft of the state domains, in swelling those large farms which were called in the eighteenth century capital farms,[10] or merchant farms,[11] and in 'setting free' the agricultural population as a proletariat for the needs of industry.

The eighteenth century, however, did not yet recognize as fully as the nineteenth the identity between the wealth of the nation and the poverty of the people. Hence the very vigorous polemic, in the economic literature of that time, on the 'enclosure of commons'. From the mass of material that lies before me, I give a few extracts chosen for the strong light they throw on the circumstances of the time. 'In several parishes of Hertfordshire,' writes one indignant person, 'twenty-four farms, numbering on the average 50 to 150 acres, have been melted up into three farms.'[12] 'In Northamptonshire and Leicestershire the enclosure of common lands has taken place on a very large scale, and most of the new lordships, resulting from the enclosure, have been turned into pasturage, in consequence of which many lordships have not now 50 acres ploughed yearly, in which 1,500 were ploughed formerly. The ruins of former dwelling-houses, barns, stables, etc.' are the sole traces of the former inhabitants. 'An hundred houses and families have in some open field villages…dwindled to eight or ten…The landholders in most parishes that have been enclosed only fifteen or twenty years, are very few in comparison of the numbers who occupied them in their open-field state. It is no uncommon thing for four or five wealthy graziers to engross a large enclosed lordship which was before in the hands of twenty or thirty farmers, and as many smaller tenants and proprietors. All these are hereby thrown out of their livings with their families and many other families who were chiefly employed and supported by them.'[13] It was not only land that lay waste, but often also land that was still under cultivation, being cultivated either in common or held under a definite rent paid to the community, that was annexed by the neighbouring landowners under pretext of enclosure. 'I have here in view enclosures of open fields and lands already improved. It is acknowledged by even the writers in defence of enclosures that these diminished villages increase the monopolies of farms, raise the prices of provisions, and produce…and even the enclosure of waste lands (as now carried on) bears hard on the poor, by depriving them of a part of their subsistence, and only goes towards increasing farms already too large.'[14] 'When,' says Dr Price, 'this land gets into the hands of a few great farmers, the consequence must be that the little farmers' (previously described by him as 'a multitude of little proprietors and tenants, who maintain themselves and families by the produce of the ground they occupy by sheep kept on a common, by poultry, hogs, etc., and who therefore have little occasion to purchase any of the means of subsistence') 'will be converted into a body of men who earn their subsistence by working for others, and who will be under a necessity of going to market for all they want…There will, perhaps, be more labour, because there will be more compulsion to it…Towns and manufactures will increase, because more will be driven to them in quest of places and employment. This is the way in which the engrossing of farms actually operates. And this is the way in which, for many years, it has been actually operating in this kingdom.'[15] He sums up the effect of the enclosures in this way: 'Upon the whole, the circumstances of the lower ranks of men are altered in almost every respect for the worse. From little occupiers of land, they are reduced to the state of day-labourers and hirelings; and, at the same time, their subsistence in that state has become more difficult.'[16] In fact, the usurpation of the common lands and the accompanying revolution in agriculture had such an acute effect on the agricultural labourers that, even according to Eden, their wages began to fall below the minimum between 1765 and 1780, and to be supplemented by official Poor Law relief. Their wages, he says, 'were not more than enough for the absolute necessaries of life'.

Let us hear for a moment a defender of enclosures and an opponent of Dr Price. 'Nor is it a consequence that there must be depopulation, because men are not seen wasting their labour in the open field…If, by converting the little farmers into a body of men who must work for others, more labour is produced, it is an advantage which the nation' (to which, of course, the people who have been 'converted' do not belong) 'should wish for...the produce being greater when their joint labours are employed on one farm, there will be a surplus for manufactures, and by this means manufactures, one of the mines of the nation, will increase, in proportion to the quantity of corn produced.[17]

By the nineteenth century, the very memory of the connection between the agricultural labourer and communal property had, of course, vanished. To say nothing of more recent times – have the agricultural population received a farthing's compensation for the 3,511,770 acres of common land which between 1801 and 1831 were stolen from them and presented to the landlords by the landlords, through the agency of Parliament?

In every country where the capitalist mode of production prevails, it is the custom not to pay for labour-power until it has been exercised for the period fixed by the contract, for example, at the end of each week. In all cases, therefore, the worker advances the use-value of his labour-power to the capitalist. He lets the buyer consume it before he receives payment of the price. Everywhere the worker allows credit to the capitalist. That this credit is no mere fiction is shown not only by the occasional loss of the wages the worker has already advanced, when a capitalist goes bankrupt,[18] but also by a series of more long-lasting consequences.[19]

Whether money serves as a means of purchase or a means of payment, this does not alter the nature of the exchange of commodities. The price of the labour-power is fixed by the contract, although it is not realized till later, like the rent of a house. The labour-power is sold, although it is paid for only at a later period. It will therefore be useful, if we want to conceive the relation in its pure form, to presuppose for the moment that the possessor of labour-power, on the occasion of each sale, immediately receives the price stipulated in the contract.

We now know the manner of determining the value paid by the owner of money to the owner of this peculiar commodity, labour-power. The use-value which the former gets in exchange manifests itself only in the actual utilization, in the process of the consumption of the labour-power. The money-owner buys everything necessary for this process, such as raw material, in the market, and pays the full price for it. The process of the consumption of labour-power is at the same time the production process of commodities and of surplus-value. The consumption of labour-power is completed, as in the case of every other commodity, outside the market or the sphere of circulation. Let us therefore, in company with the owner of money and the owner of labour-power, leave this noisy sphere, where everything takes place on the surface and in full view of everyone, and follow them into the hidden abode of production, on whose threshold there hangs the notice 'No admittance except on business'. Here we shall see, not only how capital produces, but how capital is itself produced. The secret of profit-making must at last be laid bare.

The sphere of circulation or commodity exchange, within whose boundaries the sale and purchase of labour-power goes on, is in fact a very Eden of the innate rights of man. It is the exclusive realm of Freedom, Equality, Property and Jeremy Bentham. Freedom, because both buyer and seller of a commodity, let us say of labour-power, are determined only by their own free will. They contract as free persons, who are equal before the law. Their contract is the final result in which their joint will finds a common legal expression. Equality, because each enters into relation with the other, as with a simple owner of commodities, and they exchange equivalent for equivalent. Property, because each disposes only of what is his own. And Bentham, because each looks only to his own advantage. The only force bringing them together, and putting them into relation with each other, is the selfishness, the gain and the private interest of each. Each pays heed to himself only, and no one worries about the others. And precisely for that reason, either in accordance with the pre-established harmony of things, or under the auspices of an omniscient providence, they all work together to their mutual advantage, for the common weal, and in the common interest.

When we leave this sphere of simple circulation or the exchange of commodities, which provides the 'free-trader *vulgaris*' with his views, his concepts and the standard by which he judges the society of capital and wage-labour, a certain change takes place, or so it appears, in the physiognomy of our *dramatis personae*. He who was previously the money-owner now strides out in front as a capitalist; the possessor of labour-power follows as his worker. The one smirks self-importantly and is intent on business; the other is timid and holds back, like someone who has brought his own hide to market and now has nothing else to expect but – a tanning.

Notes

*   James Steuart, *An Inquiry into the Principles of Political Economy*, Vol. 1, Dublin, 1770, p. 52.
*   William Harrison, *Description of England*, Chapter 19, 'Of Parks and Warrens', ed. G. Edelen, Ithaca, N.Y., 1968, pp. 257–8.
** This was the Edict of 1597, by which peasants who had fled from their lords could be pursued for five years and forcibly returned to them when caught.
1   In Italy, where capitalist production developed earliest, the dissolution of serfdom took place earlier than elsewhere. There the serf was emancipated before he had acquired any prescriptive right to the soil. His emancipation at once transformed him into a 'free' proletarian, without any legal rights, and he found a master ready and waiting for him in the towns, which had been for the most part handed down from Roman times. When the revolution which took place in the world market at about the end of the fifteenth century had annihilated northern Italy's commercial supremacy, a movement in the reverse direction set in. The urban workers were driven *en masse* into the countryside, and gave a previously unheard-of impulse to small-scale cultivation, carried on in the form of market gardening.
2   'The petty proprietors who cultivated their own fields with their own hands, and enjoyed a modest competence…then formed a much more important part of the nation than at present. If we may trust the best statistical writers of that age, not less than 160,000 proprietors who, with their families, must have made up more than a seventh of the whole population, derived their subsistence from little freehold estates. The average income of these small landlords…was estimated at between £60 and £70 a year. It was computed that the number of persons who tilled their own land was greater than the number who farmed the land of others' (Thomas Macaulay, *History of England*, 10th edn, London, 1854, Vol. 1, pp. 333, 334). Even in the last third of the seventeenth century, four-fifths of the English people were agriculturalists (loc. cit., p. 413). I quote Thomas Macaulay, because as a systematic falsifier of history he minimizes facts of this kind as much as possible.
3   We must never forget that even the serf was not only the owner of the piece of land attached to his house, although admittedly he was merely a tribute-paying owner, but also a co-proprietor of the common land. 'The peasant' (in Silesia) 'is a serf.' Nevertheless, these serfs possess common lands. 'It has not yet been possible to persuade the Silesians to partition the common lands, whereas in the *Neumark* there is scarcely a village where this partition has not been implemented with very great success' (Honoré-Gabriel de Riquetti, comte de Mirabeau, *De la monarchie prussienne*, London, 1788, Vol. 2, pp. 125–6).
4   Japan, with its purely feudal organization of landed property and its developed small-scale agriculture, gives a much truer picture of the European Middle Ages than all our history books, dictated as these are, for the most part, by bourgeois prejudices. It is far too easy to be 'liberal' at the expense of the Middle Ages.

5   On the private morality of this bourgeois hero, among other things: 'The large grant of lands in Ireland to Lady Orkney, in 1695, is a public instance of the king's affection, and the lady's influence…Lady Orkney's endearing offices are supposed to have been – *foeda laborium ministeria.*' (In the Sloane Manuscript Collection, at the British Museum, No. 4224. The manuscript is entitled: *The Character and Behaviour of King William, Sunderland, etc. as Represented in Original Letters to the Duke of Shrewsbury from Somers, Halifax, Oxford, Secretary Vernon, etc.* It is full of *curiosa.*)

6   'The illegal alienation of the Crown Estates, partly by sale and partly by gift, is a scandalous chapter in English history…a gigantic fraud on the nation' (F. W. Newman. *Lectures on Political Economy*, London, 1851, pp. 129–30). [Added by Engels to the fourth German edition] For details as to how the present large landed proprietors of England came into their possessions, see *Our Old Nobility. By Noblesse Oblige* (N. H. Evans), London, 1879.

7   Read for example Edmund Burke's pamphlet on the ducal house of Bedford, whose offshoot was Lord John Russell, 'the tomtit of liberalism'.

8   'The farmers forbid cottagers to keep any living creatures besides themselves and children, under the pretence that if they keep any beasts or poultry, they will steal from the farmers' barns for their support; they also say, keep the cottagers poor and you will keep them industrious, etc., but the real fact, I believe, is that the farmers may have the whole right of common to themselves' (John Howlett, *A Political Inquiry into the Consequences of Enclosing Waste Lands,* London, 1785, p. 75).

9   Sir F. M. Eden, *the State of the Poor; Or, a History of the Labouring Classes in England*, Preface [pp. xvii, xix].

10 *Two Letters on the Flour Trade and the Dearness of Corn. By a Person in Business*, London, 1767, pp. 19–20.

11 *An Enquiry into the Causes of the Current High Price of Provisions*, London, 1767, p. 111, note. This good book, published anonymously, was written by the Rev. Nathaniel Forster.

12 Thomas Wright, *A Short Address to the Public on the Monopoly of Large Farms*, 1779, pp. 2, 3.

13 Rev. Addington, *Inquiry into the Reasons for or against Inclosing Open Fields*, London, 1772, pp. 37–43 passim.

14 Dr. Richard Price, *Observations on Reversionary Payments*, 6th edn (W. Morgan, London, 1803 Vol. 2) pp. 155–6. Forster, Addington, Kent. Price and James Anderson should be read and compared with the miserable prattle of the sycophantic MacCulloch, in his catalogue *The Literature of Political Economy*, London, 1845.

15 Price, op. cit., p. 147.

16 Price, op. cit., p. 159. We are reminded of ancient Rome. 'The rich had got possession of the greater part of the undivided land. They were confident that, in the conditions of the time, these possessions would never be taken back again from them, and they therefore bought some of the pieces of land lying near theirs, and belonging to the poor, with the acquiescence of the latter, and the rest they took by force, so that now they were cultivating widely extending domains, instead of isolated fields. Then they employed slaves in agriculture and cattle-breeding, because the free men had been taken away from labour to do military service. The possession of slaves brought great gains to them, in that the slaves, on account of their exemptions from military service, could multiply without risk and therefore had great numbers of children. Thus the powerful men drew all wealth to themselves, and the whole land swarmed with slaves. The Italians, on the other hand, were always decreasing in number, worn down as they were by poverty, taxation, and military service. Even in times of peace, they were doomed to complete inactivity, because the rich were in possession of the soil, and used slaves instead of free men to cultivate it' (Appian, *The Roman Civil Wars*, Bk I, Ch. 7). This passage refers to the time before the Licinian Law. Military service, which hastened to so great an extent the ruin of the Roman plebeians, was also the chief means by which, as in a forcing-house, Charlemagne brought about the transformation of free German peasants into serfs and bondsmen.

17 [J. Arbuthnot,] *An Inquiry into the Connection between the Present Price of Provisions, etc.,* pp. 124, 129. Here is a similar argument, but with an opposite tendency: 'Working men are driven from their cottages and forced into the towns to seek for employment; but then a larger surplus is obtained, and thus capital is augmented' ([R. B. Seeley,] *The Perils of the Nation*, 2nd edn, London, 1843, p. xiv.)

18 'The worker lends his industry,' says Storch. But he slyly adds to this the statement that the worker 'risks nothing', except 'the loss of his wages…The worker does not hand over anything of a material nature' (Storch, *Cours d'économie politique*, St Petersburg, 1815, Vol. 2, pp. 36–7).

19 One example. In London there are two sorts of bakers, the 'full priced', who sell bread at its full value, and the 'undersellers', who sell it at less than its value. The latter class comprises more than three-quarters of the total number of bakers (p. xxxii in the Report of H. S. Tremenheere, the commissioner appointed to examine 'the grievances complained of by the journeymen bakers', etc., London, 1862). The undersellers, almost without exception, sell bread adulterated with alum, soap, pearl ash, chalk, Derbyshire stone-dust and other similar agreeable, nourishing and wholesome ingredients. (See the above-cited Blue Book, as also the report of the select committee of 1855 on the adulteration of food, and Dr Hassall's *Adulterations Detected*, 2nd edn, London, 1861.) Sir John Gordon stated before the committee of 1855 that 'in consequence of these adulterations, the poor man, who lives on two pounds of bread a day, does not now get one-fourth part of nourishing matter, let alone the deleterious effects on his health'. Tremenheere states (op. cit., p. xlviii) as the reason why a 'very large part of the working class', although well aware of this adulteration, nevertheless accept the alum, stone-dust, etc. as part of their purchase, that it is for them 'a matter of necessity to take from their baker or from the chandler's shop such bread as they choose to supply'. As they are not paid their wages before the end of the week, they in their turn are unable 'to pay for the bread consumed by their families during the week, before the end of the week', and Tremenheere adds on the evidence of witnesses, 'it is notorious that bread composed of those mixtures is made expressly for sale in this manner'. 'In many English agricultural districts' (and still more in Scottish) 'wages are paid fortnightly and even monthly; with such long intervals between the payments, the agricultural labourer is obliged to buy on credit…He must pay higher prices, and is in fact tied to the shop which gives him credit. Thus at Horningham in Wilts., for example, where the wages are monthly, the same flour that he could buy elsewhere as 1 s. 10d. per stone, costs him 2 s. 4d. per stone (*Public Health, Sixth Report* of the Medical Officer of the Privy Council, etc., 1864, p. 264). 'The block-printers of Paisley and Kilmarnock' (Western Scotland) 'enforced in 1833 by a strike the reduction of the period of payment from monthly to fortnightly' (*Reports of the Inspectors of Factories*…31 October 1853, p. 34). As a further nice development from the credit given by the workers to the capitalist, we may refer to the method adopted by many English coal-owners whereby the worker is not paid till the end of the month, and in the meantime receives sums on account from the capitalist, often in goods for which the miner is obliged to pay more than the market price (truck system). 'It is a common practice with the coal masters to pay once a month, and advance cash to their workmen at the end of each intermediate week. The cash is given in the shop' (i.e. the tommy shop which belongs to the master); 'the men take it on one side and lay it out on the other' (*Children's Employment Commission, Third Report*, London, 1864, p. 38, p. 192).

CHAPTER 27

The Monied Metropolis
New York City and the Consolidation of the American Bourgeoisie, 1850–1896

Sven Beckert

Introduction

On February 10, 1897, at the tail end of the most severe economic depression the United States had experienced in the nineteenth century, 700 merchants, industrialists, bankers, and professionals assembled at New York's Waldorf-Astoria Hotel for a costume ball. Invited by lawyer Bradley Martin and his wife Cornelia, the guests arrived in fancy historic costumes. Fifty celebrants impersonated Marie Antoinette, while others, according to the *New York Times,* came dressed as "Kings and Queens, nobles, knights, and courtiers whose names and personalities take up pages of history." Real estate mogul John Jacob Astor, wearing a Henry of Navarre costume, brandished a sword decorated with jewels; Ruth Hoe, daughter of printing press manufacturer Robert Hoe, "appeared in a dainty Louis XIV" costume; banker J. R. Morgan donned a Molière costume; and Caroline Astor had gems worth $250,000 sewn into her dress. Cornelia Martin, not to be outdone, wore a necklace once owned by none other than Marie Antoinette herself. To receive her guests, Cornelia Martin sat on a raised platform resembling a throne, her husband, Bradley Martin, standing next to her, wearing a "Court dress of Louis XV; white and pink brocaded satin knee breeches, white silk hose, diamond buckles on low, red-heeled shoes; powdered wig." Furthering such aristocratic pretensions, the rooms themselves were decorated to resemble the great hall of Versailles, and the guests dined on such delicacies as "Terrapene decossée à la Baltimore" and "Sorbet fin de Siècle." It was, as the *New York Times* continued to comment only one day after the ball, "the climax in this form of entertainment thus far reached in the metropolis."

Indeed, the ball was so lavish and ostentatious that it galvanized all of New York, making it the "universal and engrossing subject of interest and discussion." Cornelia Martin had justified the extravaganza as helping the country overcome the depression,

Original publication details: Sven Beckert, *The Monied Metropolis: New York City and the Consolidation of the American Bourgoisie, 1850–1896,* pp. 1–9; 12–13; 237; 256–263; 273–276; 279–283; 285–292. Cambridge University Press, 2001. Reproduced with permission from Cambridge University Press and S. Beckert.

Class: The Anthology, First Edition. Edited by Stanley Aronowitz and Michael J. Roberts.

arguing that it would "give an impetus to trade." Many New Yorkers, if we are to believe the *New York Times*, objected to such rationalizations in the midst of economic crisis, and threats of bombs kept not only New York's police but also a hired army of Pinkerton detectives on alert, watching "for thieves or for men of socialistic tendencies." As a further precaution, the first-floor windows of the Waldorf Hotel were nailed shut.

This "most elaborate private entertainment that has ever taken place in the history of the metropolis" pointed to a dramatic departure from the past. The event and the frame of mind that inspired it were part of a series of transformations that had remade the city's economic elite between 1850 and 1890, economically, socially, ideologically, and politically. Forty years earlier, New York's wealthy citizenry, steeped in the country's republican heritage and the moral imperatives of frugality and thrift, would have looked with disdain upon the ostentatious displays of wealth and conspicuous consumption that flourished at century's end. Championing northern society as the land of liberty and equal opportunity in opposition to Europe and the American South, they could not have imagined a world of such deep class hostilities evident in bomb threats, boarded windows, and Pinkertons. And in contrast to the armed-camp setting in which bourgeois New Yorkers of the 1890s displayed their social position to the world, New York's "respectable classes" forty years earlier had proudly paraded up and down Broadway each afternoon exhibiting their status to one another and to the city, a ritual in which they shared public space with other social groups. Indeed, the Martins' ball was far removed from a time when Alexis de Tocqueville observed that "in the United States the more opulent citizens take great care not to stand aloof from the people; on the contrary, they constantly keep on easy terms with the lower classes: they listen to them, they speak to them every day." The ball symbolized other changes as well. Forty years earlier, manufacturers and merchants would hardly ever have assembled at the same social occasions. And while forty years earlier "society" events usually brought only upper-class New Yorkers together, now the Martins' ball was national in scope, with "people [coming] from distant cities to attend." The ostentatious display of riches, the depth of class conflict, the national reach of social networks, and the unification of New York's upper class across economic sectors evident at the ball symbolized a significant departure from antebellum times.

Throughout the Western world, the nineteenth century saw the rise of the bourgeoisie and bourgeois society. As a result of the unfolding of capitalist economies and the emancipation of society from the state, owners of capital decisively shaped economic change and the newly emerging societies. As the first elite not to derive its status from the accidents of birth and heritage, the rising bourgeoisie worked hard, lived in modest comfort, and celebrated individual accomplishment. Accumulating ever more capital and power, this new social class gained the upper hand over an older, feudal, social elite and eventually shaped the economy, ideology, and politics of all Western nations.

In the United States, the history of this social class was exceptional. In the absence of an aristocracy or a feudal state, both bourgeois society and the bourgeoisie burst more powerfully onto the scene than anywhere else. By the end of the American Revolution, a socially distinct group of merchants had gained ever more prominence in the cities of the eastern seaboard. During the second quarter of the nineteenth century, these traders were joined by a group of artisans who had recently turned into manufacturers, and who were accumulating capital in production, not commerce. Unlike in Europe, where conflicts with an entrenched aristocracy at times drove bourgeois citizens to articulate shared identities as early as midcentury, the economic elite of the United States did not forge such bonds. While both merchants and industrialists developed social networks, cultural orientations, and institutions, as well as ideas and politics that diverged from those of farmers on the one side and workers on the other, even by as late as the 1850s they remained divided, articulating sharply different identities, creating competing social networks, and envisioning very different kinds of political economies.

By the 1870s and 1880s, however, bourgeois New Yorkers articulated a consciousness of separate class identity. In a process that accelerated during the depression of the 1870s, upper-class social life and politics increasingly manifested a new and greater distance from other groups – especially from workers, whom the economic elite perceived as a double threat to their economic and political power. As a result of these fears, many elite New Yorkers abandoned their belief in a socially cohesive society without deep class divisions and their reluctant wartime support for a state-sponsored social revolution in the South. Instead, they advocated the unquestioned primacy of unregulated markets and, most dramatically, restriction of suffrage rights in municipal elections.

Proletarianization and the overthrow of slavery drove the process of bourgeois class formation. The overthrow of slavery and the destruction of the political power of slave-holders sped the economic development of the North, benefiting industrialists and bankers while increasing the political power of the northern bourgeoisie over the federal government. It also provided the basis upon which different capitalists could find common ground. Before the war, the city's industrialists, in particular, had embraced the emancipatory promises of republicanism, seeing in the eradication of slavery, or at least its limitation, the possibility for preventing the emergence of a permanent proletariat. Merchants, in contrast, aimed at building a paternalist relationship to the city's workers, supported by the profits derived from a slave-based plantation economy. When the war destroyed slavery, it also destroyed the grounds for these arrangements.

The destruction of slavery, in effect, moved the process of proletarianization to center stage. During the war and its aftermath, those segments of New York's economic elite who based their economic activities on wage labor – namely, industrialists and financiers – became the dominant segment within the bourgeoisie itself. A coincidental challenge from the increasingly militant workers in the North compelled merchants, financiers, and industrialists to unify in defense of property rights, and to become more ambivalent about democracy, in fact, challenging some of their older assumptions about the nature of society. Many of them also increased the amount of capital they controlled, thus sharpening social inequality. As a result, the emancipatory vision of many antebellum bourgeois New Yorkers, with its universalist preoccupations, gave way to an articulation of class identities. Their political ideas focused ever more narrowly on the guarding of their own elevated social position. A new industrial liberalism replaced the producerist liberalism of antebellum manufacturers and the communitarian liberalism of merchants. New York's bourgeoisie was made and had made itself.

But before we embark on the epic story of New York City's bourgeoisie a word about *terminology*. The term "bourgeoisie" was not frequently employed by capital-rich New Yorkers during the nineteenth century, who preferred to refer to themselves at first by the specific line of business they engaged in and, later, as "taxpayers," or "business-men." Similarly, historians have employed various other terms to describe the group under review here, such as "elites," "aristocracy," "plutocracy," "ruling class," and "middle class." I believe, however, that the term bourgeoisie grasps more precisely the historical formation with which I am concerned. "Elite," for example, while a useful term, does not sufficiently distinguish the bourgeoisie as a fundamentally different kind

of elite from other elites who have come before or after. Aristocracy, while used deroga-
torily by nineteenth-century workers and lower-middle-class citizens resentful of the
wealth and power of the bourgeoisie, is problematic because it is the distinguishing
feature of United States history that no true aristocracy emerged. Plutocracy, in turn,
insufficiently grasps the totality of the bourgeoisie, calling to mind only fat, cigar-
smoking robber barons who reigned tyrannically over their enterprises and the government. Ruling class assumes the political power of the bourgeoisie instead of
investigating it. The term middle class (or middle classes), in contrast, by referring to
a distinct elite based on the ownership of capital rather than heritage and birth, as the
"estate" situated between inherited aristocracy on the one side and farmers as well as
workers on the other side, describes the group this book is concerned with quite well.
Its usage, however, has become so overwhelmed with present-day concerns that it
lacks sufficient analytical clarity. Today, "middle class" can stand either for all
Americans, past and present, who are neither extremely wealthy nor homeless, or for
a distinct social group that corresponds somewhat with the European notion of the
"petite bourgeoisie" – artisans, shop owners, and lesser professionals. For these reasons,
the term that best fits the group of people I am looking at is bourgeoisie, which I use
interchangeably with "upper class" and "economic elite." It refers to a particular kind
of elite whose power, in its most fundamental sense, derived from the ownership of
capital rather than birthright, status, or kinship. Bourgeoisie, moreover, focuses our
attention squarely on the relationships between members of the city's economic elite,
allowing us to put into the center of our investigation the question of what they did
and did not share.

To speak of the bourgeoisie in a meaningful way, then, the term must be more than a
merely descriptive term defining an economically heterogeneous group. One needs to
look beyond social structure to discover if, at certain points, something more than the
shared ownership of capital held this group of New Yorkers together. Indeed, it is only
in this specific sense that this social class, like any other, has a history. Bourgeois defines
not only a certain space in the social structure but potentially also a shared culture and
identity. And because social identities often emerge in conflict with other social groups,
it was in the process of distinguishing themselves from others, especially from workers,
but by the late century also from the lower middle class or the petty-bourgeoisie, that
bourgeois New Yorkers came to an understanding of themselves as a class and at times
were able to act collectively upon this identity.

In the emergence of this identity, culture in the broadest sense played a central role.
Especially by the late nineteenth century, a common cultural vocabulary increasingly
defined bourgeois New Yorkers, transcending divisions rooted in economic competition,
the ownership of different kinds of capital, and ethnic and religious differences. This
class culture emphasized rationality, discipline, and individual effort. It expressed itself
in shared habits and manners (such as rituals of eating at the dining room table), preferences in interior design, definitions of "high culture," and gender roles (women occupying a "separate sphere" from men). The bourgeois family, in particular, was central to
the definition and production of this bourgeois cultural world. Eventually, all these identities and inclinations were institutionalized in clubs, debutante balls, voluntary associations and museums, and, in exceptional circumstances, even in political mobilizations.
These institutions, in effect, bound different segments of the city's (and the nation's)
bourgeoisie together. By emphasizing culture as well as conflict, this book allows us
to see the creation of a bourgeoisie as the result of an active process of class formation,

not as the automatic or necessary outcome of a shared position in the social structure. It also allows us to talk about class without falling into the trap of teleology.

The formation of a bourgeoisie as a class, I argue, was neither historically necessary nor irreversible. Rather, class identities were historically contingent: merchants, bankers, and industrialists, for example, only expressed them once identities based on the ownership of a particular kind of capital had moved to the sidelines. They did so for specific reasons, most importantly their encounter with the social polarization of Gilded Age America. Furthermore, class identities expressed on one level, for example in the emergence of a shared class culture, did not necessarily have to articulate themselves in other spheres, such as politics, which is why the degree of class identity and class solidarity could change over time. And the relationship between bourgeoisie and bourgeois society, despite Marx's assertion to the contrary, was fraught with tensions: bourgeois New Yorkers were ambivalent about extending the benefits of bourgeois society to African Americans in the South during the era of the "last bourgeois revolution" (the Civil War) and later, during the 1870s, they articulated a powerful critique of liberal democracy in the North.

Studying New York's economic elite, in turn, tells us about class formation more generally. The different levels of social reality in which class can be expressed are not linked in a direct and straightforward manner, but instead can, to a certain degree, be autonomous. While bourgeois New Yorkers developed a certain sense of classness independent of outside challengers, especially in the emergence of shared manners, habits, and social institutions, it was only the confrontation with other mobilized social groups (such as the slaveholders of the South and workers in the North) that encouraged them to act collectively in the realm of politics. Furthermore, this allows us to see clearly the fundamental difference between bourgeois and working-class formation, namely, the distinct relationship between class formation and power. Workers, usually, can only exert power when they overcome divisions and act collectively, either in trade unions or in politics, whereas bourgeois New Yorkers exerted extraordinary power even without engaging in collective action, thanks to their control of capital.

Last but not least, it is important to remember that the emergence of a more cohesive bourgeoisie, the rise of a social group with shared identities, ideas, and at times politics, did not eliminate economic conflicts, social distinctions, and political quarrels. While I disagree with accounts that put ethnic and cultural divisions at the center of their analysis of New York's economic elite, these demarcations still mattered. What changed, instead, was the balance between division and cohesion. And this change, in turn, had a tremendous impact on the power of New York's bourgeoisie and, thus, on the history of the United States in the late nineteenth century.

8

The Culture of Capital

By the 1880s and 1890s, New York's merchants, industrialists, and bankers had transformed themselves more than ever before into a self-conscious class. They saw themselves and were seen by others as a distinct social group, a collective identity they articulated in numerous ways as class position and class identity corresponded to a degree unknown before. Though divisions of a cultural and political kind persisted, they did not rival those that had had their roots in slavery and the Civil War. The conflicts of the antebellum years had now finally been left behind, replaced by widespread agreement on the fundamentals of the political economy of a free-labor United States. At the same time, however, rapid industrialization deepened social cleavages, and the combined effects of rising inequality and proletarianization created tensions that, as we have seen, at times drove workers and farmers to mobilize collectively, in turn motivating upper-class New Yorkers to define themselves against these "dangerous classes." This greater sense of class identity, as well as the overcoming of the deep divisions that had characterized the age of the Civil War, enabled wealthy New Yorkers to translate their ever-growing economic power into unprecedented influence on the institutions and policies of the state. Indeed, by the last quarter of the century, their power was such that not presidents but prominent New York entrepreneurs – such as John D. Rockefeller, J. Pierpont Morgan, and Andrew Carnegie – came to represent the age.

Most basically, new class identities expressed themselves in language. Language serves as a marker of social distinction as well as self-description, and during the 1880s and 1890s, bourgeois New Yorkers began to refer to themselves in ways distinctively different than before. While in the 1850s they had regularly alluded to themselves by the specific line of business they were engaged in, such as "merchant" or "iron manufacturer," by the 1880s self-depictions as "business man" or "capitalist" had become more frequent. The *North American Review, Atlantic Monthly*, and Mark Twain all spoke of "business men" as a group of people engaged in commerce, production, and finance. In the pages of the *Commercial and Financial Chronicle*, the term "business men" now came into frequent use, replacing the term "merchant" that had regularly appeared in the pages of one of its predecessor publications, *Hunt's Merchants' Magazine*.

While "business men" turned into a generic term describing people who were engaged in manufacturing, commerce, or banking, terms such as "the better classes" and "taxpayers" entered the vocabulary to depict members of one's own class in political discourse, in contrast to the less respectable "masses" and "dangerous classes." The reform movements of the last third of the nineteenth century, as we have seen, regularly and consistently appealed to the solidarity of taxpayers.

Language, however, only expressed changes of a far-reaching kind. Upper-class social networks, habits, and institutions increasingly constructed a shared culture that overcame the divisions of the antebellum years and decisively set bourgeois New Yorkers apart from other social groups. While this bourgeois culture, with few exceptions, was predicated on access to resources that only the ownership of substantial amounts of capital made possible (that is, "culture" does not explain itself), it provided the glue that constituted the upper class and helped it to transcend the numerous economic fault lines that market competition generated. "Clothing, housing, furniture, gestures, and language, as well as opinions and beliefs" were consciously and unconsciously regulated. As Andrew Carnegie put it: "I began to pay strict attention to my language, and to the English classics, which I now read with great avidity. I began to notice how much better it was to be gentle in tone and manner, polite and courteous to all – in short, better behaved."

The bourgeois home, social clubs, food, and ways of personal interaction all helped to define the realm of the bourgeoisie. It was a realm in which bourgeois New Yorkers set rules and created boundaries, both of which were essential for the self-definition of a group that lacked legal status. Yet as the result of the principally open nature of bourgeois culture, conflicts over whom to admit and how to draw lines between different subsets were frequent, and in themselves an integral part of this bourgeois culture. Cohesion and differentiation were made from the same cloth.

The emergence of collective identities and the distancing from other social groups normally went hand in hand. Consumption was a prime example of this correspondence: Especially the richest bourgeois New Yorkers were, by late century, displaying their wealth as never before, and thus emphasizing the social gap that set them apart from the lower sort. Houses of a size and opulence unknown to earlier generations, for instance, sheltered the railroad tycoons, financial wizards, and empire-building industrialists. J. Pierpont Morgan's mansion on Madison Avenue was spacious enough to give employment to twelve servants, more than any bourgeois New Yorker had employed in the 1850s. William Vanderbilt, the son of Commodore Vanderbilt, built a mansion at Fifth Avenue and 51st Street; the interior decoration by Christian Herter alone was said to have cost $800,000. For this kind of money, Vanderbilt got a Pompeian vestibule, a Japanese parlor, and a Renaissance dining room. Alva Vanderbilt, wife of William, shortly afterward built a castle-like structure on the next block north, at a rumored cost of $3 million. Not to be outdone, George Washington Vanderbilt constructed a castle in North Carolina – including forty bedrooms, a library of 250,000 volumes, and a garden designed by Frederick Law Olmsted. The wealth and abundance of New York's bourgeoisie in the 1880s and 1890s, in turn, pervaded all forms of popular culture – ranging from novels, such as Mark Twain and Charles Ardley Warner's *Gilded Age*, to theater plays, such as *The Henrietta*.

Searching for a cultural repertoire appropriate to a rising elite, bourgeois New Yorkers increasingly turned toward European aristocratic culture. Fashion, for example, was derived from the tastes of European monarchs (truly wealthy New Yorkers had the same tailors as European rulers). Quite tellingly, when in 1897 Cornelia and Bradley Martin organized their fancy dress ball, their guests attended in the costumes of the aristocracy of yesteryear. Tiffany & Co. opened a heraldry department in the 1870s to design coats of arms. Recreational hunting, one of the favorite pastimes of the European aristocracy, found aficionados among upper-class New Yorkers, who were particularly fond of slaughtering the buffalo herds of the West. Elaborate country seats, sometimes of a size matching European castles, attracted the city's elite to the country. In these years, Newport, Rhode Island, came into its own, sporting a large number of enormous summer homes. Though August Belmont owned one of them, he also purchased more than a thousand acres in Babylon, Long Island, in the late 1860s, and built a twenty-four room house, stables, and greenhouses, as well as a one-mile racetrack.

August Belmont, like many upper-class New Yorkers, had developed a fascination for horses, another interest they shared with the European aristocracy. Since the opening of the drives in the newly built Central Park, carriage and horse riders had become the predominant users. More elaborate than the earlier promenade of the 1850s and more removed from the increasingly disorderly city, each afternoon a good number of bourgeois New Yorkers rode through the park, acknowledging each other's presence and basking in the stares of lesser spectators passing below them. Another equine pastime, albeit faster paced, was horse racing. In 1865, Leonard Jerome, August Belmont, and William Travers had formed the "American Jockey Club," and a year later, "Jerome Park" in Fordham opened, where the likes of August Belmont and Henry Ward Beecher raced their horses. On race days, New York's merchants, industrialists, and bankers took their carriages through Central Park to the tracks, the destination of "[d]ashing four-in-hands, filled with beautiful women and their attending cavaliers." The working-class public was outraged at the high entrance fees at the track that excluded poor and middling folk, but August Belmont maintained haughtily that "[r]acing is for the rich."

Collecting works of art, particularly those of European origins, further recalled the habits of ruling classes throughout history, including those of the aristocracy. After all, as sociologist Pierre Bourdieu reminds us, "[m]aterial or symbolic consumption of works of art constitutes one of the supreme manifestations of *ease*," and a life not dictated by economic necessities was one of the central attributes of the bourgeoisie. Edwin D. Morgan, the Civil War governor of New York State, described his Fifth Avenue home characteristically: "We find our Parlors, Rooms, Halls & Bed rooms so full that we have no room for more." When Morgan died, 152 art items from his estate were sold. Similarly, William Henry Vanderbilt's mansion on Fifth Avenue was crowded with paintings valued at $1.5 million. Sugar refiner Henry O. Havemeyer and his wife accumulated a huge art collection (later to be donated to the Metropolitan Museum of Art), and in their drive to acquire old European masters, unwittingly decorated their home with a number of fake Rembrandts. J. Pierpont Morgan stationed agents throughout Europe to acquire paintings, etchings, and statues. In many ways, the flow of art from Europe to the United States expressed the new economic power relations that began to evolve during these years.

Some bourgeois New Yorkers, especially of recently acquired wealth, went so far in their admiration of the aristocracy that they married their daughters to cash-poor or simply impoverished European aristocrats. The deal was straightforward: social honor in return for financial support. The trail of "dollar princesses" began in the 1870s, and by 1915 there were forty-two American princesses; seventeen duchesses; thirty-three viscountesses; thirty-three marchionesses; forty-six ladies, wives of knights, or baronets; sixty-four baronesses; and one hundred and thirty-six countesses. Jennie Jerome, daughter of Leonard Jerome, married Lord Randolph Churchill in 1874, after he had proposed to her in 1872. Prior negotiations between the families had nearly broken off when the Churchill family demanded a higher dowry from the Jeromes. Two years later, in a similar deal, Consuelo Yznaga married the Eighth Duke of Manchester, Lord Mandeville. Even Helen Stuyvesant Morton, daughter of banker and Republican Governor Levi Parsons Morton, married an aristocrat, the Comte de Perigord, Duc de Valencery. These efforts to assimilate the cultural norms of the European ruling classes of past centuries expressed the enormous confidence, power, and wealth of upper-class New Yorkers.

Just like the parlor, food and its consumption also became strong indicators of bourgeois culture. What was on the table and how it was ingested clearly set bourgeois New Yorkers apart from other social groups. Simply the management of the vast number of utensils that typically decorated bourgeois tables, including such exotic tools as "sugar tongs, Saratoga chips servers, ice cream knives, lemon forks, grape shears, oyster ladles, sardine tongs and salt spoons," was a skill that demanded training, helped along by the study of etiquette books, such as Clara Jessup Moore's *Sensible Etiquette of the Best Society*. Dinners, typically, consisted of multiple courses, and it was not unusual for a meal to include not only an assortment of appetizers but also main courses of fish, beef, and poultry. At public events, menus in French became the fashion of the day, even for such ancestor-conscious organizations as the New England Society of New York, groups of mostly small manufacturers like the printers (who enjoyed on the occasion of their 1887 convention in Chicago such delicacies as "potatoes a la Parisienne"), and the metal manufacturers and merchants who dined in 1896 on "Filet of Beef à la Moderne." Even the choice of dinner conversation demanded training in the cultural rules of one's class, which called for the evasion of such topics as "political or sectarian controversies, sicknesses, sores, surgical operations, dreadful accidents, shocking cruelties or horrible punishments." These preferences, tastes, and shared manners created boundaries that were the more important since they could not always be attained in schools and colleges.

Women as well as men were to be trained in these social skills, though this cultural capital had a significantly greater importance to women, as it was often their principal contribution to the family business. Because they had the time, inclination, and support from servants necessary to forge this class culture and transmit it to the next generation, women played dominant roles in organizing the household's social life, and it was thus not surprising that a woman, Caroline Astor, stood at the pinnacle of New York society. Bourgeois women, in effect, shaped the institutions of society, and served, as Elizabeth Blackmar and Roy Rosenzweig have argued, "as emblems of their husbands' wealth and judges of their own and others' status."

Since class formation was tightly linked to family reproduction, bourgeois women also took center stage in the transfer of this culture to their children. Though upper-class children were normally born into the material bounty of their parents' world, they still had to acquire its cultural attributes in an active process of learning. Indeed, bourgeois life was difficult to master, and the inability of most Americans to acquire these skills was one of the major lines of demarcation and one of the principal functions of this class culture. Appropriating social capital, again, was particularly important to girls. The principal goal of their education was to make them socially competent to negotiate the bourgeois world, an education, as historian Maureen Montgomery has argued, that was largely "ornamental," providing the skills to secure the right kind of husband, which, in turn, was "an important means of establishing a family's social ranking."

Schools helped out in this project: Laura Celestia Rockefeller's three daughters, for instance, were sent to the Rye Female Seminary. Barbara Guggenheim's daughters, Cora and Rosa, attended a Catholic finishing school in Paris. Diverse schools in the city itself, such as the Spence School for Girls ("pupils come from wealthy families of all sections") and the Comstock School for Girls (among its alumnae were "many of New York's most prominent society women," including Theodore Roosevelt's sister Corinne and his future wife Edith Kermit Carow) trained many of the city's daughters of wealthy families in forms of appropriate behavior, including table manners. This, in turn, helped their mothers place them well on the marriage market.

For boys, the emphasis of their upbringing was on the ethic of work. Even someone as rich and powerful as John D. Rockefeller put great weight on imbuing his children with the values and culture of his class. When at their summer home, Rockefeller's children were set to tasks such as pulling weeds from the lawn or chopping wood. Each task was paid for by the family patriarch; a wage of a penny was paid for every ten weeds pulled, at a time during which Rockefeller's Standard Oil alone would pay out dividends of nearly $14 million a year. "All home activities," remarked one of Rockefeller's biographers, "were carried on with an eye to character-building." Similarly, Joseph H. Choate told his son George early on that "the only way any man ever got on in any business... [is] by hard work, and sacrificing everything else to it."

This new class culture also provided the underpinnings for various institutions. Social clubs were the most prominent among them, and by the 1880s, dozens of exclusive clubs littered the scene, among them the Union Club, the Union League, the Manhattan Club, the Knickerbocker Club, the Calumet, the Metropolitan, the Tuxedo, the New York Yacht Club, and the Racquet Club, many of recent vintage. While their numbers had increased substantially since the 1850s, their character had not changed:

> In one corner [of the Union Club] may be seen the solid men, who have passed the age of frivolities, calmly discussing stocks, bonds, railroads, real estate, and business, failures, and defalcations. Further on politics, elections, and municipal affairs are treated from a taxpayer's standpoint. Another group again are deep in horse racing, yacht racing, pigeon shooting, mail stage coaching, and of late fox hunting.

Clubs provided institutionalized networks that now transcended the specific interests of a single economic sector. This was a major departure from the 1850s. The Union Club, once merchant dominated, for example, by late century counted among its members appliance manufacturer Thomas B. Burnham, iron manufacturers James A. Abercombie, and Dudley B. Fuller, and cordage manufacturer James M. Waterbury. The Union League Club, once the home mostly of merchants and bankers, by the 1880s had among its ranks manufacturers of oil, clothing, tobacco, hats, cotton thread, iron, machinery, and silks.

9

The Rights of Labor, The Rights of Property

While bourgeois New Yorkers had forged a shared culture, and had amassed unprecented economic power by the 1880s, their assertion of this power, their conspicuous consumption, and the striking inequality of wealth within the city and the nation propelled other social groups, particularly workers, to challenge them at the workplace and the polls. This mobilization, in turn, drove, the city's economic elite even closer together and enabled them to act at times collectively. Bourgeois class formation thus developed in relation to working-class formation; bourgeois class identities were sharpened by workers' collective action. This relationship was new, a result of the emerging dominance of industrial over merchant capital after the Civil War.

During the 1880s and 1890s, with the strife over slavery and Reconstruction left behind, concerns about wage labor moved to the center stage of bourgeois discourse. "The silver question is a bubble of insignificance," and the "tariff issue...of minor importance," compared to the "relation that prevails between labor and capital," wrote a perceptive reader to the editors of *Iron Age*. *The Nation* seconded this notion, observing that "the labor problem [received] an amount and kind of discussion from all classes such as it never received before." Indeed, *Iron Age*, the journal of iron manufacturers, discussed the "labor question" regularly and in great detail, as did the *Oil and Paint Manufacturer* and the *National Bottlers' Gazette*, and aside from discussions of new technologies and the economic outlook of the trade, it was the most important topic in their pages. A stream of more substantial publications considered the relationship between "capital and labor" as well, with titles such as *The Wage-Workers of America and the Relation of Capital to Labor; Labor; Capital and a Protective Tariff; The Duty of the Church in the Conflict Between Capital and Labor; Social Struggles;* and many more. In 1882 a journal even began to circulate with the title *Capital and Labor;* "the organ of the manufacturers on the labor question." Indeed, so fully did the conflict between workers and employers move to center stage that when the widow of department store owner Alexander T. Stewart died, the *New York Times* discussed her will in terms of its implications for class relations, noting that its provisions would spread her wealth broadly enough so that "there is nothing… to make a case for the Communists."

Labor took center stage in the political discourse of the economic elite because they were confronted by a larger and more mobilized working class. Whereas the antebellum merchants had normally employed only a few wage workers, the newly powerful industrialists depended on a large number of employees. New Yorker Meyer Guggenheim, like many others, had personally experienced this transition when he left the calmer days of trade behind and invested in Colorado silver mines, where he employed thousands of workers.

Not only were there more workers but they also struck more frequently. Indeed, just like the city's merchants, industrialists, and bankers, who had organized and become more class conscious by the 1880s, the city's workers, after the devastation of the depression, began to rebuild their organizations. The somewhat more prosperous early 1880s and the hostility of employers encouraged them to organize collectively. The number of strikes in the nation increased from fewer than 500 a year in the early 1880s to approximately 1,500 in 1886. In New York City alone, it has been estimated that between 1881 and 1900, 5,090 strikes involved 33,161 factories and 962,470 workers. These walkouts were often successful; nationwide, workers won 46.5 percent of the strikes between 1881 and 1905. And not only was the number of strikes large; American labor relations, compared to those of western Europe, also turned exceptionally violent.

Industrialists faced strikes especially frequently. William Steinway, for instance, was constantly battling his workers throughout the 1880s, conflicts he faithfully chronicled in his diary. In November 1878 there was a "[r]evolution at our factory"; in September 1879 the casemakers, machine men, and blockers successfully struck for a 10 percent raise; in early 1880 all of Steinway's workers walked out (after a bitter lockout, the strike ended in a compromise settlement); in October 1882 workers went on another four-week-long strike, during which Steinway refused to give in and discharged the strike leaders (noting on November 20, 1882, that "strike broken, feel greatly elated"); and in May 1886 Steinway defeated a strike of his workers for the eight-hour day.

Steinway's handling of strikes, quite typically, became increasingly confrontational. While he had tried in the 1860s to seek compromise, by the 1880s he battled his workers directly. During the 1880 strike he initiated a decision, backed by the Boss Piano Makers of New York, to lock out all piano workers throughout the industry. In 1882 he gave the strike leaders "a fearful talking" and planned to "in toto discharge them all." On November 10, 1882, he served "dispossess warrants … on the Astoria Strikers." Again, in 1883 during another strike, Steinway hired detectives to spy on his employees, paid the local police more than $2,000 for support during the conflict, and expelled the strike leaders from company housing in Astoria. "Our victory is complete, and the men are very much cowed down," he proclaimed triumphantly. During the 1886 eight-hour strike, he again refused to compromise. These steps, according to Steinway, brought him great support: "[A]m downtown. I am greeted everywhere," he noted in his diary in October 1882, in the wake of one strike. Though Steinway explicitly approved of the legitimacy of unions and strikes, and saw himself as a paternalistic employer, his attitude toward workers hardened. He justified his actions by blaming the "entrance of the socialistic and the communistic element in the labor unions" for the new level of hostility, a hostility he termed "terrorism" in 1883.

There was widespread agreement among bourgeois New Yorkers that the relationship between capital and labor had changed for the worse. Witnesses who appeared before the Senate Committee on Education and Labor described "a very thorough change…within the last ten or fifteen years" as employers and employees "look at each other now more or less as enemies." In somewhat exaggerated fashion, the New York machine builder John Roach even claimed that "90 per cent of all the successful men in business at the present time would be willing to go out of it now…owing to this unsettled condition of things and this feeling which is working up between capital and labor." His colleague, the iron manufacturer Abram Hewitt, agreed: When in 1878 he headed a congressional commission to inquire into the relationship of labor and capital and find ways to improve it, the *New York Times* ridiculed his hearings ("curious specimens of thought"), and Hewitt admitted that "the feeling of mutual respect and confidence and good will was rapidly diminishing." As printer Theodore Low De Vinne bemoaned, "friendly intercourse between employers and employed outside the office is becoming more restrained."

Such musings were the direct result of the precarious instability of labor relations, which easily turned into panic about the great threat that unions and workers represented. The mobilizations of 1886 especially struck fear into the hearts of upper-class New Yorkers because it was in this year that they were challenged both at the workplace and at the polls. At the core of these threats stood the Knights of Labor. Though this union's ideology still was rooted in the artisan republicanism of earlier times, its comprehensive organizational strategy and its political efforts gave it a presence no other union had ever enjoyed before. When in May 1886 the Knights called out hundreds of thousands of workers throughout the nation to demand the eight-hour day, among them Manhattan trolley car conductors, piano makers, and furniture makers, bourgeois New Yorkers closed ranks against any kind of compromise. So great was their concern about the movement that even the Chamber of Commerce, which had in prior years not taken a public position on specific strikes, called a special meeting to discuss the eight-hour movement. No fewer than fifty-seven of the Chamber's members requested the meeting, which must have originated among the city's dry goods merchants (fourteen of the twenty-three dry goods merchants who belonged to the Chamber of Commerce were present), to consider "what action … the chamber may appropriately take, with a view of sustaining and enforcing existing laws for the protection of all classes of our citizens in the peaceful pursuit of their business, and the prevention of illegal interference therewith." They resolved that "under the circumstances now existing, [the Chamber] considers it the paramount duty of every American citizen to uphold and strengthen the hands of the constituted authorities." When in early May 1886 a bomb exploded in Chicago's Haymarket, killing eight policemen during a rally held by anarchists, anxiety reached fever pitch. The *New York Times* drew a fearful portrait of a widespread plot of workers, who placed "responsibility for their poverty upon the bourgeoisie," drilling with rifles and building bombs throughout New York City, with plans to overthrow the "ruling class." From then on, "[t]he radical specter," according to historian T. Jackson Lears would, "[continue] to haunt the bourgeois imagination."

Such exaggerated fears were further fed when in the fall of 1886 the mobilization of labor – in reaction to the government's involvement in the strikes of the summer – moved into the sphere of politics. In New York City, as elsewhere, policemen during these months had escorted strikebreakers to work, had clubbed workers who tried to keep trolleys from running, and had used conspiracy laws to undermine the workers' most powerful weapon in the competitive local economy, the boycott as its "very strength ... made it necessary to forbid its use." Far from solving the conflicts that gave rise to the Knights in the first place, however, this heavy-handed response sharpened the crisis even further.

From 1886 onward, the alarm engendered by the rise of working-class political movements, strikes, and unions would become a regular feature of bourgeois discourse. Upper-class New Yorkers feared that American exceptionalism had come to an end – that a permanent proletariat had arisen quite like that of Europe, and that these workers might embrace dangerously radical ideas or even follow the example of the people of Paris. The *Commercial and Financial Chronicle* clearly recognized that the root cause of this frightening spectacle was that the relationship between employers and workers had changed fundamentally:

> The old relation has been completely destroyed, and that which has taken its place is something far different and much less satisfactory. No longer does the farmer's "hired man" live in the house of his employer and sit at his table; the journeyman carpenter or shoemaker living on terms almost of equality with the slightly more prosperous or enterprising journeyman who paid him wages, has disappeared. The causes of the change which these examples illustrate are well known. They are, first, the magnitude of modern industrial undertakings, which has led to a minute subdivision of labor; second, the substitution of corporate for individual employers; third, the growth and adoption of the spirit of modern political economy, which logically inculcates the treatment of labor with the same consideration, and no more, that is accorded to any other of the raw materials or tools of manufacture.

The world had changed dramatically and bourgeois New Yorkers had to come to terms with it. The rapidly expanding business press played an especially important role in this conversation about the nature of workers and trade unions. These publications took a central role – not only because they formulated coherent ideological positions but also because they helped employers find out what other employers where doing and thinking. In effect if not in intent, they were a central tool for collective mobilization. And these publications increasingly came to formulate "class" positions instead of those rooted in the specific exigencies of their trade. It was indeed in their discussions of the relationship to labor that they transcended most decisively older particularist identities. This was a dramatic change. In the 1850s, for example, the industrialists' free-labor position still had been most prominently articulated by a paper, the *New-York Daily Tribune*, that counted Karl Marx among its contributors. Such proximity between bourgeois and socialist thinkers was all but unimaginable during the 1880s and 1890s.

By the 1880s, notions of a mutuality of interests based on commonly experienced social mobility and transgression of the line between employers and employees, which once had dominated the discourse of manufacturers, had diminished. As the moral economy that had informed social relations in the artisanal workshop of midcentury crumbled, manufacturers increasingly saw labor as "a marketable commodity – quite as much as wheat," its price to be determined by the law of "supply and demand." So great was the distance industrialists had traveled from the free-labor ideology of antebellum times that in 1893 *Iron Age* quoted approvingly a pamphlet by a Chicago manufacturer, who asserted that "[a]ggregations of capital are beneficial to society, as they reduce the cost of production," and concluded that because "[c]apital and labor are partners, but capitalists and laborers are not...[t]he obligations of capital to share profits with labor are no greater than those of others to share their surplus with the needy." Classical liberalism now guided the city's economic elite in their understanding of the freedom of labor, a freedom that they defined as the right to enter or refuse to enter into a contract with an employer. Capitalists, they argued, "have an unquestionable right to make such contracts, rules, and regulations as may be necessary to promote the best interests of their business, as well as for the maintenance of good order." Tellingly, in 1877 the American Institute, renowned for its free-labor thinking during the 1850s, invited the silk merchant (and Republican) Elliot Cowdin to speak at its semicentennial celebration, an occasion Cowdin took to explain that workers should not envy the "seemingly wealthy man of business" because a businessman is "[l]ashed to his task by the exigencies of his business, harassed by anxieties, [a state] ruinous to his peace of mind." As a result of these trials and tribulations, Cowdin argued, businessmen were about ten times more likely to commit suicide than workers.

During the 1850s, manufacturers and others had seen propertied independence as the prerequisite of republican citizenship, but now bourgeois New Yorkers redefined republicanism itself as endorsing permanent proletarianization: while laborers still saw wage work as destroying the "independence" essential to workers as citizens, and "wage slavery" as its outcome, elite New Yorkers emphasized "freedom of contract" as the principal freedom of the Republic. For them, the "law of supply and demand" was to structure the relationship between employers and employees a "law as invariable as those of the universe." That labor refused to accept the denigration of citizens to permanent dependence was for *The Nation* the result of a peculiar "mental mood."

Mystifying the laws of the market into laws of nature allowed upper-class New Yorkers to account for their own exalted position. They explained to themselves and others that they had risen to the top of society because of their own superior intelligence, hard work, and diligence. As John D. Rockefeller put it: "It is my personal belief that the principal cause for the economic differences between people is their difference in personality." In this light, workers' collective action appeared as an effort by those with less beneficial endowments to redistribute income and power by force, undermining the pillars that kept society from sinking into anarchy and chaos. The economic elites' vision of their own beneficial role in society, in effect, allowed them to characterize challengers as threats not only to their own private wealth and power but also to the well-being of American society. Large industrialists in particular, such as Andrew Carnegie and John D. Rockefeller, assumed that natural hierarchies had put them into an elevated position from which they should steer their undertakings without outside interference. They believed, after all, that at the center of American society was the right to control and accumulate property without interference, either from the state or the propertyless. In Smithian fashion they held that what is best for the individual is best for society. Upper-class New Yorkers effectively brushed aside questions of productive versus unproductive labor, the importance of independence to republican selfhood and citizenship, and the corrupting influence of large accumulations of capital, which had been such dominant tropes in antebellum discussions, and replaced them with an emphasis on the civilizing mission of business. As Andrew Carnegie argued, inequality today guaranteed prosperity tomorrow. During the 1880s and 1890s, however, bourgeois New Yorkers failed to universalize this particular vision, encountering firm resistance from workers, farmers, and even the lower middle classes.

The belief in the "laws of supply and demand" provided an ideology that lent itself to aggressive hostility to trade unions and indeed American employers…were unusually hostile to unions. Especially during the 1880s and 1890s they conceived of workers' collective action as an essentially illegitimate interference with markets. In 1882, *Iron Age* succinctly formulated this position by claiming that strikes were a struggle against "the state of the market," a struggle "[t]he market will win every time." If economic conditions were poor, a decline in wages was "inevitable," no matter what workers did. Jay Gould seconded this thought, arguing that unions were a positive good so long as they focused on providing mutual benefits and education to their members, but not on tinkering with "the law of supply and demand." Because market laws were presumed to regulate all economic activity, higher wages or better working conditions were independent of either the collective pressures of workers or the goodwill of manufacturers. Therefore, strikes expressed a conflict not between employers and workers but of "labor against labor," that is, striking workers against strikebreakers. Wages were entirely a result of supply and demand. "No trades-unions, or riotous strikes, or leveling legislation, can suspend the operation of the inexorable law that has determined that labor ... must be sold for what it will bring," contended Elliot Cowdin.

It was at this point that employers limited the legitimate sphere of collective action by workers. As they conceived of markets as an aggregation of individual decisions, unions could dangerously alter market outcomes by organizing the individual decisions of the many into one collective voice. Quite typically, the New York Chamber of Commerce, while reaffirming the right to join unions and to strike, resolved in 1886 that the full power of the state should be employed against those who prevent "any other man from working whenever and wherever the latter may choose." By keeping strikebreakers out and by coercing workers to join unions, "workingmen...are violating the laws made for the government of the community," a violation that leaves "the officers of the law no choice but to proceed against them, even if it be necessary to invoke the aid of the military." In effect, this interpretation, by making the replacement of striking workers into a fundamental right of employers, limited unions' power to a very narrow scope. As *Iron Age* explained: "It is every man's right to sell his labor and...any man or any set of men who take it upon themselves to be the guardian of his conduct in this matter are as great tyrants as ever lived on the face of the earth." Workers' organizations and collective action thus were represented as a direct threat to the workings of the market, a convenient assertion that neglected to account for the power of aggregations of capital represented by single entrepreneurs, and moreover, by entrepreneurs who were acting collectively. In this concept of things, workers were to have little power. This, the *New York Times* remarked laconically, was "the misfortune of their position."

Bourgeois New Yorkers built their limited acceptance of unions and strikes on an assumption that legitimate unions and legitimate strikes embraced the "principles of political economy," principles that left de facto little power to trade unions. Not surprisingly, they saw any effort of workers to assert their power as stepping out of the bonds of this legitimate sphere, in turn allowing employers to call on the state to enforce the violated "laws of supply and demand." Such employers considered unions that did not follow these "laws" to be "essentially un-American" and "unnatural, founded on no principle of right or justice," and they questioned, "How long is society or a free community going to tolerate such an institution?" The greater the degree of mobilization by workers, the greater the collective outcry of employers against such "tyrannical" orders. Respectable circles viewed these strikers as the "dangerous classes," the "vagabond class," "the idle and vicious class," a "mass of envious discontent," or even a "wild beast." In 1886, during the strikes of the Knights of Labor against Gould's railway system, *Iron Age* went so far as to compare the strike to the final months of the sectional crisis of 1860, and warned that "toleration will not be carried beyond the point of safety. ...No tyranny was ever so absolute and irresistible as that which organized labor seeks to exercise over those who work without first paying it tribute." Such "tyranny," asserted the journal, called for a response: "By resorting to [the argument of force] the working man at once antagonizes the whole machinery of Government, local, State and Federal, bringing upon himself certain defeat."

Employers feared most those unions that stepped out of the traditional bounds of craft unionism, organizations employers called the "socialistic" or "communistic element." It was these unions that truly struck fear into the hearts of the city's bourgeoisie. While we might think of their reaction as overdrawn hysteria, from the vantage point of 1886 or 1892, this seemed less of an exaggeration because the conflict between labor and capital was continually sharpening, and its outcome was unpredictable.

Ideologically, bourgeois New Yorkers reconciled harsh attacks against unions and strikes on the one side and limited paternalism on the other side by drawing a sharp distinction between the group of workers who were deserving of this paternalism and those who were not. "The majority of American workingmen are law-abiding citizens, but there is a violent class among them whose brutality leads them to jump at any chance to destroy property, and if needs be, to sacrifice life. ...It is this class which can only be met with rifles," said *Iron Age*. Often upper-class discourse presented these radical unionists, socialists, and anarchists as foreign and of inferior racial heritage, thus standing outside the Republic.

As a result, many bourgeois New Yorkers combined their own sense of superiority with a disdain for immigrants. While in the early 1880s immigrants were still being lauded for bringing prosperity to the United States, the country "being enriched by the drafts we are making upon the population of the Old World," positive assessment of immigration shifted during the decade. The *Financial and Commercial Chronicle,* for example, still had asserted in 1882 that "[e]very immigrant...adds to the wealth-producing capacity of the nation," but by 1887 saw "immigration [as] far more potent for evil than for good." Immigrants allegedly brought anarchism, socialism, and "almost every danger to the organization of society peculiar to the present time." By 1889, the journal even supported restrictions on immigration. Because of "the race changes" of immigrants, they now saw them as "vicious, degraded, ignorant, amenable neither to law nor reason, [without] code of morals, know[ing] nothing about the theory of our government, and in fact abhor[ring] all government." And *Iron Age* concurred: "How America shall protect itself from the invasion of dangerous and otherwise undesirable classes of immigrants is becoming more and more a burning question." Because the majority of American workers were born overseas, many bourgeois New Yorkers combined their fears of Catholics, Jews, and African Americans with their anxiety about trade unions and radicalism. Racism, hence, became an important part of their class identity.

The coalescence of views among bourgeois New Yorkers about labor in particular and the "laws of political economy" in general was probably the most clearly articulated element of their increasing class awareness. This coalescence was also a basis of their ability to confront labor and call upon the state in support of their interests. In 1887, when the Knights of Labor's strength had already passed its peak, the *Commercial and Financial Chronicle* explained the success of employers in dealing with the movement in exactly such terms: "As the Knights of Labor grew in membership, and the number of boycotts increased, merchants and manufacturers began to feel that they had a common interest in preventing the growth of any such irresponsible power; they had a common interest in maintaining industrial order and independence which was more important than any temporary advantage to be obtained over a commercial rival." Working-class mobilization thus had engendered a greater sense of solidarity among bourgeois New Yorkers.

The jelling of a common position, in turn, enabled bourgeois New Yorkers to appeal to the state to intervene in the relationship between labor and capital. While they had political disagreements among one another and embraced different political parties, they widely agreed that the state must protect their vision of property rights. Once they had effectively narrowed the legitimate sphere of unions and strikes, and reified the laws of the market into laws of nature, it was consistent to call upon the state to step in against workers' collective action. The "state of lawlessness," which workers had presumably created, required a response by the government. Clearly spelling out this demand, *Iron Age* asked in 1886 for legislation "to suppress violence and protect life and property, and to restrain within proper bounds the exercise of the power acquired by the working classes through organizations." In 1894, on the occasion of the Pullman strike by the American Railway Union, the journal again requested "some effective remedial measure" to undercut the power of unions. Merchants concurred, accusing "the authorities" of a "strange timidity." These demands for swifter governmental response to workers' collective action increased in frequency during the 1880s and 1890s. Especially after the 1892 Homestead strike, employers called upon the state to defend their property rights. The *Manufacturer and Builder* asked for a "policy of stern repression and exemplary punishment. ...If the existing machinery of the law is inadequate effectually to cope with and check at its fountain head this rising flood of disorder and crime, then other and more efficient machinery must be invented."

Considering the importance of the state in limiting the power of their workers, employers naturally wondered how dependably a democratically legitimized state would intervene on the side of capital. Although organized expressions of antidemocratic thought had peaked in the 1870s in the effort to reintroduce property qualifications in municipal elections, concerns about democracy remained on the agenda of bourgeois New Yorkers. The Republican Club of the City of New York, for example, called upon its members "to guard and defend the purity of the ballot box" and questioned if this was best to be done by "an educational or by a property qualification, or by a residence of twenty-one years to obtain the right to the elective franchise." William E. Dodge expressed a similar anxiety when he argued that "we are still to test the problem of our republican form of government with a nation of one hundred millions, extending from ocean to ocean," many of whom were recent immigrants with their "peculiar habits and customs of their native lands." A situation such as this, he claimed, leads "the Christian patriot to fear." The *Commercial and Financial Chronicle*, in a more practical manner, suggested limiting presidential campaigns to once every six years, as the resulting stability would make politics "more responsive to the needs of commerce."

In an ironic twist, in their embrace of laissez-faire ideology, bourgeois New Yorkers called upon the state to enforce the laws of the market. Their own power depended on an institution that they saw at other times as an unnatural intervention into economic laws. In a further twist, while bourgeois New Yorkers called upon the state to defend their interests, they were hostile to efforts by the state to support those of workers. When Grover Cleveland mentioned the possibility of a federal arbitration board in April 1886, *Iron Age* feared that the federal government would get involved in labor relations, in effect recognizing "labor as an independent class." Similarly, after the electoral successes of the Farmers' Alliance, New York's economic elite observed with great relief the

Supreme Court decision that state regulations on railroads in regard to rates were subject to review by the Supreme Court, thus limiting the power of states. Bourgeois New Yorkers saw laws "to protect labor" as outright dangerous, because they thought that it was "a bad symptom...when any class comes forward with a confession of inability to protect itself, and asks the State to undertake the duty." The government, however, upon the urging of bourgeois New Yorkers, undertook faithfully the defense of a particular interpretation of property rights.

The need to call upon the state, however, was not the only tension in the upper class's ideology. As significant were their efforts at organizing employers' associations, which again violated the "iron law of the market." It was in these efforts to organize that their greater awareness of class gained another expression. Typically, when the National Association of Builders constituted itself in 1887, the delegates rejected the proposal of one of their own to change the name of the association to "National Association of Building Trades," arguing that only the term "builder" would clearly identify them as employers. No one was to confuse them with the old-fashioned trade organizations that had included workers among their members.

In the late 1870s and early 1880s, employers' associations sprang up in most New York industries, and such industry journals as the *Oil and Paint Manufacturer* did not tire of calling for further efforts at organizing. This was the age of organization, and a prominent New York lawyer, John Bleecker Miller, expressed the spirit of the age when he called for the association of "men with common material interests" in the "Business, Trade, Professional and Property-Owners Associations of the City of New York." This was a stunning departure from earlier times, as before the 1870s, most New York manufacturers had remained unorganized. By the eighties, however, all important industries, such as printing, metal, construction, furniture, and apparel, counted an employers' association, as did the carriage makers, the chandelier manufacturers, and brewers. There was the United States Bottlers' Protective Association (including the Bottlers' Protective Association of New York and Vicinity), the Boss Piano Makers of New York, the Hat and Cap Manufacturers' Association of New York, the Manufacturing Furriers' Exchange of New York, the Iron League of New York, the Shoe Manufacturers of the United States, the Iron Founders' Association, the National Association of Stove Manufacturers, and the Real Estate Owners and Builders' Association. The "employing printers" got together in 1887 and formed the United Typotethae of New York. Hardware manufacturers and dealers organized in the Hardware Club of New York "in the name of a common business interest," and by 1894, its 585 members could even sport their own clubhouse. The "temper of employers" had changed, one historian has noted aptly.

The genealogy of manufacturers' organizations followed a rather uniform trajectory: First, employers organized in the narrow segments of their specific industries on a local or regional basis. Then, they broadened their organizations to a national scope, such as among builders, manufacturers of furniture, carriages, stoves, sheet iron, steel, and boilers. In a next step, organizations joined together several smaller trade organizations under a large umbrella organization, such as the Building Trades Employers' Association of the City of New York, which brought together thirty-two trade organizations upon its founding in 1903. Eventually, some of them formed even more inclusive national organizations, such as the National Metal Trades Association and the Manufacturers' Association of Kings and Queens Counties, to represent "the great industrial interests of a locality." In January 1895, the level of organization increased even further when 583 manufacturers from throughout the United States met to organize the National Association of Manufacturers (NAM).

What really drove these associations into action, therefore, were confrontations with labor. "Organization on the part of employers is rendered compulsory, because of organization on the part of employes [*sic*]," asserted the National Founders' Association. The *Manufacturer and Builder*, a monthly journal published out of New York, agreed, arguing that "the only practical way of countermining the secret plottings of such irresponsible bands of brigands as the Knights, is by counter-organization on the part of employers, for mutual support and effective opposition." According to the National Association of Manufacturers, "it was time that the manufacturing interests of this country should be organized and consolidated. Labor was already united. ... Capital was disorganized, had no coherent force, had no definite, united policy to interpose against the aggressions that might be made upon its interests." Effective resistance against the Knights would only be possible if employers united, a goal *Iron Age* believed to be within reach because "nothing so quickly quells civil strife and unifies a people as a common danger." In some sense, the desires of employers to defend themselves against competition and to keep workers at bay were related because both were made that much more urgent by the crisis of profitability that derived from the deflationary pressures of the last decades of the nineteenth century. But it was workers in particular who "crystallized the combative sentiment of the manufacturers."

The capacity of New York's industrialists to organize was extraordinary. One historian, aptly, has termed it the "organized revolt" of employers. This capacity to organize, along with a government that was unusually hostile to trade unions, explains to a significant degree the defeat of the powerful movement of the Knights of Labor in 1886, a defeat that arguably set the conditions for the unusually weak and exclusive style of American trade unions in the decades to come. Employers' capacity to act collectively, together with their access to private and public repressive bodies, proved sufficient to weaken the labor movement in a fundamental way. It was a capacity, however, that they only enjoyed because of the state's support. It was, hence, ultimately the access to state power that helped secure and expand bourgeois power in civil society.

CHAPTER 28

Class Struggle and the New Deal
Industrial Labor, Industrial Capital, and the State

Rhonda F. Levine

Chapter One

The Capitalist State, Class Relations, and the New Deal

The Great Depression of the 1930s represented an unparalleled economic crisis in the United States. The "boom years" of the 1920s were characterized by tremendous industrial expansion both in scale and scope, the rapid concentration of social wealth, and an unequal modus vivendi between capital and labor in which the former subjected the latter to an accelerated pace of production. In retrospect, visible signs of the impending economic crisis abounded. Nevertheless, the confident optimism in business cycles that was shared almost universally came to an abrupt halt with the stock-market crash in October 1929. By 1932 the plummeting price of overvalued stocks had brought a decline of more than 38 percent in national income, more than five thousand bank failures and eighty-five thousand business bankruptcies, and an unemployment rate of 23.6 percent of the civilian labor force.[1] Representatives of small-scale capitalist firms – nonmonopoly capital – placed the blame for the profit squeeze and the expanded rate of bankruptcies among small-to-medium-sized manufacturing firms on the increased concentration and centralization of capital – monopolization – in the principal branches of industrial production. Consequently, they sought relief from the federal government in the form of revitalized antitrust legislation that would renew competitiveness and profitable opportunities and hence restore economic stability on the basis of a free-market ideology. In contrast, the representatives of large-scale capitalist firms – monopoly capital – argued quite vociferously that huge capital investments in manufacturing plants were responsible for the heightened economic prosperity of the 1920s. Hence, the domination of

Original publication details: Rhonda Levine, *Class Struggle and the New Deal*, pp. 1–3; 14–18; 22–31; 33–38; 45–46; 93–96; 99–104; 106–108. University Press of Kansas, 1988. Reproduced with permission from University Press of Kansas.

a few large firms in ever-expanding industry was certainly not the source of economic woes; it might even be the solution for them. If economic difficulties did exist, they were caused by unreliable markets. Monopoly capital sought state aid in stabilizing the market by calling for an easing of the antitrust laws and for the self-regulation of industry through price fixing and profit control.

As unemployment continued to rise during the early years of the depression, wages fell, and the hours of work increased for hundreds of thousands of employed workers. Total wages within the industrial sector had fallen some 20 percent by June 1930, and real weekly earnings of those employed in manufacturing and mining had declined by 15 to 30 percent.[2] Unemployed workers sought federal aid in relief for unemployed families as leftist political groups became more active in the struggle for relief and unemployment insurance. Employed workers concentrated on defensive goals: resisting wage decreases and demanding wage rates that would support their families. Leaders of organized labor called on the federal government to institute some sort of industrial-planning measure that would benefit workers.

The Hoover administration did virtually nothing either to restore business confidence or concretely to relieve the suffering of the impoverished and the bankrupt, believing instead that tinkering with recurrent business cycles would only exacerbate an already difficult situation. Holding on to a laissez-faire ideology, the Hoover administration declared that the depression was temporary. The result of economic recklessness, it could be overcome through voluntary measures adopted by leaders of the banking, business, labor, and agricultural communities.

The 1932 presidential election and the victory of Franklin D. Roosevelt indicated the general discontent and the overwhelming repudiation of a state administration that based its policies on laissez-faire ideological premises. As soon as Roosevelt had taken office in March 1933, his administration attempted to put into motion plans and programs for industrial economic recovery by first concentrating on a policy that would alleviate antitrust provisions, regulate production, and control prices to stimulate investments. The National Industrial Recovery Act (NIRA) stood as the centerpiece of this grandiose scheme to overcome industrial economic decline. Through the "codes of fair competition," representatives of firms within a particular branch of industry would come together and establish price- and production-control guidelines for their industrial branch. In exchange for an implicit promise of cooperation with management, the Roosevelt administration assured industrial labor that it would set minimum wage standards and maximum hours of work through specific codes of fair competition and that it would also, through section 7a of the NIRA, guarantee industrial workers the formal rights to join unions of their own choosing without management reprisals. The Roosevelt administration theorized that regulated industrial competition, in tandem with a more-or-less guaranteed standard of living, would assure the conditions of economic recovery.

The formulation of the NIRA appeared to coordinate the perceived interests of both industrial capital and industrial labor within an overall joint project to generate economic recovery. Labor leaders confidently surmised that the provisions of NIRA's section 7a provided the type of protective shield that would guarantee formal rights to form unions and to bargain collectively. It soon became evident, however, that they had misread the signals. Employers, remaining wary of the provisions of section 7a, nevertheless welcomed state-regulated price controls and production-output codes. Monopoly capital received the much-desired lifting of antitrust provisions.

Nonmonopoly capital thought that it received protection from monopolies and that it could now remain competitive in the industrial market.

Contrary to its design, the NIRA did not effectively stimulate economic recovery, it failed to adjudicate the already delicate competitive relations between monopoly and nonmonopoly capital, and it never convinced an otherwise suspicious organized labor movement that the newly created triumvirate – the partnership between capital, labor, and the state – was in its best interest. The NIRA's performance did not match its promise. While the codes of fair competition were designed to benignly coordinate the market in the interest of both monopoly and nonmonopoly capital, they actually contributed to the increased concentration and centralization of capital. Consequently, large firms found themselves in a much more favorable structural position to obtain larger market shares and to expand in size and scale. Small-to-medium capital was unable to withstand the competition. Hence, the NIRA codes of fair competition served to heighten the conflicts between fractions of monopoly and nonmonopoly capital. Moreover, the refusal of many employers to abide by the labor provisions in section 7a meant that organized labor was unable to recruit membership without conflict and confrontation. Rebuffed on the shop floor and believing that the Roosevelt administration had ignored their plight, units of industrial labor in the yet-to-be-organized basic, mass-production industries adopted new strategies and tactics to match their perceived enemies. Strike activity took on new proportions as industrial workers demanded the right to organize and join unions of their own choosing. In the face of rising working-class unity coupled with determined militancy, the industrial capitalist class appeared to lose momentum and to retreat into internecine squabbling.

The concatenation of rising labor militancy and of the erstwhile convenience that was uniting the emergent industrial union movement with the Democratic party brought together a unique convergence of social forces. In order to slow the rising tide of labor militancy and class unruliness, the Roosevelt administration enacted the National Labor Relations Act (NLRA) in June 1935. The NLRA, by guaranteeing industrial labor the right to join unions of their own choosing and to engage in collective-bargaining arrangements with employers, gave industrial labor the much-desired state machinery to enforce labor's right to organize independent unions and to protect industrial workers from employers' refusals to engage in collective-bargaining agreements with unions that were elected by a majority of workers. Moreover, this legislative enactment altered the course of the class struggle. Through the NLRA, the industrial union movement had acquired a special legal standing with both industrial capital and the state administration. In addition, organized industrial labor found a "political voice" through the medium of the Democratic party within the national political arena.

On the capitalist front, nonmonopoly capital criticized the New Deal industrial-recovery program for fostering monopoly growth, whereas monopoly capital increasingly became disenchanted with the apparent prolabor policies of the Roosevelt administration. Intracapitalist conflict increased over the "monopoly" issue, and the divisions within the class provided barriers for structural changes within the state apparatus, such as the reorganization of the executive branch.

The exigencies of the balance of class forces and uninterrupted accumulation of capital limited political decision making and the formulation and implementation of New Deal policies. The manner in which the New Deal industrial-recovery program attempted to maintain and further conditions for profitable accumulation was shaped by the dynamic of the class struggle in the United States during the 1930s.

The state is not a rational organization of political power with its own historical trajectory; rather, it is constituted by the contradictions of class society. The seemingly ad hoc fashion in which various New Deal policies were formulated had less to do with existing administrative and bureaucratic arrangements, or the fragmented character of the United States state apparatus, than it did with the nature of class relations in the United States.

A reassessment of the New Deal industrial-recovery program from a class-centered approach sheds light not only on the manner in which New Deal policies were formulated and implemented but also, and perhaps more importantly, on the extent to which New Deal policies provided conditions for a new phase of capital accumulation. The origins and implementation of New Deal policies under the Roosevelt administration represented a bold program of national economic recovery during a period of significant economic collapse, political turmoil, and ideological dissensus. Seen retrospectively, New Deal policies appear to exhibit a certain coherent logic. Yet from the perspective of those policy makers who designed and implemented them, the various policies and programs appeared as a series of ad hoc, almost desperate measures that were designed to defend temporarily against further economic decline and political rebelliousness.

When Roosevelt took office, the industrial working class was becoming increasingly restive. Unemployed workers engaged in street demonstrations and marches to demand federal relief and some form of unemployment insurance, while employed workers resisted decreases in wages and increases in the hours they were expected to work. Industrial capitalists themselves were hopelessly divided over the causes of the Great Depression and possible ways to solve it.

The shift in the balance of class forces engendered a chaotic situation in which capitalists – who themselves were increasingly being fragmented both economically and politically – were gradually losing the iron grip that during the 1920s boom period they had enjoyed over the working class in general and the increasingly restive industrial working class in particular. The various mechanisms through which capitalists had subjected labor to their discipline during the previous decade gradually became unraveled as the depression wore on. The resulting class tensions threatened to add even further to the economic chaos during Roosevelt's first term in office. By the middle of the 1930s, the growing round of strikes was the most visible sign that the industrial working class had actively intervened to determine the future course of industrial production. This intervention of the working class meant that whatever policy was pursued for economic recovery was hindered not only by the structural reality of the accumulation process but also by the activities of the industrial working class that interrupted the capital-accumulation process.

Rather than representing a coherent blueprint that by conscious design established an overall plan for economic recovery, the Roosevelt administration muddled along, tinkering with various programs – making every effort to force compromises between antagonistic interests wherever possible and simply imposing a solution when adjudication seemed impossible. The NIRA was formulated not only to overcome obstacles to accumulation but also to politically organize a fractionated industrial capitalist class. The inclusion of section 7a was an afterthought; it was only included as an effort to sidetrack the Black Thirty Hour bill and to make concessions to industrial labor simultaneously. The Black Thirty Hour bill called for the prohibition of interstate shipments of goods produced by labor that was working more than six hours a day and five days a week. Roosevelt believed that the Black bill was too rigid, that it was perhaps unconstitutional, and that it would lead to an actual drop in purchasing power because of the lack of minimum-wage provisions. The best strategy for administrating opposition to the Black bill was seen to consist of presenting a better proposal for stimulating both recovery and employment. Contrary to its design, the implementation of the NIRA only stimulated disunity among industrial capitalists and militancy among industrial labor.

Rising labor militancy combined with a significant realignment of the Democratic party, which had a strong working-class base, to stimulate the implementation of state policies that made crucial concessions to industrial labor, such as the NLRA. The class recomposition of the Democratic party, in addition to labor legislation that was favorable to segments of the industrial working class, served to diffuse labor militancy, directing the leaders of the newly emergent industrial-union movement to accept, by the end of the decade, a general consensus in support of the existing political and economic order.

The disunity among industrial capitalists persisted throughout the 1930s, as many industrial capitalists criticized a variety of New Deal programs. Yet the Roosevelt administration – because it represented the balance of class forces – attempted to put into motion plans for economic recovery that reflected compromises not only between capital and labor but also within capital itself. As a result of criticisms of nonmonopoly capital concerning the performance of the NIRA, the Temporary National Economic Committee (TNEC) was established to investigate the growth and repercussions of monopoly growth in the industrial economy. Although the TNEC documented the prevalence of monopoly growth, nonmonopoly capital was not able to alter the process of the concentration and centralization of capital. However, the conflicts within the industrial capitalist class over the best strategy for economic recovery did reveal to the Roosevelt administration that the bureaucratic structures inherited from previous administrations were inadequate to accomplish the tasks necessary to implement New Deal policies. These organizational forms constituted a structural impediment that hindered the nature and the type of recovery strategy that was historically possible. As a consequence, the Roosevelt administration was compelled to adjust, improvise, and tinker with the existing framework while it simultaneously attempted to create new structures. This process was not formalized until the administrative reorganization proposals of 1938/39.

Whereas nonmonopoly capital was not able to stimulate changes in the accumulation process, the industrial-workers' movement was able to do so. The trajectory of capitalist development took a different course as a result of the upsurge of workers' militant activities during the 1930s. Labor militancy in demanding and using collective bargaining made it possible to overcome large-scale capital's resistance to a fundamental reorganization of wages and consumption. Nevertheless, it was monopoly capital that was able to adjust to these working-class gains. Monopoly capital not only passed on to consumers the wage gains and benefits acquired by workers (both nationally and internationally); it also used collective bargaining as a way to ensure labor peace. In the process, monopoly capital was able to dominate crucial state agencies. Increased state economic intervention aided not only in the regulation of competition but also in further investment outlets. The obstacle to capital accumulation posed by too high a rate of exploitation was temporarily resolved through the institutionalization of collective bargaining and the incorporation of significant industrial unions into the national process of political bargaining. Problems of unregulated competition were temporarily resolved through state policies. The political structure was altered to correspond more closely with the imperatives of the accumulation process by having monopoly capital dominate key agencies and by having the industrial-union movement incorporated into a clearly subordinate position vis-à-vis monopoly capital on the political terrain. The incorporation of the industrial union movement into the national process of political bargaining and into a more cooperative relationship via collective bargaining with monopoly capital, the resulting ideological consensus for capitalist rule, and the unchallenged political hegemony of monopoly capital – all combined to produce the conditions for a new phase of capitalist development. By attempting to resolve class conflicts and antagonisms, New Deal industrial policies simultaneously created new structural conditions that regulated the objective conditions for capital accumulation and the conditions under which future struggles would be waged.

Chapter 2

The Process of Capitalist Development

The Tendency Toward Concentration and Centralization of Capital

The process of capitalist production and accumulation in the United States had produced a greater tendency toward the growth of monopoly capital as early as 1860. The Civil War stimulated the accelerated growth of large-scale industry through demand for war materials. This required more efficient and larger factories, the investment of more capital, and the consolidation of firms. In the period following the Civil War, declining prices and intensified competition encouraged the growth of large-scale industry. In 1847 there were 82 industrial conglomerates with a capitalization of $1 billion; in the three years 1898, 1899, and 1900, eleven conglomerates were formed with a capitalization of $1.14 billion; and the largest conglomerate of all, the United States Steel Corporation, was formed in 1901 with a capitalization of $1.4 billion.[10]

By the 1880s American manufacturing firms were beginning to grow by way of mergers. Mergers essentially involved having a number of individually owned firms join together to form one national enterprise. By the 1890s the number of mergers was increasingly rapidly – the main motive being the control of price and production schedules for a particular branch of industry. In addition to mergers, many industrial firms grew by building national and global markets and extensive purchasing organizations and by obtaining their own sources of raw materials and transportation facilities.[11] In both cases, growth in the size of firms coincided with the massive introduction of machinery, attempts to keep down the cost of production, and a greater rate of labor productivity.

Between 1860 and 1870 the total value of manufactured products increased more than 100 percent, from $1.9 billion to $4.2 billion; in the following decade the increase was less, a mere 25 percent, from $4.2 to $5.4 billion; ten years later the value of manufactured goods had increased again, this time by 75 percent; and by 1900 the total value of manufactured products amounted to $13.0 billion, almost 40 percent more than in 1890 and about seven times as much as in 1860.[12] Between 1860 and 1894, U.S.–based firms greatly increased the output of manufactured goods. The increase in the amount of capital invested in manufactured goods was even more rapid than the increase in the value of manufactured goods. Jurgen Kuczynski argues that the "means of production – machinery, buildings, etc. – became relatively more and more expensive as compared with labour power, and played an increasingly greater role."[13] Between 1860 and 1900 the rate of growth in the value of manufactured goods was outstripped by the amount of capital invested in manufacturing industries.

In general, by the end of the nineteenth century, the development of industry and the increase in manufactured output had helped make the United States an "industrialized power" within the world arena. The opening up of a vast United States domestic market, along with forces of competition, helped to produce large-scale industrial enterprises in the United States. Between 1860 and 1900 the industrial sector of the labor force grew much more rapidly than other sectors, particularly agriculture.

Between 1867 and 1900 there was the growth and expansion not only of older industries but also of what have frequently been called newer industries. In manufacturing, steel played an important role. In 1867, 1,643 tons of steel ingots were produced, and thirty years later, 7,156,957 tons were produced.[14] Basic industry developed rapidly, especially in the period 1897 to 1919. Between 1899 and 1919 the number of wage earners in manufacturing almost doubled, and the value of products increased almost six-fold.[15] The growth in manufacturing output coincided with the growth of manufacturing establishments. Between 1899 and 1919 the value of the product of each manufacturing firm increased fourfold, and the number of workers increased by 53 percent.

Not only did manufacturing firms tend to grow in size, but smaller firms also tended to decrease in importance with respect to their output. Firms with an annual output of less than $20,000 each declined in their percentage of the total with respect to the number of firms and wage earners and the value of the product. Those with an annual output of $20,000 to $100,000 declined in their percentage of the total with respect to wage earners and the value of the product. Contrary to this tendency, firms with products of $1 million or more increased notably in their percentage of the total with respect to the number of firms and wage earners and the value of the product. The 10,414 such establishments in 1919 amounted to only 3.6 percent of the total number but employed 56.9 percent of the wage earners and manufactured 67.8 percent of the products according to value.[16]

The process of concentration and centralization of capital within the industrial sector of the United States met with few obstacles in the post-World War I period. Between 1919 and 1928 more than 1,200 mergers were recorded in manufacturing, involving a net decrease of more than 6,000 independent firms by the end of 1928 and some 2,000 more by the end of 1930. Furthermore, more than 4,000 public-utilities firms were absorbed in the same period before 1929, and nearly 1,800 bank mergers caused the disappearance of an unrecorded but probably larger number of banks.[17] In addition, by 1919, chain stores were selling 27 percent of the food in the United States, 19 percent of the drugs, 30 percent of tobacco, 27 percent of clothing, and 26 percent of the general merchandise. By the end of 1929 the 200 largest business corporations possessed nearly half the corporate wealth of the United States, 38 percent of the business wealth, and 20 percent of the total national wealth.[18]

The Rise of Mass Production and Changes in the Organization of Production

The growth of large-scale industrial enterprises coincided with the massive introduction of machinery and the rise of mass-production industries. Between 1919 and 1929, capital per worker jumped by 36 percent.[19] Although mass production had been implemented in some industries as early as 1870, it did not become widespread until after World War I. In general, mass production was based on the standardization of parts and inter-changeable mechanisms, and it required technological and organizational innovations, the availability of adequate capital, and a home market large enough to absorb the prod-uct.[20] Hence, the introduction of mass-production industries required certain changes in the organization of production itself, with corresponding changes in the labor process and the conditions of labor for the working class.

Once the machine-tool industry had reached a stage where interchangeability of parts had become practical for even the most complicated machinery, large-scale industrial capitalists concentrated on the assembly aspect of production. The rapidly growing automobile industry and the Ford Motor Company, in particular, were preeminently suited for experimentation in assembly techniques. During its early years the industry was largely involved in assembling parts that had been made in various machine shops and collected at an assembly point. Ford had implemented the moving assembly line by 1913. By the 1920s, when the automobile industry was the leading industry in the United States with respect to the value of its products, Ford introduced improved methods in order to deliver work at a predetermined speed that would accomplish a small and specialized task. With assembly lines and subassembly lines and specialization by indi-viduals and crews, mass-production techniques reached their peak.[24] The net effect of the assembly line for capitalists was a reduction in labor time and labor costs.

Large-scale capital focused its attention upon the advantages of mass production dur-ing World War I and the corresponding push for wartime production. In the preparation of war materials, many capitalists narrowly specialized their factories and organized them for single purposes.[25] Massive innovations in mass-production techniques were introduced in the years following World War I. Not only were models standardized but also sizes, lengths, and thicknesses: the varieties of paving brick were reduced from 66 to 4; of sheet metal, from 1,891 to 261; of range boilers, from 130 to 13; of invoice, inquiry, and purchase-order forms, from 4,500 to 3. During a period of ten years, the Department of Commerce could report that under its guidance, more than one hundred plans for shop superintendents deteriorated and gave way to gang bosses, inspectors, and time-study men. This concentrated all the powers necessary to ensure capitalist control over the labor process and production in general. Scientific-management techniques sought to recompose the organization of work in such a way that each worker's relationship to the production process would be exclusively mediated by individual efficiency norms, rather than by work-group solidarity. In short, labor was not only subsumed economi-cally to capital – by the act of having workers sell their labor power to the capitalist – but also physically and technologically.

Another important effect of these new management techniques was the continual deskilling and fragmentation of labor itself. Although this element became more notice-able with the introduction of mass-production techniques between 1880 and World War I, scientific-management techniques had the consequence of dividing the work process. According to Michel Aglietta, scientific management

was a capitalist response to the class struggle in production in a phase when the labour process was composed of several segments, each organized on mechanical lines internally, yet whose integration still depended on direct relations between different categories of workers. The insufficient mechanical integration of the different segments meant that con-straint had to be exercised by way of rules fixing the output norm for each job as well as the nature and order of the movements to be performed. …The aim of this separation and specialization of functions was to combat the control over working conditions that the relative autonomy of jobs in the old system could leave the workers.[34]

Mass production consolidated the mechanical integration of the work process through the electrification of the factory and the introduction of the conveyor system. The new assembly line virtually eliminated the possibility of traditional forms of job control, or "soldiering." Concurrently, the resulting deskilling of large sectors of the industrial work force tended to further unify and homogenize the working class as a mass of machine operators. As early as 1919, with the growth of workers employed in factories and the rise of mass-production industry, capitalists devised new methods not only to control workers' activities, but also, to a lesser degree, to control workers themselves. Capitalists continually faced the necessity of restructuring the production process both to reduce unit costs and, even more compelling, to retain capitalist control over the class struggle. Many capitalists were forced to realize that in order to control the factory and its labor force, more was needed than changes and improvements in the physical setting, better methods of communication, and financial or social incentives to increase production – it was also necessary to deal with the workers as a group.[35]

The intensification of mass-production techniques during World War I was significant for the form of class struggle that was to take place during the interwar years. The labor shortage during the war, as well as later unemployment rates resulting from technological displacement, led many workers to resist capitalists' power advantage on the basis of industrial collectivity as opposed to craft-style organization. As Claus Offe states so clearly, "In the absence of associational efforts on the part of workers…workers would simply have no bargaining power that they could use to improve their conditions of work or wages, because each individual worker who started to make such demands would risk being replaced either by another worker or by machinery. …The formation of unions…is…a response to the 'association' that has already taken place on the part of capital, namely, in the form of the fusion of numerous units of 'dead' labour [machinery] under the command of one capitalist employer."[36] The development of industrial unionism led many capitalists and state administrators to enact various forms of labor legislation as well as private welfare programs in an effort to diminish the potential unity of working-class interests and to weaken the organizational capacity of industrial unions. In some instances, this took the form of company unions or employee-representation plans. The ultimate impact of this form of "personnel management" was that managers increased their control over production, which resulted in extended capitalist control over the worker. Moreover, the campaign to bust unions in the 1920s, "The American Plan," was successful enough to virtually eliminate gains made by labor during World War I.[37]

The Capitalist Exploitation of Labor

Simply put, the capitalist exploitation of labor refers to the process by which labor produces value for the capitalist (translated into profits) over and above the value (translated into wages) that the worker receives to reproduce his own labor power. The rate of exploitation refers to the ratio of the time that a worker spends producing value for the capitalists to the time the worker spends producing value that comes back to him in terms of wages. The extensive exploitation of labor is accomplished through a lengthening of the working day and/or the speeding up of the pace of work. The period of capitalism that is characteristic of extensive exploitation predates the introduction of mass-production techniques and labor-saving machinery. The intensive exploitation of labor is accomplished through the introduction of labor-saving machinery. The introduction of large-scale machine production during the early years of the twentieth century marked the shift from the extensive exploitation of labor to the intensive exploitation of labor within the industrial sector.[38]

Concomitant with the increase in labor productivity as a result of labor-saving machinery was the intensification of work that is referred to as the speed-up in the auto industry and the stretch-out in the textile industry. During the 1920s in particular, the rising rate in the exploitation of industrial labor was due to both intensive and extensive exploitation. The productivity of labor in manufacturing, for example, increased by 4.7 percent between 1899 and 1919, but it increased by 53.5 percent between 1919 and 1927.[39]

The Changing Composition of the Labor Force

Shifts in industrial production, the growth of large-scale corporate capital, and the introduction of mass-production techniques all combined to have profound consequences for the labor force in the United States. Along with changes in the nature of work performed, there were changes in the distribution of the working population and shifting occupational patterns. As the percentage of the total labor force that was employed in agriculture steadily declined between 1890 and 1929, the percentage of the total labor force that was employed within the industrial sector steadily increased. In 1900 the number of farm laborers and farmers was roughly equivalent to the number of wage earners. However, by 1920, farmers and farm laborers accounted for 25.5 percent of the total labor force, whereas industrial wage earners accounted for 42.4 percent.[47]

The specific characteristics of industrial expansion in the United States between the 1890s and 1929 resulted in a more nationally integrated industrial market and a more homogenized industrial labor force.[52] Yet, this result did not happen in a conflict-free environment. Capitalists in general did not merely impose new production techniques and alterations in the labor process on a docile working class, and large-scale capitalists did not assume dominance within the industrial sector without concerted opposition from smaller-scale industrial capitalists. The patterning of a new social structure of accumulation, required by the changing nature of industrial development, was, in the final instance, directed by the trajectory of the class struggle in the United States, a struggle that was itself situated within the context of changing class relations.

The Dynamic of the Class Struggle

The Struggle over Control of the Labor Process

The changes in the labor process since the late 1890s, especially the development of scientific management and the development of mass-production techniques, were not implemented merely by having capitalists impose their will on the working population. Rather, any change within the capitalist labor process was met with constant struggle from workers in an effort to maintain some control over the work process. Workers attempted to use craft unions to maintain as much control as possible over the day-to-day organization of the labor process, although by the 1920s the attempt seemed futile.

David Montgomery points out that there were essentially three levels of formal and informal organization which workers developed at the end of the nineteenth century in an effort to maintain control over the work process.[53] The first level was the functional autonomy of the craftsmen resting on their knowledge, which made them self-directing at their tasks and enabled them to supervise one or more other workers. Functional autonomy was enforced externally by strikes and slowdowns and, within the union, by either expulsion from the union or by ritual castigation carried out by dissatisfied craftsmen. The second level was the union's work rules. Work rules sought to regulate, although not eliminate, the practice of subcontracting whereby craftsmen hired helpers to assist them in production; this often involved various piece-rate schemes of petty exploitation. The third level was the mutual support of diverse trade in rule enforcements and sympathetic strikes. Montgomery's analysis of strikes indicates that craftsmen were forging important connections across locales and industries in order to enforce work rules or win union recognition. Montgomery's analysis of workers' attempts to control the labor process at the end of the nineteenth century helps to situate the rise of scientific management. Scientific management was not merely an evolution in management thought associated with the rise of mass-production industrial techniques but also a response to changing relations between capital and labor.

The craft unions of the late nineteenth century could not resist the encroachment of scientific-management techniques during the first few decades of the twentieth century primarily because they ignored the masses of unskilled, semiskilled, and, especially, immigrant workers. However, unions were extremely hostile to scientific-management techniques; the strike at the Watertown Arsenal in 1911 occurred in response to the introduction of them. Various American Federation of Labor (AFL) affiliates, led by the Molders Union and the International Association of Machinists, initiated intense lobbying efforts in Congress. The lobbying proved to be a successful attempt to pass legislation forbidding the use of federal appropriations to pay any manager who was employing time-study devices or to provide incentive bonuses to employees at army and navy arsenals. Local union leaders, through testimony before congressional hearings, remained adamant in their opposition to the efficiency experts.

Union Struggles and Antiunion Policies

Capitalist control over the labor process has provided a necessary precondition for industrial expansion since the late 1890s. Labor unions, however, have presented a direct threat to capitalist hegemony on the shop floor.[58] Labor unions provide workers with the organizational apparatus to combat capitalist attempts to further exploit labor in pursuit of higher profits, lower costs, and greater productivity. It is no surprise, therefore, that the expansion of industrial capital during the early decades of the twentieth century coincided with the concerted efforts of employers to stop the unionization of the labor force.

As early as 1903 the National Association of Manufacturers (NAM) provided employers with the leadership to launch a concerted effort to stop unionization and the implementation of the closed shop. With ample resources to engage in a propaganda campaign against unions, the NAM convinced many that the open shop was un-American and that strikebreakers were American heroes.[59] By convincing prominent members of both political and academic realms about the danger of unions, the NAM was able to strengthen the ability of small producers and local residents in particular to resist unionization and to weaken union sentiments among portions of the working class.[60] Although left-wing political organizations attempted to unify new immigrant workers with native workers through mass strikes during the early decades of the twentieth century, the use of martial law and political repression of left-wing organizers sought to cripple the trade-union movement and make more pronounced the splits within the working class between immigrant and native workers and between skilled and unskilled workers in the newly emerging mass-production industries.[61]

The trade-union movement, although it suffered significantly from antiunion attacks during the years before World War I, was able to flourish during the war years. The war created emergency conditions that required a well-disciplined labor force, thus causing both governmental officials and many industrial capitalists to endorse unionization in an effort to produce more war goods. As a result, the union movement emerged from World War I with an enlarged membership, full union treasuries, a temporary governmental guarantee of the right to collective bargaining, and numerous state agencies for adjustment and arbitration that adopted the principles not only that wages should be sufficient to support a family but also that they should rise with the cost of living.[62] Although the union movement was stronger after World War I than it had been before, unions led by the AFL made little headway into the basic mass-production industries, such as steel and automobiles. Moreover, many of the new union members were located in munitions and metal-working plants that were demobilized at the end of the war. More importantly, collective bargaining, imposed by the government upon employers, was perceived as primarily a wartime necessity.

Employers launched the "American Plan" after the war as a countermovement to the unionization drives of industrial workers. The American Plan meant, in essence, no worker self-organizations. Providing the leadership for the movement, the NAM put forth a massive literature campaign that linked unionization efforts to pro-Communist activities, making the connection between being a union member and being un-American. The sentiments that unions posed a threat to political institutions, to law, and to order were disseminated through a massive literature campaign of the 1920s that reached not only industrial employers, particularly small- and medium-sized industrial capitalists, but also politicians, clergymen, college professors, and the general population through newspapers and pamphlets. By 1929 the publicity department of the NAM reported that coverage of NAM stories had increased 100 percent in actual space covered and 50 percent in the number of clippings and columns received over the previous year. In addition to the propaganda campaign, the NAM actively lobbied for antiunion policies in the legislative realms, endorsed or condemned political candidates on the basis of their position on unions, and advocated employee representation plans as a way to impede the independent organization of workers.[63]

The educational pamphlets of the NAM were perhaps the clearest indication of the arguments against unions and the methods by which appeal was ascertained. A pamphlet in 1927 concerning the reasons for the open shop argued:

As members we favor the open shop because:

1. Rules governing plant operations are not made by men who have neither moral nor financial interests or responsibility in the success of the individual establishment.

2. It does not, by arbitrarily limiting the number of apprentices or workers who will be permitted to join unions, reduce the number of skilled workers available to industry

3. Closed shop rules which restrict the amount of daily output do not apply

4. It is possible to pay workers according to ability, securing greater production per dollar of wages than is possible under the closed shop. Lower production costs bring wider markets and larger sales. This benefits the worker by increasing the continuity of employment

5. Plants are seldom, if ever, shut down because of sympathetic strikes and jurisdictional disputes

6. Agreements by groups of employers with closed shop leaders to deprive other employers or business...are not possible. We believe that all employers should support these advantages of the open shop and energetically oppose efforts of the American Federation of Labor and its constituent unions to impose the closed shop production system of bygone centuries upon American industry. As American citizens we favor the open shop because it best represents and protects fundamental American ideals.[64]

The struggles of workers during the 1920s, although not waged in vain, were severely defeated by capitalists. Between 1922 and 1926 there was a total of 1,164 industrial work stoppages involving 688,538 workers.[66] By 1929 all of labor's wartime gains had virtually been wiped out. Union recognition and collective bargaining, which were under the protection of the state administration, had become things of the past by the mid 1920s. Moreover, the capitalist offensive against unionization compounded the internal constraints of the labor movement – the growing disunity between skilled and unskilled workers and a growing nativist reaction to immigrant workers.[67] By the end of the 1920s, industrial capital had succeeded in forging disunity among industrial workers and in retaining its hegemony on the shop floor.

The course of capitalist accumulation and the associated dynamic of the class struggle led to contradictions that are specific to the process of capitalist development in the United States. Monopoly capital accumulated at an astonishing rate as a result of the greater rate of exploitation of the industrial work force. Conditions that are favorable to the private accumulation of capital corresponded with a redistribution of wealth to the advantage of the upper layers of the capitalist class between 1920 and 1929. The top 1 percent of the population increased its share of the total national income from 12 percent to 18 percent; the top 5 percent, from 24 percent to 33.5 percent. Total income in the form of profits, interest, and rent increased by 45 percent, whereas the real wages of factory workers increased by only 2 percent. As a result, between 40 percent and 45 percent of all households were not able to participate in the market for new consumer durable goods.[86]

Growth in the concentration and centralization of capital within the industrial sector did not correspond with the necessary reorganization of wages and consumption, the regulation of competition, and an alteration in the political structure that was necessary for the new imperatives of the accumulation process. The centralization of capital required a reorganization within the industrial sector because of the massive destruction of capital as a result of a large number of business failures. This required the establishment of "new relations of competition because the destruction of one sector of industrial capital reduces the total mass of capita involved in production and gives all sections of capital new possibilities of valorization."[87] However, the need for regulated competition was blocked by a political apparatus that was not able to transcend particular fractional interests of capital. Monopoly capital, while dominant within the economic sphere, had yet to secure political dominance. The manner in which the state favored monopoly capital was established through a complex process in which state institutions underwent "changes whereby certain dominant mechanisms, modes, and decision-making centres [were] made impermeable to all but monopoly interests, becoming centres for switching the rails of state policy or for bottling up measures taken 'elsewhere' in the State that favour[ed] other fractions of capital."[88] It was the trajectory of the class struggle during the depression years that guided the process of change that the new social structure of accumulation required.

Chapter Five

The Monopoly Debate and Intracapitalist Conflict

The National Industrial Recovery Act, the cornerstone of the New Deal program of economic recovery, was an attempt by the state administration to implement the most effective form of economic recovery. The NIRA, as first formulated, was welcomed by all fractions of the capitalist class as well as by leaders of organized labor. However, as the NIRA was implemented, nonmonopoly capital objected to the dominance of monopoly capital in the implementation process, while labor objected to the lack of implementation of the labor provisions. The TNEC [Temporary National Economic Committee] investigations demonstrated that the growth of monopoly capital implied changes in the basic assumptions regarding the competitive nature of capitalist development in the United States.

The TNEC investigation, as well as the report of the National Recovery Review Board before it, bore evidence to the charges made by nonmonopoly capital with respect to the growth of monopoly capital. The findings of the Bureau of Internal Revenue revealed a higher degree of monopoly growth for 1935, the year the NIRA was declared unconstitutional. Of all corporations that reported to the bureau, 0.1 percent owned 52.0 percent of all assets. Moreover, 0.1 percent of all corporations earned 50.0 percent of their combined net income. Less than 4 percent of all manufacturing corporations that reported earned 84 percent of all net profits.[4] If the NIRA did not foster monopoly growth, it surely did not curtail the growth of monopoly capital. This documentation of monopoly growth caused members of the state administration to become quite aware of the need to regulate monopoly capital.[5] Members of the state administration sought to achieve a more unified relationship between the dominance of monopoly capital in the accumulation process and the general recovery program – including changes within the political arena.

Capital's Response to the NIRA

The NIRA initially appeared to provide benefits to all fractions of the industrial-capitalist class. Large-scale capitalists were granted a suspension of the antitrust laws, which provided the opportunity for expansion on an increased scale. Smaller-scale capitalists received price and production controls and supposedly some form of protection from unfair competitive practices of monopoly firms, which allowed them to be in a more "competitive" position within the industrial market. Capitalists were hesitant about the labor provisions of the NIRA at the time of its passage into law, but then they generally welcomed some form of state-initiated attempts at economic stabilization. However, the establishment of the NIRA and the actual implementation of the codes of fair competition left much to be desired from the frame of reference of capitalists, regardless of the size of the firm or the profitability of its enterprise. Nonmonopoly capital's disenchantment with the NIRA was centered on the accusation that the NRA and the manner of implementation of the NIRA fostered the growth of monopoly capital to the disadvantage of nonmonopoly capital. Although the implementation of the codes of fair competition was clearly in the immediate interest of monopoly capital, monopoly capitalists, "once they tasted the sweet immunity from the anti-trust acts, were irked by the growing tendency of the NRA to return to economic and legal orthodoxy, disallowing tactics that went beyond fair competition and were inimical to all competition."[6] When economic recovery for large-scale capital appeared to be under way, these same capitalists became more wary of governmental intervention.

Small-scale capitalists complained about monopoly growth during the entire period of the NIRA. These complaints began as early as six months after the official enactment of the law and continued throughout its existence. These complaints largely centered on the abuse of governmental sanctions for monopoly capital, the generalized growth of monopoly firms, and the decline of the small entrepreneur. During the final few months of the NIRA, complaints regarding the degree of monopoly growth and the degree to which the codes of fair competition placed burdens on small-scale capital were as forceful as ever. A letter from Congressman Henry C. Luckey to FDR in early 1935, stating the criticisms of the NIRA that were being expressed by Luckey's constituents in Nebraska concerning the possibility of an extension of the NIRA, exemplifies the general position of small-scale capitalists over the evaluation of the NIRA codes of fair competition:

> The multiple restrictions placed on the small business man have resulted in an unfair and unnecessary discrimination against him to the advantage of a rapidly growing, monopolistic group of big business concerns. The small business man has little time to familiarize himself with the complicated rules and regulations which change frequently, and only too often as a result of these rules, finds himself compelled to close his business rather than carry on the unequal struggle.[7]

In March 1934, less than one year after the official enactment of the NIRA, Roosevelt created The National Recovery Review Board, under the chairmanship of Clarence S. Darrow. The purpose of the Review Board was to ascertain and report to FDR whether any code or codes of fair competition were designed to promote monopolies or to discriminate against small business or whether they permitted monopolies or monopolistic practices. The Review Board was also supposed to recommend to FDR any changes in the approved codes which would rectify or eliminate the possibility of the growth of monopolies that were perceived to be detrimental to small-scale capitalists. Members of the Review Board heard complaints concerning twelve approved codes during the first five weeks of the board's existence. These complaints came from smaller-sized capitalists within each industrial branch covered by the codes. The bulk of the complaints centered on the difficulties being experienced by small-scale capitalists. The major complaint was that "small independent business men were largely ignored, both in the writing of the codes and in filling the various committees set up to enforce the codes."[8] Small-scale capitalists documented that large-scale capitalists had supervised the writing of the codes and that they then had also administered and enforced the codes of fair competition. The National Recovery Review Board suggested, after the five weeks of preliminary investigation, that further investigation be undertaken into the issue of the impact that the NIRA was having on monopoly growth.

The report of the National Recovery Review Board reinforced the charges made by small-scale capitalists that the NRA was a state agency that ruled in the interest of monopoly capital. Darrow's report found a trend toward monopoly and oppression of small business in almost all of the eight codes that it covered. The report singled out the steel and motion-picture industries, in which monopoly and monopolistic practices were extreme – to the complete detriment of smaller-scale enterprises. The report stated that only the cleaning-and-dyeing code was free of monopoly, and this code was not even being enforced by the code authorities. The report recommended that most price and production controls be eliminated and that major changes be made in the composition of the code authorities.[9]

After discussing the problems in regard to capital accumulation in an epoch in which monopoly capital was dominant within the accumulation process, Darrow and Thompson argued that it was not possible to "go back to unregulated competition" in a situation "where technological advance had produced a surplus so that unregulated competition demoralizes both wages and prices and brings on recurrent and increasingly severe industrial depression." Darrow and Thompson, in essence, argued that given the situation within the capital-accumulation process, the only way to guarantee a high standard of living and to avoid future depressions was through the socialized ownership and control of industrial production. They suggested that there were only two possible positions for state administrators to take with regard to monopoly growth. One was the regulation of monopolies by state activity, the general tendency of the policy directive of the NRA. According to Darrow and Thompson, this would mean the elimination of small business in the long run. The other choice, they argued, was a planned economy, with the socialization of the means of production. Planned economy did not mean the sanction of government to sustain profits. Darrow and Thompson were advocating a nascent form of socialism. Their final conclusions were: "The NRA is at a present stage of conflict of interest; but in proportion as the authority of government sanctions regulation by industrial combinations, the inevitable tendency is toward monopoly, with elimination of the small business."[11]

The Monopoly Debate

The implementation of the NIRA did not run counter to the process of the concentration and centralization of capital, and it provided little by way of economic recovery. Hence, small- and medium-scale capitalists, along with anti-big-business state administrators and legislators, placed the blame for the economic depression on large-scale corporate capital. After all, it appeared that monopoly capital was the only element that was able to withstand the economic crisis and even benefited within certain limits. The end of the NIRA did not subdue the debates among capitalists and state administrators over the "monopoly problem." Moreover, the 1937/38 recession brought with it a revitalization of the concern over monopoly growth within the domestic accumulation process among both capitalists and members of the state administration. As economic conditions took a turn for the worse in late 1937, members of the state administration looked toward antitrust revision as a method of handling monopoly growth and as a solution to the economic downturn. The conventional wisdom among state administrators and, more specifically, members of Congress was that the tendency toward monopoly growth in the United States meant a decline in competition that would lead to higher prices for consumer goods. Hence, a policy of antitrust revision would restore the competitive market. Moreover, after the 1937 recession, the Roosevelt administration sought an expanded spending program in an attempt to increase purchasing power so as to overcome obstacles in the accumulation process.

Roosevelt was advised that the strategy of increased spending, combined with trust busting, would aid overall capital accumulation. Leon Henderson, an economic advisor, argued that full employment and sustained production were dependent upon both a balance of prices and a balance between savings and investment. While the former could be achieved by politically dislodging monopolistic controls over the competitive market, the latter required governmental investment to offset the decline in private investment. Antitrust action, Henderson argued, would also add to the effectiveness of spending by breaking down restrictions on production and economic expansion. At the same time, spending would facilitate antitrust action by arresting deflationary forces, thus reducing the trend toward monopolization.[20]

By early 1938 the administration and liberal democratic leaders of Congress had become convinced of the need for a spending program coupled with an anti-monopoly program to combat the economic crisis. In early April 1938 Roosevelt sent a special message to Congress, in which he requested the spending or lending of more than $3 billion for relief and work programs and aid to local and state governments. In addition, he asked for the release of $1.4 billion in idle gold and the lowering of reserve requirements for Federal Reserve banks. Roosevelt was asking Congress for a Keynesian spending program in which the market forces would be manipulated in order to restore purchasing power. The proposed Recovery Relief bill was passed by Congress in mid June after a long debate. Congress thus endorsed the administration's decision to use governmental spending as a force in stimulating economic activity.[21]

Two weeks after his message to Congress, Roosevelt and his advisors worked on another message, one concerned with a revision of antitrust legislation as part of an anti-monopoly program. Although labeled "antimonopoly," the program did not seek to curb monopoly growth; rather, it was aimed at regulating the competitive practices of large-scale business concerns. The view that monopoly growth caused a decline in competition led many congressmen to believe that the process of monopoly growth had to be politically controlled. In reality, however, the process of the concentration and centralization of capital was a basic tendency within the law of accumulation; the process of monopoly growth could not be curtailed if accumulation were to continue. What might be politically controlled was competition between firms. The entire debate over the growth of monopoly firms was essentially concerned with the political regulation of competition. The so-called antimonopoly message to Congress was carefully worded so as not to lose the confidence of the business community. Henry A. Wallace, secretary of agriculture, was particularly cautious; he warned Roosevelt that "these men still controlled the bulk of flow of private capital and, at the present juncture, it was absolutely necessary to induce the flow."[22] After sixteen leading capitalists had indicated their willingness to cooperate in a policy designed to regulate monopoly growth, Roosevelt on 29 April told members of Congress that the country was controlled by a clique of private individuals who regulated and/or dominated every branch of the economy. Roosevelt implicitly argued that this tight-knit group was able to determine the performance of the economy as a whole, with little concern for anything other than their own profitability. In order to change the situation, Roosevelt asked Congress for more funds for antitrust prosecutions, further banking legislation, and $500,000 for a study of the concentration of economic power. The goal of such an antimonopoly program would be to politically restore and regulate the rhythm of capital accumulation for the country as a whole.

The investigation into economic concentration meant an investigation into the extent of the centralization of capital in the domestic process of accumulation. Concentration, as defined by the state administration, meant that fewer and fewer firms were controlling a larger share of the market and that the ownership and the control of such firms were in the hands of fewer and fewer capitalists. The TNEC was charged with investigating the degree of centralization of capital within the various branches of industry. In theory, based on the findings of the committee, legislation could be formulated to politically regulate the form that competition would take.

The experience of the TNEC was not dissimilar to that of the NRA and the National Recovery Review Board before it. The experience of the Review Board had shown that any investigation into the extent of monopoly growth and any recommendations for legislation would all be conducted within the confines that would make the accumulation of private capital profitable. The members of the TNEC were divided over the monopoly issue; they represented views as divergent as national planning, anti-big-business, and pro-monopoly capital. The TNEC mirrored the conflicts within the state apparatus itself – conflicts between those capitalists and agents of capital who stressed a more planned national economy and those who desired a return to competitive capitalism. The divergent views between members of the committee, on the one hand, and the members and researchers, on the other hand, indicated that the TNEC was split over the monopoly issue along similar lines to Congress and the administration.

The actual operations of the TNEC, like those of the NRA before it, were confused.[26] In July 1938, after having received requests from two members of the TNEC, A.A. Berle prepared a memorandum of suggestions for the investigation of business organizations and practices. In his memorandum Berle suggested that a clear goal of the investigation into the extent of monopolies be delineated so that the investigation and further recommendations of the committee would be taken seriously and would aid in the shaping of legislation.[27] Berle began by suggesting that the investigation should essentially be a search to find an organization of business that would actually work – that is, what particular form of organization would provide adequate employment, goods, and services at a fair price, eliminate waste, and assure a "fair" profit. Berle argued that all of these questions would have to be determined by actual data on various branches of industry and that some concentration of power might be more desirable in some branches than in others. He cautioned the TNEC against making incorrect assumptions about small business; he argued that small-scale enterprises were not necessarily "competitive," "humane," or "efficient." According to Berle, the charge against monopoly could not be made that size alone determined desirability with respect to economic performance. Berle also warned that the outcome of the investigation of monopolies should clearly state why an additional degree of state regulation of industrial activity should be undertaken. He suggested that the reasons should be to provide more, better, and cheaper goods; to provide more, better-paying, and steadier jobs; to continue ready access to capital financing necessary to create and maintain additional plants; and to provide for the continued development of the arts of industrial production.

Berle's memorandum in many ways outlined the position of national economic planners, of monopoly capital, and of those state agents who believed that monopoly was a normal outcome of the accumulation process and that monopolistic forms of business organization were not necessarily evil. These capitalists and state agents recognized that the purposes of the committee were essentially to gather facts and to figure out the manner in which capital could continue to accumulate at the fastest and most desirable rates. These people realized that competition could be politically regulated in order to balance the profit rate between branches of industry as well as possible. Regulated competition was perceived as the solution to industrial bankruptcies and to bottlenecks within the accumulation process.[28]

Unlike the National Recovery Review Board, the TNEC gathered facts and figures concerning the growth of monopoly capital in the United States, but their recommendations were not based upon assumptions about the need to abolish monopolies or about the desirability of a nonmonopolistic form of economic organization. Nevertheless, businessmen in general, as well as agents of capital, severely criticized the TNEC for holding an investigation that could undermine business confidence. Some persons, such as Raymond Moley, argued that business should be allowed to expand at will, rather than being politically attacked for its "successes."[29]

Monopoly Growth

In late 1938 the TNEC initiated its study and investigation of the "concentration of economic power." The TNEC met until April 1940. In the seventeen months of its existence, the committee heard 552 witnesses who filled 31 volumes with testimony and exhibits. The economists who were retained by the committee submitted an additional 43 special studies which were published separately. The reports and studies constituted the most extensive state-supported investigation into the mechanisms of capital accumulation within the industrial sector. After gathering facts upon facts, the committee presented no recommendations for major changes in the antitrust laws. In Hawley's words, "The investigation, after all, was essentially an escape mechanism, a way to deal with a fundamental policy conflict that could not be resolved. The scene of controversy was simply shifted from administrative bureaus and congressional halls to the committee hearings in the hope that somehow, by writing down all the facts, an answer might emerge."[31]

Although the committee did not make any major recommendations for legislation concerning monopoly growth, the reports and hearings of the committee did document the growth and importance of monopoly capital in the capital accumulation process. During the economic crisis itself the larger, more concentrated, and centralized firms tended to grow and profit at a much more rapid rate than smaller-scale nonmonopoly capital. The process of concentration and centralization of capital, which was so evident during the 1920s, continued during the world economic crisis of the 1930s. During the 1920s, most monopoly growth was due to mergers and acquisitions, but the increased dominance of monopoly firms during the depression was due to a higher rate of attrition among smaller firms that were less able to withstand the competition because they had smaller financial reserves. The largest 317 manufacturing corporations increased their share of net working capital from 39.0 percent in 1929 to 43.2 percent in 1933, with a further advance to 47.0 in 1938.[32]

The increased competition among capitalist firms within a given branch of industry, increased competition between branches of industry, and the negative impact of this competition on small-scale capitalist enterprises were well documented throughout the TNEC hearings. One monograph of the TNEC was devoted to the problems of small business within a generalized accumulation process dominated by monopoly capital. Frequent complaints by small-scale capitalists against the monopolistic practices of competitors were: (1) price controls; (2) the control of distribution channels; (3) labor coercion in the nature of racketeering; and (4) miscellaneous practices, including the control of location, the development of special brands, and similar devices. Small-scale capitalists complained to the Federal Trade Commission that these practices were common and that they operated unfairly against the small, independent entrepreneur, making it difficult for him or her to survive. It was further argued that state policy had been affected by business interests of large-scale corporate capital and, while seeking to protect the small-scale capitalist, had actually not helped small-scale capital at all. This was a result of the fact that state, local, and federal policies were so uncoordinated that larger-scale capitalists had a greater impact on national economic policy. The lack of coordination among pieces of protective legislation for small-scale capitalist firms was claimed to be the root cause of economic chaos and business mortality.

While many small- and medium-scale capitalist firms in the highly competitive sectors of industry suffered during the 1930s, the large, more monopolized firms actually profited during the years after the stock-market crash in 1929. For example, General Electric had a net income of $24,052,000 in 1934 and $78,207,000 in 1935; General Motors went from a net income of $110,353,000 in 1934 to $256,853,000 in 1937; the net income of Goodyear Tire and Rubber Company increased from $8,502,000 in 1934 to $11,942,000 in 1937; and United States Steel's net income grew from $11,078,000 in 1934 to $129,653,000 in 1937. Sales, profits, and profit margins for the large monopolistic firms all showed significant increases during the 1930s.[33]

Monopoly Capital, Nonmonopoly Capital, and the State Apparatus

The TNEC's investigation into the extent of the centralization of capital and the restoration of the competitive market never analyzed the process that had led to the growth of firms and to increased centralization in the first place. The committee never examined the effects of growing monopolization on economic efficiency, labor displacement, and the like. Although the TNEC was operating on the loose assumption that monopolization was the cause of economic decline and economic dislocation, the testimony gathered and the facts and figures collected simply reported the incidence of centralization without presenting an explanation or an analysis of the economic forces that lead to highly concentrated and centralized industrial sector

The TNEC did, however, recognize the growth of monopoly capital within the domestic accumulation process:

> While no final evaluation is possible concerning the amount of competition and monopoly present in our economy, certainly monopoly has greatly increased in American industry during the last 50 years because of the lax enforcement of the anti-trust laws, the impetus of price-fixing given by World War I, the tremendous development of trade associations during the twenties which increased price-fixing, the N.R.A. experience in 1933, and the great merger movements from 1898 to 1905 and 1919 to 1929.[44]

Nevertheless, the dominance of monopoly capital within the accumulation process and its increasing dominance on the political level more likely than not placed limits on the policy recommendations of the TNEC. It was nearly impossible for the TNEC to recommend major changes in the antitrust laws which would inhibit large-scale enterprises from increasing profits, since the profitability of large-scale capital had an impact on overall economic stability. The TNEC did not recommend any basic alterations in the process of capital accumulation, and it made no final evaluation of the extent of monopoly growth and its repercussions on overall economic relations in the United States. The very fact that the TNEC made no serious recommendations for reforming economic activity, after concluding that the industrial sector was highly concentrated and centralized, bears evidence that the interest of monopoly capital, as a class fraction, was gaining political dominance.

If anything, the collection of "facts" about the growth of monopoly capital within the industrial sector forced state administrators, elected officials, and the public to acknowledge the changing structure of the accumulation process. Instead of altering the process of capital accumulation, state administrators sought to alter political relationships that would coincide with the changing economic relation. Changes in the methods of production, which required state economic intervention of a new kind, had been recognized by economists and academics by the mid 1930s.[45] In the words of Arthur R. Burns:

> State participation in the administration of economic resources is urged as a means of securing greater efficiency than the partially competitive and partially monopolistic system of the past has been able to offer. It requires the frank recognition of the conflicts of interest between groups and individuals and serious effort to compromise these conflicts. This compromise can be made, however, only on the basis of a clear conception of the objectives of society. …In both the political and economic sphere the greatest of all contemporary problems is that of deciding how great a concentration of power shall be permitted. …[t]he problem is one of designing patterns for the distribution of power.[46]

This quotation from Burns illustrated the meaning of monopoly capital's dominance vis-à-vis nonmonopoly capital. The investigation into the concentration of economic power and the 1935 Supreme Court decision that ruled that the NIRA codes of fair competition were unconstitutional were the very compromises made to nonmonopoly capital at a time when monopoly capital was being organized as the dominant class fraction on the political level. The conflicts between the various fractions of capital made it clear to Burns that the political alliance of capital needed to be organized and unified by the state. Moreover, Burns's quotation illustrates his recognition that the accumulation process had changed since the turn of the century and that capital, in turn, needed to be reorganized under the hegemony of monopoly capital if the accumulation process was to continue and the long-term interest of capital as a whole was to be secure. In Nicos Poulantzas's words:

> Contradictions among the dominant classes and fractions – or in other words, the relationship of forces within the power bloc – are precisely what makes it necessary for the unity of the bloc to be organized by the State. They therefore exist as *contradictory relations enmeshed within the State.* As the material condensation of a contradictory relationship, the State does not at all organize the unity of the power bloc from the outside, by resolving class contradictions at a distance. On the contrary, however paradoxical it may seem, the play of these contradictions within the State's materiality alone makes possible the State's organizational role.[47]

The state administration did not seek to alter the profitability or the rate of accumulation for the large-scale monopoly firms; it did seek, however, to aid in altering the social relations of production within firms and the structure of the state to correspond more coherently with changes in the accumulation process. It was even acknowledged during the TNEC hearings that social relations lagged "behind developments in our economic life."[48] It appears that the state administration's strategy to rationalize economic activity in order not only to recover from the economic depression but also to prevent future economic crises favored monopoly capital. Although debates about monopoly growth continued throughout the years of the economic crisis, although the National Recovery Review Board reported a high rate of incidence of monopoly growth under the NIRA codes of fair competition, and although the TNEC verified monopoly growth, no serious political actions were taken to curb monopoly growth or the process of concentration and centralization of capital. Instead, relationships between capital and the state were altered. Monopoly capital was able to withstand political debates on the assumption that monopoly growth had been the reason and the cause for the economic decline by turning economic and political setbacks that resulted both from intracapitalist conflict and the gains made by working class struggles during the decade of the 1930s into advantages for itself in the post-World War II period. The debates and controversy surrounding the NIRA and the administrative activities of the NRA serve to support the claim that the NIRA actually provided the mechanisms that aided the process of the concentration and centralization of capital, helped to create monopolistic forms of business organization in certain branches of industry, and began the process of establishing the conditions for new social relations between monopoly capital and wage labor and between capital and the state.

Notes

Chapter One. The Capitalist State, Class Relations, and the New Deal

1   Donald Winch, *Economics and Policy* (New York: Walker, 1969), p. 219; Louis M. Hacker, *The Course of American Economic Growth and Development* (New York: John Wiley, 1970), p. 85; U.S. Bureau of the Census, *Historical Statistics of the United States, Colonial Times to 1970*, Bicentennial Edition, pt. 1 (Washington, D.C.: Government Printing Office, 1975), p. 135.

2   Bernard Bellush, *The Failure of the NRA* (New York: W. W. Norton, 1975), p. xiii.

Chapter Two. The Process of Capitalist Development: Capital, Labor, and the State, 1890–1929

10   Lewis Corey, *The Decline of American Capitalism* (New York: Covici, Friede, 1934), p. 30.

11   Alfred D. Chandler, Jr., *The Visible Hand: The Managerial Revolution in American Business* (Cambridge, Mass.: Harvard University Press, 1977), p. 286.

12   Jurgen Kuczynski, *A Short History of Labour Conditions under Industrial Capitalism, vol. 2: The United States of America, 1789–1946* (New York: Barnes & Noble, 1973), p. 71.

13   Ibid., p. 72.

14   Edward C. Kirkland, *Industry Comes of Age* (New York: Holt, Rinehart & Winston, 1961), p. 165.

15   Harold U. Faulkner, *The Decline of Laissez-faire, 1897–1917* (New York: Holt, Rinehart & Winston, 1951), p. 115.

16   Ibid., p. 155.

17 Edwin F. Gay and Leo Wolman, "Trends in Economic Organization," in *Recent Social Trends in the United States*, p. 241.

18 George Soule, *Prosperity Decade: From War to Depression, 1917–1929* (New York: Rinehart, 1947), p. 142.

19 David M. Gordon, Richards Edwards, Michael Reich, *Segmented Work, Divided Workers: The historical transformation of labor in the United States*, 1st ed, (Cambridge University Press, 1982), p. 129.

20 See Faulkner, *Decline of Laissez-faire*, p. 121; and Chandler, *Visible Hand*, p. 240.

24 Ibid., p. 123.

25 Dexter S. Kimball, "Changes in New and Old Industries," in *Recent Economic Changes in the United States*, p. 80.

34 Michel Aglietta, *A Theory of Capitalist Regulation: The U.S. Experience* (London: New Left Books, 1979), pp. 114–15.

35 Daniel Nelson, *Managers and Workers: Origins of the New Factory System in the United States, 1880–1920* (Madison: University of Wisconsin Press, 1975), p. 162; see also Griffin, Wallace, and Rubin, "Capitalist Resistance," pp. 157–61.

36 Claus Offe, *Disorganized Capitalism* (Cambridge, Mass.: MIT Press, 1985), p. 178.

37 Nelson, *Managers and Workers*, p. 121; Griffin, Wallace, and Rubin, "Capitalist Resistance," pp. 155–65.

38 For an interesting discussion of regimes of accumulation see Aglietta, *Theory of Capitalist Regulation*, pp. 68–100. For Aglietta, "A regime of accumulation is a form of social transformation that increases relative surplus value under the stable constraints of the most general norms that define absolute surplus value" (p. 68). Aglietta argues that the distinction between absolute surplus value and relative surplus value "denotes an articulation of social relations that induce different complementary practices" (p. 68). In brief, a regime of accumulation refers to the different social relations that are attributed to the different types of exploitation.

39 L. P. Alford, "Technical Changes in Manufacturing Industries," in *Recent Economic Changes in the United States*, p. 104.

47 Faulkner, *Decline of Laissez-faire*, p. 249.

52 See Gordon, Edwards, and Reich, *Segmented Work*, pp. 100–164.

53 See David Montgomery, "Workers' Control of Machine Production in the Nineteenth Century," *Labor History* 17, 4 (Fall 1976): 485–509.

58 See Larry J. Griffin, Michael E. Wallace, Beth A. Rubin "Capitalist Resistance to the Organization of Labor Before the New Deal: Why? How? Success?" *American Sociological Review*, 1986; 51:2.

59 Faulkner, *Decline of Laissez-faire*, p. 296; see Offe, *Disorganized Capitalism*, pp. 170–220, for an excellent discussion of the differences between labor organizations and associations of capitalists.

60 See Albion Guilford Taylor, *Labor Policies of the National Association of Manufacturers* (New York: Arno, 1973), passim.

61 See Mike Davis, "Why the U.S. Working Class Is Different," *New Left Review* 123 (Sept.–Oct. 1980): 3–44; Robert Justin Goldstein, *Political Repression in Modern America, 1870 to the Present* (Cambridge, Mass.: Schenkman, 1978), pp. 44–101.

62 Soule, *Prosperity Decade*, p. 187.

63 Taylor, *Labor Policies*, pp. 167–68, 91, 73.

64 National Association of Manufacturers, "Evidence for the Open Shop," 28 Feb. 1927.

66 Wolman and Peck, "Labor Groups in the Social Structure," p. 490.

67 Davis, "Why the U.S. Working Class Is Different," p. 43.

86 Michel A. Aglietta, *Theory of Capitalist Regulation* (London: New Left Books, 1978), p. 94.

87 Ibid., p. 8.

88 Nicos Poulantzas, *State, Socialism* (London: New Left Books, 1978), p. 137.

Chapter Five. The Monopoly Debate and Intracapitalist Conflict

4 U.S. Congress, Temporary National Economic Committee, *Investigation of Concentration of Economic Power: Hearings*, pt. 1: *Economic Prologue* (Washington, D.C.: Government Printing Office, 1939), p. 195.

5   See ibid., Message from the President of the United States Transmitting Recommendations Relative to the Strengthening and Enforcement of Anti-Trust Laws, p. 188.

6   Broadus Mitchell, *Depression Decade: From New Era through New Deal, 1929–1941* (New York: Holt, Rinehart & Winston, 1962), pp. 257–58.

7   Henry C. Luckey to FDR, 15 Feb. 1935, PPF 777, FDR Library.

8   John F. Sinclair to FDR, National Recovery Review Board, 14 Apr. 1934, POF 466E, box 47, FDR Library.

9   Ellis W. Hawley, *The New Deal and the Problem of Monopoly* (Princeton, N.J.: Princeton University Press, 1966), pp. 95–96.

11   Clarence S. Darrow and W.O. Thompson, *Review Board, National Recovery Act*, 3 May 1934, POF 466E, box 47, FDR Library.

20   Ellis W. Hawley, *The New Deal and the Problem of Monopoly: A Study in Economic Ambivalence, Reissue ed.* (Fordham University Press, 1995).

21   Ibid., p. 410.

22   Cited by Hawley in *New Deal and the Problem of Monopoly*, p. 411.

26   Hawley, *New Deal and the Problem of Monopoly*, pp. 416–18.

27   See "Memorandum of Suggestions: Investigation of Business Organization and Practices," A. A. Berle, Jr., 12 July 1938, Rosenman Papers, box 11, FDR Library.

28   For an enlightened discussion on the nature of competition between units of capital see Michel Aglietta, *A Theory of Capitalist Regulation: The U.S. Experience* (London: New Left Books, 1979), pp. 273–327.

29   Robert Sobel, *Age of Giant Corporations* (Praeger, 1993), pp. 119–20.

31   Hawley, *New Deal and the Problem of Monopoly*, p. 419.

32   John M. Blair, *Economic Concentration* (New York: Harcourt Brace Jovanovich, 1972), p. 67.

33   See Temporary National Economic Committee, *Investigation of Concentration of Economic Power*, monograph 17: *Problems of Small Business* (Washington, D.C.: Government Printing Office, 1941).

44   Temporary National Economic Committee, *Investigation of Concentration of Economic Power: Final Report of the Executive Secretary* (Washington, D.C.: Government Printing Office, 1941), p. 26.

45   The classic study on the nature of competition and changes in the accumulation process is Arthur Robert Burns, *The Decline of Competition* (New York: McGraw-Hill, 1936). This book was quite influential among academic economists during the 1930s.

46   Ibid., p. 565.

47   Nicos Poulantzas, *State, Power, Socialism* (London: New Left Books, 1978), p. 133.

48   Temporary National Economic Committee, *Investigation of Concentration of Economic Power*, monograph 17: *Problems of Small Business* (Washington, D.C.: Government Printing Office, 1941), p. 139.

CHAPTER 29

Scientific Management

Harry Braverman

Chapter 4

Scientific Management

The classical economists were the first to approach the problems of the organization of labor within capitalist relations of production from a theoretical point of view. They may thus be called the first management experts, and their work was continued in the latter part of the Industrial Revolution by such men as Andrew Ure and Charles Babbage. Between these men and the next step, the comprehensive formulation of management theory in the late nineteenth and early twentieth centuries, there lies a gap of more than half a century during which there was an enormous growth in the size of enterprises, the beginnings of the monopolistic organization of industry, and the purposive and systematic application of science to production. The scientific management movement initiated by Frederick Winslow Taylor in the last decades of the nineteenth century was brought into being by these forces. Logically, Taylorism belongs to the chain of development of management methods and the organization of labor, and not to the development of technology, in which its role was minor.[1]

Scientific management, so-called, is an attempt to apply the methods of science to the increasingly complex problems of the control of labor in rapidly growing capitalist enterprises. It lacks the characteristics of a true science because its assumptions reflect nothing more than the outlook of the capitalist with regard to the conditions of production. It starts, despite occasional protestations to the contrary, not from the human point of view but from the capitalist point of view, from the point of view of the management of a refractory work force in a setting of antagonistic social relations. It does not attempt to discover and confront the cause of this condition, but accepts it as an inexorable given, a "natural" condition. It investigates not labor in general, but the adaptation of labor to the needs of capital. It enters the workplace not as the representative of science, but as the representative of management masquerading in the trappings of science.

A comprehensive and detailed outline of the principles of Taylorism is essential to our narrative, not because of the things for which it is popularly known—stopwatch,

Original publication details: Harry Braverman, "Scientific Management," from *Labor and Monopoly Capital: The Degradation of Work in the Twentieth Century*, pp. 85–86; 90–91; 97–101; 107; 109–112; 139–151. Monthly Press Review, 1974. Reproduced with permission from Monthly Press.

speed-up, etc.—but because behind these commonplaces there lies a theory which is nothing less than the explicit verbalization of the capitalist mode of production. But before I begin this presentation, a number of introductory remarks are required to clarify the role of the Taylor school in the development of management theory.

[A] distinctive feature of Taylor's thought was his concept of control. Control has been the essential feature of management throughout its history, but with Taylor it assumed unprecedented dimensions. The stages of management control over labor before Taylor had included, progressively: the gathering together of the workers in a workshop and the dictation of the length of the working day; the supervision of workers to ensure diligent, intense, or uninterrupted application; the enforcement of rules against distractions (talking, smoking, leaving the workplace, etc.) that were thought to interfere with application; the setting of production minimums; etc. A worker is under management control when subjected to these rules, or to any of their extensions and variations. But Taylor raised the concept of control to an entirely new plane when he asserted as an *absolute necessity for adequate management the dictation to the worker of the precise manner in which work is to be performed.* That management had the right to "control" labor was generally assumed before Taylor, but in practice this right usually meant only the general setting of tasks, with little direct interference in the worker's mode of performing them. Taylor's contribution was to overturn this practice and replace it by its opposite. Management, he insisted, could be only a limited and frustrated undertaking so long as it left to the worker any decision about the work. His "system" was simply a means for management to achieve control of the actual mode of performance of every labor activity, from the simplest to the most complicated. To this end, he pioneered a far greater revolution in the division of labor than any that had gone before.

Taylor set as his objective the maximum or "optimum" that can be obtained from a day's labor power. "On the part of the men," he said in his first book, "the greatest obstacle to the attainment of this standard is the slow pace which they adopt, or the loafing or 'soldiering,' marking time, as it is called." In each of his later expositions of his system, he begins with this same point, underscoring it heavily.[2] The causes of this soldiering he breaks into two parts: "This loafing or soldiering proceeds from two causes. First, from the natural instinct and tendency of men to take it easy, which may be called *natural soldiering.* Second, from more intricate second thought and reasoning caused by their relations with other men, which may be called *systematic soldiering.*" The first of these he quickly puts aside, to concentrate on the second: "The natural laziness of men is serious, but by far the greatest evil from which both workmen and employers are suffering is the *systematic soldiering* which is almost universal under all the ordinary schemes of management and which results from a careful study on the part of the workmen of what they think will promote their best interests."

> The greater part of systematic soldiering…is done by the men with the deliberate object of keeping their employers ignorant of how fast work can be done.
>
> So universal is soldiering for this purpose, that hardly a competent workman can be found in a large establishment, whether he works by the day or on piece work, contract work or under any of the ordinary systems of compensating labor, who does not devote a considerable part of his time to studying just how slowly he can work and still convince his employer that he is going at a good pace.
>
> The causes for this are, briefly, that practically all employers determine upon a maximum sum which they feel it is right for each of their classes of employés to earn per day, whether their men work by the day or piece.[3]

That the pay of labor is a socially determined figure, relatively independent of productivity, among employers of similar types of labor power in any given period was thus known to Taylor. Workers who produce twice or three times as much as they did the day before do not thereby double or triple their pay, but may be given a small incremental advantage over their fellows, an advantage which disappears as their level of production becomes generalized. The contest over the size of the portion of the day's labor power to be embodied in each product is thus relatively independent of the level of pay, which responds chiefly to market, social, and historical factors. The worker learns this from repeated experiences, whether working under day or piece rates: "It is, however," says Taylor, "under piece work that the art of systematic soldiering is thoroughly developed. After a workman has had the price per piece of the work he is doing lowered two or three times as a result of his having worked harder and increased his output, he is likely to entirely lose sight of his employer's side of the case and to become imbued with a grim determination to have no more cuts if soldiering can prevent it."[4] To this it should be added that even where a piecework or "incentive" system allows the worker to increase his pay, the contest is not thereby ended but only exacerbated, because the output records now determine the setting and revision of pay rates.

Taylor always took the view that workers, by acting in this fashion, were behaving rationally and with an adequate view of their own best interests. He claimed, in another account of his Midvale battle, that he conceded as much even in the midst of the struggle: "His workman friends came to him [Taylor] continually and asked him, in a personal, friendly way, whether he would advise them, for their own best interest, to turn out more work. And, as a truthful man, he had to tell them that if he were in their place he would fight against turning out any more work, just as they were doing, because under the piece-work system they would be allowed to earn no more wages than they had been earning, and yet they would be made to work harder."[5]

The conclusions which Taylor drew from the baptism by fire he received in the Midvale struggle may be summarized as follows: Workers who are controlled only by general orders and discipline are not adequately controlled, because they retain their grip on the actual processes of labor. So long as they control the labor process itself, they will thwart efforts to realize to the full the potential inherent in their labor power. To change this situation, control over the labor process must pass into the hands of management, not only in a formal sense but by the control and dictation of each step of the process, including its mode of performance. In pursuit of this end, no pains are too great, no efforts excessive, because the results will repay all efforts and expenses lavished on this demanding and costly endeavor.[6]

From earliest times to the Industrial Revolution the craft or skilled trade was the basic unit, the elementary cell of the labor process. In each craft, the worker was presumed to be the master of a body of traditional knowledge, and methods and procedures were left to his or her discretion. In each such worker reposed the accumulated knowledge of materials and processes by which production was accomplished in the craft. The potter, tanner, smith, weaver, carpenter, baker, miller, glassmaker, cobbler, etc., each representing a branch of the social division of labor, was a repository of human technique for the labor processes of that branch. The worker combined, in mind and body, the concepts and physical dexterities of the specialty: technique, understood in this way, is, as has often been observed, the predecessor and progenitor of science. The most important and widespread of all crafts was, and throughout the world remains to this day, that of the farmer. The farming family combines its craft with the rude practice of a number of others, including those of the smith, mason, carpenter, butcher, miller, and baker, etc. The apprenticeships required in traditional crafts ranged from three to seven years, and for the farmer of course extends beyond this to include most of childhood, adolescence, and young adulthood. In view of the knowledge to be assimilated, the dexterities to be gained, and the fact that the craftsman, like the professional, was required to master a specialty and become the best judge of the manner of its application to specific production problems, the years of apprenticeship were generally needed and were employed in a learning process that extended well into the journeyman decades. Of these trades, that of the machinist was in Taylor's day among the most recent, and certainly the most important to modern industry.

Taylor was not primarily concerned with the advance of technology (which, as we shall see, offers other means for direct control over the labor process). He did make significant contributions to the technical knowledge of machine-shop practice (high-speed tool steel, in particular), but these were chiefly by-products of his effort to study this practice with an eye to systematizing and classifying it. His concern was with the control of labor at any given level of technology, and he tackled his own trade with a boldness and energy which astonished his contemporaries and set the pattern for industrial engineers, work designers, and office managers from that day on. And in tackling machine-shop work, he had set himself a prodigious task.

The machinist of Taylor's day started with the shop drawing, and turned, milled, bored, drilled, planed, shaped, ground, filed, and otherwise machine- and hand-processed the proper stock to the desired shape as specified in the drawing. The range of decisions to be made in the course of the process is—unlike the case of a simple job, such as the handling of pig iron—by its very nature enormous. Even for the lathe alone, disregarding all collateral tasks such as the choice of stock, handling, centering and chucking the work, layout and measuring, order of cuts, and considering only the operation of turning itself, the range of possibilities is huge. Taylor himself worked with twelve variables, including the hardness of the metal, the material of the cutting tool, the thickness of the shaving, the shape of the cutting tool, the use of a coolant during cutting, the depth of the cut, the frequency of regrinding cutting tools as they became dulled, the lip and clearance angles of the tool, the smoothness of cutting or absence of chatter, the diameter of the stock being turned, the pressure of the chip or shaving on the cutting surface of the tool, and the speeds, feeds, and pulling power of the machine.[7] Each of these variables is subject to broad choice, ranging from a few possibilities in the selection and use of a coolant, to a very great number of effective choices in all matters having to do with thickness, shape, depth, duration, speed, etc. Twelve variables, each subject to a large number of choices, will yield in their possible combinations and permutations astronomical figures, as Taylor soon realized. But upon these decisions of the machinist depended not just the accuracy and finish of the product, but also the pace of production. Nothing daunted, Taylor set out to gather into management's hands all the basic information bearing on these processes. He began a series of experiments at the Midvale Steel Company, in the fall of 1880, which lasted twenty-six years, recording the results of between 30,000 and 50,000 tests, and cutting up more than 800,000 pounds of iron and steel on ten different machine tools reserved for his experimental use.[8] His greatest difficulty, he reported, was not testing the many variations, but holding eleven variables constant while altering the conditions of the twelfth. The data were systematized, correlated, and reduced to practical form in the shape of what he called a "slide rule" which would determine the optimum combination of choices for each step in the machining process. His machinists thenceforth were required to work in accordance with instructions derived from these experimental data, rather than from their own knowledge, experience, or tradition. This was the Taylor approach in its first systematic application to a complex labor process.[9]

Chapter 6

The Habituation of the Worker to the Capitalist Mode of Production

The transformation of working humanity into a "labor force," a "factor of production," an instrument of capital, is an incessant and unending process. The condition is repugnant to the victims, whether their pay is high or low, because it violates human conditions of work; and since the workers are not destroyed as human beings but are simply utilized in inhuman ways, their critical, intelligent, conceptual faculties, no matter how deadened or diminished, always remain in some degree a threat to capital. Moreover, the capitalist mode of production is continually extended to new areas of work, including those freshly created by technological advances and the shift of capital to new industries. It is, in addition, continually being refined and perfected, so that its pressure upon the workers is unceasing. At the same time, the habituation of workers to the capitalist mode of production must be renewed with each generation, all the more so as the generations which grow up under capitalism are not formed within the matrix of work life, but are plunged into work from the outside, so to speak, after a prolonged period of adolescence during which they are held in reserve. The necessity for adjusting the worker to work in its capitalist form, for overcoming natural resistance intensified by swiftly changing technology, antagonistic social relations, and the succession of the generations, does not therefore end with the "scientific organization of labor," but becomes a permanent feature of capitalist society.

As a result, there has come into being, within the personnel and labor relations departments of corporations and in the external support organizations such as schools of industrial relations, college departments of sociology, and other academic and para-academic institutions, a complex of practical and academic disciplines devoted to the study of the worker. Shortly after Taylor, industrial psychology and industrial physiology came into existence to perfect methods of selection, training, and motivation of workers, and these were soon broadened into an attempted industrial sociology, the study of the workplace as a social system.

The cardinal feature of these various schools and the currents within them is that, unlike the scientific management movement, they do not by and large concern themselves with the organization of work, but rather with the conditions under which the worker may best be brought to cooperate in the scheme of work organized by the industrial engineer.[10] The evolving work processes of capitalist society are taken by these schools as inexorable givens, and are accepted as "necessary and inevitable" in any form of "industrial society." The problems addressed are the problems of management: dissatisfaction as expressed in high turnover rates, absenteeism, resistance to the prescribed work pace, indifference, neglect, cooperative group restrictions on output, and overt hostility to management. As it presents itself to most of the sociologists and psychologists concerned with the study of work and workers, the problem is not that of the degradation of men and women, but the difficulties raised by the reactions, conscious and unconscious, to that degradation. It is therefore not at all fortuitous that most orthodox social scientists adhere firmly, indeed desperately, to the dictum that their task is not the study of the objective conditions of work, but only of the subjective phenomena to which these give rise: the degrees of "satisfaction" and "dissatisfaction" elicited by their questionnaires.

The earliest systematic effort in this direction took place in the field of industrial psychology. Its beginnings may be traced back to the experimental psychology taught in nineteenth-century Germany, and in particular to the school of psychology at the University of Leipzig. Hugo Münsterberg, after receiving his training in Wilhelm Wundt's "laboratory" at that institution, came to the United States where, at Harvard, he was in a position to observe the development of modern management in its most vigorous and extensive forms, and it became his ambition to marry the methods of the Leipzig school to the new practice of scientific management. His *Psychology and Industrial Efficiency* (published in German in 1912, with an English version following the next year) may be called the first systematic outline of industrial psychology.[11] Like Taylor, Münsterberg disdained to conceal his views and aims:

> Our aim is to sketch the outlines of a new science which is intermediate between the modern laboratory psychology and the problems of economics: the psychological experiment is systematically to be placed at the service of commerce and industry.[12]

But what are the ends of commerce and industry? Münsterberg leaves that to others: "Economic psychotechnics may serve certain ends of commerce and industry, but whether these ends are the best ones is not a care with which the psychologist has to be burdened."[13] Having relieved his "science" of this burden, and having turned the task of setting the parameters of his investigations over to those who control "commerce and industry," he returns to this subject only when it is suggested that perhaps the point of view of the workers, who are also part of "commerce and industry," should be taken into consideration. So crass and vulgar an appeal to special interests arouses his horror, and he rejects it sternly:

> The inquiry into the possible psychological contributions to the question of reinforced achievement must not be deterred by the superficial objection that in one or another industrial concern a dismissal of wage-earners might at first result. Psychotechnics does not stand in the service of a party, but exclusively in the service of civilization.[14]

Having identified the interests of "civilization" not with the immense majority of workers but with those who manage them, he can now face without blanching the everyday effects of "scientific work design" upon the worker: "…the development of scientific management has shown clearly that the most important improvements are just those which are deduced from scientific researches, without at first giving satisfaction to the laborers themselves, until a new habit has been formed."[15] He sees the role of psychological science in industry as the selection of workers from among the pool offered on the labor market, and their acclimatization to the work routines devised by "civilization," the formation of the "new habit":

> …we select three chief purposes of business life, purposes which are important in commerce and industry and every economic endeavor. We ask how we can find the men whose mental qualities make them best fitted for the work which they have to do; secondly, under what psychological conditions we can secure the greatest and most satisfactory output of

work from every man; and finally, how we can produce most completely the influence on human minds which are desired in the interests of business.[16]

In this definition we have the aims—although rarely so flatly stated—of the subsequent schools of psychological, physiological, and social investigation of the worker and work. By and large, they have sought a model of workers and work groups which would produce the results desired by management: habituation to the terms of employment offered in the capitalist firm and satisfactory performance on that basis. These schools and theories have succeeded one another in a dazzling proliferation of approaches and theories, a proliferation which is more than anything else testimony to their failure.

The spread of industrial psychology in the United States was in the beginning largely due to the efforts of Walter Dill Scott, a psychologist at Northwestern University who took his doctorate at Leipzig and came to the new field by way of a prior career in advertising. During and after World War I, psychological testing was used by a number of major corporations (American Tobacco, National Lead, Western Electric, Loose-Wiles Biscuit, Metropolitan Life), and the first psychological consulting service for industry was established at the Carnegie Institute of Technology in 1915, where Scott assumed the first chair of applied psychology in an American academic institution. During the war such testing was conducted on a grand scale in the United States armed forces, also under Scott, and the popularity this gave to the new device encouraged its spread throughout industry after the war. In England and Germany the trend was similar, with Germany perhaps ahead of all others in the field.[17]

The premise of industrial psychology was that, using aptitude tests, it was possible to determine in advance the suitability of workers for various positions by classifying them according to degrees of "intelligence," "manual dexterity," "accident proneness," and general conformability to the "profile" desired by management. The vanity of this attempt to calibrate individuals and anticipate their behavior in the complex and antagonistic dynamics of social life was soon exposed by practice. The prolonged and exhaustive experiments conducted at the Western Electric plant on the west side of Chicago—the so-called Hawthorne experiments—during the last years of the 1920s crystallized the dissatisfaction with industrial psychology. In those experiments, a Harvard Business School team under the leadership of Elton Mayo arrived at chiefly negative conclusions— conclusions, moreover, which were remarkably similar to those with which Taylor had begun his investigations almost a half-century earlier. They learned that the performance of workers had little relation to "ability"—and in fact often bore an *inverse* relation to test scores, with those scoring best producing at lower levels and vice-versa—and that workers acted collectively to resist management work-pace standards and demands. "The belief," said Mayo, "that the behavior of an individual within the factory can be predicted before employment upon the basis of a laborious and minute examination by tests of his mechanical and other capacities is mainly, if not wholly mistaken."[18]

The chief conclusion of the Mayo school was that the workers' motivations could not be understood on a purely individual basis, and that the key to their behavior lay in the social groups of the factory. With this, the study of the habituation of workers to their work moved from the plane of psychology to that of sociology. The "human relations" approach, first of a series of behavioral sociological schools, focused on personnel counseling and on ingratiating or nonirritating styles of "face to face" supervision. But these schools have yielded little to management in the way of solid and tangible results. Moreover, the birth of the "human relations" idea coincided with the Depression of the

1930s and the massive wave of working-class revolt that culminated in the unionization of the basic industries of the United States. In the illumination cast by these events, the workplace suddenly appeared not as a system of bureaucratic formal organization on the Weberian model, nor as a system of informal group relations as in the interpretation of Mayo and his followers, but rather as a system of power, of class antagonisms. Industrial psychology and sociology have never recovered from this blow. From their confident beginnings as "sciences" devoted to discovering the springs of human behavior the better to manipulate them in the interests of management, they have broken up into a welter of confused and confusing approaches pursuing psychological, sociological, economic, mathematical, or "systems" interpretations of the realities of the workplace, with little real impact upon the management of worker or work.[19]

If the adaptation of the worker to the capitalist mode of production owes little to the efforts of practical and ideological manipulators, how is it in fact accomplished? Much of the economic and political history of the capitalist world during the last century and a half is bound up with this process of adjustment and the conflicts and revolts which attended it, and this is not the place to attempt a summary. A single illustration, that of the first comprehensive conveyor assembly line, will have to suffice as an indication that the wrenching of the workers out of their prior conditions and their adjustment to the forms of work engineered by capital is a fundamental process in which the principal roles are played not by manipulation or cajolery but by socioeconomic conditions and forces.

In 1903, when the Ford Motor Company was founded, building automobiles was a task reserved for craftsmen who had received their training in the bicycle and carriage shops of Michigan and Ohio, then the centers of those industries. "Final assembly, for example," writes Eli Chinoy, "had originally been a highly skilled job. Each car was put together in one spot by a number of all-around mechanics."[20] By 1908, when Ford launched the Model T, procedures had been changed somewhat, but the changes were slight compared with what was soon to come. The organization of assembly labor at that time is described as follows by Keith Sward:

> At Ford's and in all the other shops in Detroit, the process of putting an automobile together still revolved around the versatile mechanic, who was compelled to move about in order to do his work. Ford's assemblers were still all-around men. Their work was largely stationary, yet they had to move on to their next job on foot as soon as the car-in-the-making at their particular station had been taken the whole distance—from bare frame to finished product. To be sure, time had added some refinements. In 1908 it was no longer necessary for the assembler to leave his place of work for trips to the tool crib or the parts bin. Stock-runners had been set aside to perform this function. Nor was the Ford mechanic himself in 1908 quite the man he had been in 1903. In the intervening years the job of final assembly had been split up ever so little. In place of the jack-of-all-trades who formerly "did it all," there were now several assemblers who worked over a particular car side by side, each one responsible for a somewhat limited set of operations.[21]

The demand for the Model T was so great that special engineering talent was engaged to revise the production methods of the company. The key element of the new organization of labor was the endless conveyor chain upon which car assemblies were carried past fixed stations where men performed simple operations as they passed. This system was first put into operation for various subassemblies, beginning around the same time that the Model T was launched, and developed through the next half-dozen years until it culminated in January 1914 with the inauguration of the first endless-chain conveyor for final assembly at Ford's Highland Park plant. Within three months, the assembly time for the Model T had been reduced to one-tenth the time formerly needed, and by 1925 an organization had been created which produced almost as many cars in a single day as had been produced, early in the history of the Model T, in an entire year.

The quickening rate of production in this case depended not only upon the change in the organization of labor, but upon the control which management, at a single stroke, attained over the pace of assembly, so that it could now double and triple the rate at which operations had to be performed and thus subject its workers to an extraordinary intensity of labor. Having achieved this, Ford then moved to flatten the pay structure as a further cost-cutting measure:

> Before the advent of the assembly line, the company had made a general practice of dispensing more or less liberal bonuses in order to stimulate production and individual initiative. But the moment moving belt lines came into being, Ford did away with incentive pay. He reverted to the payment of a flat hourly rate of wages. The company had decided, said *Iron Age* in July 1913, to abandon its graduated pay scale in favor of "more strenuous supervision." Once the new wage policy had been put into effect, the run-of-the-mine Ford employe could expect no more variation in his earnings than in the operations which he was called upon to perform. His maximum pay was frozen, seemingly for good, at $2.34 per day, the rate of pay which was standard for the area.[22]

In this way the new conditions of employment that were to become characteristic of the automobile industry, and thereafter of an increasing number of industries, were established first at the Ford Motor Company. Craftsmanship gave way to a repeated detail operation, and wage rates were standardized at uniform levels. The reaction to this change was powerful, as Sward relates:

> As a consequence, the new technology at Ford's proved to be increasingly unpopular; more and more it went against the grain. And the men who were exposed to it began to rebel. They registered their dissatisfaction by walking out in droves. They could afford to pick and choose. Other jobs were plentiful in the community; they were easier to get to; they paid as well; and they were less mechanized and more to labor's liking.
>
> Ford's men had begun to desert him in large numbers as early as 1910. With the coming of the assembly line, their ranks almost literally fell apart; the company soon found it next to impossible to keep its working force intact, let alone expand it. It was apparent that the Ford Motor Co. had reached the point of owning a great factory without having enough workers to keep it humming. Ford admitted later that his startling factory innovations had ushered in the outstanding labor crisis of his career. The turnover of his working force had run, he was to write, to 380 percent for the year 1913 alone. So great was labor's distaste for the new machine system that toward the close of 1913 every time the company wanted to add 100 men to its factory personnel, it was necessary to hire 963.[23]

In this initial reaction to the assembly line we see the natural revulsion of the worker against the new kind of work. What makes it possible to see it so clearly is the fact that Ford, as a pioneer in the new mode of production, was competing with prior modes of the organization of labor which still characterized the rest of the automobile industry and other industries in the area. In this microcosm, there is an illustration of the rule that the working class is progressively subjected to the capitalist mode of production, and to the successive forms which it takes, *only as the capitalist mode of production conquers and destroys all other forms of the organization of labor, and with them, all alternatives for the working population.* As Ford, by the competitive advantage which he gained, forced the assembly line upon the rest of the automobile industry, in the same degree workers were forced to submit to it by the disappearance of other forms of work in that industry.

The crisis Ford faced was intensified by the unionization drive begun by the Industrial Workers of the World among Ford workers in the summer of 1913. Ford's response to the double threat of unionization and the flight of workers from his plants was the announcement, made with great fanfare early in 1914, of the $5.00 day. Although this dramatic increase in wages was not so strictly adhered to as Ford would have had the public believe when he launched it, it did raise pay at the Ford plant so much above the prevailing rate in the area that it solved both threats for the moment. It gave the company a large pool of labor from which to choose and at the same time opened up new possibilities for the intensification of labor within the plants, where workers were now anxious to keep their jobs. "The payment of five dollars a day for an eight-hour day," Ford was to write in his autobiography, "was one of the finest cost-cutting moves we ever made."[24]

In this move can be seen a second element in the adjustment of workers to increasingly unpopular jobs. Conceding higher relative wages for a shrinking proportion of workers in order to guarantee uninterrupted production was to become, particularly after the Second World War, a widespread feature of corporate labor policy, especially after it was adopted by union leaderships. John L. Lewis resolved upon this course of action shortly after the war: in return for encouraging the mechanization of the coal-mining industry and the reduction of employment, he insisted upon an increasing scale of compensation for the ever smaller and ever more hard-driven miners remaining in the pits. The bulk of the organized labor movement in production industries followed his lead, either openly or implicitly, in the decades thereafter. And these policies were greatly facilitated by the monopolistic structure of the industries in question. The workers who were sloughed off, or the workers who never entered manufacturing industries because of the proportional shrinkage of those industries, furnished the masses for new branches of industry at lower rates of pay.

If the petty manipulations of personnel departments and industrial psychology and sociology have not played a major role in the habituation of worker to work, therefore, this does not mean that the "adjustment" of the worker is free of manipulative elements. On the contrary, as in all of the functionings of the capitalist system, manipulation is primary and coercion is held in reserve—except that this manipulation is the product of powerful economic forces, major corporate employment and bargaining policies, and the inner workings and evolution of the system of capitalism itself, and not primarily of the clever schemes of labor relations experts. The apparent acclimatization of the worker to the new modes of production grows out of the destruction of all other ways of living, the striking of wage bargains that permit a certain enlargement of the customary bounds of subsistence for the working class, the weaving of the net of modern capitalist life that finally makes all other modes of living impossible. But beneath this apparent habituation, the hostility of workers to the degenerated forms of work which are forced upon them continues as a subterranean stream that makes its way to the surface when employment conditions permit, or when the capitalist drive for a greater intensity of labor oversteps the bounds of physical and mental capacity. It renews itself in new generations, expresses itself in the unbounded cynicism and revulsion which large numbers of workers feel about their work, and comes to the fore repeatedly as a social issue demanding solution.

Notes

1 It is important to grasp this point, because from it flows the universal application of Taylorism to work in its various forms and stages of development, regardless of the nature of the technology employed. Scientific management, says Peter F. Drucker, "was not concerned with technology. Indeed, it took tools and technologies largely as given." [See] Peter F. Drucker, "Work and Tools," in Melvin Kranzberg and William H. Davenport, eds., *Technology and Culture* (New York, 1972), pp. 192–93.

2 Frederick W. Taylor, *Shop Management*, in *Scientific Management* (New York and London), p. 30. See also Taylor's *The Principles of Scientific Management* (New York, 1967), pp. 13–14; and *Taylor's Testimony* in *Scientific Management*, p. 8.

3 *Shop Management*, pp. 32–33.

4 Ibid., pp. 34–35.

5 *The Principles of Scientific Management*, p. 52. In this respect, the later industrial sociologists took a step backward from Taylor. Rather than face the fact of a conflict of interests, they interpreted the behavior of workers in refusing to work harder and earn more piece rates as "irrational" and "noneconomic" behavior, in contrast to that of management, which has always behaved rationally. And this despite the fact that, in the observations made at the Hawthorne plant of Western Electric from which the "human relations" school emerged, the "lowest producer in the room ranked first in intelligence and third in dexterity; the highest producer in the room was seventh in dexterity and lowest in intelligence." (Elton Mayo, *The Social Problems of an Industrial Civilization* (Boston, 1945), p. 42.)

At least one economist, William M. Leiserson, has given a proper judgment on the workers' rationality in this connection: "...the same conditions that lead businessmen to curtail production when prices are falling, and to cut wages when labor efficiency is increasing, cause workers to limit output and reduce efficiency when wages are increasing...If the workers' reasoning is wrong, then business economics as it is taught by employers and the business practices of modern industry generally must be equally wrong." (William M. Leiserson, "The Economics of Restriction of Output"; quoted in Loren Baritz, *The Servants of Power* (New York, 1965), p. 100.) The Hawthorne investigators thought, and their followers still think, that the Western Electric workers were "irrational" or motivated by "group" or "social" or other "emotional" considerations in holding their output down, despite the fact that these very Hawthorne investigations were brought to an end by the Western Electric layoffs in the Great Depression of the 1930s, thus demonstrating just how rational the workers' fears were.

One of the most interesting inquiries into this subject was done in the late 1940s by a sociologist at the University of Chicago who took a job in the factory. He studied intensively eighty-four workers, and found among them only nine "rate busters," who were "social isolates" not only on the job but off; eight of the nine were Republicans while the shop was 70 percent Democratic, and all were from farm or middle-class backgrounds while the rest of the shop was predominantly working-class in family history. [See] William F. Whyte, *Men at Work* (Homewood, Ill.,), pp. 98–121; see also Whyte's *Money and Motivation* (New York, 1955), pp. 39–49.

6 Clearly, this last conclusion depends on Adam Smith's well-known principle that the division of labor is limited by the extent of the market, and Taylorism cannot become generalized in any industry or applicable in particular situations until the scale of production is adequate to support the efforts and costs involved in "rationalizing" it. It is for this reason above all that Taylorism coincides with the growth of production and its concentration in ever larger corporate units in the latter part of the nineteenth and in the twentieth centuries.

7 *The Principles of Scientific Management*, pp. 61–62.

8 Friedmann so far forgets this enormous machine-shop project at one point when he says: "This failure to appreciate the psychological factors in work is at least partially explained by the nature of the jobs to which Taylor exclusively confined his observations: handlers of pig iron, shovel-laborers, and navvies." (Georges Friedmann, *Industrial Society* (Glencoe, Ill., 1964) p. 63.) He was led to this error by his marked tendency to side with the psychological and sociological schools of "human relations" and work adjustment which came after Taylor, and which he always attempts to counterpose

to Taylorism, although, as we have pointed out, they operate on different levels. In general, Friedmann, with all his knowledge of work processes, suffers from a confusion of viewpoints, writing sometimes as a socialist concerned about the trends in capitalist work organization, but more often as though the various forms of capitalist management and personnel administration represent scrupulous efforts to find a universal answer to problems of work.

9   *The Principles of Scientific Management*, p. 111.

10   Personnel management, although thought of as that part of the corporate structure concerned with the worker, is usually given short shrift when a reorganization of actual work is under way. In a recent book, two prominent industrial engineers accord to almost every management level a greater role in the change in work methods than the role which they prescribe for the personnel department. They say flatly, in their recommendations for an overall "operations improvement program": "In the beginning, in most organizations, the personnel director will have no active role in the conduct of an operations improvement program." They restrict the place of this official to his value "as a sounding board for employee reactions," and to orienting new employees to the program and to answering questions and complaints. [See] Bruce Payne and David D. Swett, *Office Operations Improvement* (New York, 1967), pp. 41–42. As with personnel directors, so also with their academic counterparts in labor sociology. Charles Rumford Walker, one of the more experienced and sophisticated, as well as more "humane," of these stresses in a section of one of his papers devoted to the "Strategic Role of the Engineer," in which he recognizes that the direction of the evolution of work is determined by "managers and engineers, as architects of the future," while the role of the sociologists is that of trying to importune, press upon, and persuade the real designers of the work process to take into account the "neglected human dimension" in order to reduce discontent and increase productivity, to "seize the opportunity" offered by swift technological change, etc. [See] National Commission on Technology, Automation, and Economic Progress, *The Employment Impact of Technological Change*, Appendix Volume II, *Technology and the American Economy* (Washington, D.C., 1966), pp. 288–315, esp. section IV.

11   Loren Baritz, *The Servants of Power: A History of the Use of Social Science in American Industry* (Middletown, Conn., 1960; paperback ed., New York, 1965), pp. 26–36.

12   Hugo Münsterberg, *Psychology and Industrial Efficiency* (Boston and New York, 1913), p. 3.

13   Ibid., p. 19.

14   Ibid., p. 144.

15   Ibid., p. 178.

16   Ibid., pp. 23–24.

17   A brief history of industrial psychology is supplied in Baritz, *The Servants of Power*.

18   Quoted ibid., p. 95.

19   The actual place of industrial psychology and sociology in corporate policies was succinctly expressed by three specialists in industrial engineering at the end of an article called "Current Job Design Criteria": "It can be concluded that company policies and practices [this refers to the companies studied in the article] in job design are inconsistent with programs and policies in human relations and personnel administration. On the one hand, specific steps are taken to minimize the contribution of the individual, and on the other hand he is propagandized about his importance and value to the organization." [See] Louis E. Davis, Ralph R. Canter, and John Hoffman, "Current Job Design Criteria," *Journal of Industrial Engineering*, vol. 6, no. 2 (1955); reprinted in Louis E. Davis and James C. Taylor, eds., *Design of Jobs* (London, 1972), p. 81. But this is more than an "inconsistency," since job design represents *reality* while personnel administration represents only *mythology*. From the point of view of the corporation, there is no inconsistency, since the latter represents a manipulation to habituate the worker to the former.

20   Eli Chinoy, "Manning the Machine—The Assembly-Line Worker," in Peter L. Berger, ed., *The Human Shape of Work: Studies in the Sociology of Occupations* (New York, 1964), p. 53.

21   Keith Sward, *The Legend of Henry Ford* (New York and Toronto, 1948), p. 32.

22   Ibid., p. 48.

23   Ibid., pp. 48–49.

24   Ibid., p. 56.

CHAPTER 30

Labor and Franklin Delano Roosevelt's New Dream

Benjamin Kline Hunnicutt

Preface

Beginning in the early nineteenth century and continuing for over a hundred years, working hours in America were gradually reduced—cut in half according to most accounts—and this is true for most modern industrial nations. Few other economic or social movements lasted as long or involved as many people. Few developments excited the imaginations of so many or encouraged such hope for the future. Counted as one of the great blessings of technology, the process lasted so long that observers during the first decades of the twentieth century agreed that it was bound to continue.

No one predicted that it was going to end. On the contrary, prominent figures such as John Maynard Keynes, Julian Huxley, and Dorothy Canfield Fisher regularly predicted that, well before the twentieth century ended, a Golden Age of Leisure would arrive, when no one would have to work more than two hours a day. Humans seemed to be on the verge of meeting the ancient economic challenge. Able to ensure everyone the necessities of life at last, technology would soon present humanity with what Keynes, the best-known economist of the century, called its "greatest challenge":

> Thus for the first time since his creation Man will be faced with his real, his permanent problem—how to use his freedom from pressing economic cares, how to occupy the leisure, which science and compound interest have won for him, to live wisely and agreeably and well.[1]

However, the shorter-hour process stopped after the Great Depression. Since then we have had little or no decrease in our work. Abandoning hope for the abundant life Keynes

Original publication details: "Labor and Franklin Delano Roosevelt's New Dream," by Benjamin Kline Hunnicutt. From *Free Time: The Forgotten American Dream.* Temple University Press. © 2013 Temple University. pp. vii–x; 70–76; 109–110; 115–121; 148–150; 153–154.

so confidently predicted for us (his grandchildren), we moderns for some reason no longer expect work to ever become a subordinate part of life. We no longer look forward to gradually getting enough material goods and services so that we are able to turn our main attention to the business of living free. Unlike previous generations, we no longer worry about leisure's challenge.

What happened?

Instead of Keynes's leisure "problem," we began to face a time famine. The statistics were harder and harder to ignore. The average American was working about a month more a year in 1991 than in the mid-1970s; the trend has accelerated since the early 1990s. Now we average *five* weeks more (199 hours) than in 1973.[5]

Since the mid-1970s, we have been working longer and longer each year, about half a percentage point more from year to year—the exact reverse of what happened during the nineteenth and early twentieth centuries.[6] Moreover, because more women have entered the work force, more of us are working as a percentage of the total population. However, housework has neither magically disappeared nor been completely absorbed by the marketplace. Men have shouldered little of the extra burden. As Arlie Hochschild and Anne Machung pointed out, women routinely face a "second shift" when they get home from their paid job.[7]

Now it is commonplace for both spouses to work full time and for both to shortchange parts of their lives not connected to their paid jobs. Television talk-show hosts and their guests regularly comment on the strange fact that today it takes two parents working full time to support a family, whereas previous generations were able to survive, perhaps even thrive during the 1950s and 1960s, on one salary.

Groups in addition to women are hard pressed. The salaried middle classes, for example, have seen their yearly working hours increase by 660 hours—20 percent more than twenty-five years ago. *U.S. News and World Report* concluded in 2003 that nearly 40 percent of this group worked more than fifty hours a week.[8] Within a few years most of us will likely be working sixty hours a week if things continue the way they have since the 1980s.[9]

The pride that our nation once took in being the world leader in freeing its citizens from constant, urgent need is now but a dim memory, preserved in odd places such as bumper stickers that remind us that our labor unions represent "the people that gave us the weekend." The most recent studies from the Bureau of Labor Statistics show that workers in the United States work longer hours than those of other modern industrial nations, with the exception of South Korea.[10]

Why did the century-long shorter-hours movement end and then go in reverse? Why do the confident predictions that we would be working less than ten hours a *week* by now, made by respected, thoughtful men and women throughout the first half of the twentieth century, appear not only wrong but a bit harebrained by those of us working ten hours a *day*? Why have complaints about overwork and the frantic pace of life replaced the old debates about how best to use our coming abundant leisure? What happened to the widespread expectation that we would soon solve the economic problem and, finding it increasingly easy to make a living, get on with the much more important business of living? What happened to the seemingly irresistible movement to steadily reduce hours of labor—a movement that was once centrally important to this nation and considered by many Americans to be the essence of progress and highest expression of liberty?

4

The Eight-Hour Day

Labor from the Civil War to the 1920s

Continuing to be inspired by their vision of "the reduction of human labor to its lowest terms," American workingmen and workingwomen renewed their efforts to win the eight-hour day after the Civil War, making significant advances.[1] As Karl Marx famously observed, "The first fruit of the Civil War was the eight-hours' agitation that ran with the seven-leagued boots of the locomotive from the Atlantic to the Pacific, from New England to California."[2]

Just as it had been during the origins of the labor movement, the shorter-hours movement continued as a grassroots effort. Middle-class reformers and observers lent their support and, stirred by what workers were doing, speculated about what mechanization and the new free time might mean for America's future. Some also helped build public infrastructure to accommodate the new freedom. But the impetus continued to come from workers. They remained far ahead of middle-class reformers and moralists in imagining life in which work was put in its proper place, subordinate to the more important business of living. Daniel Rodgers observed of the late nineteenth century:

> Long in advance of the hesitant middle-class recognition of the claims of leisure, workers dreamed of a workday short enough to push labor out of the center of their lives. …How much of a man's life should work consume? No work related question was as important as this.[3]

Having consistently found strong, frequently "overwhelming" support for shorter hours in New England, researchers from the Massachusetts Bureau of Statistics of Labor concluded in 1889, "The predominant question of interest to manual workers is, at present, the shortening of the working day."[4] Labor leaders seized on the popularity of the eight-hour day to recruit new members and court politicians, reiterating that eight hours was only one step along the way.[5] Continuing laborites' identification of shorter hours with liberty, Samuel Gompers declared, "Freedom is synonymous with the hours for leisure," later adding, "Eight hours today, fewer tomorrow."[6] Bill Haywood, leader of the Industrial Workers of the World, echoed, "The less work the better."[7]

Through all the labor leaders' intricate justifications and elaborate theorizing about the economy, all the bourgeois moralizing and speculating, all the politicians' pontificating, worker motives shine clearly: they fought for shorter hours because they preferred their free time to the work created by laissez-faire capitalism and took back their time when they could afford to do so. What Daniel Rodgers called "the obvious relief from toil" is the best explanation for the century of shorter hours.[10]

Here also is the essence, the bedrock of workers' "radicalism" and class identity in America. As David Montgomery explained, "[Herbert] Gutman showed that the basic thrust of the 19th century workers' struggles entailed a rejection of economic man."[11] Nowhere is this "basic thrust" more in evidence or more important than in the struggle for the "progressive shortening of the hours of labor." Acting on the simple, powerful urge to escape the confines of modern jobs, workers choose free time for more than a century, often sacrificing wages, hoping for and often finding better things to do than be part of the "selfish system." Shorter hours not only represented the nonpecuniary, cultural motives that historians have found to be of vital importance for understanding American workers, but leisure provided the necessary means for their expression as well as for an escape from capitalism.[12]

In the autumn of 1880, the Massachusetts Bureau of Statistics of Labor surveyed textile and paper mills in Maine, New Hampshire, Massachusetts, Rhode Island, Connecticut, and New York. After "quite thoroughly" canvassing 246 manufacturing establishments and asking employees about the possibility of reducing work hours, the bureau analyzed 791 individual questionnaires, constructing frequency tables and recording pages of truncated quotes from the workers.

The listing of possible uses of leisure, ranging from everyday pleasures to lofty ones, creates a novel-like, stream-of-consciousness effect. In response to the question "What disposition would be made of leisure hours?" workers replied: "sit down and have a smoke"; "sit round the store"; "[have] more time at home"; "[take] an hour after dinner…[to] educate themselves, read the paper"; "work around the house, and improve its appearance"; "educate my children and increas[e] pleasures at home"; "go out riding with my friends"; "dress up and go visiting"; "play[] ball…[or] walk about"; "garden"; "learn to play in a band"; "[enjoy] out-door exercise and evening amusements"; "[re] store my mind"; "[seek] mental improvement."[14]

Over 85 percent of those surveyed thought that they and others would "make good use" of the additional leisure. Yet most were uncertain about specifics, saying things like "Breath[e] the pure air, and look about me to see what's going on"; "It would not be hard to find a good use for more leisure time"; "They would find use for it [leisure]"; and "Go down the street, look about me."[15] Similar to the Parisian laborers Jacques Rancière described, American workers in New England were continuing to live into their new leisure after the Civil War, experimenting with new possibilities in a kind of freedom never before available to the majority of human beings.

A New Work Ethic Emerges as the Spirit of Capitalism

Businessmen, moralists, and middle-class professionals understood the threat that worker leisure represented to the future of industrial capitalism as well as to middle-class status and morality. Specifically, they recognized the threat to the emerging *secular* "work ethic"—an ethic that Max Weber called "the spirit of capitalism," which was founded on the consumerist needs of the modern economy rather than on sixteenth-century Protestant theology.[20] Middle-class moralists and businesspeople, fearing that the nation was facing a "crisis of work," represented by labor's demand for the eight-hour day, sought to redefine and promote "full-time" jobs. They began trying to convince the nation of the glory of labor that was its own reward and that hard work, in and of itself, was the organizing principle of the individual's life and the defining virtue of the nation.[21] Thus began a process in which traditional religious worldviews and republican virtue were eclipsed by the ascendancy of a new, work-based view of the world: "the spirit of capitalism."

Just as they had done before the Civil War, workers continued to resist this new secular ethic. Well into the twentieth century, laborites persistently critiqued it and offered an alternative—an alternative implicit in "the progressive shortening of the hours of labor." Beginning with the ten-hour system, laborites repeatedly made their alternative explicit, arguing that work's perfection and true glory depended on its eventual subordination—on the shifting of life's balance from work and the market to free time.

Certainly, working-class leisure offended other parts of middle-class morality as well. Seeking to control the rowdy, indecorous behavior and sexual looseness they observed around them and intent on uplifting the leisure of masses to a standard of behavior they found acceptable, reformers set about building properly monitored public spaces: parks, beaches, playgrounds, resorts, community centers, and libraries. However, they were only marginally successful in Americanizing immigrants and uplifting the masses to the kinds of recreations they felt proper. More often they had to compromise and work with the public they were attempting to serve. More importantly, they were even less successful in convincing workers of the "glory of work"—the modern bourgeois ethic and worldview that would outlive middle-class "uplift" and Victorian squeamishness to become the dominant morality of the dominant classes by the late twentieth century.

Saloons, Dance Halls, Vaudeville, Movies

Typically, workers, careful with the little free time they had, were not overly interested in the kinds of wholesome recreations urban reformers were offering. More frequently, they found commercial facilities more to their liking. Entrepreneurs, recognizing the opportunity leisure represented, accommodated them with saloons, a favorite with older workingmen; dance halls, attractive to young women and men; and new places of amusement. Coney Island, vaudeville, nickelodeons, professional sports, and the movies began to compete for the workers' free time and extra cash.

However, the commercial parts of these establishments, the things that were ostensibly for sale (liquor, concessions, rides, spectacles), were not as socially important as the venues that were made available. The price of admission often included opportunities to find companionship, build friendships, tell stories and jokes (Mikhail Bakhtin's "festive laughter" was a hallmark of the turn-of-the-century saloon), display the latest fashion, argue and fight, and flirt and experiment with sexual boundaries and gender roles.[22] Commercial recreation, or "commercialized leisure," was a mix of commerce and leisure—of product and services together with time and occasion, with the latter often more valued than the former.[23] Indeed, this is one of the important discoveries of recent historical scholarship—that commercial recreation and consumerism were important parts of American culture in the twentieth century precisely because of their nonpecuniary content and cultural, extraeconomic function.

Mixing leisure with commerce, new establishments such as the café, dance hall, and saloon flourished at the turn of the twentieth century by offering places where, as Bakhtin observed of the Rabelaisian festival, "the people...organized in their own way, the way of the people...outside of and *contrary* to all existing forms of coercive socioeconomic and political organization."[24] Historians such as Lizabeth Cohen, Vicki Ruiz, and George Sanchez have confirmed that commercial amusements provided the places and new consumer products the accoutrements needed to express and extend ethnic cultures as well as maintain working-class identity.[25]

Just as the Lowell "mill girls" conceived and began to construct a convivial ten-hour system as an alternative to capitalism's "selfish system," workers in Worchester, Massachusetts, and other American cities began to build congenial infrastructures *contrary* to prevailing "market exchange mentality"[26] after the Civil War and did so, ironically, in the very midst of entrepreneurs' successful efforts to commodify their new leisure. Roy Rosenzweig concluded:

> The saloon was actually a "democracy" of sorts—an *internal* democracy where all who could safely enter received equal treatment and respect. An ethic of mutuality and reciprocity that differed from the market exchange mentality of the dominant society prevailed within the barroom. ...
>
> [The saloon provided] a space in which immigrants could preserve an alternative, reciprocal value system.[27]

Similarly, Kathy Peiss discovered that some turn-of-the-century New York women found a degree of personal autonomy by taking active part in commercial amusements available after work. Even though most commercial recreation continued to be divided along gender, as well as racial and ethnic, lines, in such places as dance halls and amusements parks women began to challenge "the boundaries of domesticity and female self-sacrifice," finding new ways to express themselves and relate to others. Commercial recreation also helped build communities. Entrepreneurs recruited chaperones from the neighborhoods to go on excursions and monitor dances they organized. Vaudeville and the movies attracted men and women, young and old, "decisively breaking down the segmentation of working-class recreation."[28] Agreeing with Rosenzweig, Peiss concluded that "working-class leisure...offered a refuge from the dominant value system of competitive individualism," adding that "among working women, leisure came to be seen as a separate sphere of life to be consciously protected."[29]

Randy McBee agreed that young immigrant women and men at the turn of the century found a degree of freedom from family supervision and community strictures in the popular dance halls of the era. Taking delight in their youth and bodies, they pushed against heterosexual boundaries and norms, beginning a vital process of reconfiguring gender roles and relations.[30] Nan Enstad concluded that, at the turn of the century,

> working women incorporated fashion, fiction, and film products into their daily lives. The meanings of the particular products emerged not simply from the objects themselves, but from those *social practices* that gave them currency and shared value among working women...working women embraced dime novels, fashion, and film products and used them to create distinctive and pleasurable *social practices* and to enact identities as ladies.[31]

Angela McRobbie concluded, "Mass-produced narratives and fashion can allow women to actively create leisure and personal spaces that are female-centered, and are locations for developing positive identities. ...Women are not...passive consumers."[32] Together with Worchester's saloons, New York's dance halls and amusement parks became the settings and "fashion, fiction, and film" the accoutrements for ordinary people to begin to practice and develop what Rosenzweig called an "ethic of mutuality and reciprocity that differed from the market exchange mentality...an alternative, reciprocal value system."

6

Labor and Franklin Delano Roosevelt's New Dream

Up until the beginning of World War II, organized labor and America's workingmen and workingwomen struggled to reduce their working hours. Even after the war and through the 1960s, labor pressed for the reform, continuing to fuel widespread expectations that an age of leisure would soon be a reality. Workers held fast to their traditional understanding that industrial progress meant higher wages and shorter hours. The Great Depression intensified speculation that the age of leisure was fast approaching.

The reasons given for shorter hours remained constant, with minor variations. In the place of British tyranny or Southern slavery, the image of the industrial robot came to symbolize the workers' plight. Even though progress had been made in reducing work time, the remaining hours were seen to be increasingly stressful. Modern machines and management continued to purge jobs of their nonproductive elements. Stress mingled with boredom in jobs that were so closely supervised that simple conversation was difficult; labor leaders and their supporters continued to complain of devitalized jobs.

Certainly, workers shared the widespread interest in improving jobs and making the workplace as pleasant as possible. Nevertheless, through mid-century, workers and labor leaders continued to see work's perfection in the "progressive shortening of the hours of labor," still resisting what Hannah Arendt called the "modern glorification of labor."[1]

William Green, president of the American Federation of Labor during the second quarter of the twentieth century, summed up labor's position. Arguing that the "general mechanizing process" of industry threatened to overwhelm "our social and human values" and merge "the lives of workers...with the machine until they, too, become mechanical," Green maintained that "there must be a progressive shortening of the hours of labor...to safeguard our human nature...and thereby [lay] the foundation...for the higher development of spiritual and intellectual powers."[3]

With the Lowell mill women, Fannia Cohn, and generations of labor leaders who preceded him, Green predicted the "the dawn of a new era—leisure for all," a "revolution of living." "The leisured proletariat" was gaining access to "good music, the fine arts, literature, travel, and beauty in all guises." In such "cultural use of leisure...workers find themselves...sharing in the common life of the community" and becoming "heirs of knowledge and culture of past generations." The opportunities that work used to offer, such as craftsmanship, creativity, and purpose and meaning, were being recovered in freely chosen leisure activities; the family and community were being restored and reinvigorated.[4]

Green's agenda was in keeping with the resolution passed in 1926 by the Forty-Sixth Annual Meeting of the AFL:

> Whereas under present methods of modern machine industry the workers are continually subject to the strain of mechanized processes which sap their vitality, and;
> Whereas if compelled to work for long hours under modern processes of production, the vitality, health, and very life of workers are put in serious jeopardy;
> *Resolved*, that this convention place itself on record as favoring a progressive shortening of the hours of labor and the days per week and that the Executive Council be requested to inaugurate a campaign of education and organization to that end.[5]

The coming of the Great Depression seemed to confirm labor's claim that both higher wages and shorter hours were vital to the health of the economy. To labor spokespersons it was obvious that markets were glutted because wages had not kept up with productivity and hours had not reduced fast enough to stimulate adequate demand. Overproduction and massive unemployment were the results. Henry Ford agreed with leaders of the AFL that the Depression proved that fewer working hours, in one form or another, were an inevitable part of economic growth—free time was bound to come; the only choice was unemployment or leisure.[28]

Labor proposed that the most practical and effective recovery measure the nation could take would be to shorten the hours of labor immediately. This would "take up some of the slack," drawing down the labor supply, which was obviously far in excess of immediate demand. Once the labor supply had equalized with existing demand, workers would became more confident that their jobs were secure. Finding more leisure at their disposal as well, they would begin to spend more. As economic activity quickened, workers could then demand better wages, thus stimulating the economy and leading the nation out of the Depression.

Shorter hours acted as a governor on the economy, discouraging runaway speculation and stimulating demand, thus counterbalancing the tendency of technology to replace workers with machines faster than it created new jobs. According to labor, during the 1920s speculation went unchecked—unsustainable economic growth was not slowed by sufficient reductions in working hours. Massive unemployment, as high as 25 percent, was the result. Free time, ordinarily trickling out of the economy in the form of shorter hours, had then burst forth in the tragic form of unemployment when demand slackened and inventories built.[29] To reestablish full employment, existing work needed to be redistributed. Sustainable economic growth could then resume and the historical equilibrium of progressively higher wages and shorter hours reestablished. The first response to the unemployment that defined the Great Depression was labor's call for sharing the work.[30]

Because of the national work-sharing movement, the expectation that leisure would continue to increase grew during the early years of the Depression. The expectation was further strengthened when the AFL's Executive Council drafted a bill to limit working hours to thirty a week (with severe overtime penalties attached). The bill was introduced to Congress by Senator Hugo Black of Alabama and Representative William P. Connery Jr. of Massachusetts. Initially, Roosevelt appeared to support both this legislative approach and Hoover's initiatives.[36]

In the early days of 1933 when Roosevelt was preparing to take office and the Black-Connery bill was gaining support in Congress, he and some of his advisors met with a group of prominent businessmen and industrialists in the nation's capital. Roosevelt offered to relax some antitrust regulations in exchange for their agreeing to a national six-hour-day, five-day workweek put into operation through the trade associations—thus giving Hoover's "voluntaristic system" more time to work.[37] The trust busters in the Senate, such as George Norris from Nebraska, were reportedly willing to go along with the deal.[38]

However, Roosevelt also supported labor's bill, agreeing that a mandatory thirty-hour week would provide new jobs and stabilize the economy. Roosevelt, Secretary of Labor Frances Perkins, and Democrats in Congress began to see their efforts as an improved version of Hoover's voluntaristic system, maintaining that nationwide regulation of working hours would be more effective and reliable. Moreover, legislated work sharing topped labor's political agenda, and Democrats were interested in securing their political base.[39]

A month after Roosevelt took office, the Senate passed the Black-Connery bill, prompting Secretary of Labor Frances Perkins to go before the House Labor Committee to add the administration's imprimatur to the thirty-hour legislation. After her appearance she told reporters that the committee and administration were in substantial agreement and that the legislators were ready to "clear the way for passage" of Black-Connery. Following Perkins's appearance on April 13, newspapers throughout the nation, quoting

William Green as well as Perkins, reported that the House of Representatives would pass the bill and the president would sign it before the end of April. The first nationally circulated issue of *Newsweek*, dated April 15, 1933, had for its front cover, in bold headlines, the news that the thirty-hour workweek would soon be the law of the land.[40]

Roosevelt Responds

Around the time of Perkins's meeting with the House Labor Committee, some of Roosevelt's advisors began to actively oppose work sharing—both those who favored the Republican voluntary variety and those who favored the Democratic legislative approach. Led by Rexford Tugwell and Harry Hopkins, head of the Federal Emergency Relief Administration, Roosevelt's closest advisors convinced him to mount a holding action— delaying Black-Connery, offering to give labor everything else it wanted legislatively in exchange for the holdup, buying time to come up with an alternative unemployment strategy. Subsequently and through the early days of 1935, Roosevelt's First New Deal was defined, so far as unemployment was concerned, by his trying to placate labor for his delaying passage of Black-Connery.[41]

It is far from clear what motivated Roosevelt's advisors. Certainly, business leaders were putting pressure on Roosevelt to hold Black-Connery at bay and give their voluntary efforts time to work. Hugh S. Johnson reported that business "would turn backhand somersaults against the thirty hour week."[42]

Even though there was some talk of countercyclical government spending to stimulate the economy circulating through Roosevelt's White House from the beginning, no specific unemployment strategy or guiding economic theory emerged as a clear winner and alternative to Black-Connery before 1935. Certainly, no stimulus-spending proposal had firm political support—work sharing was the only politically viable game in town. As the administration floundered, supporting the Wagner bill (known as the National Labor Relations Act when passed)[43] to appease labor and launching the National Recovery Administration (NRA) to regulate and stabilize industry, organized labor's militancy in support of Black-Connery mounted. Just before the congressional elections of 1934, the AFL, adopting a strategy being used by the Comintern Popular Front in Europe, threatened to call a national strike if the bill was not passed. As 1935 began, political support for the bill seemed insurmountable.[44]

"Salvation by Work": Roosevelt's New American Dream of Full-Time, Full Employment

In 1935 Roosevelt helped change the direction of American history. He and his administration committed the federal government to the emerging belief that progress was perpetual economic growth and Full-Time, Full Employment—the basic tenets of the new economic gospel of consumption.[45] According to the new vision, progress would no longer be understood as higher wages and shorter hours but as a constantly improving material standard of living with "full-time" (newly defined as a forty-hour week) jobs for all, supported by new government programs and policies. Roosevelt committed government to do whatever it would take to create enough new work in the public and private sectors of the economy to replace the work taken by new technology. Government would also bridge the gap created by the tendency for economic demand to lag behind increases in productivity by developing countercyclical as well as long-term spending strategies. Labor's view that shorter work hours stimulated demand and helped stabilize the economy, allowing for sustainable growth, was discarded.[46]

The federal government began to underwrite the new vision with stimulus spending, budget deficits, and liberal treasury policies. Whenever the private sector failed to generate enough work for everyone to have a "full-time" job, something it had proved repeatedly prone to, the government would step in as the employer of last resort. Identifying new social "needs," "agendas," and "crises" and inspiring national projects, or "investments in the future" (such the Tennessee Valley Authority, Hoover Dam, National Aeronautics and Space Administration, and what would become perpetual military mobilization), the federal government set about creating and funding new jobs to meet new, politically defined purposes and necessities.[47]

From 1935 until the beginning of World War II, Roosevelt put his and the business world's new dream into operation. Leon Keyserling remembered that Roosevelt began his administration with no economic strategy in mind. Consequently, the programs and policies of the "first New Deal" were "highly experimental, improvised and inconsistent." Keyserling wrote that it was the "desire to get rid of the Black bill" that prompted the administration to introduce such things as the Public Works Administration and National Recovery Administration (NRA), "to put in something to satisfy labor."[48] This same point was made by other notables in Roosevelt's administration, among them Raymond Moley and Rexford Tugwell, who concluded, "One of the reasons why NRA was sponsored by Roosevelt, and why the act was passed...was the threat of a thirty-hour law being pushed by Senator Hugo Black. It was organized labor's conception of the way to relieve unemployment."[49]

In the share-the-work issue and Black-Connery, Roosevelt and his advisors found a foil, a contrasting and coherent background of opposition that set his inchoate views in bright relief and helped disclose specific policy alternatives, which taken together revealed a guiding philosophy, what Robert Hutchins, president of the University of Chicago, would later identify as "Salvation by Work."[50] Roosevelt's new vision was simply the opposite of the old American dream—perpetual economic growth and more work instead of abundance and the opening of Higher Progress.[51] Instead of opting for expanding the realm of freedom and facing the autotelic challenge that generations of Americans, beginning with Jonathan Edwards, had struggled with, Roosevelt, and then the nation, chose the perpetual creation of needs and eternal expansion of necessity, accepting the new, daunting challenge to create sufficient work for all to have "full-time" jobs, forevermore.

One of the administration's most successful rhetorical strategies was to redefine work sharing as "sharing the poverty" or "wasting the nation's wealth." Hugh Johnson, struggling with wage and price controls, insisted that hourly wages were "the multiplier" and hours "the multiplicand" and reasoned that hours could not be reduced without impoverishing the nation.[52] With such rhetoric and new work-creating policies and programs, Roosevelt helped establish the forty-hour workweek as the enduring standard for full employment that has become "almost sacrosanct."[53] Before 1935 full employment was a sliding scale calibrated in terms of a workweek that declined from year to year. Since Roosevelt's administration, workweeks of less than forty hours have been widely understood as the loss of potential wealth and are still counted by the Conference Board as one of the nation's negative leading economic indicators.

In 1934 the Department of Commerce published its first estimates of the nation's economic health for 1929–1932. Ignoring Paul Douglas's and other economists' observations that the wealth represented by increased productivity could be spent either as shorter hours or higher wages, the department focused exclusively on what Douglas called "higher material standard of living," effectively redefining increases in leisure as lost wealth in subsequent measurements of gross national product and then gross domestic product.[54]

A similar rhetorical ploy was used in the Treasury Department by the Federal Reserve Board. Led by Marriner S. Eccles and his personal assistant, Lauchlin Bernard Currie, the Federal Reserve Board justified the taking on of substantial government debt and lowering of interest rates by arguing that these measures would help "reemploy the idleness." Instead of simply inflating the currency (the conventional view), in a period of unemployment new debt loads and low interest rates would help create new jobs. New products and services would be produced by the new work, backing the banks' paper promises. When unemployment improved, inflation threatened, and speculation escalated, then interest rates could be increased to act as a governor on unsustainable growth—hence the shorter-hour governor could be safely discarded.[55]

The events of the Second New Deal that logically followed Roosevelt's new vision are now commonplace in standard textbooks: new Treasury policies, public works, Social Security, and preparations for the coming of the war. In 1938 Roosevelt was finally able to defeat work sharing, co-opting Black-Connery with his own bill, the Fair Labor Standards Act (FLSA). Labor held out for work sharing as long as possible but at last, outmaneuvered politically by Roosevelt, fell reluctantly in line to support FLSA. Labor also adopted FDR's new American dream for the duration because the clear national purpose, winning the war, became the national priority in the closing years of the decade, far outweighing labor's claims.[56]

8

Labor Turns from Shorter Hours to Full-Time, Full Employment

After World War II, labor renewed the call for shorter hours. Using familiar arguments, some of which were over a hundred years old, laborites called for reducing weekly work hours to below forty to combat unemployment, create jobs, promote health and safety, and stimulate economic demand to make sustainable growth possible. Briefly, labor leaders challenged FDR's dream of "full employment" at forty hours a week (Full-Time, Full Employment) returning to labor's original vision of Higher Progress. The unions presented shorter hours and higher wages yet again as the roadmap for America's future.

Throughout the war, the American Federation of Labor (AFL) had reaffirmed its commitment to the thirty-hour week as its "ultimate objective" explaining that the only justified delay was winning the war.[1] As the war was drawing to a close, and with the prospect of depression returning when America's soldiers reentered the labor force, the AFL in its 1944 convention called once again for a legislated thirty-hour workweek—a call echoed throughout the nation by local union affiliates.[2] William Green repeated his claim that thirty hours was "an economic necessity…the only practical way" to avoid the return of chronic unemployment.[3] The AFL weekly news service concluded in 1946, "The 40-hour week, once labor's proudest boast, is doomed to be discarded within the foreseeable future. The 30-hour week is bound to come, opening up new opportunities for employment, and a fuller life for the working masses."[4]

As labor resumed the struggle for progressively shorter hours, President Truman and Congress reiterated Roosevelt's vision of Full-Time, Full Employment. As it was originally presented, the Full Employment Act of 1946 came close to making compensatory (countercyclical, or stimulus) spending a federal mandate and a forty-hour-week job a new individual right—enshrining Roosevelt's dream in law.[5] Truman also adopted FDR's wartime rhetoric, arguing that the newly forming Cold War and the beginning of permanent military mobilization trumped labor's call for work reductions—Eisenhower and others had linked France's poor showing during the war to its short workweek.[6]

However, as amended, the bill became more of a series of guidelines, establishing the Council of Economic Advisors and requiring the president to submit an annual report on the economy. Congress also directed the president to predict unemployment rates and take steps to promote "full employment."[7] Subsequently, the political rhetoric of jobs, jobs, jobs, as well as governmental policies and research about unemployment, with few exceptions has assumed the forty-hour week as the standard, branding anything less part-time employment.

Most exceptions occurred when labor leaders tried to reintroduce shorter hours into the national debates about unemployment after the war. Just as they had done during the Depression, laborites challenged the theory that economic growth, on its own, would sustain Roosevelt's Full-Time, Full Employment, repeatedly warning that chronic levels of high unemployment (above 5 percent) and extreme market cycles would plague the economy without the shorter-hours governor and that a national full-employment strategy had to contain a flexible definition of full-time jobs. More importantly, labor also continued to maintain that shorter hours were a "part of general national progress," and as Samuel Gompers had observed early in the century, "freedom is synonymous with the hours for leisure."[8] A resolution passed in 1959 by the American Federation of Labor–Congress of Industrial Organizations (AFL-CIO) Executive Council provides a representative example:

> [Whereas] the time has come for wide-scale reduction in hours of work so that more people may be employed[:]
>
> ...[T]here is persistent unemployment of 5 percent or more. ...
>
> ...[T]echnological change and the accompanying increasing productivity are gaining momentum. ...
>
> Unless some of the benefits of the accelerating rate of technical advance are taken in the form of shortening of time at work...unemployment will mount steadily. Technological progress is making shorter hours not only possible but essential. ...
>
> Today...there is...a general recognition that the present 8-hour day and 40-hour week...should and will be reduced as part of general national progress. ...
>
> ...[T]he plain fact is that other ways [of combating unemployment]...are not doing the job. ...
>
> ...[W]ithout a reduction in hours as a key element in an anti-unemployment program, the other measures...are not adequate...
>
> *Resolved,* That shorter hours of work must be attained as a vital means of maintaining Jobs, promoting the consumption of goods and converting technical progress into desirable increased employment rather than into increased unemployment. Our economy should and can support concurrently both shorter hours and production of additional goods and services.
>
> We call upon Congress to take as rapidly as possible the steps needed to amend the Fair Labor Standards Act to provide for a 7-hour day and a 35-hour week.[9]

Up until the mid-1950s, labor made some gains in reducing work hours in some industries. Compared to the advances made before Roosevelt's new vision gained ascendancy, however, progress was slow. Workers in the printing trades, together with some textile, telephone, mine, rubber, rail, and maritime workers, were able to reduce their hours below forty a week or mounted serious campaigns to do so. After the war, Kellogg's workers in Battle Creek, Michigan, voted more than three to one to return to six hours; Goodyear workers in Akron, Ohio, struck to reestablish their six-hour day. The International Ladies Garment Workers' Union (ILGWU) continued its leadership, winning a thirty-five-hour week by the mid-1950s. Led by Harry Van Arsdale, Manhattan's Local 3 of the International Brotherhood of Electrical Workers (IBEW) held labor's salient for a while, striking for and winning a twenty-five-hour workweek in 1962.

Workers who worked less than forty hours before 1956 were not able to hold what they had won. Ronald Edsforth points out that, after the abortive rank-and-file auto worker initiative of the 1950s and early 1960s. "UAW leaders ha[d] not renewed the labor movement's historic struggle for work time reform."[24] That labor's progress was met with fierce opposition was hardly new. What was new was the failure of labor's leadership to adequately support and actively extend the shorter-hours salient made before 1956. Also new was the failure of labor's traditional allies to lend their full support. Instead of following the examples of middle-class moralists and reformers who for over two centuries had contributed inspiring visions of what increasing leisure presaged, former supporters of shorter hours and Higher Progress such as the sociologist David Riesman and Arthur Goldberg, John F. Kennedy's secretary of labor, began to write and speak of "the problem" of leisure.[25]

While paying lip service to the reform, the AFL and major CIO unions such as the UAW and United Steelworkers (USW) made little actual progress, keeping their "shorter-hours commitments largely confined to paper." Walter Reuther opposed the Rouge River auto workers' bid for the thirty-hour week with no pay cut ("30 for 40") as "subversive."[26] For him, the choice between more money and shorter hours was no real choice at all—the need for wages always outweighed the desire for leisure: "When we get to the point that we have got everything we need, we can talk about a shorter work week."[27] John L. Lewis told mine workers, "If you want to stop eating so much and loaf more, we can get you the six-hour day."[28] Branding additional leisure as loafing, subversive, and only for "the women" became commonplace among union leaders and labor's traditional allies—an important rhetorical shift that imperiled shorter-hours advances even more than business and conservative political opposition.

After World War II, the *American Federationist*, once bristling with articles about the thirty-hour week and the promise of leisure, remained virtually silent on the subject. The *IUD Bulletin* (published by the Industrial Union Department [IUD] of the AFL-CIO) offered limited coverage. In both publications, labor's turn from shorter hours to Roosevelt's new dream was evident. Labor's publications began to fill with the rhetoric of jobs, jobs, jobs and with articles about the importance of economic growth sufficient for Full-Time, Full Employment, the need for government spending to stimulate the economy, and the necessity for new government programs and jobs to absorb whatever unemployment remained. The IUD defined labor's emerging, postwar position in a 1956 Labor Day message. With no mention of shorter hours, the *Bulletin* proclaimed, "National policy must be geared to an expanding economy, to full employment and to rapidly rising living standards."[29]

Historians have offered a variety of explanations for labor's retreat from shorter hours after mid-century: the ouster of communists and union radicals; the "countermarch of labor legislation,"[30] such as the Taft-Hartley revisions of the National Labor Relations Act; the legacy of the Depression and war; pent-up consumer demand released after the war; changing demographics; changing leadership; consumerism; and alienated or com-modified leisure. The most convincing explanation, however, is that labor abandoned shorter hours because it came to favor Roosevelt's new dream of Full-Time, Full Employment and the Keynesian governmental policies and strategies that this new ideology entailed. Ron Edsforth notes that Reuther and other UAW leaders' lack of support and abandonment of the cause was because of their turn "to a labor-oriented form of Keynesian liberalism that stressed national economic planning to create full employment and sustained economic growth."[31] Roediger and Foner confirm that labor's "alliances with liberal Democrats in support of Keynesian economic policies were much preferred [over shorter hours]…by UAW and USW."[32]

Notes

Preface

1 John Maynard Keynes, *Essays in Persuasion* (New York: Norton, 1963), 367.

5 Juliet Schor, "The (Even More) Overworked American," in *Take Back Your Time: Fighting Overwork and Poverty in America*, ed. John de Graaf (San Francisco: Berrett-Koehler, 2003).

6 Schor, "The (Even More) Overworked American," 6–11.

7 Arlie Hochschild and Anne Machung, *The Second Shift* (New York: Penguin, 2003).

8 Andrew Curry, "Why We Work," *U.S. News and World Report*, February 16, 2003, 50.

9 Schor, "The (Even More) Overworked American," 6–11; Joe Robinson, *Work to Live: The Guide to Getting a Life* (New York: Berkley, 2003), 3.

10 Susan E. Fleck, "International Comparisons of Hours Worked: An Assessment of the Statistics," *Monthly Labor Review* 132, no. 5 (2009): 3.

The Eight-Hour Day

1 William Heighton, "An Address to the Members of Trade Societies and to the Working Classes Generally," reprinted in Philip Foner, *William Heighton: Pioneer Labor Leader of Jacksonian Philadelphia* (New York: International, 1991), 69.

2 Karl Marx, *Capital: A Critique of Political Economy*, trans. Samuel Moore and Edward Aveling (New York: Modern Library, 1906), 329.

3 Daniel Rodgers, *The Work Ethic in Industrial America, 1850–1920* (Chicago: University of Chicago Press, 1979), 155.

4 Massachusetts Bureau of Statistics of Labor (MBSL), *Twentieth Annual Report* (Boston: Wright and Potter, 1889), 447. See also Rodgers, *The Work Ethic*, 157.

5 Gerald N. Grob, *Workers and Utopia: A Study of Ideological Conflict in the American Labor Movement, 1865–1900* (Evanston, IL: Northwestern University Press, 1961), 149.

6 Samuel Gompers, "Testimony before the Committee on Labor of the U.S. House of Representatives," in *The Samuel Gompers Papers, vol. 5, An Expanding Movement at the Turn of the Century, 1898–1902*, ed. Stuart Bruce Kaufman and Peter J. Albert (Urbana: University of Illinois Press, 1986), 482.

7 Bill Haywood, quoted in Rodgers, *The Work Ethic*, 156.

10   Rodgers noted that workers' interest in shortening their work hours at the time did not spring from "all the complex intellectual rationale behind the eight-hour campaign" but from an "essential… obvious appeal: the promise of the relief from toil." Rodgers, *The Work Ethic*, 160.

11   David Montgomery, "Gutman's Nineteenth-Century America," *Labor History* 19 (Summer 1978): 419.

12   Benjamin Hunnicutt, *Work without End: Abandoning Shorter Hours for the Right to Work* (Philadelphia: Temple University Press, 1988), 12–14.

14   MBSL, *Twelfth Annual Report*, 449.

15   Ibid.

20   Max Weber, *The Protestant Ethic and the Spirit of Capitalism*, trans. Talcott Parsons (1930; repr., Mineola, NY: Dover, 2003), 53, 89.

21   "Crisis of work" is James Gilbert's term. See J. B. Gilbert, *Work without Salvation: America's Intellectuals and Industrial Alienation, 1880–1910* (Baltimore: Johns Hopkins University Press, 1977), vii–xv, 31–66, 181.

22   See Roy Rosenzweig, *Eight Hours for What We Will: Workers and Leisure in an Industrial City, 1870–1920* (New York: Cambridge University Press, 1983), 54.

23   Kathy Peiss, *Cheap Amusements* (Temple University Press, 1986), 57.

24   Mikhail Bakhtin, *Rabelais and His World*, tr. Helene Iswolsky (Indiana University Press, 2009), 83, 92 (italics added).

25   Lizabeth Cohen, *Making a New Deal: Industrial Workers in Chicago, 1919–1938* (New York: Cambridge University Press, 1990), 100; Vicki L. Ruiz, *From out of the Shadows: Mexican Women in Twentieth-Century America* (New York: Oxford University Press, 1998), especially the chapter "Confronting 'America,'" 33–50; George Sanchez, *Becoming Mexican American: Ethnicity and Acculturation in Chicano Los Angeles, 1900–1943* (New York: Oxford University Press, 1993), 171–203.

26   Rosenzweig, *Eight Hours for What We Will*, 58.

27   Rosenzweig, *Eight Hours for What We Will*, 58 (italics in original).

28   Peiss, *Cheap Amusements*, 185–186.

29   Ibid., 4, 40.

30   Randy McBee, *Dance Hall Days: Intimacy and Leisure among Working-Class Immigrants in the United States* (New York: New York University Press, 2000).

31   Nan Enstad, *Ladies of Labor, Girls of Adventure: Working Women, Popular Culture, and Labor Politics at the Turn of the Twentieth Century* (New York: Columbia University Press, 1999), 16–17 (italics added).

32   Angela McRobbie, *Feminism and Youth Culture: From "Jackie" to "Just Seventeen"* (1991; repr., New York: Macmillan, 1995), 14.

Labor and Franklin Delano Roosevelt's New Dream

1   *Monthly Labor Review* 23 (December 1926): 1167; Hannah Arendt, *The Human Condition* (Chicago: University of Chicago Press, 1958), 85.

3   William Green, "Leisure for Labor: A New Force Alters Our Social Structure," *Magazine of Business* 56 (August 1929): 136–137.

4   Ibid.

5   *Monthly Labor Review* 23 (December 1926): 1167. See also C. M. Wright, "Epoch-Making Decisions in the Great American Federation Labor Convention at Detroit," *American Labor World*, 1926, 22–24; and U.S. Department of Labor, Bureau of Labor Statistics, *Handbook of Labor Statistics 1924–1926* (Washington, DC: U.S. Government Printing Office, 1927), 818.

28   Henry Ford and S. Crowther, "Unemployment or Leisure," *Saturday Evening Post* 203 (August 1930): 19; H. L. Slobodin, "Unemployment or Leisure—Which?" *American Federationist* 37 (October 1930): 1205–1208; Green, "Leisure for Labor," 136–137; W. Green, "Shorter Hours," *American Federationist* 38 (January 1931): 22.

29   Stuart Chase, *The Economy of Abundance* (New York: Macmillan, 1934), 16–22; Arthur Pound, "Out of Unemployment into Leisure" *Atlantic Review* 146 (December 1930): 784–792; William Green, "Thirty Hour Week," *American Federationist* 40 (November 1933): 1174.

30 Hunnicutt, *Work without End*, chap. 5.

36 "Labor's Ultimatum to Industry: Thirty-Hour Week," *Literary Digest* 114 (December 10, 1932): 3–4; "Labor Will Fight," *Business Week* 14–15 (December 14, 1932): 32; "The Labor Army Takes the Field: A Shorter Work Week to Make Jobs," *Literary Digest* 115 (April 15, 1933): 6.

37 Ellis Hawley, ed., *Herbert Hoover as Secretary of Commerce: Studies in New Era Thought and Practice* (Iowa City: University of Iowa Press, 1981), 44, 111.

38 *Business Week*, February 15, 1933, 3.

39 See Ellis Hawley, *Herbert Hoover and the Crisis of American Capitalism* (Cambridge, MA: Schenkman, 1973), 13, 28, 117.*

40 Hunnicutt, *Work without End*, 151–153.

41 Ibid.

42 Hugh Johnson, *The Blue Eagle from Earth to Egg* (Garden City, NY: Doubleday, 1935), 205.

43 The Wagner bill proved to be the single most important labor legislation ever enacted in the United States, granting labor the basic rights to recruit and organize.

44 Hunnicutt, *Work without End*, 220–224.

45 Just as I use "Higher Progress," capitalized, to represent the first, forgotten American dream, I use "Full-Time, Full Employment," capitalized, to represent the new dream of eternal economic growth and work without end that has eclipsed the first.

46 Ibid., 159.

47 Ibid., 191.

48 Arthur M. Schlesinger Jr., *The Age of Roosevelt, vol. 3, The Politics of Upheaval* (Boston: Houghton Mifflin, 1960), 690–692.

49 Rexford Tugwell, *Roosevelt's Revolution* (New York: Macmillan, 1977), 239.

50 Robert M. Hutchins, *The University of Utopia* (Chicago: University of Chicago Press, 1965), ix.

51 Ibid.

52 Hunnicutt, *Work without End*, 180.

53 David Roediger and Philip Foner, *Our Own Time: A History of American Labor and the Working Day* (New York: Verso, 1989), 258.

54 Milo Keynes, *Essays on John Maynard Keynes* (Cambridge: Cambridge University Press, 1980), 135–140; see also W. Nordhaus and J. Tobin, "Is Growth Obsolete?" in *The Measurement of Economic and Social Performance*, ed. M. Moss (New York: Columbia University Press, 1975). Nordhaus and Tobin developed a new "measure of economic welfare" by adding the value of leisure to the traditional GNP measurements, concluding that leisure represents over half of total consumer income.

55 Hunnicutt, *Work without End*, 207.

56 Ibid., chap. 8.

Labor Turns from Shorter Hours to Full-Time, Full Employment

1 A. H. Raskin, "AFL Reaffirms 30-Hour Week Plan," *New York Times*, November 30, 1940, 1.

2 David R. Roediger and Philip Sheldon Foner, *Our Own Time: A History of American Labor and the Working Day* (New York: Greenwood Press, 1989), 261–262.

3 "Green Says 30-Hour Week Must Come as 'Only Practical Way' to Spread Work," *New York Times*, October 26, 1944, 10.

4 William A. McGaughey, *A Shorter Workweek in the 1980s* (Minneapolis, MN: Thistlerose, 1981), 44.

5 See G. J. Santoni, "The Employment Act of 1946: Some History Notes," *Federal Reserve Bank of St. Louis Review*, November 1986.*

6 Dwight Eisenhower, *Crusade in Europe* (Baltimore: Johns Hopkins University Press, 1997), 319.*

7 Santoni, "The Employment Act of 1946."

8 Samuel Gompers, "Testimony before the Committee on Labor of the U.S. House of Representatives," in *The Samuel Gompers Papers, vol. 5, An Expanding Movement at the Turn of the Century: 1898–1902*, ed. Stuart Bruce Kaufman and Peter J. Albert (Urbana: University of Illinois Press, 1986), 482.

9 American Federation of Labor and Congress of Industrial Organizations, *Proceedings of the Third Constitutional Convention of the AFL-CIO*, vol. 1 (San Francisco: AFL-CIO, 1959), 638. See also *American Federationist* 68, no. 7 (1961): 6.

24 Ronald Edsforth, "Why Automation Didn't Shorten the Work Week: The Politics of Work Time in the Automobile Industry," in *Autowork*, ed. Robert Asher, Ronald Edsforth, and Stephen Merlino (Albany: State University of New York Press, 1995), 160.

25 A. H. Raskin, "If We Had a Twenty-Hour Week," *New York Times*, February 4, 1962, 191.

26 Roediger and Foner, *Our Own Time*, 262.

27 Edsforth, "Why Automation Didn't Shorten the Work Week," 170.

28 "Profits Face New Labor Attack," *Nation's Business*, February 1958, 70.

29 *IUD Bulletin*, September 1956, 1.

30 Roediger and Foner, *Our Own Time*, 266.

31 Edsforth, "Why Automation Didn't Shorten the Work Week," 168.

32 Roediger and Foner, *Our Own Time*, 262.

CHAPTER 31

Nixon's Class Struggle

Jefferson Cowie

H.R. Haldeman, Richard Nixon's chief of staff, called it the president's "long philosophical thing." As Washington sweltered in the hot July of 1971, a year before George McGovern would receive the Democratic nomination, Richard Nixon gathered his advisors together to explain the core premise of his domestic political strategy: winning working men to what he liked to call the "New Majority." Few issues in domestic politics stirred his passions more deeply. Although his team would go down in history most famously for the crimes of Watergate (which barely emerged in the 1972 campaign season), in the summer of 1971 they believed they were brewing a permanent realignment in the political cauldrons of the White House—one that would finally bring an end to the Roosevelt coalition.

"When you have to call on the nation to be strong—on such things as drugs, crime, defense, our basic national position," Nixon declared to the assembled political wizards gathered about him, H.R. Haldeman, John Ehrlichman, George Shultz, John Connally, and Charles Colson, "the educated people and the leader class no longer have any character, and you can't count on them." Nixon always detested the eastern elite, whom he saw as impotent and effete, and envisioned the working class as the only constituency with the "character and guts" to meet the many crises of the day. "When we need support on tough problems," he declared, "the uneducated are the ones that are with us."

In Nixon's class analysis, workers were the counterpoise to the eastern establishment for which he had nothing but bitter contempt. When the crises hit, Nixon concluded, the business and academic leaders simply "painted their asses white and ran like antelopes." The so-called managers were not what the country needed—the historical moment beckoned for what he called the "two-fisted" types. It was in workers and the labor leadership—the traditional backbone of New Deal politics—that new faith and renewal could be found for the Republican Party. They may be "shortsighted, partisan, [and] hate Nixon politically" but in the end, the president concluded, "they are men, not softies." As Nixon theorized his plans for the future, he declared, we "need to build our own new coalition based on Silent Majority, blue-collar Catholics, Poles, Italians, Irish. No promise with Jews and Negroes. Appeal not hard right-wing, Bircher, or anti-Communist." He sensed the moment and devoted his presidency to making the New Majority out of such sentiments. His sole domestic political goal was to disassemble the Roosevelt coalition and to rebuild the pieces into his own modern coalition.

Original publication details: Jefferson R. Cowie, *Stayin' Alive: The 1970s and the Last Days of the Working Class* (The New Press, 2012).

Class: The Anthology, First Edition. Edited by Stanley Aronowitz and Michael J. Roberts.

By the fall of 1972, Nixon would prove very successful in shifting what FDR called the "forgotten man" away from his bread-and-butter material concerns to the shared terrain of culture, social issues, and patriotism. This was not simply just cynical political manipulation—although there was plenty of that. Rather, it was something he really believed in: that the people's natural political alliances stemmed from their values (and that they were highly exploitable politically). "The Roosevelt coalition was just that—a coalition," he intoned to his advisors. FDR "played one against another—big city bosses, intellectuals, South, North. By contrast, our New American Majority appeals across the board— to Italians, Poles, Southerners, to the Midwest and New York—for the *same reasons*, and because of the same basic values. These are people who care about a strong United States, about patriotism, about moral and spiritual values." There may not even be consensus on what "those moral and spiritual values ought to be," Nixon confessed, "but they agree that you ought to have some." They were ironic words for a president who would have to resign in disgrace two years after the election, but they were terms he believed to be bedrock political truth. While FDR intoned against elites as the "economic royalists" who wanted to form an "industrial dictatorship," Nixon knew in his very soul that working people would rally against a new kind of elite—a liberal cultural elite "who want to take their money, and give it to people who don't work." As he concluded, "These are not just southern or ethnic notions—they're American to the core."[3]

By the 1972 campaign, he would have strategic appeals laid out to thirty-three separate ethnic voter groups ranging from the Armenians and Bulgarians to the Syrians and the Ukrainians—all united around the need for some vague sense of values. Nixon believed that he could bring those ethnicities together; surmount economic disagreements with organized labor; and, by presenting his cultural vision at his particular historical moment, become the workingman's president. And he was, to a large extent, correct.[6]

I

The origins of what Nixon's men called the "blue-collar strategy" were rooted in a more vague but famous appeal to the "Silent Majority." Barely squeaking past Hubert Humphrey and a Democratic Party in complete disarray after the 1968 Chicago convention, he turned toward sharpening his appeal to what he first called the "Silent Americans." He launched a secret group called the "Middle America Committee" in the fall of 1969 to help the Republican Party reach the "the large and politically powerful white middle class." That constituency, they reasoned, was "deeply troubled, primarily over the erosion of what they consider to be their values."[7]

As it was for Robert Kennedy and then George McGovern, the key to Nixon's political universe between 1968 and 1972 was the Wallace voter. George Wallace's oratory during his 1968 campaign, running under the banner of the American Independent Party, earned him the moniker of "Cicero of the cab driver" from one journalist because of his ability to tap into the anger, disenchantment, and racial resentments of white blue-collar America. As the governor's biographer argues, Wallace was able to draw together the social and racial problems of the late sixties and early seventies in inextricable ways. "Fears of blackness and fears of disorder—interwoven by the subconscious connection many white Americans made between blackness and criminality, blackness and poverty, blackness and cultural degradation—were the warp and woof of the new social agenda."

Working-class liberals still constituted a strong bloc, but they were growing suspicious of changes afoot and feeling forgotten in the mix. Better than many Democrats, Nixon, like Wallace, figured out that much of the backlash was a simple search for secure ground in the cultural storms.[10]

The Wallace voter offered the key to more specific plans for romancing the working class beyond the Silent Majority. Kevin Phillips, the precocious young Nixon advisor who read his computer printouts with the intensity of a biblical scholar, believed that the secret to American politics was "who hated who." The Bronx-Irish strategist understood the essential cultural conservatism of the white ethnics and boldly posited that the manipulation of race and culture would provide for what he called the *The Emerging Republican Majority* (1969). In that famous manifesto, Phillips argued that Nixon's narrow victory over Hubert Humphrey in 1968 was not the political fluke that it appeared to be; rather, it represented the beginning of a major ethnic and regional political realignment. The Wallace voters were not a one-time move away from the Democrats but part of a permanent realignment toward the Republicans. To look at simple election returns of the two major parties was to miss the point. The solid Democratic South was crumbling under the Democrats' commitment to racial equality and cultural values, he believed, and, by adding the Nixon votes to those cast for George Wallace, one could see a nation "in motion between a Democratic past and Republican future." A less prominent argument in Phillips' famous book looked beyond the Southern Strategy and considered the possibility of mobilizing the votes of northern industrial workers. "Successful moderate conservatism is also likely to attract to the Republican side some of the northern blue-collar workers who flirted with George Wallace but ultimately backed Hubert Humphrey," Phillips calculated.[11]

The problem was that working-class voters feared that a Republican administration would do away with popular New Deal programs—from social security to collective bargaining. Phillips' version of conservatism was nothing like what it would soon become; he advocated, for instance, programs ranging from national health insurance to aid for declining industrial regions. If Nixon could dispel the notion that his party and his presidency were anti-worker, cleverly manipulate the race issue, and peg the label of "elitism" on the liberals, it followed, he could build a post-New Deal coalition that transcended the Southern Strategy. As Nixon appeared soft on labor, liberals lost their bearings with (another) new Nixon. As labor insider John Herling reported in the spring of 1969, the new president "certainly is not behaving according to the pattern both friend and foe set out for him as he advanced to the White House. In the area of labor-management relations, there has been no sizzle and crackle and lopping off of heads, no snarling that 'We've got you now, bub.'" The roots of a New Right lay, Phillips contended, in the hope of "a new coalition reaching across to what elite conservatives still consider 'the wrong side of the tracks.'" The Wallace vote of 1968 was merely a "way station" for blue-collar Democrats drifting into the Republican Party—and the future of republicanism rested upon the "the great, ordinary, Lawrence Welkish mass of Americans from Maine to Hawaii."[12]

The Wallace voter was a dangerous and confusing character for any candidate. On the issues of class and economics, the Wallace voter tended to see the Democrats as the party of the center—accepting and depending upon much of the economic gains of the New Deal programs; but on race and law-and-order, that same voter would need the most conservative elements of the Republicans. The question was which element was stronger—culture or economics? As Richard Scammon and Ben Wattenberg explained in *The Real Majority*

(1970), from the hypothetical position of the ten million people who voted for Wallace in 1968, "'Law and order' beats 'bread and butter'; social beats economic. Keep your tainted federal dollars if it means putting my kid in school with the colored." For the millions of voters who originally leaned toward Wallace but voted for one of the two-party candidates in 1968, however, in the end the calculus went in the other direction—the politics of economic interest generally trumped the social issue. But, as the pugnacious liberal journalist Pete Hamill described Wallace supporters in 1968, it may have been more basic than the false binary of economics versus culture. As so often in populist movements, the Wallace movement had more than a hint of the promise of a restoration of a lost golden age. As Hamill argued,

> There was little mystery to them. They were my own people, lower middle-class people who worked with their backs and their hands, who paid dues to a union that was remote to them, people who drove a cab or tended bar one night a week to make ends meet, people who went hunting with the boys on vacations, people who handed their infant children to their wives while they applauded the candidate. Most of them seemed to make about $125 a week and were struggling to pay off GI loans on their home…. They want change; the America they thought was theirs has become something else in their own lifetimes, they want to go back. A lot of the people attracted to George Wallace are just people who think America has passed them by, leaving them confused and screwed-up and unhappy.

The vague populism of the Silent Majority, the sentiments of the Wallace followers, and the outlook of the voters Phillips scrutinized all lacked the class edge that Nixon would soon develop to his political calculations.[13]

The document that moved Nixon's thinking from these broader appeals to a more specific blue-collar strategy was another provocative essay by the liberal journalist Pete Hamill titled "The Revolt of the White Lower Middle Class." Nixon read the 1969 piece in *New York* magazine only a few months after taking office, and by all accounts he was deeply moved by its street-wise view of the issues. The article exposed the unrecognized rage coursing through the New Deal bulwark. It allowed the president to move Phillips' thinking, and the president's own impulses, from an abstract possibility to a concrete strategy by clearly identifying a set of political resentments in the urban north ready for plucking. While Hamill did not mince words about the racist expressions of white working-class anger in 1969, like Nixon, he concluded that it was less race, per se, which drove phenomena like northern blue-collar support for George Wallace, than it was workers' belief that they were not respected and that society had focused its attention and resources on other, noisier, groups. The urgency of the war, civil rights, and the rising women's movement were threatening the privileged centrality of the old New Deal base—the white ethnic working class. "It is imperative for New York politicians to begin to deal with the growing alienation and paranoia of the working-class white man," Hamill explained in this strategic Rosetta Stone; he "feels trapped and, even worse, in a society that purports to be democratic, ignored." In concluding words that must have leapt from the page into Richard Nixon's mind, the author wrote, "Any politician who leaves that white man out of the political equation, does so at very large risk."[14]

The question was, could the administration chuck the material issues it raised and succeed in winning white working-class votes solely through cultural and social appeals? Putting the pieces together, the president and his staff agreed that the political moment supported three basic, interlocking propositions. First, the white working-class vote was politically up for grabs, and Nixon could be the leader to knit them into a new political coalition—essentially giving mainstream legitimacy to Wallaceite sentiments. Second, while Mike Jerome M. Rosow's (Assistant Secretary of Labor under Richard Nixon) report brought up significant bread-and-butter issues and argued that any concern for workers had to include two million blacks "who share many of the same problems as whites in their income class," it was neither the entire working class nor its material grievances on which the administration would focus. Rather, it was the "feeling of being forgotten" among white, male workers that the administration would seek to tap. Finally, policy and rhetoric would be formulated that did not require federal expenditures or even wage increases—the politics of recognition and status would be enough. The struggle for the Nixon administration would be to ferret out non-material political responses to the "pressing needs" they knew workers experienced and, as inflation became a priority, in fact placing restraints on workers' wage demands. The key question remained for the administration: was this to be a strategy to draw out workers only or might even the unions—whose entire identity was largely wrapped up in delivering the material goods to the rank and file—also be brought on board?[17]

II

Then came the proof. Just weeks after the internal release of the Rosow Report, Richard Nixon's wildest dreams for the blue-collar strategy found their popular manifestation. Beginning in early May 1970 and lasting much of the month, New York City construction workers turned out in the streets in a frenzy of "jingoistic joy" aimed against the war protestors and "red" Mayor John Lindsay, and in support of Nixon's policies in Southeast Asia. The protests began when brightly helmeted construction workers, many wielding their heavy tools, pushed through a weak line of police and violently descended on an anti-war demonstration called after the killings at Kent Slate. The workers' goal, besides venting their rage, was to raise a flag lowered to half mast to honor the four slain students in Ohio. They then proceeded to storm the steps of City Hall, chasing student protestors through the streets of the financial district, and bloodying around seventy people in the process. While demonstrations continued on lunch hours throughout the month, the culmination of the conflicts came on May 20 when the Building and Construction Trades Council of Greater New York sponsored a rally—the previous actions had no open sponsorship—and delivered around one hundred thousand supporters in a sea of American flags, declaring their support for the war effort. Complete with a concrete mixer draped with the slogan "Lindsay for Mayor of Hanoi," and signs declaring GOD BLESS THE ESTABLISHMENT and WE SUPPORT NIXON AND AGNEW, the protests delivered to the national spotlight both the hard-hat image and the resentment Hamill pinpointed the previous year. *Business Week* called the original hard-hat revolts the "three days that shook the establishment," but it was more like three days that affirmed it.[18]

The pro-war worker was an unfair stereotype, which, upon close examination, suggests something of the class divides of the anti-war movement. Certainly there were plenty of blue-collar Americans who agreed with John Nash, a Newark printer interviewed during the protests, who chalked up support for the war as simple duty to country. "I'm backing the President all the way. My boy goes into service Dec, 7…. I'm proud of him. It's a chance we all had to take. It's his turn." But polling data belies the myth of a uniquely pro-war working class and consistently shows, in fact, that manual workers were more opposed to the war and more in favor of withdrawal than were the college educated. An amalgam of polls, interviews, and reports suggests that it was less support for the war among pro-Nixon workers than it was class resentments at the approach, privilege, and lack of duty among the protesters. With college a reasonable class signifier in the sixties, the college draft deferment tore a fairly clear class divide between those who were forced to serve and those who were not—in an era in which many families were barely more than a generation out of poverty. Thus much of the psychology of the backlash trended more toward that of class antagonisms, guilt, and victimization than an actual stand on foreign policy. As historian Christian Appy, reports, "To many veterans, the protest of college students felt like moral and social putdowns, expressions not of principle and commitment but simply of class privilege and arrogance." As one tradesman confirmed, "Here were these kids, rich kids, who could go to college, who didn't have to fight, they are telling you your son died in vain. It makes you feel your whole life is shit, just nothing."[19]

What mattered most to the Nixon administration was that the protests suddenly gave their ideas about the working class palpable imagery and potent political symbolism. "This display of emotional activity from the 'hard hats,'" argued Nixon's aide Steve Bull, provided an opportunity "to forge a new alliance and perhaps result in the emergence of a 'new right.'" Strategically, the idea was to avoid the treacherous waters of workers' inflationary wage interests by addressing a powerful and rising tide of cultural conservatism. "The emphasis," continued Bull, "would be upon some of these supposedly trite mid-America values that the liberal press likes to snicker about: love of country, respect for people as individuals, the Golden Rule, etc."[20]

The hard-hat protests and the stereotype of the hawkish working class was yet another twist in a long line of manipulations of the working-class image—whether it was the Left's revolutionary agent or the Right's neo-brown shirts. As two sociologists explained at the time, "the whole idea of the 'hard hat'—the superpatriot, the racist workingman" served to hollow out the humanity of the wearer and replace the person with a political symbol: "a thing, with an empty head hidden beneath, a part of a mass over which the 'educated' or 'enlightened' person towers." The right wing's new essentialization was as reductionist as the Old Left's equally simplistic "proletariat"—both mere instruments for others to wield for their own political purposes.[21]

The timing of the protests could not have been more fortuitous. The White House was literally and figuratively under siege in the wake of the bombing of Cambodia. Chuck Colson called the White House a "bunker" as tear gas drifted in from the streets, and the secret service resorted to ringing the grounds with buses in order to protect the president. With protestors and the press attacking the White House, the hard hats came to Nixon's aid, bolstering the sagging *esprit de corps* of the administration. The workers, Nixon exclaimed, "were with us when some of the elitist crowd were running away from us. Thank God for the hard hats!" As Haldeman noted, Nixon "thinks now the college demonstrators have overplayed their hands, evidence is the blue collar group rising up against them, and P can mobilize them," he explained optimistically as Washington lay in a fog of tear gas.[22]

Nixon seized upon the moment to uphold traditional values in the face of cultural upheaval: a discussion about manly citizens who work and support their country in opposition to the effete non-citizens who loaf, protest, and undermine the national purpose. As Peter Brennan, head of the New York building trades who helped orchestrate the hard-hat protests, explained to Colson (and Colson to the president), the "hard hats" cheering for the president did not correlate directly to votes. They did not like Nixon's economic policies and feared his push on civil rights. "What is winning their political loyalty," Brennan explained,

> is their admiration for your masculinity. The "hard hats," who are a tough breed, have come to respect you as a tough, courageous man's man. Brennan's thesis is that this image of you will win their votes more than the patriotism theme. The image of being strong, forceful and decisive will have a powerful personal appeal with the alienated voter.[23]

Many have suggested that the rampaging protests of the tool wielding tradesmen emerged from Nixon's kit of dirty tricks. Although this appears not to have directly been the case, the administration was certainly ready and willing to exploit the uprisings and, when necessary, foment more. Haldeman, aggravated by the continued presence of Viet Cong flags at the president's appearances, arranged for the illusion of spontaneous blue-collar types to descend upon flag-waving protestors so that they could be quickly removed. "The best way to do this is probably to work out an arrangement with the Teamsters Union so that they will have a crew on hand at all Presidential appearances, ready, willing, and able to remove Viet Cong flags physically." At other times Nixon approved of having Teamsters "go in and knock [protestors'] heads off." Haldeman suggested hiring "Murderers. Guys that really, you know...the regular strikebusters-types... and then they're gonna beat the [obscenity] out of some of these people." Haldeman's "to do" list in his copious yellow note pads even included "Get a goon squad to start roughing up demos" as part of the appearance of a broader revolt of the Silent Majority against the vocal minority. (There are several references to "those eight thugs" in the documents, suggesting some familiarity and use of them, and curiously Abbie Hoffman [the butt of many anti-Semitic remarks from Nixon and his advisors] did get a broken nose from unknown assailants two days before the "thugs discussion.")[24]

Whatever covert tricks the administration may have engaged in, the Nixon staff certainly made the most of *overt* operations. No sooner had the protests come to their conclusion than Nixon had invited twenty-two New York union officials, led by New York Trades Council president Peter Brennan, to the White House for a chat. The union leaders presented the president with a small metal flag for his lapel and a hard hat labeled "Commander in Chief" as well as a similar helmet for the commander in Vietnam, General Creighton W. Abrams. "The hard hat," they explained, "will stand as a symbol, along with our great flag, for freedom and patriotism to our beloved country." Nixon briefed the group on the progress of the war and "was visibly moved" when one member of the delegation, whose son had been killed in Vietnam, said "if someone would have had the courage to go into Cambodia sooner, they might have captured the bullet that took my son's life."[25]

III

Richard Nixon is often described as the "last liberal," but he, and anyone else at the time, would have chafed—if not been revolted—by the idea. "His heart was on the right," explained William Safire, "and his head was, with FDR, 'slightly left of center.'" It is only in historical perspective of the post-Reagan era that he can be seen as liberal. He was certainly the last president to function within the liberal paradigm, but it was a paradigm he sought to undo, not to promote. He was, however, not a political ideologue but a strategic opportunist, a tactical pragmatist, who made peace where he needed in order to exploit the political space between the congressional liberals and the hostility of more conservative Republicans. His domestic policy vision was mostly one of disinterest, except where it overlapped with his plans for the New Majority. On issues such as busing, his opposition allowed him to score easy points against liberals. In other areas, however, he seemed at the forefront of expanding the Great Society. He liked to compare himself to the British prime minister Benjamin Disraeli, the nineteenth-century Conservative, known for launching liberal initiatives as a way of controlling the reform process. His "liberalism" involved pre-empting liberal legislation with his own policies, while simultaneously using those more tepid liberal initiatives to draw voters to his new coalition. The president's "baffling blend of Republicanism and radicalism," in the terms of the *New York Times*, was the result: a conservative opportunist governing in a liberal paradigm with the goal of building the New Majority.[26]

The signing of the Occupational Safety and Health Act (OSHA) in December 1970 was a case in point. The new administrative office set up mechanisms for enforcement of safety and health on the job—a response to the roiling concerns about non-wage aspects of the employment relationship. President Johnson had proposed a workplace safety bill that never passed, but as the environmental and consumer safety movements took hold (the Environmental Protection Agency [EPA] was created in the same year), the momentum for OSHA grew. It was an unwelcome and intrusive intervention in the workplace for most employers and Republicans. Nixon, however, declared that it was "probably one of the most important pieces of legislation, from the standpoint of the 55 million people who will be covered by it, ever passed by the Congress of the United States." Needless to say, it dovetailed flawlessly with his desire to woo his new constituency.[27]

Perhaps the most intriguing piece of the Nixon domestic program, one that never made it to political daylight, was his welfare reform initiative known as the Family Assistance Program (FAP). Most of Nixon's domestic policy was based on his "New Federalism," which sought to increase funding but to do so by distributing power away from the federal bureaucracy and toward state and local governments. FAP, however, was slightly different. The program was based on a guaranteed annual income (of $1,600 for a family of four) that cut at the heart of the flaws in the Aid to Families with Dependent Children (AFDC) program, which was believed to penalize work and create a large bureaucracy. It had been a long-standing dream of free-market conservatives, like Milton Friedman, who called it a "Negative Income Tax." With a national guaranteed income, people could still work, and be encouraged or even required to do so, but nobody would fall below the national standard. The fundamental idea was simple, but the details were mind-bogglingly complicated and political—work requirements, break-even points, taxation rates, actual costs, the amount of assistance—all of which seemed only of interest to Democrat Daniel Patrick Moynihan, who joined the administration to try and deal with the welfare mess. Here, Nixon failed as the American Disraeli, as the bill was too much for conservatives and not enough for liberals, especially those influenced by the National Welfare Rights Organization, which demanded the most generous bill it could get. Or, perhaps, he was as shrewd as ever. As the bill stalled in Congress, Haldeman noted in his diary: "About Family Assistance Plan, [President] wants to be sure it's killed by Democrats and that we make a big play for it, but don't let it pass, can't afford it." Nixon gets the credit for the idea; Democrats get the blame for its failure.[28]

VI

Despite the flow of optimistic rhetoric and symbolic concessions, real-life labor issues plagued the administration, often putting the president in the odd position of being economically at odds with the interests of the labor movement while still allied with the AFL-CIO leadership on social issues and foreign policy. Contrary to both evidence and traditional Republican policy, Nixon's advisors pursued the blue-collar strategy even when it appeared to be failing before their eyes. The biggest problem was finding ways to continue the hard-hat angle while figuring out ways to discipline what was just beginning to compete with the administration's concerns about unemployment: inflation. And the president's staff had already decided what caused inflation—the economic demands of its hoped-for new ally, organized labor.

The building trades may have been the source of hard-hat national pride, but they were also one of the prime sources of pre-OPEC (Organization of Petroleum Exporting Countries) inflation. Wage increases in the industry were far outpacing those in manufacturing, and the powerful but fragmented craft unions prevented any easy top-down response to what was beginning to be an inflationary crisis in the industry. Nothing was more inflationary to construction users than the hated Davis-Bacon Act. The act, which required contractors working on federal construction projects to pay the highest prevailing (thus union) wages to its workers, had been regarded as an inflationary pressure in the construction industry for many years. In February 1971, Nixon suspended the act after failing to get the unions to agree to a voluntary solution to rising labor costs. Even though the *Wall Street Journal* reported that the suspension "seemed to have undone all the administration's careful cultivation of the blue collar vote," the president was not plunging into the political darkness. The suspension had been secretly vetted ahead of time with all of the major building-trades leaders as well as George Meany, Lane Kirkland, and Teamster president Frank Fitzsimmons, among over a dozen others. Although New York City building trades leader Peter Brennan felt that there were other options that could have been pursued, he was kept tightly in the loop of the administration's decisions and still promised to "deliver 90% to our side in 1972." In ending the wage guarantee in the industry, the president had the agreement that leadership would grouse but not fight, and so his crafting of his official statement on the suspension in pro-worker terms would not seem completely absurd. "While some might wish to blame management or labor unions for this inflationary syndrome, we must recognize that, in fact, they are its victims," argued the President in his official statement. "The person who is hurt most by this pattern of inflation," he explained, "is the construction worker himself. For as the cost of building increases, the rate of building is slowed—and the result is fewer jobs for the workingman."[46]

Many saw Nixon's suspension of Davis-Bacon, oddly enough, as a victory for labor. The *New York Times* editorialized that the suspension meant that "The Construction Unions Win" because the administration's solution was really a tepid response to a situation that demanded more draconian moves. True, Nixon may have pulled his punches somewhat in order to avoid alienating his new allies. The administration put the act back in place barely over a month after rescinding it, obtaining the voluntary controls it had originally hoped for as the suspension got the attention of the unions "the way a two-by-four gets the attention of a mule" explained Labor Secretary James Hodgson. The new "voluntary" controls by labor-management boards included heavy governmental pressure to control wages but gave the administration room to wiggle in order to placate friends in need. It did work, modestly, as first-year contract negotiation wage and benefits increases fell from 19 percent to 11 percent.[47]

The biggest point of conflict was controlling wages in order to keep down inflation, which came to a head with the administration's New Economic Policy (ironically, the same name as Lenin's policies for the Soviet Union in the 1920s). Controlling wages and prices were of national concern, and one of the most popular ideas was to put federal controls on both. Nixon officially opposed such drastic measures, which smacked too much of World War II era government intervention. Labor traditionally opposed freezes largely because it was much easier to control wages than prices, and, of course, it violated one of the basic functions of unions, the freedom to negotiate contracts. Controls were an immensely popular idea among voters, however, and the AFL-CIO president publicly, if tepidly, endorsed controls on the presumption that Nixon would never actually implement them. If Meany had to have controls, the type he preferred were akin to the aggressive form used during World War II in order to ensure that prices as well as wages were kept down. When the president did what the polls had been telling him was popular, and what appeared to assist his re-election hopes— declare a ninety-day wage-price freeze in August 1971 (when he also most famously took the dollar off the gold standard)—what little shared common ground there had been quickly evaporated. The unions felt that corporations would easily raise prices well beyond the level that wages were pushing them up anyway, so it was easy to assume that wage-price controls were a way of disciplining wages. When the administration ruled that 1.3 million workers scheduled to receive wage increases negotiated before the freeze would not get their pay, labor's position hardened. Leonard Woodcock, president of the UAW, declared, if the administration "wants war, it can have war."[49]

VIII

Although George McGovern was en route to a highly contested Democratic primary victory, the man that the AFL-CIO hierarchy loved for the Democratic nomination was Henry "Scoop" Jackson—cold warrior extraordinaire, the "Senator from Boeing" as he was often called. In a speech in New York City (written in part by Ben Wattenberg, co-author of *The Real Majority*), Jackson laid out the problem in a distinctly Nixonian way. "The working people are also under attack from the left fringes, by people who would like to take over the Democratic Party. If this takeover were to succeed, the Democratic Party will lose in 1972 and be in deep trouble for years thereafter." Without directly naming George McGovern, he went on, "There are some people in the Democratic Party, who, intentionally or not, have turned their backs on the working man. They are either indifferent to him or downright hostile. Their cocktail parties abound with snide jokes about 'hardhats' and 'ethnics.' They mouth fashionable clichés about how workers have grown fat and conservative with affluence, and how their unions are reactionary or racist."[58]

Nixon did his best to ensure that a cultural conservative/hawk like Jackson or a moderate like the presumed front-runner Edward Muskie would *not* get the nomination. Nixon wanted to run against an "extremist" like McGovern, so the Committee to Re-elect the President subsidized McGovern's campaign with a few surprises from the administration's bag of dirty tricks. Nixon operatives had planted the notorious "Canuck" letter that helped undermine centrist Muskie in New Hampshire by claiming he had used derogatory remarks against French-Canadians. When he went on the counter-attack, his emotions heightened while defending his wife against mean-spirited editorials. Then he appeared to weep as the New Hampshire snow fell on his cheeks. At the time, it was portrayed as a "breakdown" that made him appear fragile under stress. Also during the New Hampshire primary, the Nixon people made late night and early morning phone calls soliciting support for Muskie from people claiming to have just arrived from Harlem to help with the campaign. In Florida, Republican operatives put up posters saying "Help Muskie in Busing More Children Now" by a fictitious group called the Mothers Backing Muskie Committee. The tricks went on through the primaries and, of course, culminated in the break-in at the Watergate hotel to bug Democratic Headquarters in June 1972.[59]

The most important thing that Nixon *may* have done in the realm of dirty tricks was to make sure that George Wallace ran as a Democrat rather than an independent. The Alabama governor ran as an independent in 1968, and the race between Nixon and Humphrey was deemed too close. If Nixon could ensure that Wallace would carve votes out of the Democratic Party, and let his populism give the party fits throughout the primary process, then 1972 would be in the bag. Nixon may have made material and political contributions toward that end. A large-scale federal investigation had been launched into Wallace's taxes. It looked like indictments would be forthcoming for his campaign supporters and his brother Gerald. Then on April 30, 1971, with no explanation, federal prosecutors announced a recession in the presentation of witnesses to the grand jury. Two weeks later, Nixon and Wallace met on the presidential helicopter. Then, according to columnist Rowland Evans, Postmaster General Blount was in Alabama for discussions— allegedly over shared interests in keeping a liberal Democrat out of the White House. The Grand Jury reconvened four months later, but by then only a handful of Wallace associates were indicted—all but one of whom had already broken with Wallace. In January 1972, the Justice Department declared it was dropping its investigation of Gerald Wallace. The next day, George Wallace announced he would be running as a Democrat. Although it may never be clear exactly what happened, events made it so that the Wallace candidacy was an asset for Richard Nixon. After the attempt on Wallace's life, Nixon sent John Connally to find out if he would run then as an independent. Wallace was in no shape to do so. Connally noted, "We might well say that this was the day the election was won." Nixon agreed to pay Wallace's staff for the remainder of the year.[60]

White House operatives viewed the messiness of the 1972 Democratic Convention as the final piece in their plans to build the New Majority. "McGovern's victory is not a popular victory; it is more a coup d'etat of the Democratic Party, where a youthful leftist and suburban leftist elite has deposed and ousted the traditional Catholic and Jewish leadership of the Democratic Party," explained Pat Buchanan. Speechwriter William Safire saw it as the obverse of 1964: "As Barry Goldwater was Lyndon Johnson's gift from the Gods, George McGovern was Richard Nixon's." By the summer of 1972, Richard Nixon, the man George Meany had called a "union hater" who would "make Taft-Hartley and Landrum-Griffin (labor laws) look prolabor" back in 1968 appeared to be organized labor's new best friend.[61]

Labor leaders frequently spoke of the "kooks" and "fairies" attending the convention, but one of the more infamous of his nasty rhetorical moments came when a crusty, bitter, and immobilized George Meany described the debacle of the Democratic Convention in Miami to the national convention of the USW. Here Meany succumbed to the same cultural low-balling as Nixon, perhaps ironically contributing, in a small way, to the long-term decline of the economic dimensions of working-class identity. "We listened to the gay lib people—you know the people who want to legalize marriage between boys and boys and girls and girls," he declared in an attempt to gain support for his neutrality strategy. "We heard from the abortionists, and we heard from the people who look like Jacks, acted like Jills and had the odors of Johns about them." His snide rhetoric seems to be evidence for the idea that the New Politics-labor split was, in essence, about cultural values. It was, however, a play straight out of Nixon's book: rev up the troops for cultural battle even if the war was about political power rather than relevant issues. It did the trick. The conventioneers passed the non-endorsement resolution by voice vote, "with a considerable volume of disagreement from McGovern supporters."[62]

George Shultz, by then secretary of the treasury, increased his regular contacts and golf games with Meany in the summer of 1972 as the national campaign season approached. The conversations remained undocumented, but suggestions from the AFL-CIO hierarchy about how to campaign made it to the president through such back channels:

> The unions share Nixon's position on busing. Don't talk about defense in terms of jobs, talk about national security. Continue to fight the idea of amnesty. Don't worry about vetoing things like the clean water bill—'they don't want to be put out of jobs by environmental kooks anyway.' Run against inflation—not on the grounds that it's been solved. Most of all, they said, 'Stop pitching directly for the support of Democrats. It makes it seem like you're trying to break up the Democratic Party. You'll get more Democrats to vote for you if you don't remind them about being Democrats, or suggesting that you are a threat to the long-term continuance of the Democratic Party.'[63]

IX

Once George McGovern's nomination was secure, his candidacy gave the president the latitude necessary to portray himself as the candidate of the workingman and the Democrats as captured by the most effete and decadent elements of the permissive new liberalism. As the administration's "Assault Book" for the fall presidential contest argued,

> As the campaign progresses, we should increasingly portray McGovern as the pet radical of Eastern Liberalism, the darling of the New York Times, the hero of the Berkeley Hill Jet Set; Mr. Radical Chic. The liberal elitists are his—we have to get back the working people; and the better we portray McGovern as an elitist radical, the smaller his political base. By November, he should be postured as the Establishment's fair-haired boy, and RN postured as the Candidate of the Common Man, the working man.

Half jokingly, Buchanan and the other strategists suggested pushing even further into the lion's den, by suggesting that the Republicans take over the traditional place where Democrats launched their fall campaign: "How about RN going to Cadillac Square on Labor Day this year!!" McGovern helped by being unwise enough to tease that he would renounce his 1965 vote against the repeal of 14(b) of Taft-Hartley (the "Right-to-Work" provision), a relatively minor flaw in a pro-labor voting record that the AFL-CIO had bludgeoned him with, if Meany would proclaim that he was incorrect about Vietnam and the Cold War. This, of course, was a gold mine for the Nixon administration as all the staff had to do was wait for reporters to ask whether Meany, probably the second most prominent cold warrior in the country after Nixon, would renounce a lifetime of militant anti-communism.[64]

The proof of Nixon's newly found mettle on the labor issue came during the Republican platform fight. Ever since the New Deal, it had been Republican orthodoxy to claim to defend the nation and free enterprise against the corrupting forces of the labor bosses. They extolled the virtues of the core anti-labor laws, Taft-Hartley and Landrum-Griffin, "as if they had been written into the Constitution," explained Theodore White. When the Republican delegates on the Platform Committee gathered together to polish up the old anti-union shibboleths in 1972, however, they were stopped in their tracks by Richard Nixon. In his passionate desire to seduce the blue-collar vote away from the Democrats, he sent John Ehrlichman to oversee the crafting of the platform to ensure that the party would unilaterally end its official war with labor. As a result, the platform praised "the nation's labor unions for advancing the well-being not only of their members but also of our entire free-enterprise system." It was Nixon's less famous détente. "We salute," declared the Republican platform, "the statesmanship of the labor union movement." The man who declared he came to Congress "to smash the labor bosses" in 1947 was now declaring "There will be no anti-labor plank in this platform."[65]

However symbolic, the changes in the Republican platform were as concrete a gesture as Nixon made to his new constituency. The working-class appeal worked much like the campaign as a whole: a series of behind-the-scenes maneuvers tied together by imperial pronouncements. His nomination was more of a minute-by-minute planned coronation—complete with planned spontaneous demonstrations—and his campaign went down in history as the non-campaign, one that looked much more like a made-for-television tour. As the journalist David Broder accused, "The editors of the country and the television news chiefs ought to tell Mr. Nixon in plain terms, that before they spend another nickel to send their reporters and camera crews around the country with him, they want a system set up in which journalists can be journalists again, and a President campaigns as a candidate, not a touring emperor."[66]

As the election approached, Secretary of Labor James Hodgson tried to summarize Nixon's working-class appeal in an appearance at New York's Dutch Treat Club by arguing that "the worker's liberalism had been tied to bread-and-butter economic issues [and] when those issues were crowded from the center stage by more extraneous socio-logical concepts, the workers began to question sharply just where his self-interest lay." But even for white male workers, the Republican Party offered little of "bread-and-butter" value—comfort and solace but precious little bread. In many ways, the blue-collar strategy offered the worst type of identity politics—place of pride but place without economic substance.[67]

In the final push to get out the blue-collar vote for Nixon, the administration had one hundred thousand little stickers delivered to New York City that declared simply, "NIXON" above a hard hat emblazoned with an American flag. The campaign decals were designed to be just the right size to be placed on a workers' hard hat. There was, however, a problem: "*NO UNION BUG*" (the symbol that shows they were printed by a union firm) proclaimed a memo on one of the stickers, "*They're useless.*" The stickers never saw the light of day. While the Nixon people were able to marshal all of the symbols and pageantry of the blue-collar strategy, the underlying bedrock principle of unionism—protection of jobs and wages through solidarity—still remained an alien concept.[68]

When Richard Nixon won the largest electoral victory in American political history in 1972, he sat hidden away in his favorite office in the Executive Office Building alone with his devoted advisors, Bob Haldeman and Chuck Colson. Bob Haldeman dutifully thumbed through reams of election returns to tally the exact size of the president's landslide, calculations that would eventually lead to 62 percent of the popular vote, forty-nine states in the Electoral College, 57 percent of the manual worker vote, and 54 percent of the union vote. The increases in union and manual votes were some of the largest jumps in any category in that four-year interval, suggesting something particularly remarkable about the voting behavior of workers that year—whether due to the success of Nixon's strategy, the announcement that "Peace was at hand," the many failings of McGovern's campaign, or all three. The president himself certainly believed it was a strategic breakthrough. Basking in the private moment of a public victory, Nixon raised his scotch and soda to Charles Colson. "Here's to you Chuck," exclaimed the victorious president, "Those are your votes that are pouring in, the Catholics, the union members, the blue-collars, your votes, boy. It was your strategy and it's a landslide!"[69]

Writing in the halcyon days between Nixon's victory and the public imbroglio of Watergate, pamphleteer Patrick Buchanan claimed in a book titled *The New Majority*, that "the ideological fault that runs beneath the surface and down the center of the Democratic Party is as deep as any political division in America." The blue-collar, lower-middle-class ethnics and white Southerners "who gave FDR those great landslides" are now in rebellion against the "intellectual aristocracy and liberal elite who now set the course of their party." The 1972 election was for Nixon and the Republicans much like the 1936 election was for Roosevelt and the Democrats: the delivery of the common man to the party of Nixon. The election was, Buchanan claimed, a fundamental, semi-permanent realignment: "a victory of 'the New American Majority' over the 'New Politics,' a victory of traditional American values and beliefs over the claims of the counter-culture,' a victory of the 'Middle America' over the celebrants of Woodstock Nation".

XI

Richard Nixon was simultaneously the last president to work within the logic of the New Deal political framework of material politics, the first postwar president to try to recast the ways in which workers appeared in American presidential strategy, and the last to court labor seriously. While "struggling to change the political fortunes of the presidential Republican party by dressing it up as the congeries of the silent rather than the rich or propertied," in David Farber's formulation, Nixon helped to push the concept of "worker" out of the realm of production and helped drive a long process of deconstructing the postwar worker as a liberal, materially based concept. Knowing as he did that there was not a single working-class identity of a pure working-class consciousness, he sought to build political power out of new forms of discontent. As sociologist David Halle and others have argued, class consciousness, nationalism, and populism all have very blurry and overlapping edges; they bleed into one another and shape the presentation and representation of different sources of social identity. At any of the sources of workers' thinking about themselves, explains Halle, "there is an identity that contains the seeds of both a progressive and a reactionary response, and which one is dominant will depend on the possibilities people are presented with." Nixon grasped this basic sociology and sought to recast the definition of "working class" from economics to culture, from workplace and community to national pride. En route to his hoped-for New Majority, he paved the way for a reconsideration of labor that, in its long-term effects, helped to erode the political force, meaning, and certainly economic identity, of "workers" in American political discourse.[75]

As graceless as Nixon's ideas and plans might have been, he did attempt to fill a void in the nation's discussion of working people by drafting a powerful emotional pageantry around blue-collar resentments. In contrast, as the Democratic Party chased after affluent suburban voters and social liberals, historian Judith Stein argues, its leaders failed to "devise a modernization project compatible with the interests of their working-class base." Indeed Nixon may have been the last president to take working-class interests seriously, but his was less a "modernizing project" than a postmodernizing one. Lacking both resources and inclination to offer material betterment to the whole of the American labor force, Nixon instead tried to offer ideological shelter to those white male workers and union members who felt themselves slipping through the widening cracks of the New Deal coalition. In the end Nixon's efforts were based too much on undercutting the opposition than building his own vision, and they were too subterranean for a time that cried out for explicit leadership. He sniffed out the anger and resentment of a constituency in drift only to try to win them with his own definitions of their problems.[76]

Nixon also based his strategic reasoning on political blocs that conflated workers with unions—a hypothetical unity that Ronald Reagan would successfully bifurcate a decade later. Nixon seemed to feel that all he had to do was command his aides to do the right things, get his representatives to say what people wanted to hear, woo the right leader, and pull the right political levers to draw the right blocs into his realignment. If the project to build the New Right worker was incomplete, as Jonathan Rieder suggests, "the crafting of a new culture of the Right, one more self-consciously grounded in appeals to the working and lower-middle classes, did not occur full-blown overnight." As one Democratic strategist explained at the time, "Nixon gnaws around the edges of a worker's life. He hasn't touched the central trade union part. But he gnaws a little at the Catholic part, a little at the Polish part, a little at the patriotic part and a little at the anti-hippie part. After a while, he has an awful lot of that worker."[77]

In December 1972, still basking in the afterglow of the election, Chuck Colson telephoned the president to report that they were receiving the "damnedest fan mail" about the appointment of Peter Brennan as secretary of labor. "You mean," said Nixon, "they finally think the appointment of a working man makes them think that we're for the working man? They talk about all the tokenism—we appoint blacks and that but they don't think you're for blacks. Mexicans, they don't think you're for Mexicans. But a working man, by golly, that's really something." Yes, explained Colson, "This kind of locked it up." As Colson continued, "The fundamental dichotomy here, the fundamental cleavage within the Democratic Party is such that with what you're doing to build the New Majority, and what I hope to help you do, I think we're going to keep them split, and I'm awful bullish about what we can do in this country."

"They may not ever become Republicans," Colson summarized; "but they're Nixon."[78]

Notes

3   Raymond Price, *With Nixon* (New York: Viking Press, 1977), 121.

6   On Nixon's ethnic appeals, see "Republican Ethnic Buttons, 1972" in Collection 3334, Box 2, Political Campaigns, U.S. presidential, miscellany, 1972, KLRM.

7   Richard Reeves, *Alone in the White House*, 138–39; Dent to Nixon, 16 October 1969, President's Office Files, Box 79.

10   Stephen Lesher, *George Wallace: American Populist* (Reading, MA: Addison-Wesley 1994), 395; Dan T. Carter, *The Politics of Race: George Wallace, the Origins of the New Conservatism and the Transformation of American Politics* (New York: Simon and Schuster, 1995), 378.

11   Kevin P. Phillips, *The Emerging Republican Majority* (New Rochelle, NY: Arlington House, 1969), 463; Gary Wills, *Nixon Agonistes* (Houghton Mifflin Co, 1970), p. 265.

12   On how the Wallace issue plagued Nixon and his attempt to outflank the Alabama governor, see Carter, *The Politics of Race*, 371–414; *JHLL* 9 March 1969. As the blue-collar strategy took shape, Kevin Phillips recognized it as the "Post-Southern Strategy," *Washington Post* 25 September 1970; Phillips still believed in the liberal economic measures even as he sought to guide the nation toward social conservatism. He pushed for national health insurance, welfare reform, aid to ailing industrial and agricultural areas. Roland Evans Jr. and Robert Novak, *Nixon in the White House: The Frustration of Power* (New York: Random House, 1971), 322–23; Kevin P. Phillips, "Middle America and the Emerging Republican Majority," Box 46, Dent Files, RNP; Robert Mason, *New Majority* (The University of North Carolina Press, 2004), p. 48, 117; Philip Jenkins, *Decade of Nightmares: The End of the Sixties and the Making of Eighties America* (New York: Oxford University Press, 2006), 94.

13   Richard M. Scammon and Ben J. Wattenberg, *The Real Majority* (New York: Coward-McCann, 1970), 195–97; Pete Hamill, "Wallace," 7 *Ramparts* (7 October 1968): 44–48.

14   Pete Hamill, "The Revolt of the White Lower Middle Class," *New York Magazine*, 14 April 1969, 28–29, reprinted in *The White Majority, Between Poverty and Affluence*, ed. Louise Kappe Howe (New York: Random House, 1970), 10–22.

17   Burns to President, 26 May 1969, FF: [Welfare Book], Ehrlichman Files Box 39, RNP; "Memorandum for the Director," n.d., FF: Blue Collar, Colson Files Box 39, RNP. For another powerful iteration of the administration's thinking on the labor issue, see "The Nixon Administration and the Working Man," 11 June 1971, FF: Blue Collar, Colson Files Box 39, RNP.

18   *New York Times* 9 May 1970; *New York Times* 10 May 1970; *New York Times* 11 May 1970; *New York Times* 12 May 1970; *New York Times* 13 May 1970; *New York Times* 21 May 1970; *Business Week*, 16 May 1970; for an insightful discussion of the issue of masculinity in the hard hat image, see Joshua B. Freeman, "Hardhats: Construction Workers, Manliness, and the 1970 Pro-War Demonstrations," *Journal of Social History* 26 (Summer 1993): 726–44; see also Joshua B. Freeman, *Working-Class New York* (New York: New Press, 2000), 237–46. It is interesting to note that Hamill condemned the riots as the "work of cowards," see Vincent J. Cannato, *The Ungovernable City: John Lindsay and His Struggle to Save New York* (New York: Basic Books, 2001), 448–53.

19   *New York Times* 21 May 1970; Christian G. Appy, *Working-Class War: American Combat Soldiers and Vietnam* (Chapel Hill: University of North Carolina Press, 1993), 299; tradesman quoted in Freeman, *Working-Class New York*, 242.

20   Bull to Colson, 22 May 1970, FF: Hard Hats-Building and Construction Trades, Colson Files Box 69, RNP.

21   Richard Sennett and Jonathan Cobb, *The Hidden Injuries of Class* (New York: Knopf, 1972), 146.

22   *Haldeman Diaries*, 10 May 1970; William Safire, *Before the Fall* (Doubleday, 1975), p. 38; Charles W. Colson, *Born Again* (Old Tappan, NJ: Chosen Books, 1976), 39–40.

23   Colson to President, 26 October 1970, FF: Broder Articles, Colson Files Box 40, RNP.

24   Haldeman to Chapin, 31 July 1971, FF: 14, Chronological Files, Contested Documents, Haldeman Files Box 197, RNP; Memo from Colson to O'Hara, 21 September 1970 in Bruce Oudes, ed., *From the President: Richard Nixon's Secret Files* (New York: Harper and Row, 1989), 161; Haldeman Notes, 24 July 1970, FF: H Notes July–December '70, Haldeman Files Box 42, RNP; Colson claims that no Teamsters were hired. *New York Times* 24 September 1981; Summers, *Arrogance*, 356–57. There seemingly could be many more such ploys that may never come to light, with unresolved hints sprinkled throughout the Nixon papers such as Charles Colson's cryptic correspondence about a meeting with New York building trades leader Peter Brennan in the fall of 1970 regarding "some political chicanery that we should get going on as fast as possible."
      The only "smoking gun" that ties the administration to the revolts uncovered in this research is a small piece of correspondence between the staff member Steve Bull and one of Nixon's most trusted advisors, Charles Colson. "Obviously," Bull wrote to Colson, "more of these [hard hat protests]

will be occurring throughout the Nation, perhaps partially as a result of your clandestine activity." Biographer Anthony Summers, for instance, implies that Nixon did orchestrate the protests, and even Ehrlichman "assumed" that the some of the hard-hat attacks were "laid on" by the White House. No concrete evidence has proven the case that the original protests were directed by the White House, but it is not unlikely that the administration helped, in whatever ways necessary, to insure their continuation. Whether or not the administration actually assisted in the development of the protests, it was easy to see how, in the combination of working-class backlash, police sympathy, apparent employer support (the workers were off the job and still getting paid), and some mysterious gray-suited individuals, they added up to what *The Nation* called a pattern evincing "the classic elements of Hitlerian street tactics." See Anthony Summers, *The Arrogance of Power: The Secret World of Richard Nixon* (New York: Viking, 2000), 358, 590; Fred J. Cook, "Rampaging Patriots," *The Nation*, 15 June 1970, 712; Bull to Colson, 22 May 1970, FF: Hard Hats-Building and Construction Trades, Colson Files Box 69, RNP.

25 *New York Times* 27 May 1970; Freeman, *Working-Class New York*, 239.

26 Robert Collins, *More: The Politics of Economic Growth in Postwar America* (New York: Oxford, 2000), 103; *New York Times* 17 August 1969; Mason, *New Majority*, 57.

27 Nixon quote on OSHA in Mason, *New Majority*, 118; Charles Noble, *Liberalism at Work: The Rise and Fall of OSHA* (Philadelphia: Temple University Press, 1986), 68–98.

28 *Haldeman Diaries*; Mason, *New Majority*, 57; Joan Hoff, *Nixon Reconsidered* (Basic Books, 1994), p. 129–44; Vincent J. Burke, *Nixon's Good Deed: Welfare Reform* (New York: Columbia University Press, 1974).

46 The suspension was hotly debated by his advisors as Arthur Burns recommended Nixon "wave a big stick at the building trades unions," while Shultz, then at the Bureau of the Budget, "argued that antagonizing the hard-hat unions would be bad politics." See Evans and Novak, *Nixon in the White House*, 370–71; "Statement by the President" (suspension of Davis-Bacon Act), 23 February 1971, FF: Building and Construction Trades, Colson Files Box 39, RNP; Colson to President, 23 February 1971, FF: Building and Construction Trades, Colson Files Box 40, RNP; Colson to Chapin, 25 February 1971, FF: Hard-Hats-Building and Construction Trades, Colson Files Box 69, RNP; *New York Times* 24 February 1971 and 25 February 1971; *Wall Street Journal* 30 March 1970.

47 *New York Times* 30 March 1971; Matusow, *Nixon's Economy* (University Press of Kansas, 2998), pp. 95–96, Safire, *Before the Fall*, 587–88; for a complete discussion of the wage controversy in the construction industry, see Marc Linder, *Wars of Attrition: Vietnam, the Business Round-table, and the Decline of the Construction Unions* (Iowa City: Fanpihua Press, 1999), 304–27.

49 *New York Times* 19 August 1971; Matusow, *Nixon's Economy*, 158; Meany clarifies his stance on controls on "NBC's Meet the Press," 11 July 1971, transcript, RG 1, Box 83, FF 10, GMMA.

58 Safire, *Before the Fall*, 591–92.

59 *Washington Post* 10 October 1972; David Broder, "The Story that Still Nags at Me—Edward S. Muskie," *Washington Monthly*, February 1987; Jules Witcover, "William Loeb and the New Hampshire Primary: A Question of Ethics," *Columbia Journalism Review* (May/June) 1972, 14–27; *Manchester Union Leader* 24 February 1972.

60 The details of this potential conspiracy are laid out in Dan Carter, *From George Wallace to Newt Gingrich*, 49–51; *Haldeman Diaries*, 20 July 1972.

61 "Why Unions Are Running Scared in 1968," *Nation's Business* 56 (June 1968): 36–39; Mason, *New Majority*, 164; Taylor Dark, *The Unions and the Democrats: An Enduring Alliance* (Ithaca, NY: Cornell University Press, 1999), 87–92; J. David Greenstone, *Labor in American Politics*, 2nd ed. (Chicago: University of Chicago Press, 1977), xxv; see also, Jerry Wurf, "What Labor Has Against McGovern," *New Republic*, 5 and 12 August 1972.

62 *JHLL* 23 September 1972; *New York Times* 29 July 1972; Archie Robinson, *Meany* (Simon & Schuster, 1982), pp. 322–23.

63 Notes on the memo in Safire, *Before the Fall*, 592–93.

64 Buchanan/Kachigian "Assault Strategy," 8 June 1972, in Oudes, *From the President*, 466. On tensions between Meany and McGovern on 14(b) and communism, see *Washington Post* 28 April 1972.

65 Theodore H. White, *The Making of the President, 1972* (New York: Atheneum Publishers, 1973), 239–40; *New York Times* 15 October 1972.

66   Broder quote, ibid., 268.

67   Poll cited in Mason, *New Majority*, 187; Address by Secretary of Labor James D. Hodgson, 3 October 1972, FF: Labor (1 of 2) Barker Files Box 2, RNP.

68   *Haldeman Diaries*, 10 October 1972; Rodgers to Colson, 5 September 1972, FF: Nixon and Labor/Political, Colson Files Box 96, RNP.

69   Colson, *Born Again*, 15. Calculations made from Gallup Poll, "Vote by Groups, 1968–1972," http://www.gallup.com/poll/trends/ptgrp6872.asp. The southern vote for Nixon had the most dramatic increase of any category for Nixon—thirty-five points—but this can be attributed largely to the absence of George Wallace, who garnered 33 percent in 1968. The only other categories approaching this type of increase were the high-school-educated vote, with a 23 percent increase, but this category is not an unreasonable proxy for "manual worker." The only other substantial jump that matches these categories is in the age category thirty-to-forty-nine-year-olds, which saw a disproportionate twenty-six point increase.

75   David Farber, "The Silent Majority and Talk about Revolution," in *The Sixties from Memory to History*, ed. David Farber (Chapel Hill: University of North Carolina Press, 1994), 295; Farber applies Jean Baudrillard's post-Marxist conceptualization that controlling the means of production is less important than the means of "controlling the code"; David Halle, *America's Working Man* (Chicago: University of Chicago Press, 1984), 301, 292. See a very useful similar theoretical formulation that helps situate the politics of class with the new social movements, J. Craig Jenkins and Kevin Leicht, "Class Analysis and Social Movements: A Critique and Reformulation" in *Reworking Class*, ed. John R. Hall (Ithaca, NY: Cornell University Press), 369–92, esp. 382–84.

76   Judith Stein, *Running Steel, Running America* (Chapel Hill: University of North Carolina Press, 1998), 6.

77   "Nixon Wooing of Labor Vote Dates to 1970," 12 October 1972, FF 14, Box 031, Cope Research Files, GMMA; Jonathan Rieder, "Silent Majority," in Fraser & Gerstle, eds, *The Rise and Fall of the New Deal* (Princeton University Press,1990), p. 265; Bruce J. Schulman, *The Seventies* (Da Cappo Press, 2002), pp. 24–32; Colson, *Born Again*, 31–32. There was talk of using Nixon's biography as a "common man" to bolster the blue-collar strategy.

78   The tape is Conversation Number 153–20, 14 November 1972, Camp David Study Table, Nixon Presidential Library & Museum, Sample Conversations, Fifth Chronological Release, Part II, http://www.nixonlibrary.gov/virtuallibrary/tape excerpts/fifthchron_part_ii.php.

CHAPTER 32

The Global Reserve Army of Labor and the New Imperialism

John Bellamy Foster and Robert W. McChesney

In the last few decades there has been an enormous shift in the capitalist economy in the direction of the globalization of production. Much of the increase in manufacturing and even services production that would have formerly taken place in the global North—as well as a portion of the North's preexisting production—is now being offshored to the global South, where it is feeding the rapid industrialization of a handful of emerging economies. It is customary to see this shift as arising from the economic crisis of 1974–75 and the rise of neoliberalism—or as erupting in the 1980s and after, with the huge increase in the global capitalist labor force resulting from the integration of Eastern Europe and China into the world economy. Yet the foundations of production on a global scale, we will argue, were laid in the 1950s and 1960s, and were already depicted in the work of Stephen Hymer, the foremost theorist of the multinational corporation, who died in 1974.

For Hymer multinational corporations evolved out of the monopolistic (or oligopolistic) structure of modern industry in which the typical firm was a giant corporation controlling a substantial share of a given market or industry. At a certain point in their development (and in the development of the system) these giant corporations, headquartered in the rich economies, expanded abroad, seeking monopolistic advantages—as well as easier access to raw materials and local markets—through ownership and control of foreign subsidiaries. Such firms internalized within their own structure of corporate planning the international division of labor for their products. "Multinational corporations," Hymer observed, "are a substitute for the market as a method of organizing international exchange." They led inexorably to the internationalization of production and the formation of a system of "international oligopoly" that would increasingly dominate the world economy.[1]

Original publication details: John Bellamy Foster and Robert W. McChesney, "The Global Reserve of Labor, from *The Endless Crisis: How monopoly-finance capital produces stagnation and upheaval from the USA to China*, pp. 125–129; 131–141; 143–154. Monthly Review Press, 2012. Reproduced with permission from Monthly Press.

In his last article, "International Politics and International Economics: A Radical Approach," published posthumously in 1975, Hymer focused on the issue of the enormous "latent surplus-population" or reserve army of labor in both the backward areas of the developed economies and in the underdeveloped countries, "which could be broken down to form a constantly flowing surplus population to work at the bottom of the ladder." Following Karl Marx, Hymer insisted that "accumulation of capital is, therefore, increase of the proletariat." The vast "external reserve army" in the third world, supplementing the "internal reserve army" within the developed capitalist countries, constituted the real material basis on which multinational capital was able to internationalize production—creating a continual movement of surplus population into the labor force, and weakening labor globally through a process of "divide and rule."[2]

A close consideration of Hymer's work thus serves to clarify the essential point that "the great global job shift"[3] from North to South, which has become such a central issue in our time, is not to be seen so much in terms of international competition, deindustrialization, economic crisis, new communication technologies—or even such general phenomena as globalization and financialization—though each of these can be said to have played a part. Rather, this shift is to be viewed as the result primarily of the internationalization of monopoly capital, arising from the global spread of multinational corporations and the concentration and centralization of production on a world scale. Moreover, it is tied to a whole system of polarization of wages (as well as wealth and poverty) on a world scale, which has its basis in the global reserve army of labor.

The international oligopolies that increasingly dominate the world economy avoid genuine price competition, colluding instead in the area of price. For example, Ford and Toyota and the other leading auto firms do not try to undersell each other in the prices of their final products—since to do so would unleash a destructive price war that would reduce the profits of all of these firms. With price competition—the primary form of competition in economic theory—for the most part banned, the two main forms of competition that remain in a mature market or industry are: (1) competition for low-cost position, entailing reductions in prime production (labor and raw material) costs, and (2) what is known as "monopolistic competition," that is, oligopolistic rivalry directed at marketing or the sales effort.[4]

In terms of international production it is important to understand that the giant firms constantly strive for the lowest possible costs globally in order to expand their profit margins and reinforce their degree of monopoly within a given industry. This arises from the very nature of oligopolistic rivalry. As Michael E. Porter of the Harvard Business School wrote in his *Competitive Strategy* in 1980:

> Having a low-cost position yields the firm above-average returns in its industry.... Its cost position gives the firm a defense against rivalry from competitors, because its lower costs mean that it can still earn returns after its competitors have competed away their profits through rivalry.... Low cost provides a defense against powerful suppliers by providing more flexibility to cope with input cost increases. The factors that lead to a low-cost position usually also provide substantial entry barriers in terms of scale economies or cost advantages.[5]

The continuous search for low-cost position and higher profit margins led, beginning with the expansion of foreign direct investment in the 1960s, to the "offshoring" of a considerable portion of production. This, however, required the successful tapping of huge potential pools of labor in the third world to create a vast low-wage workforce. Expansion of the global labor force available to capital in recent decades has occurred mainly as a result of two factors: (1) the depeasantization of a large portion of the global periphery by means of agribusiness—removing peasants from the land, with the resulting expansion of the population of urban slums; and (2) the integration of the workforce of the former "actually existing socialist" countries into the world capitalist economy. Between 1980 and 2007 the global labor force, according to the International Labor Organisation (ILO), grew from 1.9 billion to 3.1 billion, a rise of 63 percent—with 73 percent of the labor force located in the developing world, and 40 percent in China and India alone.[6]

The South's share of industrial employment has risen dramatically from 51 percent in 1980 to 73 percent in 2008. Developing country imports as a proportion of the total imports of the United States more than quadrupled in the last half of the twentieth century.[7]

The result of these global megatrends is the peculiar structure of the world economy that we find today, with corporate control and profits concentrated at the top, while the global labor force at the bottom is confronted with abysmally low wages and a chronic insufficiency of productive employment. Stagnation in the mature economies and the resulting financialization of accumulation have only intensified these tendencies by helping to drive what Stephen Roach of Morgan Stanley dubbed "global labor arbitrage," i.e., the system of economic rewards derived from exploiting the international wage hierarchy, resulting in outsized returns for corporations and investors.[8] Our argument here is that the key to understanding these changes in the imperialist system (beyond the analysis of the multinational corporation itself…is to be found in the growth of the global reserve army—as Hymer was among the first to realize. Not only has the growth of the global capitalist labor force (including the available reserve army) radically altered the position of third world labor, it also has had an effect on labor in the rich economies, where wage levels are stagnant or declining for this and other reasons. Everywhere multinational corporations have been able to apply a divide-and-rule policy, altering the relative positions of capital and labor worldwide.

Mainstream economics is not of much help in analyzing these changes. In line with the Panglossian view of globalization advanced by Thomas Friedman, most establishment analysts see the growth of the global labor force, the North-South shift in jobs, and the expansion of international low-wage competition as simply reflecting an increasingly "flat world" in which economic differences (advantages/disadvantages) between nations are disappearing.[9] As Paul Krugman, representing the stance of orthodox economics, has declared: "If policy makers and intellectuals think it is important to emphasize the adverse effects of low- wage competition [for developed countries and the global economy], then it is at least equally important for economists and business leaders to tell them they are wrong." Krugman's reasoning here is based on the assumption that wages will invariably adjust to productivity growth, and the inevitable result will be a new world-economic equilibrium.[10] All is for the best in the best of all capitalist worlds. Indeed, if there are worries in the orthodox economic camp in this respect, they have to do, as we shall see, with concerns about how long the huge gains derived from global labor arbitrage can be maintained.[11]

In sharp contrast, we shall develop an approach emphasizing that behind the phenomenon of global labor arbitrage lies a new global phase in the development of Marx's "absolute general law of capitalist accumulation," according to which:

The greater the social wealth, the functioning capital, the extent and energy of its growth, and therefore also the greater the absolute mass of the proletariat and the productivity of its labour, the greater is the industrial reserve army.... But the greater this reserve army in proportion to the active labour-army, the greater is the mass of a consolidated surplus population, whose misery is in inverse ratio to the amount of torture it has to undergo in the form of labour. The more extensive, finally, the pauperized sections of the working class and the industrial reserve army, the greater is official pauperism. *This is the absolute general law of capitalist accumulation.*

Far from being a crude theory of immiseration, Marx's general law was an attempt to explain how the accumulation of capital could occur at all: that is, why the growth in demand for labor did not lead to a continual rise in wages, which would squeeze profits and cut off accumulation. Moreover, it served to explain: (1) the functional role that unemployment played in the capitalist system; (2) the reason why crisis was so devastating to the working class as a whole; and (3) the tendency toward the pauperization of a large part of the population. Today it has its greatest significance in accounting for "global labor arbitrage," i.e., capital's earning of enormous monopolistic returns or imperial rents by shifting certain sectors of production to underdeveloped regions of the world to take advantage of the global immobility of labor, and the existence of subsistence (or below subsistence) wages in much of the global South.

As Fredric Jameson recently noted in *Representing Capital*, despite the "mockery" thrown at Marx's general law of accumulation in the early post–Second World War era, "it is...no longer a joking matter." Rather, the general law highlights "the actuality today of *Capital* on a world scale."[18]

It is therefore essential to engage in close examination of Marx's argument. In his best-known single statement on the general law of accumulation, Marx wrote:

> *In proportion* as capital accumulates, the situation of the worker, *be his payment high or low*, must grow worse.... The law which always holds the relative surplus population *in equilibrium* with the extent and energy of accumulation rivets the worker to capital more firmly than the wedges of Hephaestus held Prometheus to the rock. It makes an accumulation of misery a necessary condition, *corresponding to* the accumulation of wealth. Accumulation at one pole is, therefore, at the same time accumulation of misery, the torment of labour, slavery, ignorance, brutalization and moral degradation at the opposite pole, i.e. on the side of the class that produces its own product as capital [italics added].[19]

By pointing to an "equilibrium" between accumulation of capital and the "relative surplus population" or reserve army of labor, Marx was arguing that, under "normal" conditions, the growth of accumulation is able to proceed unhindered only if it also results in the displacement of large numbers of workers. The resulting "redundancy" of workers checks any tendency toward a too rapid rise in real wages, which would bring accumulation to a halt. Rather than a crude theory of "immiseration," then, the general law of accumulation highlighted that capitalism, via the constant generation of a reserve army of the unemployed, naturally tended to polarize between relative wealth at the top and relative poverty at the bottom—with the threat of falling into the latter constituting an enormous lever for the increase in the rate of exploitation of employed workers.

Marx commenced his treatment of the general law by straightforwardly observing, as we have noted, that the accumulation of capital, all other things being equal, increased the demand for labor. In order to prevent this growing demand for labor from contracting the available supply of workers, and thereby forcing up wages and squeezing profits, it was necessary that a counterforce come into being that would reduce the amount of labor needed at any given level of output. This was accomplished primarily through increases in labor productivity with the introduction of new capital and technology, resulting in the displacement of labor. (Marx specifically rejected the classical "iron law of wages" that saw the labor force as determined primarily by population growth.) In this way, by "constantly revolutionizing the instruments of production," the capitalist system is able, no less constantly, to reproduce a relative surplus population or reserve army of labor, which competes for jobs with those in the active labor army.[20] "The industrial reserve army," Marx wrote, "during periods of stagnation and average prosperity, weighs down the active army of workers; during the period of over-production and feverish activity, it puts a curb on their pretensions. The relative surplus population is therefore the background against which the law of the demand and supply of labour does its work. It confines the field of action of this law to the limits absolutely convenient to capital's drive to exploit and dominate the workers."[21]

It followed that if this essential lever of accumulation were to be maintained, the reserve army would need to be continually restocked so as to remain in a constant (if not increasing) ratio to the active labor army. While generals won battles by "recruiting" armies, capitalists won them by "discharging the army of workers."[22]

It is important to note that Marx developed his well-known analysis of the concentration and centralization of capital as part the argument on the general law of accumulation. Thus the tendency toward the domination of the economy by bigger and fewer capitals was as much a part of his overall argument on the general law as was the growth of the reserve army itself. The two processes were inextricably bound together.[23]

Marx's breakdown of the reserve army of labor into its various components was complex, and was clearly aimed both at comprehensiveness and at deriving what were for his time statistically relevant categories. It included not only those who were "wholly unemployed" but also those who were only "partially employed." Thus the relative surplus population, he wrote, "exists in all kinds of forms." Nevertheless, outside of periods of acute economic crisis, there were three major forms of the relative surplus population: the floating, latent, and stagnant. On top of that there was the whole additional realm of official pauperism, which concealed even more elements of the reserve army.

The floating population consisted of workers who were unemployed due to the normal ups and downs of accumulation or as a result of technological unemployment: people who have recently worked, but who were now out of work and in the process of searching for new jobs. Here Marx discussed the age structure of employment and its effects on unemployment, with capital constantly seeking younger, cheaper workers. So exploitative was the work process that workers were physically used up quickly and discarded at a fairly early age well before their working life was properly over.[24]

The latent reserve army was to be found in agriculture, where the demand for labor, Marx wrote, "falls absolutely" as soon as capitalist production has taken it over. Hence, there was a "constant flow" of labor from subsistence agriculture to industry in the towns: "The constant movement towards the towns presupposes, in the countryside itself, a constant latent surplus population, the extent of which only becomes evident at those exceptional times when its distribution channels are wide open. The wages of the agricultural labourer are therefore reduced to a minimum, and he always stands with one foot already in the swamp of pauperism."[25]

The third major form of the reserve army, the stagnant population, formed, according to Marx, "a part of the active reserve army but with extremely irregular employment." This included all sorts of part-time, casual (and what would today be called informal) labor. The wages of workers in this category could be said to "sink below the average normal level of the working class" (i.e., below the value of labor power). It was here that the bulk of the masses ended up who had been "made 'redundant'" by large-scale industry and agriculture. Indeed, these workers represented "a proportionately greater part" of "the general increase in the [working] class than the other elements" of the reserve army.

The largest part of this stagnant reserve army was to be found in "modern domestic industry," which consisted of "outwork" carried out through the agency of subcontractors on behalf of manufacture, and dominated by so-called "cheap labor," primarily women and children. Often such "outworkers" outweighed factory labor in an industry. For example, a shirt factory in Londonderry employed 1,000 workers but also had another 9,000 outworkers attached to it stretched out over the countryside. Here the most "murderous side of the economy" was revealed.[26]

For Marx, pauperism constituted "the lowest sediment of the relative surplus population" and it was here that the "precarious...condition of existence" of the entire working population was most evident. "Pauperism," he wrote, "is the hospital of the active labor-army and the dead weight of the industrial reserve army." Beyond the actual "lumpen-proletariat" or "vagabonds, criminals, prostitutes," etc., there were three categories of paupers. First, those who were able to work and who reflected the drop in the numbers of the poor in every period of industrial prosperity when the demand for labor was greatest. These destitute elements employed only in times of prosperity were an extension of the active labor army. Second, it included orphans and pauper children, who in the capitalist system were drawn into industry in great numbers during periods of expansion. Third, it encompassed "the demoralized, the ragged, and those unable to work, chiefly people who succumb to their incapacity for adaptation, an incapacity that arises from the division of labour; people who have lived beyond the worker's average life-span; and the victims of industry whose number increases with the growth of dangerous machinery, of mines, chemical workers, etc., the mutilated, the sickly, the widows, etc." Such pauperism was a creation of capitalism itself, "but capital usually knows how to transfer these [social costs] from its own shoulders to those of the working class and the petty bourgeoisie."[27]

The full extent of the global reserve army was evident in periods of economic prosperity, when much larger numbers of workers were temporarily drawn into employment. This included foreign workers. In addition to the sections of the reserve armies mentioned above, Marx noted that Irish workers were drawn into employment in English industry in periods of peak production—such that they constituted part of the relative surplus population for English production.[28] The temporary reduction in the size of the reserve army in comparison to the active labor army at the peak of the business cycle had the effect of pulling up wages above their average value and squeezing profits—though Marx repeatedly indicated that such increases in real wages were not the principal cause of crises in profitability, and never threatened the system itself.[29]

During an economic crisis, many of the workers in the active labor army would themselves be made "redundant," thereby increasing the numbers of unemployed on top of the normal reserve army. In such periods, the enormous weight of the relative surplus population would tend to pull wages down below their average value (i.e., the historically determined value of labor power). As Marx himself put it: "Stagnation in production makes part of the working class idle and hence places the employed workers in conditions where they have to accept a fall in wages, even below the average."[30] Hence, in times of economic crisis, the working class as an organic whole, encompassing the active labor army and the reserve army, was placed in dire conditions, with a multitude of people succumbing to hunger and disease.

Marx was unable to complete his critique of political economy, and consequently never wrote his projected volume on world trade. Nevertheless, it is clear that he saw the general law of accumulation as extending eventually to the world level. Capital located in the rich countries, he believed, would take advantage of cheaper labor abroad—and of the higher levels of exploitation in the underdeveloped parts of the world made possible by the existence of vast surplus labor pools (and noncapitalist modes of production). In his speech to the Lausanne Congress of the First International in 1867 (the year of the publication of the first volume of *Capital*) he declared: "A study of the struggle waged by the English working class reveals that, in order to oppose their workers, the employers either bring in workers from abroad or else transfer manufacture to countries where there is a cheap labor force. Given this state of affairs, if the working class wishes to continue its struggle with some chance of success, the national organisations must become international."[31]

Global Labor Arbitrage

The pursuit of "an ever extended market" Marx contended, is an "inner necessity" of the capitalist mode of production.[34] This inner necessity took on a new significance, however, with the rise of monopoly capitalism in the late nineteenth and early twentieth centuries. The emergence of multinational corporations, first in the giant oil companies and a handful of other firms in the early twentieth century, and then becoming a much more general phenomenon in the post–Second World War years, was a product of the concentration and centralization of capital on a world scale, but equally involved the transformation of world labor and production.

It was the increasing multinational corporate dominance over the world economy, in fact, that led to the modern concept of "globalization," which arose in the early 1970s as economists, particularly those on the left, tried to understand the way in which the giant firms were reorganizing world production and labor conditions.[35] This was clearly evident by the early 1970s—not only in Hymer's work, but also in Richard Barnet and Ronald Müller's *Global Reach*, which introduced the term "globalization" to account for expanding foreign direct investment. Explaining how oligopolistic rivalry now meant searching for the lowest unit labor costs worldwide, Barnet and Müller argued that this had generated "the 'runaway shop' which becomes the 'export platform' in an underdeveloped country" and a necessity of business for U.S. companies, just like their European and Japanese competitors.[36]

Over the past half century, these global oligopolies have been offshoring whole sectors of production from the rich/high-wage to the poor/low-wage countries, transforming global labor conditions in their search for global low-cost position, and in a divide-and-rule approach to world labor. Some leading U.S. multinationals now employ more workers abroad than they do in the United States—even without considering the vast number of workers they employ through subcontractors. Other major corporations, such as Nike and Reebok, rely on third world subcontractors for 100 percent of their production workforce—with domestic employees confined simply to managerial, product development, marketing, and distribution activities. The result has been the proletarianization, often under precarious conditions, of much of the population of the underdeveloped countries, working in massive export zones under conditions dictated by foreign multinationals, such as General Electric and Ford.

Two realities dominate labor at the world level today. One is global labor arbitrage, or the system of imperial rent. The other is the existence of a massive global reserve army, which makes this world system of extreme exploitation possible. "Labour arbitrage" is defined quite simply by *The Economist* as "taking advantage of lower wages abroad, especially in poor countries." It is thus an unequal exchange process in which one country, as Marx said, is able to "cheat" another due to the much higher exploitation of labor in the poorer country.[37] A study of production in China's industrialized Pearl River Delta region (encompassing Guangzhou, Shenzhen, and Hong Kong) found in 2005 that some workers were compelled to work up to sixteen hours continuously, and that corporal punishment was routinely employed as a means of worker discipline. Some 200 million Chinese are said to work in hazardous conditions, claiming over 100,000 lives a year.[38]

It is such *superexploitation* that lies behind much of the expansion of production in the global South.[39] The fact that this has been the basis of rapid economic growth for some emerging economies does not alter the reality that it has generated enormous imperial rents for multinational corporations and capital at the center of the system. As labor economist Charles Whalen has written, "The prime motivation behind offshoring is the desire to reduce labor costs…a U.S.-based factory worker hired for $21 an hour can be replaced by a Chinese factory worker who is paid 64 cents an hour…. The main reason offshoring is happening now is because it can."[40]

How this system of global labor arbitrage occurs by way of global supply chains, however, is enormously complex. Dell, the PC assembler, purchases some 4,500 parts from 300 different suppliers in multiple countries around the world.[41] As the Asian Development Bank Institute indicated in a 2010 study of iPhone production: "It is almost impossible [today] to define clearly where a manufactured product is made in the global market. This is why on the back of iPhones one can read 'Designed by Apple in California, Assembled in China.'" Although both statements on the back of the iPhones are literally correct, neither answers the question of where the real production takes place. Apple does not itself manufacture the iPhone. Rather the actual manufacture (that is, everything but its software and design) takes place primarily outside the United States. The production of iPhone parts and components is carried out principally by eight corporations (Toshiba, Samsung, Infineon, Broadcom, Numonyx, Murata, Dialog Semiconductor, and Cirrus Logic), which are located in Japan, South Korea, Germany, and the United States. All of the major parts and components of the iPhone are then shipped to the Shenzhen, China, plants of Foxconn, a subsidiary of Hon Hai Precision Industry, Co. headquartered in Taipei, for assembly and export to the United States.

Apple's enormous, complex global supply chain for iPod production is aimed at obtaining the lowest unit labor costs (taking into consideration labor costs, technology, etc.), appropriate for each component, with the final assembly taking place in China, where production occurs on a massive scale, under enormous intensity, and with ultra-low wages. In Foxconn's Longhua, Shenzhen, factory 300,000 to 400,000 workers eat, work, and sleep under horrendous conditions, with workers, who are compelled to do rapid hand movements for long hours for months on end, finding themselves twitching constantly at night. Foxconn workers in 2009 were paid the minimum monthly wage in Shenzhen, or about 83 cents an hour. (Overall in China in 2008 manufacturing workers were paid $1.36 an hour, according to U.S. Bureau of Labor Statistics data.)

Despite the massive labor input of Chinese workers in assembling the final product, their low pay means that their work amounts only to 3.6 percent of the total manufacturing cost (shipping price) of the iPhone. The overall profit margin on iPhones in 2009 was 64 percent. If iPhones were assembled in the United States—assuming labor costs ten times that in China, equal productivity, and constant component costs—Apple would still have an ample profit margin, but it would drop from 64 percent to 50 percent. In effect, Apple makes 22 percent of its profit margin on iPhone production from the much higher rate of exploitation of Chinese labor.[42]

Of course in stipulating a mere tenfold difference in wages between the United States and China, in its calculation of the lower profit margins to be gained with United States as opposed to Chinese assembly, the Asian Development Bank Institute was adopting a very conservative assumption. Overall Chinese manufacturing workers in 2008, according to the U.S. Bureau of Labor Statistics, received only 4 percent of the compensation for comparable work in the United States, and 3 percent of that in the European Union.[43] In comparison, hourly manufacturing wages in Mexico in 2008 were about 16 percent of the U.S. level.[44]

In spite of the low-wage "advantage" of China, some areas of Asia, such as Cambodia, Vietnam, and Bangladesh, have hourly compensation levels still lower, leading to a divide-and-rule tendency for multinational corporations (commonly acting through subcontractors) to locate some sectors of production, such as light industrial textile production, primarily in these still lower wage countries. Thus the *New York Times* indicated in July 2010 that Li & Fung, a Hong Kong-based company "that handles sourcing and apparel manufacturing for companies like Wal-Mart and Liz Claiborne," increased its production in Bangladesh by 20 percent in 2010, while China, its biggest supplier, slid 5 percent. Garment workers in Bangladesh earned around $64 a month, compared "to minimum wages in China's coastal industrial provinces ranging from $117 to $147 a month."[45]

For multinational corporations there is a clear logic to all of this. As General Electric CEO Jeffrey Immelt stated, the "most successful China strategy"—with China here clearly standing for global labor arbitrage in general—"is to capitalize on its market growth while exporting its deflationary power." This "deflationary power" has to do of course with lower labor costs (and lower costs of reproduction of labor in the North through the lowering of the costs of wage-consumption goods). It thus represents a global strategy for raising the rate of surplus value (widening profit margins).[46]

The key strategic question then was, "How long will China's low wage advantage last?" His answer was that China's "enormous 'reserve army of labor'... will be released gradually as agricultural productivity improves and jobs are created in the cities."

Writing in *Monthly Review*, economist Minqi Li notes that since the early 1980s 150 million workers in China have migrated from rural to urban areas. China thus experienced a 13 percentage-point drop (from 50 percent to 37 percent) in the share of wages in GDP between 1990 and 2005. Now "after many years of rapid accumulation, the massive reserve army of cheap labor in China's rural areas is starting to become depleted." Li focuses mainly on demographic analysis, indicating that China's total workforce is expected to peak at 970 million by 2012, and then decline by 30 million by 2020, with the decline occurring more rapidly among the prime age working population. This he believes will improve the bargaining power of workers and strengthen industrial strife in China, raising issues of radical transformation. Such industrial strife will inevitably mount if China's non-agricultural population passes "the critical threshold of 70 percent by around 2020."[51]

Others think that global labor arbitrage with respect to China is far from over. Yang Yao, an economist at Peking University, argues that "the countryside still has 45% of China's labour force," a huge reserve army of hundreds of millions, much of which will become available to industry as mechanization proceeds. Stephen Roach has observed that with Chinese wages at 4 percent of U.S. wages, there is "barely...a dent in narrowing the arbitrage with major industrial economies"—while China's "hourly compensation in manufacturing" is "less than 15% of that elsewhere in East Asia" (excluding Japan), and well below that of Mexico.[52]

The Global Reserve Army

In order to develop a firmer grasp of this issue it is crucial to look both empirically and theoretically at the global reserve army as it appears in the current historical context—and then bring to bear the entire Marxian critique of imperialism. Without such a comprehensive critique, analyses of such problems as the global shift in production, the global labor arbitrage, deindustrialization, etc., are mere partial observations suspended in midair.

The data on the global workforce compiled by the ILO conforms closely to Marx's main distinctions with regard to the active labor army and the reserve army of labor. In the ILO picture of the world workforce in 2011, 1.4 billion workers are wage workers—many of whom are precariously employed, and only part-time workers. In contrast, the number of those counted as unemployed worldwide in 2009 consisted of only 218 million workers. (In order to be classified as unemployed, workers need to have actively pursued job searches in the previous few weeks.) The unemployed, in this sense, can be seen as conforming roughly to Marx's "floating" portion of the reserve army.

A further 1.7 billion workers are classified today as "vulnerably employed." This is a residual category of the "economically active population," consisting of all those who work but are not wage workers—or part of the active labor army in Marx's terminology. It includes two categories of workers: "own-account workers" and "contributing family workers."

"Own-account workers," according to the ILO, encompasses workers engaged in a combination of "subsistence and entrepreneurial activities." The urban component of the "own-account workers" in third-world countries is primarily made up of workers in the informal sector, i.e. street workers of various kinds, while the agricultural component consists largely of subsistence agriculture. "The global informal working class," Mike Davis observed in *Planet of the Slums*, "is about one billion strong, making it the fastest-growing, and most unprecedented, social class on earth."[53]

The second category of the vulnerably employed, "contributing family workers," consists of unpaid family workers. For example, in Pakistan "more than two-thirds of the female workers that entered employment during 1999/00 to 2005/06 consisted of contributing family workers."[54]

The "vulnerably employed" thus includes the greater part of the vast pools of underemployed outside official unemployment rolls, in poor countries in particular. It reflects the fact that, as Michael Yates writes, "In most of the world, open unemployment is not an option; there is no safety net of unemployment compensation and other social welfare programs. Unemployment means death, so people must find work, no matter how onerous the conditions."[55] The various components of vulnerably employed workers correspond to what Marx described as the "stagnant" and "latent" portions of the reserve army.

Additionally, many individuals of working age are classified as not belonging to the economically active population, and thus as economically inactive. For the prime working ages of 25–54 years this adds up, globally, to 538 million people in 2011. This is a very heterogeneous grouping including university students, primarily in wealthier countries; the criminal element engendered at the bottom of the capitalist economy (what Marx called the lumpenproletariat); discouraged and disabled workers who have been marginalized by the system; and in general what Marx called the pauperized portion of the working class—that portion of working age individuals, "the demoralized, the ragged," and the disabled, who have been almost completely shut out of the labor force. It is here, he argued, that one finds the most "precarious… condition of existence." Officially designated "discouraged workers" are a significant number of would-be workers. According to the ILO, if discouraged workers are included in Botswana's unemployment rate in 2006 it nearly doubles from 17.5 percent to 31.6 percent.[56]

If we take the categories of the unemployed, the vulnerably employed, and the economically inactive population in prime working ages (25–54) and add them together, we come up with what might be called the *maximum size of the global reserve army* in 2011: some 2.4 billion people, compared to 1.4 billion in the active labor army. It is the existence of a reserve army that in its maximum extent is more than 70 percent larger than the active labor army that serves to restrain wages globally, and particularly in the poorer countries. Indeed, most of this reserve army is located in the underdeveloped countries of the world, though its growth can be seen today in the rich countries as well.

Many of the workers in the vulnerably employed do not belong to the reserve army, since they are peasant producers, traditionally thought of as belonging to noncapitalist production—including subsistence workers who have no relation to the market. It might be contended that these populations are altogether outside the capitalist market. Yet this is hardly the viewpoint of the system itself. The ILO classifies them generally, along with informal workers, as "vulnerably employed," recognizing they are economically active and employed, but not wage workers. From capital's developmental standpoint, the vulnerably employed are all *potential* wage workers—grist for the mill of capitalist development. Workers engaged in peasant production are viewed as future proletarians, to be drawn more deeply into the capitalist mode.

In fact, the figures we provide for the maximum extent of the global reserve army, in an attempt to understand the really existing relative surplus population, might be seen in some ways as underestimates. In Marx's conception, the reserve army also included part-time workers. Yet, due to lack of data, it is impossible to include this element in our global reserve array estimates. Further, figures on the economically inactive population's share of the reserve army include only prime age workers between 24 and 54 years of age without work, and exclude all of those ages 16–23 and 55–65. Yet, from a practical standpoint, in most countries those in these ages too need and have a right to employment.

Despite uncertainties related to the ILO data, there can be no doubt about the enormous size of the global reserve army. We can understand the implications of this more fully by looking at Samir Amin's analysis of "World Poverty, Pauperization, and Capital

Accumulation" in *Monthly Review* in 2003. Amin argued that "Modern capitalist agri-culture—encompassing both rich, large-scale family farming and agribusiness corpora-tions—is now engaged in a massive attack on third world peasant production." According to the core capitalist view propounded by the WTO, the World Bank, and the IMF, rural (mostly peasant) production is destined to be transformed into advanced capitalist agri-culture on the model of the rich countries. The 3 billion-plus rural workers (peasant population) would be replaced in the ideal capitalist scenario, as Amin puts it, by some "twenty million new modern farmers."

In the dominant view, these workers would then be absorbed by industry, primarily in urban centers, on the model of the developed capitalist countries. But Britain and the other European economies, as Amin and Indian economist Prabhat Patnaik point out, were not themselves able to absorb their entire peasant population within industry. Rather, their surplus population emigrated in great numbers to the Americas and to various colonies. In 1820 Britain had a population of 12 million, while between 1820 and 1915 emigration was 16 million. Put differently, more than half the increase in British population emigrated each year during this period. The total emigration from Europe as a whole to the "new world" (of "temperate regions of white settlement") over this period was 50 million.

While such mass emigration was a possibility for the early capitalist powers, which moved out to seize large parts of the planet, it is not possible for countries of the global South today. Consequently, the kind of reduction in peasant population currently pushed by the system points, if it were effected fully, to mass genocide. An unimaginable 7 percent annual rate of growth for fifty years across the entire global South, Amin points out, could not absorb even a third of this vast surplus agricultural population. "No amount of economic growth," Yates adds, will "absorb" the billions of peasants in the world today "into the traditional proletariat, much less better classes of work."

The problem of the absorption of the massive relative surplus population in these countries becomes even more apparent if one looks at the urban population. There are 3 billion-plus people who live in urban areas globally, concentrated in the massive cities of the global South, in which people are crowded together under increasingly horrendous, slum conditions. As the UN Human Settlements Programme declared in *The Challenge of the Slums:* "Instead of being a focus of growth and prosperity, the cities have become a dumping ground for a surplus population working in unskilled, unprotected and low-wage informal service industries and trade."

For Amin, all of this is tied to an overall theory of unequal exchange/imperialist rent. The "conditions governing accumulation on a world scale…reproduce unequal develop-ment. They make clear that underdeveloped countries are so because they are superex-ploited and not because they are backward." The system of imperialist rent associated with such superexploitation reaches its mature form and is universalized with the devel-opment of "the later capitalism of the generalized, financialized, and globalized oligopolies."[57] Aside from the direct benefits of enormously high rates of exploitation, which feed the economic surplus flowing into the advanced capitalist countries, the introduction of low-cost imports from "feeder economies" in Asia and other parts of the global South by multinational corporations has a deflationary effect. This protects the value of money, particularly the dollar as the hegemonic currency, and thus the financial assets of the capitalist class. The existence of an enormous global reserve army of labor thus forces income deflation on the world's workers, beginning in the global South, but also affecting the workers of the global North, who are increasingly subjected to neoliberal "labour market flexibility."

In today's phase of imperialism—which Patnaik identifies with the development of international finance capital—"wages in the advanced countries cannot rise, and if anything tend to fall in order to make their products more competitive" in relation to the wage "levels that prevail in the third world." In the latter, wage levels are no higher "than those needed to satisfy some historically-determined subsistence requirements," due to the existence of large labor reserves. This logic of world exploitation is made more vicious by the fact that "even as wages in the advanced countries fall, at the prevailing levels of labor productivity, labor productivity in third world countries moves up, at the prevailing level of wages, towards the level reached in the advanced countries. This is because the wage differences that still continue to exist induce a diffusion of activities from the former to the latter. *This double movement means that the share of wages in total world output decreases*," while the rate of exploitation worldwide rises.[59]

In the advanced capitalist countries, the notion of "precariousness," which Marx in his reserve army discussion employed to describe the most pauperized sector of the working class, has been rediscovered, as conditions once thought to be confined to the third world are reappearing in the rich countries. This has led to references to the emergence of a "new class"—though in reality it is the growing pauperized sector of the working class—termed the "precariat."[61]

At the bottom of this precariat developing in the rich countries are so-called "guest workers." As Marx noted, in the nineteenth century, capital in the wealthy centers is able to take advantage of lower-wage labor abroad either through capital migration to low-wage countries or through the migration of low-wage labor into rich countries. Although migrant labor populations from poor countries have served to restrain wages in rich countries, particularly the United States, from a global perspective the most significant fact with respect to workers migrating from South to North is their low numbers in relation to the population of the global South.

Overall the share of migrants in total world population has shown no appreciable change since the 1960s. According to the ILO, there was only "a very small rise" in the migration from developing to developed countries "in the 1990s, and…this is accounted for basically by increased migration from Central American and Caribbean countries to the United States." The percentage of adult migrants from developing to developed countries in 2000 was a mere 1 percent of the adult population of developing countries. Moreover, those migrants were concentrated among the more highly skilled so that "the effect of international migration on the low-skilled labour force" in developing countries themselves "has been negligible for the most part…. Migration from developing to developed countries has largely meant brain drain …. In short," the ILO concludes, "limited as it was, international migration" in the decade of the 1990s "served to restrain the growth of skill intensity of the labour force in quite a large number of developing countries, and particularly in the least developed countries." All of this drives home the key point that capital is internationally mobile, while labor is not.[62]

If the new imperialism has its basis in the superexploitation of workers in the global South, it is a phase of imperialism that in no way can be said to benefit the workers of the global North, whose conditions are also being dragged down—both by the disastrous global wage competition introduced by multinationals and, more fundamentally, by the overaccumulation tendencies in the capitalist core, enhancing stagnation and unemployment.[63]

Indeed, the wealthy countries of the triad (the United States, Europe, Japan) are all bogged down in conditions of deepening stagnation, resulting from their incapacity to absorb all of the surplus capital that they are generating internally and pulling in from abroad—a contradiction that is manifested in weakening investment and employment. Financialization, which helped to boost these economies for decades, is now arrested by its own contradictions, with the result that the root problems of production, which financial bubbles served to cover up for a time, are now surfacing. This is manifesting itself not only in diminishing growth rates, but also rising levels of excess capacity and unemployment. In an era of globalization, financialization, and neoliberal economic policy, the state is unable effectively to move in to correct the problem, and is increasingly geared simply to bailing out capital at the expense of the rest of society.

The imperial rent that these countries appropriate from the rest of the world only makes the problems of surplus absorption or overaccumulation at the center of the world system worse. "Foreign investment, far from being an outlet for domestically generated surplus," Paul Baran and Paul Sweezy famously wrote in *Monopoly Capital*, "is a most efficient process for transferring surplus generated from abroad to the investing country. Under these circumstances, it is of course obvious that foreign investment aggravates rather than helps to solve the surplus absorption problem."[64]

The New Imperialism

As we have seen, there can be no doubt about the sheer scale of the relative shift of world manufacturing to the global South in the period of the internationalization of monopoly capital since the Second World War—and accelerating in recent decades. Although this is often seen as a post-1974 or a post-1989 phenomenon, Stephen Hymer, Harry Magdoff, Paul Sweezy, and Samir Amin, captured the general parameters of this broad movement in accumulation and imperialism associated with the development of multinational corporations (the internationalization of monopoly capital) as early as the 1970s. Largely as a result of this epochal shift in the center of gravity of world manufacturing production toward the South, about a dozen emerging economies have experienced phenomenal growth rates of 7 percent or more for a quarter century.

Most important among these of course is China, which is not only the most populous country but has experienced the fastest growth rates, reputedly 9 percent or above. At a 7 percent rate of growth an economy doubles in size every ten years; at 9 percent every eight years. Yet the process is not, as mainstream economics often suggests, a smooth one. The Chinese economy has doubled in size three times since 1978, but wages remain at or near subsistence levels, due to an internal reserve army in the hundreds of millions. China may be emerging as a world economic power due to its sheer size and rate of growth, but wages remain among the lowest in the world. India's per capita income, meanwhile, is about one-third of China's. China's rural population is estimated at about 50 percent, while India's is around 70 percent.[65]

Orthodox economic theorists rely on an abstract model of development that assumes all countries pass through the same phases, and eventually move up from labor-intensive manufacturing to capital-intensive, knowledge-intensive production. This raises the issue of the so-called "middle-income transition" that is supposed to occur at a per capita income of somewhere between $5,000 and $10,000 (China's per capita income at current exchange rates is about $3,500). Countries in the middle-income transition have higher wage rates and are faced with uncompetitiveness unless they can move to products that capture more value and are less labor-intensive. Most countries fail to make the transition and the middle-income level ends up being a developmental trap. Based on this framework, New York University economist Michael Spence argues in *The Next*

Convergence that China's "labor-intensive export sectors that have been a major contributor to growth are losing competitiveness and have to be allowed to decline or move inland and then eventually decline. They will be replaced by sectors that are more capital, human-capital, and knowledge intensive."[66]

Spence's orthodox argument, however, denies the reality of contemporary China, where the latent reserve army in agriculture alone amounts to hundreds of millions of people. Moving toward a less labor-intensive system under capitalism means higher rates of productivity and technological displacement of labor, requiring that the economy absorb a mounting reserve army by conquering ever-larger, high-value-capture markets. The only cases where anything resembling this has taken place—aside from Japan, which first emerged as a rapidly expanding, militarized-imperialist economy in the early twentieth century—were the Asian tigers (Korea, Taiwan, Singapore, and Hong Kong), which were able to expand their external export markets for high-value-capture production in the global North during a period of world economic expansion (not the deepening stagnation of today). This is unlikely to prove possible for China and India, which must find employment between them for some 40 percent of the world's labor force—and to a mounting degree in the urban industrial sector. Unlike Europe during its colonial period the emigration of large pools of surplus labor as an escape valve is not possible: they have nowhere to go. China's capacity to promote internal-based accumulation (not relying primarily on export markets), meanwhile, is hindered under today's capitalist conditions by this same reserve army of low-paid labor, and by rapidly rising inequality.

All of this suggests that at some point the contradictions of China's unprecedented accumulation rates combined with massive labor reserves that cannot readily be absorbed by the accumulation process—particularly with the growing shift to high-technology, high-productivity production—are bound to come to a head.

Meanwhile, international monopoly capital uses its combined monopolies over technology, communications, finance, military, and the planet's natural resources to control (or at least constrain) the direction of development in the South.[67]

As the contradictions between North and South of the world system intensify, so do the internal contradictions within them—with class differences widening everywhere. The relative "deindustrialization" in the global North is now too clear a tendency to be altogether denied. Thus the share of manufacturing in U.S. GDP has dropped from around 28 percent in the 1950s to 12 percent in 2010, accompanied by a dramatic decrease in its share (along with that of the OECD as a whole) in world manufacturing.[68] Yet it is important to understand that this is only the tip of the iceberg where the growing worldwide destabilization and overexploitation of labor is concerned.

The answer to the challenges facing world labor that Marx gave at the Lausanne Congress in 1867 remains the only possible one: "If the working class wishes to continue its struggle with some chance of success the national organisations must become international." It is time for a new International.[70]

Notes

1   Stephen Herbert Hymer, *The Multinational Corporation* (Cambridge: Cambridge University Press, 1979), 41, 75, 183.
2   Hymer, *The Multinational Corporation*, 81, 86, 161, 262–69.
3   Gary Gereffi, *The New Offshoring of Jobs and Global Development*, ILO Social Policy Lectures, Jamaica, December 2005 (Geneva: International Institute for Labour Studies, 2006), http://ilo.org, 1; Peter Dicken, *Global Shift* (New York: Guilford Press, 1998), 26–28.

4   Thorstein Veblen already understood this in the 1920s. See his *Absentee Ownership and Business Enterprise in Recent Times* (New York: Augustus M. Kelley, 1964), 287.

5   See Paul M. Sweezy, *Four Lectures on Marxism* (New York: Monthly Review Press, 1981), 64–65; Michael E. Porter, *Competitive Strategy* (New York: The Free Press, 1980), 35–36.

6   Ajit K. Ghose, Nomaan Majid, and Christoph Ernst, *The Global Employment Challenge* (Geneva: International Labour Organization, 2008). On depeasantization see Farshad Araghi, "The Great Global Enclosure of Our Times," in Fred Magdoff, John Bellamy Foster, and Frederick H. Buttel, eds., *Hungry for Profit* (New York: Monthly Review Press, 2000), 145–60.

7   John Smith, *Imperialism and the Globalisation of Production* (Ph.D. Thesis, University of Sheffield, July 2010), 224.

8   Stephen Roach, "How Global Labor Arbitrage Will Shape the World Economy," *Global Agenda Magazine*, 2004, http://ecocritique.free.fr; John Bellamy Foster, Harry Magdoff, and Robert W. McChesney, "The Stagnation of Employment," *Monthly Review*, 55, no. 11 (April 2004): 9–11.

9   Thomas L. Friedman, *The World Is Flat* (New York: Farrar, Strauss and Giroux, 2005). Friedman wrongly claims that his "flat world hypothesis" was first advanced by Marx. See 234–37.

10 Paul Krugman, *Pop Internationalism* (Cambridge, Massachusetts: MIT Press, 1996), 66–67. On the absurdity of expecting wage differences between nations simply to reflect productivity trends see Marx, *Capital*, vol. 1 (London: Penguin, 1976), 705.

11 On fears of an end to global labor arbitrage see "Moving Back to America," *The Economist*, May 12, 2011, http://economist.com.

18 Fredric Jameson, *Representing Capital* (New York: Verso, 2011), 71.

19 Marx, *Capital*, vol. 1, 799.

20 Marx, *Capital*, vol. 1, 764, 772, 781–94; Marx and Engels, *The Communist Manifesto*, 7; Paul M. Sweezy, *The Theory of Capitalist Development* (New York: Monthly Review Press, 1970), 87–92.

21 Marx, *Capital*, vol. 1, 792.

22 Karl Marx, "Wage-Labour and Capital," in *Wage-Labour and Capital/Value, Price and Profit* (New York: International Publishers, 1935), 45; Sweezy, *The Theory of Capitalist Development*, 89.

23 Marx, *Capital*, vol. 1, 763, 776–81, 929.

24 Marx, *Capital*, vol. 1, 794–95; David Harvey, *A Companion to Marx's Capital* (London: Verso, 2010), 278, 318.

25 Marx, *Capital*, vol. 1, 795–96.

26 Marx, *Capital*, vol. 1, 590–99, 793–77.

27 Marx, *Capital*, vol. 1, 797–98.

28 Engels deserves credit for having introduced the reserve army concept into Marxian theory, and makes it clear that what demonstrates the reserve-army or relative surplus-population status of workers is the fact that the economy draws them into employment at business cycle peaks. See Frederick Engels, *The Condition of the Working Class in England* (Chicago: Academy Chicago Publishers, 1984), 117–22, and *Engels on Capital* (New York: International Publishers, 1937), 19.

29 Karl Marx, *Capital*, vol. 3 (London: Penguin, 1981), *Capital*, vol. 2 (London: Penguin, 1978), 486–87, and *Capital*, vol. 1, 769–70; Rosa Luxemburg, *The Accumulation of Capital—An Anti-Critique*, and Nikolai Bukharin, *Imperialism and the Accumulation of Capital* (New York: Monthly Review Press, 1972), 121.

30 Marx, *Capital*, vol. 3, 363.

31 Karl Marx and Frederick Engels, *Collected Works* (New York: International Publishers, 1975), 422.

34 Marx, *Capital*, vol. 3, 344.

35 The term "globalization" was first coined in the 1930s. But the first article to use the concept in its modern economic sense, according to the *Oxford English Dictionary*, was Fouad Ajami, "Corporate Giants: Some Global Social Costs," *International Studies Quarterly* 16, no. 4 (December 1972): 513. Ajami introduced the term in a paragraph in which he was addressing Marxian notions of "concentration and centralization"—and in particular Paul Baran and Paul Sweezy's, *Monopoly Capital* (Monthly Review Press, 1966), which had pointed to the multinational corporation as a manifestation of the growth of monopolistic production at the world level. Although critical of Baran and Sweezy's analysis for its Marxian basis, Ajami (a mainstream political scientist now affiliated with the Hoover Institution and the Council on Foreign Relations) nevertheless saw what he called "the domination of multinational giants and the globalization of

markets" as emerging out of the same kinds of developments—with respect to the tendency to international oligopoly—that Baran and Sweezy had raised. Ironically, Ajami failed to notice that other theorists he drew upon in his article in contradistinction to Baran and Sweezy—Stephen Hymer, Michael Tanzer, Bob Rowthorn, and Herbert Schiller—were also Marxian and radical political economists, and in the case of the first two, authors of articles in *Monthly Review*.

36   Richard J. Barnet and Ronald E. Müller, *Global Reach* (New York: Simon and Schuster, 1974), 213–14, 306.

37   "Moving Back to America."

38   Dale Wen, *China Copes with Globalization* (International Forum on Globalization, 2005), http:// ifg.org; Martin Hart-Landsberg, "The Chinese Reform Experience," *The Review of Radical Political Economics* 43, no. 1 (March 2011): 56–76; Minqi Li, "The Rise of the Working Class and the Future of the Chinese Revolution," *Monthly Review* 63, no. 2 (June 2011): 40.

39   It should be noted that the term "superexploited" appears to have two closely related, overlapping meanings in Marxist theory: (1) workers who receive less than the historically determined value of labor power, as it is defined here; and (2) workers who are subjected to unequal exchange and overexploited, primarily in the global South. In Samir Amin's framework, however, the two meanings are united. This is because the value of labor power is determined globally, while actual wage rates are determined nationally, and are hierarchically ordered due to imperialism. In the global South therefore workers *normally* receive wages that are less than the value of labor power. This is the basis of imperial rent. See Amin, *The Law of Value and Historical Materialism*, 11, 84. John Smith and Andy Higginbottom have developed a similar approach to superexploitation based on Marx. See John Smith, "Imperialism and the Law of Value," *Global Discourse*, 2, no. 1 (2011), http://global-discourse.com.

40   Charles J. Whalen, "Sending Jobs Offshore from the United States," *Intervention: A Journal of Economics* 2, no. 2 (2005): 35. Quoted in Smith, *The Internationalisation of Globalisation*, 94.

41   William Milberg, "Shifting Sources and Uses of Profits," *Economy and Society* 37, no. 3 (August 2008): 439; Judith Banister and George Cook, "China's Employment and Compensation Costs in Manufacturing through 2008," U.S. Bureau of Labor Statistics, *Monthly Labor Review* (March 2011): 44. It is common for commentators to refer to global supply chains as global value chains, based on the concept of value added. (See, for example, Michael Spence and Sandile Hlatshwayo, *The Evolving Structure of the American Economy and the Employment Challenge*, Council on Foreign Relations Working Paper, March 2011, http://cfr.org.) This leads to the notion that the value added is much higher in high technology production engaged in the North than in the labor-intensive production now increasingly located in the South. However, more value added in this sense simply means higher relative prices and higher income. It does not tell us where the value is produced but simply who gets it (via monopoly power, imperial rent, etc.). We therefore avoid the value chain terminology in this book, and we refer, when necessary, to "high-value-capture" rather than "high-value" links in the global supply chain. The "value capture" term and a general critique of value-chain theory are presented in John Smith, *Imperialism and the Globalisation of Production*, 254–60, and "Imperialism and the Law of Value."

42   Yuqing Xing and Neal Detert, *How the iPhone Widens the United States Trade Deficit with the People's Republic of China*, ADBI Working Paper, Asian Development Bank Institute (December 2010; paper revised May 2011); David Barboza, "After Spate of Suicides, Technology Firm in China Raises Workers' Salaries," *New York Times*, June 2, 2010, http://nytimes.com. It should be noted that the assembly in China of iPhone parts and components that are produced elsewhere (heavily in other East Asian countries) is actually the dominant pattern of East Asian production. According to the Asian Development Bank, China is "the assembly hub for final products in Asian production networks." Asian Development Bank, *Asian Development Outlook, 2008* (Manila, Philippines), http://adb.org, 22; Martin Hart-Landsberg, "The U.S Economy and China," *Monthly Review* 61, no. 9 (February 2010): 18.

43   Banister and Cook, "China's Employment and Compensation," 49.

44   U.S. Bureau of Labor Statistics, "International Comparisons of Hourly Compensation Costs in Manufacturing," Table I, last updated March 8, 2011, http://bls.gov.

45   Vikas Bajaj, "Bangladesh, with Low Pay, Moves In on China," *New York Times*, July 16, 2010, http://nytimes.com.

46   Immelt quoted in Milberg, "Shifting Sources and Uses of Profits," 433. For a powerful theoretical analysis in Marxian terms of global labor arbitrage see Smith, *Imperialism and the Globalisation of Production*.

51   Li, "The Rise of the Working Class and the Future of the Chinese Revolution," 40–41, and *The Rise of China and the Demise of the Capitalist World Economy* (New York: Monthly Review Press, 2008), 87–92.

52   Yang Yao, "No, the Lewisian Turning Point Has Not Yet Arrived," *The Economist*, July 16, 2010, http://economist.com; Stephen Roach, "Chinese Wage Convergence Has a Long Way To Go," *The Economist*, July 18, 2010, http://economist.com.

53   Theo Sparreboom and Michael P. F. de Gier, "Assessing Vulnerable Employment," *Employment Sector Working Paper*, no. 13 (Geneva: ILO, 2008), 7; James Petras and Henry Veltmeyer, *Multinationals on Trial* (Burlington, Vermont: Ashgate, 2007), 70; Mike Davis, *Planet of Slums* (London: Verso, 2006), 178.

54   International Labor Organisation, *Key Indicators of the Labour Market* (Geneva: ILO, 2009), chapter 3–3; Sparreboom and de Gier, "Assessing Vulnerable Employment," 11.

55   Michael Yates, "Work Is Hell," May 21, 2009, http://cheapmotelsandahotplate.org.

56   ILO, *Key Indicators*, chapter 1-C, and chapter 5.

57   Samir Amin, "World Poverty, Pauperization and Capital Accumulation," *Monthly Review* 55, no. 5 (October 2003): 1–9, and *The Law of Worldwide Value*, 14, 89, 134; Prabhat Patnaik, "The Myths of Capitalism," *MRzine*, July 4, 2011, http://mrzine.monthlyreview.org; United Nations, *World Economic and Social Survey* (New York: UN, 2004), 3; Yates, "Work Is Hell"; Davis, *Planet of Slums*, 179; United Nations Human Settlements Programme, *The Challenge of the Slums* (London: Earthscan, 2003), 40, 46.

59   Prabhat Patnaik, "Notes on Contemporary Imperialism," *MRzine*, December 20, 2010, http://mrzine.monthlyreview.org; "Capitalism and Imperialism," *MRzine*, June 19, 2011, http://mrzine.monthlyreview.org; "Labour Market Flexibility," *MRzine*, May 9, 2011, http://mrzine.monthlyreview.org; and "Contemporary Imperialism and the World's Labour Reserves," *Social Scientist* 35, no. 5/6 (May–June 2007): 13.

61   For example, Guy Standing, *The Precariat: The New Dangerous Class* (New York: Bloomsbury Academic, 2011). On the current role of the reserve army of labor at the center of the capitalist system see Fred Magdoff and Harry Magdoff, "Disposable Workers: Today's Reserve Army of Labor," *Monthly Review* 55, no. 11 (April 2004): 18–35.

62   Ghose, et al., *The Global Employment Challenge*, 45–49.

63   On the interrelation of these two negative elements affecting employment in the advanced capitalist countries see Foster, "The Stagnation of Employment."

64   Baran and Sweezy, *Monopoly Capital*, 107–8.

65   Michael Spence, *The Next Convergence* (New York: Farrar, Strauss and Giroux, 2011), 19–23, 48, 53–54, 85–86, 107; "China's Urban Population Exceeds Countryside for First Time," Bloomberg.com, January 17, 2012.

66   Spence, *The Next Convergence*, 100–3, 194–98.

67   Samir Amin, *Capitalism in the Age of Globalization* (New York: Zed, 1977), 4–5.

68   Louis Uchitelle, "Is Manufacturing Falling Off the Radar?" *New York Times*, September 11, 2011, http://nytimes.com.

70   Samir Amin, "The Democratic Fraud and the Universalist Alternative," *Monthly Review* 63, no. 5 (October 2011): 44–45, *The World We Wish to See* (New York: Monthly Review Press, 2008).

CHAPTER 33

The End of Retirement

Teresa Ghilarducci

An esteemed colleague read three paragraphs of news clip on employer pensions before he realized it was from the satirical newspaper *The Onion*. The tip off was the interview with an eighty-seven-year-old machine shop worker struggling with widowhood, high stress, and early stage Alzheimer's at General Electric. Early stage Alzheimer's was the first clue, not the eighty-seven-years of age. Satire writers must have a holy grail of seconds before the earnest reader starts chuckling; my colleague's delay might be a record. It takes three seconds to know "Cindy Sheehan loses second son in Katrina" is a lampoon. The reason it took so long to laugh at a news story that GE was adopting a new policy of "lifetime" jobs and a new forty-five-year vesting period for their pensions is that it is credible; the signs of the end of retirement are all around.

Scarcely a day passes without a new pension nightmare: Social Security privatization, pension terminations by corporations that are household names (such as Delphi and United Airlines), household saving reaching another new low, canceled retiree health benefits, and 401(k) accounts becoming "201(k)s" while replacing traditional pensions. Airlines were able to use bankruptcy courts to abandon their defined benefit obligations. Most of the pensions were protected by the Pension Benefit Guaranty Corporation (PBGC), but future accrual was scrapped. The PBGC will not be able to handle many more obligations without more defined benefit plans coming in. That is why efforts to enhance the defined benefit system are so crucial—they grow or die [see box].

These nightmares reflect an unpleasant reality. What we need to know is what has caused reality to change. The changes in the retirement future of Americans stem from the decline of union contracts, a dramatic shift in presidential and congressional attitudes about government responsibility for social insurance, and the substitution of defined contribution or 401(k)-type accounts for traditional defined benefit pensions.

The current federal policy of promoting an "ownership society" means shifting risks that were once spread out among many workers and employers to individuals, who are now expected to manage individual accounts: their 401(k) plans, their health savings accounts, and, if powerful forces get their way, Social Security individual accounts. None of this bodes well for working people. Twenty years of experience with 401(k) plans reveal that workers will never be able to accumulate enough assets in individual accounts and choose payout options that will provide a steady stream of income for life

Original publication details: Teresa Ghilarducci, "The End of Retirement," *Monthly Review*, 58:1. *Monthly Review*, May 2006.

Defined Benefit Plan

An employer pension plan in which a retired employee receives a specific amount based typically on salary history and years of service. The employer determines the investments and bears the investment risk and return, agreeing to pay the stated benefit. Investment gains or losses do not affect the benefit payable to the plan participant at retirement.

Defined benefit plans usually pay out benefits in the form of a life annuity. Due to the Employee Retirement Income Security Act (ERISA) of 1974, most defined benefit plans are further guaranteed with insurance under a program administered by a government agency called the Pension Benefit Guaranty Corporation (PBGC).

Defined Contribution Plan or 401(k) Plan

A retirement savings plan administered at the workplace that sets aside a certain amount of money each year for an employee. Employers do not have to contribute to the plan; but they do administer it. The employee determines how much to contribute subject to limitations. These contributed funds are invested in investment products containing stocks, bonds or other securities. The employer chooses the investment products but the worker decides how their funds are allocated among them. Some plans restrict the bulk of the investments in the employer's stock. The plan's accumulated value at retirement or termination represents the total value of all contributions made and investment income earned or lost. The investment results of a defined contribution plan are not guaranteed, and there is no guaranteed amount paid at retirement. Such plans are commonly referred to by the tax code number they are defined by, such as a 401(k) in the for-profit sector and 403(b) in the not-for-profit sector.

after retirement. This means that Americans will turn to the option that American adults have always relied on—contingent, low-paying jobs—and will lose one of the few remaining accomplishments of the American working class, retirement.

Whither Retirement?

The concept of retirement changed in the post-Second World War period, when U.S. workers, through their collective power, won retirement time. This meant that workers' households spent more time in a period of life called retirement, which opened up to the working class a way of life heretofore reserved for the wealthy.

The expectation of time off at the end of one's working life is a concept that has evolved, just as have other entitlements to time off, such as "the weekend" and the eight-hour workday. The entitlement developed through compromises among workers, organized labor, business firms, and the government. Throughout the post-Second World War period, workers, mainly those in unions, negotiated for holidays, vacations, and leaves, trading these for lower pay or increased productivity. That unionized workers wanted free time is evidenced by the fact that some of the most famous strikes in the 1950s were over pension benefits. Just last year, transit workers in New York City stranded millions of commuters in chilly December over a proposed cutback in benefits. Workers and their organizations came to regard pensions as one way to achieve middle-class status.

Despite corporate and political arguments to the contrary, pensions are as affordable as they were thirty years ago. The nation can still afford retirement, or more precisely, the ability of older people to choose not to work. Everything really depends on the distribution of power in the labor market. The loss of pensions and the ability to choose to work on one's own terms coincided with the loss of union bargaining power, which began in the 1980s. We must be clear that workers losing the bargaining power to secure pensions is not the same thing as the economy losing the ability to pay for them. Those who argue that the elderly should work more imply that we cannot afford the same levels of retirement time because a growing number of retirees must be supported by fewer workers. But demography is not destiny: economic bargaining power is.

The Erosion of the U.S. Retirement Security System

For the first time in U.S. history, every source of retirement income is under siege: Social Security, personal savings, and occupational pensions.[2]

Social Security: The cornerstone of national retirement security is Social Security which currently pays benefits to more than 47 million people, including retired workers, disabled workers, the spouses and children of retired and disabled workers, and the survivors of deceased workers. It is the largest single source of income to retirees. Although Social Security helps keep most retirees out of poverty, it is not sufficient to provide a middle-class worker with their accustomed standard of living. The system replaces about 41 percent of income for workers who earn average wages throughout their careers; financial planners recommend replacing 70 percent of pre-retirement income. Alicia Munnell at Boston College found that the already low 41 percent replacement rate will fall in two decades to 30.5 percent as normal retirement age creeps up to age 67, which reduces income for those collecting at earlier ages, as do income taxes, and Medicare premium increases.

Personal Saving: For the first time since the Great Depression, at the end of 2005, Americans spent more than they received: American workers are now, on average, consuming all of their income and more. Just twenty years ago workers (aged 25–55) were saving 10 percent of their income. Brookings Institute economists Barry Boswell and Lisa Bell found that the United States ranks last among any industrialized country in personal saving rates, with other developed nations having rates as high as 12 percent.

The fact that nearly all saving by households is now in the form of contractual, institutionalized, "pension savings" is well-known. American spendthrift spending habits (household saving started to decline in the 1980s) are legendary, but up until the 1990s, contractual or institutionalized savings, again mainly pensions, helped staunch the red ink. Today a deep decline in contractual savings—especially by employer-financed defined benefit pension plans—explains a large part of the savings rate decline, because employers had to allocate funds in advance to fulfill the promises made for workers' pensions, and if the firm provided a defined benefit pension, almost everyone at the firm was included.

The decline in defined benefit plans has corresponded with a rise of defined contribution plans. However, twenty years of experience with such plans show clearly that workers have been either unwilling or unable to fill the savings gap. An extensive survey by Vanguard found that only one-third of workers were on track to achieve a 70 percent retirement replacement rate. Further, 40 percent of households at risk of not having enough income in retirement would need to double their savings rates or defer retirement until age 70 to maintain living standards.

There is little evidence that average- and lower-income workers have the capability to anticipate, manage, and save enough money to retire. Generally, workers who report having reasonable expectations and a retirement plan to meet those expectations have higher incomes in the first place. This relationship between income and retirement preparation is partially rooted in public policy. A major impetus for retirement planning stems from the tax code's exemption of income that is diverted into retirement accounts such as 401(k) plans, individual retirement accounts (IRAs), and similar savings vehicles. Since they have more income and because income taxes are progressive, it is the higher-income quintiles that have the greatest financial incentive to take advantage of professional counseling to maximize their tax-preferred retirement savings.

The bottom line is that automatic institutionalized pension saving, particularly through defined benefit plans, are the critical ways workers save for retirement.

Employer Pensions: After Social Security, employer-based pensions are the second largest source of retirement income, providing almost 20 percent of the income received by elderly households. These contractual forms of savings are key ways middle-income workers retain "middle-class status" in retirement. The amount of taxes not collected because pensions get a tax break equaled a full fourth of total annual Social Security contributions—$114 billion in 2004. Yet, despite taxpayers forgoing a huge amount of revenue in the form of federal tax breaks to pensions, coverage has stagnated for the last decade, with participation of only about 60 percent of the workforce.

Chief among the causes for pension stagnation is the decline in union density and the corresponding reduction in collective bargaining agreements. Compared to the compensation of nonunion workers, union compensation consists of less cash and more insurance and employee benefits. Unions inform and educate members about the importance of insurance and pensions, and more senior workers tend to have more say in setting union priorities than the marginal, younger worker just hired, who likely prefers cash relative to insurance. Unions form communities, and communities often lengthen time horizons and expand the concerns of their members beyond individual consumption and competition. Instead of striving for positional goods—those that set a person apart from another—individuals in communities tend to put more value on public goods and longer-term security. Whatever the reasons, union workers have almost twice the coverage rates for the lower-income workers and over 10 percent more for higher-paid workers.

Along with the overall stagnation of pension coverage is the development of the increasing dominance of defined contribution plans over defined benefit plans. The number of single-employer defined benefit plans has declined significantly, from about 95,000 in 1980 to fewer than 35,000 in 2002, while the number of active defined benefit plan participants—employed workers covered by a defined benefit plan—has declined as a percent of all national private wage and salary workers from 27.3 in 1980 to about 15 percent in 2002.

Explaining the Shift from Defined Benefit to Defined Contribution Plans

Explanations for the trend toward defined contribution plans and away from defined benefit plans range from those that emphasize the shift as an inevitable evolutionary development in a global economy and those that view the result as a consequence of policies that created a hostile environment for defined benefit plans to grow. The first view implies that defined benefit plans are dinosaurs that did not adapt to the environment. The other view is that defined benefit plans are pandas, a worthwhile species endangered by short-sighted policies and decisions. The dinosaur interpretation argues that employees have come to prefer the 401(k)-type defined contribution plans. Yet, despite much popular wisdom, there is little evidence that defined benefit pensions are stagnating because workers do not want them. Rather, defined contribution plans are, to many workers, a second-best option given the uncertainty and the lack of commitment to defined benefit plans displayed by employers.

The panda interpretation is that defined benefit coverage rates are stagnating because many companies are adopting 401(k)-style plans to take advantage of temporary changes in accounting standards and the economy in order to reduce pension costs, not to respond to supposed worker preferences for defined contribution plans, or to changes in labor processes and technology. A sponsor's pension costs may also be reduced by 401(k) plans because a substantial number of workers choose not to participate in a defined contribution plan, even when it means foregoing the sponsor's contribution match. Extrapolating from a detailed study of large companies, economist Bridgett Madrian and her colleagues calculate that between 2002 and 2004, if all eligible workers participated in their employers' 401(k) plans, employers would have had to contribute 26 percent more—for an annual total of $3.18 billion.

The Implications for Workers

Most workers who have 401(k) plans have not saved nearly enough for retirement, nor could they ever do so, even if a 401(k) was their only plan. The median annual salary deferral into a 401(k)-type plan was just $1,896 in 2004—an adequate retirement savings rate would be twice that. (Financial planners recommend saving 12 percent of salary in a retirement account; $5,400 is required per year for workers earning the median salary of $45,000.) Further, the share of workers in 401(k) plans who say they cannot afford to save has risen from 15 percent in 1998 to 19 percent in 2003.

The several decades of experience with 401(k) type plans—since 1978—do not instill hope that savings behavior will improve. The average size of defined contribution account balances remains quite low. As of 2004, the mean value for 401(k) plans was $53,600 for near retirees (those aged 55–64) with a far lower median value of $23,000. These accounts may not seem small, but the annuities they would generate are. A $50,000 lump sum would buy a 65-year-old person less than $50 per month if indexed for inflation. Low incomes, low savings, the potential to borrow from the accounts, and the ability to consume the account balance upon switching employers, despite the tax penalties, are all likely suspects in the current weak balance accumulation performance of defined contribution plans.

Why are people not accumulating sufficient balances? Besides low incomes, at least some individuals are hampered by events and human traits that interfere with increased retirement asset accumulation. Unexpected emergencies, the desire for increased consumption, or simple shortsightedness can lead to decisions that favor placing more immediate priorities and desires ahead of retirement saving. For example, even if people save a lot in their 401(k) plan, they may tend to spend down or borrow against their 401(k)s to pay for costs associated with job changes—over half of people who change jobs spend their 401(k) plan balances—health emergencies, home purchases, and financing a child's education. Seventy-two percent of workers have 401(k) plans that allow 401(k) loans (which reduce accumulations), and 10 percent of participants borrowed from their 401(k)s. The median outstanding balance of a loan from a 401(k) plan is $2,000. Such temptation is not only common, it is popular among plan participants. The Government Accountability Office found that the ability to borrow from one's 401(k) plan was a key incentive in workers choosing to participate in the plan.

That people can spend their 401(k)s when they leave employment makes 401(k)s, ironically, a problem in a mobile society. The seemingly attractive portability feature of 401(k) plans can become counterproductive for retirement saving because half of workers participating in 401(k) plans cash them out when they change jobs rather than roll them over for retirement. In such instances, 401(k) plans may actually serve as severance plans that help alleviate the costs associated with being out of work and changing jobs. There are other leakages from the 401(k) retirement system that also diminish needed accumulations. Many workers use 401(k) plans to pay for their children's education, household expenses, and housing needs. Although such leakage is often more a consequence of broader weaknesses in the social safety net—low unemployment insurance benefits, the lack of health insurance, etc.—it nevertheless erodes the basic goal of pension plans, which is to help provide an adequate retirement income.

[Those] who had defined benefit accumulations will have more at retirement than 401(k) holders. 401(k) participants pay higher retail money management fees, while defined benefit plan sponsors pay wholesale fees. The level of fees crucially affects overall financial returns, a 1 percentage point fee can lower returns by 20 percent. Typical fees charged to defined contribution accounts can reduce account values by 21–30 percent depending on the size of the account.

Defined benefit plans also typically pay annuities, and workers cannot access pension income before retirement. Defined contribution participants usually are paid in a lump sum. But annuities provide more piece of mind to retirees: a Boston College and Rand study found that retirees having both a defined benefit plan and a 401(k)-type plan report an 8 percent boost in satisfaction. However, just having a 401(k)-type defined contribution plan alone does not improve an elderly persons' self-reported satisfaction with life.

The reasonable interpretation is that the elderly would rather have an equivalent level of income coming from a defined benefit plan or a combination of a defined benefit and a defined contribution plan, rather than just from a defined contribution plan. This is because retirees, like many of us, would trade some income for security.

The employer, rather than the employee, bears the risk of investment loss and employers can bear the risk better than individuals—they typically have a longer time horizon, have more financial resources, can tap expert advice more easily, and can bargain for cheaper investment fees than individual workers can. Defined benefit plans are especially valuable to middle-aged workers, who are poised to experience the largest rates of accrual under traditional defined benefit plans. On the other hand, workers like defined contribution plans because they are easier to understand and are portable. To the extent that workers use their accounts as a form of general savings, it is also nice to have savings to fall back on in emergencies. The problem is that many emergencies occur before the golden age of retirement.

Pension Reform

The right kinds of policies can encourage plans with the favorable characteristics of both defined benefit and defined contribution plans. For example, cash balance plans have increased in number over the last twenty years. These plans resemble 401(k) accounts, and their value is expressed similarly, but the employer invests the funds and bears all the performance risk. Under cash balance plans, the sponsor guarantees a return on the employer's contributions and is obligated to pay the balance when the individual retires and benefits are insured by the Pension Benefit Guaranty Corporation. Although cash balance plans express their benefit as in 401(k)s and in fact are touted as offering participants a lump-sum option, these plans are also required to offer an annuity option. The notional balances of the cash balance plans cannot be spent or borrowed against by the employee.[3]

Cash balance plans, properly designed, could provide adequate benefits for all workers, especially if they ban lump sum payments. Some unions, like the Communication Workers of America, have negotiated cash balance plans for some of their members.

The other major type of hybrid is over seventy years old—the defined benefit multi-employer pension plan. Multi-employer plans cover approximately 20 percent of defined benefit participants and exist in industries where workers are often skilled and mobile, for instance in the mining, needle trades, trucking, and construction sectors. TIAA-CREF, the largest pension plan in the nation, which covers research, university, and college professionals, is a type of multi-employer plan incorporating many defined benefit and defined contribution characteristics.

Through collective bargaining, the union representing mechanics and other workers at US Airways agreed to a new defined benefit plan after the old one was terminated in bankruptcy in the summer of 2005. When that single-employer defined benefit plan failed, the International Association of Machinists' multi-employer plans stepped in as a replacement, offering better benefits than the airline's proposed defined contribution plans for the same contribution. The plan is comparatively more stable for the workers, because it is a defined benefit plan that includes the other airlines. These workers could lose their jobs at US Airways or any other airline, but as long as they obtained employment at another carrier participating in the plan, they could maintain active membership in their pension plan.

In the late 1990s, nurses in a New Jersey hospital finally achieved their longstanding demand to join the multi-employer pension plan of the hospital's operating engineers. Why a multi-employer plan? Why the operating engineers? The hospital had changed ownership so many times that each single employer plan ended when another firm bought the hospital. The employees didn't move—it was the employers who were mobile. Joining the multi-employer plan—the only remaining plan at the site—allowed the nurses to build up credits in one defined benefit plan and provided for a more secure retirement.

Jobs and the Older American

Under what conditions can society provide jobs that older people want, not jobs that older people have to take? Currently it seems employers are offering jobs to older people that employers have previously reserved for other marginal workers. Instead of sixty being the new thirty if would be the new seventeen as older people fill the area with the predicted largest growth in new jobs—retail clerks. This seems to be the direction in which we are going.

Since 1949, men and women over age sixty-five have said "ciao" to the labor market in recessions, and men withdrew from the labor force at the average yearly rate of 2.4 percent and women by 1.5 percent. Yet, in the most recent recession, men over age sixty-five still said "ciao" by 3.9 percent; but women said "hello" by increasing work effort by 5.3 percent. The labor force participation rate for slightly younger men and women, aged fifty-five to sixty-four, was higher over the most recent business cycle. However, if we remember our economics lessons, labor force participation and working are not the same thing. AARP analyst Sara Rix characterized 2002, the year the upturn began, as a mixed year for older workers. Despite the rapid increase in labor force participation, many of the elderly found unfavorable working conditions. If the elderly were laid off, they had half as much chance of being reemployed as younger people. The average duration of unemployment is higher for older workers and rose in 2002; the average search for job seekers over age fifty-five was sixteen weeks, up from 12.7 in 2001. Significantly, older men's job security has gotten much worse. Their median years of tenure—the number of years a person has been employed by their current employer—has fallen dramatically, by almost 50 percent from 15.3 years for men aged 55–64 to just 10.2 years. (The decline is much smaller for women, from 9.8 years in 1983 to 9.6 years in 2002.)

Just because some of us will expect to live longer than our parents does not mean that people should work longer. The logic is based falsely on the assumptions that workers do not value free time, that older people can do the new jobs, and that improved longevity is not related to retiring sooner. The first is obviously false; as the nation grew richer work hours fell and vacation time soared. Second, there is little evidence that the ability of older people to work longer has improved. Since 1981, the share of older workers reporting limitations in the ability to work stayed steady at about 15–18 percent. Jobs demanding heavy lifting, stooping, and kneeling, and overall physical effort are declining, especially for men. But, older workers report an over 17 percent increase in their jobs involving a lot of stress and intense concentration. Older women report an over 17 percent increase in their jobs requiring good eyesight. Only magical thinking can conclude that the computer has made jobs easier for older workers.

That older people found jobs harder to get, more difficult to perform, and unemployment duration much longer suggests that older people are forced onto the labor market because of eroding pensions. The unemployment rate for older women went up faster than any other's in the recession, and older men's and women's unemployment rate recovered less than younger people's in the expansion.

The U.S. system of retirement security is in transition. Despite their limitations in providing retirement without significant reform, defined contribution plans are here to stay. However, there is barely a regulatory framework in place to protect the public interest. Sensible protections that already govern the investment behavior of defined benefit plan fiduciaries could be a good place to start. The percent of a portfolio that is allowed to be in the employee's company's stock could be limited; lump sum payments could be banned; and worker representation on pension boards could be mandated.

Ultimately, it matters less what vehicles we use to get to a secure national retirement system than that we ensure a secure retirement for all American workers and their families. Unions, progressive activists, advocates for the elderly (principally the AARP), and the Democratic Party were impressively united against Social Security privatization. The puzzle is why the same solid coalition is not being built around diminishing pension expectations and the chipping away of good pensions. The answer may be that many workers are settling for individual accounts, and most workers do not have access to either 401(k) or defined benefit plans. The only way most workers get pensions is to unionize and organize. In order to have a balanced work life—with adequate pay, time off, security, and safety—it seems to always come down to that same ineluctable reality.

Notes

2   The declining availability of retiree health insurance and the rise of housing costs are critical issues in American retirement security but are outside the scope of this essay.

3   See *Cooper v. IBM Pers. Pension Plan*, F. Supp 2d.1010 (S.D. Ill. 2003). Cash balance plans are controversial. Over the last ten years, many employers converted DB plans to cash balance plans to save money, and many older workers lost expected benefits. One recent district court case has ruled that such plans are age discriminatory and the Internal Revenue Service has placed an effective moratorium on the applications for approval of cash balance plan designs.

CHAPTER 34

The Politics of Austerity and the Ikarian Dream

Kristin Lawler

As a longtime fan of the leisurely aspect of European culture, I am always thrilled whenever it makes its way onto the radar screens of Americans, who are, it is clear, grievously overworked by comparison. Too often, images of Europe are portrayed in the context of a grim new discursive "common sense" about the European lifestyle that say it is (a) an unsustainable anachronism and (b) onerous and not something Americans would want anyway. When more celebratory images of Euroleisure emerge, I like to think that Americans wonder why we cannot have what European workers have successfully pressed for – long vacations, relatively short hours of work, and the generous social wage that makes free time enjoyable rather than stressful. And when Americans start asking themselves these questions, all kinds of liberatory possibilities open up. In the context of the current continental battle over austerity, which is more than anything a speed-up imposed on the European lifestyle, these images and their reception here in America become especially important.

This is why the buzz around one recent article in particular really warmed my heart. On October 24, 2012, the *New York Times Magazine* profiled a small Greek island where, as the title proposes, "People Forget to Die." The author investigates the extraordinary health and longevity of the residents of the island, Ikaria, and finds that their secret is pretty simple – in addition to eating a plant-based, legume-heavy, locally sourced, generally organic diet, the residents of Ikaria are just amazingly chill.

Ikarians have no alarm clocks; they just start the day when they wake up. They work at a leisurely pace and take long lunch breaks and daily naps. Meals are always an occasion for socializing and wine. Life, according to this profile, is relatively carefree and filled with the pleasures of friends and family. The Ikarians' relationship to time is the polar opposite of ours – whereas in the "developed" world, the abstraction of the clock dominates the concrete reality of each moment, in Ikaria, it is the reverse. A typical resident is quoted:

> "People stay up late here…we wake up late and always take naps. I don't even open my office until 11 a.m. because no one comes before then." He took a sip of his wine. "Have you noticed that no one wears a watch here? No clock is working correctly.

Original publication details: Lawler, 2013. Reproduced with permission from K. Lawler.

When you invite someone to lunch, they might come at 10 a.m. or 6 p.m. We simply don't care about the clock here."

http://www.nytirnes.com/2012/10/28/magazine/the-island-where-people-forget-to-die.html?pagewanted = all&_r = 0

The article points out that the typical Ikarian has never really experienced the stress of being late.

In terms of the incredible longevity of the Ikarian people, there are a number of inter-locking factors at work: exercise and healthful food are integral to everyday life, a feeling of communal solidarity leaves no one at the mercy of isolation and loneliness (unlike in the United States, where we warehouse our elderly in grim wards), everyone gardens and walks a lot, but most important, I think, is the simple fact that the central pursuit of Ikarians seems to be enjoying life. Where Ikarians make pleasure – relaxing, eating and drinking wine with friends, dancing – the center of their lives, Americans have accepted the idea that relaxation and pleasure must be marginal to the real center of life, paid labor and its associated stresses.

The differential effects in terms of health and happiness are clear – the article begins with a story of an Ikarian immigrant to the United States who was diagnosed with termi-nal lung cancer, moved back to the island, stopped stressing and started hanging out with his old friends, and regained his health. Here in the United States, we see this kind of lifestyle as "unrealistic." What is realistic to Americans, though, is actually quite unrea-sonable – overwork, stress, and an epidemic of preventable disease. Maybe it is time to rethink our definition of realistic.

The Ikaria article was widely e-mailed and discussed, and the affluent nutrition-obsessed sector of Americans were quick to consume other articles, like "How to Eat Like an Ikarian." And although almost all of the online commentary waxed nostalgic about this seemingly idyllic, premodern lifestyle, not one commenter made the connection between the Ikarian lifestyle and the struggle currently raging in Greece.

Which is strange, given the fact that it is a more modern and cosmopolitan version of just the kind of relaxed lifestyle identified in the Ikaria article that is *precisely* the object of the European banking troika (the European Commission, the European Central Bank [ECB], and the International Monetary Fund) and its insanely punishing auster-ity policies. The very week that the Ikaria article came out, the *Times* coverage of the Greek crisis included a story on the attempt by the troika to link changes in Greek labor law to a new round of so-called "aid" from the ECB (85 percent of which goes to recapitalize banks, not to the people who are made to pay for it). In exchange for billions of euros that will keep Greece tied to its European lenders, the government is to continue to sell off public assets, raise taxes, raise the retirement age, cut pensions and public services, and "streamline" "rigid" labor laws that keep the country from being "competitive."

In the midst of the heated negotiations going on between the Greek government and the troika, the Greek people themselves continue to demonstrate and resist. Sadly, the American people, potential allies similarly subject to policies of public-sector austerity and the imperatives of private-sector "competitiveness" (also known as profitableness for corporations and banks), seem to be buying the bankers' analysis of the crisis in the Eurozone. According to this analysis, the Greeks, in the streets striking and rioting against this punishment, are somehow just being unreasonable. This logic insists that they should stop complaining, suck it up, and get to work.

It is not surprising: all of the "legitimate," supposedly unbiased news sources approach the issue with the same tone of disdain for the Greeks, who, in this narrative, actually *caused* the entire European crisis with their lazy, profligate ways. According to the story told by the *New York Times*, NPR, and the rest of the mainstream media, Greece lied its way into the Eurozone, borrowed beyond its means, blew all the money, and is now in the streets refusing to work off its debts.

This story, of a lazy and irresponsible culture, is best told by influential lightweight Michael Lewis, in his *Boomerang: Travels in the New Third World*. His chapter on Greece, disparagingly titled "And They Invented Math," identifies Greek dishonesty and over-borrowing as the problem, and Greeks buckling down to pay the piper as the only possible solution: "But this question of whether Greece will repay its debts is really a question of whether Greece will change its culture, and that will happen only if Greeks want to change." Lewis calls what's happening in Greece in the wake of the crisis a "total moral collapse" of the society and ends the chapter with a crescendo of paternalistic moralizing: "Even if it is technically possible for these people to repay their debts, live within their means, and return to good standing inside the European Union, do they have the inner resources to do it? Or have they so lost their ability to feel connected to anything outside their small worlds that they would rather just shed the obligations?"

The only major challenge to this obnoxious discourse in the mainstream media has come from reliably Keynesian lefty economist and *NYT* columnist Paul Krugman, who, importantly, corrects the narrative regarding the responsibility of the European banks for the crisis in Greece, but only at the expense of leaving Greek culture out of the matter entirely. And, it seems to me, the culture of the Greek working class is precisely the point.

And although Krugman mistakenly takes the austerity hounds at their word that the policies are therapeutic rather than disciplinary – even in the face of the reality that austerity is actually increasing Greek debt by shrinking the economy – he points out some basic facts that everyone should understand, first and foremost:

> Fifteen years ago Greece was no paradise, but it wasn't in crisis either. Unemployment was high but not catastrophic, and the nation more or less paid its way on world markets, earning enough from exports, tourism, shipping and other sources to more or less pay for its imports.
> http://www.nytimes.com/2012/06/18/opinion/krugman-greece-as-victim.html

In other words, before central bankers in Germany and France decided that money could be made by bringing Greece and other mellow European countries into the Euro, Greece was fine. Unemployment was relatively high, but unemployment is a far less threatening matter when extended families live together, government pensions are generous, and "unemployed youth" are happily sipping coffee at the café with their friends all day. "Greek culture" simply was not anybody's problem; in fact, it was a major tourist draw. The country basically had enough to pay its own way and distribute its surplus however its internal class struggle determined. Which was, given the militance of the Greek working class, pretty generous as far as the people were concerned. This was never anyone else's business, until Greece joined the Euro, was flooded with cheap money, and spent it. Now, the logic goes, the Greeks must suffer for their sins.

Anthropologist and organic intellectual of the Occupy movement David Graeber, in his 2011 *Debt: The First 5,000 Years*, lays out the ways in which debt has traditionally been used by those in power to accomplish two things: to make people work and to create markets.

This was especially true of the European colonial powers taxing their subjects, but Graeber's analysis traces this dynamic to the economic beginnings of the colonial powers themselves. Debt has always been used as a mechanism to bring people to heel.

Today's massive lending and its aftermath, the drying up of credit, is working to have precisely this effect. Like the Third World debt that preceded it, Greek debt is a means to compel the Greek people to work harder and longer now that the Euro has linked the largely self-sufficient Greek economy to the larger market of Europe much more intensely. Cheap money and economic integration encouraged Greece to import all kinds of new goodies as well as necessities like food that used to be produced at home, and the withdrawal of credit by international markets is, as we are all witness to today, resulting in a punishing burden of austerity, the object of which is twofold.

First, austerity in public budgets means that public services become unsustainable and selling them off to the highest private bidder seems the only possibility (sound familiar?). From water to airports to government services, the Greeks are indeed being pressured to sell off public assets to pay their bills. So creating indebtedness is, in this case and others, a privatization strategy, attempting to transform public goods into privately profitable ones. Second, the artificially-produced scarcity that austerity policies induce functions as a means to compel populations to work, and work harder. Scarcity breeds desperation, and desperation kills cultures like the one in Ikaria, in which people work to live instead of living to work. So indebtedness and the austerity that results leave only two possibilities for its subjects: stop enjoying life and start hustling to work off the debt. Or resist.

In light of all this, Krugman's analysis of Greece as victim of the Euro, and his resulting anti-austerity position, is a...welcome corrective to the moralizing about Greek culture that stands in for economic analysis in the American mainstream press. It can help Americans to understand that the Greeks did not break Europe – if anything, Europe broke the Greeks. Thus, it is not really fair to extract payment for northern European lenders off the backs of the Greek people.

However, Krugman's position, in a classic progressive mistake, discounts the cultural question to avoid "blaming the victim," but at the expense of understanding the important contours of the struggle. The class struggle, in Greece and elsewhere, rages between the logic of capital on one side and on the other, the counterlogic of the working class, which dreams of life on Ikaria, among other things. Culture is central to the economic battle raging in Greece and around the world; in fact, the culture of leisure and pleasure and people's autonomy over their own time is precisely what opposes the imperatives of capital to make every moment of life and every iota of the lifeworld into a means to the end of profit.

The story of the struggle against austerity in Greece, and the attitude that similarly-situated Americans ought to have toward Greek resistance, can best be understood when we are thinking about how smart the Ikarians are to enjoy their lives with friends, food, wine, and plenty of rest and sunshine, and how stupid we are, to waste our precious lives stressed out and working ourselves to death. Gardening your own food is not for everyone, and many of us prefer big-city life to the old-fashioned village. But these are cultural preferences that come to the fore when people are free to constitute time on their own terms. The Ikarians are an image of a culture that privileges pleasure over labor, and that is the key political point, in Europe and beyond.

Simply put, there is a hidden politics to Ikarian culture that goes even beyond the fact, unmentioned in the New York Times magazine, that Ikaria is one of the most consistently

Communist-voting blocs in all of Greece, and among the most militant in the nation in resisting the new taxation schemes designed to pay bank debts out of the people's incomes, which are already estimated to be down by 30–40 percent. If you dig Ikaria, whether you know it or not, you support their anti-austerity cultural politics as well as their left-wing electoral politics.

In tracing the origins of capitalism, Karl Marx explains the centrality of human desperation to the ability of capital to generate profit, that is, to exist. From the British enclosure movements that privatized common village lands and thus left the peasants little choice but to look for work to survive, to the contemporary privatization of public goods all over the world, especially in the United States (frequently framed as a result of the necessity to pay back debt), capital needs a population with nothing but their labor-power to sell on the market in order to have a reliable, reliably profitable, working class. Artificially created scarcity breeds docile workers; austerity is the creation of this scarcity. Overworked, stressed-out Americans would do well to understand how much the fight against austerity is our fight too.

This is also the story of what's happening in Greece right now. George Caffentzis explains it best in his recent dispatch from the struggle there:

> This experiment [austerity] is being run because the last century of social and class struggle in Europe has made the rate of exploitation and profit too low for capitalists in the Europe of the 21st century. The introduction of the Euro a decade ago was a failed experiment aimed at increasing the profitability of European capital (i.e., capital employed in Europe), it has been a grave disappointment to capitalists. The currency manipulation and the cutting of "transaction costs" the Euro allowed were not able to challenge the structures that workers over many strikes, street demonstrations, and eventually war have built to make their lives safer, less risky and longer (and cut the profits of their bosses).
>
> For European capitalism to survive this period of globalization, wages must be reduced, public property, instead of becoming common, must be privatized and whatever wealth workers have accumulated to deal with emergencies must be taxed away to pay the national debt that has been generated to prevent bank failures! Workers of all sorts, industrial and service, skilled and unskilled, undocumented and documented, material and immaterial must be made to cut their demands and accept the minimum (with thanks!). This crisis experiment is a desperate move on the part of the capitalists, of course, but its success depends on treating each country and working class one-at-a-time and keeping them separated as much as possible.
>
> http://blog.occupiedlondon.org/2012/08/26/george-caffentzis-summer-2012-a-report-from-greece/

One way to keep the working class of each country separated is to make sure that they never see their struggles as one and the same. The manipulation of the German public into an us-and-them discourse vis-à-vis the Greeks has been a victory for the ruling class on this front; the increasing popularity of the fascist anti-immigrant right in Greece itself is a troubling if not exactly surprising result of us-and-them divisions. However, the rejection of this strategy by the French, who decisively refused the divisive politics of austerity and its scapegoating of the Greeks in their spring 2012 presidential election was a victory for anti-austerity forces and the solidarity they require. And a recent daylong continent-wide general strike to protest austerity policies is an exciting sign that the European working class is resisting the divide-and-conquer strategy of an always quite solidaristic capitalist class.

What the anti-austerity forces need now is for the Americans to see their own budding struggles – for the eradication of student debt and for a restoration of decimated public services especially – as part of an international movement. Painting the Greek people as "irresponsible" for refusing the austerity that would make them desperate and thus docile workers, while encouraging Americans to identify with the interests of corporations, banks, and the seemingly impartial "economic growth," has been a pretty effective cultural strategy to subvert this potential solidarity.

But every now and then, another account slips through the official organs – this time, in the "Body Issue" of the *NYT Magazine*.

Americans ought to read articles like the one about the health and happiness of the Ikarian people with the understanding that the goal of capitalist austerity is precisely to bring an end to these last places of freedom, to make us all believe that it's simply not realistic, that killing ourselves working rather than enjoying life with friends and family and good food and wine and dancing is the way life just *has* to be.

Michael Lewis ends his book with a chapter on America, which he says is next in this whole debt to austerity cycle. Of course, the European situation and the American one are different in key outlines, but Lewis is right on this one. Public and consumer debt – run up to finance wars, tax cuts for the rich, and massive bonuses for Wall Street shell-game scammers – is now being used as a stick to discipline the American working class into working harder for less in the context of increasingly starved-out and then sold-off public services. But this is only the most recent salvo in capital's decades-long project to use outsourcing, union-busting, debt, and privatization to attack the working-class share of the social product in America and all around the world.

I submit that Americans will only have a fighting chance in the face of this attack if they take impulses like the happy fascination with the people of Ikaria and translate them into a politics of life and freedom against the austerity for the working class that makes profit for corporations.

What if Americans saw the Greeks' insistence on privileging life over labor as something to celebrate? If we saw our own dreams in the culture of mellow Europe that the Ikarian image is an exaggerated version of? Judging by the reception of the profile of these free-living, fun-loving Ikarians, perhaps we are beginning to. The Occupy uprising of a year ago was a good start, and those movement activists have always been connected to European anti-austerity movements. Now that cross-border organizing needs to go really big. The Europeans are already doing it. It is certainly too soon to hope that a majority of Americans will join them. But, I think, working to reframe for Americans the meaning of austerity and anti-austerity struggles, and our place in them, is a step in the right direction. Nurturing our Ikarian dreams is a start.

Selected Bibliography

Aronowitz, Stanley and DiFazio, William. (1994) *The Jobless Future: Sci-Tech and the Dogma of Work* (Minneapolis, MN: University of Minnesota Press).

Baran, Paul A. and Sweezy, Paul M. (1966) *Monopoly Capital: An Essay on the American Economic and Social Order* (New York: Monthly Review Press).

Beckert, Sven. (2001 [1993]) *The Monied Metropolis: New York City and the Consolidation of the American Bourgeoisie, 1850–1896* (New York: Cambridge University Press).

Bousquet, Marc. (2008) *How the University Works: Higher Education and the Low-Wage Nation* (New York: New York University Press).

Braverman, Harry. (1974) *Labor and Monopoly Capital: The Degradation of Work in the Twentieth Century* (New York: Monthly Review Press).

Brecher, Jeremy. (1997) *Strike!* (Cambridge, MA: South End Press).

Brenner, Aaron et al. (2010) *Rebel Rank and File: Labor Militancy and Revolt from Below in the Long 1970s* (London: Verso).

Cohen, Lizabeth. (1990) *Making a New Deal: Industrial Workers in Chicago, 1919–1939* (Cambridge: Cambridge University Press).

Cowie, Jefferson. (2010) *Stayin' Alive: The 1970s and the Last Days of the Working Class* (New York: The New Press).

Cutler, Jonathan. (2004) *Labor's Time: Shorter Hours, the UAW, and the Struggle for American Unionism* (Philadelphia, PA: Temple University Press).

Dalla Costa, Mariarosa. (1975) *The Power of Women and the Subversion of Community* (Falling Wall Press).

Davis, Mike. (1975) "The Stop Watch and the Wooden Shoe: Scientific Management and the Industrial Workers of the World Movement," in *Radical America*, Volume 8, Number 6, pp. 69–96.

Enstad, Nan. (1999) *Ladies of Labor, Girls of Adventure: Working Women, Popular Culture and Labor Politics at the Turn of the Century* (New York: Columbia University Press).

Foster, John Bellamy and McChesney, Robert W. (2012) *The Endless Crisis: How Monopoly-Finance Capital Produces Stagnation and Upheaval from the U.S.A. to China* (New York: Monthly Review Press).

Foster, John Bellamy and Magdoff, Harry. (2009) *The Great Financial Crisis: Causes and Consequences* (New York: Monthly Review Press).

Geoghegan, Thomas. (2004) *Which Side Are You On? Trying to Be for Labor When It's Flat On Its Back* (New York: The New Press).

Ghilarducci, Teresa. (2006) "The End of Retirement," in *Monthly Review*, Volume 58, Number 1.

Glaberman, Martin. (1973 [1952]) *Punching Out* (Detroit, MI: Bewick Editions).

Glickman, Lawrence B. (1997) *A Living Wage: American Workers and the Making of Consumer Society* (Ithaca, NY: Cornell University Press).

Gutman, Herbert G. (1977) *Work, Culture, and Society in Industrializing America: Essays in American Working-Class and Social History* (New York: Vintage Books).

Class: The Anthology, First Edition. Edited by Stanley Aronowitz and Michael J. Roberts.
© 2018 Stanley Aronowitz and Michael J. Roberts. Published 2018 by John Wiley & Sons Ltd.

Harrison, Bennett and Bluestone, Barry. (1988) *The Great U-Turn: Corporate Restructuring and the Polarizing of America* (New York: Basic Books).

Heifetz, Robert. (2000) "The Role of Professional and Technical Workers in Progressive Social Transformation," in *Monthly Review*, Volume 52, Number 7, pp. 26–39.

Hoberk, Andrew. (2005) *Twilight of the Middle Class* (Princeton University Press).

Hunnicutt, Benjamin Kline. (1988) *Work Without End: Abandoning Shorter Hours for the Right to Work* (Philadelphia: Temple University Press).

Hunnicutt, Benjamin Kline. (2013) *Free Time: The Forgotten American Dream* (Philadelphia: Temple University Press).

Kracauer, Siegfried. (1998 [1929]) *The Salaried Masses: Duty and Distraction in Weimar Germany*, translated by Quintin Hoare (London: Verso).

Kelley, Robin D. G. (1996) *Race Rebels: Culture, Politics, and the Black Working Class* (New York: The Free Press).

Krugman, Paul. (2012) *End This Depression Now!* (New York: Norton).

Larson, Magali Sarfatti. (1977) *The Rise of Professionalism: A Sociological Analysis* (Berkeley, CA: University of California Press).

Lawler, Kristin. (2012) "The Politics of Austerity and the Ikarian Dream." http://slackerpolitics. com/2012/11/16/pleasure-politics-and-ikarian-dreams/

Levine, Rhonda. (1988) *Class Struggle and the New Deal: Industrial Labor, Industrial Capital, and the State* (Lawrence, KA: University Press of Kansas).

Mallet, Serge. (1975) *The New Working Class*, translated by Andre and Bob Shepherd (Nottingham: Spokesman Books).

Marx, Karl. (1991 [1981]) *Capital: A Critique of Political Economy, Volume Three*, translated by David Fernbach (New York: Penguin Books, in association with New Left Review).

Marx, Karl. (1990 [1976]) *Capital: A Critique of Political Economy, Volume One*, translated by Ben Fowkes (New York: Penguin Books, in association with New Left Review).

Mason, Paul (2012) *Why It's Kicking Off Everywhere: The New Global Revolutions* (London: Verso).

McNeill, George. (1887) *The Labor Movement: The Problem of Today* (Boston: A. M. Bridgman & Co.).

Mills, C. Wright. (1953) *White Collar: The American Middle Classes* (New York: Oxford University Press).

Mills, C. Wright. (2000 [1956]) *The Power Elite* (New York: Oxford University Press).

Mogensen, Vernon L. (1996) *Office Politics: Computers, Labor and the Fight for Safety and Health* (New Brunswick, NJ: Rutgers University Press).

Moore, Ryan. (2009) "The Unmaking of the English Working Class: Deindustrialization, Reification and Heavy Metal," in *Heavy Metal Music in Britain*, edited by Gerd Bayer, pp. 143–162 (London: Ashgate).

Piven, Frances Fox, and Cloward, Richard A. (1993 [1971]) *Regulating the Poor: the Functions of Public Welfare* (New York: Vintage Books).

Preis, Art.(1972) *Labor's Giant Step* (New York: Pathfinder Press, 1972).

Roberts, Michael J. (2009). "The Dialectic of Labor and Capital in Globalization: How the Historical Formation of the American Labor Movement Influenced the Course of Globalization," in *Globalization and the Prospects for Critical Reflection*, edited by Jung Min Choi and John W. Murphy (Delhi: Aaakar Books).

Roberts, Michael J. (2014) *Tell Tchaikovsky the News: Rock'n'Roll, the Labor Question and the Musicians' Union, 1942–1968* (Durham, NC: Duke University Press).

Roediger, David R. (1991) *The Wages of Whiteness: Race and the Making of the American Working Class* (London and New York: Verso).

Rosenzweig, Roy. (1985) *Eight Hours for What We Will* (Cambridge: Cambridge University Press).

Ross, Andrew. (2000) "The Mental Labor Problem," in *Social Text*, 18.2, 1–31.

Stiglitz, Joseph E. (2012) *The Price of Inequality* (New York: Norton)

Thompson, E. P. (1963) *The Making of the English Working Class* (New York: Pantheon Books).

Thompson, E. P. (1967) "Time, Work-Discipline, and Industrial Capitalism," in *Past and Present*, Number 38, pp. 56–97.

Tomlins, Christopher. (1985) *The State and the Unions: Labor Relations Law, and the Organized Labor Movement in America, 1880–1960* (New York: Cambridge University Press).

Veblen, Thorstein. (1963) *The Engineers and the Price System* (New York: Harcourt, Brace & World Inc.)

Weber, Max. (2011) *The Protestant Ethic and the Spirit of Capitalism*, translated by Stephen Kalberg (New York: Oxford University Press).

Wilentz, Sean. (1984) "Against Exceptionalism: Class Consciousness and the American Labor Movement," in *International Labor and Working Class History*, Number 26, pp. 1–24.

Index

Page numbers in *italics* refer to Figures